# VOLUME 1

# CHOICE AND COST UNDER UNCERTAINTY

# THE COLLECTED WORKS OF
# Armen A. Alchian

## VOLUME 1

## CHOICE AND COST UNDER UNCERTAINTY

EDITED AND WITH AN INTRODUCTION BY

DANIEL K. BENJAMIN

LIBERTY FUND

Indianapolis

This book is published by Liberty Fund, Inc.,
a foundation established to encourage study of the
ideal of a society of free and responsible individuals.

The cuneiform inscription that serves as our logo and
as the design motif for our endpapers is the earliest-known
written appearance of the word "freedom" (*amagi*), or "liberty."
It is taken from a clay document written about 2300 B.C.
in the Sumerian city-state of Lagash.

© 2006 Liberty Fund, Inc.
Frontispiece © 2000 Cascade Photographics. Used by permission.
Jacket and cover photograph courtesy of Armen A. Alchian
All rights reserved
Printed in the United States of America

10  09  08  07  06  C  5  4  3  2  1
10  09  08  07  06  P  5  4  3  2  1

Library of Congress Cataloging-in-Publication Data
Alchian, Armen Albert, 1914–
Choice and cost under uncertainty / Armen A. Alchian ; edited and with an introduction by
Daniel K. Benjamin.
p. cm. — (The collected works of Armen A. Alchian ; v. 1)
Includes bibliographical references and index.
ISBN-13: 978-0-86597-632-0 (alk. paper)
ISBN-10: 0-86597-632-5 (alk. paper)
ISBN-13: 978-0-86597-633-7 (pbk. : alk. paper)
ISBN-10: 0-86597-633-3 (pbk. : alk. paper)
1. Economics. 2. Cost. 3. Inflation (Finance) I. Benjamin, Daniel K. II. Title.
III. Series: Alchian, Armen Albert, 1914– Works. 2006; v. 1.
HB171.A427 2006
330.01—dc22          2005044682

LIBERTY FUND, INC.
8335 Allison Pointe Trail, Suite 300
Indianapolis, Indiana 46250-1684

# CONTENTS

# INTRODUCTION

This is the first of two volumes that compose the Collected Works of Armen A. Alchian. Together the volumes include all his major scholarly articles, some shorter papers published in nontechnical periodicals, and several unpublished papers, many dating from his years at the RAND Corporation in the 1950s. Not included in the Collected Works are his famous textbooks with William R. Allen, *University Economics* and *Exchange and Production*. Also excluded are a few unpublished papers for which some or all pages are missing, some book reviews, and a few comments written by Alchian about the work of others, papers that are not fully intelligible taken out of context. These two volumes are thus both a replacement for, and a supplement to, *Economic Forces at Work*, an earlier Liberty Fund publication that brought together a selection of Alchian's earlier papers. The Collected Works differs from that earlier book in that it includes numerous papers excluded from it, as well as many papers written by Alchian in the intervening years.[1]

This first volume, *Choice and Cost under Uncertainty*, is the more eclectic of the two volumes, for the topics covered range from the meaning of utility measurement to effects of inflation.[2] Despite their enormous scope, there is a remarkable coherence to the papers included, a point to which I shall return. The second volume, *Property Rights and Economic Behavior*, is much more narrowly focused. Alchian is generally regarded as (along with Ronald H. Coase and Harold Demsetz) one of the founders of the economic study of property rights. This second volume makes it clear that this reputation is fully justified.

Alchian continues to work, even as I write these words, so his contributions to the literature are contemporary in every sense of the word. Indeed, his papers, even those published more than five decades ago, continue to garner

---

1. Armen A. Alchian and William R. Allen, *University Economics* (Belmont, Calif.: Wadsworth, 1964); *Exchange and Production* (Belmont, Calif.: Wadsworth, 1969); *Economic Forces at Work: Selected Works by Armen A. Alchian* (Indianapolis: Liberty Fund, 1977).

2. Armen A. Alchian, "The Meaning of Utility Measurement," *American Economic Review* 43 (March 1953): 26–50; Reuben Kessel and Armen A. Alchian, "Effects of Inflation," *Journal of Political Economy* 70 (December 1962): 521–37.

citations in research taking place on the current frontiers of economics. Thus, even if I were charged with setting out Alchian's place in history—which I am not—I would be unable to do so. In fact, as Alchian himself might remark, that is a task better left to the marketplace of ideas. What I can do is attempt to place the papers in the context in which the work was conducted and show how the ties between seemingly unrelated strands of research reveal much about Alchian's intellectual focus and enormous range.

Three themes unify Armen Alchian's work on economics. Together they outline both a coherent methodology for doing economics and a view of the world that celebrates the importance of individual liberty. For Alchian, the unit of analysis is always the individual; hence, the theory must be consistent with each person acting as an individual utility or wealth maximizer. This view compels us to recognize that the responsibility for choices lies with the individual, who is thus the ultimate source of all human power—whether that power happens temporarily to reside in a set of democratic institutions or in the hands of a dictator.

In Alchian's view, economic theory must be as general as possible. It must apply to both sides of the market, to markets for all types of goods and services, and to the decisions of all economic agents. Alchian is unremitting in demanding that economics be ruled by theory rather than by theorist, thus insisting on the general applicability of any proposition that purports to be economic theory.

Finally, in Alchian's view, both theory and theorist are constrained, indeed governed, by the facts: Theory must always confront and conform to the facts. It must yield refutable implications, and if these are in fact refuted, it is the theory—not the facts—that must yield. The purpose of theory is never theory in and of itself; it is instead to help individuals understand the world around them. In this sense, the ultimate consumers of economic theory are the people whom it describes.

I have cast the opening paper of this volume, Alchian's "Principles of Professional Advancement," as a preface, for it includes a description of the events leading up to three of Alchian's most insightful papers, all of which are included in this volume.[3] In "Professional Advancement" Alchian also describes an unpublished paper, "The Stock Market Speaks," which was arguably the first empirical demonstration of the power of markets to incorporate into

---

3. Armen A. Alchian, "Principles of Professional Advancement," *Economic Inquiry* 34 (July 1996): 520–26.

asset values all relevant information about those values—even information that may be top secret. Sadly, this paper is not included in the Collected Works because it no longer exists: Written at the RAND Corporation in the early 1950s on the topic of the hydrogen bomb, the original manuscript and all copies were confiscated and, as far as anyone can determine, destroyed.

There is an important sense in which all of the papers in part 1 of this volume, "Uncertainty and Information Costs," can be traced to an extraordinarily simple idea: Information, like all goods, is scarce—which is to say, it is costly to acquire and to disseminate. Will my trading partner do what she says she will? Will the good I am purchasing perform as it is claimed to perform? And will any of this be true tomorrow or next year? Efforts to answer questions such as these drive a broad array of the economic behavior we observe around us, ranging from advertising to unemployment. Alchian was among the first to recognize the fundamental importance of treating information as we treat all other scarce goods; as a result, several of the papers in this section have helped shape major strands of the literature in the years since he wrote them.

Part 1 of this volume begins with Alchian's first published professional paper, "Uncertainty, Evolution and Economic Literature." He wrote this paper initially not for publication, but simply to help himself and his graduate students understand the issues more clearly. Only at the suggestion of, and after considerable prodding by, Stephen Enke did Alchian consider submitting it for publication; even then, it took some very encouraging remarks by Milton Friedman (who had seen a copy) to induce Alchian to follow Enke's advice. The paper brought an entire line of inquiry (or mode of thinking) to a grinding halt: economists had been struggling with the question, How do people think? Alchian made it clear that this matters not. What is relevant is how they behave: This is all we can observe and is all that will determine the outcome of their decisions. The paper also got Alchian's career off to a fast start. As Kenneth Arrow (who was a colleague of Alchian's at RAND in the 1950s) has remarked, "What made Armen really famous was his paper in 1950 on evolution."[4] The paper continues to be cited by economists and lawyers working on topics ranging from securities markets to marriage.

Another paper in this section, "Information Costs, Pricing and Resource Unemployment," was undertaken at a time when economists were reexamining the

---

4. Armen A. Alchian, "Uncertainty, Evolution and Economic Theory," *Journal of Political Economy* 58 (June 1950): 211–21; Kenneth Arrow, ISNIE *Newsletter* 3 (Fall 2001), p. 6.

foundations of the literature that had grown up in the footsteps of John Maynard Keynes's *General Theory*.[5] Alchian's contribution to this literature was notable in at least two respects. First, it demonstrated that it was possible to think about macroeconomic issues using microeconomic tools. Just as important, this paper made it clear that unemployment—whether of people or of nonhuman resources—was, in fact, productive activity and could be thought of as the outcome of choices made by individuals in a world in which information is a scarce good.

Alchian's work at the RAND Corporation, where he was a consultant while a faculty member at UCLA, played a crucial role in stimulating much of his early research. The work in part 2, "Cost," illustrates this clearly. During the late 1940s at RAND, Alchian tried to determine what it actually cost to produce airplanes. The data were held by the engineers at RAND, and in the course of his work on costs, he found that the engineers looked at costs much differently than did economists. In his efforts to "correct" the engineers' thinking, Alchian discovered that they had insights into the production process and the nature of costs that he and other economists had completely missed: Not just the rate of production was important; so, too, was the intended volume of the production run. Although the results of Alchian's work circulated internally at RAND during the late 1940s, because of national security concerns it was not until a decade later that any of it appeared in the published literature.

The papers in this section highlight an important enigma. I think it is fair to say that everyone who is familiar with Alchian's work on costs believes that it is both innovative and fundamentally superior to the conventional treatment of the issues. Yet the work has had almost no impact on the literature. Why? A small part of the story may be that although "Costs and Outputs" was originally accepted for publication in the *American Economic Review*, Alchian chose instead to have it published in a *Festschrift* for Bernard Haley, one of his Stanford professors. But this cannot be the whole story, because the importance of this paper is recognized widely enough that it has been reprinted several times. Moreover, the other major published paper in this section, "Reliability of Progress Curves in Airframe Production," appeared in the prestigious journal *Econometrica*.[6] Even though many fundamental aspects of the production pro-

---

5. Armen A. Alchian, "Information Costs, Pricing and Resource Unemployment," *Economic Inquiry* 7 (June 1969): 109–28; John Maynard Keynes, *The General Theory of Employment, Interest and Money* (New York: Harcourt Brace, 1935).

6. Armen A. Alchian, "Costs and Outputs," in *The Allocation of Economic Resources: Essays in Honor of Bernard Francis Haley*, by Moses Abramovitz et al. (Stanford: Stanford University

cess cannot be understood without focusing on the intended volume of the production run, economists continue to write almost exclusively about the rate of production.

Alchian's work with Reuben Kessel on inflation was stimulated by the latter's arrival at the RAND Corporation in the mid-1950s. Kessel had written his dissertation on the topic at the University of Chicago, and Alchian admired Kessel's way of thinking, as well as the data he had acquired.[7] At Alchian's suggestion, Kessel successfully applied for funding to work further on inflation, and the result was a series of papers that transformed how economists view the consequences of inflation. Many of these papers focus on who gains and loses from inflation, with conclusions that not merely changed the way people thought about the problem but also—once again—highlighted the importance of uncertainty and information costs in determining those gains and losses.

This volume closes with a series of papers in which Alchian explicitly focuses on the semantics and the methods that we use in conducting economic analysis. Despite the absence of formalism from much of his work, Alchian's graduate training included large doses of mathematical statistics that incorporated the pioneering work of R. A. Fisher, J. Neyman, and E. S. Pearson. Indeed, when he arrived at UCLA for his first job, Alchian had the option of going to the statistics department or the economics department, and he ended up teaching mostly statistics at first. His training in both economic theory and statistics helped spur Alchian toward precision in thinking and in writing. And while this precision is evident in all his work, the papers in this section particularly highlight that aspect of his approach to economics.

Two of these papers warrant particular mention because of the historical context in which they were written. The rapid pace of technological change during and immediately after World War II induced the Army Air Forces (AAF) to have the RAND Corporation study the rate at which durable equipment should be replaced. The result was "Economic Replacement Policy," which is, to my knowledge, the first systematic study of this issue.[8] It was written at a

---

Press, 1959), 23–40; Armen A. Alchian, "Reliability of Progress Curves in Airframe Production," *Econometrica* 31 (October 1963): 679–93.

7. Reuben A. Kessel, "Inflation and Wealth Redistribution: An Empirical Study" (Ph.D. diss., University of Chicago, 1954).

8. Armen A. Alchian, "Economic Replacement Policy," RAND Corporation R-224, April 12, 1952.

time when computing was in its infancy. Analogue computers, favored by engineers, were the fastest machines then available; the slower digital machines were the choice of scientists because of their greater accuracy. Alchian did the computations for his study using RAND's REAC analogue computer (one of only a handful in the country at the time), and the original version of the study published by RAND includes the wiring diagram for the REAC.

The paper entitled "Analysis Procedures" was written by then-Captain Armen A. Alchian while he served in the Army Air Forces during World War II.[9] Early in the war, the AAF became concerned about the large number of candidates who were failing to complete air-crew training. After a year and a half of trial and error in devising methods of screening candidates, the AAF in November 1943 instituted standardized testing procedures. These screening procedures substantially reduced failure rates in the training program by weeding out unsuitable candidates ahead of time. Although the statistical procedures used by Captain Alchian are the stuff of today's undergraduate texts, they were, at the time, the most advanced available—methods that proved their worth in wartime practice.

Many of the papers contained in the Collected Works are coauthored. Alchian is, at every opportunity, effusive in his praise of his coauthors and colleagues; I would be remiss if I did not emphasize his gratitude and appreciation for their contributions and their friendship. Alchian is also deeply grateful to Liberty Fund for its attention and support over the years.

My debt to Liberty Fund in this endeavor is lengthy and large. Indeed, one might argue that the origins of this project can be traced back to 1975, when Liberty Fund decided to assemble a selection of Alchian's works in honor of his then-upcoming sixty-fifth birthday and asked me to edit what became *Economic Forces at Work*. Naturally, I was delighted when Liberty Fund decided to publish the Collected Works, and even happier when they asked me to participate in its preparation.

Special thanks are also due to Armen and Pauline Alchian's daughter, Arline Alchian Hoel. She undertook much of the drudgery of tracking down many of the papers appearing here, especially the previously unpublished manuscripts. In many cases, it took repeated trips to files that had remained undisturbed for

---

9. Armen A. Alchian, "Analysis Procedures," in *Records, Analysis, and Procedures*, ed. Walter L. Deemer (Randolph Field, Texas: Army Air Force School of Aviation Medicine, 1947), 445–509.

many years. Hoel also transcribed the five-plus hours of videotapes created in producing the Intellectual Portrait Series, a prodigious effort that enabled me to harvest many of the bits of history recounted here. And finally, she has served as a valuable sounding board for me as I have sought to organize Alchian's work in a manner that would be useful and has at all times encouraged me in my efforts.

My greatest personal and intellectual debt is to Armen Alchian himself. He showed me the beauty and power of economics and demonstrated that both could be transmitted in the classroom and through the written word. The science of economics is an enriched discipline because of Armen Alchian, and I am a different person. Most important, I believe that the world is a better place because he has graced us with his wisdom, his kindness, and his love of liberty.

Daniel K. Benjamin
*Clemson University*
2005

# INTRODUCTION TO *ECONOMIC FORCES AT WORK*

## RONALD H. COASE

Economists treat their heroes well. All our great men have had their works collected in volumes which are treasured and studied. It was therefore to be expected that the economics profession would want to see Armen Alchian's major papers gathered together and published as a book. Such a collection makes it much more convenient for those who wish to study his thought (as many do, and will), but even more important, it exhibits, in a way no single article can, the essential character of his approach.

Keynes tells us that Edgeworth, after the publication of his *Collected Economic Papers*, was genuinely surprised, and pleased, to learn the extent of his international reputation. Armen Alchian will, I am sure, experience a similar surprise, and also pleasure. It was remarked by Sir James Mackintosh that he had known Adam Smith, Ricardo, and Malthus, and that it said something for economics that "its three greatest masters were about the three best men I ever knew." It would be difficult to add some modern economists to this list without changing the wording. But this would not be necessary with Armen Alchian. He is classical in manners as well as thought. The publication of this book offers us an opportunity to pay honor to a colleague who has enriched our subject but who never stooped to conquer.

Armen Alchian was born on April 12, 1914, in Fresno, California. He was brought up in a tightly knit Armenian community, a community which was subject to intense discrimination. This discrimination, which does not now exist, was not the result, Armen Alchian believes, of any natural unfriendliness or unreasonableness on the part of the other inhabitants of Fresno but was due to the strangeness of the Armenians' manners and customs, which, because they were unusual and not quickly altered, were not understood or tolerated initially. This personal experience with discrimination led Armen Alchian to distrust efforts to prevent or remove discrimination by political means.

Armen Alchian was educated in the Fresno school system and in 1932 went

Reprinted from Armen A. Alchian, *Economic Forces at Work* (Indianapolis: Liberty Fund, 1977), 7–10, by permission of Ronald H. Coase.

to Fresno State College. Two years later he transferred to Stanford, where he obtained his B.A. in 1936. He continued at Stanford for graduate work, obtaining his Ph.D. in 1944, the thesis topic being "The Effects of Changes in the General Wage Structure." Armen Alchian's teachers at Stanford included Elmer Fagan, Bernard Haley, Edward S. Shaw, and Allen Wallis. While working for his Ph.D., Alchian was a teaching assistant in the Department of Economics from 1937 to 1940, held a Social Science Council Fellowship at the National Bureau of Economic Research and Harvard in 1940 and 1941, and, for a period in 1942, was an instructor in economics at the University of Oregon. In 1942, he joined the U.S. Army Air Forces, in which he served until 1946. From 1943 until the end of the war, he was engaged in statistical work for the Air Forces.

The war over, Armen Alchian joined the economics department of the University of California, Los Angeles, where he has been ever since, becoming a full professor in 1958. In 1946, he also became associated, at the instigation of Allen Wallis, with the RAND Corporation, a connection which was to have a profound influence on his work in economics. It enabled him to see how economics could be used to illuminate and solve practical problems. It also brought him into close contact with Reuben Kessel, Jack Hirshleifer, and William Meckling, and from his collaboration with them much important work sprang.

Armen Alchian's first publications were an outgrowth of his statistical work with the U.S. Army Air Forces. His later publications were undoubtedly influenced by his work at RAND and his interaction with his colleagues there. But it would be wrong to think of Armen Alchian's contribution to economics as a fortuitous result of the RAND connection. In 1950, he published his paper on "Uncertainty, Evolution and Economic Theory" (reprinted in this volume), a paper of striking originality, whose importance was immediately perceived and which gained him international recognition. It was clear that economics had a new master. The power which that article revealed would have served economics whatever the circumstances of Armen Alchian's life. But it was our good fortune that fate led him in the particular direction it did.

Armen Alchian has made important contributions to the economic analysis of inflation and unemployment, and to the theory of costs and of the firm. He has played the leading role in the development of a theory of property rights. His writing is distinguished by his ability to disentangle the essential from the trivial and, above all, by his skill in showing how the same basic economic forces are at work in a wide variety of apparently completely different social settings. And if the operation of these forces seems to produce sometimes satis-

factory and sometimes unsatisfactory results, this does not come about because the individuals concerned are better or worse but because the environment within which they make their choices is not the same. This is true whether
one is dealing with discrimination in Fresno or with the behavior of university
teachers, government officials, or businessmen.

Alfred Marshall considered that it was an essential task of an economist to
demonstrate "the Many in the One, the One in the Many." No modern economist has been more successful in accomplishing this than Armen Alchian.

I am grateful to Mrs. Pauline Alchian, Dean William Meckling, and Professors Wytze Gorter, Harold Demsetz, and Jack Hirshleifer for their assistance in
the preparation of this introduction.

Special thanks are also due to Professor Daniel K. Benjamin of the University of Washington, who selected the essays included in this volume.

# PRINCIPLES OF PROFESSIONAL ADVANCEMENT

You've finished your Ph.D. ordeal, and luckily you're now in your first year as a real member of the faculty. The expected relief from the burden of completing the dissertation is quickly replaced by the burden of publishing. But then you realize it's the same pressure again. You've already extracted what little there might have been in the dissertation. What can you do next, something really on your own?

You may not know now, but in a few decades, predictably, you'll have more than you can complete. Unfortunately, by then you'll have less desire to publish. The capital value of another publication will have become pretty small. So you'll find yourself passing ideas to, and encouraging, the younger members of the department, wondering if they'll be so fortunate as you were in early publishing an article that really helped your career.

These reflections by an older, retired, out-of-date person—one who has succeeded far above the "expected value" of entrants to the profession—are a sort of confession of "How I did it." Or more honestly, maybe, "How it was done to me!" Perhaps it will inspire hope in new entrants, particularly with respect to publications.

I emphasize that the opening part of this essay is not entirely a conjectural story. It's mine, with a couple of minor exceptions. I'll confine my major comments to three papers I wrote some time ago, and with which I remain pleased today (for reasons I'll explain). I hope the comments will be of some interest to economists, especially in those moments when everything seems a bit confused, though not hopeless. I won't resist the temptation to reminisce and pontificate, the privilege of the emeriti.

## Background

Although I was officially awarded the Ph.D. in 1944, while in the United States Air Force, I actually had finished my doctoral work by 1942, just before entry into the military. My dissertation was on the presumed effects of a gen-

Reprinted from *Economic Inquiry* 34 (July 1996): 520–26, by permission of Western Economic Association International.

eral cut in wage rates across the economy. Like most dissertations, it should have been addressed to my supervisors with the label "For Your Eyes Only" and then forgotten—as mine properly has been. It had nothing to do with my subsequent work, happily. But the USAF engagement meant that between the dissertation and the first academic job there were several years in the military, with time to wonder what the point was in being what is called an "economist."

Fortunately, I had a major sub-discipline as required in the 1930s: statistics. I had learned a few things about inference, probability, random walks, and stochastic, evolutionary processes. I learned them from a few extraordinary teachers, among them Allen Wallis, Edward Shaw, and Holbrook Working. And during military service I got to use what I had learned. At the USAF Training Command from 1942 to 1945, I did statistical evaluation of the validity of entry-level test scores of Air Force cadets, for their training as pilots, navigators, or bombardiers.

### Principle of Professional Advancement No. 1

Upon return to civilian life in 1946 in my new teaching job at UCLA, I again started to read the journals in economics with my superb graduate students (the majority of them relatively mature ex-military men in their mid-twenties). In that way I began to relearn economics. For economists, Principle of Professional Advancement No. 1 is, "Have super students!" The value of good students is evidenced by publications. All three of the articles I will discuss below were developed during classroom exposition and discussion with my students.

### "Uncertainty, Evolution and Economic Theory"[1]

In my early years of teaching, a pair of confrontational articles by a Professor Richard Lester and a Professor Fritz Machlup, published in the leading journal, the *American Economic Review*, were dutifully studied with disappointment and distress. Current readers will be astonished to know that the debate was about whether business people "really" used marginal productivity and profit-maximization analysis in making decisions! Lester said "no"; Machlup said "yes." Of course, both were right and both were wrong, but their reasoning and defenses were easily demolished by each other.

If that was the quality of analysis passing for economics, I should have

---

1. Armen A. Alchian, "Uncertainty, Evolution and Economic Theory," *Journal of Political Economy* (June 1950): 211–21.

stayed in the military I thought. So, one day in class I explained what I had read. Then a bit testily, I complained about the quality of the articles, all in the privacy of the classroom. I then explained what I thought the two economists should have said. They should have said, "Read Darwin! It's not what you think you are doing or how you rationalize your choice of that action. It's whether the action has survival value. And if outside analysts can identify the reasons the chosen action had survival value, and in what direction changes in the environment (constraints) affect survival conditions, economists don't have to worry about how people discover by thought or luck what are the new best conditions. Competitive trial and error will evolve toward the fittest—whom economists characterize as profit maximizers."

Word of my comments passed to my colleague Professor Stephen Enke, as sensible and practical an economist as you would ever want to know. He remarked that the comments would make a publishable article. I scoffed that it was all too obvious and trivial, and appropriate only for a class lecture, not as a publishable article. He nevertheless urged me to write it at least for future classroom handouts.

I did. He read it, and liked it enough to demand that I send it to a journal. I didn't know of one minor enough to warrant a chance for publication. He persevered, saying I should not send it to the AER, where the original two had been published. Instead, he brazenly suggested and insisted that I send it to the *Journal of Political Economy*.

To my genuine surprise, a very encouraging letter was quickly (by current standards) received from a Professor Milton Friedman, of whom I had heard. The paper would be published if a few suggested extrapolations and minor modifications were made. The article quickly appeared. It was my first article.[2] I proudly fondled the issue and sent reprints to close friends, expecting they might respond by saying "Thanks, I'll read it sometime soon." I could not at that time believe that evolutionary competitive principles were so forgotten or ignored.

## Principle of Professional Advancement No. 2

I have since begun to realize that I was exceptionally fortunate to have had a father who thrust my nose into Darwin's *Origins* when I was in high school. Then, in college, I had a course in biology which was all Darwin and evolution.

---

2. I had published a small, minor comment in the *Journal of the American Statistics Association* on someone else's paper.

Finally, at the graduate level, I was fortunate to have worked with Professor Wallis, who introduced me to R. A. Fisher's *Statistical Methods for Biological Research*, and to have studied with Professor Working, whose chief interest was random walks in wheat futures prices. With that training, evolutionary interpretations were virtually genetic. So Principle No. 2 is, "To advance your career, you have to be smart enough to have had the right teachers."

### Principle of Professional Advancement No. 3

That's also how, by great foresight and research, you can be at the right place at the right time. The article on evolution and economics happened to appear at a time of reviving interest in, and a more rigorous formulation of, the evolutionary processes. That the approach helps relieve economists from squirming and hedging in futile attempts to assess what business people were "really doing" was probably a reason why the article was so well received and why it has remained a relatively well-cited paper. Principle of Professional Advancement No. 3 is, "Plan to be at the place where your training happens to be useful—at the right time."

I'm still astonished at the success of the article on evolution and economics. As I look back—the privilege granted to those who survive for a long time—I see that the idea had an enormous effect. But not because of the article I wrote. It was because of the idea itself, taken from Darwin. I just happened to be the person who brought the news to economics, as a middleman brings goods from manufacturers to consumers. If I hadn't done it, many others would have.

I would regard the article as having contributed to a major revision in the science if there had followed a strong interest and research in the genetics of economic behavior. For example, while economists treat the "individual" as the unit of analysis, a more general and (I conjecture) more powerful analysis of economic behavior can be founded on "genes" as the unit of analysis or, more exactly, as the competing units. Certainly the convex preference map is a convex survival map, mapping points of equal survival probability. Is it not true that all forms of life have indifference survival curves that are convex, etc.? Using a biological approach—economics is a life science!—economists would look at competition beyond the benevolent type.

Jack Hirshleifer's recent work is an example of this thrust into ignored economic behavior. Someplace in my 1950 article on evolution (or perhaps elsewhere), I argued that biology and economics ultimately would merge. My colleague Professor Hirshleifer now appears to be manipulating a takeover of the one by the other.

## "Costs and Outputs"[3]

My ability to apply Principle of Professional Advancement No. 3—being at the right place at the right time—was illustrated by my decision to join UCLA, close to where the RAND Corporation would later be created. RAND would (at the instigation of Allen Wallis) invite me to be their first resident consulting economist. I happened to join the UCLA faculty in 1946; it happened that RAND was set up in Santa Monica in 1945. Allen happened to know General "Hap" Arnold well. So it was all happenstance—like the birdies I make in golf.

RAND was not sure what an economist would do. I certainly didn't know either. But I learned a lot about "big real world problems"—too big to comprehend, usually. Since it wasn't clear at first what an economist could do that was pertinent, the task was to snoop around, look at the problems being analyzed (defense problems, usually), and try to see how economics could help.

What we economists did first was detect how economics was being ignored, in particular how costs and interest rates were ignored in making military-strategy decisions. Another "complicated, surprising" proposition was that for assigning nuclear material to the Air Force versus the Navy, it was not deemed necessary to know whether it was more important for the Navy or the Air Force to have more fissile material. But of course, that would be very desirable to know. With the idea of indifference curves between nuclear material and labor (as inputs), marginal rates of substitution between the two in the Navy and also in the Air Force would indicate directions in which to revise the allocations. That "revelation" gave the economics group some extra clout.

I cite these as two examples of how the simplest concepts and propositions in economics have megaton power. In that vein, I like to brag that I did the first "event study" in corporate finance, back in the 1950s and 1960s. The year before the H-bomb was successfully created, we in the economics division at RAND were curious as to what the essential metal was—lithium, beryllium, thorium, or some other. The engineers and physicists wouldn't tell us economists, quite properly, given the security restrictions. So I told them I would find out. I read the U.S. Department of Commerce Year Book to see which firms made which of the possible ingredients. For the last six months of the year prior to the successful test of the bomb, I traced the stock prices of those firms. I used no inside information. Lo and behold! *One* firm's stock prices rose, as

3. Armen A. Alchian, "Costs and Outputs," in *The Allocation of Economic Resources*, ed. M. Abramovitz et al. (Palo Alto: Stanford University Press, 1959), 23–40.

best I can recall, from about $2 or $3 per share in August to about $13 per share in December. It was the Lithium Corp. of America. In January, I wrote and circulated within RAND a memorandum titled "The Stock Market Speaks." Two days later I was told to withdraw it. The bomb was tested successfully in February, and thereafter the stock price stabilized.

In the economics division I was working with Stephen Enke, under the strong support and leadership of Charles Hitch.[4] One thing we discovered was that engineers didn't quite understand why "cost" had something to do with a choice of armaments. To help them learn how and why costs and things like interest rates weren't just financial shenanigans, we collected cost data on production and operations of airplanes. I quickly noticed that the production engineers kept saying marginal costs decreased and continued to decrease, lower and lower. To the contrary, as every economist knew, marginal costs begin to rise at some stage. And our textbook diagrams and cost theory proved it.

So what mistake were the engineers making? After too long a time, with embarrassment, I discovered that "output" meant something entirely different to production engineers than it appeared to mean to economists. Output to engineers was measured in units of accumulated total output, not in rate of output. Simple, but spectacularly different. Yet, not a single economics textbook, advanced or elementary, mentioned that. In fact most of the time the texts left unclear what was meant by "amount of output." The engineers were explicitly clear—it was the accumulated number of units produced, with nothing whatever about the rate of production of that aggregated volume of output. Economists, judging by the relations posited to exist with "output," had, if anything, the "rate of output" in mind, unconscious of the importance of the difference between rate and volume of produced output.

Which group was correct? It was a draw. The engineers were right in that marginal costs of volume decreased with volume; economists still could be

4. As a Rhodes scholar, Charles Hitch had been a friend of John Williams, the chief of the division at RAND in which the mathematicians were located, and where I was placed for lack of knowing what an economist could do. Williams invited Hitch to Santa Monica for a month on the beach, which fortunately helped to persuade Hitch to be the head of an economics division. In addition to myself and Hitch, the economics division included my UCLA colleague Roland McKean, who co-authored a book with Hitch based on some of the work being done at RAND. (Charles J. Hitch and Roland N. McKean, *The Economics of Defense in the Nuclear Age* [New York: Atheneum, 1960].)

allowed to presume marginal costs of increased speed of output were rising. But the economists were obviously right more generally in emphasizing costs in the choice of alternative weaponry. And in measuring cost, it was capital value, the present value of a stream of future activities, that was pertinent, not just the initial year's flow of "cost."

The important points were, first, that investment decisions for output involved contemplated total amount, or volume, as well as the rate. Second, the cost had to be in terms of capital values—the present value of the contemplated outlay in the future. By confining one's thoughts to rates of output, the capital value measure was hidden, resulting in overly narrow attention on variable, fixed, and marginal costs of changes in the rate of output. I thought that was important. At least it matched the procedure being initiated in the Kennedy administration's five-year military costing conception.

I was allowed to summarize the situation in some memoranda on learning and "progress curves," as the engineers dubbed the cost-output relations.[5] A summary of implications was written, called "Costs and Outputs," which was accepted for publication in the *American Economic Review*. But then I was asked instead to include it in a collection of papers being prepared by Moses Abramovitz and others in honor of their Stanford colleague—and my old teacher—Professor Bernard Haley. I declined the invitation to publish "Costs and Outputs" in the AER in favor of the Haley festschrift. I regret that it did not get into the AER where more people would have seen it. But I don't regret having had that opportunity to express appreciation for the help Professor Haley gave me while I was a student at Stanford.

The paper—henceforth a festschrift book chapter—has been reprinted several times.[6] Still, the paper seems to have had no effect on anything. After all, who bothers to read festschrifts? No texts, so far as I could discover, were changed in any way to avoid the confusions in the meanings and measures of output and of the pertinent measure of cost. I was disappointed. Why were the implications ignored?

A possible answer soon dawned. If capital value concepts of cost and ag-

---

5. That work also led to my writing an article on the reliability of progress curves in airframe production ("The Reliability of Progress Curves in Airframe Production," *Econometrica* [October 1963]: 679–93).

6. For example, in *Readings in Microeconomics*, 2nd ed., ed. William Breit and Harold M. Hochman (New York: Holt, Rinehart and Winston, 1971).

gregate output were on the supply side, should something not appear on the demand side to make the analysis compatible? Demand was conventionally viewed as a rate of demand, not as an aggregated total volume. Until modified, the demand-and-supply analysis would continue to limp along on one foot.

But an article appearing recently in *Economic Inquiry* asked and answered the question of why firms persist in intentional mispricing, that is, in keeping prices too low when demand increases transiently.[7] Why are shortages and rationing deliberately chosen over a more profitable, higher, market-clearing price? And which customers are favored? The basis of the answer, when stripped of all surrounding detail, is, I believe, that demand and price must be viewed not simply one-dimensionally as the current rate, but as the anticipated aggregated volume. More precisely, price is not just the current dollar price for a unit now, but is the anticipated capital value of all future business from the customer. For example, which is a greater demand: (a) a rate of 1000 a day lasting one week, or (b) a rate of 100 a day lasting a year? The rate over time is certainly an important dimension of the demand vector. More attention is paid to that vector of "demand price" than to the current flow price. This is especially important for items like CD disks, computers, computer programs, and drugs, where marginal costs of extra units of volume are very small compared to the total cost of development.

If I were a young assistant professor today, there's no doubt as to what puzzles and issues I'd tackle. There is much more work to be done in tying the volume-demand effect to the stochastic nature of demand. Applications of such models to a wide range of pricing problems will be very fruitful, I believe; Art De Vany is doing such work with theatrical exhibitions and pricing. The "zero" marginal cost of extra units of things like software, drugs, and patented ideas likewise poses interesting pricing and contractual problems.[8]

7. David D. Haddock and Fred S. McChesney, "Why Do Firms Contrive Shortages? The Economics of Intentional Mispricing," *Economic Inquiry* (October 1994): 562–81. In essence, Haddock and McChesney argue that once demand is viewed more broadly, in more dimensions of "size," the implied market-clearing competitive pricing concept is altered. What appears to be irrational, inefficient pricing is seen to be economically efficient.

8. The biological-genetic work mentioned above is also of great interest, although this area is too technical for many people trained as economists.

## "Information Costs, Pricing and Resource Unemployment"[9]

Perhaps mistakenly, I like to regard this paper as my best. It posed the simple question, why is there unemployment? In attempting to answer the question, the article owes its genesis to a casual comment by George Stigler one day during a round of golf.[10] That particular day, I inquired of George, "Economists don't have an explanation of unemployment. Why does it occur?" Stigler, a man who could recognize a serious question even when trying to extricate himself from a bunker, responded, "Did you ever think of the reasons for, and costs of, search?"

That showed I knew how to apply Principle No. 2: have the right teachers. As with the article on evolution and economics, the paper sparked by George's comment was at first intended as an exposition just for my own information and understanding. It ultimately appeared in *Economic Inquiry* (then the *Western Economic Journal*) while Professor Harold Somers was editor.[11]

I stated above that I think this paper my best. It tackles a clearly important problem, one on which I had seen much nonsense—and still do. It was an attempt to put in plain English what economists know about things like search, and to dispose of explanations based on "monopoly," "price rigidities," "unions," and so forth. Because the exposition was simple but the ideas themselves powerful, the paper has had wide readership.

9. Armen A. Alchian, "Information Costs, Pricing and Resource Unemployment," *Western Economic Journal* (June 1969): 109–28.

10. George was an avid golfer. He lived next to Flossmoor Country Club, where I was lucky enough to play with him a couple of times. I also visited George at his summer home on Lake Muskoka in Canada, where we boated across the lake to alternate golf courses. And we played a few holes at Princeton (where I first met George at a conference), with Milton Friedman as our caddy.

It is unclear whether golf and economics are complements or substitutes. Bob Crawford and I used to talk a lot about economics as we were developing our ideas about opportunistic behavior (Benjamin Klein, Robert G. Crawford, and Armen A. Alchian, "Vertical Integration, Appropriable Rents, and the Competitive Contracting Process," *Journal of Law and Economics* [October 1978]: 297–326), but bad golf was sometimes the result.

11. Somers, retired from the UCLA economics department and my current officemate, is also the man who brought Ronald Coase from England to Buffalo.

## Principles of Professional Advancement Nos. 4 and 5

Two more Principles of Professional Advancement remain. Principle No. 4 is, "Make frequent use of co-authors." They keep you on the "straight and narrow." If you can survive as friends after a joint paper, you are doubly lucky. It has been a boon to me to have co-authors like Robert Crawford, Harold Demsetz, Reuben Kessel, Benjamin Klein, Roland McKean, William Meckling, and Susan Woodward. (I hope I have not forgotten any.) Oh, I also have a William Allen as co-author of a textbook that was forty years ahead of its time, in which he claims I wrote all the odd words while he wrote the even ones.[12]

I'm not going to comment on how the jointly-authored articles were initiated and co-authored. The co-authors would have to co-author any current recollections. But a common theme has been the structure and role of types of property rights. All the persons mentioned have remained good friends to this day, except that Kessel and McKean, most sadly, died far too early. I want to seize this rare opportunity to pay tribute to Reuben Kessel, whom I met at RAND, and with whom I worked most intensively. He was a natural-born economist, and he was *Homo economicus*. My error rate in economics diminished rapidly after a few years of friendship with him, and my horizon of understandable events widened.

Finally, and in that vein, be sure you have helpful, smart colleagues, ones who are willing to spend hours trying to demolish your argument while trying to help you reach a better understanding, or suggesting ideas for you. I followed that advice. Fortune favored me not only with excellent graduate students and co-authors, but also with other colleagues who are superb economists. Of course, although it's not publicized, colleagues who aren't co-authors with you often contribute more to your career than co-authors. Being smart enough to have cooperative colleagues like that is not just luck. I was deeply involved in recruiting for the department. So in closing, I commend Principle No. 5, "Have superb and cooperative colleagues."

12. Armen A. Alchian and William R. Allen, *University Economics: Elements of Inquiry*, 3rd ed. (Belmont, Calif.: Wadsworth, 1972).

# 1

## UNCERTAINTY AND
## INFORMATION COSTS

# UNCERTAINTY, EVOLUTION
# AND ECONOMIC THEORY[1]

A modification of economic analysis to incorporate incomplete information and uncertain foresight as axioms is suggested here. This approach dispenses with "profit maximization"; and it does not rely on the predictable, individual behavior that is usually assumed, as a first approximation, in standard textbook treatments. Despite these changes, the analytical concepts usually associated with such behavior are retained because they are not dependent upon such motivation or foresight. The suggested approach embodies the principles of biological evolution and natural selection by interpreting the economic system as an adoptive mechanism which chooses among exploratory actions generated by the adaptive pursuit of "success" or "profits." The resulting analysis is applicable to actions usually regarded as aberrations from standard economic behavior as well as to behavior covered by the customary analysis. This wider applicability and the removal of the unrealistic postulates of accurate anticipations and fixed states of knowledge have provided motivation for the study.

The exposition is ordered as follows: First, to clear the ground, a brief statement is given of a generally ignored aspect of "profit maximization"; that is, where foresight is uncertain, "profit maximization" is *meaningless* as a guide to specifiable action. The constructive development then begins with an introduction of the element of environmental adoption by the economic system of the *a posteriori* most appropriate action according to the criterion of "realized positive profits." This is illustrated in an extreme, random-behavior model without any individual rationality, foresight, or motivation whatsoever. Even in this extreme type of model, it is shown that the economist can predict and explain events with a modified use of his conventional analytical tools.

This phenomenon—environmental adoption—is then fused with a type of

Reprinted from Armen A. Alchian, *Economic Forces at Work* (Indianapolis: Liberty Fund, 1977), 15–35. This article was previously published in *Journal of Political Economy* 58 (June 1950): 211–21.

1. I am indebted to Dr. Stephen Enke for criticism and stimulation leading to improvements in both content and exposition.

individually motivated behavior based on the pervasiveness of uncertainty and incomplete information. Adaptive, imitative, and trial-and-error behavior in the pursuit of "positive profits" is utilized rather than its sharp contrast, the pursuit of "maximized profits." A final section discusses some implications and conjectures.

## I. "Profit Maximization" Not a Guide to Action

Current economic analysis of economic behavior relies heavily on decisions made by rational units customarily assumed to be seeking perfectly optimal situations.[2] Two criteria are well known—profit maximization and utility maximization.[3] According to these criteria, appropriate types of action are indicated by marginal or neighborhood inequalities which, if satisfied, yield an optimum. But the standard qualification usually added is that nobody is able really to optimize his situation according to these diagrams and concepts because of uncertainty about the position and, sometimes, even the slopes of the demand and supply functions. Nevertheless, the economist interprets and predicts the decisions of individuals in terms of these diagrams, since it is alleged that individuals use these concepts implicitly, if not explicitly.

Attacks on this methodology are widespread, but only one attack has been really damaging, that of G. Tintner.[4] He denies that profit maximization even makes any sense where there is uncertainty. Uncertainty arises from at least two sources: imperfect foresight and human inability to solve complex problems containing a host of variables even when an optimum is definable. Tintner's proof is simple. Under uncertainty, by definition, each action that may be chosen is identified with a *distribution* of potential outcomes, not with a unique outcome. Implicit in uncertainty is the consequence that these distributions of

---

2. See, e.g., J. Robinson, *Economics of Imperfect Competition* (London, Macmillan, 1933), p. 6, for a strong statement of the necessity of such optimal behavior. Standard textbooks expound essentially the same idea. See also P. Samuelson, *Foundations of Economic Analysis* (Cambridge: Harvard University Press, 1946).

3. In the following we shall discuss only profit maximization, although everything said is applicable equally to utility maximization by consumers.

4. "The Theory of Choice under Subjective Risk and Uncertainty," *Econometrica* 9 (1941): 298–304; "The Pure Theory of Production under Technological Risk and Uncertainty," ibid., pp. 305–11; and "A Contribution to the Nonstatic Theory of Production," *Studies in Mathematical Economics and Econometrics* (Chicago: University of Chicago Press, 1942), pp. 92–109.

potential outcomes are overlapping.[5] It is worth emphasis that each possible action has a *distribution* of potential outcomes, only one of which will materialize if the action is taken, and that one outcome cannot be foreseen. Essentially, the task is converted into making a decision (selecting an action) whose potential outcome *distribution* is preferable, that is, choosing the action with the *optimum distribution*, since there is no such thing as a *maximizing* distribution.

For example, let each of two possible choices be characterized by its subjective distribution of potential outcomes. Suppose one has the higher "mean" but a larger spread, so that it might result in larger profits or losses, and the other has a smaller "mean" and a smaller spread. Which one is the maximum? This is a nonsensical question; but to ask for the optimum distribution is not nonsense. In the presence of uncertainty—a necessary condition for the existence of profits—there is no meaningful criterion for selecting the decision that will "maximize profits." The maximum-profit criterion is not meaningful as a basis *for selecting* the action which will, in fact, result in an outcome with higher profits than any other action would have, unless one assumes nonoverlapping potential outcome distributions. It must be noticed that the meaningfulness of "maximum profits"—a realized outcome which is the largest that could have been realized from the available actions—is perfectly consistent with the meaninglessness of "profit maximization"—a criterion for selecting among alternative lines of action, the potential outcomes of which are describable only as distributions and not as unique amounts.

This crucial difficulty would be avoided by using a preference function as a criterion for selecting most preferred distributions of potential outcomes, but the search for a criterion of rationality and choice in terms of preference functions still continues. For example, the use of the mean, or expectation, completely begs the question of uncertainty by disregarding the variance of the distribution, while a "certainty equivalent" assumes the answer. The only way to make "profit maximization" a specifically meaningful action is to postulate a model containing certainty. Then the question of the predictive and explanatory reliability of the model must be faced.[6]

---

5. Thus uncertainty is defined here to be the phenomenon that produces overlapping distributions of potential outcomes.

6. Analytical models in all sciences postulate models abstracting from some realities in the belief that derived predictions will still be relevant. Simplifications are necessary, but continued attempts should be made to introduce more realistic assumptions into a workable model with an increase in generality and detail (see M. Friedman and L. Savage,

## II. Success Is Based on Results, Not Motivation

There is an alternative method which treats the decisions and criteria dictated by the economic *system* as more important than those made by the individuals in it. By backing away from the trees—the optimization calculus by individual units—we can better discern the forest of impersonal market forces.[7] This approach directs attention to the interrelationships of the environment and the prevailing types of economic behavior which appear through a process of economic natural selection. Yet it does not imply that individual foresight and action do not affect the nature of the existing state of affairs.

In an economic system the realization of profits is the criterion according to which successful and surviving firms are selected. This decision criterion is applied primarily by an impersonal market system in the United States and may be completely independent of the decision processes of individual units, of the variety of inconsistent motives and abilities, and even of the individual's awareness of the criterion. The reason is simple. Realized positive profits, not *maximum* profits, are the mark of success and viability. It does not matter through what process of reasoning or motivation such success was achieved. The fact of its accomplishment is sufficient. This is the criterion by which the economic system selects survivors: those who realize *positive profits* are the survivors; those who suffer losses disappear.

The pertinent requirement—positive profits through relative efficiency—is weaker than "maximized profits," with which, unfortunately, it has been confused. Positive profits accrue to those who are better than their actual competitors, even if the participants are ignorant, intelligent, skillful, etc. The crucial element is one's aggregate position relative to actual competitors, not some hypothetically perfect competitors. As in a race, the award goes to the relatively fastest, even if all the competitors loaf. Even in a world of stupid men there would still be profits. Also, the greater the uncertainties of the world, the greater is the possibility that profits would go to venturesome and lucky rather than to logical, careful, fact-gathering individuals.

The preceding interpretation suggests two ideas. First, success (survival)

---

"The Utility Analysis of Choices Involving Risks," *Journal of Political Economy* 56, no. 4 [1948]: 279).

7. In effect, we shall be reverting to a Marshallian type of analysis combined with the essentials of Darwinian evolutionary natural selection.

accompanies relative superiority; and, second, it does not require proper motivation but may rather be the result of fortuitous circumstances. Among all competitors, those whose particular conditions happen to be the most appropriate of those offered to the economic system for testing and adoption will be "selected" as survivors. Just how such an approach can be used and how individuals happen to offer these appropriate forms for testing are problems to which we now turn.[8]

### III. Chance or Luck Is One Method of Achieving Success

Sheer chance is a substantial element in determining the situation selected and also in determining its appropriateness or viability. A second element is the ability to adapt one's self by various methods to an appropriate situation. In order to indicate clearly the respective roles of luck and conscious adapting, the adaptive calculus will, for the moment, be completely removed. All individual rationality, motivation, and foresight will be temporarily abandoned in order to concentrate upon the ability of the environment to *adopt* "appropriate" survivors even in the absence of any adaptive behavior. This is an apparently unrealistic, but nevertheless very useful, expository approach in establishing the attenuation between the ex-post survival criterion and the role of the individual's adaptive decision criterion. It also aids in assessing the role of luck and chance in the operation of our economic system.

Consider, first, the simplest type of biological evolution. Plants "grow" to the sunny side of buildings not because they "want to" in awareness of the fact that optimum or better conditions prevail there, but rather because the leaves that happen to have more sunlight grow faster and their feeding systems become stronger. Similarly, animals with configurations and habits more appropriate for survival under prevailing conditions have an enhanced viability and will with higher probability be typical survivors. Less appropriately acting organisms of the same general class having lower probabilities of survival will find survival difficult. More common types, the survivors, may appear to be

---

8. Also suggested is another way to divide the general problem discussed here. The process and rationale by which a unit chooses its actions so as to optimize its situation is one part of the problem. The other is the relationship between changes in the environment and the consequent observable results, i.e., the decision process of the economic *society*. The classification used in the text is closely related to this but differs in emphasizing the degree of knowledge and foresight.

those having *adapted* themselves to the environment, whereas the truth may well be that the environment has *adopted* them. There may have been no motivated individual adapting but, instead, only environmental adopting.

A useful, but unreal, example in which individuals act without any foresight indicates the type of analysis available to the economist and also the ability of the system to "direct" resources despite individual ignorance. Assume that thousands of travelers set out from Chicago, selecting their roads completely at random and without foresight. Only our "economist" knows that on but one road are there any gasoline stations. He can state categorically that travelers will *continue* to travel only on that road; those on other roads will soon run out of gas. Even though each one selected his route at random, we might have called those travelers who were so fortunate as to have picked the right road wise, efficient, foresighted, etc. Of course, we would consider them the lucky ones. If gasoline supplies were now moved to a new road, some formerly luckless travelers again would be able to move; and a new pattern of travel would be observed, although none of the travelers had changed his particular path. The really possible paths have changed with the changing environment. All that is needed is a set of varied, risk-taking (adoptable) travelers. The correct direction of travel will be established. As circumstances (economic environment) change, the analyst (economist) can select the types of participants (firms) that will now become successful; he may also be able to diagnose the conditions most conducive to a greater probability of survival.[9]

### IV.   Chance Does Not Imply Nondirected, Random Allocation of Resources

These two examples do not constitute an attempt to base all analysis on adoptive models dominated by chance. But they do indicate that collective and individual random behavior does not per se imply a nihilistic theory incapable of yielding reliable predictions and explanations; nor does it imply a world lacking in order and apparent direction. It might, however, be argued that the facts of life deny even a substantial role to the element of chance and the associated adoption principle in the economic system. For example, the long lives

---

9. The undiscerning person who sees survivors corresponding to changes in environment claims to have evidence for the "Lysenko" doctrine. In truth, all he may have is evidence for the doctrine that the environment, by competitive conditions, selects the most viable of the various phenotypic characteristics for perpetuation. Economists should beware of economic "Lysenkoism."

and disparate sizes of business firms and hereditary fortunes may seem to be reliable evidence of consistent foresighted motivation and nonrandom behavior. In order to demonstrate that consistent success cannot be treated as prima facie evidence against pure luck, the following chance model of Borel, the famous French mathematician, is presented.

Suppose two million Parisians were paired off and set to tossing coins in a game of matching. Each pair plays until the winner on the first toss is again brought to equality with the other player. Assuming one toss per second for each eight-hour day, at the end of ten years there would still be, on the average, about a hundred-odd pairs; and if the players assign the game to their heirs, a dozen or so will still be playing at the end of a thousand years! The implications are obvious. Suppose that some business had been operating for one hundred years. Should one rule out luck and chance as the essence of the factors producing the long-term survival of the enterprise? No inference whatever can be drawn until the number of original participants is known; and even then one must know the size, risk, and frequency of each commitment. One can see from the Borel illustration the danger in concluding that there are too many firms with long lives in the real world to admit an important role to chance. On the contrary, one might insist that there are actually too few!

The chance postulate was directed to two problems. On the one hand, there is the actual way in which a substantial fraction of economic behavior and activity is effected. On the other, there is the method of analysis which economists may use in their predictions and diagnoses. Before modifying the extreme chance model by adding adaptive behavior, some connotations and implications of the incorporation of chance elements will be elaborated in order to reveal the richness which is really inherent in chance. First, even if each and every individual acted in a haphazard and nonmotivated manner, it is possible that the variety of actions would be so great that the resulting collective set would contain actions that are best, in the sense of perfect foresight. For example, at a horse race with enough bettors wagering strictly at random, someone will win on all eight races. Thus individual random behavior does not eliminate the likelihood of observing "appropriate" decisions.[10]

Second, and conversely, individual behavior according to some foresight and motivation does not necessarily imply a collective pattern of behavior that is different from the collective variety of actions associated with a random selection of actions. Where there is uncertainty, people's judgments and opin-

10. The Borel gamblers analogue is pertinent to a host of everyday situations.

ions, even when based on the best available evidence, will differ; no one of them may be making his choice by tossing coins; yet the aggregate *set* of actions of the entire group of participants may be indistinguishable from a set of individual actions, each selected at random.[11]

Third, and fortunately, a chance-dominated model does not mean that an economist cannot predict or explain or diagnose. With a knowledge of the economy's realized requisites for survival and by a comparison of alternative conditions, he can state what types of firms or behavior relative to other possible types will be more viable, even though the firms themselves may not know the conditions or even try to achieve them by readjusting to the changed situation if they do know the conditions. It is sufficient if all firms are slightly different so that in the new environmental situation those who have their fixed internal conditions closer to the new, but unknown, optimum position now have a greater probability of survival and growth. They will grow relative to other firms and become the prevailing type, since survival conditions may push the observed characteristics of the set of survivors toward the unknowable optimum by either (1) repeated trials or (2) survival of more of those who happened to be near the optimum—determined ex post. If these new conditions last "very long," the dominant firms will be different ones from those which prevailed or would have prevailed under other conditions. Even if environmental conditions cannot be forecast, the economist can compare for given alternative potential situations the types of behavior that would have higher probability of viability or adoption. If explanation of past results rather than prediction is the task, the economist can diagnose the particular attributes which were critical in facilitating survival, even though individual participants were not aware of them.[12]

11. Of course, the economic units may be going through a period of soul searching, management training, and research activity. We cannot yet identify mental and physical activity with a process that results in sufficient information and foresight to yield uniquely determinate choices. To do so would be to beg the whole question.

12. It is not even necessary to suppose that each firm acts as if it possessed the conventional diagrams and knew the analytical principles employed by economists in deriving optimum and equilibrium conditions. The atoms and electrons do not know the laws of nature; the physicist does not impart to each atom a willful scheme of action based on laws of conservation of energy, etc. The fact that an economist deals with human beings who have sense and ambitions does not *automatically* warrant imparting to these humans the great degree of foresight and motivations which the economist may require for his customary analysis as an outside observer or "oracle." The similarity between this argu-

Fourth, the bases of prediction have been indicated in the preceding paragraph, but its character should be made explicit. The prediction will not assert that every—or, indeed, any—firm necessarily changes its characteristics. It asserts, instead, that the characteristics of the new *set* of firms, or possibly a set of new firms, will change. This may be characterized by the "representative firm," a purely statistical concept—a vector of "averages," one dimension for each of the several qualities of the population of firms. A "representative firm" is not typical of any one producer but, instead, is a set of statistics summarizing the various "modal" characteristics of the population. Surely, this was an intended use of Marshall's "representative firm."

Fifth, a final implication drawn from consideration of this extreme approach is that empirical investigations via questionnaire methods, so far used, are incapable of evaluating the validity of marginal productivity analysis. This is true because productivity and demand analyses are essential in evaluating relative viability, even though uncertainty eliminates "profit maximization" and even if price and technological changes were to have no consciously redirecting effect on the firms. To illustrate, suppose that, in attempting to predict the effects of higher real wage rates, it is discovered that every businessman says he does not adjust his labor force. Nevertheless, firms with a lower labor-capital ratio will have relatively lower cost positions and, to that extent, a higher probability of survival. The force of competitive survival, by eliminating higher-cost firms, reveals a population of remaining firms with a new average labor-capital ratio. The essential point is that individual motivation and foresight, while sufficient, are not necessary. Of course, it is not argued here that therefore it is absent. All that is needed by economists is their own awareness of the survival conditions and criteria of the economic system and a group of participants who submit various combinations and organizations for the system's selection and adoption. Both these conditions are satisfied.[13]

As a consequence, only the method of use, rather than the usefulness, of economic tools and concepts is affected by the approach suggested here; in fact, they are made more powerful if they are not pretentiously assumed to be necessarily associated with, and dependent upon, individual foresight and adjustment. They are tools for, at least, the diagnosis of the operation of an

---

ment and Gibbsian statistical mechanics, as well as biological evolution, is *not* mere coincidence.

13. This approach reveals how the "facts" of Lester's dispute with Machlup can be handled with standard economic tools.

economic system, even if not also for the internal business behavior of each firm.

## v. Individual Adapting via Imitation and Trial and Error

Let it again be noted that the preceding extreme model was designed to present in purest form only one element of the suggested approach. It is not argued that there is no purposive, foresighted behavior present in reality. In adding this realistic element—adaptation by individuals with some foresight and purposive motivation—we are expanding the preceding extreme model. We are not abandoning any part of it or futilely trying to merge it with the opposite extreme of perfect foresight and "profit maximization."

Varying and conflicting objectives motivate economic activity, yet we shall here direct attention to only one particular objective—the sufficient condition of realized positive profits. There are no implications of "profit maximization," and this difference is important. Although the latter is a far more extreme objective when definable, only the former is the sine qua non of survival and success. To argue that with perfect competition the two would come to the same thing is to conceal an important difference by means of a very implausible assumption. The pursuit of profits, and not some hypothetical and undefinable perfect situation, is the relevant objective whose *fulfillment* is rewarded with survival. Unfortunately, even this proximate objective is too high. Neither perfect knowledge of the past nor complete awareness of the current state of the arts gives sufficient foresight to indicate profitable action. Even for this more restricted objective, the pervasive effects of uncertainty prevent the ascertainment of actions which are supposed to be optimal in achieving profits. Now the consequence of this is that modes of behavior replace optimum equilibrium conditions as guiding rules of action. Therefore, in the following sections, two forms of conscious adaptive behavior are emphasized.

First, wherever successful enterprises are observed, the elements common to these observable successes will be associated with success and copied by others in their pursuit of profits or success. "Nothing succeeds like success." Thus the urge for "rough-and-ready" imitative rules of behavior is accounted for. What would otherwise appear to be merely customary "orthodox," nonrational rules of behavior turns out to be codified imitations of observed success, e.g., "conventional" markup, price "followship," "orthodox" accounting and operating ratios, "proper" advertising policy. A conventionally employed type of behavior pattern is consistent with the postulates of the analysis employed, even though the reasons and justifications for the particular conventions are not.[14]

Many factors cause this motive to imitate patterns of action observable in past successes. Among these are: (1) the absence of an identifiable criterion for decision making, (2) the variability of the environment, (3) the multiplicity of factors that call for attention and choice, (4) the uncertainty attaching to all these factors and outcomes, (5) the awareness that superiority relative to one's competitors is crucial, and (6) the nonavailability of a trial-and-error process converging to an optimum position.

In addition, imitation affords relief from the necessity of really making decisions and conscious innovations, which, if wrong, become "inexcusable." Unfortunately, failure or success often reflects the willingness to depart from rules when conditions have changed; what counts, then, is not only imitative behavior but the willingness to abandon it at the "right" time and circumstances. Those who are different and successful "become" innovators, while those who fail "become" reckless violators of tried-and-true rules. Although one may deny the absolute appropriateness of such rules, one cannot doubt the existence of a strong urge to create conventions and rules (based on observed success) and a willingness to use them for action as well as for rationalizations of inaction. If another untried host of actions might have been even more successful, so much the worse for the participants who failed, and even for those who missed "perfect success."

Even innovation is accounted for by imitation. While there certainly are those who consciously innovate, there are those who, in their imperfect attempts to imitate others, unconsciously innovate by unwittingly acquiring some unexpected or unsought unique attributes which under the prevailing circumstances prove partly responsible for the success. Others, in turn, will attempt to copy the uniqueness, and the imitation-innovation process continues.

14. These constructed rules of behavior should be distinguished from "rules" which, in effect, do no more than define the objective being sought. Confusion between objectives which motivate one and rules of behavior is commonplace. For example, "full-cost pricing" is a "rule" that one cannot really follow. He can try to, but whether he succeeds or fails in his objective of survival is not controllable by following the "rule of full-cost pricing." If he fails in his objective, he must, of necessity, fail to have followed the "rule." The situation is parallel to trying to control the speed of a car by simply setting by hand the indicator on the speedometer.

Innovation is assured, and the notable aspects of it here are the possibility of unconscious pioneering and leadership.

The second type of conscious adaptive behavior, in addition to imitation, is "trial and error." This has been used with "profit maximization," wherein, by trial and ensuing success or failure, more-appropriate actions are selected in a process presumed to converge to a limit of "profit maximization" equilibrium. Unfortunately, at least two conditions are necessary for convergence via a trial-and-error process, even if one admits an equilibrium situation as an admissible limit. First, a trial must be classifiable as a success or failure. The position achieved must be comparable with results of other potential actions. In a static environment, if one improves his position relative to his former position, then the action taken is better than the former one, and presumably one could continue by small increments to advance to a local optimum. An analogy is pertinent. A nearsighted grasshopper on a mound of rocks can crawl to the top of a particular rock. But there is no assurance that he can also get to the top of the mound, for he might have to descend for a while or hop to new rocks. The second condition, then, for the convergence via trial and error is the continual rising toward some *optimum optimorum* without intervening descents. Whether decisions and actions in economic life satisfy these two conditions cannot be proved or disproved here, but the available evidence seems overwhelmingly unfavorable.

The above convergence conditions do not apply to a changing environment, for there can be no observable comparison of the result of an action with any other. Comparability of resulting situations is destroyed by the changing environment. As a consequence, the measure of goodness of actions in anything except a tolerable-intolerable sense is lost, and the possibility of an individual's converging to the optimum activity via a trial-and-error process disappears. Trial and error becomes survival or death. It cannot serve as a basis of the *individual's* method of convergence to a "maximum," or optimum, position. Success is discovered by the economic system through a blanketing shotgun process, not by the individual through a converging search.

In general, uncertainty provides an excellent reason for imitation of observed success. Likewise, it accounts for observed uniformity among the survivors, derived from an evolutionary, adopting, competitive system employing a criterion of survival, which can operate independently of individual motivations. Adapting behavior via imitation and venturesome innovation enlarges the model. Imperfect imitators provide opportunity for innovation, and the survival criterion of the economy determines the successful, possibly because imperfect, imitators. Innovation is provided also by conscious willful action, whatever the ultimate motivation may be, since drastic action is motivated by the hope of great success as well as by the desire to avoid impending failure.

All the preceding arguments leave the individual economic participant with imitative, venturesome, innovative, trial-and-error adaptive behavior. Most conventional economic tools and concepts are still useful, although in a vastly different analytical framework—one which is closely akin to the theory of biological evolution. The economic counterparts of genetic heredity, mutations, and natural selection are imitation, innovation, and positive profits.

### vi. Conclusions and Summary

I shall conclude with a brief reference to some implications and conjectures.

Observable patterns of behavior and organization are predictable in terms of their relative probabilities of success or viability *if* they are tried. The observed prevalence of a type of behavior depends upon both this probability of viability and the probability of the different types being submitted to the economic system for testing and selecting. One is the probability of appearance of a certain type of organization (mutation), and the other is the probability of its survival, or viability, once it appears (natural selection). There is much evidence for believing that these two probabilities are interrelated. But is there reason to suppose that a high probability of viability implies a high probability of an action's being taken, as would be implied in a system of analysis involving some "inner-directed urge toward perfection"? If these two probabilities are not highly correlated, what predictions of types of action can the economist make? An answer has been suggested in this paper.

While it is true that the economist can define a profit-maximization behavior by assuming *specific* cost and revenue conditions, is there any assurance that the conditions and conclusions so derivable are not too perfect and absolute? If profit maximization (certainty) is not ascertainable, the confidence about the predicted effects of changes, e.g., higher taxes or minimum wages, will be dependent upon how close the formerly existing arrangement was to the formerly "optimal" (certainty) situation. What really counts is the various actions actually tried, for it is from these that "success" is selected, not from some set of perfect actions. The economist may be pushing his luck too far in arguing that actions in response to changes in environment and changes in satisfaction with the existing state of affairs will converge as a result of adaptation or adoption toward the optimum action that should have been selected, if foresight had been perfect.[15]

In summary, I have asserted that the economist, using the present analytical tools developed in the analysis of the firm under certainty, can predict the more adoptable or viable types of economic interrelationships that will be induced by environmental change even if individuals themselves are unable to ascertain them. That is, although individual participants may not know their cost and revenue situations, the economist can predict the consequences of higher wage rates, taxes, government policy, etc. Like the biologist, the economist predicts the effects of environmental changes on the surviving class of living organisms; the economist need not assume that each participant is aware of, or acts according to, his cost and demand situation. These are concepts for the economist's use and not necessarily for use by individual participants, who may have other analytic or customary devices which, while of interest to the economist, serve as data and not as analytic methods.

An alternative to the rationale of individual profit maximization has been presented without exorcising uncertainty. Lest isolated arguments be misinterpreted, let it be clearly stated that this paper does not argue that purposive objective-seeking behavior is absent from reality, nor, on the other hand, does it endorse the familiar thesis that action of economic units cannot be expressed within the marginal analysis. Rather, the contention is that the precise role and nature of purposive behavior in the presence of uncertainty and incomplete information have not been clearly understood or analyzed.

It is straightforward, if not heuristic, to start with complete uncertainty and

---

15. An anomalous aspect of the assumption of perfect foresight is that it nearly results in tautological and empty statements. One cannot know everything, and this is recognized by the addendum that one acts within a "given state and distribution of the arts." But this is perilously close, if not equivalent, to saying either that action is taken only where the outcome is accurately foreseen or that information is always limited. The qualification is inserted because one might contend that it is the "*constancy* of the state and distribution of arts" that is necessary as a *ceteris paribus*. But even the latter is no solution. A large fraction of behavior in a world of incomplete information and uncertainty is necessarily directed at increasing the state of arts and venturing into an unknown sphere. While it is probably permissible to start with a prescribed "distribution of the knowledge of the arts," holding it constant is too restrictive, since a large class of important and frequent actions necessarily involves changes in the state and distribution of knowledge. The modification suggested here incorporates this search for more knowledge as an essential foundation.

nonmotivation and then to add elements of foresight and motivation in the process of building an analytical model. The opposite approach, which starts with certainty and unique motivation, must abandon its basic principles as soon as uncertainty and mixed motivations are recognized.[16] The approach suggested here is intellectually more modest and realistic, without sacrificing generality. It does not regard uncertainty as an aberrational exogenous disturbance, as does the usual approach from the opposite extreme of accurate foresight. The existence of uncertainty and incomplete information is the foundation of the suggested type of analysis; the importance of the concept of a class of "chance" decisions rests upon it; it permits of various conflicting objectives; it motivates and rationalizes a type of adaptive imitative behavior; yet it does not destroy the basis of prediction, explanation, or diagnosis. It does not base its aggregate description on individual optimal action; yet it is capable of incorporating such activity where justified. The formalization of this approach awaits the marriage of the theory of stochastic processes and economics—two fields of thought admirably suited for union. It is conjectured that the suggested modification is applicable to a wide class of events and is worth attempts at empirical verification.[17]

16. If one prefers, he may believe that the suggestions here contain reasons why the model based on certainty may predict outcomes, although individuals really cannot try to maximize profits. But the dangers of this have been indicated.

17. Preliminary study in this direction has been very convincing, and, in addition, the suggested approach appears to contain important implications relative to general economic policy; but discussions of these are reserved for a later date.

# BIOLOGICAL ANALOGIES IN
# THE THEORY OF THE FIRM
## COMMENT

Edith Penrose's "Biological Analogies in the Theory of the Firm" appearing in the December 1952 issue of this *Review* criticizes an article of mine appearing in the *Journal of Political Economy* on the ground that it rests on the theory of biological evolution.[1] A brief reply may serve to bring out some points of scientific value.

The presently relevant aspects of my original article can be summarized briefly. Economics predicts the observable effects of change in exogenous and endogenous factors impinging on the operation of the economic system. It analyzes the economic effects of these various factors upon the optimal conditions of firms and other basic units. From these deduced changes in optimal conditions, it predicts that the constellation of firms found in a new environment will have characteristics closer to the new optimal conditions than to the old. It does not (or should not) assert that any or all of the firms in the original circumstances will adjust or modify themselves to achieve the conditions which are optimal for the new conditions. What it does (or should) say is that in the new environment the observed characteristics of the population of firms will be found to have changed toward the new optimal conditions. And this will have happened whatever the wisdom, perspicacity, or motivation of the individual firms. Those who like to think that firms are able to make the required adjustments are free to do so; others, among whom the author is to be counted, can be less restrictive in their axioms and still get similar predicted observable circumstances.

These less restrictive axioms do not assert that businessmen try to maximize profits, since, with uncertainty, no definite meaning can be attached to that

Reprinted from *American Economic Review* 43 (September 1953): 600–603.

1. Edith T. Penrose, "Biological Analogies in the Theory of the Firm," *Am. Econ. Rev.*, Dec. 1952, 42, 804–19; Armen A. Alchian, "Uncertainty, Evolution and Economic Theory," *Jour. Pol. Econ.*, June 1950, 57, 211–21.

prescription of behavior. It is true that there is some situation which, if achieved, would, *ex post*, have yielded a larger profit than any other would have. But this situation is unknowable; hence the lack of prescriptive content. But the economist can, from certain generalized production functions and demand functions, infer the directions of changes in the optimal values of the variables of these functions if these values are now to approach the conditions of the new rather than the old optimum. The economist can do this not because he has greater knowledge than the individual firm but because he is analyzing changes in the optimum conditions of generalized functions. The business-man requires much more than this; he needs to know his particular values, not merely the directions of changes between two different optima derived from generalized functions.

The significant point is that the new optimum is approached even in the absence of foresighted appropriate adaptive behavior of individual economic units. It can be induced by differential growth, viability, or profit rates in a com-petitive regime in which (1) realization of profits is a necessary condition for survival, and in which (2) there is a diversity of adjustments manifested in the variety of factor-service input ratios or consumption patterns.

Economic analysis is therefore not merely a theory of the behavior of indi-viduals; it is a theory of the operation of an economic system, and it yields pre-dictions about the effects of certain changes in both endogenous and exoge-nous factors affecting the economy. To regard it as a theory of individual behavior is fatal.[2]

With this prologue I now turn to Mrs. Penrose, who says she is "not so much concerned to present an analytical critique of the theory as to discuss the ap-plicability of the biological analogy and the implications involved in its use."[3]

---

2. For example, see the prolonged exchange of views on profit maximization and marginalism beginning with R. A. Lester, "Shortcomings of Marginal Analysis for Wage Employment Problems" (Mar. 1946), and F. Machlup, "Marginal Analysis and Empirical Research" (Sept. 1946), and continuing for three years in this journal. Machlup's defense of profit maximization and marginalism against those who were trying to test axioms rather than theorems would have been airtight if he had (a) defended profit maximization analysis as based on a set of axioms postulating accurate foresight and from which theo-rems about the operation of the economic system are derived rather than as a theory of in-dividual entrepreneurial behavior, (b) pointed out the difference between testing axioms and testing theorems, and (c) not defended marginalism or profit maximization as a ba-sis for describing individual behavior in the presence of uncertainty.

3. Penrose, op. cit., p. 811.

This is a bit puzzling. The theory I presented stands independently of the biological analogy. Criticisms of the latter are irrelevant to the theory. Mrs. Penrose seems, at the same time, not to have noted another distinction—that between (1) the foundations and development of a theory and (2) the methods of exposition and presentation of it. In my original article every reference to the biological analogy was merely expository, designed to clarify the ideas in the theory.[4]

Having said this much, I could stop if Mrs. Penrose had criticized only the analogy, for then her criticisms would have been irrelevant. But some of her criticisms are directed at the theory, and they are incorrect.

Some of her criticisms rest on logical errors.[5] Most of her criticisms rest on a misconception of what I wrote. In an extremely revealing footnote, she misconstrued the logic of my position, which she restated as follows: "Economists can know the conditions of survival. . . . Therefore economists can know what firms must do to make zero or positive profits. Therefore economists can know how maximum profits can be obtained."[6] Not only do the second and third sentences represent a *non sequitur*, but in addition they exactly reverse my position. Let me explain this by a little analogy(!) A football coach knows that the condition of winning is making more points than his opponent. Does knowing this imply that the coach can know what his team must do in order to win? Does the coach know how this can be done? Defining a desired condition is not the same thing as knowing how to achieve that condition. The confusion between desired conditions and the methods of achieving those conditions is a confusion

4. Readers of an earlier draft, containing no references to the biological similarity, urged that the analogy be included as helpful to an understanding of the basic approach. My conviction that they were right has been strengthened by Mrs. Penrose, for, paradoxically, she has revealed that the analogy is even better than I had suspected.

5. For example, she confuses necessary and sufficient conditions in saying that if we "abandon the assumption" that "businessmen . . . strive to make as much [money] as is practicable" and that "if we assume men act randomly, we cannot explain competition, for there is nothing in the reproductive processes of firms that would ensure that more firms would constantly be created than can survive." Op. cit., p. 812. Except for her insisting on the analytical use of the biological analogy, such inferences on her part would be unjustified. Conditions for competition in the two areas, biology and economics, need not be the same; and in any event, desire to make a profit is not profit maximization, and furthermore, random behavior was not assumed; I repeatedly stated that it was used as a starting point for the complete exposition. See also p. 815 where "long run" is interpreted as an actually realized situation.

6. Penrose, op. cit., p. 813, footnote 26.

which I attempted to expose in my original article. Profit maximization purports to be a definition of a situation, not a statement of a method of achieving that condition. That is what Enke meant when he said it was a description, not a prescription.[7] That distinction is fundamental. Ability to prescribe behavior is not necessary—however helpful it is—for the economist to perform as an economist. I started my presentation in the original paper with an extreme model of "random" behavior in order to emphasize that such special knowledge is not necessary. Subsequently, motivated purposive behavior was introduced—without implying profit maximizing, because this could not be defined. It was then stated that even with varied motivations, the economist had a method for predicting the types of new situations or firms which would have higher probability of survival and thus tend to become the dominant surviving type. It was denied that the economist could predict which particular firms would survive and what adjustments each particular firm ought to make. Thus all of Mrs. Penrose's criticisms on pages 813–15 miss the point.

Finally, she asserts that "the biological framework in which he cast his model has led him to underestimate the significance" of the precise rôle and nature of purposive behavior in the presence of uncertainty and incomplete information.[8] Whether I am right or wrong in my implicit estimation of the significance of certain undefined types of purposive behavior cannot be judged by examining the axioms from which theorems are derived. Only by testing its predictive value by empirical investigation can the theory and its implications about the significance of a particular type of purposive behavior be evaluated properly.

Surely some of her criticisms must hit their target: but this target is one of her own creation—the utilization of strictly analogous reasoning in which the concepts, conditions, and interpretations of a theory in one discipline are blindly picked up and applied in another discipline. Neither Enke nor I did that. And there is a grave danger in shooting so many arrows toward this straw target. Economics may gain much, as it already has, from the concepts and methods of analysis of other disciplines.

7. Stephen Enke, "On Maximizing Profits: A Distinction Between Chamberlin and Robinson," Am. Econ. Rev., Sept. 1951, 41, 566–78.

8. Penrose, op. cit., p. 816.

# REVIEW OF *THE INVESTMENT DECISION:*
# *AN EMPIRICAL STUDY*

The findings of this empirical study "can be reduced to two salient points: The investment decision is subject to a multiplicity of influences, and evidences different behavior under different environmental circumstances and in different time periods. The most suggestive of these differences is the clear tendency for liquidity and financial considerations to dominate the investment decision in the short run, while, in the long run, outlays on plant and equipment seem geared to maintenance of some relation between output and the capital stock."[1] (The short run is that period during which there is no technological change.) Investment is measured by the authors' gross of depreciation; the major measure of liquidity used is depreciation expense as reported to the SEC by some 750 firms in twelve manufacturing industries in 1946–50. From those data the authors sought to learn about the process of entrepreneurial decisions to purchase capital assets. A review of the existing literature suggested to them three principal explanations: "(1) the profit motive, which is the fundamental propelling drive in both static marginal theories and the more recent adaptations of marginalism . . . , (2) the technical need for greater capacity to meet an increase in demand for final product, which is the accelerator in its original and strictest construction; and (3) the desire to keep or increase one's share of the market. . . ."[2] The authors recognize that their sample is of limited coverage, and they say the scope of generalization is therefore immediately limited, since different explanatory hypotheses might be required for these unincluded sectors. The authors claim to have found "some support" for each of these three "hypotheses." At times, one worked well, and, at times, some others worked well. "The only economic hypotheses about investment behavior for which little direct confirmation could be found were those relating to the influences

Review of John Meyer and Edwin Kuh, *The Investment Decision: An Empirical Study* (Cambridge: Harvard University Press, 1957), reprinted from *Journal of Business* (July 1959): 287–88.

1. P. 192.
2. Pp. 3 and 4.

of various price variables. While there was some evidence that a good market for corporate equities tended to increase investment outlay, this result has to be interpreted cautiously because of the close interrelationship between increases in stock prices and improvements in sales levels."[3]

A large amount of energy has gone into the data condensation and statistical analysis. When it is recognized that the authors wrote this book as graduate students at Harvard, one must recognize their great energy and initiative. Yet it is doubtful whether that is sufficient to excuse loose and erroneous statistical and economic interpretation. For example, the following is a very small sample of the kinds of statements that can be found throughout the book, which, with greater care and analysis, would undoubtedly have been substantially changed.

"A theory so general as to encompass all situations in different economic environments will ordinarily have little to say about any particular milieu."[4] Does this mean that the theory of gravity is so universal that it will ordinarily have little to say about any particular milieu? Does it say that the fundamental demand theorem of economics—that more of a good is wanted at a lower price—is so general as to be of no value in any particular milieu? If so, then what is a theory supposed to be good for?

Another example, "However, the unanimity of responses from hundreds of firms suggests that investments marginal to the interest rate are or have been negligible."[5] It is harder to imagine a more fallacious statement. There are two fundamental errors. One involves methodology and the economic reasoning: What is important is not what a person *says* motivates him, but what *in fact* does motivate him. Asking people why they do things is not reliable evidence as to the absence of a motive, even if that motive is never mentioned. Ask a politician why he runs for office. Does he say, "I'll be better off if I win"? Ask a businessman why he is in favor of a tariff. How many, if any, will reply, "It will reduce the competitive supply of what I am producing so that its price will be high enough to enable me to match the higher wages that my more productive American competitor employers offer"? Failing to get such answers, should I conclude that those factors are not at work? Economic analysis is not something that can be replaced by the interview and majority opinion technique. A second error is also evident: Economic analysis suggests that interest rates do ration available savings among alternative investments and expenditures. Fur-

3. P. 192.
4. P. 4.
5. P. 9.

thermore, it suggests what these allocations will be if interest rates rise or fall. Does not the quoted statement mean that no firm revises its investment or borrowing plans as the bond market weakens? Does it not imply that no borrower pays attention to financing charges—interest payments—involved in borrowing? Does it not imply that the lending terms have no effect on decisions to build houses rather than business buildings? If the demand should increase in the West relative to the East, does the quotation mean that there will not be a transfer of funds from East to West? These are exactly what the quotation implies. That the implications are wrong seems to need little emphasis or new evidence for readers of a business journal.

Another example: "Like the quantity theory of money, the acceleration principle has little or no motivational content."[6] It will come as a surprise to businessmen to learn they have no motive for holding money or for making investments when business picks up. Apparently they just act from the force of habit and instinct.

A final quote: "For one thing, if parameter estimates fail to pass probability tests, they are not likely to be of substantial importance. At the other extreme, should the estimates prove highly significant, it is unlikely that the bias of selectivity and nonrandomness will nullify the findings based on a probability approach."[7] If I tested the hypothesis that smoking and cancer were not correlated and found that the results failed to pass probability tests, meaning that the hypothesis was not rejected, would the estimate be of no substantial importance? Or if I tested whether food intake and weight were correlated and found that the results were consistent with the hypothesis of no effect, would that establish that the effect was not likely to be of substantial importance? Not at all; it depends upon the size of the sample or, more precisely, upon the power of the test. It depends upon the probability that if the parameter value is of substantial size, the sample estimate will be consistent with the hypothesis of small parameter value. And that depends upon the sample size, not upon the fact of observance of an insignificant sample estimate. The authors have confused the effect of sample size with the fact of observance of an insignificant statistic. But there is still a second sentence in that quotation, and it, too, is in error. A statistically significant result is one that is very improbable under the tested hypothesis; but, if obtained, it does not suggest that bias or non-randomness was not present in producing the observed statistic. In fact, it should always serve

6. P. 14.
7. P. 47.

as an incentive to re-examine one's procedures, since biases and selectivity are just the kind of events that will nullify the applicability of the probability tests.

Unfortunately, the book is replete with similarly defective statements reflecting the same weak methodological, economic, and statistical reasoning. Especially noteworthy is the inadequate attention devoted to the fact that a correlation of gross investment and depreciation expense involves self-correlation. Furthermore, the interpretation of investment rates for small and large firms contains the regression fallacy, and it may be sufficiently strong to upset the conclusion drawn, but no hint of recognition of this could be found in the discussion.

Admittedly, this reviewer's impression is not very favorable, for the reasons given. Against his judgment must be set the judgment of the Harvard Economics Department which awarded this book the David Wells Prize for 1954–55—a prize offered annually to Harvard students of not more than three years of graduate standing for the best essay in certain specified fields of economics.

# THE MEANING OF UTILITY MEASUREMENT

Economists struggling to keep abreast of current developments may well be exasperated by the resurgence of measurability of utility. After all, the indifference curve analysis was popularized little over ten years ago amidst the contradictory proclamations that it eliminated, modified, and strengthened the rôle of utility. Even yet there is confusion, induced partly by careless reading and exposition of the indifference curve analysis and partly by misunderstanding of the purposes and implications of utility measurement. This paper attempts to clarify the rôle and meaning of the recent revival of measurement of utility in economic theory and of the meaning of certain concepts and operations commonly used in utility theory.

*Measurement* in its broadest sense is the assignment of numbers to entities. The process of measurement has three aspects which should be distinguished at the outset. First is the purpose of measurement, second is the process by which one measures something, i.e., assigns numerical values to some aspect of an entity, and the third is the arbitrariness, or uniqueness, of the set of numerical values inherent in the purpose and process. In the first part of this paper, we briefly explore the idea of arbitrariness, or uniqueness, of numbers assigned by a measurement process. In Part II we state some purposes of utility measurement. In Part III we examine a method of measuring utility, the purpose of the measurement, and the extent to which the measurement is unique. In Part IV we look at some implications of the earlier discussion.[1]

Reprinted from *American Economic Review* 43 (March 1953): 26–50.

The author wishes to acknowledge gratefully the aid of Norman Dalkey and Harry Markowitz, both of The RAND Corporation. The patient explanations of Dalkey in answering innumerable questions overcame early impulses to abandon the attempt to understand recent utility literature. Markowitz detected several ambiguities and errors in earlier drafts of this exposition. Since neither has seen the final draft they must be relieved of responsibility for remaining errors and ambiguities.

1. The explanation assumes no mathematical background and is on an elementary level. This paper is not original in any of its ideas, nor is it a general review of utility and demand theory. It is merely a statement of some propositions that may help the reader separate the chaff from the wheat. It may even make clear to the reader, as it did to the

TABLE I. *Illustration of types of measurement*

| Entities | Alternative Measures of "Utility" | | | | | | | | |
|---|---|---|---|---|---|---|---|---|---|
| | 1 | 2 | 3 | 4 | 5 | 6 | 7 | 8 | 9 |
| A | 1 | 2 | 6 | 11 | 2 | 6 | 5 | 6 | 3 |
| B | 2 | 4 | 7 | 12 | 4 | 12 | 7 | 10 | 7 |
| C | 3 | 5 | 8 | 13 | 6 | 18 | 9 | 14 | 13 |
| D | 4 | 8 | 9 | 14 | 8 | 24 | 11 | 18 | 21 |
| E | 5 | 11 | 10 | 15 | 10 | 30 | 13 | 22 | 31 |
| F | 7 | 14 | 12 | 17 | 14 | 42 | 17 | 30 | 43 |
| G | 11 | 22 | 16 | 21 | 22 | 66 | 25 | 46 | 57 |
| H | 14 | 28 | 19 | 24 | 28 | 84 | 31 | 58 | 73 |
| I | 16 | 33 | 21 | 26 | 32 | 96 | 35 | 66 | 91 |
| J | 17 | 34 | 22 | 27 | 34 | 102 | 37 | 70 | 111 |

## I. Degree of Measurability

The columns of Table I are sequences of numbers illustrating the concept of the "degree of measurability." The entities, some aspect of which we wish to measure, are denoted by letters. Later we shall discuss the meaning of these entities. Our first task is to explain the difference between monotone transformations and linear transformations. We shall begin with monotone transformations and then come to linear transformations via two of its special cases, additive and multiplicative constants.

*Monotone Transformations*

Let there be assigned a numerical magnitude (measure) to each entity concerned. For example, in Table I, for the ten entities, A–J, listed in the extreme left-hand column, nine different sets of numbers are utilized to assign nine

------

writer, one meaning of utility. Most of the material presented here is contained in J. Marschak, "Rational Behavior, Uncertain Prospects and Measurable Utility," *Econometrica* (April 1950), 18, 111–41, an article written for the mathematically mature. A bibliography is included, to which those who might wish to read more deeply should refer. Excellent starting points are M. Friedman and L. J. Savage, "The Utility Analysis of Choices Involving Risk," *Jour. Pol. Econ.* (Aug. 1948), 56, 279–304, and J. Marschak, "Why 'Should' Statisticians and Businessmen Maximize 'Moral Expectation'?" *Proceedings of the Second Berkeley Symposium on Mathematical Statistics and Probability* (Berkeley, University of California Press, 1951), pp. 493–506.

different numbers to each of the entities. If two sets of numbers (measures) result in the same ranking or ordering of the entities (according to the numbers assigned), then the two sets are *monotone transformations* of each other. In Table I it will be seen that all nine measures give the same ranking, thus all nine measures are monotone transformations of each other. If this property holds true over the entire class of entities concerned, then the two measures are monotone transformations of each other for that class of entities. The possible set of monotone transformations obviously is very large.

### Linear Transformations: Additive Constants

We shall approach the linear transformation by considering two special forms. Look at the numbers in column 3. They are the same as those in 1 except that a constant has been added, in this case 5, i.e., they are the *same "up to"* (except for) an *additive constant.* The measure in column 4 is equivalent to that in column 1 with 10 added. Columns 1, 3, and 4 are *transforms* of each other "up to" (by means of) *additive constants.* This can also be expressed by saying they are equivalent except for an additive constant. The term "up to" implies that we may go through some simpler types. For example, all the transforms up to an additive constant are also contained in the larger, less restricted class of possible transforms known as monotone transforms. An additive constant is a quite strong restriction, even though it may not seem so at first, since there is an unlimited number of available constants. But relative to the range of possibilities in the general linear transformations, this is very restrictive indeed.

### Linear Transformations: Multiplicative Constants

Now look at column 5. It is equivalent to column 1 except for multiplication by a constant, in this case, 2. Column 5 is a monotone transform of column 1, and it is also a "multiplicative by a constant" transform of column 1. Column 6 is column 1 multiplied by 6. This, while columns 1, 5, and 6 are monotone transforms of each other, they are also a more particular type of transform. They are transforms up to a multiplicative constant. These are special cases of linear transformations which we shall now discuss.

### General Linear Transformations

The numbers of column 7 are equivalent to column 1 except for multiplication by 2 and addition of 3. Letting $y$ denote the numbers or "measures" in column 7, and $x$ those of column 1, we have $y = 2x + 3$. Column 8 is derived similarly from column 1; the multiplier is 4, and the added constant is 2. Column 8 is given by $4x + 2$, but a little inspection will show that column 8 can be derived from column 7 by the same process of multiplying and adding. In this case column 8 is obtained from column 7 by multiplying by 2 and adding $-4$. Columns 1, 7, and 8 are thus "linear transforms" of each other. This is also expressed by saying that they are the same measures "up to a linear transformation"; that is, any one of these measures can be obtained from any other one by simply selecting appropriate constants for multiplication and addition.

There is a particular property of the linear transformation that has historical significance in economics. Look at the way the numbers change as one moves from entity to entity. For example, consider columns 1 and 7. The numerical change from entity E to entity F has a value of 2 in the measure of column 1, while in the measure of column 7, it has a numerical value of 4. From F to G the change is 4 in measure 1, and in measure 7 it is 8. If the increment is positive, it will be positive in all sequences which are linear transforms of this particular sequence. But this is true also for all monotone transformations—a much broader class of transformations or measures. Of greater significance, however, is the following attribute of linear transforms: if the differences between the numbers in one of the sequences increases (or decreases) from entity to entity, then the differences between the numbers of these same entities in all of its *linear* transformations will also be increasing (or decreasing). In general, the property of increasing or decreasing increments is not affected by switching from one sequence of numbers to any linear transformation of that given sequence. In mathematical terms, the sign of the second differences of a sequence of numbers is invariant to linear transformations of that sequence.[2] The significance of invariance will be discussed later, but we should note that this property of increasing (or decreasing) differences between the numbers assigned to pairs of entities is nothing but increasing marginal utility—if one christens the assigned numbers "utilities."

## II. Purpose of Measurement

*Order*

In the nine columns of Table I are nine "different" measures of some particular aspect of the entities denoted A, B, C, . . . J. How different are they? We have already answered this. Which is the "right" one? This depends upon what one wants to do with the entities and the numbers. It would be more useful to

2. In monotonic transformations the sign of the *first* differences only are necessarily left undisturbed.

ask which one is a *satisfactory* measure, for then it is clear that we must make explicit for what it is to be satisfactory.[3] For example, if my sole concern were to predict which of the entities would be the heaviest, the next heaviest, etc., I could, by successively comparing pairs in a balancing scale, completely order the entities. Having done so, I could then assign the numbers in *any* one of columns 1 through 9 so long as I assign the biggest number to the heaviest, and so on down. This means that for the purpose of indicating *order*, any one of the monotone transforms is acceptable.

The remaining task is to determine whether the order is "correctly" stated; the fact that the order is the same, no matter which one of the above transforms is used, does not imply that the order is correct. What do we mean by "correctly"? We mean that our stated or predicted order is matched by the order revealed by some other observable ordering process. You could put the entities on some new weighing scales (the new scales are the "test"), and then a matching of the order derived from the new scales with our stated order is a verification of the correctness (predictive validity) of our first ordering. Any monotone transform of one valid ordering number sequence is *for the purpose* of this illustration *completely equivalent* to the numbers actually used. That is, any one of the possible monotone transformations is just as good as any other.

We may summarize by saying that, given a method for validly ordering entities, any monotone transformation of the particular numerical values assigned in the ordering process will be equally satisfactory. We may be technical and say that "all measures of order are equivalent up to (except for being) monotone transformations." Or, in other words, a method of validly denoting *order* only, is not capable of uniquely identifying a particular set of numbers as *the* correct one. Any monotonic transformation will do exactly as well. The degree of uniqueness of an ordering can also be described by saying it is only as unique as the set of monotone transformations. Thus, we often see the expression that "ordering is unique up to a monotone transformation."

### Ordering Groups of Entities

But suppose our purpose were different. Suppose we want to be able to order *groups* of entities according to their weights. More precisely, suppose we want to assign numbers to each of the component objects so that when we combine

---

3. A pause to reflect will reveal that there is a second problem besides that of deciding what "satisfactory" means. This second problem, which we have so far begged, is: "How does one assign numbers to entities?" It is deferred to the following section.

the objects into sets or bundles we can order the weights of the composite bundles, knowing only the individually valid numbers assigned to each component, by *merely adding* together the numbers assigned to each component. And we want to be able to do this for any possible combination of the objects. Fortunately, man has discerned a way to do this for weights. The numbers which are assigned by this discovered process are arbitrary up to a multiplicative constant (of proportionality), so that the numbers could express either pounds, ounces, tons, or grams. That is, we can arbitrarily multiply all the numbers assigned to the various components by any constant we please, without destroying the validity of our resulting numbers for this particular purpose. But we can not use any monotone transformation as we could in the preceding case where our purpose was different.

If we were to add an arbitrary constant to each component's individually valid numerical (weight) value, we would not be able to add the resulting numbers of each component in order to get a number which would rank the composite bundles. Thus, the numbers we can assign are rather severely constrained. We can not use any linear transformation, but we can use a multiplicative constant, which is a special type of linear transformation. And if we were to "measure" lengths of items so as to be able simply to "add" the numbers to get the lengths of the items laid end to end, we would again find ourselves confined to sequences (measures) with a multiplicative constant as the one available degree of arbitrariness.

### Utility and Ordering of Choices

The reader has merely to substitute for the concept of weight, in the earlier example about weight orders, the idea of "preference," and he is in the theory of choice or demand. Economics goes a step further and gives the name "utility" to the numbers. Can we assign a set of numbers (measures) to the various entities and predict that the entity with the largest assigned number (measure) will be chosen? If so, we could christen this measure "utility" and then assert that choices are made so as to maximize utility. It is an easy step to the statement, "you are maximizing your utility," which says no more than that your choice is predictable according to the size of some assigned numbers.[4] For analytical convenience it is customary to postulate that an individual seeks to maximize something subject to some constraints. The thing—or numerical measure of

---

4. The difficult (impossible?) psychological, philosophical step of relating this kind of utility to some *quantity of satisfaction, happiness, goodness,* or *welfare* is not attempted here.

the "thing"—which he seeks to maximize is called "utility." Whether or not utility is some kind of glow or warmth or happiness is here irrelevant; all that counts is that we can assign numbers to entities or conditions which a person can strive to realize. Then we say the individual seeks to maximize some function of those numbers. Unfortunately, the term "utility" has by now acquired so many connotations that it is difficult to realize that for present purposes utility has no more meaning than this. The analysis of individual demand behavior is mathematically describable as the process of maximizing some quantitive measures, or numbers, and we assume that the individual seeks to obtain that combination with the highest choice number, given the purchasing power at his disposal. It might be harmless to call this "utility theory."[5]

### Three Types of Choice Predictions

*Sure Prospects.* Before proceeding further it is necessary to indicate clearly the types of choice that will concern us. The first type of choice is that of selecting among a set of alternative "riskless" choices. A riskless choice, hereafter called a sure prospect, is one such that the chooser knows exactly what he will surely get with each possible choice. To be able to predict the preferred choice means we can assign numbers to the various entities such that the entity with the largest assigned number is the most preferred, the one with the second largest number is the next most preferred, etc. As said earlier, it is customary to christen this numerical magnitude with the name "utility."

An understanding of what is meant by "entity" is essential. An entity denotes any specifiable object, action, event, or set or pattern of such items or actions. It may be an orange, a television set, a glass of milk, a trip to Europe, a particular time profile of income or consumption (e.g., steak every night, or ham every night, or steak and ham on alternate nights), getting married, etc. Identifying an entity exclusively with one single event or action would lead to unnecessary restrictions on the scope of the applicability of the theorem to be presented later.[6]

*Groups of Sure Prospects.* A second problem of choice prediction would be that of ordering (predicting) choices among riskless *groups* of entities. A riskless

---

5. The author, having so far kept his opinions submerged, is unable to avoid remarking that it would seem "better" to confine utility "theory" to attempts to explain or discern why a person chooses one thing rather than another—at equal price.

6. For example, see H. Wold, "Ordinal Preferences or Cardinal Utility? (with Additional Notes by G. L. S. Shackle, L. J. Savage, and H. Wold)"; A. S. Manne, "The Strong Independence Assumption—Gasoline Blends and Probability Mixtures (with Additional

group consists of several entities, all of which will be surely obtained if that group is chosen. The problem now is to predict the choice among riskless groups knowing only the utilities assigned to the individual entities which have been aggregated into groups. Thus if in Table I we were to assemble the entities A through J into various groups, could we predict the choice among these groups of entities knowing only the utility numbers that were assigned to the component entities for the purpose of the preceding choice problem? Of course we ask this question only on the assumption that the utilities previously assigned to the component entities were valid predictors of choice among the single sure prospects.[7]

*Uncertain Prospects.* A third type of problem is that of ordering choices among risky choices, or what have been called uncertain prospects. An uncertain prospect is a group of entities, only one entity of which will be realized if that group is chosen. For example, an uncertain prospect might consist of a fountain pen, a radio, and an automobile. If that uncertain prospect is chosen, the chooser will surely get one of the three entities, but which one he will actually get is not known in advance. He is not completely ignorant about what will be realized, for it is assumed that he knows the probabilities of realization attached to each of the component entities in an uncertain prospect. For example, the probabilities might have been .5 for the fountain pen, .4 for the radio, and .1 for the automobile. These probabilities sum to 1.0; one and only one of these entities will be realized. An uncertain prospect is very much like a ticket in a lottery. If there is but one prize, then the uncertain prospect consists of two entities, the prize or the loss of the stake. If there are several prizes, the uncertain prospect consists of several entities—the various prizes and, of course, the loss of the stake (being a loser).

But there is another requirement that we want our prediction process to satisfy. Not only must we be able to predict the choices, but we want to do it in a very simple way. Specifically, we want to be able to look at each component separately, and then from utility measures assigned to the elements, as if they were sure prospects, we want to be able to aggregate the component utility measures into a group utility measure predicting choices among the uncertain

Notes by A. Charnes)"; P. Samuelson, "Probability, Utility, and the Independence Axiom"; E. Malinvaud, "Note on von Neumann-Morgenstern's Strong Independence Axiom," *Econometrica* (Oct. 1952), 20, 661–79.

7. For an illustration of this problem of rating a composite bundle by means of the ratings of the ratings of the components, see A. S. Manne, op. cit.

TABLE II. *Examples of uncertain prospects*

| | Probabilities of Getting | | |
|---|---|---|---|
| Uncertain Prospect | Pen | Radio | Automobile |
| 1 | .5 | .4 | .1 |
| 2 | .58 | .30 | .12 |
| 3 | .85 | .0 | .15 |
| 4 | .0 | .99 | .01 |

prospects. For example, suppose the uncertain prospects consisted of a pen, a radio, and an automobile as listed in Table II.

Are there utilities which can be assigned to the pen, the radio, and the automobile, so that for the purpose of comparing these four uncertain prospects the same numbers could be used in arriving at utility numbers to be assigned to the uncertain prospects? In particular, can we assign to the pen, the radio, and the automobile numbers such that when multiplied by the associated probabilities in each uncertain prospect they will yield a sum (expected utility) for each uncertain prospect, and such that these "expected utilities" would indicate preference?

Before answering we shall briefly indicate why choices among uncertain prospects constitute an important class of situations. Upon reflection it will be seen to be the practically universal problem of choice. Can the reader think of many cases in which he *knows*, when making a choice, the outcome of that choice with absolute certainty? In other words, are there many choices—or actions—in life in which the *consequences* can be predicted with absolute certainty? Even the act of purchasing a loaf of bread has an element of uncertainty in its consequences; even the act of paying one's taxes has an element of uncertainty in the consequences involved; even the decision to sit down has an element of uncertainty in the consequence. But to leave the trivial, consider the choice of occupation, purchase of an automobile, house, durable goods, business investment, marriage, having children, insurance, gambling, etc., ad infinitum. Clearly choices among uncertain prospects constitute an extremely large and important class of choices.

### III. Method of Measurement

So far we have discussed the meaning and purpose of measurement. We turn to the method of measurement recognizing that for each type of choice prediction the method of measurement must have a rationale as well as a purpose. For a moment we can concentrate on the rationale which is properly stated in the form of axioms defining rational behavior.

## Sure Prospects

Let us start with a rationale for the first type of choice. We postulate that an individual behaves consistently—i.e., he has a consistent set of preferences; that these preferences are transitive—i.e., if B is preferred to A, and C to B, then C is preferred to A; and that these preferences can be completely described merely by attaching a numerical value to each. An implication of these postulates is that for such individuals we can predict their choices by a numerical variable (utility). Asking the individual to make pairwise comparisons, we assign numbers to the sure prospects such that the choice order will be revealed by the size of the numbers attached. The number of pairwise comparisons that the individual must make depends upon how fortunate we are in selecting the pairs for his comparison. If we are so lucky as first to present to him a series of pairs of alternatives of sure prospects exactly matching his preference order, the complete ordering of his preferences will be obtained with the minimal amount of pairwise comparisons. Any numbering sequence which gives the most preferred sure prospect the highest number, the second preferred sure prospect the second highest number, etc., will predict his choices according to "utility maximization." But any other sequence of numbers could be used so long as it is a *monotone transformation* of the first sequence. And this is exactly the meaning of the statement that utility is *ordinal* and not cardinal. The transitivity postulate enables this pairwise comparison to reveal the complete order of preferences, and the consistency postulate means he would make his choices according to the prediction. Thus if he were to be presented with any two of ten sure prospects, we would predict his taking the one with the higher utility number. If our prediction failed, then one of our postulates would have been denied, and our prediction method would not be valid. A hidden postulate is that the preferences, if transitive and consistent, are stable for the interval involved.[8] Utility for this purpose and by this method is measurable up to a monotonic transformation; i.e., it is ordinal only.

8. Some problems involved in this assumption and in its relaxation are discussed by N. Georgescu-Roegen, "The Theory of Choice and the Constancy of Economic Laws," *Quart. Jour. Econ.* (Feb. 1950), 64, 125–38.

*Groups of Sure Prospects*

The second type of choice, among *groups* of sure prospects, can be predicted using the same postulates only if we treat each group of sure prospects as a sure prospect. Then by presenting pairs of "groups of sure prospects" we can proceed as in the preceding problem. But the interesting problem here is that of predicting choice among groups of sure prospects (entities) only by knowing valid utility measures for choices among the component sure prospects. Can these utility numbers of the component entities of the group of sure prospects, which are valid for the entities by themselves, be aggregated to obtain a number predicting choice among the groups of sure prospects? In general the answer is "no." Hence, although utility was measurable for the purpose of the kind of prediction in the preceding problem, it is not measurable in the sense that these component measures can be aggregated or combined in any known way to predict choices among *groups* of sure prospects. Utility is "measurable" for one purpose but not for the other.[9]

*Uncertain Prospects*

We want to predict choices among uncertain prospects. And we want to make these predictions solely on the basis of the utilities and probabilities attached to the elements of the uncertain prospects.

Without going into too many details, an intuitive idea of the content of the axioms used in deriving this kind of measurability will now be given.[10] For ex-

9. It is notable that the usual indifference curve analysis is contained in this case. Any *group* of sure prospects (point in the xy plane of an indifference curve diagram) which has more of each element in it than there is in another group of two sure prospects, will be preferred to the latter. And further, if one group of sure prospects has more of one commodity than does the other group of sure prospects, the two groups can be made indifferent by sufficiently increasing the amount of the second commodity in the other group of sure prospects. The indifference curve (utility isoquant) approach does not assign numbers representing utility to the various sure prospects lying along either the horizontal or the vertical axis and then from these numerical values somehow obtain a number which would order choices among the groups of prospects inside the quadrant enclosed by the axes.

10. This is the method developed by J. von Neumann and O. Morgenstern, *The Theory of Games and Economic Behavior* (Princeton University Press, 1944). A very closely analogous method was suggested in 1926 by F. Ramsey, *The Foundations of Mathematics and Other Logical Essays* (The Humanities Press, N.Y., 1950), pp. 166–90. The neatest, but still very difficult, exposition is by J. Marschak, op. cit. Still another statement of essentially the same set of axioms is in Friedman and Savage, op. cit.

pository convenience the statement that the two entities A and B are equally desirable or indifferent will be expressed by A = B; if, however, A is either preferred to or indifferent to B, the expression will be A ≥ B.

(1) For the chooser there is a transitive, complete ordering of all the alternative possible choices so far as his preferences are concerned. That is, if C ≥ B
and B ≥ A, then C ≥ A.

(2) If among three entities, A, B, and C, C ≥ B, and B ≥ A, then there is some
probability value $p$, for which B is just as desirable as the uncertain prospect
consisting of A and C, where A is realizable with probability $p$, and C with
probability $1 - p$. In our notation, if C ≥ B and B ≥ A, then there is some $p$ for
which B = (A, C; $p$), where (A, C; $p$) is the expression for the uncertain prospect
in which A will be realized with probability $p$, and otherwise, C will be realized.

(3) Suppose B ≥ A, and let C be any entity. Then (B, C; $p$) ≥ (A, C; $p$) for any $p$.
In particular, if A = B, then the prospect comprising A and C, with probability
$p$ for A and $1 - p$ for C, will be just as desirable as the uncertain prospect comprised of B and C, with the same probability $p$ for B , and $1 - p$ for C.

(4) In the uncertain prospect comprising A and B with probability $p$ for A, it
makes no difference what the process is for determining whether A or B is received, just so long as the value of $p$ is not changed. Notationally, (A, B; $p_1$), B;
$p_2$) = (A, B; $p_1 p_2$).

To help understand what these axioms signify, we give an example of behavior or situation that is inconsistent with each, except that I can think of no
totally unreasonable behavior inconsistent with the first axiom. Behavior inconsistent with the second axiom would be the following: suppose C is two
bars of candy, B is one bar of candy, and A is being shot in the head. Form an
uncertain prospect of C and A with probability $p$ for C. If there is no $p$, however
small or close to zero, which could possibly make one indifferent between the
uncertain prospect and B, the one bar of candy, he is rejecting axiom (2). Are
such situations purely hypothetical?

The third axiom, sometimes called the "strong independence assumption,"
has provoked the most vigorous attack and defense. So far no really damaging
criticism has been seen. It takes its name from the implication that whatever
may be the entity, C, it has no effect on the ranking of the uncertain prospects
comprised of A or C, and B or C. This kind of independence has nothing whatever to do with independence or complementarity among groups of commodities. Here one does not receive both A and C, or B and C. He gets either A
or C in one uncertain prospect, or he gets either B or C in the other. Even if

A and C were complements and B and C were substitutes, the ordering would not be affected—this is what the postulate asserts.[11]

Axiom (3) is inconsistent with a situation in which the utility of the act of winning itself depends upon the probability of winning or, more generally, if probability itself has utility. For example, at Christmastime, one does not want to know what gift his wife is going to give him; he prefers ignorance to any hints or certainty as to what his gift will be. This is a type of love for gambling. Conversely, one may be indifferent to whether he gets roast beef or ham for dinner, but he does want to know which it will be purely for the sake of knowing, not because it will affect any prior or subsequent choices.

Axiom (4) is inconsistent with a concern or difference in feeling about different ways of determining which entity in an uncertain prospect is actually received, even though the various systems all have the same probability. For example, suppose an uncertain prospect had a probability of .25 for one of the entities. It should make no difference whether the probability is based on the toss of two successive coins, with heads required on both, or whether it is based on the draw of one white ball from an urn containing one white and three black. But consider the case of the slot machine. Why are there three wheels with many items on each wheel? Why not one big wheel, and why are the spinning wheels in sight? One could instead have a machine with covered wheels. Simply insert a coin, pull the handle, and then wait and see what comes out of the machine. Does seeing the wheels go around or seeing how close one came to nearly winning affect the desirability? If observation or knowledge of the number of steps through which the mechanism must pass before reaching the final decision makes any difference, even if the fundamental probability is not subjectively or objectively affected, then axiom (4) is denied.

Implied in the stated axioms is a method for assigning numerical utility values to the various component entities. The method is perhaps explained best by an illustration of the method using the entities of Table I. Take one entity, A, and one other, say B, as the two base entities. Between these two entities you choose B as preferable to A. Now I arbitrarily assign (i.e., choose any numbers I wish so long as the number for B exceeds that for A) the number 2 to B, and some smaller number, say 1, to A. You then consider entity C, which you assert you prefer to A and to B. The next step is rather involved: I now form an uncertain prospect consisting of C and A. You are now offered a choice between B, a sure prospect, and the uncertain prospect comprised of "A or C," where you get

11. See the literature listed in footnote 6.

A or C, depending upon the outcome of a random draw in which the probability of A is $p$; otherwise you get C.

You are asked to, and you do, select a value of $p$ which when contained in the uncertain prospect leaves you indifferent between B and the uncertain prospect, "A or C."[12] If $p$ were set at nearly zero, you would choose the uncertain prospect, since C is assumed here to be preferred to B; choosing the uncertain prospect would mean that you would almost surely get C. The converse would be the outcome if $p$ were set at nearly 1. Therefore, someplace in between, there is a value of $p$ which would leave you indifferent between B and the uncertain prospect of "A or C." After you indicate that value of $p$, I assign to the uncertain prospect the same number, 2, I did to B since they are equally preferred by you.

Now we may determine a number for C by the following procedure. Treat the probability $p$ and its complement $1 - p$ as weights to be assigned to the numbers for A and C such that the weighted sum is equal to the number 2, which has been assigned to the uncertain prospect. If, for example, you were indifferent when $p$ was equal to .6, then we have the following definitional equation, where we let U(A) stand for the number assigned to A, U(B) for the number assigned to B, and U(C) for the number assigned to C:

$$U(B) = p \cdot U(A) + (1 - p) \cdot U(C)$$
$$\frac{U(B) - p \cdot U(A)}{(1 - p)} = U(C) = 3.5$$

Using this convenient formula, we can assign numbers to the entities D, E, F by appropriately forming uncertain prospects and letting you determine that value of $p$ which produced indifference. These revealed numbers will completely order the entities. If E has a larger number than G, E will be preferred over G. This assignment of numerical value is made without ever comparing E and G directly. Each has been compared with a base entity. A brief pause to reflect will reveal that in this paragraph we have been specifying a convenient method for manipulating, or combining, the "utilities" or "choice indicator numbers" as well as specifying a process of attaching numbers (utilities) to the entities.

It happens that if we insist on using the simple formula above, rather than some more complicated one, the numerical magnitudes assigned by this pro-

---

12. It is important to notice that the sure prospect must not be preferred to both of the components of the uncertain prospects, for in that event no probability value would induce indifference.

cess are unique up to a linear transformation. For example, suppose that by our process of assigning numbers, we obtained the set of numbers in column 3 of Table I for entities A to J. Now, instead of assigning 7 and 6 to B and A, had we decided in the first place to assign a value of 7 to entity B and a value of 5 to entity A, we could have obtained, instead, the sequence in column 7. Column 7 is a linear transformation of column 3. In other words, we may arbitrarily, at our complete discretion, assign numbers to *two* of the entities; once that has been done, our method will determine the remaining unique numbers to be assigned. But all the various *sets* of numbers (utilities) that could have been obtained, depending upon the two initial numerical values, are linear transformations of each other. Thus, our measurement process is unique "up to" a linear transformation.

If the preceding method of assigning numbers does predict correctly the choice a person actually makes among uncertain prospects, then we have successfully assigned numbers as indicators of choice preferences. We have successfully measured utility and have done it with the convenient computational formula above. Furthermore, every linear transformation of our predicting numbers, "utilities," would be equally valid—or invalid.

In summary, (1) we have found a *way* to assign numbers; (2) for the way suggested, it so happens that the assigned numbers are unique up to linear transformations; (3) the numbers are convenient to manipulate. All this was implicit in our set of postulates. Before asking whether the numbers predict actual behavior, we shall discuss some side issues.

### Diminishing or Increasing Marginal Utility

Recalling our earlier exposition of the mathematical properties of linear transformations, we see that in all of the columns (except 2 and 9, which are not linear transformations of the others) the pattern of *increments* between the numbers assigned to entities is similar. For example, between pair H and I on scale 7, the increment is 4, and between pair I and J it is 2. Moving from H through I to J, we have a diminishing increment in the numerical magnitudes assigned. In more familiar terminology we have diminishing marginal utility among H, I, and J.[13] Similarly, all the linear transforms of scale 7 will retain this diminishing marginal utility over the range of entities H, I, and J. And the sug-

---

13. More strictly we should also have some scale for measuring the amount of H, I, and J, either in weight or volume, etc. While the process for assigning these scales also is a complex one, we may pass over it in order to concentrate upon the "utility" measure.

gested way of assigning numbers to the component entities assigns numbers (utilities) which are equivalent up to a linear transformation; that is, any one of the linear transformations will be just as good—for our purposes—as any other of them. By implication we can determine whether there is diminishing or increasing marginal utility.

### Maximization of Expected Utility

By this method of assigning utilities, we have ordered all the entities. However, our purpose was more than this; otherwise the uniqueness of the numbers up to a linear transformation would have been an unnecessary restriction. As we know, any monotonic transformation would leave order unaffected. The linear transformation restriction is imposed by our desire to predict choices among uncertain prospects from the utilities and probabilities of the component entities and to do it in a convenient form, viz., according to maximization of expected utility.[14]

Implied in our set of postulates is not only the preceding method of assigning numbers for utilities but also (in fact the two are merely two aspects of the same implication) a method for combining the utilities of the component entities into a utility number for the uncertain prospect.

This method is based on the implication that a person who behaves according to the axioms will choose among uncertain prospects according to expected utility. Expected utility is merely the sum of the weighted utilities of the components of the uncertain prospects where the weights are the probabilities associated with each component. In symbolic form

$$U(A \text{ or } B, p) = p\, U(A) + (1 - p)\, U(B)$$

where the expression $U(A \text{ or } B, p)$ denotes the utility of the uncertain prospect of entities A and B, in which A will be received with probability $p$, and B otherwise. For example, we could from any one of our measures in Table I (except columns 2 and 9) predict what one would do when faced with the following choice: he is presented, first, with an uncertain prospect containing entities B and C. If he chooses this prospect, his probability of getting B is one-half; otherwise, he will get C. The other uncertain prospect which he is offered contains entities A and E, and if he chooses this prospect, his probability of getting E is one-fourth—otherwise, he gets A. Our individual will choose the first

14. It is not dictated by any nostalgia for diminishing marginal utility.

prospect, no matter which of our acceptable measures we use. We obtain this prediction by multiplying (weighting) the "utility" measures of each entity in each prospect by the probability of that entity. If we use the utility measure of column 8, we have for the first prospect $(^1/_2 \times 14) + (^1/_2 \times 10) = 12$, and for the second prospect, $(^3/_4 \times 6) + (^1/_4 \times 22) = 10$. The first prospect has the larger expected "utility" and will be chosen.[15] How can we justify this procedure of adding the products of probabilities and "measures of utilities" of entities in an uncertain prospect and calling the result "the utility" of the uncertain prospect? The axioms of human behavior on which it is based are those which earlier gave us the procedure for "measuring utility" up to a linear transformation.[16]

Another way to express this implication that a rational person chooses among uncertain prospects so as to maximize expected utility is in terms of the implied shapes of indifference curves in the plane of *probabilities* of the various components of the uncertain prospects.

Suppose that I am indifferent between receiving a watch and receiving $30.00. In Figure 1a, the horizontal scale measures the probability with which I will get $30.00, and the vertical axis measures the probability with which I will get the watch. The origin represents the point at which I am sure to get nothing. The point W on the vertical axis presents the situation in which I am sure to get the watch and not get the $30.00. The point M on the horizontal axis represents the situation in which I am sure to get the money and am sure not to get the watch. A straight line drawn from W to M represents all the various uncertain prospects in which I might get the watch or I might get the money, where the probabilities are given by the horizontal distance for the money and the ver-

---

15. If column 9 had been used, the chooser would have been declared indifferent; i.e., the two combinations have equal utility. This is inconsistent with the utility value and predictions derived from the measures in the other columns.

16. If our task is merely to order choice among the uncertain prospects, we could, after obtaining the expected utility of the prospect, obviously perform any monotonic transformation on it without upsetting the order of choices among the uncertain prospects. However, there seems little point in doing so, and there is good reason not to do so. In particular one might wish to predict choices among groups of uncertain prospects where, in each group of prospects, the entities are themselves uncertain prospects. This combination of several uncertain prospects into one resultant uncertain prospect is a consistent operation under the preceding postulates, and the utility measures attached to it will have an implied validity if the utility measures attached to the component prospects, derived in the manner indicated earlier, are valid.

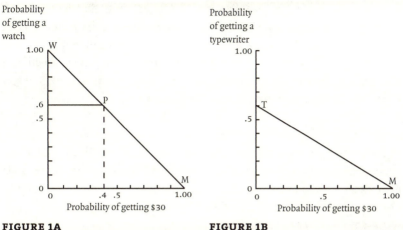

**FIGURE 1A**                                   **FIGURE 1B**

tical distance for the watch. Thus, the point P represents the prospect in which I will get the watch with probability 0.6, or otherwise the money (with probability 0.4). The preceding axioms imply that this straight line is an indifference line, or utility isoquant. In other words, the utility isoquant is a *straight* line in the space of probabilities, in this case a straight line from one sure prospect (the watch with certainty) to the other equally sure prospect (the $30.00 with certainty).

The straight line utility isoquants need not go from sure prospect to sure prospect, as can be seen from a second example. Suppose that I am indifferent between receiving $30.00 with certainty (sure prospect of $30.00) and the uncertain prospect in which I will get a particular typewriter with probability .6 and nothing with probability .4. In Figure 1b, this latter uncertain prospect is T on the vertical axis. Since I am indifferent between this uncertain prospect T and the $30.00 with certainty (point M), a straight line, TM, is a utility isoquant, and all prospects represented by the points on that line are indifferent to me— have the same utility. In summary, in any such figure, a straight line through any two equally preferred prospects will also contain all prospects (certain and uncertain) that are equally preferred to the first two. This can be generalized into three and more dimensions, in which case the straight line becomes a plane surface in three or more dimensions.

The additivity of the simple weighted (by probabilities of the components of the entities) "utilities" enables us to call this composite utility function a linear utility function. This means that the measure of "utility" of uncertain prospects (in a probability sense) of entities is the sum of the "expectation" of the "utilities" of the component entities; it does not mean that our numerical indicators (measuring utility) assigned to the entities are linear functions of the physical amounts (e.g., weights or counts) of the magnitude entities. Here linearity means that the utility of the uncertain prospects is a linear function of the utility of the component entities; incidentally, the utility function is also a linear function of the probabilities of the entities.

## IV.  Validity of Measurement

Has anyone ever succeeded in assigning numbers in this way, and did the sequence based on past observations predict accurately the preferences revealed by an *actual* choice among new and genuinely available prospects? The only test of the validity of this whole procedure, of which the author is aware, was performed by Mosteller and Nogee.[17]

The essence of the Mosteller-Nogee experiment was to subject approximately 20 Harvard students and National Guardsmen to the type of choices (indicated above on pages 38–40) required to obtain a utility measure for different entities. In the experiment, the entities were small amounts of money, so that what was being sought was a numerical value of utility to be attached to different amounts of money. After obtaining for each individual a utility measure for various amounts of money, Mosteller and Nogee predicted how each individual would choose among a set of uncertain prospects, where the entities were amounts of money with associated probabilities. Although some predictions were incorrect, a sufficiently large majority of correct predictions led Mosteller and Nogee to conclude that the subjects did choose among uncertain prospects on the basis of the utilities of the amounts of money involved and the probabilities associated with each, i.e., according to maximized expected utility. Perhaps the most important lesson of the experiment was the extreme difficulty of making a really good test of the validity of the implications of the axioms about behavior.

Whether this process will predict choice in any other situation is still unverified. But we can expect it to fail where there are pleasures of gambling and risk-taking, possibly a large class of situations. Pleasures of gambling refers not to the advantages that incur from the possibility of receiving large gains, but rather to the pleasure of the act of gambling or act of taking on extra risk itself. There may be an exhilaration accompanying sheer chance-taking or win-

---

17. F. Mosteller and P. Nogee, "An Experimental Measurement of Utility," *Jour. Pol. Econ.* (Oct. 1951), 59, 371–404.

ning, per se, as distinct from the utility of the amount won. Even worse, the preference pattern may change with experience.

### v. Utility of Income

We can conclude our general exposition with the observation that although the preceding discussion has referred to "entities," we could have always been thinking of different amounts of income or wealth. The reason we did not was that we wanted to emphasize the generality of the choice problem and to emphasize that utility measures are essentially nothing but choice indicators. However, it is useful to consider the utility of income. How do the numerical values (utilities) assigned by the preceding method vary as income varies? Now this apparently sensible question is ambiguous, even after our preceding discussion which we presume to have eliminated confusion about the meaning of "measurability of utility." For the question still remains as to whether the utility measure assumes (1) a utility curve that stays put and along which one can move up and down as income varies or (2) a utility curve whose shape is definable only on the basis of the current income as a reference point for change in levels of income. The former interpretation emphasizes dependence of utility on levels of income, while the latter emphasizes the dependence of utility on the changes in income around one's present position.

The most common type of utility curve has been one whose shape and position are independent of the particular income actually being realized at the time the curve of utility of income is constructed. For example, Friedman and Savage draw a utility curve dependent primarily upon levels of income rather than upon changes in income, and it is presumed that individuals choose as if they were moving along that curve.[18] The generic shape of the curve postulated by Friedman and Savage is shown in Figure 2.[19] This shape is supposed to explain the presence of both gambling and insurance. How does it do this?

Reference back to our method of predicting choices among uncertain prospects reminds us that choices will be made so as to maximize expected utility. A graphic interpretation is very simple. In Figure 2, let the income position now existing be A; let the individual be faced with a choice of staying where he is or of choosing the uncertain prospect of moving to income position B, with probability .999, or of moving to income position C, with probability .001. Position A represents paying fire insurance, while positions C and B form the

18. Op. cit.
19. The utility curve is unique up to a linear transformation.

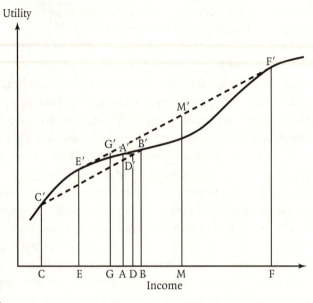

**FIGURE 2**

uncertain prospect where C is the position if a fire occurs with no insurance, and B is the position if no fire occurs with no insurance. Will he choose the uncertain prospect or the sure position A? The basis for the choice as implied in our postulates can be described graphically as follows: From point B′ draw a straight line to point C′. This straight line gives the expected utility of all uncertain prospects of the incomes B and C as the probability attached to C varies from zero to one. The point on this straight line yielding the expected utility of our uncertain prospect can be found by computing the expected *income*, D, and then rising vertically to point D′ on the straight line B′C′. The ordinate DD′ is the expected utility of the uncertain prospect. If the length of DD′ is less than AA′, as it is in our example, where AA′ denotes the utility of the income after taking insurance, then the person will choose the insurance and conversely.

It is apparent that if the utility curve were always convex, as in the first and last part of the curve in Figure 2, a person would never choose an uncertain prospect whose expected income was no greater than the insured-income position. And if the curve were concave, a person would always choose the uncertain prospect where the expected income was at least equal to the present insured position.

If the curve has the shape postulated by Friedman and Savage, it is possible to explain why a person will take out insurance and will, at the same time, engage in a gamble. To see how the latter is possible, suppose a person were at position A. At the same time that he might be willing to take out insurance, he might also be willing to gamble by choosing an uncertain prospect of ending up at E or F, despite its lower expected income at G, because the expected utility GG' of the uncertain prospect is larger than the utility AA' of position A. Friedman and Savage tentatively attempt to lend some plausibility to this shape of utility curve by conjuring that economic society may be divisible into two general income-level classes, the lower one being characterized by the first convex part of the curve, and the higher one by the upper convex section. An intermediate group is in the concave section.

H. Markowitz has pointed out certain unusual implications of the Friedman-Savage hypothesis.[20] A person at the point M would take a fair bet with a chance to get to F. This seems unlikely to be verified by actual behavior. Secondly, if a person is at a position a little below F, he will not want insurance against small probabilities of large losses. Further, any person with income greater than F will never engage in any fair bet. But wealthy people do gamble. Is it solely the love of risk taking? To overcome these objections, Markowitz postulates that utility is related to *changes* in the level of income and that the utility function has three inflection points. The middle one is at the person's "customary" income level, which, except in cases of recent windfall gains and losses, is the present income. The income interval between the inflection points is a nondecreasing function of income. The curve is monotonically increasing but bounded; it is at first concave, then convex, then concave, and finally convex.

Markowitz's hypothesis is consistent with the existence of both "fair" (or slightly "unfair") insurance and lotteries. The same individual will both insure and gamble. The hypothesis implies the same behavior whether one is poor or rich.

Markowitz recognizes that until an unambiguous procedure is discovered for determining when and to what extent current income deviates from customary income, the hypothesis will remain essentially nonverifiable because it is not capable of denying any observed behavior. The Markowitz hypothesis reveals perhaps more forcefully than the Friedman-Savage hypothesis, that utility has no meaning as an indicator of a level of utility. Utility has meaning only for changes in situations. Thus, while I might choose to receive an increase in income rather than no increase, there is no implication that after I have received

20. H. Markowitz, "The Utility of Wealth," *Jour. Pol. Econ.* (April 1952), 60, 151–58.

it for a while I remain on a higher utility base—however interpreted—than formerly. It may be the getting or losing, the rising or the falling that counts rather than the actual realized position. In any event, Markowitz's hypothesis contains no implications about anything other than changes in income.

Our survey is now completed. We started with developments after the Slutsky, Hicks, Allen utility position in which utility is measured up to monotone transformations only. This meant exactly no more and no less than that utility is ordinal. In other words, the numerical size of the increments in the numbers in any one measure (column of numbers in Table I) is without meaning. Only their signs have significance. Utility translation: marginal utility has meaning only in being positive or negative, but the numerical value is meaningless, i.e., *diminishing* or *increasing* marginal utility is completely arbitrary, since one can get either by using the appropriate column.[21]

The first postwar development was the von Neumann and Morgenstern axioms which implied measurable utility up to a linear transformation, thus reintroducing diminishing or increasing marginal utility,[22] and which also implied a hypothesis or maxim about rational behavior. This was followed by the Friedman and Savage article and Marschak's paper. These papers are essentially identical in their postulates and propositions, although the presentation and exposition are so different that each contributes to an understanding of the other. The Friedman and Savage paper, however, contains an added element: they attempt to prophesy the shape of the curve of utility of income that would be most commonly revealed by this measurement process. Mosteller and Nogee then made a unique contribution in really trying to verify the validity and applicability of the postulates. Most recently, Markowitz criticized the Friedman and Savage conjecture about the shape of utility of income curve, with his own conjecture about its dependence upon income changes. And that is about where matters stand now.

A moral of our survey is that to say simply that something is, or is not, measurable is to say nothing. The relevant problems are: (1) can numerical values be associated with entities and then be combined according to some rules so as

---

21. It is a simple task—here left to the reader—to find current textbooks and articles—which will be left unnamed—stating that the indifference curve analysis dispenses with the concept of utility or marginal utility. Actually it dispenses only with *diminishing* or *increasing* marginal utility.

22. Incidentally, the *Theory of Games* of von Neumann and Morgenstern is completely independent of their utility discussion.

to predict choices in stipulated types of situations, and (2) what are the transformations that can be made upon the initially assigned set of numerical values without losing their predictive powers (validity)? As we have seen, the currently proposed axioms imply measurability up to a linear transformation. Choices among uncertain prospects are predicted by a simple probability-weighted sum of the utilities assigned to the components of the uncertain prospect, specifically from the "expected utility."

And now, to provide emotional zest to the reader's intellectual activity, the following test is offered. Imagine that today is your birthday; a friend presents you with a choice among three lotteries. Lottery A consists of a barrel of 2000 tickets of which 2 are marked $1000, and the rest are blanks. Lottery B consists of another barrel of 2000 tickets of which 20 are marked $100, and the rest are blanks. Lottery C consists of a barrel of 2000 tickets of which 1 is marked $1000, and 10 are marked $100. From the chosen barrel one ticket will be drawn at random, and you will win the amount printed on the ticket. Which barrel would you choose? Remember there is no cost to you; this is a free gift opportunity. In barrel A the win of $1000 has probability .001, and the probability of getting nothing is .999; in barrel B the probability of winning $100 is .01, and getting nothing has probability .99; in barrel C $1000 has probability .0005, $100 has probability .005, and winning nothing has probability .9945. For each barrel the mathematical expectation is $1.00. The reader is urged to seriously consider and to make a choice. Only after making his choice should he read the footnote.[23]

23. Only the reader who chose C should continue, for his choice has revealed irrationality or denial of the axioms. This can be shown easily. He states he prefers C to A and to B. First, suppose he is indifferent between A and B; he doesn't care whether his friend chooses to give him A or B, just so long as he gets one or the other. Nor does he care how his friend decides which to give. In particular, if his friend tosses a coin and gives A if heads come up, otherwise B, he is still indifferent. This being so, a 50-50 chance to get A or B is equivalent to C, as one can see by realizing that C is really equivalent to a .5 probability of getting A and a .5 probability of getting B. Thus if A and B are indifferent, there is no reason for choosing C.

Second, the reader choosing C may have preferred A over B. We proceed as follows. Increase the price in B until our new B, call it B', is now indifferent with A. From the uncertain prospect of A and B' with probability of .5 for A. This is better than C, since C is nothing but an uncertain prospect composed of A and the old B, with probability of .5 for A. Where does this leave us? This says that the new uncertain prospect must be preferred to C. But since the new uncertain prospect is composed of .5 probability for A and .5 for B',

## Conclusion

1.  Some readers may be jumping to the conclusion that we really can use *diminishing* or *increasing* marginal utility and that the "indifference curve" or "utility isoquant" technique has been superfluous after all. This is a dangerous conclusion. The "indifference curve" technique is more general in not requiring measurability of utility up to a linear transformation. But its greatest virtue is that unlike the earlier "partial" analysis of demand of a single commodity the indifference curve analysis by using an extra dimension facilitates intercommodity analyses—the heart of price analyses. But does the more "precise" type of measurement give us more than the ordinal measurement gives? Yes. As we have seen, measurability "up to a linear transform" both implies and is implied by the possibility of predicting choices among uncertain prospects, the universal situation.

2.  Nothing in the rehabilitation of measurable utility—or choice-indicating numbers—enables us to predict choices among groups of sure prospects. The "utility" of a group of sure prospects is not dependent on *only* the utility (assigned number) of the *entities* in the combination. It is dependent upon the particular *combination of entities;* i.e., we do not postulate that the utility of one sure element in a group of sure things is independent of what other entities are included. We think it obviously would not lead to valid predictions of actual choices. Therefore, it must be realized that nothing said so far means that we could measure the total utility of a market basket of different entities by merely adding up the utilities of the individual component entities. No method for aggregating the utilities of the component entities for this purpose has been found; therefore, for this purpose we have to say that utility is not measurable.

3.  Is the present discussion more appropriate for a journal in psychology or sociology? If economists analyze the behavior of a system of interacting indi-

---

the chooser of C must be indifferent between the uncertain prospect and A. (In axiom 3 let A and B be indifferent, and let C be identically the same thing as A. In other words, if the two entities in the uncertain prospect are equally preferred, then the uncertain prospect is indifferent to one of the entities with certainty.) The upshot is that A is just as desired as the new uncertain prospect, which is better than C. Thus A is preferred to C, but the chooser of C denied this. Why? Either he understood and accepted the axioms and was irrational in making a snap judgment, or else he really did not accept the axioms. He may now privately choose his own escape. This example is due to Harry Markowitz.

viduals operating in field of action—called the economic sphere—by building up properties of the system from the behavior aspects of the individuals composing the system, then the economists must have some rationale of behavior applicable to the individuals. An alternative approach is to consider the whole system of individuals and detect predictable properties of the system. The classic example of this distinction is in physics. One approach postulates certain laws describing the behavior of individual molecules, or atom particles, while the other starts with laws describing the observable phenomena of masses of molecules. Apparently, most economists have relied upon the former approach, the building up from individuals—sometimes referred to as the aggregation of micro-economic analysis into macro-economic analysis. On the other hand, those who are skeptical of our ability to build from individual behavior find their haven in postulates describing mass behavior. The current utility analyses aid the former approach.

4. The expression "utility" is common in welfare theory. For demand theory and the theory of prediction of choices made by individuals, measurability of the quantity (called "utility") permits us to make verifiable statements about individual behavior, but there is as yet no such happy development in welfare theory. "Measurability up to a linear transformation" does not provide any theorems for welfare theory beyond those derivable from ordinality. I mention this in order to forestall temptations to assume the contrary. The social welfare function as synthesized by Hicks and Scitovsky, for example, does not require the "utility" (choice-ordering numbers) of each individual to be measurable up to a linear transformation. It is sufficient that the individual's utility be measurable up to a monotone transformation—or, in other words, that it have merely ordinal properties. Ordinal utility is adequate in this case because orderings are made of positions or states in which, as between the two states compared, everyone is better off in one state than in the other. The welfare function does not enable a ranking of two states in one of which some people are worse off.[24] This would require an entirely different kind of measure of utility for each person because of the necessity of making interpersonal aggregations of utilities. As yet no one has proposed a social welfare function acceptable for this purpose, nor has anyone discovered how, even in principle, to

24. Absolutely nothing is implied about taxation. For example, justification of progressive income taxation by means of utility analysis remains impossible. The best demonstration of this is still E. D. Fagan, "Recent and Contemporary Theories of Progressive Taxation," Jour. Pol. Econ. (Aug. 1938), 46, 457–98.

measure utility beyond the linear transformation. Even more important, the various elements in the concept of welfare (as distinct from utility) have not been adequately specified. In effect the utility whose measurement is discussed in this paper has literally nothing to do with individual, social, or group welfare, whatever the latter may be supposed to mean.

5. A brief obiter dictum on interpersonal utility comparisons may be appropriate. Sometimes it is said that interpersonal utility comparisons are possible, since we are constantly declaring that individual A is better off than individual B. For example, "a rich man is better off than a poor man." But is this really an interpersonal utility comparison? Is it not rather a statement by the declarer that he would prefer to be in the rich man's position rather than in the poor man's? It does not say that the rich man is happier or has more "utility" than the poor man. Even if the rich man has a perpetual smile and declares himself to be truly happy and the poor man admits he is sorrowful, how do we know that the rich man is happier than the poor man, even though both men prefer being richer to being poorer? If I were able to experience the totality of the poor man's situation and the rich man's and preferred the rich man's, it would not constitute an interpersonal comparison; rather it would be an intrapersonal, intersituation comparison.

It is hoped that the reader now has at his command enough familiarity with the meanings of measurability to be able to interpret and evaluate the blossoming literature on utility and welfare, and that this exposition has made it clear that welfare analysis gains nothing from the current utility analysis, and conversely.

# INFORMATION COSTS, PRICING
# AND RESOURCE UNEMPLOYMENT

Economic theory of exchange often appears to imply that demand changes induce instant wage and price adjustments to maintain full resource use. But unemployment, queues, rationing, and idle resources refute any such implication. And macroeconomic theory does not explain why demand decreases cause unemployment rather than immediate wage and price adjustments in labor *and* nonhuman resources. Instead, administered prices, monopolies, minimum wage laws, union restrictions, and "natural" inflexibilities of wages and prices are invoked.

This paper attempts to show that economic theory is capable of being formulated—consistently with each person acting as an individual utility, or wealth, maximizer without constraints imposed by competitors and without conventions or taboos about wages or prices—so as to imply shortages, surpluses, unemployment, queues, idle resources, and nonprice rationing with price stability. The theory implies massive correlated fluctuations in employment of both labor and capital in response to aggregate demand decreases—in a context of open market, individual utility maximizing behavior. The theory is general in that it applies to nonhuman goods as well as to human services. Though my primary motivation to explain "unemployed" resources arose from labor market behavior, the analysis is best exposited initially without special reference to labor markets.

The key, which, till recently, seems to have been forgotten, is that *collating information about potential exchange opportunities* is costly and can be performed in various ways.[1] Nobody knows as much as he would like (at zero cost) about

Reprinted from Armen A. Alchian, *Economic Forces at Work* (Indianapolis: Liberty Fund, 1977), 37–71. This article originally appeared in *Western Economic Journal* 7 (June 1969): 109–28, and is reprinted by permission of the author.

Acknowledgment for substantial aid is made to the Lilly Endowment, Inc., grant to UCLA for a study in the behavioral effects of different kinds of property rights.

1. A study of G. J. Stigler ("Information in the Labor Market," *Jour. Pol. Econ.*, Supplement 70 [October 1962]: 94–105) will reveal this paper to be a development and application of the fundamentals of that paper. See also, for earlier interest in this problem,

everyone else's offers and demands (including the properties of goods offered or demanded), but at a cost, more information can be acquired. Two questions guide our analysis. First, what are the means of providing information more efficiently? Second, given that information is costly, what kinds of substitute arrangements are used to economize on search costs?

## 1. Theory of Exchange, Unemployment, and Price Stability

In equilibrium everyone has equal marginal rates of substitution, but how is that equilibrium equality approached? It is not rational to expect a person to exchange with the first person he happens to meet with a different subjective value. It will pay to seek a higher "bid" or a lower "ask." Discovery of the variety of bids and offers and the best path or sequence of actual exchange prices toward an "equilibrium" requires costly search over the population. Institutions facilitate and economize on that search. The marketplace is an example. A large and costly portion of so-called marketing activity is information dissemination. Advertisements, window displays, sales clerks, specialist agents, brokers, inventories, catalogues, correspondence, phone calls, market research agencies, employment agencies, licensing, certification, and aptitude testing services (to name a few) facilitate the spread and acquisition of knowledge about potential demanders and suppliers and their goods and about prices they can expect to see prevail.

Marketing includes many activities: (a) "extensive" searching for all possible buyers or sellers; (b) communication of information about characteristics of the goods of each party—the "intensive" search;[2] (c) contract information; (d) contract enforcement; (e) "buffer inventories" by sellers; (f) queueing of buyers; and (g) provision of price predictability. Two propositions about the costs of production or market opportunity information will be critical in the ensuing analysis.

(1) *Dissemination and acquisition (i.e., the production) of information conforms to the ordinary laws of costs of production—viz., faster dissemination or acquisition costs more.*

------

A. Rees ("Wage Determination and Involuntary Unemployment," Jour. Pol. Econ. 59 [April 1951]: 143–44, and "Information Networks and Labor Markets," Am. Econ. Rev., Supplement 56 [May 1966]: 559–66). K. J. Arrow and W. M. Capron ("Dynamic Shortages and Price Rises: The Engineer Scientist Case," Quart. Jour. Econ. 73 [May 1959]: 292–308) used the difficulty of knowing the true market demand and supply as a reason for individual delays in adapting to the equilibrating price and output.

2. This terminology is taken from Rees, "Wage Determination."

A simple, fruitful characterization of the search for information is sampling from a distribution of "offers" (or "bids") with some mean and dispersion. As the sample is enlarged, the observed maximum value will increase *on the average* at a *diminishing* rate. Assuming search (sampling) at a constant rate, with time thereby measuring size of sample, the expected (mathematical expectation of the) maximum observed value will rise from the median at a diminishing rate toward the upper limit of the distribution.[3] That limit will exceed the past actual price, since there is no necessity for the past sale to have been negotiated at the highest possible price (with exhaustive prior sampling, regardless of cost).

(2) *Like any other production activity, specialization in information is efficient. Gathering and disseminating information about goods or about oneself is in some circumstances more efficiently done while the good or person is not employed, and thus able to specialize (i.e., while specializing) in the production of information.* If seeking information about other jobs while employed is more costly than while not employed, it can be economic to refuse a wage cut, become unemployed, and look for job information.[4] The deeper the wage cut in the old job, the cheaper the choice of unemployment in order to ferret information. Without this proposition of *differential* search costs, the theory would not be able, consistently with wealth maximizing choices, to account for the fact that some people refuse to accept a low wage while acquiring and comparing job information.

The fact that being employed is itself a recommendation to a prospective employer does not deny that it may pay to forsake that recommendation in view

---

3. For example, if potential prices are normally distributed with mean, m, and with variance, $\sigma^2$, then the expected maximum observed bid $W(n)$ at the n-th observation is approximately $m + \sigma(2 \log n)^{1/2}$. $W(n)$ starts at m and increases at a decreasing rate with n. If we assume one observation every $\lambda$ units of time, then we can replace n by $\lambda t$, and obtain $W$ as a function of time of search.

$$W(t) = m + \sigma(2 \log \lambda t)^{1/2}$$

Further, if we increase expenditures on search, the rate of search can be increased per unit time, whatever is the environment of search; in other words, the effective $\lambda$ is a function of the environment, $V$, and of the expenditures on search $E(t)$: $\lambda = f[V, E(t)]$. A larger expenditure implies a larger $\lambda$ and if we let a larger $V$ denote a more costly search environment, then a larger $V$ implies a smaller $\lambda$.

4. This proposition is added to those contained in Stigler and is crucial to much that follows.

of the large wage cut required to obtain it. The value of such a recommendation would imply acceptance of greater wage cuts to keep jobs. However, the question here is why anyone would choose to forsake that lower wage and accept unemployment—not why wages are sometimes cut to hold jobs.

Our choice of words is deliberate when speaking of seeking "job-information" rather than seeking "jobs." Jobs are always easily available. Timely information about the pay, working conditions, and life expectancy of all available jobs is not cheap. In a sense, this kind of unemployment is self-employment in information collection.

This applies to nonhuman resources as well. For example, the automobile on a used car lot—out of "normal" service (unemployed)—facilitates cheaper information to potential buyers. Similarly, unoccupied apartments and houses (like cars and people) are cheaper to show to prospective clients.[5]

A graph of some characteristics of search and its costs is shown in Figure 1. Time is on the horizontal scale, and price or wage on the vertical. For any constant rate of search over the population of potential buyers, time and scope of search can both be measured on the horizontal scale. If some good were sold to the first found offerer at $t_0$, the price would be $P_0$. The height of curve $P_0P_t$ is the "expectation" of the maximum discerned available contract price found by time $t$—assuming discerned options do not disappear or decay with time. The line rises at a decreasing rate, rather than being horizontal at $P_t$, as it would be if information about all potential offers were costless (and if all people knew all the characteristics of the good). As the sample (information) increases, the expected maximum discerned available price increases by successively smaller increments. In terms of costs, there are increasing marginal costs of unit increments of expected maximum ascertained price.[6] The curve for an unemployed searcher will be above that for an employed searcher—if unemploy-

---

5. We can now identify a "perfect" market—one in which all potential bids and offers are known at zero cost to every other person, and in which contract enforcement costs are zero. Characteristics of every good need to be known perfectly at zero cost. A "perfect" market would imply a "perfect" world in which all costs of production, even of "exchanges," were zero. It is curious that while we economists never formalize our analysis on the basis of an analytical ideal of a perfect world (in the sense of costless production), we have postulated costless information as a formal ideal for analysis. Why?

6. If we subtract the cumulated search costs over the search interval from the then best observed sales bid price, the net price line, now net of search costs, will hit a peak after which it will decrease, assuming no "decay" in value of earlier perceived options.

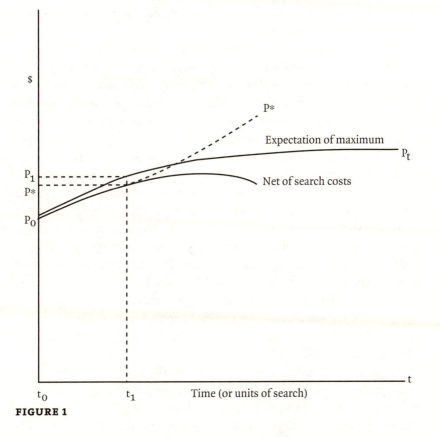

**FIGURE 1**

ment is to occur. By identifying characteristics that will affect the shape and position of the curves we can reduce unemployment patterns.

*Liquidity.* The analogy to liquidity is obvious. Liquidity concepts can be portrayed by the same diagram. The ratio of $P*$ to $P_t$ is one dimension of the liquidity *vector*. Another, for example, is the time to $t_1$.

The expectation of discerned maximum offers is a function of amount of expenditures (of all types) for acquiring information up to any moment. A potential (expected maximum discerned) *gross* price will be higher, as of any time t, if more is spent on hastening the information-acquiring process. The seller nets a reward equal to $P_1$ minus his search costs, and the buyer pays $P_1$ plus his search costs. A perfectly liquid asset is one for which $P_0P_t$ is horizontal at height $P_t$ with no search costs. Money is typically regarded as a resource fulfilling these criteria.[7] It enters into almost every exchange because it provides the most economical vehicle of exchange.

*Brokers and Middlemen.* The $P_0P_t$ curve reveals an opportunity for exchange with an intermediary broker. Since this analysis is applicable to nonhuman goods as well as to labor, it will be profitable for a "middleman" or "broker" to offer at the initial moment, $t_0$, a price higher than $P_0$ if he believes the discerned resale value of the good (net of his search costs) will increase at a rate greater than the interest rate and greater than that of the existing possessor of the good. The price he would offer at $t_0$ would be, at most, the present value of the expected maximum discerned bid price for the time his discerned price line (net of his search costs) was rising at a rate equal to the interest rate. This can be illustrated by inserting an "iso-net-present value" $P*P*$, the height of which at the vertical axis ($t = 0$) shows the maximum present net discounted value as of $t_0$ of any future net amount available (net of the middleman's search costs). The price that would be offered now by the middleman is $P*$. The difference between the present-value price $P*$ and the future selling price $P_1$ is essentially the retail-wholesale price spread, or the bid-ask spread of brokers, wholesalers, or retailers. Since the middleman is a successful specialist in search, his search costs are, by definition, lower, and hence his $P*$ is higher than for a nonmiddleman, nonspecialist.[8]

*Price Stability: Economizing on Information and Market Adjustment Costs.* Aside from the obvious ways to produce information (e.g., advertising and specialist middlemen), there are less well recognized ways involving price stability, unemployed resources, and queues (in which costs are incurred to *reduce* search and other marketing costs even more). Inventories economize on costs of information. Inventories may appear to be idle, excess, or unemployed resources, but they can be interpreted as an economical use of resources.[9] An oversimplified but suggestive example is the problem faced by a newsboy who sells an average of 100 copies of a daily paper—but not always 100 each day. The more accurately he tries to predict and the more quickly he adjusts to imperfectly predictable fluctuations in the flow of demand, the greater are the costs of his action. Potential customers may prefer that he stock an excessive number on

7. For an illustration of the application of information and search costs to money and liquidity, per se, see H. L. Miller, "Liquidity and Transaction Costs," *Southern Econ. Jour.* 32 (July 1965): 43–48.

8. H. Demsetz, "The Cost of Transacting," *Quart. Jour. Econ.* 82 (February 1968): 33–53.

9. T. L. Saaty, *Elements of Queueing Theory* (New York, 1961).

the average with instant availability from inventories, despite higher costs caused by unsold copies. The higher cost may be manifested to customers as a lower quality of product, fewer sellers, or a higher price. But this extra cost (of the unsold papers) will be less than if the newspaper sellers attempted to obtain complete information about demands at each future moment or to make instantaneous adjustments in the number of papers without an inventory. In brief, the costs of unsold items are incurred to reduce even more the information costs in marketing.

Another option exists. The seller could change price instantly to always clear the market when demand fluctuates and thereby never have an inventory of unsold goods awaiting purchasers.[10] Retailers would not be awaiting buyers. Retailers could avoid reservations and queues by varying price instantly with the random fluctuations of appearance of customers. Why don't they? After all, that is what happens, or seems to happen, in the futures markets and stock markets.[11]

Consider the consequences. Patrons appear at random intervals, though the probability density of the rate may be predictable. Would patrons prefer to see the market instantly cleared with no queues whatsoever—but only with price fluctuations to do the rationing? Not necessarily. That might *induce more search elsewhere* than under queueing. Customers may prefer more predictable prices with enhanced probability of some queues and less search. Unpredictable prices, as well as queues, impose costs on patrons; there is no reason why only

10. The expression "demand fluctuation" covers a great amount of mischievousness. For a more rigorous conceptualization, a "probability distribution of latent offers" is better. Reference to the mean and variance of that distribution of potentially discernible or revealed offers would provide some specification of the demand confronting a seller. Furthermore, there is not a *given* flow of *revealed* demanders. Offers could be emitted or received at a slower or faster rate. The analogy to emissions of particles from radioactive elements is apt. The emissions have a "mean" and a "range" of values (voltages) and a random time between emission, i.e., the "rate" of emission. These "randomly spaced" emissions of market offers can be characterized by a probability distribution. The *rate* at which offers are discerned by the seller can be increased or decreased by engaging more information activity (i.e., marketing activity). This paper is not trying to specify some special underlying distribution rigorously. Some progress toward this is to be found in Stigler, "Information in the Labor Market."

11. As a matter of fact, even on the futures markets and stock exchanges, there are specialists and "scalpers" who stabilize price by providing a buffer inventory (H. Working, "Tests of a Theory Concerning Floor Trading on Commodity Exchanges," *Food Research Institute Studies: Supplement* 1 [1967]: 5–48).

*one* should be avoided regardless of the cost of the other. Retailers must balance (a) costs of search induced by unpredictable prices and of inventories against (b) costs of queues and of waiting in queues. If prices of all sellers were known, extensive persistent search could be reduced (there would still be search for small queues), and the gross cost could fall, even though the money price were higher. This is basically one of the economic defenses of manufacturer-imposed retail prices.

A seller who eliminates a nonpredictably fluctuating, transient, market-clearing price could offer his patrons a saving in costs of search. He could make price more predictable by carrying a larger inventory to buffer the transient demand fluctuations, and customers would reduce search costs with the assurance of a stable (i.e., predicted) price if they accepted some costs of waiting in a queue.

The queue length could vary with constant price so long as the *mean* rate of purchases is matched by the production rate. The greater the variance in the transient rate of appearance of shoppers, the greater will be the variation in the length of the queue and *also* the longer will be the average length of the line. An alternative to customer queues is "queueing" of an inventory as a buffer to eliminate customer queues while price is constant. Among these options—transient and instant price changes, customer queues, inventories, and continued market search for better options—what determines the efficient extent of each?

Customers engage in repeat purchases; in making purchase plans, predictability of price is conducive to closer adjustment to optimal purchases. Revising purchase plans and actions is costly. If one finds a dinner price transiently and unexpectedly high because of randomly high demand at the moment he appears in the restaurant, he will have been led to inappropriate action. Ex post his action was not optimal. To avoid such losses, he will, thereafter, prior to concluding a purchase, engage in more search among sellers to discover unusually, transiently low prices. This extra search is less costly than taking one's chances as to what price he will face in a transiently fluctuating market.

In general, smaller and more frequent random fluctuations in demand (i.e., with a fixed expectation in the probability density function), greater search costs, greater value of the buyer's time, and less burdensome forms of queueing or rationing will all increase the incidence of price stability. If the demand probability density function shifted *predictably*, prices would vary—as they do for daytime and evening restaurants and theaters for example. A lower cost of holding inventories relative to the value of the product will increase the relative size of inventories and increase price stability and shorten queues for any frequency and size of random demand fluctuations.[12]

Accordingly, we should expect to see some prices maintained relatively rigidly over time and among retail stores (with so-called Fair Trade Laws) as *manufacturers* seek to assure final customers of the lower *overall* costs of purchasing their items for high quality, but low value, items purchased by people whose time is relatively valuable (i.e., high wage groups).

An obvious application of the analysis is to shop hours. Stores are open during known hours and stay open even when there are no customers in sight. A store could have lower prices if customers were to ring a bell and wait for the owner to open the store, but this would impose waiting costs on the patrons. I presume the advantage to the store operator (with lower pecuniary prices to customers) in closing his store when no customers are in sight is smaller than the convenience to shoppers.

More apartment units are built than the owner expects, on the average, to rent. This, of course, assumes that *revealed* demand to *him* for his apartments is neither continuous nor costlessly and perfectly predictable. It pays to build more apartments to satisfy *unpredictable* vagaries in "demand fluctuations" if such demand fluctuations cannot be accommodated by costless reallocation among demanders or "no inconvenience" from immediate rent changes. The apartment owner could always keep apartments fully rented at a lower, quickly revised rental; or at higher stable rentals, he could have vacancies part of the time. A landlord, faced with an empty apartment, could cut the rent sufficiently to induce immediate rental to the first person he happened to see, if he ignored marketing (including moving) costs. But in view of costs of transactions, contract revision, and displaying and arranging for new higher paying tenants of already *occupied* premises, it sometimes yields greater wealth to forgo transient rent revision that would keep apartments *always* rented. In maintaining vacancies, he is responding to renters' preferences (a) to examine apartments, to have rental predictability, and to move more spontaneously rather than (b) to continually adjust to rental changes, or (c) to make plans and reservations in advance if there were price predictability *and no* inventory of vacant apartments. The "vacancies" serve as inventories; as such, they do not warrant rent reductions.

12. Had this paper been devoted also to the conditions that induce non-market-clearing prices, even with predictable demand, it would have included a discussion of forms of property rights in the goods being sold.

If instant production were no more costly than slower production or adjustment, people could always produce whatever was wanted only at the moment it was wanted. In fact, however, producing in advance at a less hasty, less expensive rate and holding an "excess" for contingent demands economizes in having more services at a cost that is worth paying, taking into account the value of being able to adapt to changed demands without long-range, advance "reservations-type" planning. The situation is the same for a home with enough bathrooms and dining space to accommodate more visitors than one will ordinarily have. To say there is "idle," "wasted," or "unemployed" bathroom or dining room capacity is to consider only the cost of that extra capacity while ignoring its infrequent-use value and the greater costs of other ways of obtaining equally high convenience or utility.

The foregoing considerations suggest that in a society with (a) costs of obtaining information about sellers' "asking" prices, (b) costs of sellers' obtaining information about customers' demand, and (c) a tendency for unpredicted price changes to induce extra search by buyers and sellers, the "ideal" market will not be characterized by prices that instantly fluctuate so as always to clear the market without queues by buyers or sellers. Instead, to reduce the losses consequent to unpredictable delivery times if prices were perfectly stable, it pays (a) sellers to hold inventories, (b) buyers to accept some queueing—as means of purchasing at predictable prices and avoiding higher search costs that would be induced if with instant price adjustments there were no queues and inventories, and (c) buyers sometimes to continue shopping before making a contract. The stable price accompanied by queues and inventories will be slightly higher than if it were not stabilized by queues and inventories—but the higher pecuniary price can save on search and disappointed, incorrect price anticipations. This higher price to the buyer is lower than the sum of the average lower fluctuating price plus search and inconvenience costs to the buyer.

Before leaving the question of price stability as an information-economizing device, it is useful to try to complete the catalogue of reasons for price stability in the sense that some prices are persistently below or above the market-clearing level. This can be done by introducing considerations of the property rights held by the allocator of the goods, of price controls, and of transaction-enforcement costs. Attenuated property rights as prevail in nonprofit enterprises, not-for-profit institutions, or publicly owned enterprises induce prices below the market-clearing level. They do so because the higher income or wealth derivable with a higher price at a market-clearing level does not become the private property of the allocator or principal to whom it may be responsible.

Transactions costs also induce price inflexibility and rationing at a zero price. If the value of the item being rationed is less than the costs of collecting a fee and enforcing the contract (as in parking space or street use), the price will be chronically too low. Or if the change in price to a market-clearing level is less valuable than the costs of enforcing that changed price, the price will lag on non-market-clearing levels.[13]

## II. Labor Markets

Though most analyses of unemployment rely on wage conventions, restrictions, and controls to retard wage adjustments above market-clearing levels, Hicks and Hutt penetrated deeper. Hicks suggested a solution consistent with conventional exchange theory. He stated that "knowledge of opportunities is imperfect" and that the time required to obtain that knowledge leads to unemployment and a delayed effect on wages.[14] It is precisely this enhanced significance that this paper seeks to develop, and which Hicks ignored when he immediately turned to different factors—unions and wage regulations, placing major blame on both for England's heavy unemployment in the 1920s and 30s.

We digress to note that Keynes, in using a quantity-, instead of a price-, adjusting theory of exchange, merely postulated a "slow" reacting price without showing that slow price responses were consistent with utility or wealth maximizing behavior in open, unconstrained markets. Keynes's analysis was altered in the subsequent income-expenditure models where reliance was placed on "conventional" or "noncompetitive" wage rates. Modern "income-expenditure" theorists assumed "institutionally" or "irrationally" inflexible wages resulting from unions, money illusions, regulations, or factors allegedly idiosyncratic to labor. Keynes did not assume inflexibility for only wages. His theory rested on a more general scope of price inflexibility.[15] The present paper may in part be viewed as an attempt to "justify" Keynes's presumption about price response to disturbances in demand.

13. See A. A. Alchian and W. R. Allen, *Exchange and Production: Theory in Use* (Belmont, Calif., 1969), 153–79; Arrow and Capron, "Dynamic Shortages"; and M. Friedman, "The Monetary Studies of the National Bureau," *The National Bureau Enters Its Forty-Fifth Year, Forty-Fourth Annual Report* (Washington, 1964), 14–18.

14. J. R. Hicks, *The Theory of Wages*, 2d ed. (London, 1963), 45, 58. And he added another type—"the unemployment of the man who gives up his job in order to look for a better."

15. For a thorough exposition and justification of these remarks on Keynes, see A. Leijonhufvud, *On Keynesian Economics and the Economics of Keynes* (Oxford, 1968).

In 1939 W. H. Hutt exposed many of the fallacious interpretations of idleness and unemployment. Hutt applied the analysis suggested by Hicks but later ignored it when discussing Keynes's analysis of involuntary unemployment and policies to alleviate it.[16] This is unfortunate, because Hutt's analysis seems to be capable of explaining and accounting for a substantial portion of that unemployment.

If we follow the lead of Hicks and Hutt and develop the implications of "frictional" unemployment for *both* human and *nonhuman* goods, we can perceive conditions that will imply *massive* "frictional" unemployment and depressions in open, unrestricted, competitive markets with rational, utility maximizing, individual behavior. And some tests of that interpretation can be suggested.[17]

*Unemployment.* The preceding analysis shows why an employee will not necessarily accept a pay cut to *retain* a job, even though some current wage income is better than "none." An employee correctly and *sensibly* believes he can, with some search and evaluation of alternatives, get approximately his old wage at some other job; after all, that is why he was getting what he did at his current job. If looking and "finding out" is more costly while employed, he may have reason to choose temporary unemployment as an efficient form of "producing" or investing in information.

There is reason for rejecting even a "temporary" wage cut. A subsequently restored demand will not be immediately revealed to the employee-seller at zero cost; he will continue at the lower wage than he could get elsewhere, if only he had incurred costs to "find out." Of course, employer competition

---

16. W. H. Hutt, *The Theory of Idle Resources* (London, 1939), 165–69.

17. Many labor economists have used elements of this approach in their writings. In that sense, nothing said in the preceding is new. But we are attempting to collate and assemble these elements into a general theory of pricing and exchange of goods and service in which labor is included. For example, see H. Kasper, "The Asking Price of Labor and the Duration of Unemployment," *Rev. Econ. Stat.* 49 (May 1967): 165–72; A. C. Pigou, *Lapses from Full Employment* (London, 1945); R. V. Rao, "Employment Information and Manpower Utilization," *Manpower Jour.* 1 (July–September 1965): 7–15; L. Reynolds, *Labor Economics and Labor Relations*, 4th ed. (Englewood Cliffs, N.J., 1964); A. M. Roose, "Do We Have a New Industrial Feudalism?" *Am. Econ. Rev.* 48 (December 1958): 903–20; H. L. Sheppard and A. H. Belitsky, *The Job Hunt: Job-Seeking Behavior of Unemployed Workers in a Local Economy* (Kalamazoo, 1965); V. Stoikov, "Some Determinants of the Level of Frictional Employment: A Comparative Study," *Intl. Lab. Rev.* 93 (May 1966): 530–49.

would not reveal subsequent demand increases instantly; employers also have costs of getting information about alternatives. The cost of learning about all potentially available bids and offers (for employers, as well as employees, and the attributes of the goods being offered) restricts the speed of price adjustments. In sum, a refusal to cut wages to retain continuous present employment is neither nonoptimal behavior nor adherence to a convention as to "proper" wages.[18]

Any firm experiencing a demand decrease could try to lower costs (to maintain output) by offering less to its inputs. But if providers of inputs know, or believe, they have undiminished opportunities elsewhere they will not accept the cut.[19] It seems exceedingly unlikely that all providers of inputs would know that all their alternatives had deteriorated (if, indeed, they had) so as to induce them to accept a cut sufficient to retain their current employment. The larger the portion of the providers of inputs who do not regard their alternative discoverable

18. For an indication of the difficulties in formulating as well as solving the optimal search problem, see J. MacQueen and R. G. Miller, Jr., "Optimal Persistence Policies," *Oper. Res. Jour.* 16 (March–April 1968): 362–80; J. J. McCall, "The Economics of Information and Optimal Stopping Rules," *Jour. Bus.* 38 (July 1965): 300–317; and, especially, J. J. McCall, "Economics of Information and Job Search," RM-5745-OEO, Santa Monica, 1968.

19. A seller faced with decreased demand by a buyer does not regard it as a reliable indicator of similar changes in demand by all other demanders for that service. Yet such behavior has been described as an irrational holding of "less than unity (or even zero) elasticity of price expectation." A decrease in price available from a buyer does not mean all other buyers have reduced their offer prices. To the extent we see only a part of the potential "market" at any one time, it is rational to believe that a decrease in price here does not imply all potential offers will have fallen elsewhere. Keynes, in assuming inelastic price expectations, could have been arguing that a decrease in wages from a current employer or a small set of them is not sufficient to warrant the expectation they are lower every place as well. The contrast with securities is especially striking. Insofar as the securities market is a cheaper market—that is, insofar as it reflects more cheaply a larger, more complete sample of bids and offers of the population—any fall in an observed price is more likely indicative of a decrease in other potential offers as well; the elasticity of expectations about yet-to-be discerned available prices with search should be higher. Thus there is nothing inconsistent in assuming different price expectations elasticities in different markets; in fact there is much to be gained in detecting factors that make them different. See J. Tobin, "Liquidity Preference as Behavior Towards Risk," *Rev. Econ. Stud.* 25 (October 1957): 65–86, and W. Fellner, *Monetary Policies and Full Employment* (Berkeley, 1946), 141–51, for examples of failures to make the distinction.

opportunities as having deteriorated, the larger is the required price cut an employer must ask the complementary inputs to accept if he is to continue their employment in current jobs.[20]

*Layoffs.* There remains a phenomenon that obscures the present interpretation. For example, General Motors lays off men when demand for cars drops, without any negotiations about a temporary wage cut. It is tempting to blame unions or to conclude that no wage, however low, would enable GM profitably to maintain employment, or that lower wages were impossible because of pressure from those workers who are not laid off. But suppose there were no such pressure and no union contracts. What would evolve as the "sensible" response when GM's demand fell? Employers learn that wage cuts sufficient to justify profitable maintenance of the prior rate of output and employment would be too low to keep employees, given their beliefs about alternatives. And so layoffs are announced without fruitless wage renegotiations.

If there are job-switching costs, but a man's search costs are not far greater when he is employed than unemployed, a *temporary* wage cut is more likely to be acceptable. If the *temporarily* reduced wage offer is too low to make work worthwhile, the result is a "temporary layoff" taken without an intent of changing jobs. Insofar as onset and duration of "temporary" conditions are *predictable*, the situation is a recognition of normal working hours (e.g., not working at nights or on weekends) at *predictable* intervals because the worker prefers leisure to the wages available during those hours. If the onset of the decreased demand is unpredictable (building workers), but if its probability is believed known, this is again akin to weekend rest—and the wage rate is adjusted to reflect that. Building workers are an example; "casual" labor is another. If the demand reduction persists longer than expected, the person will begin a job-information search.

If job-information costs depend upon whether one is employed or unemployed, then unemployment can occur (with or without moving costs). If there are moving costs also, the *length* of unemployment will be longer. But *differential* information costs are necessary for the incidence of unemployment. A *common* (i.e., undifferentiated) cost of search and job switching would only mean a

---

20. The deeper the wage cut necessary to retain the old job, the greater the incentive to embark on job information search while unemployed. The greater the degree of seniority, the greater the wage cut that could be imposed before unemployment, for equally high seniority elsewhere cannot be obtained by a job change. The greater threatened wage cut is fought by the requirement that lower seniority men be dropped first.

greater reduction of wealth of employees, not their unemployment as a result of unexpected demand decreases.[21]

*Irrelevancy of Atomistic vs. Monopolistic Market Types.* Resources sold in atomistic markets (devoid of all monopolistic or "impure" competition) experience unemployment. In any market—even in a price taker's atomistic market, free of all price "administration" or constraints—if demand falls, some sellers will be unable immediately to sell their output at the price at which others are selling, because marketing (i.e., information) is costly. Although hazardous, it is tempting to push the analysis into the foundation of pure, perfect, and monopolistic markets; the idealized polar extreme, pure competition market assumes zero costs of market information and product identification. If costs of either are significant, some sellers would sell less at a higher price to cater to buyers who deem it not worthwhile looking further for lower price sellers— given the costs of convassing the population. To attribute unemployment to monopolistic markets or to administered conventional wages and prices is to assume that market information costs the same amount no matter how it is produced.

*Job Vacancies: Search by Employers.* Information is sought by employers also. Job vacancies, with search for best employees, are the counterpart to unemployment. An employer searching (i.e., competing) for more employees knows that a higher wage will get more employees—or that it costs more to more quickly find out who will work at the same wage with the same talent. Employer search activity will increase the incidence of job changes without the employees' having experienced unemployment, because employers will seek currently employed labor and offer better wages.

Uncertainty of the employer about the quality of a potential employee induces a lower initial wage offer. The best perceived offer to a prospective employee will reflect both the applicant's costs of canvassing all employers *and* the

---

21. Some of the preceding ideas can be summarized in terms of general economic theory by explicitly treating information as a good that is demanded and supplied. The sum of excess demands and supplies for all goods should be zero by definition. We may say that during unemployment there is an increased demand for and supply of information about market opportunities. Or we may say the market for each good is in equilibrium, but the production of market-opportunity-information has increased, leaving other production at equilibrium rates lower than would have existed had resources not been diverted to production of more market-opportunity information. This method of formulating the structure of the analysis saves Say's Principle that the sum of excess demand equals the sum of excess supplies—always.

employer's cost of learning more about the applicant. The more homogeneous the class to which the employer believes the applicant belongs—or the less the variance of the possible marginal productivity of the applicant—the closer will the applicant's discerned offers be to the maximum. He will more quickly settle on a new job.

*Interproduct Shift vs. "Depression" Unemployment.* The greater the rate of interproduct demand shifts, the larger will be unemployment. We could talk of interproduct demand shift unemployment and also of aggregate demand decrease (depression) unemployment, without any reference to *full* employment.[22] We shall occasionally use the term "full" employment to admit of unemployment in the absence of *aggregate* demand shifts. In such cases interproduct demand shifts will determine the degree of unemployment that is associated with "full" employment. That source of unemployment is usually called "frictional." But if aggregate demand changes, there is a change in the degree of unemployment, whatever it be called.

*Output per Unit of Input.* Faced with demand decreases that are regarded as transient, employers will retain employees and equipment because there is a cost of finding new employees as replacements. (Of course, any layoff probably involves loss of some employees.) Keeping "excessive" employees on the payroll is analogous to having empty apartments to allow for economic adjustment to transient unpredictable shifts in demand. Therefore, decreases in demand for an employer's products can imply a less than equivalent reduction in employment and a resultant apparent "higher cost" per output. This is more economical (efficient) than quickly adjusting the size of the work force.

*"Depression" Unemployment.* It is not necessary here to explain decreases in aggregate demand. Our purpose is to concentrate on the consequences of aggregate demand decreases without attention to feedback effects of unemployment on aggregate demand. A decrease in general demand causes an increase in unemployment because more people will accept unemployment to engage in search, and each unemployed person will look longer. Wage earning opportunities will diminish in the sense that lower wages are available elsewhere. People use time to *learn* that the failure to find other equally good job options as quickly as they thought they would reflects *diminished* alternatives in general, not unlucky search. The discerned maximum offers will be lower than if the structure of alternatives had not decreased. The lower level and slower rate of rise of best observed options is at first taken as an unlucky string of searches,

22. Hutt, *Theory of Idle Resources,* 35.

and so unemployment is extended in the expectation of "shortly" finding that elusive best option. And with each person looking longer, the total number of unemployed at any one time will be larger. (Incomes fall and feedback effects occur.) Each now has the added task of revising his whole pattern of expectations. Whereas he was formerly searching for a higher clearly formulated expected wage, now he must learn that the "best" has deteriorated.

If the decrease in aggregate demand is a continuing affair (induced, we shall assume for concreteness, by a continuing fall in the quantity of money), unemployment will persist at the higher level during the continuing decrease in demand, which must be continually "discovered." The greater the rate of decrease of general demand, the greater the extent and average duration length of unemployment. Thus a *continuing* decrease in the community's stock of money is associated with a continuing decrease in general demand and with continuing unemployment of human (and nonhuman) resources. Holding general demand at its *new* level would reduce unemployment. But the costs of that mode of recovery may be greater than action designed to increase aggregate demand back to the demand beliefs that people hold.

Conversely, if the rate of increase in the quantity of money accelerates (unanticipated), the general increase in demand will increase job vacancies, increase job information dispersal activity by employers, and increase the search by employers for information about available employable resources. "Jobs are easier to get," meaning the alternatives are better than they (as well as the present job) formerly were thought to be.

Changes in aggregate demand confuse the public. Each seller notices a changed demand for his current product, but he cannot tell if that is a change also in aggregate demand which affects options elsewhere. Whether he should shift to another option, as he should not if the demand change is general, or stay where he is and change price, is the question to be answered. Should an employee switch jobs upon receipt of a superior offer or should he look over the market more fully? Given interproduct fluctuations, any person who refuses unemployment search for the best alternative option can be misled into accepting another job too soon. He will, because of increasing demand, more easily find a job with higher wages than he now gets. Yet he should have held out longer, since the upward shift means he could have done better. Unemployment will be less than "optimal"—*given* the extent of *interproduct* demand shifts and of the differential costs of knowing other job potentials. In speaking of "optimal" unemployment, we are not suggesting that unemployment per se is desirable. We mean that *given the fact of differential search costs and demand shifts* it pays to engage in some search more economically while not employed. The opportunity to search while not employed is better than the lack of an opportunity to move to unemployment as a more efficient means of search. Given interproduct demand shifts, without unemployment the extent to which resources are in their most valuable uses is reduced, because the public is fooled into believing they have found the best available jobs, when, in fact, they have failed to invest in enough search to find "best" available jobs.

One cautionary note: Constant per capita aggregate demand is consistent with falling prices of final products. Falling consumer good prices in this case reflect lower costs of production, not reduced profitability of production. Resource prices will not fall. If there is an unanticipated inflation trend, the increased (unanticipated) aggregate demand (per capita) will reduce unemployment and maintain it at a lower level. If inflation is correctly anticipated, the change of unemployment implied for any given rate of change of aggregate demand will be lower than for unanticipated inflation, and it will be independent of the anticipated rate.

*Lag of What Behind What?* The analysis can be expressed more conventionally, but *not* as follows: "A reduction in demand involves a lag of wage rate decreases behind prices—which is a rise in real or relative wage rates. This rise implies lower employment because of diminishing marginal returns to labor inputs." That is not contained in the present analysis; wage rates and all other prices can fall at the *same* rate. But the lag that does occur is a lag of the *discernment* of the best available prices behind the new, as yet undiscerned, best (i.e., the new, unascertained lower *equilibrium*) prices which *when* discovered would restore employment. In Walrasian terms, the auctioneer does not instantaneously reveal the new equilibrium price vector. (Even in an actual auction, the time for bidders to reveal the best price is not trivial.) The "lag" is the *time for discovery*. The lag terminology tends to confuse a lag of wages behind other factor or product prices with the "lag" of discernment of the best opportunities behind the (undiscerned) equilibrating price—a price that is not freely or instantly revealed to the world. It follows that a general economywide demand decrease does not imply a correlation between real wage rates and depressions (and recoveries). Wage rates can fall as fast as other prices; *that* lag is not necessary for unemployment.[23]

---

23. An intriguing intellectual historical curiosum may be explainable by this theory, as has been brought to my attention by Axel Leijonhufvud. Keynes's powerful, but elliptical, definition of involuntary unemployment has been left in limbo. He said men were in-

Reduced employment of human *and nonhuman resources* when coupled with the conventional production function implies nothing about real output per employed input. Suppose that resources when faced with a demand decrease in present jobs *immediately* accepted the first available job—foregoing search for a better job. Job allocations would be "inefficient." Better allocations could be discerned with search, at a cost. The destruction of a former equilibrium is not followed by a costless immediate new equilibrium. But the faster it is sought the greater the costs. There is some optimal rate. Insofar as resources take interim jobs, while "inefficiently" searching for better jobs, or failing to search,

———

voluntarily employed if, ". . . in the event of a small rise in the price of wage-goods relative to the money-wage, both the aggregate supply of labor willing to work for the current money wage and the aggregate demand for it at that wage would be greater than the existing volume of employment" (Kasper, "The Asking Price of Labor," 15). To see the power and meaning of this definition (not *cause*) of unemployment, consider the following question. Why would a cut in money wages provoke a different response than *if* the price level rose relative to wages—when both would amount to the same change in relative prices, but differ only in the money price level? Almost everyone thought Keynes presumed a money-wage illusion. However, an answer more respectful of Keynes is available. The price-level rise conveys *different information*: money wages everywhere have fallen relative to prices. On the other hand, a cut in one's own money wage does not imply options elsewhere have fallen. A cut only in one's present job is revealed. The money versus real wage distinction is not the relevant comparison; the wage in the present job versus the wage in all other jobs is the relevant comparison. This rationalizes Keynes's *definition* of involuntary unemployment in terms of price-level changes. If wages were cut everywhere else, and *if* employees knew it, they would not choose unemployment—but they would if they believed wages were cut just in their current jobs. When one employer cuts wages, this does not signify cuts elsewhere. His employees rightly think wages are not reduced elsewhere. On the other hand, with a rise in the price level, employees have less reason to think their current real wages are lower than they are elsewhere. So they do not immediately refuse a lower real wage induced by a higher price level, whereas they would refuse an equal money wage cut in their present jobs. It is the revelation of information about prospects elsewhere that makes the difference. And this is perfectly consistent with Keynes's definition of unemployment, and it is also consistent with his entire theory of market adjustment processes (J. M. Keynes, *The General Theory of Employment, Interest and Money* [London, 1936]), since he believed wages lagged behind nonwage prices—an unproved and probably false belief (R. A. Kessel and A. A. Alchian, "The Meaning and Validity of the Inflation-Induced Lag of Wages Behind Prices," *Amer. Econ. Rev.* 50 [March 1960]: 43–66). Without that belief a general price-level rise is indeed general; it includes wages, and as such there is no reason to believe a price-level rise is equivalent in real terms to a money-wage cut in a particular job.

the "total" output vector will be smaller. In other words there is an optimal rate of unemployment *given* the rate of demand changes and *given* the differential costs of search. Very low unemployment resulting from inflationary forces can be socially inefficient, because resources mistakenly accept new jobs with too little search for better ones.

## III. Potential Tests of the Theory

Empirical tests of the theory can be sought by identifying characteristics of resources that increase the length and frequency of unemployment. Or situations in which the parameters of search conditions have changed can be compared to see if the implied changes in unemployment are observed. Since the class of alternative theories is open-ended, we shall simply indicate some implications of the present theory, letting the reader conjecture whether any alternative theory contains so broad a class of phenomena.

A discriminatory test of the theory lies not in its implication of "cyclical" labor unemployment fluctuations but in its implication of unemployment, price stability, and queueing for *all* types of resources—as suggested in the preceding pages.

One aggregative unemployment feature that is implied by this analysis is a positive correlation between extent of recovery in employment from a depression with the extent of the preceding decline; a *zero* correlation is implied between the magnitude of an expansion with the subsequent decline. Absence of tendencies to restore employment would imply no correlation between either pair of movements. There is, in fact, a positive correlation of magnitude of rises with the preceding decrease, and none between contractions and preceding rises.[24]

Resources with *less differentiated* costs (while employed or unemployed) of obtaining or dispersing information will have lower incidence, as well as shorter periods, of unemployment. Since an employer knows more about his own employees than about those of other employers, the probability of job changes (in tasks and grades) should be greater within a firm than among firms—especially in the upward direction. But the excess probability should decrease in the higher paid tasks, since extra search is more economic the higher the marginal product of an employee's position.

Readily (i.e., cheaply) recognizable, divisible (time, place, etc.), portable (more quickly moveable at a given cost), durable (more long-lived so as to re-

24. Friedman, "Monetary Studies of the National Bureau."

duce contracting costs) resources should display shorter length of unemployment.[25] What characteristics of goods yield low costs of information? Market demands and offers of homogeneous goods ("easily and cheaply recognized") should be cheaper to survey. Tract houses built by one builder should be easier to sell or rent than custom-built houses. "Easier" to sell or buy means that for given cost of search the realized price is closer, more quickly, to the best possible price obtainable (i.e., to the price that would have resulted if every potential buyer or seller had been canvassed and if each had full information about the product). An observable magnitude correlated with search costs should be the bid-ask spread, or markup, between the buying and selling price.[26] Thus inventories should be a smaller ratio to sales for low-information-cost items than for high. Frequent, repeated purchases by buyers should be correlated with knowledge about the item and alternative sources of purchases so that the bid-ask spread is lower. Goods sold in a formal market should have lower price spreads, reflecting the lower cost of information provided by formal markets. For example, over-the-counter stocks should have a larger bid-ask spread than stocks on more-organized markets.[27] New goods, we conjecture, involve higher information-dispersal costs and, hence, inventories relative to sales and wider price spreads.[28]

Apartments built in standard designs will have lower vacancy rates, because their characteristics are more cheaply understood, being already commonly known. At one time in Southern California, homes with swimming pools were so unusual as to fall in the higher information-cost category. Brokers' fees should therefore be larger in percentage terms.

Corporation stocks and bonds can be categorized by extent of knowledge by the public about the companies. If only a few people are informed, and unless they are more easily discovered, the market will be "thin," implying longer search periods or larger bid-ask spreads. The fewness of buyers or sellers is not, per se, a source of thinness or high information costs. Rather it is the higher cost of finding those few potential buyers among the larger population.

---

25. The preceding sentence reminds us of the attributes of money, and who can doubt that money has a very low "unemployment" rate? The suggestive analogy is, in fact, precisely to the point.

26. Demsetz, "The Cost of Transacting."

27. Ibid.

28. H. Demsetz, "Exchange and Enforcement of Property Rights," *Jour. Law Econ.* 7 (October 1964): 11–26.

Thus new "unseasoned" stocks and bonds should be markedly different in the bid-ask spread from older established stocks and bonds.[29]

Price stability with transient demand fluctuations is provided in the commodity and stock exchanges by floor traders. They trade on the "uptick and downtick" out of personal inventories, so as to reduce the variance of prices in response to what these traders regard as transient, random fluctuations in revealed market demands and supplies.[30]

The highest and the lowest priced variant of any class of goods will have a longer inventory period and larger retail-wholesale price spread than the typical or modal variant. We assume the extremes are less familiar types; information acquisition and disbursing costs will be larger. Special purpose machine tools should have a longer unemployment period than general purpose widely used types of equipment. Their inventory to sales ratio should be larger.

Standard types of used automobiles should have a shorter inventory interval (and lower ratio of inventory to sales) than do unusual used cars because information about the standard type of car is more common among potential buyers.

The larger the dispersion of potential bid prices among buyers, the greater the gross gain from continued search. The *absolute* (not relative) increment of discerned maximum price is larger if the dispersion is larger. Assuming that more unusual items (like paintings or works of art) are subject to a larger variance in valuation by the population, we expect a longer search period or larger markup.

The fewer the major employers in any community, the shorter will be the length, and the lower will be the incidence, of unemployment. Information about jobs is more readily available if there are fewer employers to search and to be told of one's talents. Wages should be more quickly adjusted in areas with only one employer. It has been suggested that the Negro in the South is faced with a smaller number of employers in the small towns than in the North and that he would therefore spend less time in job search in the South.[31]

If the highly skilled worker has a higher ratio of wages per hour to the value of self-generated income from extended job information search, then the highly paid laborer will resort more to employment agencies to economize on his relatively valuable search time. And he will use private more than public em-

29. Demsetz, "The Cost of Transacting."
30. Working, "Test of a Theory."
31. Suggested by H. Gregg Lewis.

ployment agencies, because private agencies, by being able to charge higher fees for higher salaried employees, have an incentive to devote more resources to placement of such people than do public agencies. Public agencies are closer competitors of private agencies for lower wage job applicants. (This does not mean low wage workers are not served by private agencies.) Looking at the employment problem from the point of view of the buyer or employer, one implication is that job vacancies for the expensive, heterogeneous executive will be longer-lived than for lower productivity and standard types of laborers. Some evidence of this should be revealed by employment agency fees, which, according to the present analysis, should be larger than for lower paying jobs.

Consider an employer looking for a manager and for a janitor. The value of a manager's services is higher than a janitor's, so a dollar spent for information about managers has a larger expected net marginal product. Because a better measure of the probability of the marginal product of high-marginal-product employees is worth more than a better measure of the probability of a lower-marginal-product employee, the employer will find it profitable to incur greater costs to get information about potential managers than for janitors. If skin color, eye shape, or sex is cheaply observable and believed to be correlated with quality or performance, the physical traits provide cheap (though incomplete) information about the quality of the person. For higher salaried jobs an extra dollar of costs for information about the potential employee is more likely to be profitable. The extra information will supplement the skin, eye, or sex indicator of quality. As a result, for higher paying jobs, the cheap information will be supplemented by other information. "Discrimination" solely according to eye shape, sex, skin color, and ethnic group is less profitable and, hence, less probable in higher paying jobs.[32]

If the evidence were to conform to all the foregoing implications, could this

---

32. The example of this paragraph was developed by A. De Vany. The same principle applies to short- versus long-term employees. This test is not relevant for the *differentiated* (according to employed or unemployed) search cost, but instead is derived from presence of search costs as such. One index of discrimination is the extent to which similar types of people work in clusters. Janitors are more likely to be mostly of the same types, but managers are more likely to be of a mixed group. Discrimination by cheaply observed traits should be less frequent for managers. My impression is that, in fact, for lower paying jobs there is greater concordance or uniformity of physical types than in higher paying jobs. A. A. Alchian and R. A. Kessel, "Competition, Monopoly, and the Pursuit of Pecuniary Gain," in *Aspects of Labor Economics*, Universities–National Bureau Committee for Economic Research Conference (Princeton University Press, 1962), 156–83.

interpretation be consistent with the events of 1929–39? There is no doubt that aggregate demand decreased rapidly from 1929 to 1932. Money stocks fell by about fifteen percent in 1929, 1931, and 1932. That does imply decreasing aggregate demand and abnormal unemployment. But it is the prolonged high unemployment after 1932 and the slow recovery, when aggregate demand stopped decreasing, that appears inconsistent with the theory. After 1932 national income and money stocks were increasing, and it is hard to believe that the rate of unemployment should not have decreased more rapidly. Even if the money stock had not increased, the convergence toward the full equilibrium price vector should have progressed more rapidly, if one is allowed to make *ad hominem* conjectures as to the expected rate of recovery.[33]

One thing that can save the proposed interpretation despite the prolonged unemployment is the imposition of arbitrary restrictions on permissible prices. Another factor that would help to explain the prolonged unemployment without rejecting the proposed interpretation is a sequential injection of depressing policy actions.

In other words a prolonged unemployment—without decreasing aggregate demand—would be consistent with the present interpretation of price behavior and unemployment if actual permissible (not the equilibrium) wages or prices were arbitrarily or exogenously increased. Events that support this interpretation have been chronicled by Roose and by Friedman.[34] A *sequence* of measures by the government (NIRA, Guffey Coal Act, agricultural price support, and the Labor Relations Act, minimum wages) arbitrarily and successively raised prices and wages over the period—not once and for all in 1932. In the absence of these autonomous factors pushing up permissible (though not the

---

33. There is one restraining factor in the unrestored quantity of money. If the quantity of money is not increased, the recovery of output and employment will imply still lower "full employment" equilibrium prices. The increased real output with constant stock of money requires still lower prices. This continuing deflationary pressure on prices would retard the return of production and employment to "full-use" levels. A sufficient increase in money stocks would have avoided the necessity of a fall in prices and wages and thereby would have speeded the rate of resource reallocation and, hence, the restoration of employment and output, by eliminating the cost of discerning the continuing reduction of potentially available prices and wages in all other opportunities. This was, of course, Keynes's advocated policy.

34. K. D. Roose, *The Economics of Recession and Revival* (New Haven, 1954), 45–57; M. Friedman, *A Monetary History of the United States, 1867–1960* (Princeton, N.J., 1964), 493–99.

equilibrating) wages and prices, 1933–37 would have shown greater employment and output. Roose attributes the low recovery to restrictive policies such as higher wages of NIRA codes, National Labor Relations Act, minimum wage enactments, imposition of social security taxes, and unemployment and old age security taxes on employment.[35] In the same interval other policies involving new regulatory agencies are believed to have temporarily restrained capital goods production. Securities and exchange acts, separation of investment from commercial banking, public utility holding company restrictions, the encouragement of labor strikes, and a general attack on businessmen all contributed to a lower capital goods equilibrating price—whatever their merits. To these factors add the 1937 monetary legal reserve debacle. If all of these factors had occurred once and for all in, say, 1932, the subsequent recovery rate should have been more rapid. But they, in fact, did occur in sequence over several years. If these considerations are accepted, the delayed recovery until 1941 in the face of nondecreasing aggregate demand is consistent with the differential-cost-of-information-about-best-available-job-opportunities theory of unemployment.

35. Roose, *Economics of Recession*, 45–57.

# WHAT IS THE BEST SYSTEM?

## I. Introduction

RAND's official purpose is to recommend preferred instrumentalities of air warfare between the United States and other continents. Our systems analyses, in seeking this end, combine the individual contributions of many specialists. However, specialized knowledge and extensive computations are insufficient to indicate which systems are better or worse than others. The best of many alternative systems cannot be determined unless a valid criterion is employed.

The purpose of this paper is partly negative and partly positive. Negatively, it can be shown that certain "criteria" are logically incorrect and will not discriminate between good systems and bad, except perhaps by accident. Section V—"Invalid Criteria and Their Consequences"—demonstrates, for example, the dangers implicit in maximizing output per unit of some single input. More positively, this paper indicates the nature of the logically correct criterion, but it also explains some of the practical difficulties that prevent its pure employment.

The essence of the criterion problem is that we do not know how to define and measure what might be loosely termed the utility and disutility functions. Thus, in actual practice, we can never distinguish with confidence the *optimum optimorum*. However, there are both reasonable and practical ways of approximating this ideal that are more logical and justifiable than other standards that might have been and that have been used. It is these realistic optima that RAND must discover from its systems analyses and recommend to Air Staff.

## II. The Logical Criterion

Ideally, to select preferred weapons or techniques, we require a social utility function. In fact we have no such function and do not know how to derive it.[1] We must therefore resort to suboptimizing procedures which give incomplete answers but are consistent—so far as they go—with the optimal function.

"What Is the Best System?" RAND Corp., January 4, 1951. Reprinted by permission of the RAND Corporation and the author.

1. The problems associated with the existence and measurement of a social utility function are discussed by K. J. Arrow, "Social Choice and Individual Values," RM-291.

A method of obtaining consistent, if not complete, functional relationships, is to use the principle of separation of variables. In the complete social utility function, there are determining variables which have positive coefficients (i.e., positive first derivatives of social utility with respect to these variables), and there are variables with negative coefficients. We may call those in the latter class the *cost* variables and those in the former the *objectives* variables.[2] Suboptimizing by this process means incomplete optimization; i.e., we are able to identify and measure only *some* of the variables *and* their coefficients. Nevertheless, we can, for variations in the alternative sets of the values of the variables and coefficients which we *can identify and measure*, determine those sets which yield highest utilities. And even if we cannot *measure* some of the identified variables, or if we do not know the values of their coefficients, we can hold them constant and maximize social utility by selecting either (a) the appropriate values of variables with known positive coefficients or (b) the appropriate values of variables with known negative coefficients. The latter case is called minimizing costs for given objectives, and the former is called maximizing returns for given costs. The economist, when referring to "cost minimization," is expressing indirectly the idea that social utility is being maximized by the appropriate selection of a set of values for the variables with negative coefficients.

If we are able to separate the variables into two *additive* functions, one containing all the variables of the class of variables with negative coefficients, and the other function containing all the variables with positive coefficients, we shall designate the latter as the objectives function and the former as the cost function. In the more general case treated above we assumed merely that we have a function $U(x, y)$, $x$ and $y$ being vectors characterizing the objectives and cost variables, respectively; here we are, in addition, imposing the restriction that $U(x, y)$ be separable into two functions $O(x)$ and $C(y)$, $U(x, y) = O(x) - C(y)$. As is easily seen, in this case one maximizes $U(x, y)$ by maximizing the difference $O(x) - C(y)$. In most of the discussion that follows, it is not, in principle, essential that we be able to separate the function in this way, and thus our arguments do not depend upon this assumption in a crucial way. In practice, however, as most of the examples included in the text will show, this separation of the one function into an objectives and a cost function greatly simplifies analysis as well as substantive work.

---

2. For example, in an offensive systems analysis the objectives series might be targets destroyed, and the costs series might be economic resources required to procure and operate the system.

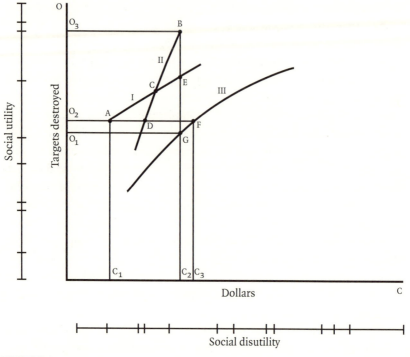

**FIGURE 1**

Figure 1 may render this all less abstruse. The vertical axis represents Soviet targets destroyed (O) and is the objectives dimension, since we assume that higher O values are associated with higher social utilities. The horizontal axis represents the cost function of the offensive bombing system (C) measured in dollar units. We assume that higher costs are associated with reductions in social utility. The three curves in Figure 1 represent the estimated target versus dollar combinations attainable through each of three alternative bombing systems; for instance, System I may represent a SNARK system, II a roundtrip unrefueled B-47 system, and III a one-way bomber system. What then is the best system?

One important point is that the superiority of one system over another may depend upon the scale of operation. According to the illustrative graph, System I is superior to System II between A and C, but System II is superior to System I between B and C. System III, however, is inferior to both the others at all practicable scales of operation.

Apparently a preferred system would be any one that placed us somewhere along ACB. Unfortunately, we cannot, from these limited assumptions about the social utility function, determine whether point A is preferable to point B, or conversely. It is true that the B combination involves the destruction of more targets than that of A; however, it also costs far more. If the additional target destruction had only a minor effect upon the war, while the economic resources diverted had great potential utility elsewhere—say in increasing Tactical Air Command (TAC) strength—A might well be preferable to B.

In general, it will be impossible for RAND to optimize explicitly on the scale of operation, and so in effect we shall be limited to determining constrained maxima. We can seek to discover either the most destructive system at any dollar level or the least expensive system at any destruction level. For example, at $C_2$, System II is the best, and at $O_2$, System I is the best. Alternatively, a number of dollar levels might be considered, and A, B, and F would then be revealed as superior to D, E, and G. And, if a number of destruction levels were considered, B, A, and G would be revealed as superior to E, D, and F. A combination of these two investigations shows that F and G must be definitely rejected as inferior to A and B. Once again, the complete utility function is necessary in order to calculate a preference between A and B. Not knowing the function, RAND calculations must defer to political/military judgment.

Difficulties increase if we cannot represent all the "good" aspects of a system along a unique objectives dimension, or all the "bad" aspects of the same system along a unique costs dimension. For example, for the same costs, with Defense System I we may lose 89 U.S. plants and suffer 8 million civilian casualties to Soviet attacks, whereas with Defense System II we may lose 143 plants but suffer only 3 million civilian casualties. Both industrial capital and lives seem so important that we cannot ignore one and concentrate exclusively upon the other, but it is extremely difficult to find any satisfactory basis for combining them in a single objectives index.

RAND will certainly undertake projects where either some objectives or some costs appear incommensurate. Consider a case in which there are two objectives variables A and B and two cost variables X and Y. Two competing systems might (where 1 indicates a higher order than 2) rank along these dimensions as follows:

| System | Objectives | | Costs | |
|--------|------------|--------|--------|--------|
| I | $A_1$ | $B_2$ | $X_1$ | $Y_2$ |
| II | $A_2$ | $B_1$ | $X_2$ | $Y_1$ |

This case represents complete stalemate as far as explicit systems calculations are concerned. Judgment must be exercised either at RAND or by a constitutionally competent higher authority on the ultimate question of social utility; i.e., the relative importance of A and B and of X and Y. In practice, of course, the differential importance of the various dimensions may be so great and so obvious as to justify the project officer in excluding all save one objectives and costs dimension from consideration.

Even where two important and incommensurable objectives must be considered, the difficulties can be circumvented to some extent. In most RAND problems, as will be explained in Section IV below, all costs can usually be expressed in terms of economic resource costs measured in dollars. Where there are two objectives variables, the scales of operation of competing systems can usually be juggled until the two systems are indifferent with respect to one of the objectives. Then we have:

| System | Objectives | Costs |
|--------|------------|-------|
| I | $A_1$ $B_1$ | $C_1$ |
| II | $A_1$ $B_2$ | $C_2$ |

In this case System II differs from System I only in that the latter accomplishes more of B and also costs more resources.[3] The problem is then essentially no more difficult than the choice between point A or B in Figure 1. While the preferred system cannot be calculated, the alternatives are presented in the most convenient form for the exercise of judgment.

Usually, with care and ingenuity, we can define a single objectives and a single costs dimension. We then either (1) minimize C, for each of several O levels, and/or (2) maximize O, for each of several C levels. The selection of an appropriate objectives function that is monotonically related to social utility requires judgment and should not be undertaken casually (see Section III). In a majority of cases the costs dimension can be expressed in dollars (see Section IV).

---

3. For example, I might be a surface-to-surface missile system and II might be an aircraft bombing system. The missile system might, having a higher aiming error, consequently have larger "bang" weapons and destroy far more square miles of urban area ($B_1$) incidental to its destruction of the same industrial targets as the aircraft system ($A_1$). If the missile system also costs more ($C_1$), there would then be the problem of deciding whether this "bonus damage"—if really positive—is worth the extra cost.

It follows from the foregoing that there is no way of distinguishing good systems from bad when *both* the objectives level and the costs level are *assumed*. In fact, for any given objectives or cost level, there will usually be only one "economical" system. In a few special cases (e.g., at point C in Figure 1), there may be two or more systems at a given O and C level. If the suboptimization has been correctly made, the choice between them will be a matter of indifference, although there will be a temptation to assert a preference on the basis of some relatively insignificant consideration. Overspecification, in this sense, prevents rather than aids the discovery of preferred instrumentalities of warfare.

Because of the obscure nature of social utility and disutility it is not possible to apply a pure criterion and so determine the perfect system. However, the impossibility of perfection is no excuse for resorting to criteria possessing little, if any, logical justification. RAND should always seek to employ those criteria that most nearly approximate the ideal and yet are practical. In short, having carefully chosen the objectives and costs dimensions, maximize O, given C; or minimize C, given O.

## III. The Objectives Function

The validity of the criterion will depend in part upon the wisdom with which the objectives variables, which are monotonically and positively related to social utility, are selected. In making this selection there can be no escape from the need for judgment. Frequently the judgment required is of the kind which exists in the Social Science Division.

All weapons systems have as their ultimate purpose the fundamental political goals for which the nation prepares or undertakes war. These goals, even if they are fully understood by the Administration and the public, will usually be categorical and unamenable to numerical analysis. The RAND scientist must then, depending upon the mission of the military operations being analyzed, seek some objectives or "output" dimension for the system that judgment suggests will co-vary with the attainment of the apparent national goals.

For example, the mission of a strategic air offensive may be to prevent the flow of war material to the Soviet armed forces. Possible types of objectives variables, any one of which might be most appropriate for some RAND systems analysis, include the following:

1. Reductions in the outputs of specific military end products, as an objectives vector.

2. Reduction in an index of Soviet military production, using appropriate weights for different military products.
3. Reductions in the outputs of the specific industries bombed, as an objectives vector.
4. Weighted number of targets destroyed, using some measure of relative importance as weights.
5. Number of targets destroyed, unweighted.

There would be, of course, many variants under each of these type headings. The selection of the most appropriate objectives variable or variables for any particular analysis will depend upon the scope of the analysis and the degree of refinement in other components, upon the sensitivity of the results to the characteristics of the target system, upon our knowledge of the Russian economic system and of Russian strategic plans, etc., etc.[4]

It is, of course, important that the adopted objectives dimensions co-vary with national goals throughout the scale of operations considered.[5] If satiety is suspected, it may be useful to substitute a single fixed objective rather than adopt an objectives function that supposedly co-varies with national utility. For instance, one may not be sure that the destruction of 400 Soviet plants will contribute any more to "winning the war" than the destruction of 300, and yet one may feel confident that the destruction of 300 plants will contribute more to "winning the war" than the destruction of none. In such a case, a fixed objective for which we minimize costs would appear to be a more useful approach than maximization of an objectives function for given costs.

It is almost inconceivable that we shall ever be unable to select some single objective that is "good" for the nation. It is to be hoped that, in general, we can do more than this and find an objectives function that co-varies with progress toward national goals. This selection must be made as carefully as possible, utilizing the best judgment of the most highly qualified people.

---

4. A useful by-product of an aircraft bombing system, probably not possessed by a missile bombing system, is that the attacking planes chew up defending interceptors. If this consideration is not to be ignored, some objectives vector will be required. When different carrier systems accomplish their main task in different ways, occasioning different by-product damage, we have what might be termed an objectives overlap problem.
5. Under certain circumstances it may be possible to overbomb, for instance.

## iv.  The Cost Function

Inasmuch as the cost dimension must be monotonically related to social disutility, the problem is to find some series that will satisfy this requirement. In the main, the cost to society of achieving its objectives can be measured in dollars. The dollar cost of a military system, if proper costing methods are employed, is usually a fairer representation of its real cost than any other single series and frequently an adequate measure for RAND systems analyses.

### Real Costs and Money Costs

If the U.S. government decides to create, maintain, and operate a weapons system costing $X, the real, as distinct from money, costs of doing so are some combination of the following:[6]

a.  A reduction in the supply of goods and services to civilians; or
b.  An increase in employment (or hours of work), which, in the aggregate, is unrewarded; or
c.  A reduction in the scale of some other weapons system.

The distribution of real costs among these three categories depends upon circumstances and higher political decisions. If the military budget is freed in peacetime, or if we are "fully" mobilized in war, the real costs will be wholly of category C. In any case the market valuation of the real costs will be approximately $X.

The dollar budget allocated to a military system is a generalized claim upon the current resources (e.g., labor, services of capital) and the existing stocks (e.g., petroleum and U-235 reserves) of the nation. In connection with the achievement of any given objective, we should attempt to minimize the expenditure of these resources and stocks. In general, we accomplish this by minimizing the dollar cost of commanding these resources and stocks. The dollar prices of economic goods and services represent, with some qualifications, the value placed on these scarce items by society. This value reflects the intensity of civilian, business, and government demands; the scarcity of resources and stocks; and the difficulties of production.

If a military system ignores dollar costs and uses high-priced items where low-priced ones are equally satisfactory, a higher budget will, of course, result.

6.  We are ignoring the depression or chronic underemployment case in which it may be possible to increase military expenditure with no real cost.

This would be unfortunate for the nation—not because *dollars* are scarce but because this means that the system in question is employing scarcer rather than more plentiful resources, more intensely demanded instead of less intensely demanded goods, or items difficult to produce instead of ones easy to produce. The dollars we needlessly waste will be a reflection of needlessly wasted economic resources.

A somewhat more detailed and technical justification for the acceptance of dollar costs as a roughly satisfactory measure of social costs (for the limited purposes we have in mind) is attached as Appendix A.

There may be some unwillingness to believe that dollars are an index of fundamental physical constraints because of the ever current possibility that the military establishment may at some future date find itself confronted by an unexpected emergency. The actual and most stringent limitation may then not be generalized resources but some specific lack of equipment, men, or, perhaps, bombs. Clearly, this is always a possibility, but it is probably irrelevant for long-range planning decisions. If the unexpected does occur, the system recommended by RAND on the basis of some unrealized but expected development will not be optimum. One cannot plan to cope optimally with all possible contingencies.

### Costing Economic Goods

The costing of military systems cannot proceed very far without distinguishing between supply stocks and production flows. In most instances, the goods that will be used during a war will come partly from current production and partly from existing stocks; but during a period of preparedness there will usually be a slow rate of use, and most production will go into stocks. In wartime, the probable length of the war is most important—it affects the rate at which stocks should be depleted. During preparedness, the remaining peace period's length is most important—it affects the rate at which stocks must be built up. Hitherto, RAND's systems analyses have mostly concerned themselves with the peacetime creation of military systems, and this is the situation assumed in most of the following discussion.

It will be helpful to distinguish three kinds of goods. First, "old" goods; these are goods that already exist at the time some military system requiring them is selected, and of which no more are produced, such as B-29 planes today. Second, "new" goods; these are goods that do not exist at the time plans are adopted, and which must be entirely procured, such as SNARK missiles. Third, goods that are neither "old" nor "new"; these are goods that already exist, but in insufficient quantities, so more units must be produced. Most military goods are of this third type; examples are B-47 planes, A-bomb, and aviation gasoline.

Also it is most important to distinguish between what might be called the budget cost and the implicit price of certain goods. The budget cost indicates how much some weapon system should be charged for using a good. The implicit price indicates how freely or frugally a particular good should be combined with others in some weapon system.

A final distinction is between goods that are useful to a military system but have no alternative civilian or military uses, and goods that have a more general usefulness.

The most general case in costing is that of a good or service having multiple uses that already exists in such inadequate quantities that it must also be procured. This is the case that will first be considered. Certain special cases will then be examined.

*The General Case.* If a good already exists but is also being rationally procured, it can be inferred that of all the most important uses the existing goods can be put to the least pressing is still sufficiently important to justify the incremental costs of further production. Normally these incremental costs will be higher, the more rapid the rate of production. If war is expected within a year, rather than at the end of five years, production rates and incremental costs will be high. Rationally, the level of incremental costs should reflect the expected date at which the goods in question will be used, and if these expectations are realized, incremental costs will be equal to estimated marginal use values.

For example, Figure 2 illustrates, perhaps, the case of U-235, assuming an existing stock of OA at the start of 1951. The D curve, after the manner set forth in the footnote, is indicative of marginal military worth in different uses.[7] $S_{1951}$ indicates the incremental costs attached to increasing the stockpile by differ-

---

7. The D curve in Figure 2 might be obtained in the following way. First, it might be determined that U-235 could be used to advantage in operations A, B, C, and D, etc. That is to say, it would involve less cost to undertake these operations, using U-235, than by using some other substitute such as TNT. A "good"—but not an optimum—scale for each of these operations might be arbitrarily established. The saving resulting from the use of each kilogram of U-235 in each system might be estimated. If these uses in alternative operations were ranked according to descending importance and potential economies, some continuous curve such as D in Figure 2 might be fitted to this array.

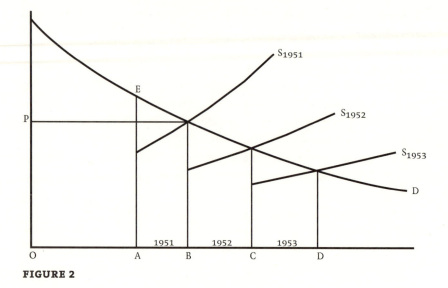

**FIGURE 2**

ent amounts by the end of 1951. If the C.I.A. were to convince the National Security Council (NSC) that war would begin at the end of 1951, the economical rate of production would be AB during the year. If the NSC always expected war at the end of the year, but peace always continues, production should be AB in 1951, BC in 1952, and CD in 1953. The appropriate production rate depends upon the expected date of war.

Many problems are resolved if it is possible to accept the rationality of current production rates and incremental costs. The economic value of, say, U-235 is then reflected by its incremental costs. Use value and production costs are equal at the margin. The implicit price—which helps to determine the proportions in which this good should be combined with others—is then OP in 1951. The budget cost—which should be charged against the system using this good—should be OP multiplied by the number of units previously allocated to this weapon system.[8]

*New Goods with Alternative Uses.* In this case there are no existing stocks at the outset. Production rates reflect war expectations. Implicit prices and budget costs depend upon incremental costs as explained above.

---

8. However, if war had unexpectedly begun at the start of 1951, the economic value of one kilogram more or less of U-235 would be AE, which is higher than incremental costs.

*Old Goods with Alternative Uses.* The existing stocks of old goods are not augmented, by definition. Lack of production rationally implies that more economic substitutes will be available for all military operations that are considered to be worthwhile. Incremental costs therefore provide no yardstick. The marginal use value—which, although not readily determinable, will be less than incremental costs—sets the implicit price. However, so long as each weapon system uses this good as economically as this implicit price dictates, the budget cost of this good to the economy should be considered zero.[9] Historical costs of procurement are immaterial for the economy if additional production is irrational.

*No Alternative Uses.* If the good is a "new" good, the budget cost of the good should be its production cost, and the implicit price should be its incremental or marginal cost. If the good is an "old" good, the budget cost and the implicit price are zero. In the case of a good that was a new good in, say, 1951 but becomes an old good in 1954, the passage of time has the effect of reducing the budget cost of the military system that employs it.

If a good having no alternative uses is both stockpiled and currently procured, implicit prices are incremental costs, and the budget cost is equal to prospective, but not historical, production costs.

*The Cost Expression*

The total budget cost of a weapons system is given by the expression

$$\text{Expenditures} + \text{Opportunity Costs} - \text{Salvage Value}$$

*Expenditures.* The expenditure which should be charged to a system, such as a strategic bombing campaign, is the part of the national budget which, cutting across all organizational lines, can fairly be ascribed to the bombing campaign. For example, if bombing is carried on from overseas bases which require defense by the Army or Navy, the cost of this defense is part of the total cost of the bombing campaign even though they do not appear on the official budget of the Strategic Air Command (SAC) or the Air Force.

——————

Plans would then have to be revised to cope with this unexpected situation. Businessmen are continuously forced to make unexpected short-run adjustments to longer-run plans, and military organizers will frequently have to do the same.

9. Because opportunity costs are counted separately in the cost expression. See below.

This allocation of the national budget among different theoretical systems involves many difficulties because, while the annual budget of the SAC is a fairly well defined quantity, the total cost of a Phase I bombing campaign can be estimated only with uncertainty. What proportion of the cost of the Military Air Transport System (MATS) or of the Air Force overhead should be ascribed to this bombing campaign? Rule-of-thumb answers to such questions will, of course, be imperfect. Fortunately, however, the largest dollar expenditures tend to be specific variable costs.

The principles of charging costs for procurement, training, and maintenance are well known. We must charge the full cost of everything which must be procured for the weapons system in question; this includes the cost of new air bases and of additional atomic bombs. We must also charge for all such maintenance and indirect costs as the expense of Army or Navy protection of bases.

*Opportunity Cost.* The various physical assets of a bombing system will be, in part, inherited from previous systems. Accordingly, the true economic cost of a bombing system will differ from the current budget disbursements for it. In this section we will examine the question of valuing the inherited assets used in the system.

First, let us suppose that the inherited assets have no alternative uses. It is then clear that we need not economize on them, so long as we do not use more than the original stockpile. Solutions of the systems analysis using more of the inherited assets are no more expensive than solutions using less. A resource with no alternative use can therefore be used without cost up to the limit of the stockpile, even if it was originally very costly to procure and even if the resource is militarily very potent (see "Costing Economic Goods").

Second, let us suppose that the inherited assets have alternative uses and that this type of good is also currently being procured. Then the use of such inherited goods by a system will occasion additional costs for extra production. The cost of using such a good should then be based upon marginal production costs.

Third, let us suppose that the inherited assets have alternative uses which are not sufficiently important to justify further production. The problem is then a difficult one. Other systems and operations might have more or less urgent uses for the good in question. As a practical matter, we want to be able to cost goods to one system and operation without having simultaneously to consider alternative uses in many other systems and operations. Here, perhaps, is a case where the exercise of judgment, rather than the employment of some mechanical formula, is unavoidable.

*Salvage Value.* Salvage values are the obverse of opportunity costs. What is a salvage value for an earlier system may be an opportunity cost for a later system. The same principles apply to the determination of salvage values as of opportunity costs.

If there are no subsequent uses for the equipment that will survive some operation, there is no salvage value. If it is expected that this same kind of good will still be produced for other systems after the completion of the operation under consideration, surviving equipment should be valued at incremental production costs. The real difficulty, once again, is to determine the salvage value of surviving equipment that will have subsequent uses but that will not be produced.

In this latter case, incremental production costs establish an upper bound while zero provides a lower bound. Between these limits a number of values can be obtained by using any one of several plausible formulae (see RM-476). What is theoretically required is the price at which all commanding generals, responsible for different operations, would collectively demand no more nor less than the probable future stock of this "old" good. As commanding generals do not do their own purchasing out of set budgets, this figure will be very difficult to estimate in practice.

The magnitude of the salvage value problem may not be as great as once supposed. In general, even allowing full production-cost salvage values for surviving equipment, the least costly systems will usually be those that leave little surviving equipment. The most important term of the cost expression will normally be the expenditure term.

### The Real Cost of Human Losses

A military operation obviously involves human costs in addition to dollar costs. The question arises whether or not personnel losses are to be considered as a cost over and beyond the dollars invested in their training or required to procure and train replacements. The answer to this question *must be in the affirmative;* in our society, personnel lives do have intrinsic value over and above the investment they represent. This value is not directly represented by any dollar figure, because, while labor services are bought and sold in our society, human beings are not. Even so, there will be some price range beyond which society will not go to save military lives. In principle, therefore, there is some exchange ratio between human lives and dollars appropriate for the historical context envisaged in any particular systems analysis. Needless to say, we would be on very uncertain ground if we attempted to predict what this exchange ratio should be.

Occasionally we may have to state the cost of any particular system in terms of both dollar cost and human cost. To do some given job, we should first indicate the minimum dollar cost and the number of human lives involved and then list several higher levels of dollar cost required to do the same job with fewer casualties. The choice among the different systems represented by the various combinations of dollar costs and human costs can then be left to a higher political level. The choice made will involve an explicit or implicit selection of an exchange ratio between dollars and personnel or, in effect, between human lives and other forms of social sacrifice.

However, personnel losses will not normally affect the results of RAND systems analyses. This is due to the enormous disparity, especially for atomic bombing, between the small numbers engaging actively either in attack or in defense and the magnitude of expected casualties. Before we spend money to save military personnel, we must examine what that amount of money would purchase in terms of attack or defense. Suppose that we could carry on a certain bombing campaign at a minimum cost of $4 billion spent and 1,000 crew lives lost, and that we could save 500 of the 1,000 men by doing the same job at a cost of $8 billion. Before we decide to save the men, we must examine what we could get for the additional $4 billion in the best alternative use. It seems very likely that the additional $4 billion could be used in offense to increase the number of targets destroyed and so indirectly save a number of American lives probably far greater than 500; it seems almost certain that $4 billion additional spent on defense of our cities against air attack could directly save far more than 500 lives. It would be unwise to spend any more than the minimum cost for the sole purpose of saving personnel lives, since the additional expense could save more lives in alternative uses. The issue is really lives *versus* lives.

It might be maintained that it is *necessary* to save additional crew lives in a bombing system, perhaps for morale reasons. However, if the physical danger of carrying out a bombing strike actually occasions greater bombing errors and aborts, these repercussions can be included as a dollar cost. In order to maintain morale, it may be necessary to limit a tour of duty to a few strikes, but this can also be translated into more crews and a higher dollar cost. Crew losses can thus be converted into a dollar dimension in terms of the operational costs of lowered morale or the training costs of short tours of duty.

Our conclusion must be either that crew losses can be translated directly into economic costs or that the dollar cost of saving *these* lives will be so great that net lives lost will tend to be minimum when the minimum budget system is adopted. In presenting a systems analysis we can always list crew losses as a special kind of cost. But the best system, especially in this atomic age, is not that which minimizes crew losses but rather that which minimizes real resource costs, including crew costs.

## v. Invalid Criteria and Their Consequences

It has been argued above that the proper criterion for a systems analysis is to maximize O − C when the O and C scales have been chosen to represent social utility and disutility. Nevertheless, there is a widespread feeling that alternative, or even preferable, criteria exist. Among the alternatives which have been suggested, and sometimes actually used, are such ratios as target damage to number of planes (crews) lost, target damage to pounds of aircraft lost, etc. It is explained below why we believe these criteria have been proposed, what their relations are to true maximizing, and their general relevance to systems analysis problems. The position taken will be that these criteria are for the most part irrelevant and misleading. Under certain circumstances some of them may become logically equivalent to the correct criterion (that is, they may also lead to a true optimum); in such cases, however, the alternative criteria are redundant. Except at very few points, the arguments leading to this conclusion involve only logical issues.

### The Concept of Engineering Efficiency

Engineering efficiency measures are essentially ratios of some output to some input. Thus, labor efficiency is often conceived of as output per units divided by input hours. Some "criteria" proposed in the past are of this general form. For instance, the ratio of target damage to planes lost is a measure of the average efficiency of a plane that is lost in use.

Since the selection of a measure of engineering efficiency is largely a matter of convention, one can see why many persons believe that a number of equally valid and alternative criteria exist for systems analysis. Unfortunately, despite any intuitive plausibility which they may possess, engineering efficiency measures do not answer the questions which systems analyses seek to solve. We want to know which of several alternative combinations of weapons and strategies is best for doing a certain type of job, where there are states of the world we would like to bring about (objectives function), and which we can only bring about at a certain cost to ourselves (cost function). Regrettably, the aims of engineering efficiency are almost never completely consistent with the goals of what might be called economic efficiency. The efficiency the engineer concentrates upon refers only to one factor in the whole production process, and past a point, its efficient utilization can only be increased at the expense of decreased efficiency in the utilization of other factors.[10] For example, if a wheat farmer arranged his operations in such a way as to secure the absolute maximum possible bushel yield per acre of land, he would very likely soon pass into bankruptcy, and the 2,000-odd employees he had employed on his quarter-acre farm would soon be job hunting. Similarly, industrial engineers who organize factories so as to raise the output per machine may also succeed in raising the dollar costs per unit of output, so the most efficient firms in an engineering sense are often too inefficient economically to survive.[11]

Following the goals of engineering efficiency to their logical conclusion must lead to arrangements that are economically inefficient except under the most unusual conditions. The validity of this statement rests upon the almost universal physical fact of diminishing returns. Economics and engineering efficiency could coincide only if, with a given state of the arts, and holding all factors but one constant, it were possible to obtain double the final output indefinitely by doubling the input of a selected factor.[12] It is unlikely that any systems analysis will ever consider such a strange circumstance.

It may be instructive to consider the probable consequence of adopting just one of the several engineering criteria which have been suggested as criteria for systems analyses. If one adopted the ratio of target damage to bombs used—and suboptimized by assuming a given damage level—the resultant bombing system would be enormously expensive in its use of all other resources. The air

10. "The correct definition of efficiency is the ratio, not between 'output' and 'input' but between *useful* output and total output or input. Hence efficiency, even in the simplest energy transformation, is meaningless without a measure of usefulness or value. In any attempt to understand economic efficiency, the notion of value is more obviously crucial since most economic problems are concerned with a number of kinds both of outlay and of return, and there is no conceivable way of making comparisons without first reducing all the factors to terms of a common measure" (Frank H. Knight, *The Economic Organization*, pp. 8–9).

11. See A. S. Dewing, *The Financial Policy of Corporations*, vol. 4, pp. 16–17.

12. For a more complete exposition, see G. F. Stigler, *The Theory of Competitive Price*, pp. 116–46.

would have to be filled with escort and decoy planes. Such a criterion would be valid only if all these planes and their crews occasioned no costs and were, in effect, free.

It is noteworthy that several alternative engineering criteria can almost never be satisfied at the same time. They are compatible neither with one another nor with the criterion derived from the concept of an economic optimum.

Much of the plausibility of the answers obtained by using these alternative criteria derives from the very halfhearted manner in which they are applied. This halfheartedness automatically occurs, since the range of plane characteristics over which the maximization takes place does not, in general, contain the extreme types which would produce the absolute possible maximum for the criterion in question. If we really believe in these criteria, we should follow where they lead us—even to extreme planes. Thus, suppose we wish to maximize the ratio of target damage to aircraft lost. Then, it is clear that the true maximum (allowing both damage and losses to vary) might be obtained by buying a one-plane air force which flies so high (or is sent on such specially selected missions) that it cannot be shot down. It will, then, sustain zero losses while imposing some positive damage. It may, perhaps, ruin some of the enemy's wheat crops more or less accidentally (its bombing accuracy will, of course, be terribly low), and so the damage/loss ratio $= C/o = \infty$.

Engineering criteria will generally lead to some such ridiculous result if really used. Furthermore, it makes no sense to restrict the results to a "plausible" range and then to use a local maximum of the criterion; the results have been constrained to be "plausible," but they still may not be *correct*. Ad hoc patching up of these supposedly alternative criteria will not save them. They are wrong, root and branch. Economic optimizing is not equivalent to the indiscriminate maximizing of technological efficiency.[13]

---

13. "Technology and economics are concerned with the same data, means and ends. But whereas the economist is concerned with the best allocation of scarce means among competing ends, the technologist studies the best means to attain a specific end. Economic factors will influence the selection of the best means, however. If land is free and labor expensive, it is a matter only of technique to decide how much land to use with a given amount of labor, i.e., the amount of land which will produce maximum output per worker. But if land also has a cost, then the technologist alone cannot determine the best means for producing the product, for this will obviously depend in part on prices." G. F. Stigler, op. cit., p. 15.

*The Doctrine of Harmony or Agreement*

It has occasionally been stated or implied that a specific system is to be preferred if all alternative criteria indicate it to be best. This may be called the strong form of the doctrine of harmony. As will be pointed out below, in the section on the efficient point proposal, this is formally true. But in actual fact, if any one engineering criterion were taken seriously and the system designed to satisfy it so far as possible, that selected system could not simultaneously maximize any of the other alternative criteria. We would assert then that almost certainly the technological possibilities are such that no dominant system in this sense exists, though if it did it would, of course, be the optimum system.

It is virtually certain, for instance, that a system that minimizes the number of bombs used could not also minimize the number of planes lost. It is also evident that the tactics that would be selected to minimize bomb losses would be different from the tactics selected to minimize plane losses. In fact, every assumption regarding specifications, mixes, and operations that would satisfy one criterion as perfectly as possible almost certainly could not simultaneously satisfy other criteria perfectly. In its strong form, the satisfaction of the doctrine of harmony is a physical impossibility.

A somewhat weaker version of the harmony doctrine is also possible and might be termed the doctrine of majority rule. This doctrine would assert that if a *majority* of criteria are satisfied by some one plane or missile or system, it is the preferred one. Here again it should be pointed out that if a system were designed to satisfy only one engineering criterion and enough systems were considered, no one system could satisfy several criteria, and each system would find itself in a minority position. However, quite apart from this consideration, it is evident that military planning should not proceed according to selection procedures that permit the swamping of a good method of selection by the introduction of numerous unsound criteria.

Of course, if a system is initially overspecified, by stipulating both its cost and the job done, it becomes impossible to apply our economic criterion. Selection of a preferred system must then depend upon some noneconomic element. The bewildered systems designer is then confronted with a difficult choice, and it is not surprising if under these circumstances he succumbs to the guiles of such doctrines as harmony and majority rule. The solution in such a case should be to remove the overspecification of the system and to permit either the job done to rise or the cost level to fall.

A ratio criterion can lead to the selection of the same preferred system as the economic criterion in two circumstances. First, if either the level of the job or the cost is fixed, and the ratio criterion is the ratio of job to cost, then agreement is certain, since this criterion is logically equivalent to the economic criterion; however, the ratio criterion is then redundant. Second, if all factors except A are free goods, maximizing the ratio of job done to units of A expended is equivalent to an economic maximum whether or not the job done is fixed or allowed to vary. This last qualification is of little practical significance though. It is most unlikely that any system, having all inputs free save one, will ever be evaluated by RAND.

## vi. The Efficient Point Proposal

There have been a few suggestions within RAND that an efficient point approach to the selection problem would relieve us of some of our valuation difficulties. Although at present no well worked out proposal for implementing this suggestion exists, a few comments can be made concerning it. If we quickly review the efficient point concept, some of these will stand out more clearly.

Let

$x$ be a $1 \times n$ vector of inputs

$y$ be a $1 \times m$ vector of outputs

A be an $m \times n$ matrix of input-output ratios (technological coefficients)

and $Ax' = y'$. If we for the moment consider $x$ as a fixed vector, or if we know the prices of the components of $x$ and let Budget $= px'$ be fixed, then the problem is to choose A so as to maximize $y$. One specific vector of output $y_0$ is greater than another vector of output $y_1$ if every element of $y_0$ is greater than or equal to the corresponding element of $y_1$ with at least one greater than relation holding. In general, in the real world, no unique maximum vector $y$ (Max) will exist. A set of efficient vectors $y_i$ will exist, however, and a corresponding set of matrices $A_i$. A vector is said to be efficient if no other vector has uniformly larger elements. It is easily seen that similar partial orderings of the input vectors $x_i$ exist for a fixed vector of output $y$.

Several comments can be made. First, with regard to the doctrine of harmony, we see that if there exists a matrix $A_0$, such that each of its elements is the maximum over all the matrices, then $A_0 x' = y_0' > y_i' = A_i x'$ for every i. On technological grounds we have ruled out this possibility.

Second, one of the current suggestions for the use of efficient point procedures is to use as elements of the output vector various alternative criteria of the engineering efficiency type discussed above. This appears to us to be wrong, since the input-output ratios are elements of A and not of y. The elements of the vector should be outputs, i.e., targets destroyed, planes left over, etc. Once one sees this, one also sees that the number of reasonable elements may be rather small. At any rate it is clear that the efficient point procedure does not, in general, involve the maximization of A (input-output ratios) but rather the maximization (partial ordering) of y (outputs).

It has been suggested earlier that in comparing lives and dollar costs, a vector analysis may have to be employed. For a given job, alternative combinations of dollar costs and human losses can then be shown, one for each contemplated system. A series of so-called efficient input points will then be obtained. These points will represent all those systems for which lower dollar costs cannot be obtained without sacrificing lives, and conversely. Presumably it will be the responsibility of the Air Force or the Joint Chiefs of Staff to select one of the points as the most sensible one. Of course, any such selection implies a definite exchange ratio between lives and dollars. If this ratio could be revealed to the designers of bombing systems at an early stage they could explicitly determine the most effective system in terms of job done for a given combined cost. While probably impossible in this particular case, we ought to avoid whenever possible the presentation of results only in efficient combination form. This yields the weakest possible ordering of the results given minimal rationality assumptions. All efforts should be made to utilize whatever information we have about the relative values of the various inputs. We shall usually know more about the world than that more of everything good is better than less of everything good.

### VII. Conclusions

Despite our ignorance of social utility and disutility functions, the designer of a RAND systems analysis should be able to select an objectives function and a cost function that are monotonically related to social utility and disutility, respectively. He will then not be able to optimize on the scale of the operation—e.g., the best number of targets to destroy—but he will be able to discover the least expensive way of doing some job or the most effective way of using some resource budget. It should be possible to rank alternative systems according to objectives accomplished (given cost) or costs saved (given objectives). Costs can usually, as a first approximation, be measured in dollars.

The economic criterion will not select the same "best" system as will engineering criteria. Different hardware criteria, if applied with vigor over the widest possible range of performance characteristics, are likely to lead to the selection of widely different systems. The maximization or minimization of the ratio of some physical output to some physical input will normally result in the selection of an economically inefficient system. There are two major reasons why this will be so. First, diminishing physical returns are an almost universal fact of life; holding all other inputs constant, one can hardly ever indefinitely redouble output by redoubling one input. Second, more than one input will almost certainly be an economic good or service; it will then be impossible to attain maximum output per some input without wasting other scarce goods and occasioning unnecessarily higher total costs.

Every RAND systems analysis implicitly and inevitably comprises a set of hardware relations within a software framework. The physical relations established by the hardware divisions must be related to what is "good" and "bad" if "better" systems are to be distinguished from "worse" ones. The external scale of representative social values must be determined carefully by those most competent to do so. However, whatever these physical relations and social values may be, there is only one logical criterion that will combine them so that preferred instrumentalities of intercontinental warfare will stand revealed.

## Appendix A: The Measurement of Social Cost

The social costs of achieving given objectives are measured by the resources of our society (including labor services and capital services as well as natural resources) which we are forced to expend in attaining the ends we seek. More correctly, the social costs are not the resource expenditures *per se*, but the alternative uses (among which we may classify leisure) which we must forego when we employ these resources for military purposes. This section indicates that expenditures in dollars for military purposes are the best available estimate of these social costs, though they are by no means a perfect measure of them.

To make clear the extent to which dollar expenditures represent social costs, it will be necessary to have some idea of the ideal social function of dollar prices. Price, of course, depends upon supply and demand. Demand, in turn, depends upon the intensity of desires, given the distribution of wealth and income. Supply is related, inversely, to scarcity of resources and to other obstacles to production. A relatively high price for a good indicates intense demand or scarcity of the resources or difficulty of the process required to make it; a relatively low price indicates limited demand or plentiful resources and easy processes.

In a competitive situation if there is an imbalance in which demand exceeds supply at the going price, then the price does not give proper weight to scarcity or difficulty of production in combination with the intensity of demand; an increase in price will then restrict the less intense demands and encourage production to the point where supply and demand are brought into balance. The reverse is true where supply exceeds demand at the given price.

In either case, the competitive market tends to bring about the corrective operation automatically. In this way, the market enforces the allocation of scarce resources into those lines of employment which satisfy the most intense demands. It can be shown, in fact, that the competitive market economic solution is an "efficient" one, in the sense that no redistribution of goods or reallocation of resources is possible which will improve the situation of any individual without harming the position of some other or others.

In all of this, price has a crucial role. Briefly, price does three things: it *registers*, *rations*, and *guides*. Price registers and signals the changing intensities of demand and scarcities or difficulties of supply by going up and down; it rations limited supplies of goods and resources by excluding that part of the market whose demand is less intense; it guides production through the profit motive into those lines where the demands are strongest relative to the supplies available.

It is the *registering* function of price which is the most immediately interesting to us. The process described above values a good in terms of the community's desire for it as compared with other goods which could also be manufactured with the community's limited stock of resources; the market price is clearly a *social valuation*. The aggregate of military expenditures ideally represents, therefore, the total social sacrifice which the community is willing to make for the military effort.

We will now examine briefly the qualifications which we must attach to the aggregate of military expenditures as a measure of social cost. First of all, the picture of Congress voting a military budget with the intention of making an equivalent social sacrifice is far too idealistic a view. Congressmen and administrators have less trouble getting together in appropriating and spending vast quantities of dollars for military purposes than in imposing the equivalent sacrifice by siphoning off as much purchasing power from elsewhere in the economy. This in turn leads (in the absence of a considerable reserve of unemployed resources) to inflation—as military and private sectors bid resources away from one another. If prices were allowed to rise freely, the aggregate social sacrifice would then be represented not by the original dollar military expenditures but by the proportion of military expenditures to the total national product after the latter has been increased by the price inflation. The process is likely, however, to lead to price controls of a general or selective type, priorities for military production, and other controls which will make it more and more difficult to measure the aggregate social cost of the military effort. Fortunately, the budget expenditures we are concerned with in systems analysis take place during the preparedness period, during which a free price system is more likely to govern. Even in the worst case, however, aggregate military expenditures will probably provide a better measure of social cost than any other available.

A second objection to price as an indicator of social valuation turns upon the fact that the price mechanism gives answers in terms of pecuniary demands rather than human needs. A rich man's desire will have more weight in the price scale than a poor man's. This is certainly true and to some extent undesirable. It must be admitted, however, that the status quo with respect to the distribution of wealth and income in the United States can claim some social sanction. Furthermore, it seems unlikely that any politically conceivable redistribution will change the price structure very greatly—and certainly the range of politically conceivable distributions of income can claim great social sanction.

A final objection to price as a measure of social cost turns upon the existence of monopolies, oligopolistic indeterminacies, disequilibrium situations, and so forth, all of which disturb the ideal competitive solution in the real world. Here there is a grave danger of not seeing the forest for the trees. While industrial organization in the United States is far from an ideal state of pure competition, the price structure is less affected by monopolistic elements than might be supposed—despite a few egregious cases. The reasons for this are complex, but some will be listed here: extreme price behavior is prevented by, among other things, the fear of new competition entering the industry, the fear of losing ground to established competitors within the industry or in industries producing possible substitutes, the fear of government antitrust procedures or other punitive actions, the American business tradition of social service and of mass volume, the desire to expand operations and to build empires rather than to exploit a smaller market mercilessly, etc. It may, in fact, be a safe generalization to say that monopoly price situations exist in the United States only where the government actively supports their development (regulated public utilities, patent laws, protective tariffs, agricultural price supports). Here the government support might be presumed to provide social sanction for any price anomaly which exists.

The objections to price as a social valuation on the grounds of the existence of disequilibria and indeterminacies are unimportant in the context of the other uncertainties of a systems analysis; they are only surface ripples which can hardly obscure the true shape of things for long. Other minor divergencies between social cost and dollars exist where the private costs of a certain process do not reflect the total cost (e.g., where an industrial process produces grime and smoke which harmfully affect an entire neighborhood), but these may also be classed as unimportant. Potentially much more important are Office of Price Administration–type controls which, of course, prevent prices from continuing to perform their social function. In that case, dollars would still be a good measure of social cost when controls are first introduced, but would become more and more inferior as a measure as conditions arise to which free prices would adjust but frozen prices cannot.

It may be reasonably concluded, then, that dollar prices do substantially measure social costs, though it is impossible to give any quantitative indication of the reliability of the measure, and that there is no practical alternative.

### Appendix B: The Effect of Imperfect Data

It may be thought that, since we must often use very unsatisfactory data, some of the alternative criteria rejected above become more acceptable. For this argument to be valid, it must be shown that the airplane characteristics which maximize any, all, or some subset of these efficiency measures are closer to the true maximum values of these parameters than the estimated values obtained by the maximization of the economic criterion. More explicitly, our position may be exemplified as follows: Let us suppose for a bombing system that we have a fixed number of targets to destroy in Phase I and so the objectives function is constant. Our object, then, is to minimize cost, where cost is equal to budget minus salvage value, neglecting the opportunity costs involved. Writing these two variables explicitly as functions only of those parameters in which we are immediately interested, let

$v$ = velocity as plane characteristic
$h$ = altitude as plane characteristic
$(v, h)$ = is sufficient to define a plane
$B(v, h)$ = true resource cost
$S(v, h)$ = true salvage value of the expected number of planes remaining after Phase I. We are assuming here that salvage value is represented adequately by an average salvage value obtained from a probability distribution of various states of the world in Phase II and the particular salvage values of these states.

We do not know these true values, however, and have only

$$B^\star(v, h) = B(v, h) + \delta(v, h)$$
$$S^\star(v, h) = S(v, h) + e(v, h),$$

where $\delta$ and $e$ are error terms. Let $\hat{v}$ and $\hat{h}$ be the values of $v$ and $h$ which minimize

$$B(v, h) - S(v, h)$$

and $v^\star$ and $h^\star$ those which minimize

$$B^\star(v, h) - S^\star(v, h).$$

We assert that there is no presumption that

$$[(\hat{v} - v^\star)^2 + (\hat{h} - h^\star)^2] \geq [(\hat{v} - v')^2 + (h - h')^2]$$

for values of $v'$ and $h'$ minimizing or maximizing any set of technological efficiency ratios. The above measure of the discrepancy between the true and estimated minimizing values is the square of the distance in the $v, h$ plane between the two points. As our knowledge of $B(v, h)$ and $S(v, h)$ increases, $(v^\star, h^\star)$ approaches $(\hat{v}, \hat{h})$; other estimates do not and are in the limiting case wrong with probability one. It is a very dubious argument which proposes that we use inconsistent estimates because we have poor or inadequate data. Compounding ignorance with inconsistency surely cannot improve our position.

Another problem which arises when we have inadequate data is as follows. An analysis, when carried out as suggested, may show one plane to be optimum, but several other planes may do almost as well according to our criterion. This conclusion is based upon estimates of varying degrees of accuracy, and it may be asked, what assurances do we have that the ordering of planes given by the estimates is the true ordering? No explicit assurances can be given, but unless the estimates of the component variables can be shown to be systematically biased from their presumed true values in such a way as to favor one plane or another, no reasonable alternative ordering of the planes is available. Another way of putting this is to point out that although our estimate of the cost of Phase I $[B^\star(v, h) - S^\star(v, h)]$ may have a large variance for an individual plane, the co-variance between planes may be large. In this case errors in the ranking of the planes may be relatively infrequent.

### Appendix C: Risk, Uncertainty, and Ignorance

We have introduced in the preceding Appendix B certain problems center-
ing about our ignorance of the correct values to insert into the components of
the correct selection criterion. For many reasons large elements of the contingency must necessarily enter into our consideration of the problems for which
systems analyses are prepared. Some of the reasons for this are intrinsic to the
problems in the sense that the outcome of a bombing campaign is a random
variable having a probability distribution depending upon initial conditions.
Other reasons are related to the fact that we are to some extent unable to foresee the initial conditions which will apply five or six years in the future. A complete discussion of the various ways in which contingency enters and how it
ought to be treated would be either too long or too difficult for us here, but the
following outline will serve as an introduction to these problems:

1. It may be that the outcome of the activity we are concerned with is a random variable. Thus, given that we knew everything we possibly could, the outcome of, say, a multiple-strike A-bomb campaign is uncertain, and this can be
completely characterized by a conditional probability distribution depending
upon certain initial conditions. This sort of contingency will be called *uncertainty*.

2. Or it may be that the parameters and initial conditions which determine
the conditional distribution function above are not completely known to us.
This we will call *ignorance*, and it may, of course, be of various degrees. This
ignorance is again of two kinds:

   (i) Time-independent ignorance. With regard to some of the parameters which may be thought of as constants of nature, our ignorance
   is essentially independent of time in any direct sense, since it will
   remain the same except for fundamental changes in our knowledge.

   (ii) Time-dependent ignorance. The explicit or exact initial conditions
   under which the multiple-strike campaign indicated above will take
   place must remain to some extent unknown to the long-range plan-
   ner. This ignorance will, of course, not entirely vanish by the time
   the campaign is to be launched, but clearly it must considerably diminish.

3. A somewhat different contingency consideration concerns the probability of war. The risk of war must also be taken into account in our discussion of
just how we shall prepare for war, but until now it has been neglected in systems
analyses. This particular form of contingency should enter into our decision
primarily with regard to the scale of preparedness. We are interested not only

in the probability of war as such, but also in the probability of defeat or the occurrence of other unpleasant states of the world associated with war. Thus, we are interested in the probability of war and the conditional probability of defeat given war. Both of these will probably be functions of the relative strengths of the United States and the U.S.S.R. Our estimates of these probabilities will have elements of uncertainty and ignorance in the senses of the above two paragraphs and can be analyzed further from those points of view. In this paper no more will be said about the probability of war problems.

Thus, in some sense, we may say that there are two kinds of contingency. There is an irremediable kind called here uncertainty and another kind called ignorance, which time and science may cure.

Just how these various forms of contingency can be handled is an important and very difficult problem. To a great extent bracketing procedures have been used for the solution of the ignorance problem. The results have been rather promising. In general this would seem to be an area in which Bayes or minimax procedures might be used. Uncertainty has been handled in a much more summary fashion. The current situation is roughly as follows: If we let $x$ be the random outcome of the campaign with a distribution function $F(x)$ and $U(x)$ be the utility of the outcome, then the quantity entered into our criterion should be the expected utility.

$$E(U(x)) = \int_0^\infty U(x)\, dF(x).$$

Systems analyses thus far have tended to use instead $U(E(x))$, the utility of the expected outcome. An important improvement in current practices which should be attempted is the use of $E(U(x))$. A first step in this direction would be to obtain an estimate of the variance of $x$.

# MARKET VALUE EFFECTS OF TAKE-OVERS?

## AN ALL-OR-NOTHING TENDER OF CONJECTURES

ARMEN A. ALCHIAN, HENRY MANNE, AND SUSAN WOODWARD

Evidence collected on effects of take-overs and mergers has concentrated on the behavior of stock prices of the companies. That evidence strongly supports an increase in the value of the affected firms (stock plus bond values), but it is received with skepticism. For example, some critics argue that stock-value changes are short-run effects; others using accounting data have found no lasting effect. However, we argue that the results have been misinterpreted because of inadequate economic analysis of the forces at work.

We first digress to reformulate the first of the above-mentioned criticisms. The contention that stock values represent short-run effects and are unreliable evidence of the longer-run effects of the take-overs can be interpreted in two ways, one wrong and one right. It is an error to contend that they represent the market value of only the immediate effects. Stock prices are capital values and reflect all presently foreseeable and anticipated effects indefinitely far into the future. However, the contention would be correct if it meant the effects of the take-over and mergers will not be reliably known until much later, so that the immediate stock price change is an immediate *estimate* of imperfectly anticipated and estimable future effects. The immediate estimates will in the distant future be corrected. The immediate estimates are virtually certain to be incorrect, even if unbiased. If they are unbiased, then for evidentiary purposes, a large sample of stock-price changes as evidence of the long-run effect is not subject to this criticism.

There is a criticism of the general economic logic analysis in interpreting the results of take-overs or mergers. Even if stock prices showed on average *no* abnormal (market-adjusted) gain over all take-overs, that would not imply that take-overs were economically and socially valueless. Many financial economists start with the premise that positive value effects are a critical criterion of

This previously unpublished, undated article appears here by permission of the author.

net economic gains. However, zero net gains are also consistent with valuable economic effects that would deem take-overs economically useful. Only losses might be evidence of economic loss. The underlying nature of the argument can be suggested, but not rigorously established, with a simple analogy.

If from 1000 lottery tickets for a $1000 single prize, 10 were selected as first-stage "qualifiers" from which one was on the next day to win the prize, each of the 10 first-stage qualifiers would jump in value to about $100 each. But after the next day, 9 would fall back to zero, and one would rise to $1000. We interpret the immediate stock-price rise as analogous to the first-stage lottery selection. More significantly, of all the lottery tickets worth initially about $1 each, 90 would, after the first-stage drawing, fall to zero. Over the whole episode the total value of all the tickets ($1000) remained unchanged, with only the distribution changed (assuming, of course, no risk aversion).

Or try another, possibly redundant, analogy. If oil were possibly present in some land, held as separate parcels by separate owners, the value of each parcel would reflect the anticipated expected value of the oil. Each parcel would be selling for a higher price than if oil were definitely known to be not present. Let us now suppose additionally that each parcel was deemed initially to have a 10% chance of containing oil (regardless of what was found on other parcels). If some prospector, using whatever surface detection was newly available, should be seen to purchase an option on a particular parcel, the land value of that parcel would jump. Under our assumption, the one parcel will show an abnormal price rise. The effect of the purchase of the option is a price rise.

Suppose the explorer drills and finds only rock. That land's price will fall below its initial value (the others may fall or rise, depending on the side assumptions mentioned earlier). But suppose the explorer had been correct and oil was discovered. The price of that land would rise even higher. Suppose all other parcels are drilled and one in 10 did find oil in the expected amount. The average price effect over all the explorations would be zero, because the initial anticipations were correct. That is, the land market was efficient and unbiased. The reader can surely, by now, fill in the rest of the argument. But to test our own ability to do so, we continue.

Though the average value effect of drilling is zero, the value of drilling is not zero, nor is the value of the discovered oil zero. These values had already been imputed into the land prices. These values have been reshuffled and more accurately reallocated among the parcels of land. Who would argue that the drilling and discovery were therefore worthless? Their value had already been imputed into land values (and so had the drilling and exploratory costs).

Only an average negative price change would be significant. That would have meant that (a) the market had initially overestimated the value of the oil or (b) drilling in and of itself was an unexpectedly economically harmful action. A negative price change is evidence consistent with either. Or one could argue that the market had underestimated the oil value but that the drilling was unexpectedly harmful for other unanticipated reasons. (The variations on this theme of offsetting expectations are not worth pursuing further, at least not to us.) The main point here is that a zero stock-price effect now or over the future after the dust has settled is consistent with economic value of drilling. The oil value is now accurately apportioned among the parcels of land, and we know where it is. That reduction in uncertainty may raise the average value of all the land (risk aversion), but then it may lower it, depending upon the opposite of risk aversion, where lottery tickets command a premium. What can one say about oil value prospects? In any event, whether zero or slightly positive, the price effect over all drilling (and by analogy, over all take-overs) is an ambiguous indicator of the economic value of the activity.

### Takeovers—A Means for Introducing Innovations

Proceed now to take-overs (hereafter including mergers and spin-offs). These are here interpreted to be *means of introducing innovations* or revisions in the operation of the affected firms. Newcomers acquire control and displace management or change financial and capital structure or operating policy. The innovations are fundamentally no different than those introduced by incumbent management when products are revised (new auto models, advertising agencies are switched, manufacturing processes altered, employees displaced by newcomers, new plant locations created, etc., etc.). Innovations occur virtually continuously. Some pay off, others do not. They are speculative alterations with a stochastic outcome. Of course, take-overs and mergers are not the only way innovations are introduced into a firm's operation. But what does distinguish take-overs is a pair of differences.

First, they are easily publicly noted, whereas the other types are rarely noted or heeded except by those making, and those immediately affected by, an innovation. In contrast, internally introduced innovations are not revealed by such clear signals. This has led economists to concentrate on the effects of one particular *means* (tender offers) of introducing innovations, instead of on the innovations themselves (with few exceptions, e.g., M. Jensen on free-cash flows and bonds). In other words, we treat take-overs as means of introducing innovations. Since this method of introducing innovations can introduce an enormous variety of innovations, it seems dangerous to try to guess what the inno-vation or change or feature is that makes the take-over economically useful.

Second, this form of introducing innovation is accompanied by an *antecedent* or *public advance notice* of an introduction of an innovation. The fact is that these innovators buy some stock of the acquired company, thereby driving up its value. We needn't here digress into the effectiveness of this method of in-troducing innovations, where such antecedent notice is required to be made even more public than the innovator would like, as with legislation like the Williams Act.

Combine these considerations with the strongly held presumption that in-novations are implemented in expectation of profit. Add the fact that competi-tion exists in investigating and seeking to detect and implement profitable innovations. Add that competition results in a normal rate of return to that activity. Therefore, if all innovations could be identified and the results to-talled, the gain would equal only the normal competitive return on that risk class of activity. Add, finally, that the stock market is "efficient" in the sense that future possible events are stochastically capitalized into present values. What follows? Stock prices will on average over all innovations, or even over a subset of a particular kind of innovation, yield just the normal rate of return, because the effects of potential future innovations have been capitalized into the stock prices, much (but not exactly) as land prices include the expectational value of future possible oil and mineral discoveries.

Apply this to take-overs. Not all attempted innovations will be successful—no more than every hole dug for oil is a success. Competition plus optimal search and risk taking will result in some losers and winners with a marginal return matching the normal rate of return already incorporated in asset prices. Competition among potential innovators will reduce the average to the mar-ginal return, or else supramarket return would be available to newcomers. This is simply the result of standard competitive behavior. If all innovations of one particular type were evaluated, say all new television series or changes of actors or changes of advertising agencies or changes in location of business, or what-ever, the average should be the normal rate of return—no excess over the mar-ket (all other assets).

Repeat the argument. Initially, before any particular take-over or innovation is proposed, all stocks have values incorporating an expectational value of the prospect of profitable innovations (including that by take-over). When some particular firm is subjected to a tender offer (with increased *prospects* of realiz-ing some successful innovation), its stock value is increased. Others fall, if the prospecting competing innovators, like oil prospectors, now believe them to be less likely capable of innovative improvement. Total value over all firms would be constant, though the stock value of tender-involved firms rises. Alternatively, it could be contended that the average over all firms would show no excess return if the stock prices of firms not involved in tender offers did not initially include any prospective innovative value that required a tender offer or merger for implementation, and therefore are unaffected when others are not selected. This would mean that the subset of tender-related innovations would on average show just a normal ultimate rate of return. Later, as the implemented innovations in the tender-offer firms are more fully tested and assessed, some will have failed, and their prices will fall to below the pre-tender-offer value (former pre-tender prospects destroyed), while the successes rise some more. So, the total value is unchanged over all firms as a set. Competition among innovators results in the normal rate of return for innovative activity over the set of all engaging in innovative endeavour.

Neither analysis implies that tender offers are unproductive in the absence of excess rates of return. Instead, the stock-price behavior shows that the future expected value of such activity was correctly (expectationally) already incorporated into the initial prices. Absence of an excess rate of return for tender-related firms does not refute the value of the tender-related innovations; that value may already be in the prices. Therefore, if security markets "really" are "efficient," we expect zero abnormal long-run stock market excess price effects.

In summary, innovations from and on the outside are constantly occurring in a process called "market competition" with no effect on aggregate stock values beyond a normal rate of return. So it is also with take-overs and the market for corporate control.

We are embarrassingly aware that the foregoing analysis lacks a rigorous formulation or model of the innovation-generation process. We have made implicit and unknown (to us) assumptions, which if known would probably affect our analysis. We leave it to others of greater and more elegant talent to discern or modify them.

### Implied "Conjectures"

1. Proposed innovations are, we conjecture, more likely to be successful where the proposer "puts money before mouth"; because an innovator is likely to risk one's own wealth, the more likely or the more probable are profitable prospects. Take-overs financed by the innovator's own personal wealth are more likely to involve innovations that have higher prospects of being profit-

able and are more likely to show excess (or larger) returns to the initial stock-holders (than those financed by nonpersonal wealth, e.g., junk bonds)—and probably, but not necessarily, a larger expected return to the tenderers them-selves. This does not imply that junk bond–financed tender receivers will on average obtain less than the risk adjusted normal rate of return to the bond-holders or to the stockholders of the involved firms. This is a readily testable conjecture, isn't it?

2. If it be true that the take-over is a new means of introducing innovation, it might be (and we believe is) true that the take-over as a means of introducing innovations is itself an innovation in the means of implementing innovations. On this basis the market as a whole, not just firms "taken over," should show positive value changes reflecting the value of that new effective way of intro-ducing innovations. But once the take-over is discerned to be an economic de-vice, that value will be imputed to all stocks on an expectational basis and re-sult in a higher average of all stocks, and thereafter will not be evidenced by a *change* in stock prices over all take-overs. Pursuing this line of analysis, part of the rise in the whole stock market from the time of the demonstration of the effectiveness of the take-over, as a new competitive device enhancing the effec-tiveness of monitoring management and introducing useful innovations, can be the imputed value of the new device, the take-over. If such be the case, prices should have risen more for those stocks that are more easily and cheaply ex-posed to a take-over threat and should have risen less for those that are not so exposed to that threat (regulated utilities, radio and TV stations, railroads). The change in the airline industry from regulated to unregulated, which is here as-sumed to facilitate take-overs, suggests that airline stocks should have risen.

3. Greenmail is consistent with our interpretation. A "raider" enters and is bought out after revealing the proposed innovation. Why not just sell the inno-vation to the firm's management? Implementing may be more feasible by the existing management. But how can one ensure that the firm will pay, once the idea is revealed. The answer is that by buying a block, especially a block large enough to influence management, three effects are achieved. (A) The innova-tion, if profitable, will have its value reflected in the stock-price appreciation of all the shares including the block purchased by the innovator. Some reward for a good idea is assured. (B) But the stock-price rise on the shares held by the in-novator and the reward thereby received by the innovator is only a small portion of the value generated by the innovator. Greenmail (buying the stock back from the "innovator-raider" at premium) is a more complete reward of the value of the innovator's idea. All existing shareholders are getting a free ride. (C) The

block of stock held by the raider-innovator is large enough to ensure payment of the more complete reward, in the form of a side payment, or else the block will be used to "unsettle" the management that refuses to more fully reward the innovator.

4. Psychological conjecture innovators tend to be arrogant, confident disturbers of the status quo. Because many of the innovations fail, one can readily see why challenged managers, just as they are infuriated by innovative challenges by competition of other firms, are infuriated by challengers who presume to know more about how to run the firm. The innovator may not know how to run the firm but may be able to introduce a desirable innovation.

Enough . . . our tender is made.

# INFORMATION, MARTINGALES AND PRICES

I begin by distinguishing two statistical, stochastic series called (a) Martingales and (b) random sampling, the latter being my terminology. In the random sampling series, the values are generated by independent draws from a *fixed*, *unchanging* probability distribution. Sampled values above the mean are more likely to be followed by decreased values in the next observations. The successive values regress toward the mean. The *differences* between successive values are negatively correlated. A plus change is more likely to be followed by a negative change than by a positive change. In stock market jargon such a presumed response is often called a "technical correction." However, this random series model is inappropriate for stock prices, for reasons we shall study. The more appropriate model seems to be more like a Martingale.

Why the model called a Martingale is given that name will be ignored here. The name is also the name of a gambling system for making bets—that of doubling the stake after each loss in a fair game betting situation.

## 1. Martingales

For our purpose a Martingale series is one in which the population being sampled *shifts* with every observation. In particular, it shifts so as to have its mean *equal* the last observed value. Thus the mathematical expectation of the next population sampled is equal to the most recently observed value. Symbolically and more briefly,

$$E(X_{t+1}) = X_t$$

where E denotes "expectation," and t denotes time. No other restrictions are placed on the distribution being sampled. It may change in *any* other respect from moment (observation) to moment. For example, its variance may change. In contrast, the random sampling series is characterized by saying that X is a

Reprinted from *Swedish Journal of Economics* 76 (1974): 3–11, by permission of Blackwell Publishing.

random variable drawn from a probability distribution with an unchanged "expectation."

A more general conception of a Martingale can be presented. Instead of saying that the means shifts so as to equal the past observed value, we can say it shifts so as to always equal some *pre-specified function of the most recent* observation. For example, the mean for the next observation's probability distribution may be always 10 percent greater than the last observed value, rather than equal to it. Any pre-specified (before the next price is agreed to) nonrandom relationship between the current observed value and the expectation of the next moment's probability distribution is permissible. Then the next observation is drawn at random from that next moment's distribution independently of the prior observation.

As another example, the projected population expectation may be projected by a sine curve fixed in time with the *expectation* of the next being given by the present sampled value projected forward on a sine wave function, using time as the argument in the sine wave—much as if the predicted moment-to-moment change were a seasonal variation. Thus a seasonal pattern or an interest rate growth effect is includable in the Martingale series.

In contrast, I repeat, the random sampling series from a fixed population is one whose mean does not shift, or does not shift in the manner that defines the Martingale.

We assert: "All prices are Martingales." And we conjecture a second proposition: "No quantity variables are Martingales." The first can be argued from current economic theory and has substantial corroborative evidence. The second may be regarded as a half-serious, not entirely ludicrous proposition. We shall see later that the distinction is crucial and has been ignored in important parts of economic theory.

Price *stability* could mean (a) the series is a Martingale, or (b) it is a constant sequence or (c) one with very small changes from observation to observation. In other words, the variance of differences is insignificant. But what shall we say of a series that predicts perfectly in the sense that though the future is always changing it is perfectly foreseen? What would that sequence of prices look like when the future is perfectly known? That would depend upon the relative demands and supplies and their transferability over the future. Such a "correctly foreseeing" series would leave no profitable arbitrage opportunities, because people would have bid up prices at times when it appeared that prices would be too low; bid them down at other times. If demand and supply were

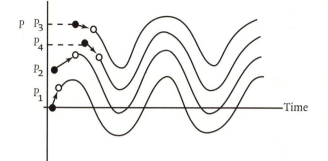

**FIGURE 1.** $P_1 - P_2, P_2 - P_3, P_3 - P_4$ *are independent in sign and have expectation of zero, when adjusted for projection.* ● *denotes actual price,* $P_i$; ○ *denotes projected expectation.*

constant over time, the price series would be constant. And if demand and supply were shifting, the prices at any pair of times could not differ by more than the costs of transporting goods, or substituting in consumption between one time to another. In any event no one would permit any one else to complete any profitable transaction; he would outbid them, so the opportunity for profitable arbitrage would be eliminated by appropriately patterned prices over time. The observed change of prices would be explained by transfer (storage, transport, consumption, substitution and insurance). All the remaining price change would just cover costs.

Diagrammatically, the predicted prices are those along an upward- or downward-shifted projection curve, as in Fig. 1. Any observed *price* change that exceeds the former *price* projection is interpreted as a change in the projected price sequences.

All this says that if a price has unexpectedly increased, it will tend to stay there. The mathematical expectation of the next value is its present price (adjusted by the predictable transfer cost).

This seems also to say that for purposes of predicting the next price, the only price worth knowing is the present price, while all preceding prices are useless. In statistical terms, the bias, if any, in the prediction will not be removed by knowing earlier prices, and the variance of the predicted price will not be reduced by knowing any earlier prices. All information available is captured or reflected by the *present* price. What *past* prices may contribute is an estimate of two factors: (a) the variance of the price changes and (b) the transfer costs. The bias in prediction of the next price is zero—if in fact the present price eliminates profit prospects from arbitrage operations. Could it not be that people persistently underestimate the next price? Yes, conceivably, but the evidence is that they do not.

## 2. Martingales and Information

Present negotiations result in a contract price differing from a future anticipated price by not more than transport or transformation costs—nor by less—if arbitrage is operating. And it is; for that is what middlemen, at least, are doing. In the same way that prices of a good rise when passing through channels of distribution, prices will show a predictable change over time—reflecting carrying costs either of the goods or of productive facilities for those goods. (Good economics compels us to note that prices *fall* as one moves from the consumer back through the chain of intermediaries—falling by the costs of the services provided by each intermediary. The temptation to view final prices as being built up by additions of costs induces people erroneously to think intermediaries cause price to be higher to the consumer—and to be lower to the producers "earlier" in the production chain. The opposite is in fact true.)

While it is permissible and correct to speak of present events as implying or causing future consequences, it is not permissible to say present prices cause future prices to be what they will be. For physical events that may occur now, it is permissible to say that present *events* cause or determine future events, and future prices, which are used to set present prices. The entire set of prices (intertemporal or geographical) is simultaneously determined—no one determines the others. It is a failure to understand this aspect of price relationships—so fully exposited in capital value theory—that leads to frequent misinterpretations or confusions about behavior in prices.

Fully adjusted prices leave no sure profit prospects. In this sense they are efficient and fully reflective of *complete* knowledge. But price changes do permit realized profits and losses, even though each price change yields a zero difference *expectation*. In other words, no one could, *on the average*, make a profit or loss from the next price change. This is a consequence *and a cause* of the statement that the price series is a Martingale or that the expectation of the next price is the present price. Some holders of wealth will obtain profits and some losses. Profit *prospects* remain because the next price is not perfectly predictable—it is predictable only in the "average" or "mean" or "mathematical expectation" sense.

Does the next price, on the average, equal the present price? And if so, is this good? The evidence is overwhelming for a large class of asset prices (stock markets, futures markets, commodity prices) that the Martingale property holds: present prices are unbiased estimates of the next price. What of the variance or average (absolute) error? Large errors are indicative of poor forecasting, even if unbiased. Large errors mean profits and losses will be realized but not on a predictable basis. It may seem remarkable that the expectation is not *presumed* to be zero—in prospect. Whether in fact it is zero is an empirical issue. In hindsight, of course, a *persistent* bias in present prices would indicate reliable profit or reliable loss predictions.

Before accepting the evidence for the unbiased nature of asset prices, I would make a test of the predictability of *particular identifiable* forces, rather than of forces in general. For example, in particular, I would like to know if there is a systematic bias in the predictability of wheat fungus. It could be that in every instance of wheat fungus, the futures markets overestimated the crop damage and consequent price rise. Similarly, it could be that in every or most inflations, the public has underestimated the extent of the future inflation so that prices have not behaved as Martingales during inflations. I say it "could be," not in the sense that it is conceivable—for what is not?—but in the sense that some specifiable factors have been systematically misestimated by market prices, i.e., by the public. Certainly, the evidence is that the inflations and deflations in the U.S. were seriously underestimated in all five major cases. While randomizing over all possible events that will cause prices to change and though getting unbiased estimates of the whole set, it does not necessarily follow that effects of each identifiable factor are estimated in an unbiased fashion. I offer "inflation" as one.

Nor do I find it warranted to call the stock market "efficient" in any pertinent sense just because the present price is an unbiased estimate of the forthcoming price. I would rather call it unbiased. The sampling, or control error, is so large that the power of the test of unbiasedness is weak. Past prices tell us nothing beyond what the present price tells us, and the present price appears to be a *minimum* variance unbiased estimate of the next price.

At the risk of being excessively pedantic, I emphasize that present prices reflect future price beliefs, rather than future prices reflecting or being derived from the present price. Capital value theory makes that abundantly clear. So a more intriguing way of putting the issue is to reverse one's stance and ask if today's prices are on the average equal to tomorrow's actual revealed price. This would be expressed as

$$E(P_t) = P_{t+1}$$

which is a reverse temporal Martingale. If the evidence does not satisfy this condition, would I be forced to assume that foresight is on the average biased?

### 3. Price Flexibility or Predictability?

The Martingale property of prices does not in any way indicate the degree of error of forecasting. Nor does it say anything about the usefulness of price constancy or variability. Prices could be constant or could move in a perfectly predictable seasonal pattern because of perfect foresight. An *unbiased* nature of prices does not indicate anything about the size of the forecasting error or of the extent to which prices would change from moment to moment. The variance can be large or it can be small. Nevertheless, economics argues both that great price flexibility (as measured by frequency of price change and by size of change) is desirable *and* undesirable. The argument for flexibility suggests that quick price adjustments permit greater market clearing and fuller use of resources. The argument for price constancy suggests that the future has been more fully forecast and that plans can be made more appropriately in the light of future prices and costs. One has only to glance at the literature on foreign exchange rate flexibility and at studies of prices of large industries to get conflicting views. And one can cite innumerable allegations that price inflexibility or "imperfect" flexibility in labor markets is bad. Or that it is excessive in futures and stock markets.

What is meant by "imperfect" flexibility or by "perfect" flexibility? That unemployed or idle resources occur? Foresight was imperfect? Whatever it may mean, I shall bypass that here and examine factors conducive to a narrower range of price fluctuation in a given interval of times—though the price may later change over a larger range or more abruptly, to "catch up," than if it had changed earlier and quickly in a shorter interval. Statistical measures of frequency or of size of price change in any given interval will not serve as tests of the performance of markets, without some economic theory of how market prices are determined and what their functions are.

Let me illustrate. In the futures and stock markets there are middlemen, just as there are used car dealers in the used car exchange markets. These middlemen, called scalpers and specialists, buy at wholesale and sell at retail. That is, they stand ready to buy at a "tick" below the last price or to sell at a "tick" above the last price. The bid-ask spread is a way of revealing this price difference. It is similar to the wholesale-retail price difference, *not to a range of prices* offered by potential customers. If one looks at stock market prices and sees variations in prices, he is seeing a mixture of wholesale and retail prices—not a series of retail or homogeneous price changes. The ticker tape gives a mixture of retail and wholesale prices. The main point I am getting to is not that ticker tape prices are heterogeneous but that the markets contain people who, by their middle-men market-making activities, make the prices at retail (or at wholesale) less changing in response to momentary transient deviating, fluctuations in buyers who enter the market with different market demands. An inventory serves as a buffer to clear the market at prices that do not change or do not change as much as they would have. Consequently, buyers sometimes buy for more and some-times for less than if the market did not have these inventories to buffer out the "random" appearance in the markets of buyers and sellers. This kind of price stability in the stock market is probably of small magnitude relative to the price, yet it is present. Is it desirable? Can we judge its desirability by its relative magnitude of stability? I think not. Not, in any event, independently of the rea-sons for the price being made stable or of the reasons for the inventory being provided.

Price stability in a free open market in which participants are allowed to ne-gotiate any price that is mutually agreeable is often regarded as a defect of the exchange process. By stability I refer to a price that does not change in the face of what we can assume are correctly interpreted as demand or supply changes of a transient type. Yet it is a fact that price predictability (and a stable price is one way to make it more predictable) is desirable. It permits plans for future ac-tions to be made earlier and more economically—if desired amounts of sup-plies can be obtained or sold at the predicted prices. Elsewhere I have elabo-rated at some length on the ways that predictability and stability can be obtained and on some of the factors that make it easier or harder (see *Western Economic Journal*, 1969, "Information Costs . . ."). Certainly it is profitable for the supplier to provide that stability, and the consumer is willing to pay for it rather than incur the higher costs that would be involved in search and quick readjustment—as well as the greater liquidity available in resalable assets.

More importantly, the role of price and wage predictability has been given greater scope and significance in work by Donald Gordon in expanding on the costs of information and in the consequent adjustment in employee-employer arrangements. He asserts that employees can accept wage fluctuations to ob-tain work stability or can accept work fluctuations to accept wage stability. But, he asserts, there is no reason to assume one of these is paramount. The em-ployee can obtain more wage stability at the cost of less employment stability. More significantly, the employee can obtain both wage *and* employment *pre-dictability* and *stability* if he is willing to accept a lower wage on average. However, he could choose to risk the average of the wage fluctuations and be acting like a gambler who is not risk averse—in the sense of not being averse to fluctuations in the wage rate and thinking he can surely realize "the" average. The capital market access or the wealth required to finance one's self through the low-wage intervals may be provided more readily by employers who, like insurance companies, will bear the fluctuations whilst assuring the employee of a given wage and employment over a significantly long span of time. This kind of arrangement will result in what could be interpreted by one who did not understand the situation as wage inflexibility in the face of increased or decreased demand. During periods of reduced demand, refusals to hire new replacements at lower wages than those being paid incumbent workers would be superficially regarded as irrational. But Gordon's interpretation is that these are long-term arrangements in which the employees on their part agree to work during periods of higher demand without immediately insisting on higher wages available elsewhere on short-term contracts and to work harder during such periods. In turn during lower-demand intervals, the employees retain their income even though work they do is less or of some other less-productive value to the employer. One need merely discern how retail clerks work in a store during the week to note periods of excess demand or deficient demand. Yet no one is surprised that there are too many clerks at some hours and too few at others, at constant wages.

The same pattern seen over a week or a month can be observed over a few years by large companies who, because of their heterogeneity of assets and product demands, can more cheaply provide the kind of insurance. What appears as inflexible wages are merely long-term contract prices—with *newly* formed contract prices being different. It does not follow that such contracts are socially undesirable in that they appear to cause unemployment when some people who are not party to such agreements can not induce employees to break those contracts with incumbent employees by cutting wages. The role of tenured or higher security employees is explainable in these terms. Yet this is often regarded as imperfect price or wage inflexibility. I can see why it is so regarded, but I can also see why it should not be so regarded. Our whole theory of wage-rate setting and unemployment could well stand re-examination and with it much of our so-called countercyclical policy.

Should one interpret those long-term arrangements as efficient responses to the higher costs of getting more information about the future, one could (a) pay higher costs for more reliable information about the future, or (b) simply suffer the consequences of poor information and bear the oscillations and fluctuations or (c) make risk-sharing agreements. All are responses to the costs of getting more information about the future. And in each the price behavior will be different. Before condemning or evaluating price behavior *per se* we must be careful to understand the kinds of contracts being formed and which of the alternatives have been selected.

### 4. Transient or Permanent Values?

We conjectured that all prices are Martingales, even prices of labor, services and perishables. If they weren't, there would be predictable profits. The Martingale property of price series probably now does not seem so strange—it merely amounts to completely arbitraged series, which should come as no surprise. Yet what does come as surprise is the extent to which physical quantities are assumed to be Martingales. The most notorious case is the consumption function in which current consumption was assumed to be a function of *current* rate of income, as if each moment's rate of income were the future's expectation, or as if present consumption would be geared to current income regardless of what income might be expected to be in the future. By now we know better; the permanent income, or life cycle, consumption function is basically a revision of the income concept to one that is a Martingale. The observable momentary income accrual is not a Martingale. Income is, we conjecture, a random sampling series. For decision purposes, for purposes of a variable to put into a functional relationship, it is the artifact, constructed "Martingale" conception of permanent income that is used. Insofar as the independent variables in a function are pure prices, no problem would arise. If they are not pure prices, it is doubtful one should regard the *dependent* variable as varying with the "transient" value of the independent variable. Yet is this done in all the models you use? In the investment function, is investment a function of income? Which income conception? What is investment at each moment? Not a Martingale. What about the money series? In terms of "information" which deviations or changes are regarded as conveying no information or as conveying information that the mean of the probability distribution or stochastic generator has remained unchanged, as in a "quality control" statistical series?

### 5. Lag Weighted Forecasts?

If the foregoing description of price series as Martingales is correct, how can one explain the usefulness of lag weighted past prices as predictors of future prices? Do they contribute to a smaller error of prediction than if only the present price is used? That may be one function; but I doubt it, for that would leave predictable profit opportunities. Another may be that the earlier prices, insofar as they have any use, serve to identify the seasonal or predictable pattern of prices while the present price identifies the level of price or price from which the pattern can be projected. In any event, to continually revise the pattern, as is done in these formulations, is to violate the Martingale property and also to convert the result into a "descriptive" rather than analytic summary.

## 6. Information Loss, Coordination and Price Behavior

My last observation concerns the breakdown of prices as an information conveyor. More precisely, I mean that the future has become so clouded as events transpire that the confidence placed in present prices is eroded. General reductions in demand, when perceived, leave current sellers, be they business employers, investors or employees, with less information about the future. Current events are, by a wide margin, different from what was expected. What then are the new best options hereafter? As recent prices become more obsolete, the induced search for more reliable information in response to the new situation—depression-inducing decreases in demand—induces search activity not only by employees but also by employers and investors. What are the now best options? If old products no longer sell profitably, what will hereafter? If only somehow the patterns of demand and prices that would be viable could be discerned, people could make adjustments in prices to those equilibrating prices. But they are not so well anticipated now. A general reduction in coordinated information induces a major redirection of activity toward that information search activity.

# WHY MONEY?

Ignorance of availability of goods and of their terms of trade and attributes will provoke efforts to reduce that ignorance in order to achieve more trade. Several institutions have evolved to reduce those costs: money, specialist middlemen who are experts in assessing attributes of goods and who carry inventories and whose reliability of assurance is high, specialized market places, and even unemployment. This paper concentrates on the way in which that ignorance leads to the use of money and how money requires concurrent exchange with specialist, expert middlemen of high reputability. It will be seen that the use of money does not rest on a bookkeeping, debt-recording function. The recording function could be done by any good without specialized markets if goods were perfectly and costlessly identifiable in all relevant, present and future, attributes including future terms of trade. We mean by money a commodity used in all or a dominant number of exchanges.

Imagine society to be composed of people with different goods but without costlessly perfect knowledge of characteristics or attributes of each good. Any exchange proposed between two parties with two goods will be hindered (be more costly) the less fully informed are the two parties about the true characteristics of the proffered goods. We assume: Interpersonal differences exist in degrees of knowledge about different goods—either by fortuitous circumstance or by deliberate development of such knowledge. Goods differ in the costs of determining or conveying to others their true qualities and attributes. Reputability of people as sources of reliable information about goods differs, and their ranking is different among goods. People differ in their costs of not only assaying goods but in searching out potential profferers of the good.

Reprinted from Armen A. Alchian, *Economic Forces at Work* (Indianapolis: Liberty Fund, 1977), 111–23. This article was previously published in *Journal of Money, Credit and Banking* 9 (February 1977): 133–40, and is reprinted by permission of Ohio State University Press.

The best way I can indicate respect for my long association with Karl Brunner and admiration for his work is to report as a secretary-reporter the gist of some ancient joint discussions when we were willing to admit we had a lot to learn. My hope is that he will find the report faithful, while others may find it interesting and instructive. Brunner cannot be absolved from blame for errors nor credit for merit.

These differences may be fortuitous or may be developed in response to economic motives, a point to which we shall return. With these conditions it can be shown that:

a. People will specialize in certain goods in providing information and availability to searching buyers.
b. Specialist purveyors (or buyers) of goods will be reputable (low variance) sources of estimates of the quality of what is being purchased from or sold to that specialist.
c. People who have developed lower costs of identifying characteristics of goods will be specialists in selling, buying, inventorying, and giving information about the good.
d. Trade between a specialist and a novice will involve lower transactions costs than trade between two nonexperts.
e. If some good was sufficiently and most cheaply identifiable so that everyone was like an expert in it, exchange cost of that good for any other good would be less than if a more costly to identify good were offered, and it would become a money.

Consider a world of four goods: diamonds, wheat, oil, and the one called just C. Not all are immediately identifiable in all their true characteristics at insignificant costs, and some are more expensive to identify than others. The community consists of people most of whom are novices, or nonspecialists, in these goods. Imagine (and this begs a question initially) four people who are experts respectively in one of the four goods.

Prior to completing an exchange of diamonds for oil between two novices in diamonds and oil, each will incur the costs of identifying the other's product attributes, including legal entitlements, quantity, and all aspects defining the rights and the quality and quantity of the good being transferred. The net value transfer after subtracting those costs will be less than if they knew costlessly the true characteristics of these goods.

Table 1 shows the proportions of value *remaining* after "transactions" costs between all pairs of traders with various goods. For example, if a novice in diamonds were to trade some of his diamonds (no matter why!) for the diamonds of another novice in diamonds, only four percent of the (perfect knowledge) value would be remaining, as stated in row one. Why? Each party knows the quality of only his own diamonds. Each would assess the quality of the other's diamonds. Assume the costs of the assay amount to 80 percent of the diamonds tested—a sort of destructive test in which four out of five good diamonds were destroyed

TABLE 1. *Net value after exchanges*

| Single Party after Inspection Value | | Novices | | | | Experts | | | |
|---|---|---|---|---|---|---|---|---|---|
| | | D | O | W | C | D | O | W | C |
| Novices | | .2 | .4 | .6 | .95 | .85 | .90 | .95 | .99 |
| D | .2 | .04 | .08 | .12 | .19 | .85 | .18 | .19 | .20 |
| O | .4 | .08 | .16 | .24 | .38 | .34 | .90 | .38 | .40 |
| W | .6 | .12 | .24 | .36 | .57 | .51 | .54 | .95 | .59 |
| C | .95 | .19 | .38 | .57 | .90 | .81 | .86 | .90 | .99 |
| Experts | | | | | | | | | |
| D | .85 | .85 | .34 | .51 | .81 | 1 | 1 | 1 | 1 |
| O | .90 | .18 | .90 | .54 | .86 | 1 | 1 | 1 | 1 |
| W | .95 | .19 | .38 | .95 | .90 | 1 | 1 | 1 | 1 |
| C | .99 | .20 | .40 | .59 | .95 | 1 | 1 | 1 | 1 |

for each one determined to be good. Instead of a destructive test, one can think of the costs of determining the quality as being equal to 80 percent of the value of the diamond. If offered 100 diamonds on a one-for-one basis (prior to tested quality), then *net* of examination costs he is receiving 20 proven diamonds for his 100. The second party, also a novice, will incur the same costs in examining the first party's stones. He will net only 20 of the 100 diamonds he would receive. So, knowing his own proffered diamonds are good, the first party would be willing to offer only 20 of his diamonds for the 100 untested ones of the other party. The second, who would receive 20 untested diamonds, would end up with four tested, proven diamonds after he incurs his tests. So the second party would have given 100 of his diamonds to get back four tested ones—a loss from exchange of 96 percent of the value of what he gave up. An exchange is less likely.

If a pair of novices were to make an agreeable exchange of a diamond for some oil, their costs of ascertaining the qualities of the two products to be purchased would, according to Table 1, amount to 92 percent of the value of the goods. Only eight cents on the dollar would be remaining. Unless at least one of the parties had a very high marginal personal value for one of those goods, no trade would occur. A very large part of that net potential gain would be dissipated in the transactions costs.

If a diamond novice were to trade his diamond for wheat from a wheat novice, 12 percent of the value of the two goods remains.

By definition of C, trade between a novice in diamonds and one in C would lose less than between novices trading diamonds and any other good, as can be seen from the first row, left side. The first row is pertinent to a novice in diamonds who proposes to sell a diamond. The right half of the row is the result of trades made by our diamond novice with experts in diamonds, oil, wheat, or C. An expert is defined as one who has a lower cost function for identifying attributes of a good. (We temporarily beg the question of why some are more expert than others.)

A transaction with an expert will cost less if the novitiate buyer of the product from the expert will rely on the expert's word. The expert's word will have value if he develops a reputation for honesty and reliability in his assessment. Experts will then sell their knowledge at a price lower than the cost for a buyer to get such information in other ways. It is not necessary that the expert be the seller of the good in which he has expertise. He could be an independent assayer, but for reasons to be discussed later, experts will tend to be dealers in the commodity in which they are experts—and dealers will tend to be experts in the goods in which they deal.

The right-hand half of row one indicates that a diamond novice trading with a jeweler (diamond expert), where the novice trades his diamond for some from the expert (no matter why such a trade would be made), will experience a lower loss of value than if the diamond were sold to an expert of any other good. A diamond for a diamond will get better terms because the expert is an expert in what he is both getting and giving (here just one kind of good), whereas though a diamond by a novice for oil from an oil expert will save on oil identification costs, it will not save on diamond identification. Hence the costs of transactions between a novice and an expert in the same commodity are less than those between a novice and an expert in a different good.

The matrix is completed, with some redundancy, by filling in the row cells in the bottom half, representing sales by experts in diamonds, wheat, oil, and C to novices (in the left-hand half of those rows). Exchanges between pairs of experts, one in each commodity, are represented in the lower right-hand half. We assume experts are perfectly knowledgeable in the commodities in which they specialize and are 100 percent honest. This assumption may be too strong, but we make it.

Less loss occurs with trade between two novices where one exchanges diamonds for C than when he trades diamonds for wheat. It may be tempting, but erroneous, to conclude that trades should occur of diamonds for C, and then with the C to buy wheat. That is not quite correct.

To test that, try to find how a *novice* in one good could trade for another good with a novice and gain by going through an intermediary good. It can't be done in the upper left-hand portion of the table, because the costs of recognizing the intermediate good are an added cost incurred by use of an intermediary trading good. The costs of identifying the two "basic" goods are not reduced, while an extra cost identifying the intermediate good is added.

Using the specialist expert involves an extra exchange, a cost of identification of another good—the one offered to him, in which he is not an expert. An expert is an expert in one good only, not in all *pairs* of goods. Hence the problem of identification costs persists. Now, if there is some good in which identification costs are both (a) *low* and (b) low for *everyone*, that will permit purchase of product identification information cheaply from the specialized intermediary expert. If his costs of identifying that offered (money) good are less than the reductions in costs by using the specialist for information about the basic goods, the total costs of identification can be reduced.

The cost of identifying that intermediary good is less than the reduced costs by use of a specialist who provides information about the basic good at a low cost. That double event, (1) a low identification cost to everyone about the intermediate commodity *and* (2) specialist-experts who provide quality assurance and information more cheaply than novices can provide for themselves, explains the use of a low identification cost commodity as a general intermediary medium of exchange—money. It permits purchase of information from lower cost sources, a cost reduction that exceeds the added cost of using an intermediary good for indirect exchange. No double coincidence of wants is pertinent. Indeed, it is a general prevalence of double coincidence of information by both parties that would avoid use of money.

The matrix illustrates the above propositions. For example, consider some alternative routes of exchange for a novice with diamonds, who wants some wheat.

1. Diamonds to wheat, novice to novice ($D_n \rightarrow W_n$). A diamond novice exchanges diamonds for wheat with a wheat novice. The net value obtained by the diamond novice, according to the matrix of information-transaction costs, is .12.

2. Diamonds to oil to wheat, all through novices ($D_n - O_n - W_n$), yield .0196 ($= 1 \times .08 \times .24$). This is less than .12 because of an extra pair of identification costs of oil.

3. Diamonds to C (cash) to wheat, all through novices ($D_n - C_n - W_n$). The

result is a net value of .108 (= 1 × .19 × .57). Though better than through any other mediary because cash, C (because identification costs are less than for oil), it is not as cheap as either direct barter or route 4.

4.  Diamond novice to wheat with wheat specialist. The net result is .19. Contrasting this with the prior route shows the gain from using the specialist for wheat. The difference is the saving to the diamond novice in identifying the wheat, because the wheat specialist offers him "wheat assurance" at a lower cost. And the wheat specialist's word, his reputable reliability, is a source of income. A dishonest specialist would lose a source of income if he destroyed his credibility. So an established wheat merchant has more incentive to make honest statements about the quality of his wheat than does a transient novice.

5.  Interposing the intermediary good, C, into route 4 will worsen matters because the costs of identifying an intermediary good, C, are added to the process, with no reductions in any other costs. For example, going from a diamond novice through a C novice—or even a C expert—rather than through a diamond expert first won't help. Some buyer of the novice's diamonds still has to value them. Whether a wheat specialist or anyone else (except a diamond specialist) does so won't reduce costs. And introduction of C as another good only adds another identification cost. The net value of a route from diamond novice through C through a wheat specialist is .1715, compared to .19 for a direct barter via route 4 without intermediate goods.

6.  A gain would arise if the lower cost services of a *diamond* expert could be used in the exchange process. So what does permit further lowering of costs through an intermediary good is the use of *two* specialists—in wheat and in diamonds. The diamond novice sells to a diamond expert (who assesses qualities more cheaply than any other buyer could), and then our novice takes the proceeds of C and purchases wheat from a wheat specialist, relying on the specialists' reputations and knowledge as a cheaper substitute for the demand and wheat assessment costs by novices. The extra costs of using C are offset by the expert's lower diamond assessment costs.

In our matrix we can compute the net value (.767) of the intermediate-good, two-middlemen route wherein a diamond novice goes to a diamond specialist and then to a wheat specialist using the good C as the medium between specialists. The value is .767, as the product of .85 × .9025, the values, respectively, of (a) the diamond specialist who receives C, and (b) the entry in the cell for the C novice (the former diamond novice who now offers C to the wheat specialist) selling C to the wheat specialist.[1] This increase in value to .767 is the result of ability to get quality assurance at a lower cost from the diamond specialist and from the wheat specialist without imposing on them the higher costs of identifying goods other than C, in which most people are nearly experts.

The feature emphasized here (without excluding others) is the use of the pair of specialists in diamonds and wheat to reduce information costs. With only one specialist no intermediary good helped. (See routes 2 and 3.) The intermediary good C would be of no use in this context if *two* (or more) specialists were not used as economical sources of quality assurance. It is both (1) the presence of *more* than one specialist and (2) the generally low identification cost good, C, that enable indirect exchange to reduce quality ascertainment costs. Use of C as the intermediary good with the lowest *general* identification costs enables obtaining the conveying information more cheaply from several specialists.

What properties of the matrix of information costs are critical? First, specialists permit lower costs, as indicated by the larger numbers in the cells in the upper right-hand or lower left-hand quadrants. Second, the row and column of C for novices is larger uniformly than any other row or column, and the corresponding rows and columns for experts are also dominant. It is the dominance of the *row* of C both for the novice and for the experts in other goods that seems critical. The ability of everyone to assess the qualities of C enables it to be used as a low-cost means of purchasing information about other goods from specialists without imposing offsetting high costs on the experts to identify the good C.

An alternative view of the reason for use of a common medium of exchange is in its presumed role of avoiding the necessity of a double coincidence of wants. But any commodity used as an intermediary would do that. If goods were perfectly identifiable at zero costs, rights to goods could be transferred, and any commodity would serve as measure of debt. This would then leave

---

1. Where does the diamond specialist get C to pay the diamond novice who offers diamonds? From a C specialist. The diamond specialist will have an inventory of C on hand because that will economize on the novice's information costs the novice induces with the wheat specialist when the novice purchases wheat from the wheat specialist. Of all the intermediary goods to be used by a novice between successive specialists, the best is C, a generally easily recognizable good. Try interposing others, and the poorer results will be demonstrated with the data of the matrix.

some goods as presumably less volatile in value so that the exchange value of units of those goods would be preferred. But this confuses the store of value with the medium of exchange. The two need not be the same good.

Another presumed rationale is the case of search over the population of potential demanders of a good. If everyone uses a good, it is more likely that it could be a medium of exchange. But, again, everyone uses bread or milk. Generality of use aids, but is neither a sufficient nor a necessary precondition. Generality here is a result of people using it as a medium of exchange, not a cause of the good becoming a medium. For example, chocolate candy and nylons became a near money during price controls in the absence of other "money." The items were cheaply identifiable by many people—not necessarily consumed by everybody.

Costs of identifying qualities of a good are what counts. If costs for some good are low and generally low across members of society, the good will become a medium through which information costs can be reduced and exchange made more economical. But it will rise only with the rise of chains of specialists in various goods and commodities, who know the goods cheaply, whose reputation for reliability of evaluation is high, who because of that knowledge and cheapness of assurance to buyers become specialist middlemen in the good as both inventory carriers and buying and selling agents. Other explanations of the occurrence and use of money are silent or vacuous on the existence of specialists and their reliability and activities.

This analysis explains the use of money, which good becomes money, why it is not necessarily also the store of value, the existence of two or more specialists in the sequence of exchanges with money, the reputability of specialists as an integral part of their capital values, and the reason specialists are also dealers.

This model is also consistent with the explanation of unemployment as a search and selection process for best work opportunities during demand shifts among potentially performed activities. Commodities or services that are more difficult to assess in qualities will experience greater losses or changes in values consequent to demand shifts. That higher cost tends to act like specificity of a good to particular tasks. The higher costs of assessing their attributes are like a tax on transfer. Hence the larger gains (or avoidance of loss) from more expensive search in the event of a demand shift (with a large change or high variance of next best known opportunities) induce greater or longer search. It is not simply a task of searching out best opportunities, but also a search for potential demanders to assess productive qualities. Those costs of becoming informed about what a good or service or rented good will do raise transfer costs and also reward longer or greater searching activity by potential buyers or employers. Commodities or services with qualities that have high costs for other people to ascertain will tend to be held longer in inventories awaiting sale and will suffer greater costs of exchange—as evident by larger bid-ask spreads, wholesale-retail spreads, or "unemployment" lengths. Since the commodity used as money will have low cost in these respects, we conclude money will have the lowest "unemployment" rate.

It is not the absence of a double coincidence of wants, or of the costs of searching out the market of potential buyers and sellers of various goods, or of record keeping, but the costliness of information about the attributes of goods available for exchange that induces the use of money in an exchange economy—if some good has low recognition costs for a large segment of the population while other goods do not. A result is the use not only of money but of knowledgeable experts, with high reputability, who deal in the goods in which they are specialists.

Because most of the formal economic models of competition, exchange, and equilibrium have ignored ignorance and lack of costless full and perfect information, many institutions of our economic system, institutions that are productive in creating knowledge more cheaply than otherwise, have been erroneously treated as parasitic appendages. The explanation of use of money, expertise with dealing in a good as a middleman specialist with a trademark or brand name, reputability or goodwill, along with advertising of one's wares (and even unemployment) is often misunderstood. All these can be derived from the same information cost factors that give rise to use of an intermediary medium of exchange.

# TRADING STAMPS

## ARMEN A. ALCHIAN AND BENJAMIN KLEIN

Inefficiency of trading stamps—green, blue, or gold—as a medium of exchange is beyond doubt. Their persistence is therefore often condescendingly attributed to irrational, acquisitive instincts of shoppers. An alternative explanation, based on straightforward economic analysis, without appeal to irrational behavior was offered by Otto Davis; stamps permit price discrimination among customers of differing demand elasticities.[1] Davis has not followed with an *application* of the analysis. How is price discrimination accomplished with stamps? Which attributes of a person put him in one or the other class? What refutable implications will test this interpretation against others? These are the questions answered in this paper.

## 1. The Theoretical Analysis

Assume, to avoid irrelevancies, that all consumers have the same *consumption* demand. When faced with a definite known price, the rate of consumption would be the same for all customers. But let customers differ in their *shopping* (i.e., market search and purchase activity) costs: (a) some can more cheaply search for lower-priced sources; (b) some have lower costs of negotiating and completing purchases from those sources; (c) some differ in their demand elasticity to a *particular* seller. That is, some buyers prefer a seller more than do other buyers.

For example, richer housewives devote less time to daily searching out sellers who on that day have the lowest prices than do poorer women. Also they devote less time in actual purchasing. A rich one values time released from shopping arrangements more (relative to monetary wealth) than does a poor one—since the rich have more pecuniary wealth relative to time than do the poor. A woman who earns her monetary income in the market will likely devote less time to price searching for daily or weekly purchased goods and to arranging purchases than does a wife with the same income from her husband.

This previously unpublished, undated article appears here by permission of the author.

1. "The Economics of Trading Stamps," *Journal of Business* 32 (April 1959): 141–50.

Since transaction costs include the cost of searching over the market for better prices, for knowledge of characteristics of goods, and for completing the sale contract, the value of time enters into the calculus of behavior. A person whose time is more valuable relative to money will substitute more money to save the time of shopping or discovering prices and contract negotiation. That person's demand in a *given* store will be less elastic to a higher price than for a person with a lower value of shopping time.

Suppose the price of some good is predictably constant over time and uniform among all retailers (and known to be by all customers). Who would pay more to have this situation prevail? Who would prefer to have prices fluctuate over time and among stores—with, say, the same average over time as the constant price? Clearly, a predictably constant price over time and among retailers is more highly valued by "richer" persons and, hence, is more likely for items purchased exclusively by them. For example, if higher-quality brands are more likely to be bought by the rich, we should expect more resale price fixing by the manufacturers of those higher-quality brands as a means of economizing on their customers' shopping (price-search) costs.

It would be profitable to the retailer to charge a higher price to a less elastic demander who is less likely to reduce his purchase rate from this retailer, since "shopping around" costs are higher or because the cost of going to some other lower-price store is higher. If all prices were always constant, there would be no point in shopping around and, hence, no induced difference among customers in elasticities of demand for *a particular retailer's* items. In addition to effects of the fluctuating price over time and among stores, even if prices were constant and known, rich people near some store find it not worthwhile to go to more distant, less convenient stores in view of their high value (costs) of time. The retailer would want to charge a higher price to the less-elastic-shopping-demand customers and a lower price to the more elastic shopping demanders.

How can he reduce the price to only the people with the more elastic demand for purchasing at his store? He offers a right to a rebate of, say, 3 percent and even offers the rich person a similar right which, however, the rich person doesn't bother to collect, because the costs (measured by value of time required) for collecting, preserving, and redeeming the rights are too expensive for him. He offers stamps which must be stuck in books and redeemed, which is more costly for the rich. But those costs are not too expensive for the poorer people (or those with children who provide cheap labor for collecting and putting stamps in a book). It is not costless to preserve small low-value rebate coupons for later redemption. Poorer people (here used as a proxy for elastic demanders) get a discount via the value of goods from redeemed stamps, while the rich (less elastic) non-preservers of stamps get no discount. The gross money price (*ignoring* stamp redemption value) is higher to both buyers, but the poor people get a more-than-compensating rebate via the coupon's redemption value—one that is too costly for a rich person to get. Thus stamps lower net costs to the more elastic shopping demanders and raise them to the less elastic shopping demanders.

It is *not* necessary to assume that all non-redeemers refuse to take stamps. It is sufficient that they do not bother with redeeming all of them.

So long as customers decide whether to accept and redeem the stamps, the costs of detection of differing demand elasticities is reduced. The remaining cost to achieve discrimination is the cost of creating, distributing, and redeeming the stamps. The cost of redemption centers is a normal cost present in any regular retail outlet and, hence, is not an extra cost of distribution of goods to consumers. (However, as we shall indicate later, there are in addition to the cost of making and distributing the stamps some other "free-ride prevention" costs that arise when *some* retailers use tactics to benefit themselves at the expense of other stamp-issuing retailers.)

Will the economics or mathematics really work out? Yes. We assume either that (a) only those customers who will redeem the stamps take them, while the less elastic demanders do not, or that (b) the less elastic demanders redeem a smaller fraction of the stamps they do take or hold them longer. Either is sufficient. If no stamps are taken by non-redeemers, the merchant can buy stamps for 1 cent each and give them to *only* the redeemers who turn them in for 1 cent redemption value in terms of the goods they get at the redemption center. If non-redeemers take stamps, the retail cost of an issued stamp will be reduced below its redemption value to those who redeem. Under these conditions (i.e., not all customers take or not all taken stamps are redeemed) the retailer is lowering price to one class of customers relative to the other. It is well established from the theory of pricing to different classes of customers that charging different prices to customers of different demand elasticity can result in greater profits to the sellers, in lower prices to some customers (high elasticity of demand in response to price differential), and in higher prices to others—if the scheme for detecting demand differences and enforcing different prices is not prohibitively costly. This is simply price discrimination.

In the pure model, the price to the less elastic shoppers is raised, while the net price to the more elastic shoppers is reduced. Usually price discrimination models are presented as if the price is raised to one group and lowered to another relative to the uniform price. In fact, it is profitable to raise the price to one group *or* lower it to the other, even though doing both would be even more profitable. For the present, we are assuming (and believe) that both price changes occur. Whether in the trading stamp case both effects occur or only a higher price occurs for non-stamp takers or only a lower net price for stamp redeemers is not possible to determine from the pure theory of price discrimination. A systematic comparison of data on net prices to redeemers with the prices they would pay without stamps is required for that conclusion.

## II. Implications

1. Savings coupons or stamps are more common for retailers catering to heterogeneous (differing elasticities) customers than for those catering to only non-stamp-redeeming or only stamp-redeeming customers.

2. Stamps would be issued more in those stores for types of goods for which prices over time, and among retail outlets, are less predictable, i.e., fluctuate more. This follows from the differential costs of getting information about prices at various stores and times.

3. Stamps will be used only where small (absolute) discounts are optimal, because their effectiveness is correlated with the *differential* costs of preserving and redeeming stamps. For large percentage discounts (i.e., large stamp redemption value), the cost of redemption would be relatively smaller, and everyone would take and redeem stamps.

4. Stamps are less likely to be issued if the total value of each single-purchase transaction is large. The more stamps a person gets at one purchase, the easier it is for him to thereby *collect* a sufficient amount worthy of redemption; part of the costs inhibiting redemption are the costs of keeping track of the few stamps at each purchase. Thus if an enormous value is issued at one transaction, the purchaser has significantly less cost of achieving a quantity of stamps warranting the remaining costs involved in redemption—or sale or gift to others.

5. If customers obtain extensive specific personal or special services in the process of purchase or use of the good, then the more these vary among customers, the more will the service difference be a substitute for price discounting or discrimination. Barber and beauty shops with specific personal services are examples of service places that are unlikely to profit from stamps. Tipping and stamps are negatively correlated. Stamps should be less likely in stores that can adapt services among specific customers, that engage in bargaining, and that utilize tipping, all of which permit discrimination.

6. A retailer who operates his own store and knows which customers have low elasticity and which have high elasticity can provide personal services of varying quality to engage in price (or product) discrimination—not by changing the price (as with bargaining at each purchase) but by varying the service. But if the retailer has an employee negotiating each sale, the owner cannot watch each sale and accompanying services. The incentive for the employee to discriminate in the same way is weaker than for the owner. We ignore here the fact that it will pay the employee to discriminate in other ways the weaker the employer's surveillance or the weaker is competition by potential employees for that employee's job. We would expect, therefore, stamps and coupons to be more commonly given in stores with more employees handling the customers than in stores operated by "Mom and Pop." For the same reason that bargaining is more likely by an owner of a store than by employees, we would expect stamps to be more likely in larger employee-type stores than in owner-operated stores. Incidentally, in Hong Kong camera and photo shops, employees are sometimes permitted to buy items in stock from the employer and then sell the item in the store for whatever price the employee can negotiate with prospective customers. This initial sale by the owner to the employee involves some bargaining in anticipation of eventual sales price, but the incentive system is neat. Customer discrimination is increased; total proceeds to the store are increased and shared between employer and employee. Do used car or even new car dealers do that with their salesmen? With their best salesmen? Permitting employees to work for tips is a variant of this, insofar as high-elasticity customers will tip less for a given service. All this is independent of any variation of amount of service for which tipping is also awarded.

7. Items sold with return of used items will less likely have stamps, since the allowance on a used item permits price discrimination. With turn-ins, the retailer, *insofar as he can discern to whom* price cuts are more appropriate, can adjust the allowance.

8. A stamp-issuing retailer will post a conspicuous sign saying he gives stamps, but ideally he would not thrust them at the customer. Instead he would give them to those who ask. This would economize on his costs of stamps. Of course, so long as *every* retailer using a given type of stamp thrusts them on every customer, the advantage to any one retailer of not thrusting them at every customer diminishes. (The reason is that the cost of a stamp to a retailer reflects the national average rate of redemption of issued stamps, and not just that of the one retailer. By not thrusting stamps, an individual retailer saves on the costs of stamps not issued. If all retailers thrust, then the cost of a stamp

will be lower relative to its redemption value, since more of the issued stamps will not be redeemed.) Either, then, every retailer of a given type of stamp, say Blue Chip, should be encouraged by the stamp company to thrust the stamps at every customer as a matter of policy, or every retailer should be required to wait until the customer asks—if one retailer is not to take advantage of other retailers using the same brand of stamps. Employee-operated and self-service (i.e., uniform-service) firms will thrust stamps, but owner-operated firms will not.

9. Stamp-issuing and -redeeming companies should avoid schemes that *equate* or *raise* stamp redemption costs to *all* customers. The costs of redeeming stamps should be higher for those who are the less-elastic-demand customers. Since customers do not fall into two widely disparate classes according to greatly differing elasticities of demand, it is not possible to make the costs of redemption for one class strictly inapplicable to the other class. Placing redemption centers nearer the homes of the elastic-demand customers and having redeemers stand in lines—to economize on the clerical costs of operating the redemption centers—would enable greater redemption value of stamps to those willing to stand in lines—presumably the high-elasticity demanders. Requiring stamps to be pasted in books also adds a differential cost.

So we should expect to see the redemption centers concentrated more heavily in areas of poorer, more-elastic-demand customers and the incidence of lines and queues greater than in conventional retail stores. Also, the hours of operation will be hours less convenient to the low-elasticity demanders—say from 9 to 4 on weekdays. Redemption by mail would not be permitted except for those who live in communities without centers—say those in a town at least 50 miles from a redemption-center town. Ideally, if somehow less elastic demanders were not to redeem stamps, no matter what, then redemption centers would have incentive to provide better service to redeemers.

10. A scheme for making stamp collection costs different is to issue stamps to those who walk to a special counter for stamps. (Personal observations indicate about half of the customers collected stamps.) This helps screen out inelastic (high-time-value) customers. But it *raises* costs also to high-elastic demanders and hence reduces their desire for stamps. Ideally the stamp company wants the *difference* larger, but primarily by raising the redemption costs to the less elastic demanders.[2]

---

2. In this example, this particular retail store is reducing its stamp costs by ensuring that only the most sure to redeem will collect stamps. The store makes more effective use

Stamp companies should object to intermediaries who offer to purchase stamps for cash, or exchange one brand of stamp for another. If every stamp were made *equally* costly and valuable in redemption to *every* customer so that differential probability of acceptance and redemption could be eliminated, retailers could not use stamps to charge different effective prices. (See the next implication for a special kind of easier but differential redemption that would not destroy stamp issue.)

11. Would stamp companies object to a cash discount if stamps are not taken? Introduction of the option of a cash discount will reduce the issuance rate, but it will increase the *redemption* rate of stamps that are issued. Only those customers most likely to redeem stamps will now decide to take them in lieu of cash. Therefore, if only some retailers adopt this practice, we once again have the problem of inter-retailer "cheating." All retailers share the higher cost of a particular outlet's higher redemption rate. This problem is minimized if, for example, differential prices were charged by the stamp companies to individual retailers as a function of particular issuing practices or redemption rates[3] (which would be extremely difficult to police), or if all retailers adopted the practice. If the "cheating" problem is not significant, the cash discount option gives each retailer the power to alter the degree of price discrimination.

12. Price discrimination will not be eliminated as long as the discount for not taking stamps is less than the stamp value to those who do take them. Let the retailer charge 41 cents a gallon for gas if stamps are taken. Assume collecting and redeeming stamps is worth 2 cents to customers who *do* take stamps. Now let the retailer offer a 1 cent per gallon cash discount to those who decline stamps (because to the decliners, stamps are worth nothing—or at most less than 1 cent). The cash price to the stamp *refuser* is 40 cents, and to the stamp *taker* the *effective* pecuniary price (net of stamp redemption value) is 39 cents—which is at worst no less than the net amount received by the retailer after paying for the issued stamp. (If every stamp issued were redeemed, the retailer's cost of stamps would equal the 2 cent redemptive value of the stamp, so

---

of the fewer stamps it *does* issue—so that as compared to all other retailers, it is getting greater value per stamp. Of course, it is not greater value per stamp issued that counts; it is profits of the store. The stamp company should object to this system, unless *all* retailers adopt it.

3. Note that a cash discount option may, in fact, push a retailer's redemption rate to the average industry- (or economy-) wide level and would be unobjectionable to the stamp company.

the retailer would be paying 2 cents for the stamps and netting 39 cents.) The price to stamp collectors and redeemers is *lower* than from merchants who do not offer stamps and do not discriminate with lower prices to high-elasticity shoppers. This means, however, that *non*-stamp customers would be getting a lower cash price (40 cents) from this retailer than from other stamp-issuing merchants who charge 41 cents and do not offer cash rebates. This would take inelastic-demand customers away from the no-cash-discount stamp-issuing retailers, whose incentive to use stamps would be *reduced* but not removed. Even if every retailer were thereby to offer cash discounts to stamp refusers, the system of cash discounts for not taking stamps would work, for there are still different net prices to the two classes of customers. Stamps would survive.

13. If some retailers offer greater multiples of stamps per dollar of purchase than other retailers to attract collectors, a larger fraction of stamps issued by *these* merchants would be redeemed. This increases the fraction of *all* stamps issued that are redeemed and would ultimately require a higher cost of a stamp to each participating merchant. Pending that adjustment, the disproportionate stamp giver is gaining wealth from the retailers who give stamps in standard amounts or whose issued stamps are redeemed in the average or less proportion. Either the stamp company accepts lower profits, or it raises stamp prices to all retailers. Retailers whose issued stamps are less likely to be redeemed are paying a disproportionately higher price for each stamp that is redeemed.

Perhaps more important is that giving a greater multiple of stamps permits a greater price difference between the two classes of customers. The optimal degree may differ among retailers.

14. If stamp redemption value exceeds the cost of a stamp to the merchant (which means *some* stamps must be unredeemed), merchants would like to use them even in homogeneous-type-customer stores where all customers are stamp redeemers, say in low-income areas. But the stamp company will find this not profitable, since these stores, by raising the proportion of stamps that are redeemed, reduce the difference between merchant cost and redemption value. The fact that stamps are issued in retail stores where all customers take and redeem stamps suggests that in the aggregate not all stamps are redeemed. Recall that it is not necessary that some stamps not be redeemed; it is sufficient that some (less-elastic-demand) customers do not take stamps.

In sum, retailers will issue stamps or are more likely to find them profitable the less predictable are their prices of each good temporally, the more are prices likely to vary among stores, the smaller the size of each customer's purchase, the less is customer-unique service provided, the less heterogeneous are its customers with respect to their value of time relative to money wealth, the less likely tipping is involved as part of the purchase cost, the less there is bargaining and higgling about the price at each purchase (and the greater are the expense-account customers who can keep the stamps rather than handing them over to the expense-account payer).

### iii. Two Predictions

1. A potential prediction may soon be testable. Self-service gasoline stations should result in more elastic demanders using self-service with lower prices (on assumption that more elastic demanders are those more willing to serve themselves). Will the price spread between self- and full services equate marginal revenues—or only reflect marginal cost differences? Will full-service customers have less elastic demands for full service and hence be subjected to a greater price differential than the marginal costs? One is tempted to answer in the negative on the grounds that competition among stations would wipe that out. But the negatively sloped demand curves to each gasoline station still persist, so some price differentiation should be potentially profitable among self- and full services. Probably the greater homogeneity within the class of full-service customers and within the self-service customers would make stamps less effective, since the price difference is already being effective. This suggests the *prediction* that stamps will be less common (if not totally absent) in stations with self- and full-service options.

2. Some supermarkets found that small-purchase customers were being lost because of the time required waiting at the check stand. Safeway has opened express lines. We assume that express-line customers have less elastic demands and "could" be charged a higher price. How? By giving stamps *only* in non-express lines.

These are some implications of the price discrimination hypothesis initiated by Davis. It takes a better theory—not a fact—to displace a theory. What do the alternative interpretations have to imply?

### iv. Alternative Attempts at Interpretations

1. "People are crazy or stupid and don't realize they would be better off without stamps." Answer: Why are they crazy when shopping in a grocery store but not in the barber or beauty shop?

2. "It's a battle of sexes. Stamps provide a means for women to collect wealth that their husbands can't use." Implication: Redemption centers redeem

stamps for goods used by women or henpecked husbands and not for goods used by the family as a whole or for widows or widowers. Nor would stamps be issued in stores that catered primarily to men, but in those that cater primarily to women—like beauty shops—where they are rare to extinction.

3. "There is . . . a threshold problem with price cutting. Reducing prices in a supermarket by the cost of stamps would mean an average reduction per item of one-half to three-fourths of a penny. Many customers would not perceive such a price cut. Others, who notice the change, may not respond. After all, in total, a 2 percent price cut amounts to only ten or twelve cents on the average customer's transaction. But the same 2 percent means fifty or sixty stamps, which turns out to be a highly visible and dramatically attractive incentive for many shoppers."[4] That this kind of argument could be advanced seriously is a testimony to the kinds of analysis devoted to the subject. On that interpretation's own ground, its advocates should have said . . . No (rather than not many) customers would perceive the price difference, and that none *will* (not may) respond. Yet those who propound this interpretation go on to assert that many customers *do* recognize that attempts to create the illusion of lower prices, on the average, by a few cuts on some items are recognized after a short while. It's a "tails I win, heads you lose" argument. As it stands, this so-called explanation is irrefutable by any observable events and therefore leads a long and sterile life.

4. "Price cutting is easily imitated. Stamp use is typically on a franchised basis. Thus stamps provide distinctiveness, but customer acceptance varies considerably among stamp brands, and the store with the best stamp and the best program for promoting stamps has an edge." If we understood that, we might be able to respond. And stamp companies would encourage easy instant cash redemptions of their stamps!

5. "Most women (and even most men) like to save them. Most consumers think of stamps as discretionary spending power—a way to provide extras for the home—perhaps an easier way than putting aside nickels and dimes. Many customers seem to prefer stamp saving to other promotional extras. . . . So trading stamps continue to thrive in America not because they are generally more efficient than money but because they are more efficient in meeting the special competitive needs of some retailers and because they bring satisfactions to many customers that could not readily be realized in other ways."[5]

4. E. Beem and L. Isaacson, "Schizophrenia in Trading Stamp Analysis," *Journal of Business* 41, no. 3 (1968): 340–51, at 341.

5. Ibid.

That is empty, hence impregnable. We are still left with the question of *why* that form of lower price is viable, and why stamps bring "satisfactions" to many customers that could not readily be realized more efficiently by cash. In what sense are they more efficient? The proffered statements assert rather than explain the incidence of stamp issue or conditions placed on their redemption.

6. "Trading stamps permit price cutting on price-maintained items." Then why are they used most extensively by retailers of grocery and gasoline, where nearly nothing is price maintained? While this cannot be denied as an ancillary factor, it is noteworthy that it fails to explain the pattern of stamp issuance and therefore could not by itself account for stamp profitability—whereas price discrimination can.

7. "Trading stamps are low-cost savings account receipts." The trading stamp is basically a claim to a later repayment *with interest* like a savings account, except that the stamps permit small deposits to be made daily and at lower cost than accumulating a larger sum in cash and then depositing it. This is certainly a logical and economically consistent possibility. But it faces two difficulties. The amount of interest paid is very loosely correlated with the length of time stamps are held and secondly, fails to explain the kinds of stores and purchases with which stamps are issued. In sum, the explanation is internally consistent, but empirically refuted.

8. "Originally stamps were issued as discounts for cash." Perhaps they were, but their success cannot be explained by that factor alone, especially with stamps issued extensively by stores that do not accept credit sales. And in any event, why not just give a cash discount?

# THERE REALLY IS A FREE SERVICE

## 1. Summary

Any seller with prices in excess of marginal cost has a potentially unexploited profit which he could obtain if he could sell extra units without a cut in price on former units. Multipart pricing and fee-plus-marginal-cost pricing are standard examples of procedures to do that, as well as to try to capture more of "exchange surplus." This note indicates another method which seems to be used for this purpose but which has been interpreted as "price discrimination" of the usual type, wherein a seller achieves marginal revenue (not price) equality among customers. The tactic is simple: entice an extra buyer or purchaser by giving a free ancillary service, the cost of which is less than *the excess of price over the marginal cost of the extra unit thereby sold.*[1] This increases the output closer to where price equals the full marginal cost of the extra unit including the "free service." The consumer and the seller are better off, and the so-called monopoly seller inefficiency is reduced or eliminated. *No prices are raised.*[2] See Figure 1.

If special ancillary services or items can attract some *new* customers or *new* sales without price cuts on existing sales (at the marginal revenue equals marginal cost output), a seller will offer these services either free or at less than their cost. This is *not* below-cost pricing. The "last" package is priced at its marginal costs; the price of the complete package sold covers the total cost of the complete package, including the ancillary peripherals taken. Without peripherals the price at the smaller output was above marginal costs because of the negatively sloped demand in which price exceeds marginal revenue.

---

This previously unpublished August 1979 article appears here by permission of the author.

1. The *usual* mathematical relation between elasticity and marginal revenue/price is broken by cutting price on *only* the extra unit (if that can be arranged), which makes the marginal revenue equal to price.

2. Indeed, some are reduced, i.e., those that are offered "free."

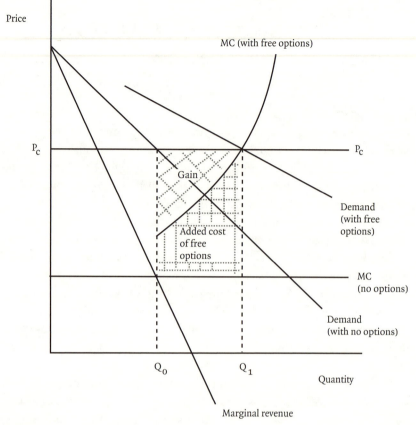

**FIGURE 1**

## II. Details

*Non-price Competition*

Seller A produces and sells a package of goods and services, denoted by the vector of elements $(x_1, x_2, \ldots, x_m)$. Assume every purchaser from this seller always takes a package with elements $x_1$ through $x_g$, called the basic package, in which $x_1$ is the basic good and $x_2, \ldots, x_g$ are the basic services. In addition, the seller offers elements $(x_h, \ldots, x_m)$ at no extra charge, *and not all* purchasers take every one of those extra elements with every purchase. We call this the option vector. The customer is offered a package and has some choice with respect to which of the options to take. For example, he may read the advertising or ignore it; he may ask for gift wrapping or ignore it; similarly for return privileges, free delivery, credit, time of salesclerks, inspection of large inventories, parking lots, and on and on through a long list of "free" options.

We denote (1) price competition as intercustomer or intertemporal *variations* in the price charged for the basic package. We denote as (2) non-price competition the activity of permitting customers to select the options $x_h, \ldots, x_m$ to have at no extra charge. Both price and non-price competition can occur simultaneously. Denote as (3) "variable non-price competition" the *altering of* the service vector $x_h, \ldots, x_m$, possibly by expanding it or reducing the set.

Queries: (a) Why is there a set of elements $x_2, \ldots, x_g$ along with the basic element $x_1$? (b) Why are optionals, $x_h, \ldots, x_m$ offered *at no extra* charge? The answer to (a) is that the services in that set are less expensive to provide than if purchased by separate negotiation with other specialists in those services. For example, the purchase of groceries is accompanied by their being placed in paper bags provided by the seller. (Ever go shopping in Europe?) The costs of separately purchasing the service are too high, so it is priced in the package.

An answer to (b) is that the options, $x_h, \ldots, x_m$, are means of selling *extra* units of $x_1$ without cutting prices on all units. This achieves a marginal revenue closer to price. Providing one customer with free credit in order to get more of his business does not require a price cut (or equal cost) to all other customers or on all that customer's purchases. The seller gets that extra sale without cutting price on all units sold, so the achieved marginal revenue is higher than if price is cut on all units. It is the price received on that sale. See Figure 1.

These free options need not raise the prices to any buyers. The key to the apparent mystery of no higher prices is the unexploited excess of price over marginal cost. That excess of price over marginal cost is a latent source of profit and also of consumer gain if somehow those extra units could be sold without cutting price on the other units. The option enables that gain to be realized so long as the cost of the option taken with the extra sale at the initial price is covered by the excess of that price over marginal cost. Larger, more valuable output is made achievable. Neither price nor costs of the former units are increased. Only the cost of the extra units is increased, but that still is less than the price received on that extra unit. The latent "efficiency loss of monopoly" is reduced—for those interested in "welfare." If every buyer has the same *price* elasticity of demand for the basic package of elements $x_1, \ldots, x_g$, but different demand elasticities for $x_1, \ldots, x_g$, with respect to the options $x_h, \ldots, x_m$, the price of the packages need not be increased to any purchasers.

### III. Applications?

Advertising may attract a new set of customers heretofore unaware of the product. Free silverware or traveller's checks can attract new accounts to a bank. These are usually thought to be ways of getting around fixed interest rate ceilings, but they also are ways to get new customers or more sales without cutting price on all units.

Trading stamps should have this power to push quantity to marginal cost equals price, and without raising price to any buyers. Trading stamps are also a price discrimination device (i.e., they help achieve marginal revenue equality among buyers).

Free delivery, free parking, and discount coupons (not offered to everyone) should also be effective. Less obvious services include permitting sales clerks to devote a large amount of time to selling a particular customer, while not giving a lower price to those who purchase with less use of the clerks' time. Large inventories are more useful to some buyers than to others. Staying open at all hours and not charging more to customers during high-cost periods is a means of attracting customers who would not otherwise have purchased. Typically these are separated by specialty shops that charge more and do more of their business at the expensive times (nights and weekends), while the low-price shops close down at the times costs of operation are high or demand is low. Free trials of goods are another example. Warranty service to people who are high risks at the same price as to low-risk people gets extra sales. (Credit cards?) "Loss" leaders are an example; but there is no loss, even though those sellers (not producers) of these options who are outcompeted will object to "below-cost" pricing. (Is there any commodity sold by any seller that does not have a set of associated "optional" services included in the price? Conjecture: If you find a case, it will be a case of pure competition.)

### IV. Some Free Optional Reflections on the Theory of Markets

The pure competition model (marginal revenue equals price equals marginal cost) has several uses: e.g., meaning of scarcity and costs, prices and property rights as systems of control, specialization and comparative advantage, inflation, capital values, effects of taxes, tariffs and price controls. But nothing in the formal logic of the competitive model or even the monopoly model explained or implied advertising, brand names, warranties, inventories, exclusive franchises, "free" optional services, or even the use of money in the economy.

It is a defensible proposition that the existence of costs of communicating or discovering information about properties of goods—and of bids and offers, and of negotiating transactions—and the uncertainty about the future implies a negatively sloped demand curve facing each seller. To reduce or economize on those costs includes the tactics just mentioned. It is misleading to assume (though convenient for some problems which are validly analyzed with the pure competition model) that any cut in price is sufficient to attract consumers from all other producers as if they immediately knew of the lower price and knew that the product package was the same. Products are rarely identical; indeed it is rare that goods are sufficiently identical to make consumers willing to take any unit from any seller of a "given" product at random (at essentially zero inspection costs) at the same price, or to be willing to take whichever one may have the lower price—without any further examination. Rather than assume that differences in products are consciously created, we reverse the assumption and assume that cheap recognition of identical products is the exception. Why test drive a Ford to see if you want that particular car, or probe a piece of meat in the supermarket, or sample a bottle of wine after it is uncorked, or sample a carload of wheat? Full and costless knowledge—or uniformity—is a rare thing in economic goods.

Prior beliefs or accumulated (but necessarily incomplete) knowledge about various goods, sellers, or people is valuable, though erroneous. We correctly hesitate to assume that items that might be different, or not known to necessarily be identical, are really identical. If information is neither perfect nor costless, we will not switch to another seller or another item of that "same" good (which in fact may be identical or just as good) at the slightest difference in price. Doubts are valuable and are not priced at zero. We do not respond to every slightest difference in price between two goods that might be the same.

1. Items that are really different, but about which people are in a complete state of ignorance as to whether there is any difference, or about which they incorrectly believe there is no difference, will experience reductions in elasticities of demand as more information reveals differences between the classes of goods. A greater difference in price between the price of a good in one class of the items will be required to make a switch to an item of the other class, now perceived to be different.
2. Items that are really the same, but about which differences are believed to exist, or about which there is uncertainty of performance, will have increased elasticity of demand as more information is available attesting to their greater-than-initially-perceived similarity.

Why are brand names used to identify suppliers or producers? If products were recognizable in their quality characteristics and traits at trivial inspection costs, and if cost of purchase were also trivially determinable, brand names would serve no purpose. They would add nothing of informative value to prospective purchasers. The particular producer or supplier would be irrelevant, because knowledge of who the maker or supplier was would add nothing to what could be ascertained at trivial cost.

However, let the quality characteristics or price not be ascertainable at low cost prior to commitment to purchase (with later consequences, if unfavorable, capable of being a serious loss to the purchaser). In this circumstance a potential buyer will devote costs to becoming informed about these features—if he believes the costs will be less than the buyer's surplus he would achieve upon discovery of this information and purchase of the product. Alternatively, the seller would devote resources to trying to inform potential customers of the quality or price of a product. The seller or supplier has a better knowledge of the probability that a customer would want to buy his product if he were fully informed, and the supplier knows better who is likely to be a customer. The seller is therefore more likely to make the investment in providing prepurchase information services. And that, of course, is typically what happens. Sellers display wares, sellers advertise features of what they have to offer, and they maintain stores. Buyers do not advertise, and buyers do not maintain stores at which they buy.

Buyers take a risk in quality and price when making a purchase. If information of all the characteristics of a good and its price is cheap and accurate, the risks to buyers are small. If not, the sellers will undertake to provide information to reduce those risks, because the seller, who can be presumed to know about the quality and price of offerings, will be better informed as to whether there is a high likelihood the customer would regard discovery and availability of this supplier's goods as inducing a purchase.

This previously unpublished, undated article appears here by permission of the author.

Suppliers will take the risk of providing information to purchasers prior to any commitment to purchase by a customer. Suppliers also will be willing to invest in warranty and guarantee of performance and price if they know more about the performance probabilities than consumers. Sellers will have a better idea as to actuarially sound risk premiums. But if consumers easily affect the performance quality, then the consumer may have a better idea as to the probability of satisfactory performance with the economic degree of care. In this case, he will bear the risk.

Explicit warranties are not sufficiently detailed to cover all contingencies. But the supplier can be motivated to provide good service by the prospect of future income. Define a "good" service or a "good" product as one that the customer, after consumption, deems worth having purchased and does so by repeat purchase or recommendations to his friends. The product is one he would have purchased if he had foreknowledge of exactly what did in fact happen. In other words, he would have bought it again. All of this rests on the presumption that the customer does not know costlessly, prior to purchase, exactly what he would be getting.

What sources of information can he rely on? Aside from the personal knowledge (very expensive) and the explicit warranty, he can rely on the reputation of the supplier, a reputation based on past performance—a performance he projects into the future. In other words, if a customer can predict that the supplier will continue to perform in the future as he has in the past, he will use the past performance as information. The reputation of the supplier is based on past continued performance. The supplier is identified by his name. His name is his brand name, his trademark.

The value of that brand name, as a source of information to customers, corresponds to the informative value obtained by knowing who the supplier is. The greater the value of the product to the consumer, the greater the direct costs the customer would have to incur to ascertain those qualities, and the greater is the probability that the supplier can be counted on to continue to provide the kind of product rendered in the past, the greater is the value of that name as a means of identifying or finding that supplier. The brand name, then, is a direct substitute for firsthand, expensive expertise by the customer about the costs and qualities that the supplier provides. The better the product of the supplier and the harder it is to identify those desirable qualities by direct personal observation prior to purchase, the greater will be the value of knowing who is the supplier of a good whose quality is already known from past demonstrated experience and who can be believed to continue to perform at the same standard. That is why brand names are so valuable to the consuming public and why they are so valuable to the supplier. They rest on (1) high costs of direct personal ability to detect quality and price of a product prior to commitment to purchase, (2) the value of assurance and quality to the customer, and (3) the probability that the supplier will continue to provide that reputed quality and price of service.

Implications of the analysis are easily tested and are supported by the facts. Items such as lettuce, carrots, celery, grapes, and potatoes rarely have brand names. They are easily knowable by the customer. Further, the prices are readily known and the seriousness of a "failure" is not great. The name of the supplier would be of little value. Some items are more difficult to test by feel, weight, or looks, and for these a trade or brand name is more likely to develop—oranges, bananas, canned goods (ever try to look inside and sample it?). Automobiles are expensive and are difficult to evaluate by personal expertise. The brand name is more important.

# THE CHEF, GOURMET AND GOURMAND

## I. Introduction

The weapon phasing problem—the influence of the preceding and succeeding weapons upon a particular weapon's usefulness and efficiency, and the importance of its particular date or time of potential utilization—remained intractable until the purposes of RAND recommendations *vis-à-vis* the Air Forces' actual decisions were clarified. The following discussion of those recommendations and decisions will meet with agreement or with criticism. In either event, more accurate specification of pertinent problems will be the result.

Whether RAND's interest be intercontinental war, comparison of weapon systems, or research in methods of war, its major effort is devoted to the search for new ideas and weapons. Of the two standard motives for research and learning, the satisfaction of intellectual curiosity and the necessity of choosing a course of action, the latter is of immediate concern to RAND and the Air Force. These choices can be separated, analytically and temporarily, into two interdependent classes.

## II. The Procurement Decision

The procurement decision is the choice of weapons to order now for later military operational use. For example, if we assume that the stock of strategic bombing weapons to be on hand by 1954 is firmly determined by present commitments, short of war, then the current procurement decisions will affect our 1955 operational capabilities. As an example of the present procurement choice, we have the problem of whether we should switch from B-47B's to B-47C's with or without Rascals, or to B-52's with air-refueling or with overseas ground refueling bases, or to Snarks, etc. A standard procedure seems to have consisted of a comparison of the potency of weapon A with weapon B in 1955–58. Then, by considering costs, one of the systems is recommended. Everyone recognizes that there is a possibility that the comparison of two weapons at a particular interval of time may give misleading information. There is the pos-

Reprinted from RAND Corp., RM-798-PR, March 24, 1952.

sibility that the relative superiority of the various weapons will depend upon the system in use prior to the considered weapons and upon the systems that may be available subsequently. Even more, the relative superiority may depend upon the particular contemplated time of operational availability. In a nutshell, weapon superiority may be a function of weapon dating and sequencing.

### III. The Research and Development Decision

Whether or not the desirability of a weapon depends upon its inheritance, its endowment, its life length, and its date of life, we can be certain that the current procurement decision is affected by past, present, and future amounts and allocations of Research and Development funds. The amount and division of these funds critically affects the set of weapons available and their availability dates. Hence, we should regard these future dates and weapon potentialities as variable and should investigate the effect of shuffling them around, moving projected weapons forward or back, and changing them. Thus, the second decision to which attention must be directed is the Research and Development budget size and allocation.

### IV. Factors Affecting Decisions

An extended discussion of these two different, but interdependent, actions is appropriate since the distinction between (a) the decision to initiate research, design, and development and (b) the decision to procure large numbers for operational use in the AF is fundamental to Air Force Planning. These two decisions are very different in their timing, in the information required, in their criterion of proper decision, and in their intended effects.

1. I have collected information (primarily from the Aircraft Responsibility Chart of HQ AMC MCGO; June 1949 and supplements) about the time intervals involved in Research and Development, in procurement, and readiness for operations. Table I presents, in number of months before and after decisions to procure large quantities for operational use, the times at which design was suggested, experimental prototype production was started, first production model was completed, and peak rate of output and operational availability. I believe that the numbers are accurate to three or four months.

Each reader will attach significance to different facts in this table. (1) Bombers seem to require a longer R & D period, meaning a longer time from design initiation to first experimental flight testing, than do fighters. (2) The period between procurement decision and operational use is only very little, if any, longer for bombers than for fighters. The interval was about four years (if we

TABLE I. Time intervals for bomber and fighter development and procurement, centered on date of initial service testing (in months)

| | Plane | | | | | | | | | |
|---|---|---|---|---|---|---|---|---|---|---|
| | B-47 | T-28 | B-52 | B-45 | F-89 | B-57 | F-84 | F-94 | F-86 | C-124 |
| 1. AF requests designs | 80 | 30 | 92 | 68 | 66 | x | 48 | 19 | 48 | 36 |
| 2. Spec. approved | 74 | 25 | 86 | 60 | 60 | x | x | 17 | 36 | 28 |
| 3. Mock-up inspection | 56 | 17 | 66 | 52 | 50 | x | x | 16 | x | 20 |
| 4. First X flight | 36 | 4 | 28 | 27 | 27 | x | x | 8 | 17 | 4 |
| 5. Quantity order | 27 | 21 | 30 | 30 | 25 | 24 | 25 | 17 | 26 | 24 |
| 6. Service test | 0 | 0 | 0 | 0 | 0 | 0 | 0 | 0 | 0 | 0 |
| 7. Peak output rate | 10 | x | x | 12 | 12 | 6 | 6 | 5 | 3 | 2 |
| 8. 1st operational group | 12 | x | x | x | x | x | x | x | x | x |
| 9. 2nd operational group | 18 | x | x | x | x | x | x | x | x | x |

Source: Responsibility Charts & Supplements, issued by HQ, AMC, MCGO.

x = not available in reference document

allow one year to accumulate substantial numbers in the force). (3) The decision to procure was made much later than the decision to initiate research, design, and development. It was made at about the same time the experimental model was tested; in fact, more often it came prior to first flight. (4) It is apparent that decisions to procure did not have to wait for a complete verification of the aircraft producer's performance capability promises. (5) For emphasis, I repeat that the interval between design initiation (and also between procurement decisions) and operational availability date has been very long.

2. The separability in time of these two decisions, the research and the procurement decisions, is very fortunate, for even though the general type of information required for each is similar, the accuracy of available predictions may be different. For the Research and Development decision, part of the required information pertains to the feasibility of designing a producible weapon which will have specified performance characteristics. But this is not enough; a second kind of essential information is the type of performance that is wanted. The kind of performance that is wanted depends upon the kind of war to be fought and the enemies' capabilities. If both these kinds of information—that is, (1) the future state of the enemies' capabilities and intentions and (2) the design and production feasibility of new weapons—were known with certainty, we could concentrate our Research and Development effort on the optimal weapon. But, since we suffer from predictive myopia in both eyes,

either we can guess and then design what we hope will be the optimal, or a good, weapon—or we can truthfully admit we don't know and obtain insurance by designing several alternative weapons, one for each possible contingency. The Research and Development effort is intended to create designs of new weapons which will form our confirmed and broad set of weapons available for procurement. It must be recognized that R & D is directed toward providing a set of available choices rather than toward providing the one weapon that *ex post* best collates with the realized state of the world ten years hence. To assume that our foresight is adequate for this purpose is the error of not knowing how blind we really are. R & D not only advances us technically—it is also our only assurance of flexibility and wide range of choice in the future. An intelligent R & D program must satisfy *both* objectives.

3. The major, if not decisive, element in the procurement decision is, on the other hand, uncertainty about the enemy capability and intentions and the type of war that may have to be fought in the period contemplated. The shorter the period between procurement and operational use, the less will be this uncertainty. The procurement decisions need more information about costs, enemy capabilities and intentions, and the types of war that are possible. With these necessarily narrower or pinpointed conjectures, the procurement office selects from the menu of available weapons the optimal weapon if it has already been made available through Research and Development. Research and Development decisions are those of the Chef, who concocts new dishes and plans a menu of available alternative dishes from which the Gourmet, at a later time, has the privilege of choosing in light of his tastes, companions, and income. A good Chef provides a broad menu—thereby assuring the Gourmet the opportunity to make the best selection. The difference between the tasks of the Chef and the Gourmet must be kept strictly distinct. To confound the two is as disastrous in the military as in the restaurant business.

Equally disastrous is the failure to see the vital interdependence between them. Thus, the R & D activities—which we have, under ideal foresight, confined to only a single weapon—are, in fact, made with a range of possibilities to characterize the future. We, therefore, must recommend the development of a menu of several alternative weapons, guaranteeing that ignorant or malevolent critics will be able to show that a large majority of them were "useless" and "wasted" millions of dollars but assuring ourselves flexibility in order to have safety and economy with optimal weapons systems in actual use. The essential conditions for this procedure are, first, that the cost of this flexibility be small relative to the cost of procuring and maintaining the operational weapon system; second, that the cost, minute though it is, enable us to save enormously larger amounts by choosing optimal systems rather than being forced to use the only system available; and third, that we be only partly, not completely, blind in our foresight so that we can select sensible R & D allocations.

## v. Implications

Now all of this, while perfectly correct, may appear to be very trite and obvious. With this I am inclined to quarrel.

First, it appears that in some studies with which RAND has been associated, there has not been a sufficient distinction made between the two decisions, or, at least, not in their timing. For example, a recent study conducted by RAND recommended bombing systems for 1956–60. In this study the period 1960 was regarded as still "in the blue." But for the type of weapons studied, it was exactly this "blue" period that was relevant. We simply couldn't have the recommended weapons until then. For the 1956 time period, one should have been concerned with procurement contracts, not Research and Development contracts. Design development of bombers should pay no attention to the 1950's. It's already too late.[1] It is also easy to find several other examples in which the question posed related to a Research and Development decision, but in which the time period was relevant only if a procurement decision was pertinent.

Second, it is perfectly correct, but totally irrelevant, that anyone with a modicum of imagination can suggest what ought to be invented. The question to be answered is not what ought to be invented, but instead what ought we try to invent. Given our limited knowledge and resources and conjectures about the future possible states of affairs, a great deal of "analysis" and "judgment" is needed in discerning what directions of inventive effort have the highest need and promise of fruition.

Third, the time of Research and Development projects must be specified. It has been alleged that in some of the projects the target date has not been set, or has been set so far away that a lackadaisical spirit pervades them. Unfortunate though a lackadaisical spirit may be, it is not nearly so mischievous as the direct consequence of inadequate time-scheduling for the completion of complementary projects. Errors will result in bottlenecks or wasted efforts which

1. What is the analogous date for sighting systems, fighters, and other components?

might have produced useful results in other projects. The moral is that our studies must seek to determine not only what is worth doing, but also the time value of achieved accomplishments.

Fourth, the amount of money devoted to Research and Development is so small (about 5%) compared with procurement, operating, and training costs that it might appear that commensurably less effort or attention is required for wise Research and Development recommendations. However, the real test is the total magnitude of expenditures ultimately affected or eliminated by Research and Development decisions—not merely the amount spent on Research and Development itself. From what I have seen and read of the justification and allocation of Research and Development funds, it is impossible to escape the impression that the role of Research and Development is grossly underestimated and misunderstood. The only alternative interpretation open is that the allegations of a shortage of trained personnel, equipment, and facilities are true; but this I believe is a misunderstanding of the facts and one which will do naught but ensure a continuation of inadequate Research and Development efforts. But to explore here this particular problem would lead us astray.

I would only argue that I fear we shall all soon cease to be economizing Gourmets with à la carte menus and become expensive, undernourished table d'hôte Gourmands.

By its nature the phasing problem cannot confine its attention to merely the currently available weapons; it must ask which weapon *and when*. That is, it must decide when to initiate procurement contracts. It can do this only by ascertaining what weapons it can order next year and the year after. To look at the phasing problem as merely a question of whether we should start replacement now with what new weapon is sensible and difficult. But for it to be done at RAND in so narrow a context would be to throw away all justification for doing it here rather than elsewhere.

In brief, the actions affected by this study would be actions about (1) R & D and (2) procurement. There will not result a specific *series* of particular steps which *must* be taken each year. The only firm decision now is the one applying to steps taken in the first year. Actions of succeeding years, while conditioned by the chosen moves in this year, are to be selected from the choices available in later years, in the following way. As a result of present decisions, there will be a realized situation a year hence, the exact nature of which cannot be foreseen now, but which, nevertheless, can be characterized as one of a foreseen set of eventualities. To evaluate a present action, we try to foresee the range of possible future eventualities a year hence, and the then available moves with the subsequent set of potential consequences that follows from each of the possible moves that may at that time be taken. And *ad inf.* In a nutshell, we seek a strategy for selecting actions as the need arises; we do not seek a particular series of actions to be committed to now.

# 2

COST

# COSTS AND OUTPUTS[1]

Obscurities, ambiguities, and errors exist in cost and supply analysis despite, or because of, the immense literature on the subject. Especially obscure are the relationships between cost and output, both in the long run and in the short run. Propositions designed to eliminate some of these ambiguities and errors are presented in this paper. More important, these suggested propositions seem to be empirically valid.

## Costs

Costs will be defined initially as the change in equity caused by the performance of some specified operation, where, for simplicity of exposition, the attendant change in income is not included in the computation of the change in equity. Suppose that according to one's balance sheet the present value of his assets is $100, and suppose that at the end of the operation one year later the value of his assets is expected to be $80, not counting the sale value of the product of the operation. The present value of $80 a year hence (at 6 percent) is $75.47, which yields a cost in present capital value (equity) of $24.53. Because of logical difficulties in converting this present value concept into a satisfactory rate (per unit of time) concept, we defer a discussion of this problem and, for convenience, measure costs in units of present value or equity. Hereafter, the unmodified expression "costs" will always mean the present worth, capital value concept of cost, i.e., the change in equity.

Reprinted from Armen A. Alchian, *Economic Forces at Work* (Indianapolis: Liberty Fund, 1977), 273–99. This article was previously published in M. Abramovitz et al., *The Allocation of Economic Resources: Essays in Honor of Bernard Francis Haley* (Stanford: Stanford University Press, 1959), 23–40.

1. Indebtedness to William Meckling of the RAND Corporation, who gave many long hours to discussion of the points raised herein, even before the first of several drafts, is very great. Although my egoism prevents sharing the authorship with him, I cannot absolve him from responsibility for any errors that still remain and likewise for any merit the paper may have.

## Output

All the characteristics of a production operation can affect its cost. In this paper we want to direct attention to three characteristics:

1. The rate of output is typically regarded in economic analysis as the crucial feature. But it is only one feature, and concentration on it alone has led to serious error, as we shall see.

2. Total contemplated volume of output is another characteristic. Is accumulated output volume of 10,000 or 100 or 1,000,000 units being contemplated? Whatever may be the rate of output, the total volume to be produced is a distinct feature with important effects on cost. Of course, for any rate of output, the larger the total accumulated volume to be produced, the longer the operation will continue. Hence, incorporated in this description of total output is the total time length of the programmed production. Will it span one month or one year, or (at the other extreme) is the contemplated total volume so large that at the rate of output an indefinitely long time is allowed to the production run?

3. The programmed time schedule of availability of output is a further characteristic. For a point output, the programmed date of the output availability is sufficient, but for outputs which continue over time, the time profile (delivery schedule) of the output replaces a single date. We shall call these three distinct aspects the output *rate*, the contemplated *total volume*, and the programmed delivery *dates*.

These three characteristics can be summarized in the following definition, which also defines a fourth characteristic, m, the total length of the programmed schedule of outputs:

$$V = \sum_{T}^{T+m} x(t)dt.$$

In this expression, V is the total contemplated volume of output, $x(t)$ the output rate at moment t, T the moment at which the first unit of output is to be completed, and m the length of the interval over which the output is made available. Of these four features, only three are independently assignable; the fourth is then constrained. Unless specific exception is made, in the following we shall always discuss changes in only one of the features V, $x(t)$, and T, assuming the other two to be constant and letting the full compensatory adjustment be made in m.[2]

---

2. We note that time or dating enters in a multitude of ways: there is the date at which the delivery of output is to begin; there is the period of time used as a basis for the mea-

## Propositions about Costs and Output

Our task is now to make some propositions about the way costs are affected by changes in these variables. Letting $C$ denote costs (i.e., the change in equity), we have

$$C = F(V, x, T, m)$$

subject to the definition of $V$, which constrains us to three degrees of freedom among the four variables.

Proposition 1

$$\frac{\partial C}{\partial x(t)} \bigg|_{\substack{T = T_o \\ V = V_o}} > 0$$

The left-hand expression is the derivative of the costs with respect to $x$, when $T$ and $V$ are held constant, letting $m$ make up the adjustment. It shows the change in costs when the rate of output is increased without increasing $V$ and without changing the delivery date, but with an appropriate reduction of $m$. Proposition 1 states that the faster the rate at which a given volume of output is produced, the higher its cost. We emphasize that cost means the change in equity, not the *rate* of costs.

Proposition 2

$$\frac{\partial^2 C}{\partial x^2} \bigg|_{\substack{V = V_o \\ T = T_o}} > 0$$

The increment in $C$ is an increasing function of the output rate. This is a proposition about increasing marginal cost in present value measure and is usually derived as an implication of efficient allocation of scarce heterogeneous resources among alternative uses.

---

sure of the rate of output, i.e., so many units per day, per week, or per year; and there is the total time over which the output is to be made available.

Its validity, however, does not depend upon the validity of the premises of the classical model. For example, inventories need not increase in proportion to the rate of output if the variance of random deviations in output rates does not increase more than proportionally to the expected output rate. In this event, a sufficient condition for Proposition 2 as derived by the classical model would be upset. But destruction of sufficient conditions does not eliminate the possibility of all necessary conditions being fulfilled; thus, even if the classical model's assumptions are upset, the proposition could still be true. Whether or not it is, in fact, true cannot be settled by an examination of the model from which it is derived. For present purposes, Proposition 2 can be regarded, if one wishes, as a postulated proposition.[3]

Proposition 3

$$\frac{\partial C}{\partial V}\bigg]_{\substack{x = x_0 \\ T = T_0}} > 0$$

C increases with V for given x and date of initial output, T. At a constant output rate, for example, this will require a longer program of production, a larger m.

Proposition 4

$$\frac{\partial^2 C}{\partial V^2}\bigg]_{\substack{x = x_0 \\ T = T_0}} < 0$$

Increments in C diminish as V increases, for any rate of output, x, and initial output date, T. Thus, for any constant rate of output, as the total planned output is increased by uniform increments, costs (changes in equity) will increase by diminishing increments. The "reasons" for this proposition will be given later.

3. See T. M. Whitin and M. H. Peston, "Random Variations, Risk and Returns to Scale," *Quarterly Journal of Economics* 68 (November 1954): 603–14, for a longer discussion of some forces that could reverse the inequality of Proposition 2. Some of their suggested forces, e.g., relation between stocks of repairmen and number of machines, are circumvented by the ability to buy services instead of the agents themselves. Another weakness is the association of size of output with the number of independent random forces.

Proposition 4 also implies decreasing cost *per unit* of total volume, V. We shall state this as a separate proposition.

Proposition 5

$$\frac{\partial C/V}{\partial V}\bigg]_{\substack{x = x_o \\ T = T_o}} < 0$$

## Graphic and Numerical Illustrations of Propositions 1–5

### 1. Graphic Illustration

The above properties are shown by the cost surface in Figure 1. Proposition 1 describes the slope of a slice on the cost surface where the slice is parallel to the *Cx* plane. Proposition 2 states that the slope of the path of such a slice on the cost surface increases with *x*. Proposition 3 is portrayed by the slope of a slice along the surface parallel to the *CV* plane—going back into the page. The slope of this slice decreases as V increases. Proposition 4 describes the decreasing

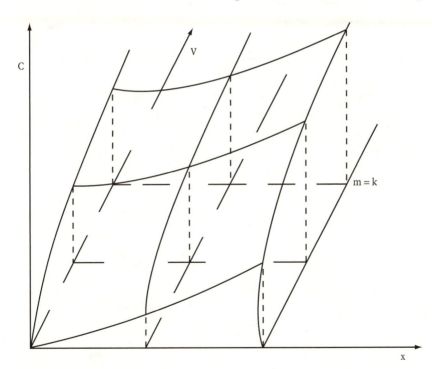

**FIGURE 1.** *Cost Surface as Function of* x *and* V

rate at which this surface of costs increases along this slice. Movements in other directions can be visualized. For example, one possible path is to start from the origin and move out some ray. This gives costs as a function of proportional increase in both the rate and the total output for a fixed interval of production, m, but the behavior of the cost slope of this slice, except for the fact that it is positive, cannot be derived from these propositions.

### 2. Tabular, Arithmetic Illustration

For an output rate, x, of one per year, beginning at some specified T, production must continue for one year to get a total volume, V, of one, for two years to get two, for three years for three, etc. For a production rate of two per year, production must last one year to get two units, two years to get a total of four, etc. The present value of costs for an output rate, x(t), of two a year for a total V of four in two years is $330 (which, at 6 percent, is equal to a two-year annuity of $180 a year).

Proposition 1 is illustrated by the increase in the numbers (costs) in cells down a given column. Proposition 2 is illustrated by the increases in the differences between these cell entries. These differences increase as the rate of output increases, for a given total output. This represents increasing marginal costs (remember that cost is a present-value capital concept) for increments in the rate of output. Proposition 3 is illustrated by the behavior of costs along a row (given output rate) as total volume of planned output changes. Proposition 4 states that the increment in C is a diminishing increment as one moves across a row, i.e., as total volume of output is larger. For example, in the first row, the output rate is one a year. The first cell is therefore an output operation lasting one year, because only one is produced, at the rate of one a year. The total cost

TABLE 1. *Costs, volume of output, and rates of output*

| Rate of Output, x (per year) | Volume of Output | | | |
| --- | --- | --- | --- | --- |
| | 1 | 2 | 3 | 4 |
| 1 | 100 | 180 | 255 | 325 |
| 2 | 120 | 195 | 265 | 330 |
| 3 | 145 | 215 | 280 | 340 |
| 4 | 175 | 240 | 300 | 355 |

is $100. For a total contemplated output of two units, at a rate of one per year, the operation will take two years, and the cost is $180. The marginal cost of one more unit of total volume of output—not of one unit higher *rate* of output—is $80. For a total output of three units in three years the cost is $255, an increment of $75, which is less than the previous increment of $80. Here the increments in cost are associated not with increments in rates of output, but with increments in total volume of output. *Proposition 5* is illustrated by dividing the cell entries in a row by the output quantities at the head of each column. The quotient, cost per unit of output quantity, decreases as V increases.

### 3. Economic Illustration

A comparison that could be made is the following: imagine a person to contemplate a total volume of output of one unit at the rate of one a year. But he subsequently revises his plans and produces one more in the next year at the rate of one a year, again planning to produce a total volume of just one unit. Compare the total costs of that operation with an operation in which two units of total output were initially planned at the rate of one a year. Both take two years, but the cost of the latter is $180, while the former's present value is $100 plus $100 discounted back one year at 6 percent, or a total of $194. Thus it is cheaper to produce from a *plan* for a two-year output of two units at the rate of one a year than to produce two by repetition of methods which contemplate only one total unit of output at the same rate of one a year.

From this example it would appear that a reason for Proposition 4 is that better foresight enables one to see farther into the future and make more accurate forecasts; but this is not the reason, however helpful better foresight may be. A larger planned V is produced in a different way from that of a smaller planned V. A classic example is the printing press. To get 300 copies of a letter in one day may be cheaper with mimeograph than with either typewriter or offset printing. The mimeograph method may be so much superior that, even if the rate of output were stepped up to 300 in an hour (instead of in a day), mimeographing might still be cheaper than typing. This does not deny that higher rates of output imply higher costs, as for example, that 300 in an hour will cost more than 300 in two hours. The method of production is a function of the volume of output, especially when output is produced from basic dies— and there are few, if any, methods of production that do not involve "dies." Why increased expenditures on more durable dies should result in more than proportional increase of output potential is a question that cannot be answered, except to say that the physical principles of the world are not all linear (which may or may not be the same thing as "indivisible").[4] Different methods of tooling, parts design, and assembly are the usual explanation given in the production engineering literature.

Proposition 4 seems not to be part of current economic principles. Yet it may be the key to seeing the error in some attempts to refute Proposition 2, which applies to increased *rates* of output for constant total volume of output (or, as we shall see later, for perpetuity durations of output). Propositions 2 and 4 refer to two counterforces, rate of output and total planned volume of output. What would be the net effect of increases in both cannot be deduced from the present propositions. All that can be said is that if the rate of output is increased for a given total contemplated volume of output, the increment in cost will be an increasing function of the rate of output. Proposition 4, on the other hand, implies diminishing increments as V increases, and it implies a lower per-unit cost for a larger total volume of output. Thus, we have the possibility that higher rates of production might be available at lower unit costs if they are associated with a larger volume of output, because this latter factor may be sufficient to overcome the effects of the higher output rate.

A larger volume of output could, of course, be obtained by both longer time and faster rates of production, but the relationship between time and volume should not be allowed to mask the fact that it is total contemplated volume of output—not the longer duration of output—that is here asserted (maybe erroneously) to be the factor at work in Propositions 3 and 4.

If both the *volume* and the *rate* of output change in the same direction, the two effects on costs are not in the same direction, and neither the net effect on the rate of change of *increments* in the cost nor even the effect on the costs per unit of total volume of output is implied by these or any other accepted postulates. It has been said, for example, that if some automobile manufacturer were to cut V, the volume of cars produced of a given year's model, from 1,000,000 to 500,000, costs per car would increase. This statement could refer either to a reduction in V achieved by producing for half the number of months at an unchanged monthly rate of output or to a simultaneous and parallel reduction in both V, the volume, and x, the monthly rate of output. If it refers to the former, it is a restatement of Proposition 5; if it refers to the latter, it is a statement that

---

4. Could it be that the term "indivisibility" has been meant to cover this phenomenon? A yes or no answer to that question is impossible because of the extreme vagueness and ambiguity with which the term has been used. Furthermore, the question is probably of little, if any, significance.

cannot be deduced from our propositions, which imply merely that costs would be lower if both $V$ and $x$ were reduced than if $V$ alone were lowered.

Even returns to scale seem to have been confused with the effect of size of output. It is conjectured that a substantial portion of the alleged cases of increasing returns to scale in industries or firms is the result of ignoring the relation of costs to volume (rather than to rate) of output. The earlier discussions of automobile production and printing costs are simple illustrations of how this confusion can occur.

How many of the cases of alleged decreasing costs to *rates* of output are really decreasing costs to *volume* of output is an open question. Is it too much to expect that all of them can be so explained? Or that the realm of such cases can be greatly reduced by allowing for $V$, instead of letting $x$ be the only variable? But that dirty empirical task is left for later and more ambitious efforts.

The observed concentration on a standardized model, e.g., four or five different sizes of tractors as distinct from a much greater possible range, is explained by the effect of volume of output on cost. Although an infinite range is possible, the concentration on a smaller set of fewer alternatives is more economical for most problems. The only way economic theory heretofore could explain this apparent anomaly was to invoke a falling cost curve for small output rates, in turn dependent upon some kind of unidentified indivisibility or returns to scale. Now the explanation may be contained in Propositions 4 and 9.

## More Propositions

Four more propositions remain. Proposition 6 is given in a footnote because its implications will not be suggested in this paper.[5] Propositions 7 and 8 con-

---

5. Proposition 6

$$\left. \frac{\partial^2 C}{\partial x \partial V} \right|_{T = T_0} < 0$$

This says that the marginal present value-cost with respect to increased rates of output decreases as the total contemplated output increases. This can be regarded as a conjectural proposition, whose implications will not be developed in this paper. And the same proposition can be re-expressed as

$$\left. \frac{\partial^2 C}{\partial V \partial x} \right|_{T = T_0} < 0$$

This states that marginal present-value costs of increased quantity of output decrease as the rate of output increases.

Of interest is the relationship between these postulates and the implied shape of the

cern the effects of changes in T, the time between the decision to produce and the delivery of output.

Proposition 7

$$\frac{\partial C}{\partial T}\bigg]_{\substack{x = x_o \\ V = V_o}} < 0$$

This is not shown in the graph or in the table, but it says that the longer the time between decision to produce and delivery of output, the less the cost.

If we think of a single output point, then T is relatively unambiguous. If the output is to be made available over a period of time, then T could be defined as the beginning moment of output. But many different output programs are possible, even when they all extend over the same interval. One might be tempted to use some sort of average T, say, the date of output weighted by the rate of output. However, such an average T cannot be used for our purposes, because any particular value of T can be identified with an infinite variety of output patterns. Since we are talking about partial derivatives, the whole problem is easily avoided. All we need do is to state that, if one moves any output program or schedule closer to the present (or farther into the future) by a simple time shift, T will have decreased (or increased). Whatever the shape of the output sched-

---

production possibility function, where the rate and the volume of output are the two output alternatives. The cost isoquant with $x$ and $V$ as the arguments can be convex or concave. Usually a concave function is implied when rates of output of two different products are the arguments. However, J. Hirshleifer ("Quality vs. Quantity: Cost Isoquant and Equilibrium," *Quarterly Journal of Economics* 64 [November 1955]: 596–606) has pointed out that convex production possibilities are implicit in many engineering cost functions when quality and quantity are the alternative outputs. Hirshleifer, as it seems from his context, is really discussing cases where his quantity variable refers to volume and not to rate of output. Had he really meant rate of output rather than volume, his results might not have been so "reasonable." The convexity or concavity of the cost isoquant, it may be recalled, is given by the sign of

$$\frac{d^2x}{dV^2} = \frac{F_{xx}F_y{}^2 - 2F_{xv}F_xF_v + F_{vv}F_x{}^2}{F_v{}^3}$$

Substituting our postulated conditions shows that the expression may be of any sign, hence the indeterminacy of the concavity or convexity property. However, concavity of the cost isoquant where the two arguments are rates of production for two different products is still implied.

ule, a reduction of the interval between the present moment and the beginning of the output date (a sort of uniform timewise shifting) will increase cost. A more deferred output schedule (whatever its unchanged shape) will mean a lower cost.

Proposition 7 is really a corollary of Proposition 2. The slower the rate at which inputs are purchased, the lower their price because the lower are the costs to the seller, when Proposition 2 is applied to the seller.

Not only do the supply curves of inputs fall (or shift to the right) as more time is allowed, but the rates of shifting differ among inputs. The supply curves of some inputs are more elastic than those of others; and the rate at which the price elasticity of supply increases with T differs among inputs. Thus, while in an immediate period the price elasticity of supply of input $x$ may be low relative to that of input $y$ (and it may always be lower than that of $y$), the *ratio* of the costs of increments in $y$ to the costs of increments in $x$ may change with deferred purchase. If the ratio decreases, deferred purchases of $y$ relative to purchases of $x$ will be economical. In other words, it is not merely the slope of the supply curve or the price elasticity of supply that determines which inputs are going to be increased earliest. Rather, it is the rate at which these price elasticities *change* with deferred purchase that is critical. Thus, as stated earlier, the input $x$ with a very low price elasticity of supply will vary more in the immediate period than the input of $y$ with a higher price elasticity if the deferment of purchases by, say, a month would lower the cost of $y$ more than that of $x$. As an extreme, if the supply curves of two inputs, $x$ and $y$, were both horizontal, the input of one of them would be increased less if with deferred purchase the price or supply curve would become lower—though still horizontal. That input whose price would become lower with a deferred purchase would be increased in quantity later, with the relatively heavy present increase concentrated on that input whose deferred purchase price would not be as much lower.

Proposition 8

All the derivatives in Propositions 1–5 are diminishing functions of T, but not all diminish at the same rate. This proposition asserts a difference in the extent to which inputs will be varied in the immediate, the short, and the longer period.

*Short and long run.* Statements to the effect that certain inputs are fixed in the short run are frequent and characteristic. In fact, there is no such fixed factor in any interval other than the immediate moment *when all are fixed.* Such statements may represent a confusion between revealed choice and technological constraints. There are no technological or legal restraints preventing one from varying any of his inputs. Even in Viner's classic statement of the short- and long-run cost curves, the short run is defined in terms of some *fixed* inputs and other inputs which can be varied as desired.[6] He stated that the long run is the situation in which all the inputs are "freely" variable. One need only ask, "What do the desires to adjust depend upon in the short run?" and, "What does 'freely' variable mean?" The first is answered by "costs" and potential receipts of the variations, and the second by noting that "freely" does not mean that costs of changes are zero. The fact is that the costs of varying the inputs differ among inputs, and the ratios of these costs vary with the time interval within which the variation is to be made. At any *calendar* moment, T, the producer will choose which input to vary according to *economic costs* and not because of technical or legal fixities that prevent the changing of some inputs.[7]

Debate over definitions or postulates is pertinent only in the light of their purpose. The purpose of the short- and long-run distinction is, presumably, to explain the path of prices or output (x or V?) over time in response to some change in demand or supply. The postulate of fixed inputs, and others more variable with the passing of time, does imply a pattern of responses that seems to be verified by observable evidence. On that count, the falsity of the postulate is immaterial. But if there are other implications of such a postulate that are invalidated by observable evidence, the postulate becomes costly. The question arises, therefore, whether it is more convenient and useful to replace the fixity postulate by a more general one that yields all the valid implications that the former one did and more besides, while at the same time avoiding the empirically false implications. It appears that the proposed alternative is cheaper in terms of logical convenience, more general, and more valid in its implications. But that is a judgment which is perhaps best left to the reader.

The differences between a short-run (near T) and a long-run (distant T) operation imply differences in costs, and these costs are pertinent to an explanation of the path of prices or costs over time in response to a lasting change in demand or factor availabilities. For example, for a lasting increase in de-

6. J. Viner, "Cost Curves and Supply Curves," *Zeitschrift für Nationalökonomie* 3, no. 1 (1931): 23–46.

7. The nearest, but still different, presentation of the immediate, short run, and long run found by the author is that contained in Friedman's unpublished lecture notes. Other statements may exist; an exhausting search of the literature failed to clarify exactly what is meant by the long run and short run.

mand, the output made available at more distant dates is producible at a lower cost; this means that the supply at a given cost will be larger and the price lower in the more distant future as the longer-run operations begin to yield their output. These outputs, having been planned for a later T date, are lower in cost. Output will be larger for a given price, thus reducing price in the market. This longer-run lower cost is the phenomenon whose explanation has usually been sought by resort to fixity of some particular inputs in the short run. The above argument suggests that this phenomenon can be explained without the fixity assumption that in turn leads to other, empirically wrong, implications.

The implication of our proposition is worth emphasizing here. It is that we define a "short run" and a "long run" not as differing in the fixity of some inputs; instead, we use T as the length of the run, and then from Proposition 8 derive the implications that were sought by the fixity assumption.

Most important, however, Proposition 8 makes it clear that there is not both a "long-run" and a "short-run" cost for any given output program. For any given output program there is only *one* pertinent cost, *not* two. Unambiguous specification of the output or action to be costed makes the cost definition unambiguous and destroys the illusion that there are two costs to consider, a short- and a long-run cost for any given output. There is only one, and that is the *cheapest* cost of doing whatever the operation is specified to be. To produce a house in three months is one thing, to produce it in a year is something else. By uniquely identifying the operation to be charged, there results one cost, not a range of costs from immediate to short- to longer-run costs. There is a range of operations to be considered, but to each there is only *one* cost. The question is not, What are the long-run or short-run costs of some operation? but, instead, How do total, average, and marginal costs vary as the T of the operation is changed? Answer: They decrease as T increases, according to Propositions 7 and 8.

The significance of this should be evident in the debate about marginal cost pricing policies for "optimal" output. Also the use of short-run and long-run costs as alternatives in public utility pricing appears to be a ripe area for clarification of concepts.

What the relationship is between the presently suggested effects of T, which we have just called a short- or long-run effect, and the common short run or long run in the standard literature is not entirely clear. Rather vague and imprecise implications about short and long run are available. Hence, rather than assert that the T effect is here being proposed as a substitute for the standard short-run analysis, the reader is left free to supply his own interpretation of the conventional "run" and to supplement or replace it, however he chooses, with the present proposition.

Proposition 9

The preceding propositions refer to costs of outputs for a given distribution of knowledge, F, at the present moment, to situations where technology is held constant.[8]

Proposition 9 is "As the total quantity of units produced increases, the cost of *future* output declines." The cost per unit may be either the average cost of a given number of incremental units of output or the cost of a specific unit. This is not identical with the earlier Proposition 4 referring to the effects of the larger planned V. There the effect was a result of varying *techniques* of production, not of changes in technology. Here we are asserting that knowledge increases as a result of production—that the cost function is lowered. It is not simply a matter of a larger V, but rather a lower cost for any subsequent V, consequent to improved knowledge. This distinction should not be attributed necessarily to all the explanations of the learning curve. Some describers of the learning curve bring in the effect of different techniques consequent to different-sized V. Others also mention that, as output is produced and experience acquired, improved knowledge is acquired. Thus, even if one continually planned to produce small batches of output, so that the V was constant but repeated, the costs would nevertheless be falling. In the present presentation, we have chosen to separate these two effects in logic and principle, attributing the first effect, that of technique, to changes in planned V but with a given state of knowledge (as in Proposition 4), while the second effect, that of increased knowledge consequent to accumulated production experience, is isolated in Proposition 9. A review of industrial and production management literature will show that both effects are adduced and incorporated in the learning curve discussion, contrary to our decision to separate them. This proposition about the rate of change in technology is accepted in industrial engineering. Usually the proposition is known as the "learning curve" or "progress curve."[9]

---

8. Technology, the state of distribution of knowledge, is different from techniques of production, which can be changed at any time, even with a constant technology.

9. Sometimes the curve is called an 80 percent progress curve, because it is sometimes asserted that the cost of the 2nth item is 80 percent of the cost of the nth item. Thus the fortieth plane would involve only 80 percent of the direct man hours and materials that the twentieth plane did.

Several factors have been advanced as a rationale for this proposition: job familiarization, general improvement in coordination, shop organization and engineering liaison, more efficient subassembly production, and more efficient tools. An extensive literature on this proposition has been developed, but it seems to have escaped integration with the rest of cost theory in economics.[10]

Nevertheless, the proposition is a well-validated proposition and is widely used in industrial engineering. The significant implication of this proposition is that, in addition to rate of output, an important variable in determining total costs is the total planned output, for two reasons: first, because of changes in technique via Proposition 4, and, second, because the larger is the planned and ultimately realized output, the greater is the accumulated experience (technology) and knowledge at any point in the future via Proposition 9. Thus, the average cost per unit of output will be lower, the greater is the planned and ultimately experienced output. A more complete discussion of the evidence for this proposition would require a separate paper.

## On the Advantages of the Capital Value Measure

Use of capital values enables one to avoid misleading statements like "We are going to operate at a loss in the near future, but operations will be profitable later," "In the short run the firm may operate at a loss so long as receipts exceed variable costs," "A firm operates with long-run rather than short-run objectives." All of these statements are incorrect if liabilities or assets (other than money) are owned by the enterprise. What seems to be meant when a person talks about expecting to have losses for a while before getting profits is that cash flows will be negative for a while, but it is difficult to see how this is in any relevant sense a situation of losses. And, similarly, when a person talks about expecting losses, it appears that he means he expects future events to occur which are unfavorable; and in this case the changed belief about the future is immediately reflected in current values if not in current money flows—as many a stockholder has learned. Any periods during which expectation about future events becomes more favorable are periods of increasing equity (i.e., of profits), even though the period in which the more favorable events will occur is in the future. When a

10. See W. Hirsch, "Manufacturing Progress Functions," *Review of Economics and Statistics* 34 (May 1952): 143–55. A less accessible, but more complete, reference to the published material is given in H. Asher, *Cost-Quantity Relationships in the Airframe Industry* (RAND Corporation, Santa Monica, Calif.), July 1956. But see P. A. Samuelson, *Economics* (New York: McGraw-Hill, 1948), p. 473, where it is mentioned but left unincorporated.

firm reports that it operated during the past quarter at a loss, it means simply that the net present value of assets decreased during that period, even though the future cash receipts and outlays have not yet been realized. The profits are in the present moment—the increase in equity—as some stockholders have joyously learned. The presently anticipated increase in *future* receipts relative to future outlays means an increase in *present* equity values, profits.

Statements to the effect that a firm would willingly and knowingly operate at a loss in the short run are consistent only with an identification of costs with money flows, and are certainly inconsistent with the postulates of seeking increased wealth (or utility) as a goal or survival attribute. Such identification of costs with money flows eliminates capital theory from the theory of the firm and from much of price theory. There is no cause to pay this price, since it is just as easy not to abandon capital theory, and if one retains it, more useful implications will be derived.

Yet, in economic texts, costs are almost always measured as *time-rates*, and only rarely as capital values. At first blush this would seem to be an irrelevant or trivial distinction, since capital values are merely the present values of *receipt* or *outlay* streams. But what about going from capital values to time rates of *cost* streams? New problems arise in this effort. Suppose that the outlay stream for some operation is used as the basis for cost calculations. If, and only if, *no* other assets or liabilities are involved can money flows be identified with costs; otherwise they represent, in part, accumulations of assets or liabilities. As soon as assets and liabilities are admitted, money flows are not synonymous with costs, and changes in values of assets or liabilities must now be included. With the break between money outlays and costs, the measure of costs becomes the change in present value of net equity consequent to some action (ignoring receipts, for present purposes).

If a firm signed a contract and committed itself to produce some quantity of output, then the cost it has incurred in signing the contract and obligating itself to produce the output is its decrease in equity, say $E_a - E_b$. At moment $a$, prior to the contract, the equity or net wealth of the firm is $E_a$. At this moment the firm considers entering into some production plan. If it does so, what will happen to its equity at the end of the plan, or how will the equity change over that interval? If, for the moment, we ignore the receipts or income from that plan, the decrease of equity by moment $b$ would be the measure of cost of the output operation which it is obligated to perform. The difference, $E_a - E_b$, between the equity ($E_a$) at the beginning and the *present* value ($E_b$) of the equity ($E_t$) at the end of the operation, is the total cost, $C$, of the operation.

The time rate of costs (of change in equity) is given by $dE/dt$, the slope of the line from $E_a$ to $E_t$, which is quite different from $C$. The former, $dE/dt$, is a derivative, a time rate of change. The latter, $C$, is the integral of the former. It is a finite difference, $E_a - E_t$, obtained from two different points on the E curve, while the former is the slope of the E curve and can be obtained only after an E curve is obtained. What is the meaning of the E curve in such a case? Presumably it means that, if the firm decided at any moment to stop further output, under this contract it would find itself with an equity indicated by the height of the line $E_aE_t$. Ignoring the contractual liability for obligation to produce according to the contract, the equity declines along the E line; but if one does regard the contract performance liability, the equity does not change as output is produced, because there is an exactly offsetting reduction in contractual liability as output is produced. The equity of the firm stays constant over the interval if the outlays and asset values initially forecast were forecast correctly.

If the rate of cost, $dE/dt$, or if the E curve is plotted not against time, but against the output rate, we do not get a curve similar in interpretation to the usual total cost curve in standard cost curve analysis. The rate of cost, $dE/dt$, can be converted to average cost per unit of rate of output by dividing the rate of cost, $dE/dt$, by the associated rate of output at that moment, and the marginal time rate of cost is obtained by asking how the slope of the equity curve $dE/dt$ is affected by changes in $x$, i.e., $(d^2E/dt\,dx)$.

The difference between this curve, where $dE/dt$ is plotted against $x$, and the usual time rate of cost curve analysis is that our current analysis is based on a larger set of variables, $x(t)$ and $V$, and, hence, $dE/dt$ cannot be drawn uniquely merely against the rate of output, $x(t)$. A new curve must be drawn for each output operation contemplated; even worse, there is no assurance that such a curve of $dE/dt$ drawn against the rate of output on the horizontal axis would have only one vertical height for each output rate. The curve might fold back on itself and be multivalued because one value of $dE/dt$ might be associated with a particular rate of output early in the operation and another different value later in the operation, even though at both moments the output rates were the same.

The number of cost curves that could be drawn is greater by at least an extra factor, $V$. In fact, we have at least two families of curves, one for different values of $V$ and one for different time profiles of $x(t)$, and it is not clear what is usually assumed about these in the standard cost curve analysis. One possibility is to assume that the length of the production run, $m$, or the contemplated total output, $V$, does not affect the rate at which equity changes for any given output rate.

The difficulty with this position is not merely that it is logically wrong but that it leads to implications that are refuted by everyday events.

A kind of average or marginal cost can be defined on the basis of the approach suggested earlier. For any given contemplated operation, the change in equity implied can be computed and evaluated in present worths. If this cost is divided by the total contemplated volume of output, $V$, the result is present value cost per unit of product (not time rate per unit *rate* of output). If the same total output were to be produced at a higher output rate, $x$, and thus within a shorter time interval, $m$, the total cost (change in equity) would be greater, and so the cost per unit of total volume of output would be higher. As noted in the first part of this paper, the increase in total present value cost, $\partial C/x$ (not $d^2E/dt\,dx$), is the marginal cost, consequent to an increased rate of output. By varying the contemplated rates of output $x$ for any given total output plan ($V$ and $T$), one can get different total capital costs. These changes in total capital costs can be called the marginal capital costs. But it is important to note again that there are as many such marginal capital value cost functions as there are different possible total output patterns that can be contemplated, and these marginal capital costs are not time rates of costs.

## Conclusion

Four features have been emphasized in the foregoing pages. First, the distinction between rate and quantity of output; second, changes in technology as distinct from changes in technique; third, the use of calendar time dates of output instead of technical fixity for distinguishing output operations; fourth, the use of capital value concepts instead of rates of costs.

The first and second features (and the ones that are emphasized in this paper) enable us to capture within our theory the lower costs attendant on larger quantities of output—not rates of output. Everyday experience where large rates of output are available at lower prices could be explained as a movement down the buyer's demand curve as the seller, in order to sell a larger amount, lowers price. But this seems to be incapable of explaining all such situations. Another explanation usually advanced is the economies of scale, where scale is related to *rate* of output. However, an alternative explanation suggested here is the lower cost resulting, not from higher *rates* of output per unit time, but from larger planned volume of total output quantities. An examination of the production management and engineering literature reveals much greater emphasis on batch or lot size as contrasted to the rate of output. Frequently the latter is not much of a variable in each particular firm's decision.

This means that the extent to which rate of output is varied may be slight—not that it can't be varied or that its significance is slight. That there has been confusion between the rate of output and the batch size or quantity planned is sure. How much cannot be known.

The third feature—that of identifying each output operation with a calendar date and then postulating that the more distant the date the smaller the change in equity (the smaller the cost)—provides a way to escape the unnecessary bind imposed by the definition of short-run costs as that which results from fixed inputs. The ambiguous idea of two different costs, a short-run and a long-run cost for a given output, disappears and is replaced by one cost for each different program of output.

What must have been assumed in our present literature about the factors mentioned here? Was the rate of output profile assumed to be a constant rate extending into perpetuity? The answer could not be ascertained from an exhausting reading of the literature nor from analogically implied conditions. Certainly the standard cost curve analysis does not envisage a perpetuity output at some given rate, nor does it seem to specify the effects of shorter-length runs at any output. For example, Stigler, in his well-known paper on the effects of planning for variations in the rate of output, imagines one to be moving along a given cost curve appropriate to the case in which output varies. This desirable attempt to modify the cost curve analysis would have been more successful if the output had been further specified or identified in terms of $V$ and $T$. Then the conventional curves would have disappeared, and many logical inconsistencies and ambiguities could have been removed from the standard analysis. But merely drawing the curve flatter and higher does not avoid the problems of appropriate interpretation of costs for unspecified values of the pertinent variables.

Finally, introduction of a new variable, $V$, complicates the equilibrium of demand and supply, for now there must be a similar element in demand which will determine the equilibrium size of $V$, if such there be. Suffice it to say here that even though consumers may not act or plan consciously in terms of $V$, their actions can be interpreted in terms of a resultant aggregative $V$. Producers, in contemplating the demand for their products, will be required to think of capital value or present value of income with the rate of output integrated into a $V$—possibly a break-even $V$—on the basis of which they may make production plans. A simple rate of output, price relationships, will not be sufficient. But this remains to be developed later, only if the present propositions prove valid and useful.

# COST

In economics, the cost of an event is the highest-valued opportunity necessarily forsaken. The usefulness of the concept of cost is a logical implication of choice among available options. Only if no alternatives were possible or if amounts of all resources were available beyond everyone's desires, so that all goods were free, would the concepts of cost and of choice be irrelevant. If choices are made on anything other than a random, purposeless basis, a criterion of choice is implied. Whatever the criterion, the chosen option will involve a loss of the highest-valued forsaken option. This implies that only if one chooses actions so as to maximize the value realized will cost be covered.

Failure to appreciate the purpose of the concept of cost can lead to confusing the concept of cost with the undesirable attributes of some event. For example, when one builds a swimming pool, the toil and trouble of digging it and the nuisance of noisy, disobedient neighborhood children and uninvited guests who use it are undesirable attributes of the pool. They are not the costs of creating and having a pool. This distinction between (a) undesirable attributes inherent in some event and (b) the highest-valued forsaken option necessary to realize that event is fundamental, for only the latter is cost as the term is used in economics.

We can illustrate. The construction and possession of the pool involve an amalgam of undesirable and desirable attributes. But if, in some sense, the desirable exceed the undesirable, it does not follow that one would choose to have the pool. One might choose something else instead, say having an extra car, and that too would involve desirable and undesirable attributes. The decision-maker must choose among events that are amalgams of "goods and bads." He cannot choose all events whose desirable features more than offset their undesirable ones, given the limited resources at his disposal. A comparison among all the *available* options (each consisting of an amalgam of good and

Reprinted from Armen A. Alchian, *Economic Forces at Work* (Indianapolis: Liberty Fund, 1977), 302–33. This article was previously published in *International Encyclopedia of Social Sciences*, 3:404–15 (New York: Macmillan, 1968), © 1968 Macmillan, and is reprinted by permission of The Gale Group.

bad) yields for each option a rank-indicating measure of value. The cost of one amalgam is the best of the forsaken amalgams. It is not necessary for each event that the good and bad attributes be separated and that there be assigned a measure of the undesirable attributes and also a measure of the desirable. Such a procedure would indicate only that many events are desirable on net, and a criterion of choice among these would still be needed.

We can illustrate with the person deciding whether or not to have a swimming pool. He determines that the "good" consequences of a pool are worth what we shall call "100 units," while the "bad" are equivalent to the loss of "70 units." The best alternative to having a pool is, let us say, to take action "A," with "good" attributes valued at 50 and "bads" valued at a loss of 10. The pool has a net value of 30, while event A is worth 40. The cost of the pool is 40 (not 70), while the cost of A is 30 (not 10). What is lost if the pool is selected is the 40 units of value otherwise available by opting for A.

Business usage encourages the temptation to think that because events are *valued* by comparing the good attributes with the bad, cost must be the bad attributes. Businessmen weigh revenues (as good consequences) against expenses or costs. Considering these costs as the bad attributes overlooks the distinction between *valuation* and *costing*. The *value* of a given event is obtained by weighing its good and bad consequences against each other—if one wants to think in terms of good and bad rather than less or more desirable—but the *cost* of that event is still not revealed. The highest-valued forsaken option must still be ascertained in order to determine the cost. Even in the businessman's calculation, what his cost really measures, as shown below, is not the bad consequences of an action but the highest-valued forsaken opportunity.

It is sometimes fallaciously thought that if building a pool involved even more pain or other undesirable consequences, its costs surely must be higher. But the costs of the pool are not higher unless the best alternative is affected. More pain in building a pool may or may not affect my alternative opportunities. If an extra hour of work is involved, then my alternatives are changed, because I lose another hour of other desirable uses. The definition of cost does not deny that the pain and time and trouble of producing some event are influential in the measure of cost. But it does show that these aspects enter into costs only by affecting the value of the best forsaken opportunities.

This can be seen more clearly if we consider the following situation in which the alternatives are not affected. Suppose that in building the pool, the pain to be suffered during a given time was to be more intense—but not longer-lived. In this case, the increase in intensity of pain (assuming that recovery is immediate upon the cessation of the work) does not affect the alternative opportunities. These stay the same. What this more intense pain does is *reduce the value of the pool, not raise its cost.*

Another example of an increase in undesirable attribute that does not increase costs is one that increases that attribute uniformly for *all* opportunities. In this case, the feature cannot be avoided no matter what one does. A uniform reduction in the value of all options reflects the lower level of "utility" now generally available. One could even call this effect a *decrease* in costs—since the best-valued options are now lower-valued. The costs are lower because the values are lower, for that is what cost reflects.

Clarification of the logical role of the concept of cost in order to explicate clearly the distinction between the two ideas—the value of forsaken alternatives and the so-called undesirable attributes—was begun by the Austrian school of economics in the nineteenth century and was further developed by Frank Knight.[1]

## Money Costs in a Society

The preceding is relatively unambiguous for choices or selections of options in a one-person world. But in a society, selection among options involves not only different options for the same person but also different options available to different people. Therefore an interpersonal value measure is necessary. A society in which choices are made in accord with a single dictator's preferences resembles the one-person world. In a pluralistic (individualist) society, an interpersonal value measure can be based on interpersonal exchange rates. Voluntary market exchanges among individuals reveal the highest values of available options and, hence, their costs in terms of values of forsaken options. These market prices, to which all people can adjust their choices, provide a common measure of the value of increments of one event relative to others.

For example, a market exchange rate of 1 Coca-Cola for 2 ounces of chocolate indicates the relative value of each. The optional event—having 1 more Coke—is compared with the option of having 2 more ounces of chocolate. In an open market—one in which all people have access to all goods—the exchange rate, or price, of Cokes must at least equal the highest-valued alternatives to 1 more Coke. If the price does not equal the highest-valued alternative, those who value a Coke at more than the market exchange price will prefer, and

---

1. Frank H. Knight, "Some Fallacies in the Interpretation of Social Cost," *Quarterly Journal of Economics* 38 (1924): 582–606.

will be able, to enter the market and offer more for a Coke. And this will raise the exchange rate to at least the highest-valued alternative. Rather than expressing the values of alternatives to 1 Coke in terms of the amounts of chocolate, beer, or other individual goods that are as much desired as 1 Coke, convenience dictates agreement on a common measure of value. Since almost all formal contractual exchanges are conducted with the medium of money, all exchange rates typically are measured in units of money—as so many dollars or cents per Coke. The use of money prices does not mean that money is all that counts, or that people love money. It means simply that money is the medium of exchange and therefore is the convenient denominator of interpersonal exchange values of events or options.

In sum, because goods are substitutable sources of utility, and because substitution is facilitated by exchange via money, it is possible to measure the value of a forsaken option in money terms. When goods can be obtained not only by interpersonal trade but also by production, at the "cost" of other things that could have been produced, the costs incurred in production choices will be related to the market prices of interpersonal exchanges if producers have access to markets in which to offer their products.

## Market Prices and Cost

The preceding discussion implies that cost in an exchange economy is based on market-revealed values. If some productive resources are used in ways that yield less than their highest achievable alternative, or "opportunity," values, these uses will not cover cost. The incentive to increase one's wealth induces shifts of resources to their higher-valued use until their cost is at least matched by the value of their currently yielded product. As the output of the service now being produced at a higher rate increases, the value of additional increments will fall until there is no further shifting of resources from other uses. By drawing resources from lower-valued to higher-valued uses, the value of a producible good or service influences the allocation of resources and so the rate of output of the good or service itself.

This adjustment or reallocation of resources among various uses is often expressed less rigorously. For example: (a) "Lower-cost resources are shifted to their higher-valued uses." (b) "If costs of production are less than potential values of output, low-cost resources will be shifted to increasing the output of the higher-priced goods, thus inducing a lower price of that good, until ultimately no disparity exists between costs and values of output." Both of these formulations, while explaining the shift in resource uses, are misleading in that they refer to "lower-cost" resources. The resources are not really lower-cost; rather, they are being used in lower-valued uses. It is only the lower value of their use that makes them appear to be lower-valued or lower-cost resources. Strictly speaking, the cost of the use of any resource is never less than the highest-valued opportunity for its use; it is always equal to the amount bid by the most optimistic (highest) bidders in the market for that resource.

No matter how any particular set of resources is used, the cost of their use will be the same—only the realized value of the output, or event yielded, will be affected. If resources are used in less than their most valuable ways, their cost will not be covered, and the difference will be an economic loss. This suggests the query, Is it possible for resources to yield a value in excess of their cost? The answer is yes, in the sense that the current market values do not reflect the future value of the resources—which depends upon unforeseen events or actions. For example, if the use of a resource is changed so as to expose a preferred result to the market, the market value of the resource will be raised. This increase in value of the resource above the former market value is initially a profit. With the unforeseen revaluation, however, costs will be revised upward. In effect, profits are capitalized by the market into costs of subsequent use of the resources.

We may digress to note that we can now interpret the principles underlying the categories "demand" and "supply" as applied to factors affecting price, allocation, and value. *Demand* reflects the value of different amounts of available resources in a particular class of use, say to produce A, while *supply* represents the value of the resources in all *other* potential uses. The demand function indicates a negative relationship between the rate at which good A is made available and the value of another unit of availability of A; the supply function indicates an increasing value of all *other* opportunities of use as more and more of them are forsaken in order to increase the amount of resources devoted to the production of A. If another unit of A has a value greater than the highest value of other necessarily forsaken options (costs on the supply function), the output of A will increase, thereby lowering its unit value and increasing the "costs" (value in *other* uses only) until the two are brought to equality.

The meaning of costs in the demand for and supply of A refers to the value in the *second* or next best use—not in the overall best use. As long as the value of resources in other uses is lower than in the production of good A, more resources will be shifted to A until the value of another unit of A falls to a level that is no greater than that of its component resources in the *next* best other use. At this point the transfer of resources stops, and the rate of output of A will not increase further. But this supply schedule reflects costs *only* in the *other* uses; it does not reflect cost of resources in the sense of *best* opportunities for use over *all* opportunities, including A. The demand-and-supply classification is satisfactory for investigating factors that affect the output of particular goods relative to other goods, but it is not a satisfactory analytical classification for understanding the meaning of the cost concept in its wider range of application and function.

## When Are Costs Incurred?

Forsaken alternatives to a current choice are not necessarily composed only of present events. A decision to build a pool can involve a commitment to a sacrifice of future events. In general, a sacrifice of present consumption is valued more highly than the sacrifice of an equivalent future good is valued *now*. The relationship between the present value of two events, identical except in their time of availability, defines a rate of interest. A rate of interest of 10 percent per year means that a unit of good A, which would be worth $1.00 if available now, will, if it is available only a year hence, have a value *now* (referring to the time of valuation, not to the time of availability) of $.909. It follows that if an event A involves the sacrifice *both* of an alternative good available and worth $1.00 now and of a good available in one year and worth $1.00 at *that* time (but only $.909 now), the present-value cost of the compound event A is $1.909—the sum of the *present* value of the present item ($1.00) plus the *present* value ($.909) of the future item. The cost of event A is therefore the present value of the implied chain of sacrificed options, whether they are realizable now or later.

From this it is tempting to try to draw distinctions such as the following: The present event A involves costs that, although incurred now, are not experienced now. That this distinction is not meaningful can be seen by carefully considering the meaning of incurring a cost. The individual incurs a cost by choosing event A in the sense that his choice makes unavoidable the loss of some otherwise available alternatives. Even if these alternatives were otherwise realizable only far in the future, the cost is incurred now if the present choice of the event A eliminates these future possibilities. The cost is incurred now in the sense that the current choice of the event has meant the irretrievable loss of certain alternatives.

Although the cost is incurred now, the consumption loss can be in the future. For example, a person who buys a car now incurs a cost, but by borrowing he can shift the reduction in consumption to the future. There is no necessity for the reduced consumption to be simultaneous with the incurring of the cost. This is especially true for an individual; borrowing from other people will permit him to transfer the consumption loss to any time he wishes within the limits of the borrowing and repayment schedules available to him.

The cost of a *decision* to perform some event is not always the same as the cost of the *event*. For example, if I decide to build a swimming pool that will cost $3,000, does my making a commitment to build a pool involve the entire cost? Not if I can change my mind tomorrow. Thus, the cost of the *contracting* for a swimming pool may be only $500, in that if subsequently I change my mind, I lose only $500. If, then, the cost of the current commitment to build a pool is $500, when are the remaining $2,500 of costs incurred? They are incurred as work progresses and the successive options are irretrievably lost. In sum, the cost of the decision *and the completion* of a swimming pool is $3,000. At any moment the whole $3,000 cost may not have been incurred, and has not been incurred to the extent that one can still avoid the loss of the subsequent options included in the $3,000 that would have been lost had the work progressed to completion. What is emphasized in this paragraph is the need to avoid ambiguity in the meaning of the *events* being costed—e.g., the decision is one event, and the execution of the project may be a series of subsequent events. Exactly to what event the costs apply should be made unambiguous.

### Examples of Measures of Cost

Principles underlying the measurement of cost as defined above are simple and will now be illustrated, but it must be emphasized that in actual practice the measurement is very imprecise in that it involves estimates of uncertain future events. We shall consider first the cost of *purchasing* (obtaining and retaining ownership of) a car, and then the cost of *using* the car. Its purchase price is $3,000. If we retain the car until it becomes worthless (and if we incur no other costs), the cost of ownership for the indefinite future is $3,000. Assume that we could sell the car immediately for $2,500. At the moment of purchase, then, we have incurred a cost of $500, the cost of acquiring ownership. If we retain the car, we will gradually incur the remaining $2,500 of cost; however, since we can always sell the car, the cost of ownership up to any moment is not the $2,500 but only that portion which cannot be recovered by resale. If a month later we can sell the car for $2,300, the cost of acquiring and retaining ownership for one month is $500 plus $200.

Suppose now we plan to keep the car for two years and then sell it (without using it in the meantime) for $2,000. Of course, $2,000 two years hence does not have the same value as $2,000 now. At a 10 percent rate of interest, the pres-

TABLE 1

|  | Beginning of year 1 | Beginning of year 2 | End of year 2 |
|---|---|---|---|
| Purchase price | $3,000 | $ — | $ — |
| Taxes and insurance | 150 | 150 | — |
| Resale value | (2,500) | (2,200) | −2,000 |
|  | $3,150 | $150 | −$2,000 |
| 10% present-value factor | (1.00) | (.909) | (.826) |

Present-value cost: $1,634.35 = $3,150.00 + $136.35 − $1,652.00

ent value of $2,000 deferred two years is $1,652. The present-capital-value measure of the cost of owning a car for two years is equal to the purchase price minus the present value of the resale price two years hence: $3,000 − $1,652 = $1,348. The decrease in the value of the car from the $3,000 purchase price to the $2,000 resale value is called *depreciation* (for expository simplicity we ignore maintenance expenditures, which are assumed to be optimal). If the reduction were greater than expected, the excess would be called *obsolescence*.

Ownership of a car usually involves more than the costs of acquisition of ownership, even though the car is never to be driven. For example, there are the costs of taxes and insurance. If these total $150 yearly, to be paid at the beginning of each year, the cost of ownership for two years is reckoned as shown in Table 1.

The cost of obtaining and retaining (insured) possession for two years is $1,634.35. By rearranging the data, we can express this cost as the sum of depreciation (purchase price minus resale price, adjusted to present value) plus the other ownership costs (taxes and insurance), as in Table 2.

Operating the car will involve more costs and a lower resale value, $1,700 rather than $2,000. Suppose outlays for gasoline, maintenance, and such amount to $500 in the first year and $400 in the second year. (Let these outlays be payable at the end of each year.) The costs of ownership and operation are now $2,667.05, compared with the cost of $1,634.35 for ownership only (see Table 3).

Events are rarely indivisible; instead, the magnitude of the event can be varied. Thus, in the automobile example, we could consider a set of alternative output programs, e.g., running the car zero miles in two years, one mile in two

TABLE 2

| | | |
|---|---|---|
| Purchase price | $3,000 | |
| Resale value | −1,652 | (present value of $2,000 deferred two years) |
| | ——— | |
| Depreciation | $1,348 | |
| Taxes and insurance | 150 | (first year) |
| Taxes and insurance | 136.35 | (present value of second year's payment) |
| | ——— | |
| Present-value cost | $1,634.35 | |

years, two miles in two years, etc., up to, say, 20,000 miles in two years. Suppose that for each of these we can determine the costs. The difference in costs between adjacent alternative programs is the incremental or marginal cost for the mileage increment. That is, the difference in cost between two-year programs of 19,999 miles and 20,000 miles is called the marginal cost of a mile of travel at 20,000 miles; it is the increment in cost for a 20,000-mile program over the cost for a 19,999-mile program. If we computed the cost for one mile of distance, for two miles, etc., up to 20,000 miles, we could compute a series of marginal costs at, or associated with, one mile more than no miles, one mile more than one mile, one mile more than two, etc. The sum of all these (including the cost of zero miles with two-year ownership) will total to the cost of ownership *and* 20,000 miles of travel. The concept of marginal cost is relevant for deciding among available programs because it tells by how much the cost of one program differs from that of adjacent available programs.

In the comparison of mileage programs, we do not mean that one performs the program of, say, 10,000 miles of travel and then, *after* completing that program, asks how much one more mile would cost. Instead, initially one considers the cost of a proposed 10,000-mile program and the cost of a proposed 10,001-mile program. The difference in cost between the proposed programs is the marginal cost. (To run one more mile as the result of a last-minute decision may involve a higher extra cost than if one had planned for that extra mile from the beginning. In the extreme situation one might have to buy another car in which to do it.)

TABLE 3

|  | Beginning of year 1 | Beginning of year 2 | End of year 2 |
|---|---|---|---|
| Purchase price | $3,000 | $ — | $ — |
| Taxes and insurance | 150 | 150 | — |
| Gas, oil, and maintenance | — | 500 | 400 |
| Resale value | — | — | −1,700 |
|  | $3,150 | $650 | −$1,300 |
| 10% present-value factor | (1.00) | (.909) | (.826) |

Present-value cost: $2,667.05 = $3,150.00 + $590.85 − $1,073.80

For any event there are two associated concepts of cost—total and marginal (the latter referring to a comparison between one particular event and another differing by one unit in some dimension of the event). For every alterable dimension there is a marginal cost of increments in that dimension. Two important dimensions in most output programs are the *rate*, or speed, of output and the total *volume* to be produced. We shall confine our subsequent discussion to changes in these rate and volume dimensions.

The present-capital-value measure of total (or of marginal) cost can be converted into a variety of other equivalent measures for expressing that cost. For example, the present capital value can be reexpressed as a *future* capital value with the future value measure (t units of time in the future) in the ratio $(1 + i)^t$ to the present value, where i is the rate of interest. Alternatively, the present capital value can be converted to a *rate* of costs over some interval. For example, a present-capital-value cost of $1,000 is, at 10 percent per year, equivalent to a perpetual rate of cost of $100 per year, or to a rate of $263 per year for five years.

If the event being costed consists of a group or collection of homogeneous units, e.g., the production of pianos, or the production of miles of service from a car, or the production of bushels of wheat, the cost can be prorated or expressed as an average cost per unit of each item. In the automobile example, the event consisted of owning and driving a car 20,000 miles in two years, the cost of which was $2,667.05. This can be expressed as $2,667.05/20,000 = 13.3 cents per mile of distance. This is the prorated amount that, if received *now* for each future mile of service, will enable the receipts to cover the cost.

Sometimes the rate at which revenues must be received in order to cover costs is measured not by dividing the capital-value measure of costs by the total volume of output, but instead by dividing an annual rate of costs by an annual rate of performance or output. For example, the present-value measure of cost in the above illustration was $2,667 (for a two-year program of 20,000 miles of travel at the rate of 10,000 miles per year). The $2,667 present value can be re-expressed as an equivalent-valued continuous-flow annuity for two years, at 10 percent per year compounded continuously. This steady-flow or rate measure is $1,479 per year for two years (and since there are 8,760 hours in a year, this is equivalent to $1,479 per year/8,760 hours per year = 16.9 cents per hour). The speed of service, at the rate of 10,000 miles per year for two years, is equivalent to 10,000 miles per year/8,760 hours per year = 1.14 miles per hour. If we divide one annual (or hourly) rate of costs by the other annual (or hourly) rate of service (i.e., $1,479 per year/10,000 miles per year, or 16.9 cents per hour/ 1.14 miles per hour), we get 14.8 cents per mile. Therefore, if costs are to be covered by revenues received concurrently with the service performed, the receipts must be 14.8 cents per mile of distance. (This differs from the earlier cost measure of 13.3 cents per mile paid at the beginning of the entire two-year program, because the 14.8 cents is paid later and includes interest on the *average* delay.)

Extreme care must be taken to ensure that rates are divided by rates or that present-capital-value measures are divided by volume measures of the output. Confusion will result if rate (flow) measures of output are divided into capital-value (stock) measures of cost. That would yield cost per unit of speed of output (e.g., miles per year), not per unit of output (e.g., miles). Since outputs are usually sold or priced in units of output or volume, rather than in units of speed of service, it is more useful to consider the covering of costs by receipts per unit of volume of output rather than per unit of speed or of rate of production.

### Fixed and Variable Costs

The preceding discussion distinguished among events being costed according to whether they involved (a) the ownership of some good, (b) the operation of that good to produce some service, or (c) a unit expansion of the event, giving a marginal cost. For some purposes a classification of costs may be useful. It may be relevant to know, for a chosen output program, what costs have been incurred even if we were, at some subsequent moment, to abandon the program. As was seen in the automobile example, at the moment of purchase we have incurred some loss of resale value, e.g., $3,000 − $2,500 =

$500. That "cost" is "sunk," or "historical." Once we purchase the car, the sunk cost cannot be escaped. It should play no role (except as a help in forecasting costs of similar future events) in any subsequent decision, for regardless of what we do, that historical "cost" has been incurred, and is inescapable and unaffected. For any ensuing decision only the escapable, or "variable," costs are relevant.

Having separated sunk, or historical, "costs" (which really are no longer costs) from future costs, we can proceed to classify future costs into invariant and variable costs. Suppose a person can choose among a restricted set of output programs but that associated with all those options there is a common set of activities or inputs, the cost of which is therefore common to each option in the subset. The cost of these common activities is sometimes called a "fixed" cost. Regardless of which option in the subset he chooses, he cannot avoid those "fixed" costs. But since the real range of options is greater, he really can escape the "fixed" cost by choosing an option outside that subset. Therefore that "fixed" cost is not a "sunk" cost. Fixed cost is a useful concept, for example, in situations in which there can be delegation of authority to choose within some subset. So long as the selection is to be made within that subset, only the costs other than the "fixed" costs are relevant. But for the larger range of options, the "fixed" costs are not "fixed" and are relevant for comparing options. To avoid the impression that "fixed" costs are fixed upon a person as an inescapable loss, it seems appropriate to use the name "invariant" rather than "fixed," but this is not yet a generally accepted terminology. (Fixed, or invariant, costs would be "sunk" if and only if the subset was in fact the entire set of possible options, for then regardless of what one did, one could not avoid the sacrifice of those alternatives.)

## Law of Costs

So far, we have classified costs according to differences in the event being costed, and also in terms of various ways of expressing the costs of a specified event or output program. The question to which we turn now is whether there are any laws or general propositions that relate the magnitude of costs to the characteristics of output programs. But first it is pertinent to identify the relevant characteristics or dimensions of an output, or production, program. As suggested earlier, the total volume and the rate or speed of production are two important dimensions of such a program. A third is the timing of the output. We may denote these three variables as follows: $V$ is the volume of output, $v(t)$

is the rate of output at moment t, $T_o$ is the present moment, and $T_m$ is the terminal moment. An increase in $v(t)$ will either increase V or, for fixed V, will decrease $T_m$ (move it closer to $T_o$). Let C denote the capital-value measure of cost of the entire program. Several laws can now be stated in terms of these symbols.

(1) It is a well-recognized and validated law that cost is larger, the larger V is (whether V is increased by increasing $v(t)$ or by increasing $T_m$). Simply put, a bigger output costs more than a smaller one. Symbolically this means $\partial C/\partial V$ is positive, even for fixed or unchanged $v(t)$. The expression $\partial C/\partial V$ is called the marginal cost with respect to volume.

(2) Another proposition is that $\partial C/\partial V$ is smaller (but always positive), the larger V is (again with the rate of production held constant and with the increased V being obtained by increasing $T_m$). In symbols, $\partial^2 C/\partial V^2$ is negative. This effect is sometimes referred to as the lower-costs effect of mass or large-volume production. A larger output can always be produced by replicating the technique for a smaller output. However, sometimes a larger output can be produced at lower cost through the use of different techniques (e.g., metal dies instead of sand casting for forming metal), but this cheaper method cannot be subdivided proportionately for smaller volume. It follows that larger volume will at most involve proportional increases in total cost (by replication of the cheapest methods for small volumes) and may permit utilization of lower-cost methods. Learning and improvement in methods with a larger volume of output are also predictable. Both effects, substitution of cheaper methods for larger volume and learning, contribute to the decrease in increments of total cost for increments in volume.

The two laws relating costs to volume of output imply that (3) the average cost per unit of volume of output decreases, the larger the volume—a widely recognized phenomenon. This lower unit cost with larger volume is manifested in the extensive standardization of products, in contrast with the less common individually styled, custom-built goods, which would be preferable if the costs were no higher. This lower cost with larger volume (along with the gains from specialization in production resulting from the greater heterogeneity of productive resources) is one reason why larger markets and population areas permit lower costs per unit.

(4) A law relating cost to the *rate* (not volume) of output is that the cost, C, is a positive function of $v(t)$ for any given V; that is, $\partial C/\partial v$ is positive. The more rapidly a volume of output is produced, the higher its cost.

(5) Another, possibly less general, law is that the marginal cost with respect

to rate, $\partial C/\partial v$, while always positive, increases for larger $v$ (that is, $\partial^2 C/\partial v^2$ is positive). This law is possibly less general because the evidence is contradictory for "very low" rates of output, at which it is sometimes claimed that increases in the rate might lead to decreasing increases in total cost. Nevertheless, a general and universally valid law is that for every volume of output there exists an output rate beyond which the marginal cost with respect to rate always increases. This is commonly called the law of increasing marginal costs and reflects the well-known law of diminishing marginal returns with respect to rate of output. If expressed in terms of average costs per unit of *volume* of output, the effect of higher rates of production of *that* volume is persistently to raise the average cost—after a possible initial fall in average cost for very low output rates.

(6) Instead of increasing the rate at which some constant volume is produced, output programs can be different in that both the rate *and* the volume are proportionally larger over a specified interval of time. Joint proportional increases in both the rate and the volume (over the given interval of production) will, of course, raise total costs. The effect on the cost per unit of product is not predictable except for "high" rates of output. Unlike proposition (3), concerning per-unit cost, proposition (6) involves an increase in the rate of output as well as in the volume. These two work in opposite directions on the per-unit cost, with the higher rate increasing unit costs while the larger volume decreases them. The rate effect ultimately will dominate as programs with higher rates are considered. For production programs arrayed according to the rate and volume of output (both varying strictly in proportion to each other), it follows that the average cost per unit of volume of output can be decreasing for small outputs. But as larger outputs are considered, the average cost will, beyond some output rate, begin to rise persistently and with increasing rapidity until a limiting rate of production is realized—at which all the resources of the world are devoted to this one program over that given time interval.

### Short-Run and Long-Run Costs

We are now in position to examine another classification—short-run and long-run. Although it is common to see references to the short-run and long-run costs of some production program, there is in fact only *one* cost for any program. The short-run–long-run cost distinction rests on two concepts that are sometimes confounded with each other. A short-run cost is sometimes used to refer to a short, as contrasted with a long, program of production. At other times it is used to refer to the cost of doing something more quickly rather than less quickly. Yet in each case the shorter output and the quicker output both involve higher per-unit costs than do the longer output and the later output. Sometimes the higher per-unit short-run cost (no matter in which of the two different senses) is attributed to an alleged fixity in some of the productive units. In fact, of course, no producer is stuck with literally fixed inputs (except in the sense that momentarily it is hardly possible to increase anything). What is true is that it is more expensive to vary some inputs in any given interval than to vary others. That differential cost of adjusting various inputs is often oversimplified into an extreme bipolar classification of fixed and variable inputs.

The purpose of the long-run–short-run distinction is to note the differences in cost between *different* output programs, those achieved in the more immediate future in contrast with those undertaken later, when one can get the advantage of less expensive, less hasty adjustments. For example, if the demand for some good increases, producers will be able to respond immediately, but at a higher cost than for less hasty revisions of output. Although the "same" good is being produced (except, of course, for the important difference in the time of its availability), the cost is lower for the later output. To trace the impact of a demand change on output and prices, one will want to recognize the difference in the output and price with the passage of time. Instead of tracing out a continuous history or sequence of subsequent developments, it is convenient to divide the history arbitrarily into two episodes: the relatively immediate response (the short run) and the limiting ultimate response (the long run). The difference between these two "runs" indicates the path and direction of effects subsequent to the initial event.

While the long-run–short-run distinction serves as a convenient two-stage analysis of a sequence of effects, obviously there are as many "runs" as one wishes to consider. However, in analyzing total effects, three states or runs are usually considered: the "market period" (referring to that period of adjustment in prices which occurs before there is any change in output), and the aforementioned short run and long run, during both of which output is changed.

### Joint Products and Unallocable Costs

Suppose that an output program yields several joint products, e.g., wool, meat, and leather from sheep; or gasoline and kerosene from crude oil; or heat and light from electrical energy; or passenger miles and freight miles from an airline. What is the cost of each of the joint products? Depending upon which one is called the residual, or by-product, a different allocation of costs can be obtained. By calling meat the "basic" product and attaching most of the costs to it, the costs of wool can be made small, and conversely. It is tempting to jump to the conclusion that something must be wrong with the concept of cost or with the economic system if such indefiniteness can result. After all, if costs cannot be uniquely allocated, how can one tell what prices are right? How can one tell on which of the joint products he is making a profit? If costs cannot be assigned, how can one tell which to produce or what prices to charge? In fact, however, the presence of cost that cannot be allocated uniquely among the joint products does not upset anything or prevent unique prices.

If we recall the purpose of the cost concept—that of enabling choices among alternatives according to some criterion of preference—we see that what is required is a way of assessing the consequences of *changes* in the output. If the airline program is revised to transport more passengers and less freight, or revised so as to transport more passengers with the same amount of freight, what happens to cost? Comparing the costs of alternative programs gives marginal costs, which, with the marginal value of the revised output, give a basis for a decision. There is no possibility and no necessity for allocating costs into uniquely identifiable parts for each product in order to determine what to produce and what prices to ask. The prices set will be those which allocate the amount produced among the competing claimants and yield a maximum wealth to the producer of the joint products. His power to maximize his wealth will, of course, depend upon competitors' access to the market. The function of inducing output does not require an assignment of portions of total cost to each of the joint outputs. What is necessary is a comparison of the total cost of the set of joint products with its value. If the market value of the *set* does not cover the cost, in an open market, the loss of wealth will induce reduced production (of some or all the joint outputs) and higher prices, until the value of the set of joint products covers the costs. (If joint products can be produced only in fixed combinations, then not even marginal costs of each output can be ascertained; nevertheless, everything said in the preceding two sentences is still valid and applicable.)

## Private and Social Allocations of Costs

Throughout the preceding discussion the costs of a choice were assumed to be borne by the chooser; none of the forsaken options are forsaken by anyone else. If Smith builds a swimming pool, the forsaken options—the costs—are all borne by him. The options open to the rest of the community or to any of its members are in no way reduced. So we assumed. If, however, Smith builds a pool and in doing so creates a "nuisance" for his neighbor, Jones, Smith has taken away Jones's peace and quiet. If Smith's pool overflows and harmfully floods Cohen's land, Cohen has had options removed from his range of choice. Being less careful and thereby letting water run over into a neighbor's land, or having a more riotous time and disturbing the peace, is less costly for Smith if he does not incur the costs of being more careful in watching the water level or in soundproofing his play area.

The situation is similar to that of the factory owner who "dumps" smoke, waste, smells, noises, and night lights on other people's land. By doing so he keeps his land in better condition and avoids the cost of filtering his smoke, collecting and disposing of his own garbage, etc. He makes others bear some of the costs, instead of bearing them himself. His actions involve a sacrifice of alternative uses of goods, which sacrifice, instead of being borne by the decision-maker, is in part borne by or imposed on other people.

"Property rights are not private" is another way to express this situation. The use of "one's" resources is not subject solely to the owner's voluntary control, but is in fact and *de jure* controllable in part by other people. This ability to "use" other people's resources for one's benefit, and thereby remove their options, enables one to make other people bear part of the costs of one's decisions. The costs are divided between the decision-maker and outsiders. This division or separation is called a divergence between private and social costs—where social costs are treated as the whole of costs as defined in the earlier portions of this discussion, with private costs being the portion of those costs borne by the decision-maker or owner of the resources directly concerned. Social and private costs are not two different costs—they are merely classifications according to the bearer of the cost. If there is no divergence, so that all social costs are private costs, then all the costs of use are borne by the person choosing or authorizing the choice of action. The divergence between private and social costs is also characterized as the presence of "external" costs.

Parallel reasoning is relevant on the side of benefits. The *value* of a resource in this use may be incompletely revealed or have incomplete influence on decisions if that value is dispersed so that only a part of it accrues to the decision-maker. This is a divergence between private and social value in this use. If the value measure assigned to any particular potential use by the chooser is less than the total value in that use, then there will be a divergence between his private valuation and the social valuation. In this case, values of some uses of resources are not as fully revealed and available as inducements to the competing resource users as are the values of other uses. As a result, the values of some uses will be understated, which encourages more of other kinds of use by leading to an underestimation of their cost. Thus the analysis of external versus private or of social versus private values or costs is an essential part of the analysis of the meaning and role of costs.

But whatever they are called, such effects are commonplace and well-nigh universal. For example, every voluntary act of exchange involves a choice of use of resources that benefits the other party as well as oneself. However, the external effect is "internalized" as an inducement on the acting agents. If you give me "that," I will do, or give you, "this"; and what you give me reflects the gains you will get from what I do. The external effects of my actions are made internal or effective by your ability to offer me a gain reflecting the value to you. The external costs of my acts are internalized or made effective in controlling my behavior by laws prohibiting my imposing any such costs on you unless I pay you an acceptable amount for the right to do so. Our laws of property and the right to engage in exchange help to make private costs also contain the social costs, and to make private gain reflect social gains. In other words, external effects are usually internalized.

In every society the extent of a divergence between private and social costs (or the presence of external effects) for some resource use depends upon the technological facts *and* upon the legal structure of property rights. The costs of defining, policing, and enforcing various types of property rights vary. Private property rights, defined as those in which external physical effects are not permissible, may be too expensive to enforce with respect to some effects. But if there is a cheap way to internalize external effects or to make the private costs equal the social costs, then the use of resources will respond more fully to the cost or values of use. If there were some cheap means of excluding other people from enjoyment of some use I may make of my resources, then I could charge them for the availability of that enjoyment and thereby make that value of use effective in my decision as to how to use resources. This is a means of internalizing external effects or of making external effects "inducive" with respect to my choices about resource uses.

Often the costs that must be borne in order to internalize external effects exceed the value of those external effects but may nevertheless be worth incurring if they involve associated revenues and a more profitable, larger enterprise. For example, a golf course provides benefits to neighboring landowners. A golf course builder could buy enough land to build a course and to build homes on the surrounding property, thus internalizing a higher value from proximity to the golf course. Another example is that of the apartment building in which the rental includes the cost of maintenance of common gardens and recreation areas, rather than having each tenant maintain his own area. The purchase of cemetery lots includes a payment for upkeep of the whole cemetery. By such devices, neighborhood effects are made the owners' effects.

Another important means of internalizing or making external effects "inducing effects" is the development corporation, which enables a larger venture to be undertaken so that more of the benefited resource owners can be included in the unit of ownership that provides the benefits. If all the land of a suburban shopping center is owned by one enterprise, there can be more complete response to the total value of the shopping center, which includes values external to the component units resulting from their proximity. Similarly, department stores with several departments in one building are a means of "internalizing" values or of making private and social effects converge. Signal decoders and wire transmission systems for television, fences around athletic pavilions to keep out nonpaying spectators, and walls around theaters are examples of devices (not costless) for internalizing and increasing the value of the service to those who provide it, and so are "inducive" to that resource use.

In other cases the value of complete suppression of external effects may be less than the cost. For example, automobile exhaust suppressors and smoke filters are not universally required. As a result, those who create smoke and smog thrust part of the costs of their actions on other people. An especially instructive example is provided by the problem of noisy airplanes. If an airport owner had to compensate the nearby landowners for the noise made by the airplanes using his airport, the landowners would in effect be selling rights to that particular use of their land, and the airport owner could in turn charge the airplane owners. Instead, one of the following solutions is usually adopted: (1) There is no compensation for the noise. (2) The planes are prohibited. (3) The neighboring land is bought up and people are prohibited from living there—even though many would prefer to do so, if they could buy the land at a low enough price to reflect the value of the lost quiet. These extreme policies are sometimes explained by an incorrect presumption that it is impossible or undesirable to buy the rights to "dump" noise on neighboring land; in fact, they are used because neighboring landowners do not have a legally recognized right to the undisturbed use of their land.

As the preceding remarks have indicated, often our *legal structure* of property rights is such that decisions are made in which only part of the costs are operative in affecting the choice. This may be a result of a deliberate attempt to attenuate the role of costs in decision-making, or, because of technological features, it may be the result of the difficulty (cost) of defining, policing, and enforcing rights to resources in such a way that private and social costs do not diverge much. Laws may be what they are because those most influential in affecting them may want resources to be used with less regard to the exchange-value measure of costs. It may be thought that the values the people of the society would express in the way they would use resources are inappropriate or improper and therefore should not be so influential in affecting resource allocations. If so, choices about uses of resources should be insulated from those alternative use values (i.e., costs). This can be achieved by suppressing a marketplace in which market prices would reveal alternative use values, or it can be achieved by not sanctioning private property rights, so that no one can negotiate an exchange that would reveal alternative use values (that is, resources would not be "owned," in the sense of being salable).

Policing and enforcing of property rights is not performed exclusively by the government. In many cases other forms of control are effective. Etiquette and socially accepted codes act as determiners of rights. These institutions serve, in part, to restrict the extent to which a person can impose the costs of his choices on others. That is, they are often means of inducing behavior of a type that would occur if resources involved were "privately" owned and exchangeable. Custom and etiquette, along with property rules, affect the degree of concentration of costs on decision-makers.

### External Value Effects and Costs

Still another source of confusion is the confounding of the external *price* effects of some event with its costs. Cost has been defined as the highest-valued option necessarily sacrificed consequent to action A. Suppose that I open a restaurant near yours and, by virtue of my superior cooking talents, attract customers away from you, with a consequent loss of wealth by you of, say, $50,000. So far as *you* are concerned, my effect on you is as bad as if I had burned your uninsured $50,000 building for the joy and excitement this afforded me. From an analytical point of view, the *former* loss of $50,000 of value is not a cost, whereas the destruction of the building would have been a cost. Why the difference? Simply that opening a restaurant does not necessarily involve a sacrifice to society at large, while the destruction of the building does. My superior cooking skills do not involve a sacrifice of $50,000 of alternatively valuable output, whereas my enjoying the fire would. My superior cooking may impose a *loss of wealth* on you because I outcompete you in providing services to third parties. But the $50,000 loss to you is more than matched by the gain in the value of service to the third parties who were formerly your customers but who have shifted to me, and by the increase in my own wealth. No formerly available options are forsaken by society as a whole. Everything that could be done before I opened my restaurant still can be done. That $50,000 is not a sacrificed opportunity—instead, it is a measure of a *transfer of wealth* from you to two other parties, me and the customers. The distinction between the transfer of rights to uses of resources and the costs of use of goods should be kept clear. For example, when I open a new restaurant service, and the public offers less for your goods and more for mine, they are telling you that the exchange rights formerly attached to your goods—their market value—are being transferred by them to my goods.

The transfer of rights of choice of use and the revision of exchange values consequent to changes in offers by competitors, or consequent to changes in tastes by customers, do not reduce the total set of alternative use options. The transfer changes the person authorized to control the decision as to use. When my superior culinary talents reduce the exchange value of your services (without affecting their physical attributes in any way) and so reduce your wealth, society could, in principle, take away some of my gains and those of my customers (who gain by accepting my offers rather than yours) and fully reimburse you, while still leaving me and the customers better off than before I entered the market. Such compensation is not possible for true costs.

The person who loses wealth via either transfer of goods or the reduction of their exchange value is suffering a real loss of wealth, but not a cost. That loss is different in principle, in kind, and in fact from a cost. From the private point of view both sources of loss of wealth are "bad" for him. Both are losses of opportunities to him, though only a cost is a loss to the *community as a whole*. What he loses in the pure price revaluation case, someone else gains.

There are many examples of the use of public policy to reduce such transfers. Taxes have been imposed on innovations or on new products in order to reimburse owners of resources formerly used to produce the displaced products. Sometimes laws are passed prohibiting new, cheaper devices, in order to preserve the marketable wealth of users of older, more costly methods. Sometimes general taxes are imposed to aid those whose wealth is reduced by new methods, e.g., government financing of retraining of displaced workers and low-interest loans to business firms in distressed areas. Taxes on innovations make the innovators count the taxes as part of their costs. The "costs" of innovation are thereby biased upward, with a resultant attenuation of the incentive to introduce new methods or products that would produce a larger total wealth.

Although wealth transfers via market revaluations are not costs, they may influence behavior. For example, if such market revisions of wealth are (somehow) deemed undesirable, steps can be taken to restrain people from taking actions that revise the distribution of wealth, or steps can be taken to redistribute the wealth again so as to restore the *status quo ante* wealth for each individual. Social policy (laws of property) may be evolved to insulate decisions from these effects or, conversely, to make them more sensitive. But in neither case are these market-price side effects on wealth components of costs.

We conclude by returning to the initial theme. The costs of some event are the highest-valued options necessarily forsaken. We have seen that he who is to forsake those options and he who makes the decision about the chosen option may or may not be the same person. Furthermore, the privately borne costs may be less or greater than the true costs, depending upon laws and upon the structure of property rights.

## BIBLIOGRAPHY

Böhm-Bawerk, Eugen von. *Capital and Interest.* 3 vols. South Holland, Ill.: Libertarian, 1959. First published in German. See especially vol. 2, pp. 248–56, "The Law of Costs," and vol. 3, pp. 97–115, "On the Value of Producers' Goods and the Relationship Between Value and Costs."

Clark, John Maurice. *Studies in the Economics of Overhead Costs.* Univ. of Chicago Press, 1962.

Coase, R. H. "The Problem of Social Cost." *Journal of Law and Economics* 3 (1960): 1–44.

Demsetz, Harold. "The Exchange and Enforcement of Property Rights." *Journal of Law and Economics* 7 (1964): 11–26.

Knight, Frank H. "Some Fallacies in the Interpretation of Social Cost." *Quarterly Journal of Economics* 38 (1924): 582–606.

Stigler, George J. *The Theory of Price.* Rev. ed. New York: Macmillan, 1960. First published (1942) as *The Theory of Competitive Price.*

Viner, Jacob. "Cost." *Encyclopaedia of the Social Sciences,* vol. 4, pp. 46–75. New York: Macmillan, 1931.

———. "Cost Curves and Supply Curves." Pp. 198–232, in American Economic Association, *Readings in Price Theory.* Homewood, Ill.: Irwin, 1952.

# RELIABILITY OF PROGRESS CURVES
# IN AIRFRAME PRODUCTION[1]

## Summary

The airframe manufacturing progress curve estimates direct labor per pound of airframe needed to manufacture the Nth airframe, from N, the cumulative number of planes of a given model produced at a given facility. The relation is customarily written as a linear function between the logarithm of direct labor per pound and the logarithm of the Nth airframe. Statistical tests of the similarity of the functions among various airframe manufacturers, on the basis of reported World War II data, have been made in this paper. An assessment has also been made of the reliability of predictions made with these curves.

The functions are shown to differ among the various airframe types and manufacturing facilities in both the amount and rate of change of required direct labor per pound of airframe.

Nevertheless, for practical purposes it may be appropriate to use an average of individual progress functions. One such practical purpose would be the prediction of total direct labor requirements for the first 1,000 airplanes of a particular model. The average error of prediction is shown to be about 25 percent.

Reprinted from Armen A. Alchian, *Economic Forces at Work* (Indianapolis: Liberty Fund, 1977), 335–60. This article was previously published in *Econometrica* 31 (October 1963): 679–93, and is reprinted by permission of the Econometric Society.

1. In 1948, when seeking estimates of costs of alternative weapon systems, the potentially embarrassing error of relating costs to rates of output while ignoring another relevant variable, quantity of items produced, was made obvious by access to the airframe production data analyzed in this paper. By 1949 the present paper had been completed for the RAND Corporation, but reliance on "military classified" data and sources prevented open publication at that time. Although the sources and data have been declassified for several years, it seems appropriate to publish the paper in its original form now that the phenomenon is being incorporated in formal economic theory. Any views expressed in this paper are not to be interpreted as necessarily reflecting the views of the RAND Corporation or the official opinion or policy of any of its governmental or private research sponsors. Acknowledgment is made to Charles Hitch, who encouraged and aided the study.

For the entire output of any particular airframe model produced in one facility the error of prediction is also 25 percent.

If specific curves are fitted to the past performance of a particular manufacturing facility in order to predict its future requirements, the margins of error of prediction average about 20 percent. All these margins of error, while averaging about 20 to 25 percent, represent specific errors which in .9 of the cases range between −40 and +70 percent. An illustration of the possible practical significance of such errors is given.

Finally, functions with other variables, in addition to N, are briefly considered.

## General Problem and Hypotheses

The "progress function," or "learning curve," is one of the instruments of planning, scheduling, and forecasting used in the aircraft industry and the U.S. Air Force. It is designed to express the relation between the amount of direct labor required to produce an airframe and the number of airframes produced. It associates the number of direct man-hours per pound of airframe used in the production of a specific airframe with the number of airframes of that particular type produced in a specific production facility. The relationship, in general, indicates that the required number of direct man-hours decreases as more airframes are produced.

Direct labor is the number of direct man-hours that, so to speak, are congealed in the Nth airframe. It is the direct[2] labor that was expended in the production and fabrication of the component parts and their assembly into that particular airframe. The N of the Nth airframe is the cumulative number of airframes accepted up to and including the Nth airframe. N is not the rate of production per unit of time.

The form of the relationship between direct labor per pound (hereafter called m) of airframe for the Nth airframe, and the Nth airframe, is usually formulated as

$$\log_{10} m = a + b \log_{10} N$$

subject to $a > 0$ and $-1 < b < 0$ where $a$ and $b$ are parameters of the linear form. Graphically on double-log paper the equation plots as a straight line with negative slope.

---

2. Defined below.

A statistical study of the reliability of this function for certain types of estimates is presented in this report. It is indisputable that lower direct labor costs occur as the number of items produced increases; the evidence on this point is overwhelming. Questions can be raised, however: (1) How long does this reduction continue? (2) Can it be represented by a linear function on double-log scale? (3) Does it fall at the same rate for all different airframe manufacturing facilities? (4) How reliably can one predict marginal and total labor requirements for a particular production facility from an industry average progress curve derived from the experience of all airframe manufacturers? (5) How reliably can a curve fitted to the experience of all bomber (fighter) production predict labor requirements for a specific type of bomber (fighter) produced in a particular facility? (6) How reliable is a single manufacturing plant's own early experience for predicting its later requirements for producing a particular type of airframe? (7) What may be the consequences of the margins of error involved in these estimating methods?

The general order of analysis follows the sequence of the above questions. These questions are investigated on the assumption that the estimates are made for a period in which general production conditions are the same as those which prevailed during World War II.

It must be emphasized that this study is concerned with the various types of estimates and predictions that might be made from the assumed *linear* form of the relationship. No attempt is made here to evaluate other forms of relationships that might be used for certain types of predictions. Nor is there any discussion here of the reasons for the decline in labor requirements. Both of these questions may be analyzed in subsequent reports.

### Source of Information

All information used was derived from the *Source Book of World War II Basic Data; Airframe Industry, Vol. I*, prepared by AAF Matériel Command, Wright Field (undated). The data reported in the *Source Book* were, in turn, derived from the Aeronautical Monthly Progress Reports (AMPRs). The reliability of the AMPRs has been subject to a good deal of speculation and remains a moot point. The following description of the data is based entirely on the statements contained in the *Source Book* itself. The AMPRs provided data on acceptances, direct man-hours per unit and direct man-hour expenditure for the report month, subcontracting, etc. Prior to December 1942 direct man-hours were obtained from letters submitted by facilities or by district offices.

The following definitions were adopted by the AMPRs:

*Direct man-hours per pound of airframe*, m (on-site plus off-site), are obtained by dividing direct unit man-hours for the Nth airframe by its unit weight.[3]

*Direct man-hours for the entire airframe* are the "facility's best estimate of the total number of direct hours which would be required to perform the entire airframe manufacturing operation within the reporting facility."[4] This estimate is, in turn, the sum of two estimates: (1) "The estimated direct man hours it would require to perform within the facility that part of the airframe . . . being produced outside the plant or plants of the reporting facility," and (2) direct man-hours per unit on-site.[5]

*Direct man-hours per unit on-site* are the "contractor's best estimate of (1) the direct unit hours expended within the reporting facility (including feeder plants) prior to acceptance on the last unit for which complete records are available in the report month, or (2) the average direct man-hours cost of the last lot produced for which complete records are available in the report month."[6] That is, the direct man-hours relate either to a single unit or to an average of a lot—in either case it is the last unit or last lot for which complete records are available. Man-hours per unit include all hours necessary to complete an airframe, whether these hours are spent during the month of completion (report month) or over a period of several months.

"*Direct man hours charged to a model* normally are obtained from shop or work orders and not from payroll records."[7] Man-hours included are hours expended on the airframe manufacturing process, which includes machining, processing, fabricating, assembling, and installing all integral parts of the airplane structure, flight operations (but not test piloting), and reworking prior to acceptance.[8] Not included are hours expended in the production of raw stock, equipment items, spare parts, and reworking after acceptance.[9] Direct man-hours are not the same as *productive man-hours*. The latter include also hours expended in mold loft, in jig fixture and tool production, in inspection, shipping, receiving, and warehousing.[10]

It is important to note that the observations are the contractor's best esti-

3. *Source Book*, p. 37.
4. Ibid.
5. Ibid.
6. Ibid.
7. Ibid.
8. Ibid.
9. Ibid., p. 23.
10. Ibid., p. 1.

mates of the direct labor used. The methods of making these estimates varied considerably among the manufacturing facilities. It is believed that in some cases very crude estimates were presented. This does not affect the validity of the present study, which is designed to test the predictive utility of progress curves based on reported data. If the progress curves had been derived from exact data, their reliability might be either higher or lower. As long as present and future methods of obtaining data are basically similar to those used in the past, it makes no difference how they were obtained.

*Cumulative plane number, N.* Through April 1944 these are total *acceptances* for each model from a given manufacturing facility as reported to the Air Matériel Command Statistical Division in "Special Historical Report of Airframe Weight" or in letters submitted by the facilities. Beginning with May 1944 the source of these data is the AMPR, #2, or the corrections thereto submitted by the facility or the district office.[11]

All model-facility combinations in the *Source Book* that satisfied the following criteria were used in the analysis:

1. More than 1,000 airframes of a given model were produced in the facility.
2. Data for airframes with N of less than 100 were available for the facility.
3. More than 60 percent of direct labor in any given month was on-site production in the facility provided the cumulative N had reached 100.

The model-facility combinations that satisfied these criteria were:

1. B-29 Boeing, Wichita
2. B-18 Boeing, Seattle
3. B-24 Ford, Willow Run
4. B-24 Con-Vult., Ft. Worth
5. B-25 N. American, Inglewood
6. B-26 Martin, Baltimore
7. A-20 (DB-7) Douglas, Santa Monica
8. A-30 Martin, Baltimore
9. A-26 Douglas, Long Beach
10. TBM Eastern, Trenton
11. P-40 Curtiss, Buffalo
12. P-39 Bell, Buffalo

11. Ibid., p. 37.

13. P-51 (A-36) N. American, Inglewood
14. P-51 N. American, Dallas
15. RP-63 A & C Bell, Buffalo
16. FM1 Eastern, Linden
17. F6F Grumman, Bethpage
18. PT-13-17 (N2S) Boeing, Wichita
19. C-46 Curtiss, Buffalo
20. C-47 Douglas, Oklahoma City
21. AT-6 (SNJ) N. American, Dallas
22. AT-10 Beech, Wichita

The above facilities were classified into four groups: bombers, fighters, trainers, and transports.

## Statistical Analysis

Question 1: *How long does the decline continue?* In every case there was no evidence of any cessation of a decline. This conclusion is based on visual examination of the graphs presented in the *Source Book*. No elaborate statistical analysis appears to be needed to answer this question, given the available data. Whether or not the decline would cease for substantially larger N could not, of course, be determined.

Question 2: *Does the progress curve correspond fundamentally to a linear function on double-log scale?* The purpose of this study is to evaluate the reliability of the learning curve as commonly used in its linear form. Furthermore, a test for linearity would require specification of some alternative nonlinear functional forms for comparison. Since it appeared that the observations would not be sufficient to give a very powerful test of the linear hypothesis with respect to some acceptable alternative, it was believed best to postpone such possible tests until more adequate observations were available. For the rest of this study linearity is simply postulated.

The appropriateness of the linear function as a descriptive device for the accumulated data is indicated by the coefficients of correlation. These exceeded .90 in sixteen of the model-facility combinations and exceeded .80 in the six other cases.

Question 3: *Is the progress curve slope or height the same for all the model-facility combinations?* For the first three categories of airframe the following hypotheses were tested for *each category separately*: $H_1$—The k samples from the bombers (k = 9), fighters (k = 8), and trainers (k = 3) are samples from populations with

TABLE 1. *Analysis of variance test of* $H_1$
$H_1$: *The samples from each category (bombers, fighters, trainers)*
*are from populations with equal intercepts; $A_o$ (unspecified)*

| Category | Source of variation | Sum of squares (a) | Degrees of freedom (b) | Mean square (a/b) | F |
|----------|---------------------|--------------------|------------------------|-------------------|---|
| Bombers | (1) among MFC | 26.24 | 8 | 3.28 | |
| | (2) within MFC | 1.3400 | 300 | .00447 | |
| | | | | | 733 |
| Fighters | (1) among MFC | 22.1007 | 7 | 3.157 | |
| | (2) within MFC | .88806 | 248 | .00358 | |
| | | | | | 882 |
| Trainers | (1) among MFC | 46.042 | 2 | 23.021 | |
| | (2) within MFC | .2757 | 122 | .00226 | |
| | | | | | 11.371 |

Note: $F_{.01}$ exceeded in all cases.

constant height, $a_o$ (unspecified). $H_2$—The $k$ samples are from populations with slope $b_o$ (unspecified). Transports were not tested since there were only two acceptable model-facility combinations (hereafter called MFCs).

One difficulty in applying standard statistical tests to these hypotheses is that the residuals around the progress function are serially correlated. This reduces the number of degrees of freedom and almost always understates the size of the internally estimated error. Crude allowance can be made for this effect by assuming that the degrees of freedom are equal to a fraction of the number of observations. In this study the fraction is one-fourth, which is believed to err on the side of making it more difficult to deny the two hypotheses.

Table 1 presents the analysis of variance of $H_1$ for each of the three categories. Table 2 summarizes the analysis of covariance for $H_2$ for each of the three categories.

Because of the qualifications expressed above about the available degrees of freedom, the critical F ratios for .05 and .01 probability are degrees of freedom estimated at one-fourth of the number of observations.

In every case the hypotheses $H_1$ and $H_2$ are very clearly denied. This means that question 3 has a negative answer. One may conclude that if a linear relationship between log m and log N exists, it exists only uniquely for each par-

TABLE 2. *Analysis of variance test of* $H_2$

$H_2$: *The samples from each category (bombers, trainers, fighters)*
*are from populations with equal slopes, $\beta$ (unspecified)*

| Category | Source of variation | Sum of squares (a) | Degrees of freedom (b) | Mean square (a/b) | F |
|---|---|---|---|---|---|
| Bombers | (1) among individual regression coefficients | 1.57685 | 8 | .19711 | |
| | (2) within sample individual regression coefficient residuals | 2.09592 | 300 | .00698 | |
| | | | | | 28.2 |
| Fighters | (1) among individual regression coefficients | 1.2467 | 7 | .17811 | |
| | (2) within sample individual regression coefficient residuals | 1.11903 | 248 | .00451 | |
| | | | | | 39.49 |
| Trainers | (1) among individual regression coefficients | 1.24 | 2 | .62008 | |
| | (2) within sample individual regression coefficient residuals | .4847 | 122 | .00397 | |
| | | | | | 156.2 |

Note: $F_{.01}$ exceeded in all cases.

ticular MFC. The relationships differ in slope and height even among the various facilities producing the same general type of airframe (bombers, fighters, or trainers). The denial of $H_1$ and $H_2$ also constitutes a denial of homogeneity of the $a_i$ and $b_i$ where the MFCs are not classified according to bomber, fighter, and trainer types.

This means that it is wrong to regard all the individual MFCs as having the same progress function. It is wrong in the sense that if there are linear functional relationships between log $m$ and log $N$ within individual MFCs, they do not have the same heights or slopes. But just as we do not require that everything be equal before considering them fundamentally alike for practical purposes, so one may talk of an average of the curves. Whether the use of the average as typical is appropriate or adequate can be judged only in terms of the margins of error resulting when one uses this averaging technique. It is these margins of error which will now be evaluated.

### Margins of Error

The margin of error depends upon what is being predicted. One may predict the direct labor per pound of a given type of airframe or the cumulated direct labor requirements for the production of a given number of airframes of a particular type. The latter was selected for study as more important. The margins of error will be relatively smaller for cumulative requirements than for marginal requirements, since variations in marginal requirements will offset each other and tend to cancel out when cumulated into a sum of direct labor requirements. It might be added that if one were to seek a method of estimating cumulated direct labor requirements, he would ordinarily obtain a prediction equation directly between cumulated direct labor and N, rather than between marginal direct labor, m, and N. This particular study, however, was directed toward an examination of the progress curve concept as postulated in the *Source Book*.

The margin of error also depends on the type of progress curve used, of which there are at least three: (1) An industrywide average progress curve is one in which the a coefficient and b coefficient are obtained by combining all the data into one heterogeneous set. (2) The airframes can be classified on some basis, such as type of airframe (bomber, fighter, trainer), and for each class, the a and b coefficients can be computed by pooling the data for that set. (3) The various MFCs can be kept separate, and a and b can be derived for each from the early buildup part of its operations (to an approximate peak rate—usually occurring 1 to $1^1/2$ years after the tenth frame was produced). Questions 4, 5, and 6 deal with predictions made from each of these three progress curve types, respectively.

It is essential to note that because $H_1$ and $H_2$ were denied, which means that progress curve types (1) and (2) are really averages of heterogeneous concepts, there is no readily available method of deriving from the internal error variance the margin of error of any of the estimates that might be made with these two types of curve. Therefore an alternative procedure was used for estimating the margin of error. For each facility predictions of direct labor requirements were made by means of the progress curves and compared with realizations as given in Table 3 of the *Source Book*.

*Question 4: How reliable are the predictions derived from an industrywide average progress curve?* An industrywide average progress curve was obtained by combining all the observations from the twenty selected MFCs (excluding transports) into one large sample. The resulting progress curve was integrated from zero to 1,000 to obtain an estimate of the cumulated direct labor requirements for the first 1,000 airframes in any MFC. Since these requirements are on a per-pound basis and since weights of airframes differ from type to type, the cumulated direct labor requirements per pound were multiplied by the weights of the airframes. Adjustments were made for changes in the weights of airframes due to modifications in design. Thus for each MFC an estimate was obtained of the required cumulated direct man-hours for the first 1,000 airframes.[12] The prediction of direct labor requirements was confined to 1,000 airframes because it was presumed that by the time 1,000 airframes had been made the particular MFC could use its own experience for further prediction. Table 3 presents the resulting predictions and realizations. It will be seen that the absolute differences between predicted and actual values[13] average 25 percent of the actual.

*Question 5: How reliable are the predictions derived from a general airframe-type progress curve?* With the airframe-type curve (bomber, fighter, trainer), predictions for each MFC were made for both zero to 1,000 airframes and for the entire run of airframes produced by the various MFCs. The bomber-type curve was obtained by combining the observations from the nine bomber MFCs into one large sample. That is, the observations were pooled but not the sample covariances. The fighter-type coefficients were obtained by similarly combining observations on the eight fighter types, and the trainer coefficients were obtained from the three trainer types. For each MFC prediction, the corresponding type curve was integrated over the appropriate range. This integral, when multiplied by the weight of the plane, is the predicted cumulated direct labor requirement.

Predictions and realizations are given in Table 3 for the first 1,000 airframes. The percentage of error is defined as the ratio of the difference between predicted and actual values to the actual. The weighted average of these errors (nonalgebraic) is 25 percent. This failure to obtain a smaller margin of error by using type curves rather than the industry average curve suggests that there is

12. In the cases of a few models, the estimate had to be made for a range starting a little beyond the first plane and extending to the 1,000th airframe. This was necessitated by the lack of check data for early production.

13. Weighted by actual man-hours.

TABLE 3. Predictions of direct labor requirements for first 1,000 planes (less $N_o$) by industry progress curve and by airframe-type progress curve

| j | Model-facility combination | $N_o$ | Man-hours (Millions) | | | $P_r - A_t/A_c$ (Percent) | |
|---|---|---|---|---|---|---|---|
| | | | Predicted by | | Actual reported | Industry curve | Airframe-type curve |
| | | | Industry curve | Airframe-type curve | | | |
| | *Bombers* | | | | | | |
| 1 | B29 Boeing, Wichita | 0 | 107 | 99 | 76 | +41 | +30 |
| 2 | B17 Boeing, Seattle | 45 | 48 | 40 | 52 | −8 | −23 |
| 3 | B24 Ford, Willow Run | 0 | 52 | 48 | 35 | +49 | +37 |
| 4 | B24 Con Vult, Ft. Worth | 79 | 43 | 37 | 25 | +72 | +48 |
| 5 | B25 N. Amer., Inglewood | 0 | 28 | 26 | 18 | +56 | +44 |
| 6 | B26 Martin, Baltimore | 0 | 34 | 31 | 30 | +13 | +03 |
| 7 | A20 (DB7) Douglas, Santa Monica | 0 | 21 | 19 | 21 | 0 | −10 |
| 8 | A30 Martin, Baltimore | 0 | 20 | 19 | 19 | +5 | 0 |
| 9 | A26 Douglas, Long Beach | 0 | 32 | 30 | 28 | +14 | +07 |
| | Error per bomber facility | | | | | 29 | 22 |
| | Weighted average* per bomber facility | | | | | 29 | 24 |
| | *Fighters* | | | | | | |
| 10 | TBM Eastern, Trenton | 7 | 15 | 17 | 17 | −12 | 0 |
| 11 | P40 Curtiss, Buffalo | 9 | 7 | 8 | 7 | +9 | +22 |
| 12 | P39 Bell, Buffalo | 0 | 8 | 9 | 9 | −7 | +4 |
| 13 | P51 (A36) N. Amer., Inglewood | 0 | 10 | 11 | 7 | +41 | +57 |

| | | | | | | |
|---|---|---|---|---|---|---|
| 14 | P51 N. American, Dallas | 0 | 10 | 11 | 7 | +37 | +52 |
| 15 | RP63 A & C Bell, Buffalo | — | — | — | — | — | — |
| 16 | FM1 Eastern, Linden | 23 | 7 | 8 | 13 | -41 | -34 |
| 17 | F6F Grumman, Bethpage | 22 | 12 | 13 | 12 | -3 | +9 |
| | Error per fighter facility | | | | | 21 | 25 |
| | Weighted average* per fighter facility | | | | | 20 | 21 |
| | Trainers | | | | | | |
| 18 | AT6 N. American, Dallas | 0 | 6 | 7 | 3 | +73 | +87 |
| 19 | AT10 Beech, Wichita | 19 | 7 | 8 | 4 | +58 | +71 |
| 20 | PT13-17 Boeing, Wichita | 20 | 3 | 3 | 5 | -45 | -40 |
| | Error per trainer facility | | | | | 59 | 66 |
| | Weighted average* per trainer facility | | | | | 56 | 62 |
| | Transports | | | | | | |
| 21 | C46 Curtiss, Buffalo | 0 | 53 | — | 55 | -04 | — |
| 22 | C47 Douglas, Oklahoma City | 0 | 28 | — | 23 | +22 | — |
| | Weighted average* per transport facility | | | | | 09 | — |
| | All Facilities | | | | | | |
| | Error per facility (nonalgebraic average) | | | | | 28 | 29 |
| | Weighted* error per facility (nonalgebraic) | | | | | 25 | 25 |

*Weighted by actual man-hours.

—Not computed.

no significant difference between the average *a*'s and *b*'s by airframe types. Table 4 contains the results for the complete run for each MFC. In this latter set of predictions the error averages 26 percent.

*Question 6: How reliable is a single MFC's own early buildup progress curve for predicting its subsequent direct labor requirements?* For each particular MFC, a progress curve was estimated from the buildup portion (usually lasting about one year) of its own production experience. With this equation, predictions were made of the direct labor requirements for the rest of the production run. Predictions were obtained by integrating the progress curve and multiplying by airframe weight. These predictions were then compared with realizations. Coefficients of the "buildup" progress curves are presented in Table 5. The results of the predictions are presented in Table 6. The average margin of error (ratio of absolute error to actual requirements) is about 22 percent. Inspection of the results does not indicate any correlation of the relative size of the error or prediction with either the number of airframes for which direct labor is predicted, or the type of the airframe. Figure 1 (p. 220) is a graphic summary of the results.

*Question 7: What are some possible consequences of these errors of estimate?* The consequences of the errors of estimate in predicting cumulated direct labor requirements can be determined only in the context of some specific problem. As an illustration the following example is presented. If 1,000 airframes have been produced and if a total of 5,000 is to be produced, one may estimate the required amount of labor for the next 4,000 airframes. Suppose that the slope of the progress curve had been computed to be −.32.[14] Now suppose it is discovered that the predicted amount of direct labor required was 20 percent less than that actually required. How many planes would have been produced by the time the predicted amount of direct labor had been used? Only 3,100, or 22 percent less than the extra 4,000 required. If instead the prediction had overstated the required amount, then utilization of the predicted amount would have resulted in 5,030 airframes, or 27 percent too many.[15] A review of the figures given in the earlier part of this report will indicate that the above example is not an unusual one. In general, an error in estimating direct labor requirements implies a greater discrepancy between actual and expected airframe production.

14. This is equivalent to an 80 percent progress curve.
15. See Appendix for mathematical derivation.

TABLE 4. *Predicted and actual direct labor requirements for total production based on airframe-type progress curves*

| j | Model-facility combination | $N_o$ | $N_z$ | Direct man-hours | | $\dfrac{P_r - A_c}{A_c}$ |
| | | | | Predicted based on type curve | Reported actual | |
| --- | --- | --- | --- | --- | --- | --- |
| | | | | (Millions) | | (Percent) |
| | *Bombers* | | | | | |
| 1 | B29 Boeing, Wichita | 0 | 1606 | 132 | 94 | +40 |
| 2 | B17 Boeing, Seattle | 45 | 6949 | 151 | 179 | −21 |
| 3 | B24 Ford, Willow Run | 0 | 8238 | 169 | 108 | +56 |
| 4 | B24 Con. Vult., Ft. Worth | 79 | 1927 | 60 | 37 | −62 |
| 5 | B25 N. Amer., Inglewood | 0 | 3180 | 52 | 47 | +11 |
| 6 | B26 Martin, Baltimore | 0 | 3677 | 71 | 71 | 0 |
| 7 | A20 (DB-7) Douglas, Santa Monica | 0 | 5685 | 58 | 81 | −20 |
| 8 | A30 Martin, Baltimore | 0 | 1566 | 25 | 25 | 0 |
| 9 | A26 Douglas, Long Beach | 0 | 1107 | 31 | 29 | +07 |
| | Error per bomber facility | | | | | 24 |
| | Weighted error* per bomber facility | | | | | 27 |
| | *Fighters* | | | | | |
| 10 | TBM Eastern, Trenton | 7 | 7190 | 73 | 72 | +01 |
| 11 | P40 Curtiss, Buffalo | 9 | 13686 | 63 | 87 | −28 |
| 12 | P39 Bell, Buffalo | 0 | 9407 | 46 | 56 | −18 |
| 13 | P51 (A-36) N. Amer., Inglewood | 0 | 9872 | 60 | 38 | +58 |
| 14 | P51 N. Amer., Dallas | 0 | 4650 | 35 | 19 | +84 |

(continued)

TABLE 4. (continued)

| j | Model-facility combination | $N_o$ | $N_z$ | Direct man-hours Predicted based on type curve | Reported actual | $\dfrac{P_r - A_c}{A_c}$ |
|---|---|---|---|---|---|---|
| 15 | RP63 A & C Bell, Buffalo | — | — | — | — | — |
| 16 | FM1 Eastern, Linden | 23 | 5715 | 30 | 35 | −14 |
| 17 | F6F Grumman, Bethpage | 22 | 12211 | 86 | 71 | +21 |
| | Error per fighter facility | | | | | 32 |
| | Weighted error* per fighter facility | | | | | 25 |
| | Trainers | | | | | |
| 18 | AT6 N. Amer., Dallas | 0 | 12811 | 41 | 35 | +17 |
| 19 | AT10 Beech, Wichita | 19 | 1700 | 11 | 7 | +64 |
| 20 | PT13-17 Boeing, Wichita | 20 | 8419 | 14 | 20 | −30 |
| | Error per fighter facility | | | | | 37 |
| | Weighted error* per trainer facility | | | | | 27 |
| All facilities | | | | | | |
| | Error per facility | | | | | 29 |
| | Weighted error* per facility | | | | | 26 |

*Weighted by actual man-hours.
—Not computed.

TABLE 5. First and second portion progress curves—individual model-facility combinations

| j | Model-facility combination | Range of product 1st portion | Progress curve for 1st portion | | Progress curve for 2nd portion | | Range of production for 2nd portion |
|---|---|---|---|---|---|---|---|
| | | | intercept | slope | intercept | slope | |
| 1 | B29 Boeing, Wichita | 0–267 | 1.41 | .48 | 2.21 | .78 | 268–1606 |
| 2 | B17 Boeing, Seattle | 45–385 | 1.87 | .58 | 1.45 | .43 | 386–6949 |
| 3 | B24 Ford, Willow Run | 0–769 | 1.69 | .61 | 1.62 | .55 | 770–8238 |
| 4 | B24 Con. Vult., Ft. Worth | 79–711 | 1.25 | .43 | 1.94 | .68 | 712–1927 |
| 5 | B25 N. Amer., Inglewood | 0–242 | .64 | .19 | 1.14 | .35 | 243–3180 |
| 6 | B26 Martin, Baltimore | 0–409 | 1.17 | .35 | 1.54 | .47 | 410–3677 |
| 7 | A20m Douglas, Santa Monica | 0–623 | 1.14 | .30 | — | — | 624–5685 |
| 8 | A30 Martin, Baltimore | 0–651 | .88 | .21 | — | — | 652–1566 |
| 9 | A26 Douglas, Long Beach | 0–402 | 1.24 | .38 | 1.20 | .35 | 403–1107 |
| 10 | TBM Eastern, Trenton | 7–1335 | 1.23 | .32 | 1.86 | .49 | 1336–7190 |
| 11 | P40 Curtiss, Buffalo | 9–8494 | .81 | .16 | .13 | .08 | 8495–13686 |
| 12 | D30 Bell, Buffalo | 0–1073 | 1.05 | .26 | .99 | .22 | 1074–9407 |
| 13 | P51 N. Amer., Inglewood | 0–910 | .77 | .21 | — | — | 911–9872 |
| 14 | P51 N. Amer., Dallas | 0–1248 | 1.04 | .32 | 3.19 | .97 | 1249–4650 |
| 15 | RP63 Bell, Buffalo | — | — | — | — | — | — |
| 16 | FM1 Eastern, Linden | 23–1215 | 1.65 | .42 | 2.14 | .57 | 1216–5715 |
| 17 | F6F Grumman, Bethpage | 22–2097 | 1.27 | .35 | 1.43 | .39 | 2098–12211 |
| 18 | AT6 N. Amer., Dallas | 0–2089 | .52 | .15 | .97 | .26 | 2090–12811 |
| 19 | AT10 Beech, Wichita | 19–560 | 1.11 | .39 | — | — | 561–1700 |
| 20 | PT13-17 Boeing, Wichita | 20–720 | 2.19 | .63 | 1.37 | .33 | 721–8419 |
| 21 | C46 Curtiss, Buffalo | 450 | .63 | .06 | — | — | 451–2526 |
| 22 | C47 Douglas, Oklahoma City | 1384 | 1.50 | .48 | .90 | .31 | 1385–5190 |

—Not computed.

TABLE 6. Predicted and actual direct labor requirements for 2nd portion of production based on individual model-facility combination progress curves (1st portion)

| j | Model-facility combination | Second portion range of cumulative production | Predicted direct labor man-hours based on MFC curve of first portion (millions) | Reported actual (millions) | $\dfrac{P_r - mA_c}{A_c}$ |
|---|---|---|---|---|---|
| 1 | B-29 Boeing, Wichita | 268–1606 | 67 | 56 | +.20 |
| 2 | B-17 Boeing, Seattle | 386–6949 | 125 | 154 | –.19 |
| 3 | B-24 Ford, Willow Run | 770–8238 | 59 | 78 | –.24 |
| 4 | B-24 Con. Vult., Ft. Worth | 712–1927 | 25 | 19 | +.31 |
| 5 | B-25 N. Amer., Inglewood | 243–3180 | 44 | 41 | +.07 |
| 6 | B-26 Martin, Baltimore | 410–3677 | 64 | 57 | +.12 |
| 7 | A-20 (DB-7) Douglas, Santa Monica | 624–5685 | 68 | 64 | +.06 |
| 8 | A-30 Martin, Baltimore | 652–1566 | 16 | 12 | +.31 |
| 9 | A-26 Douglas, Long Beach | 403–1107 | 14 | 15 | –.07 |
| 10 | TBM Eastern, Trenton | 1336–7190 | 50 | 50 | .00 |
| 11 | P-40 Curtiss, Buffalo | 8495–13686 | 29 | 31 | –.06 |
| 12 | P-39 Bell, Buffalo | 1074–9407 | 42 | 47 | –.11 |
| 13 | P-51 (A-36) N. Amer., Inglewood | 911–9872 | 41 | 31 | +.32 |
| 14 | P-51 N. Amer., Dallas | 1249–4650 | 14 | 11 | +.26 |
| 15 | RP-63 A & C Bell, Buffalo | * | * | * | * |
| 16 | FM1 Eastern, Linden | 1216–5715 | 23 | 21 | +.10 |

| 17 | F6F Grumman, Bethpage | 2098–12211 | 50 | 51 | –.02 |
| 18 | AT-6 (SNJ) N. Amer., Dallas | 2090–12811 | 26 | 28 | –.07 |
| 19 | AT-1o Beech, Wichita | 560–1700 | 3 | 4 | –.27 |
| 20 | PT-13-17 (N2S) Boeing, Wichita | 721–8419 | 9 | 16 | –.44 |
| 21 | C-46 Curtiss, Buffalo | 451–2526 | 134 | 62 | +1.16 |
| 22 | C-47 Douglas, Oklahoma City | 1385–5190 | 32 | 29 | +.10 |
| | Error per facility | | | | .21 |
| | Weighted error per facility | | | | .22 |

*Not computed.

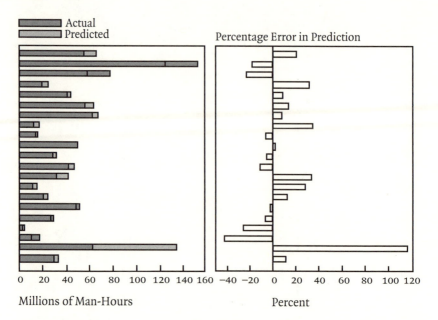

**FIGURE 1.** *Predicted and actual direct labor requirements (after production buildup); predictions by each model-facility combination's progress curve during buildup period.*

## Alternative Progress Functions

Alternative relationships between direct labor per pound of airframe, cumulative N, time and rate of production have been suggested and investigated with the present data. The results cast doubts on any of the alternatives being better fits than the usual progress curve. The principal reason that little improvement would be expected is the presence of very high correlation among time, N, and ΔN. The various other relationships considered for each particular MFC were:

   a. $\log m = a_2 + b_2 T$, where T is time.
   b. $\log m = a_3 + b_3 T + b_4 \Delta N$, where ΔN is rate of production per month.
   c. $\log m = a_4 + b_5 \log T + b_6 \log \Delta N$.
   d. $\log m = a_5 + b_7 T + b_8 \log \Delta N$.
   e. $\log m = a_6 + b_9 T + b_{10} \log N$.
   f. $\log m = a_7 + b_{11} \log N + b_{12} \log \Delta N$.

## Conclusion

The preceding analysis has been concerned with the margin of error to be expected when estimating direct labor requirements and cumulative airframe production by the linear progress curve if the basic assumption of historical similarity of production conditions is fulfilled. The virtual certainty of non-fulfillment of some part of the basic assumption would increase the magnitude and seriousness of error. In each case there should be an investigation of the range of uncertainty in prediction (e.g., acceleration curves and program feasibilities, which are in part derived from and based on "progress curves") before making decisions. This follows from the fact that reliable decisions can be made only among those alternative programs that are disparate beyond the range of uncertainty of error of estimate of the predictive method.

## Appendix[16]

The basis for the calculations for question 7 is as follows.

Labor expended in the production of the first $n_o$ items is $A_o$. Total labor, $A_e$, required for the production of a total required number, $n_r$, is estimated by the formula

$$A_e = A_o \left( \frac{n_r}{n_o} \right)^{1-m}$$

The total labor actually required for the production of $n_r$ is some quantity $A_r = A_e$.

Assuming the formula is correct, but that the estimation of the value of $m$ is in error, what would have been the actual production, $n_a$, had the estimated labor, $A_e$, been expended? This is given by

$$\log n_a/n_r = \frac{-(\log n_r/n_o)\,(\log A_r/A_e)}{(1 - m)\,(\log n_r/n_o) + \log A_r/A_e}$$

where the logarithms are taken to any convenient base.

In terms of the additional labor estimated, $B_e$, and the additional labor required, $B_r$, to build the additional $n_r - n_o$ items,

$$\frac{A_r}{A_e} \frac{A_o + B_r}{A_o + B_e} = 1 + \left[ 1 - \left( \frac{n_o}{n_r} \right)^{1-m} \right] \frac{B_r - B_e}{B_e}$$

In terms of P, the "slope of the progress curve,"

$$m = \frac{-\log P}{\log 2}$$

16. This mathematical derivation was made by H. Germond.

The ratio of the difference between actual and required output to the required additional output is

$$\frac{n_a - n_r}{n_r - n_o} = \sum_4 \left( \frac{n_a}{n_r} - 1 \right)$$

*Example:* Suppose $n_r = 5 n_o$, and P is erroneously estimated to be 80 percent. Then

$$m = \frac{-\log 0.80}{\log 2} = .0321928,$$

$$\frac{A_r}{A_e} = 1 + [1 - (0.2)^{0.678072}] \frac{B_r - B_e}{B_e}$$

$$= 1 + 0.664225 \frac{B_r - B_e}{B_e},$$

$$\log_{10} n_a / n_r = \frac{-0.69897 \log_{10} A_r / A_e}{0.47395 + \log_{10} A_r / A_e},$$

and

$$\frac{n_a - n_r}{n_r - n_o} = \frac{5}{4} \left( \frac{n_a}{n_r} - 1 \right)$$

Suppose, now, the estimated labor for the production of the $n_r - n_o$ additional units is found to be in error by 20 percent, depending upon (1) $B_e = 1.2 B_r$, or (2) $B_e = 0.8 B_r$. Carrying out the computation yields the results given in the text.

# 3

## THE SOURCE AND MEASUREMENT
## OF INFLATION

# ON A CORRECT MEASURE OF INFLATION

## ARMEN A. ALCHIAN AND BENJAMIN KLEIN

Two commonly cited and newsworthy price indices are the Bureau of Labor Statistics' Consumer Price Index and the Commerce Department's GNP deflator. These indices have become an important part of our economic intelligence and are frequently considered to be the operational counterparts of what economists call "the price level." They, therefore, often are used as measures of inflation and often are targets or indicators of monetary and fiscal policy. Nevertheless, these price indices, which represent measures of current consumption service prices and current output prices, are theoretically inappropriate for the purpose to which they are generally put. The analysis in this paper bases a price index on the Fisherian tradition of a proper definition of intertemporal consumption and leads to the conclusion that a price index used to measure inflation must include asset prices. A correct measure of changes in the nominal money cost of a given utility level is a price index for wealth. If monetary impulses are transmitted to the real sector of the economy by producing transient changes in the relative prices of service flows and assets (i.e., by producing short-run changes in "the" real rate of interest), then the commonly used, incomplete, current flow price indices provide biased short-run measures of changes in "the purchasing power of money." The inappropriate indices that dominate popular and professional literature and analyses are thereby shown to result in significant errors in monetary research, theory, and policy.

Reprinted from Armen A. Alchian, *Economic Forces at Work* (Indianapolis: Liberty Fund, 1977), 481–513. This article was previously published in *Journal of Money, Credit, and Banking* 5 (February 1973): 173–91, and is reprinted by permission of Ohio State University Press.

The authors are indebted to Michael DePrano, Michael Hamburger, Joseph Ostroy, Earl Thompson, Jai Hoon Yang, and participants at seminars at the University of Washington, Carleton University, and the National Bureau of Economic Research for helpful comments and to Irene Abramson for able research assistance. Financial assistance was provided by the National Bureau of Economic Research and by the Lilly Foundation, Inc., grant to UCLA for the study of property rights. This work has not undergone the full critical review accorded National Bureau Studies and is not a National Bureau publication.

## I. An Iso-utility Price Index with Intertemporal Consumption

A well-recognized principle is that the appropriateness of a price index depends on the question to which an answer is sought.[1] For many situations we are interested in measuring the *money* cost of a fixed-welfare or constant-utility vector of goods as money prices change. This iso-utility price index, often called a cost-of-living or fixed welfare index, was first discussed formally by Könus. However, as early as 1906 Irving Fisher (and others earlier, we conjecture) pointed out that an iso-utility vector included claims to future consumption. And more recently, Samuelson elegantly restated the significance of wealthlike measures (instead of current income) in comparisons of welfare. We, therefore, regard the utility or preference ordering of any situation as a function of a vector of claims to present and future consumption,[2]

---

1. See, for example, R. Frisch, "Annual Survey of General Economic Theory: The Problem of Index Numbers," *Econometrica* 4 (January 1936): 10; W. C. Mitchell, *The Making and Using of Index Numbers*, U.S. Bureau of Labor Statistics Bulletin no. 656, 3rd ed. (Washington, 1938), 23; J. M. Keynes, *A Treatise on Money*, book II, vol. 1 (London: Macmillan, 1930; reprinted, 1938), 23; and M. J. Ulmer, *The Economic Theory of Cost of Living Index Numbers* (New York, 1949), ch. 2. Fisher, on the other hand, considered the problem of constructing a price index independent of purpose and concluded that "from a practical standpoint, it is quite unnecessary to discuss the fanciful arguments for using 'one formula for one purpose and another for another' in view of the great practical fact that all methods (if free of freakishness and bias) *agree!*" (I. Fisher, *The Making of Index Numbers: A Study of Their Varieties, Tests and Reliability*, 3rd ed. [Boston, 1927], 23; his italics). However, Fisher (*The Purchasing Power of Money* [New York, 1911], ch. 10) earlier stated that the correctness of an index depended on its purpose, and he emphasized the theoretical importance of not basing an index of purchasing power to be used in long-term loan contracts solely on consumer service prices. Using an analysis similar to our own, he argued that

> Borrowers and lenders, in other words, may be more interested in purchasing factories, railroads, land, durable houses, etc., which yield services during a long future, than in purchasing more or better food, shelter and entertainments, which yield immediate satisfactions. To base our index number for time contracts solely on services and immediately consumable goods would therefore be illogical.

Although he asserts that the practical differences may be inconsequential, the broad-based index which he concludes is best to use as the P in his equation of exchange is similar to our index in terms of its inclusiveness.

2. A. A. Könus, "The Problem of the True Index of the Cost of Living," *Econometrica* 1 (January 1939): 10–29 (first published in Russian in 1924); I. Fisher, *Nature of Capital and Income* (New York, 1906); P. A. Samuelson, "The Evaluation of 'Social Income': Capital For-

$$U = U([q(i, t)]) \tag{1}$$

where the $q(i, t)$ element represents the quantity of the ith consumption service flow at time t.

Assume, initially, that markets exist for every consumption service flow to be delivered at every moment of time. At any moment an individual is assumed to be constrained by a scalar $W$ (wealth), which he allocates over claims to present and future consumption flows at present prices quoted on these markets. If at each (current and future) moment there are n consumption services, then

$$W_A \equiv \int_0^\infty \left[ \sum_{i=1}^n q_A(i, t)\, p_A(i, t) \right] dt; \tag{2}$$

where $W_A$ is the individual's current nominal wealth, $p_A(i, t)$ is the current rental price of the ith consumption service for moment t (i.e., present prices include prices of present claims to future consumption), and $q_A(i, t)$ is the magnitude of the ith consumption service flow at moment t which at the current price vector and wealth level maximizes the individual's intertemporal utility. All of these values are described as given under condition A.[3]

------

mation and Wealth," in *The Theory of Capital*, ed. F. A. Lutz and D. C. Hague (London, 1961), 32–57. Samuelson notes that A. C. Pigou (*The Economics of Welfare*, 4th ed. [1932; London, 1960], 37) explicitly recognized that economic welfare depends upon "total consumption" and not solely upon "immediate consumption." See any recent mathematical price theory textbook, for example, J. M. Henderson and R. Quandt (*Microeconomic Theory* [New York, 1958], 229–40), for a formal statement of this commonly accepted proposition.

While we consider present and future consumption as the sole elements in the utility function and emphasize wealth as claims to future consumption, we do not deny the possibility that individuals are willing to hold wealth in, and of, itself. See, for example, D. Dewey (*Modern Capital Theory* [New York, 1965]) for an analysis where consumption is not the sole end of economic activity. This alternative view is not inconsistent with the analysis of this paper.

3. This model, like the standard microeconomic model under which the usual price indices are derived, assumes the absence of all information or transaction costs and therefore lacks a theoretical justification for the value of a price index. (Introduction of uncertainty by the use of costlessly made contingency contracts—e.g., K. J. Arrow, "The Role of Securities in the Optimal Allocation of Risk Bearing," *Review of Economic Studies* 31 [1964]: 91–96—where all transactors know the true state of the world when it occurs, is also economically equivalent to a world of perfect information with no rationale for a price index.) We will here ignore this fundamental question and concentrate solely on defining what is

Let present flow prices, including present prices of future consumption services, change and describe this new state as condition B. The question we are asking is whether prices, measured by a constant-utility index, have risen or fallen. We can, in principle, compute at the new set of present prices, $[p_B(i, t)]$, the cost of an iso-utility consumption service vector, $[q_B(i, t)]$. If, for example, the new cost under price condition B, $W_B$, is greater than under the initial price condition A, we can say that the money cost of an iso-utility vector of goods has risen.[4] The iso-utility price index implicit in this can be represented by

$$P_{AB} \equiv \frac{W_B}{W_A} \equiv \frac{\int_0^\infty \left[ \sum_{i=1}^n q_B(i, t)\, p_B(i, t) \right] dt}{\int_0^\infty \left[ \sum_{i=1}^n q_A(i, t)\, p_A(i, t) \right] dt} \tag{3}$$

where $q_B(i, t)$ represents the $(i, t)$ element in the minimum cost consumption vector that yields the same condition A utility at the new condition B price vector. If $P_{AB}$ is greater than one, the nominal money cost of condition A utility has increased; an inflation has occurred.

To emphasize the intertemporal nature of this price index and the fact that it does not refer solely to the cost of the current moment's consumption, it could less misleadingly be called the current "cost-of-life" index. Current instantaneous prices of current consumption flows enter this index, but insignificantly.

## II. Futures and Asset Prices

Current cash prices (to be paid now) for future consumption services are here called futures prices.[5] Any price index that fails to include these current futures prices is deficient in not including the cost of all relevant elements of the utility function. Its incompleteness can result in a severe (negative or positive)

---

commonly considered to be a fixed welfare price index, recognizing that the usefulness of this or any other index depends crucially on the particular information and transaction costs assumed.

4. But we cannot, with a fixed quantity weighted index, say it has risen. The analysis is exactly parallel, indeed is identical, to the standard price index theory where $q$ is interpreted as current services. See R. G. D. Allen, "The Economic Theory of Index Numbers," *Economica* 16 (August 1949): 197–203.

5. The current futures price of the ith consumption service at moment t, $p(i, t)$, is related to the future (or forward) price currently anticipated at moment t, $f(i, t)$, by an im-

bias of indicated change in the money price level of "life." Prices of current services may rise, while futures prices (present money prices of claims to future services) fall more than enough to lower the money cost—or the opposite may happen.

The major difficulty in making our index operational is that separate futures markets or contracts do not exist for all future consumption services.[6] As a result, some futures prices required for a complete iso-utility price index will not be directly observable in explicit market prices. But since assets are sources of future services, asset prices provide clues to prices of present claims on future consumption. Current wealth can be represented by the sum of all asset values or, equivalently, interpreted as the sum of all present valued claims to all consumption service flows over time. Symbolically, if there are $m$ assets, wealth is denotable by:

$$W_A \equiv \sum_{j=1}^{m} P_A(j)\, Q_A(j) \equiv \int_{0}^{\infty} \left[ \sum_{i=1}^{n} q_A(i, t)\, p_A(i, t) \right] dt \tag{4}$$

------

plicit market rate of interest, $r(i, t)$; $p(i, t) = f(i, t)e^{-r(i, t)}$. If interest rates are assumed not to vary over different consumption service flows, equation (2) restated in terms of forward, rather than futures, prices is therefore:

$$W_A = \int_{0}^{\infty} \left[ \sum_{i=1}^{n} q_A(i, t)\, f_A(i, t) \right] e^{-\int_{0}^{\infty} r_A(t)\, dt} dt \tag{2}$$

Our terminology here may be somewhat confusing, since "futures" conventionally refers to the price paid later but agreed to now in a futures contract on a commodity exchange, while "forward" price is also often used to refer to a price to be paid in the future upon future delivery but agreed to now. With apologies to our readers, and on the assumption that forewarned is forearmed, we use the word "futures" to denote a price agreed to now, "payable now" for services to be received in the future.

6. H. S. Houthakker ("The Scope and Limits of Futures Trading," in *The Allocation of Economic Resources*, ed. Abramovitz et al. [Stanford: Stanford University Press, 1959], 134–59) theoretically examines why futures markets exist only for a rather small number of commodities. The answer to this important question must be based on the transaction costs of purchasing and selling particular commodities. These costs are determined, in part, by the costs of obtaining information about "characteristics" of assets and the distribution of such information among transactors in society (where "characteristics" is an economic and not a physical concept) and have implications for the essential properties of money (cf. K. Brunner and A. H. Meltzer, "Some Further Investigations of Demand and Supply Functions for Money," *Journal of Finance* [May 1964]: 240–83).

*where* $W_A$ is the individual's current nominal wealth and $[Q_A(j)]$ is the current vector of asset quantities that would yield his intertemporal utility-maximizing consumption service stream $[q_A(i, t)]$. If assets are standardized in terms of their present and future service flows, the current vector of asset prices $[P_A(j)]$ can therefore be used as a proxy for current futures prices, $p_A(i, t)$.

When relative prices change, one can, in principle, determine the vector of assets $[Q_B(j)]$, which will yield the minimum cost iso-utility consumption service stream $[q_B(i, t)]$ at the new set of asset prices $[P_B(j)]$ and implicit futures prices $p_B(i, t)$. Current asset prices can therefore be used to construct our constant welfare price index

$$P_{AB} \equiv \frac{W_B}{W_A} \equiv \frac{\sum_{j=1}^{m} P_B(j)\, Q_B(j)}{W_A} \tag{5}$$

where $W_B$ is the nominal cost of the vector of assets that will yield a flow of present and future consumption services equal in utility to the initial condition A consumption service stream.

It is crucial to emphasize that the vectors $[Q_A(j)]$ and $[Q_B(j)]$ must include all assets—consumer and producer, durable and nondurable, tangible and intangible, financial and nonfinancial, human and nonhuman. All sources of present and future consumption services must be considered. The vectors do not represent the actual assets held by the representative individual, but the asset combination that would yield the individual's desired consumption service flows. An individual may hold some assets that yield the exact pattern of consumption service flows that he demands over time—for example, a house that yields his present and future desired housing service flow. But, more generally, due to transaction costs, individuals will hold some assets not because they yield services that coincide with their consumption plans, but because they are an efficient form in which to hold wealth. The services from these assets or the assets themselves are later sold and exchanged for desired consumption services. Human capital is the most obvious example.

Since our asset price index is not constructed on the basis of assets actually owned by an individual, we are therefore not measuring whether the individual is better or worse off after a change in prices, only whether he requires more or less money to reach the same utility level. We must distinguish between actual shifts in the budget constraint with corresponding welfare changes and changes in our measure of inflation. $W_B$ is compared with $W_A$ to determine the change in the individual's money cost of a constant utility level. The individual's actual nominal wealth under condition B must be compared with $W_B$ to determine if he is better or worse off under the new set of prices. An individual, for example, may own a coal mine not because he consumes the coal yielded by the mine over time, but because the coal mine is an efficient form in which to hold his wealth. He sells most of the coal for income to purchase other consumption flows, and he intends to sell the mine and retire to an Hawaiian resort in a few years. If under condition B the only change is an increase in the price of coal, the individual's current wealth will rise more than $W_B$; he is better off while he experiences an inflation. Alternatively, if the price of Hawaiian land increases under condition B, the individual's nominal wealth remains unchanged (if he did not own any of the land) while $W_B$ increases; he is worse off and experiences an inflation. Any combination of inflation or deflation and better off or worse off is possible.

### III. The Systematic Bias of Current Service Flow Price Indices

A money price index based on considerations we have outlined is fundamentally different from the CPI, which is constructed on the basis of prices of *current* consumption services. The CPI considers the prices of only a part of the utility function and is therefore inadequate in principle as a constant utility money price measure. The CPI attempts to measure changes in the cost of only the iso-utility current consumption flows and therefore supplies an answer to a question distinct from whether the present money cost of consumer utility has changed.[7]

Current service flow prices are related to asset prices by implicit real rates of interest, and therefore our iso-utility price index is logically equivalent to an index based on current service flow prices and a broadly defined interest rate vector. If our representative individual moved to a new society where current

7. It is interesting to note that a major gap between a theoretically correct constant utility price index and the actual CPI is often said to be the improper inclusion of some consumer durable prices, such as new and used automobiles and houses, in the index. The proper price for these durables is said to be the current rental price or current cost of using the services from the asset and not the purchase price of the asset itself (cf., e.g., P. O. Steiner, "Consumer Durables in an Index of Consumer Prices," in U.S. Joint Economic Committee, *Government Price Statistics*, part 1, *The Price Statistics of the Federal Government: Review, Appraisal and Recommendations*, 305–35. We would claim, on the other hand, that the CPI is inappropriate because of the emphasis on current prices and the insufficient weight given to asset prices.

service flow prices are identical but where real interest rates are higher, our iso-utility price index would fall. The individual would substitute future consumption for present consumption, and his money cost of life would decrease.[8]

If we assume that society's equilibrium rate of time preference and real productivity of investment remains constant, is there any reason to suppose that use of a current service flow price index provides a deceptive measure of inflation? If real interest rates remain constant and the prices of current services and the prices of current assets move together, then, as a practical matter, a current service price index can be used as a perfect proxy for the theoretically correct wealth price index. There is, however, reason to expect a major systematic discrepancy in the transitory movement of a current service flow price index and a current asset price index. And it is this discrepancy which makes a current service flow price index an especially poor short-run indicator and target of monetary policy.

Changes in the quantity of money cause a "nonadiabatic" adjustment process in the money market which is terminated when all prices have changed proportionately. The initial price changes will depend upon how the monetary change is accomplished; but, ignoring distribution effects among individuals which may cause permanent changes in relative prices, the initial changes will "*diffuse* themselves equally after a certain time through all price levels alike."[9] But all prices may not change at the same rate. Keynes emphasized the possibility that price levels might not be rapidly "diffused" and that the failure of different price levels to move in the same way was a crucial element in the explanation of short-period fluctuations. Differential adjustment speeds among prices, of consumption goods and capital goods (or of service flows and durable assets) in particular, formed a cornerstone of his theory of the trade cycle.[10]

The behavior of current service flow prices relative to asset prices as a crucial element in the transmission process between monetary stock changes and

---

8. On the contrary, *nominal* interest rates (current mortgage rates) enter the CPI positively. An increase in nominal interest rates due to an increase in anticipated future (or forward) prices which leaves real rates and current futures prices unchanged will not alter our price-of-wealth index.

9. Keynes, *A Treatise on Money*, 90.

10. Ibid., ch. 7; Leijonhufvud's recent interpretation of Keynes emphasizes the importance Keynes placed on an "inappropriately" low relative price of assets (or high interest rate) as a "cause of unemployment" (A. Leijonhufvud, *On Keynesian Economics and the Economics of Keynes: A Study in Monetary Theory* [New York: Oxford University Press, 1968], 335–38).

economic fluctuations has also been emphasized by Friedman and Schwartz.[11] They maintain that monetary changes temporarily affect real income by producing transient changes in the interest-rate structure, defined by the ratio of current rental prices of services to the price of current assets as sources of the services, that is, by changing wealth relative to income. A decrease in the supply of nominal money, for example, decreases the demand for and prices of financial and nonfinancial assets as individuals adjust their portfolios by attempting to add to their depleted cash holdings. This causes asset prices to fall relative to service flow prices and relative to the cost of producing new assets. (The general fall in the asset price level is a rise in "the" real interest rate; wealth falls relative to income.) In turn, the reduced profitability of producing new assets decreases their production (i.e., leads to a fall in the rate of "investment"), and the higher interest rate implicit in the current rental asset price ratio stimulates asset purchases relative to rentals (i.e., leads to a rise in the rate of "saving"— in the sense that consumption of current services is reduced).[12]

If such an "interest-rate" mechanism actually operates, then short-run effects on "the purchasing power of money" of a change in the rate of growth of money will be underestimated by a current service flow price index compared with an index that also includes asset prices. But, unfortunately, we have not been able to verify the existence of such a mechanism. Very little reliable information exists on transaction prices of used assets and almost none on a quarterly or monthly basis.[13] Given the assumed importance of asset prices in the transmission of monetary changes, this deficiency in the data

11. M. Friedman and A. J. Schwartz, "Money and Business Cycles" (1963), in *The Optimum Quantity of Money and Other Essays* (Chicago: University of Chicago Press, 1969), 229–31.

12. In addition to asset prices generally adjusting more rapidly than current flow prices, prices of "liquid" (low transaction costs) assets will adjust more rapidly than prices of "illiquid" assets.

Even if relative prices are not affected by the monetary change, real income will be affected if anticipations about market clearing prices lag behind changing reality—which is costly to detect and adjust to instantly. See A. A. Alchian, "Information Costs, Pricing, and Resource Unemployment," in *Micro-economic Foundations of Employment and Inflation Theory*, ed. E. Phelps (New York: Norton, 1970), 27–52 (originally published in *Western Economic Journal* 7 [June 1969]: 109–28).

13. R. W. Goldsmith and R. E. Lipsey (*Studies in the National Balance Sheet of the United States*, vol. 1 [Princeton: Princeton University Press, for NBER], 1963) have constructed an annual wealth price index in the context of estimating a national and sectoral balance sheet. The components of their index, however, are not based on transaction prices but

and lack of any previous systematic empirical analysis of the behavior of asset relative to flow price is truly shocking. Some suggestive evidence on the existence of this cyclical relative price process can be obtained, however, by examining recent movements in common stock price indices relative to flow price indices and by examining movements in estimates of "the" real rate of interest. Although there are significant problems in the interpretation of the movement of stock prices (see section VI), they should be included in our iso-utility price index since they implicitly measure current prices of capital assets owned by corporations and represent the only readily available data on current market prices of assets. And changes in the real rate of interest can be considered an indirect measure of changes in the relative prices of service flows to capital stocks.[14]

The sharp decrease in the growth rate of money during 1969 provides a classic example of the bias involved in measuring inflation by considering only, for example, movements in the CPI. Narrowly defined money, which had grown at a 7.6 percent annual rate over the two previous years, grew at only a 2.9 percent annual rate from January 1969 to February 1970. (Most of this restraint, as

---

on owner estimates of the market value of their property (for farm real estate and for most of the single-family house data) and on construction costs (for commercial, industrial, and residential structures and for producer and consumer durables). Reliance on cost data limits our indices solely to measures of new asset prices. Over long periods this procedure may not yield biased price estimates of all existing assets but will most certainly yield misleading current asset price measures in a short-run cyclical context when reproduction costs are considerably more rigid than market prices. L. Grebler, D. M. Blank, and L. Winnick (*Capital Formation in Residential Real Estate* [Princeton: Princeton University Press, for NBER, 1956], appendix C), for example, compare the market "prices" (i.e., owner estimates) of houses with the construction costs for the 1890–1934 period and conclude that, although there is close conformity between the two series over decade-long periods, market prices fluctuate more widely than construction costs, and there are significant divergencies between the series over shorter periods of several years.

Market transaction price data for used assets are available in trade publications and dealer catalogues for cars, trucks, and farm equipment; and less complete price data possibly may be collected by other trade associations.

14. It should be noted that although our discussion emphasizes that movements in asset and service prices differ largely because of differing rates of adjustment to cyclical monetary disturbances there may also be a significant secular bias due to changing equilibrium real asset yields. (The apparent increase in real rates of interest over the years is ignored in our discussion.)

recorded in the figures revised for the unusually large volume of Eurodollar borrowing in early 1969, came in the second half of 1969.) Although real magnitudes were clearly affected, this policy was generally considered to have been a failure in curbing the rate of inflation. The CPI, which rose at a 5.8 percent annual rate during the second half of 1969, showed no sign of decelerating and rose at a 6.0 percent annual rate during the first half of 1970. Absence of any perceived response of prices in the face of rising unemployment led to the total abandonment of monetary restraint during 1970 and early 1971 and ultimately to the imposition of wage and price controls. But there is some evidence that asset prices responded almost immediately and quite dramatically to the change in policy.

Standard and Poor's Composite (500) Common Stock Price Index started to decline in early 1969, and by June 1970 had fallen nearly 30 percent, to the level of early 1964. In addition, the real rate of interest as measured by the Federal Reserve Bank of St. Louis (the nominal corporate Aaa bond yield minus the average annual rate of change of the GNP deflator over the previous twenty-four months) rose about one percentage point during the last half of 1969 and the first half of 1970—from 2.3 percent in June 1969 to 3.3 percent in June 1970.[15] This evidence suggests that asset prices declined relative to flow prices over the period and that movements in the CPI severely underestimated the deflationary effects of the tight money policy.

15. The Federal Reserve Bank of St. Louis discontinued publishing their real rate series shortly after this episode. Although their measured real rate showed remarkable stability over the 1960s, this unique precipitous rise should have been expected as part of the normal relative price reaction to monetary disturbances. What might have been misleading is that the previous tight money episode of 1966, although similar in magnitude to 1969, did not produce such severe relative price changes. (The money stock showed no change from April 1966 to January 1967 after rising at about a 6 percent annual rate over the previous year. This produced a clear deceleration of the rate of increases in the CPI, which rose at a 4.5 percent annual rate from January to August of 1966 and only a 1.6 percent annual rate over the following six months; while stock prices, which fell more than 13 percent from January to August 1966, quickly recovered and rose more than 8 percent over the next six months, the St. Louis real rate remained essentially unchanged over the period, rising less than ten basis points from April to August 1966 and then quickly falling back to and then below its original level.) This dramatic difference in the relative price movement between the two most recent contractionary episodes may explain why the downturn in economic activity was much milder in 1966–67 than in 1969–70, but the surprising flexibility of flow prices in 1966 remains unexplained.

## IV. Current Output Flow Prices, Stock Prices, and the Demand for Money

Another commonly employed index of inflation is the GNP deflator, which measures the price of current output flows. This price index includes the prices of newly produced assets but does not include the prices of previously existing items of wealth and therefore is conceptually distinct from our iso-utility wealth price index. Therefore, although it is useful for other purposes, a current output price index also provides a biased estimate of changes in the money cost of consumer utility. The theoretical considerations outlined above with regard to the bias in the movement of the CPI compared with a wealth price index also suggest a similar systematic bias in the movement of the GNP deflator relative to a wealth price index. Prices of already produced assets will, we conjecture, generally be more flexible than prices of currently produced goods, which are based on current costs that are often made less flexible by long-term contracts. And given the rigidity of current production costs relative to asset prices, a fall in the rate of growth of money decreases the profitability (and therefore the rate) of new asset production. Concern during 1969–70 about the rigidity in the rate of rise of current output flow prices should therefore be based on the evidence this gave us on the extent of the recession, not on the extent of the inflation.[16]

The GNP deflator is incorrectly used not only as a measure of inflation, but also almost universally used as the deflator of nominal money balances in demand for money studies. If, however, money is considered to be a capital asset and the demand for money treated as an application of the general theory of wealth constrained intertemporal portfolio choice, the purchasing power of money is more meaningfully measured in terms of our price of wealth index.[17]

16. In a crude "monetarist" model such as Anderson and Carlson's (L. C. Anderson and K. M. Carlson, "A Monetarist Model for Economic Stabilization," Federal Reserve Bank of St. Louis, *Review* 52 [April 1970]: 7–25), changes in money imply changes in nominal income; and the movement of current output prices, which depends on past output price changes, determines the division of the nominal income change between real income and prices. Therefore, the flexibility of current output flow prices is an important determinant of cyclical economic activity.

17. One of the major developments in monetary theory in the postwar period has been the integration of monetary theory with capital theory and the recognition of money as an asset in an optimum wealth portfolio (see, e.g., M. Friedman, "The Quantity Theory of Money: A Restatement" [1956], in *The Optimum Quantity of Money and Other Essays* [Chi-

Final choice of the proper price deflator in the demand for money, however, is conditional upon the particular structural specification from which the demand for money is derived. An explicit theory of the demand for money is necessary before we can determine the price index that should be used. If money is alternatively considered, for example, solely as a medium of exchange and the demand for money derived on the basis of an inventory-transactions-type model, the use of the GNP deflator as the relevant price variable in the demand for money function remains theoretically unjustified. Money is used to purchase assets of varying durability and age. The demand for money therefore cannot be dependent solely on the prices of current output flows which represent only a part of what money can buy. Hence, within the context of a transactions demand framework or a wealth portfolio choice framework, the GNP deflator is incomplete, and the purchasing power of money could be more meaningfully measured in terms of our more inclusive price of wealth index.[18]

If nominal money balances are deflated by our asset price index, then the connection between income (not wealth) velocity of money and the demand for real cash balances is no longer as direct as once thought. The ratio of our asset price index to the current output price index that is used to deflate nominal income now enters as an additional variable; that is, both asset prices and current output prices enter the velocity function. Since asset prices are gener-

---

cago: University of Chicago Press, 1969], 51–67; and J. Tobin, "Money, Capital, and Other Stores of Value," *American Economic Review* [May 1961]: 26–37). Friedman's empirical work explicitly takes account of the fact that money holders "judge the 'real' amount of cash balances in terms of the quantity of goods and services to which the balances are equivalent, not at any given moment of time, but over a sizable and indefinite period" (M. Friedman, "The Demand for Money: Some Theoretical and Empirical Results" [1959], in *The Optimum Quantity of Money*, 121) by deflating nominal balances by "permanent" or "expected" prices. But this price variable is merely a weighted average of current and past GNP deflators and does not properly consider anticipated future prices as embodied in current asset prices.

18. Keynes (*A Treatise on Money*, ch. 6) defines two price indices, a cash-transactions index and a cash-balances index, that may be superior deflators of nominal balances within these theoretical frameworks. Both of these indices, like our iso-utility wealth price index, include all objects of possible expenditure, but the weights applied to the objects are significantly different. The cash-transactions index weights objects in proportion to the amount of money transactions to which they give rise per-unit time, and the cash-balances index weights objects in proportion to the demand for money they occasion, representing the $P$ in the Fisher and Cambridge quantity equations, respectively.

ally more flexible than output prices, if "real" balances are (incorrectly) defined in terms of a current output price index (and asset prices ignored), a decrease in the nominal stock of money leads to an overestimate of the initial resultant decline in real cash balances and hence to an "unexplained" increase in velocity. Movements in the relative prices of assets to flows may explain the initial offsetting changes of velocity in response to monetary changes without invoking a presumption of a short-run disequilibrium (i.e., slow adjustment). The introduction of a vector of interest rates (to reflect relative prices of current services and wealth) in an incorrectly specified demand for "real" money may then serve as a proxy for the more complete price of wealth deflator. This implies that use of the incomplete current output price index as the price deflator in the demand for money induces, to some extent, the observed existence of a significant interest rate effect on the demand for "real" cash balances. If a wealth price index were employed instead, interest rates would then implicitly enter in a more general way, while "the" observed interest rate effect would be reduced and possibly eliminated.[19]

The question is essentially an empirical one of whether the commonly used interest rates on financial assets are sufficient to pick up this short-run "liquidity" effect of changes in money on the relative prices of existing stocks and flows. The significance of the dividend yield in the demand for money may, in fact, be reflecting the inability of the prices of financial assets to completely pick up this relative price movement.[20] As shown in equation (1.1), the dividend yield is statistically significant in a quarterly demand for money regression over the 1951–71 period.[21]

19. This factor is taken account of most fully in Brunner and Meltzer's empirical work (e.g., Brunner and Meltzer, "Some Further Investigations," and A. H. Meltzer, "The Demand for Money: The Evidence from the Time Series," *Journal of Political Economy* [June 1963]: 219–46). They, however, use a price index for nonhuman wealth not as a measure of the purchasing power of money, but as a deflator of the wealth constraint. They assume the relevant deflator of nominal balances is the GNP deflator, and it is therefore entered as an additional variable in the demand for money.

20. M. J. Hamburger, "The Demand for Money by Households, Money Substitutes, and Monetary Policy," *Journal of Political Economy* 74 (December 1966): 600–623.

21. $M_1$ equals currency plus demand deposits, P is the GNP deflator, Y is nominal GNP, $r_s$ is the four- to six-month commercial paper rate, $r_D$ equals Standard and Poor's dividend yield of corporate stock, log refers to natural logarithm, $\bar{R}^2$ is the coefficient of determination adjusted for degrees of freedom, DW is the Durbin-Watson statistic, and SE is the standard error of estimate. The values in parentheses are the t-values of the estimated

$$\Delta \log (M_1/P) = -.0011 + .3096 \, \Delta \log (Y/P) - .0044 \, \Delta \log r_s - .0359 \, \Delta \log r_D$$
$$\qquad\qquad\qquad\qquad (4.66) \qquad\qquad\quad (0.78) \qquad\qquad (2.87)$$

$$\bar{R}^2 = .295 \qquad DW = 1.06 \qquad SE = .0058 \qquad\qquad\qquad\qquad (1.1)$$

But the significance can be attributed solely to the variability of real stock prices and not to the variability of real dividends. If, as in equation (2.1), we substitute stock prices deflated by the GNP deflator for the dividend yield in the above regression (where S refers to Standard and Poor's 500 Common Stock price index), we observe that stock prices actually enter slightly more significantly than the dividend yield. This implies that, if anything,

$$\Delta \log (M_1/P) = -.0011 + .2914 \, \Delta \log (Y/P) - .0053 \, \Delta \log r_s + .0369 \, \Delta \log (S/P)$$
$$\qquad\qquad\qquad\qquad (4.29) \qquad\qquad\quad (0.95) \qquad\qquad (2.91)$$

$$\bar{R}^2 = .297 \qquad DW = 1.03 \qquad SE = .0058 \qquad\qquad\qquad\qquad (2.1)$$

changes in dividend payments go in the "wrong direction." Further, as shown in (2.1a), stock prices become insignificant when the same regression is run over the same period using annually averaged data.[22] Both of these pieces of evidence suggest that the dividend yield enters the demand for money function not as a measure of the direct cost of holding money but as a proxy for the short-run movement of asset prices relative to the GNP deflator.[23] In addition,

---

regression coefficient. The regression is reported in first-difference form since $r_D$ enters a level regression highly positively with a DW less than .2, indicating that clearly a variable is missing. Even in the first-difference form, the autocorrelation of the residuals remains disturbingly high.

22. Our hypothesis implies that cycle average data would reduce the statistical significance even further. The annually averaged regression for the dividend yield indicates slightly better results.

$$\Delta \log (M_1/P) = -.0129 + .5757 \, \Delta \log (Y/P) - .0217 \, \Delta \log r_s - .0420 \, \Delta \log r_D$$
$$\qquad\qquad\qquad\qquad (3.57) \qquad\qquad\quad (1.36) \qquad\qquad (1.42)$$

$$\bar{R}^2 = .463 \qquad DW = .871 \qquad SE = .0134 \qquad\qquad\qquad\qquad (1.1a)$$

23. Similarly, changes in the quantity of money can be expected to influence stock prices in the short run not, as commonly believed, because stocks are close substitutes for cash balances or because the short-run liquidity effect influences the rate at which future earnings are discounted, but because of the differential flexibility of stock prices to the monetary change. Fisher (The Purchasing Power of Money, ch. 9) outlined a similar mechanism in the context of the transactions version of the quantity theory. He emphasized that

the significance of stock prices in a short-run but not in a long-run demand for money regression also provides evidence against the hypothesis that stock prices enter as a wealth variable as, for example, Thompson and Pierce maintain.[24]

$$\Delta \log (M_1/P) = -.0127 + .5767 \, \Delta \log (Y/P) - .0266 \, \Delta \log r_s + .0282 \, \Delta \log (S/P)$$

$$(3.36) \qquad\qquad (1.68) \qquad\qquad (0.98)$$

$$\bar{R}^2 = .429 \qquad DW = 1.01 \qquad SE = .0138 \qquad\qquad\qquad (2.1a)$$

### v. Policy Implications

Nearly fifty years ago Keynes emphasized the fundamental policy mistakes risked by the use of an inappropriate price index. He claimed that Churchill returned England to the gold standard in 1925 at the prewar parity primarily because Churchill was "gravely misled by his experts" who, by using the inappropriate but commonly employed wholesale-price index, significantly underestimated the extent of the necessary deflation.[25]

An analogous situation may exist today. Presently employed price indices are improper measures of the change in the money cost of an iso-utility consumption package. Reliance on these biased numbers as an indicator or target of monetary policy makes it difficult for the monetary authorities to know what

——

many prices are rigid and are likely to change less than in proportion to monetary fluctuations in the short run, and, therefore, other prices must change more than in proportion in the short run for the quantity equation to hold; and he noted that stock prices are likely to be the most "supersensitive" of these other prices to changes in the quantity of money. Since the quantity equation is now generally stated in income form, where "the" price level that is determined does not include existing items of wealth, this mechanism cannot be recognized.

24. T. D. Thompson and J. R. Pierce ("A Monthly Model of the Financial Sector," presented at the Konstanzer Seminar on Monetary Theory and Policy, Konstanz, West Germany, June 1971) use a total public wealth variable based on Goldsmith and Lipsey's work in a monthly demand for money study. But month-to-month changes in their variable are dominated by stock price changes. In addition, Thompson and Pierce fail to distinguish between nominal and real values of wealth and money and assume (as most macro models do) that the money market can only be cleared by movements in a small subset of interest rates on financial assets, ignoring the possible short-run adjustment of a broader spectrum of asset prices.

25. J. M. Keynes, "The Economic Consequences of Mr. Churchill" (1925), in *Essays in Persuasion* (New York: Norton, 1963; reprinted, 1938), 249–50.

they are doing, let alone what they should be doing. And action on the basis of these numbers can lead to inappropriate decisions; policy changes will often come too late and move too far. Recent monetary policy provides an instructive example. The authorities' preoccupation with the movement of inappropriate flow price indices to the almost complete exclusion of asset prices was partially responsible for a monetary policy that was too easy for too long a period (1967–68) and then a policy that was too tight for too long a period (1969) followed by a policy that was once again too easy (1970–early 1971). A crude modification of the CPI with, say, an index of stock prices would have provided a much more useful indicator and target for price level stability.[26]

Our discussion also helps explain the general reluctance of contracting parties to adopt escalator clauses. If long-term contracts were set in "real" terms, that is, tied to "the price level," economic uncertainty would seem to be decreased.[27] But "the price level" must be made operational by a particular, arbitrary, and incomplete price index. And the fact that price indices are not generally used in long-term contracts (or a tabular standard not adopted) provides some evidence that the indices are poor measures of "the price level." Only if the variance of future anticipated price change is high will the use of, for ex-

26. H. C. Simons ("Rules versus Authorities in Monetary Policy," in *Readings in Monetary Theory*, ed. F. A. Lutz and L. W. Mints [Homewood, Ill., 1951], 349), in discussing the feasibility of a monetary policy designed to stabilize a price index, notes that the particular price index chosen "must be highly sensitive; otherwise, the administrative authority would be compelled to postpone its actions unduly after significant disturbances."

Realization of our ignorance about movements of the appropriate iso-utility price index does not necessarily imply that we should adopt a monetary rule. Discretionary monetary policy can still be based on income and employment statistics, and, of course, the inappropriate flow price indices could be used if we knew and took cognizance of the differing lags of adjustment of prices to monetary disturbances. In this context, our discussion may supply some support for those that believe that "money market conditions" (i.e., the behavior of interest rates) are a relevant short-run indicator of monetary policy. If the acceleration of the money supply is not considered, the inclusion of short-run interest rate movements with price movements may provide a much less misleading monetary indicator than price movements alone, since price anticipations are probably relatively rigid over the short term, and therefore short-run changes in market interest rates will be related to short-run changes in real rates and short-run changes in the relative prices of assets and current flows.

27. And a rationale for administrative wage-price "jawboning," that it is necessary to convince negotiating parties that the government intends to reduce the future rate of inflation, would be eliminated.

ample, a CPI price escalator clause decrease the anticipated variance of the real payoff. This may explain the more frequent use of price escalators in foreign countries that have experienced great price variability, and the recent trend towards increased use of price escalators in the United States (see J. V. Conti, "Price Escalators Gain in Popularity as Means to Pass on Cost Hikes," *Wall Street Journal*, June 3, 1971).

Strictly speaking there is no such thing as a "correct" price index. As we stated initially, the appropriateness of an index can be judged only by the answer it supplies to a particular decision problem. Our price index answers the standard textbook question of whether an individual needs more or less money to remain at the same level of satisfaction. An individual in attempting to determine how much money wealth he now needs for a particular level of present and future consumption would use our index.

But why, then, isn't there a demand for a price index that includes asset prices and why do movements in the CPI appear to be politically important?[28] Within the context of our model it is difficult to find a rationale for the fact that rising consumer service flow prices are generally unpopular, while falling asset prices are generally unpopular. The relevance of our intertemporal iso-utility index appears to be seriously questioned by common attitudes. One possible explanation may be that individuals fail to recognize that price changes of assets they do not own may significantly affect their money cost of life and their welfare. While individuals that, for example, own houses are aware of the decrease in their wealth when prices of houses fall, individuals that do not own houses do not appear to recognize that such a price change also affects them by lowering future housing service prices. Individuals are more fully aware of changes in their nominal wealth than of changes in the nominal cost of future consumption, possibly because an intertemporal consumption index is not now published. Alternatively, the CPI may be a politically relevant index because many individuals have utility functions that only contain current consumption service flows. Old individuals who do not have the real quantity of wealth they can leave their heirs as an important argument in their utility function, and housewives who do not make any capital transactions or budgeting

28. G. H. Kramer ("Short-Term Fluctuations in U.S. Voting Behavior, 1896–1964," *American Political Science Review* [March 1971]: 131–43) found that movements in the CPI, holding real income and some other variables constant, had no significant effect on the division of the national vote for the U.S. House of Representatives over the 1896–1964 period.

decisions within the family, for example, will both be myopic in terms of the time horizon of consumption services prices they are concerned with. This is the major unanswered question we are left with. Is the focus that is presently placed on the CPI as a measure of inflation merely an historical "accident," or are individuals narrowly concerned only about movements in prices of a small subset of the goods in their utility function?[29]

Would a redefinition of our concepts and the replacement of what is now commonly called "inflation" by "current consumer service flow price inflation" alter any of the recent discussions of many journalists, politicians, and economists of the extreme rigidity of the rate of price change and the need for some form of wage-price controls?[30] We will be able to answer these questions more satisfactorily after a price of wealth index is constructed and employed.

## VI. Can the Iso-utility Price Index Be Measured?

Our imprecise statements indicate what we think should ideally be (1) the modification in present measurements of the impact of monetary polity on the rate of inflation using an asset and service price index and (2) how they would influence monetary theory and policy. Although the direction of effect seems obvious to us, our conjecture that presently employed numbers yield misleading conclusions can be verified only by the construction of a superior index number (i.e., it takes a number to beat a number).

The desired constant utility price index, however, is difficult (expensive) to make operational. As we have already noted, without future contracts in all commodities, the explicit futures prices and quantities needed for construction of a wealth price index are unavailable. Current prices of assets of different life lengths provide a theoretical substitute, since they embody present prices of expected future service flows. But both the asset prices and asset quantities necessary for this index are extremely expensive to determine. We must have prices of a very broad spectrum of assets on which we presently have very little information. Our data must include prices of generally nonmarketable assets, such as human capital, and of assets of varying durability, so that we are able to produce the exact optimum current and future consumption service flows by ad-

---

29. Historically, the original price indices were narrowly based on internationally traded commodities (e.g., spices and grains).

30. It is particularly interesting to note that many of the important prices in our wealth price index (e.g., land and security prices) are not covered under the recent wage-price controls.

justing the asset mix. We may not be able to determine all these prices with any reasonable expenditure of resources, but surprisingly little reliable information exists on current prices of assets, and given the assumed importance of these prices in the transmission of monetary impulses, some effort in this direction would seem to be clearly economic. Collection of transaction price data on land, commercial and residential structures, producer and consumer durables and other tangible and financial assets, and the construction of a crude quarterly wealth price index would probably be worthwhile.[31]

Determination of the asset quantity vectors is also extremely difficult. As we have already noted, the assets actually held by an individual cannot be used as an index of the individual's desired future consumption. Some way of determining the composition of the individual's desired intertemporal consumption services—that is, of specifying his utility function or fixing particular constant asset weights—must therefore be devised. In addition, a more complete specification of the constraints on the individual's intertemporal transactions is also necessary to determine the relevant asset weights. An individual may, for example, demand a particular time stream of housing services under conditions of costless perfect futures or asset markets, but due to transactions costs actually buy and sell houses over time and consume a housing service flow that does not coincide with this "ideal" service flow.

And finally, even if asset prices and quantities were available, we would have significant problems in the interpretation of asset price changes. A change in the market value of an asset may reflect (i) a change in the price of an unchanged future service flow from the asset, (ii) a shift in preferences for this assets service relative to other assets, (iii) a shift in preferences for present consumption relative to future consumption, or (iv) a change in the anticipated magnitude of service flow from the asset. Any or all of these changes are likely

---

31. Stigler's price statistics committee (U.S. Congress Joint Economic Committee, *Government Price Statistics* [Washington, 1961], part 1, app. C, 95–99) makes a similar proposal. Considering the resources expended on the collection of price data on, for example, current food prices, which are such a small element in the relevantly defined utility vector, a reallocation of funds would seem to have a payoff in terms of providing a relevant answer to the question of determining price-level-induced changes in consumer welfare. Carl Snyder's attempt to measure "the general price level" (defined essentially as the P in the equation of exchange) included realty values, security prices, and equipment and machinery prices in addition to the standard cost-of-living items and was a movement in the correct direction ("The Measure of the General Price Level," *Review of Economic Statistics* [February 1928]: 40–52).

to be occurring simultaneously, and therefore the cause of a change in a particular asset price is difficult to determine. Changes (ii) and (iii) represent a shift in tastes while (iv) represents a change in asset quality; however, they are not conceptually different from the problems encountered in constructing the presently used indices. Changes in the preference or utility maps are ruled out in the presently used consumption service cost-of-living indices.[32] And the quality-change problem, whereby a change in the price of a given service flow must be distinguished from changes in the service flow, is also present in current indices and has already been handled in an innovative way for transactions prices of used cars (see P. Cagan, "Measuring Quality Changes and the Purchasing Power of Money: An Exploratory Study of Automobiles," *National Banking Review* 3 [December 1965]: 217–36).

For example, consider changes in common stock prices. The prices of common stock are included in our index because whether an asset such as a house is owned by a single proprietor or owned by him as a corporation should have no effect on the price of the house as manifest in the price of the stock. If the corporation represented not just the house but, as is typically the case, the services of a manager who rented and maintained the house, then the stock price would reflect also the manager's specific talents. Changes in the price of common stock would reflect changing prices of two things: the house services and the manager's talents specific to this activity. So much the better, for we have included human and nonhuman assets; the physical service flow being priced now has a second dimension, the flow of human services, and that may change just as a house may deteriorate. Stock prices contain no more conceptual problems than do the prices of any assets—or, for that matter, of current service flows in which one has to separate quantity changes and quality changes from price changes.

Although some of the conceptual problems in constructing a wealth price index are similar to those encountered in presently used flow price indices, the practical problems in the interpretation of asset price movements are more difficult. What would one do, for example, with the drop in common stock prices of 1969–70? Did it reflect claims to reduced real future services (a de-

---

32. This is not to say that there is, in principle, no computable index, for there is. One needs to know the equivalent utility vectors under the shifted preference map. But the base weighted indices (and all other for that matter) no longer can be interpreted as they are now. The difficulty posed by shifting preferences is no greater than for the present incomplete indices.

crease in quality), or lower prices of unchanged flows of future services (a deflation), or a shift in demand towards more present consumption relative to future consumption due to higher real rates of interest (brought about by "tight" monetary policy or by increased uncertainty leading to an increase in the rate of time preference), or perhaps a combination of all of these forces? For business corporation stocks, the price decrease reflects, at least in part, reduced or deferred outputs of future services. Fewer future cars will be produced or more will be deferred. The stockholder may think of anticipated future money earnings; they have fallen not necessarily because future (i.e., forward) prices (not futures) are expected to fall but possibly because of reduced anticipated profitability—much as if a tree would be expected to yield fewer apples as less fertilizer is applied in the coming years with lower demand expected for apples. If, however, all prices were expected to be lower in the future, the reduced earnings reflected in lower present stock prices would be truly a reduced price level of unchanged real claims. We conjecture both factors were present in the stock price fall—a reduction in present prices of given future services and a reduction in the future anticipated output and earnings relative to what it was before.[33] In other words, real future services are reduced and also the present price of a unit of future service has decreased. It is the latter we want to measure.

We can attempt to approximate the division of an asset price change into these two components by estimating changes in real rates of interest. A rise in the real rate would indicate a fall in future prices relative to current service prices. But we observe only nominal interest rates, which reflect the anticipated future rate of inflation. Market estimates of changes in the currently expected rate of change of future prices can be obtained by examining the ratio of stock prices of net monetary neutral firms to bond prices.[34] Alternatively, we could examine the movement of money interest rates relative to forward price spreads, quoted on commodity exchanges. The usefulness of these sugges-

33. These two factors are related. Since the prices of primary factors (especially labor) purchased by a firm are generally the most rigid, an unexpected decrease in the prices of future services sold by the firm will reduce future anticipated earnings.

34. Movements in the stock price to bond price ratio will not, however, represent solely a changing price anticipations effect. If the change in the anticipated rate of change of prices alters the demand for and quantity of real cash balances and hence the savings function, real interest rates will change. Stock prices of net monetary neutral firms will therefore not remain unchanged, but will move in the same direction as the anticipated rate of price change movement.

tions for obtaining market measures of anticipated inflation can only be determined by further empirical work.

The empirical problems involved are enormous. But whatever efforts may be made in this direction and whatever the results, we believe it is an error to assign all of the change in common stock and other asset prices to changes in anticipated future service flows with no change in present prices of such future flows . . . which is what is implicitly done now in commonly used price indices that ignore asset prices.

It may be cheaper to make empirical judgments about quality and quantity changes of current service flows than for future service flows. But what has been added is essentially a significantly larger number of items that should be priced; and weights for assets in the "typical" man's portfolio of possession of claims must be ascertained. This is not a new theoretical problem—it is an enlargement of an existing task. And we believe that the marginal cost of improving a price index along these lines is less than the marginal gains of improved monetary and fiscal policy consequent to less misleading indicators of inflation.

## ADDITIONAL REFERENCES

Hoover, E. D. "Index Numbers: Practical Applications." In *International Encyclopedia of the Social Sciences*, vol. 7. Ed. D. L. Sills, 159–63. New York: Macmillan, 1968.

Ruist, E. "Index Numbers: Theoretical Aspects." *International Encyclopedia of the Social Sciences*, vol. 7. Ed. D. L. Sills, 154–59. New York: Macmillan, 1968.

# BE WARY OF THE CPI COMMISSION REPORT!

## ARMEN A. ALCHIAN AND HAROLD M. SOMERS

The proposed elimination of quality improvements from the CPI for adjusting Social Security benefits to retirees constitutes an alarming breach of contract with the current and all future retirees! The proposal would deny to retirees, current and future, their current rights to automatically obtain, with the rest of society, the continuing improvements in quality even for goods that have not risen in price.

The explanation is simple. Everyone, retired or not, automatically receives the benefits of general societywide improvements in quality of goods and services, whether or not their prices change. The receipt of those benefits in quality is in no way affected by any changes in the price level. The Commission, by suggesting that the quality improvements be eliminated from the CPI, are, in fact, suggesting that these universal rights be expropriated from all retirees with benefits adjusted by the proposed CPI version.

Normally there are and have been and will continue to be improvements in quality of goods and services. These will occur often without any rise in the dollar price of the item. All consumers normally, over the years, get more for their dollar. The proposed adjustments for quality would expropriate those benefits from the dollar—from only the retirees' dollars.

We submit that the social commitment to all people under Social Security does not remove from retirees (as represented, for instance, by ourselves) this continuing social benefit obtained by everyone as a part of the progress made by the economic system. The commitment was that they would continue to enjoy, with everyone else, the benefits of those improvements. For example, cleaner air is part of that improvement and so are better TV reception and hip transplants.

This proposed expropriation of rights to the economic-progress value of the dollar would occur, not just for retirees, but for all people with contracts containing cost-of-living adjustments—even for the new U.S. Government Price-level Index Bonds!

This previously unpublished, undated article appears here by permission of the author.

# THERE'S ONLY 1 CAUSE FOR INFLATION

"What's causing inflation?" "What can be done about it?" and "Where will it all end?" The answer to the first question is easy. The second is much harder. And the third isn't important.

To see what causes inflation, it is necessary to know what is, and what is not, meant by inflation and also what is meant by "cause." Inflation usually means a continuing general rise in most prices, not a one-time jump in most prices without a continuing rise. The difference is important; they are caused by different events.

The second can be caused by any disaster which reduces production, such as a crop failure, a drought, invasion, war, plague of insects, or earthquake. In these cases, with a smaller stock of goods and the same amount of money in the society, prices will rise. The same amount of money chases fewer goods, to speak allegorically. These events usually are transient, and in that case, when output returns to normal, prices fall back to predisaster levels.

A recent example of a non-transient change is the reduced output of oil. That means a smaller total output. With the same amount of money, prices of goods would rise and then stay at that higher level. That is essentially a once-and-for-all change.

None of those events will cause a continuing rise in the price level, as has occurred in the United States since the mid '60s. The necessary and sufficient condition for a persisting, increasing price level is that the quantity of money be increasing relative to the stock of real goods and service. That and only that is the source of a persisting inflation.

History records no instances of a persisting (several years) inflation without the amount of money increasing relative to real goods, and no cases of steady increases in money relative to real goods without a similar inflation of prices. In every case, the increase in money relative to goods occurred because the supply of money persistently increased—not because the amount of goods persistently decreased with a constant supply of money. And that is true for the present one.

Reprinted, by permission of the author, from *Los Angeles Times*, 1979.

That pushes the question back to "What causes money to increase?" The answer is easy at one level of interpretation but extremely complicated at a deeper level. At the superficial level, it increases because the Federal Reserve of the United States prints money faster than before the 1960s and is printing it about 3% to 10% per year faster than goods can be increased. It follows by logic and in fact that the inflation could and would be stopped whenever the Fed stops creating more money so rapidly—the greenbacks which you have in your purse.

(Those who are knowledgeable in banking practices would add that the commercial banks, which you and I use for checking purposes, also create money. True, but the amount they can create depends, for reasons that are not important here, on how much paper money the Fed prints and spends.)

Inflation is not (I repeat not) caused by government spending more or taxing less or by unions seeking higher wages or by businessmen wanting bigger profits. Politicians blame businessmen for inflation. Businessmen will blame government and unions. Union leaders will blame businessmen, etc. But the blame rests solely on the excessive rate of increase in money. These incorrectly alleged causes have been around for generations, and yet there have been long periods of no inflation. But never has the amount of money persistently risen without an inflation, and never has a persisting inflation occurred without that money increase. So say it again: inflation is a result only and always of increased money relative to goods.

Another interpretation error occurs when people who measure prices say that inflation occurred this month because rents and meat prices rose, while last month it was gasoline and medical care. This interpretation confuses the fact and measure of inflation with the cause. Price rises don't cause inflation. They are the inflation of prices. They occur because money, and hence money demand for goods, has increased more rapidly than the amount of goods.

If you know of a way to persuade Federal Reserve Board Chairman G. William Miller and the rest of the board's members to restrain that increase, you would stop inflation. To do that you'd have to know what causes them to inflate the money so rapidly. But you'd have a hard time persuading them.

First, some members of the Fed don't even understand or admit the validity of the preceding simple facts and analysis. Second, those who are more informed are not prepared to reduce the rate of inflation of the money supply. They fear congressmen would complain that they were not accommodating the government's expenditure of more than was being taken in with explicit, specific taxes.

The Fed prints money to help the federal government spend more than the federal government collects in taxes, exactly the same way I would print money in my basement (if I had one of those money printing machines) to cover my shortfall of income below expenditures. Congress is not about to give up that privilege of having money printed for it.

Of course, the government could borrow existing money from the public, just as I could borrow to cover my personal deficit, and that would avoid an inflation of money and, hence, of prices, because the Fed would then not be printing more money for the convenience of the federal government. Borrowing existing money from the public to finance a deficit would not create inflation. And that is why it is not the federal government's deficit that creates inflation.

The printing of new money too rapidly for any reason or purpose is the culprit. If all of us had printing presses in our basements to run whenever we wanted to spend more than our income, you can imagine what a phenomenal rate of rise of prices would be occurring. But the federal government does have the right to create money, not surprisingly, and it doesn't hesitate to use that right. Indeed, every government, to be a dominant government, must exclusively have two things: the military and the money printing press.

To make more respectable their unwillingness to restrain the creation of more new money, the Fed argues (and they even have official committees of economists to lend credibility) that (1) restraint would cause a depression and unemployment, and (2) the inflation is necessary to maintain full employment.

The latter point is simply false, but I won't explain why here. And the first is a cop-out. Restraint will cause a depression only because the promise of restraint would not be believed by the public, given the past record of the Fed.

We all now believe the Fed will not reduce the rate of creation of money, despite its pompous statements about restraints. With that record of credibility, actual restraint in the rate at which money is being created would indeed be surprising. But once that reduced rate of money creation became reliable and once the public believes that policy of non-inflationary expansion of the money supply is the actual fact, and will so continue, then prices will not be raised, interest rates will fall, employment will be restored. A transient decrease in output and employment would be the probable consequence of the unexpected revisions in the rate of money creation, a revision that is becoming harder and harder to convince the public will take place this year or next year.

In sum, blaming government spending, unions, businessmen, or greediness misses the point. It is the increased money created by the Fed that is the culprit. That's easy to verify. What is more difficult, indeed, impossibly difficult so far, is to figure out a way to restrain the Fed from such large increases. But that's a different issue and should not confuse the creation of too much money as a "cause" of inflation in the technical economic sense with the political forces that are "causing" the Fed to print money at that inflationary rate. The former is easy to understand. The latter is much harder.

# PROBLEMS OF RISING PRICES

I believe inflation is inevitable as a long-run trend, with transient, decade-long interruptions of stable or falling prices. That forecast reflects my view of government. Inflation is a tax on money. Like any tax, it will be used. The more subtle, the less detected, and the less avoidable the tax, the better it is for those with predominant political power and the more surely it will be used. I join Keynes in at least part of the following: "progressive deterioration in the value of money through history is not an accident, and has had behind it two great driving forces—the impecuniosity of governments and the superior political influence of the debtor class."[1]

Since Keynes has been dead wrong in interpreting the effects of inflation, I cite him for eloquence, not authority. Furthermore, the "superior political influence of the debtor class" is not clearly significant. But impecuniosity of governments, that is, their desire to spend more and their ability to do so by creating money, is, I believe, irresistible for any government. And when we add the recent priestly dogma that increasing the money stock is a means of assuring high employment, there is no doubt that inflation at a transient varying rate is a way of life.

By inflation I mean either a single-shot rise in the price level or a continuing rising price level. Thus, I can interpret a rising price level as a sequence of factors, possibly overlapping, causing single-shot rises, though possibly so overlapping that one is unable to distinguish their putt-putt forces from a continuous jet stream.

Reprinted, by permission, from *Governmental Controls and the Free Market: The U.S. Economy in the 1970's*, ed. Svetozar Pejovich (College Station: Texas A&M University Press, 1976), 19–40.

1. J. M. Keynes, *Tract on Monetary Reform* (London, 1923; reprint New York: St. Martin's Press, 1971), p. 12. Is it a definition of government to say that any possessor of the dominant military power and monopoly of the base money is a government?

## Sources of Inflation

I turn first to sources of inflation. Two already have been mentioned—the ability to print money and the dogma that more *should* be printed to reduce unemployment. As causes of inflation, two factors should be distinguished: (1) changes in the ratio of money supply to money demand, and (2) factors that induce changes in that ratio—that is, that induce us to embark on an inflationary policy. An increased supply of money relative to demand creates higher prices. But the factor that persuaded the money suppliers to increase the supply of money is what induced us to embark on a monetary policy that creates inflation. Monetary policy is a *means* of creating inflation; the objective of the policy is the *reason* for resorting to inflation. Both are often called "causes." The increased money stock relative to demand creates inflation, whatever the reason ("cause") for embarking on the inflationary increase in the supply of money. Unless we keep those things distinct, we aren't going to get anywhere.

The supply of money can increase in a variety of ways. Gold or silver discoveries, development of new, more efficient forms of money (bank demand deposits) used along with the existing money, or the simple printing of more money by the official money printer for the "impecunious" government all are increases.

Certain interesting factors, events, or goals induce the government to spend more than its explicit tax income. To identify them, ask, "What do governments do?" The answer is, "More than before." That reply is especially valid when the costs can be spread over a wide range of people and their impact can thereby be attenuated below the individual's costs of preventing them. A larger fraction of national income will be taxed, and the larger that fraction, the greater the extent to which the printing press will be used to "balance the budget." That is the Keynesian "impecuniosity."

In addition, it has recently become respectable to create money by twisting the Keynesian doctrine that government should increase the money supply to counter major monetary contractions. That original Keynesian monetary prescription has been twisted particularly by political aspirants, for whom it is a congenial way to enhance their political status or use of government power. The new dogma is that employment is to be maintained—or, more accurately, efforts are to be exerted to try to maintain it—above that level maintainable in a free, liberal society in which people not assigned to jobs could investigate and choose those they themselves deem best. In other words, each person has the right to refuse to work for wages he, and he alone, deems unacceptable because of opportunities he believes to be discoverable elsewhere or available later. If we announce that action will be taken to assure current jobs at wages greater than those acceptable to both parties, we are announcing a policy of trying to maintain an impossibly low average rate of unemployment by assuring jobs and incomes to people whose services consumers think are not worth their asking price. The policy is to induce employers to buy their employees' services by increasing the employers' demand for their services and in turn by increasing the demand for those employers' products. This is not the desirable policy of avoiding monetary contractions; instead, monetary expansion is recommended for *any* reduction in actual employment.

The source of the (erroneous) belief that monetary expansion would assure such jobs—that is, that it would hold unemployment below that rate consistent with changed demands and with costs of getting information about new opportunities and costs for entrepreneurs to ascertain to what other tasks or outputs they should convert their productive facilities (I shall return to this point later)—is a result of confused analysis and misread empirical evidence. The employment acts in the United States and Britain simply assumed that we could somehow keep employment at that natural "full employment" rate, presumably by pure fiscal policy. But transient shifts in demand among firms and industries and products will induce higher rates of unemployment in some and lower rates in others. To prevent all unemployment increases in every sector is to attempt the impossible in a free, liberal society—a fact that still seems to escape most people. That doctrine was given an aura of respectability by the delusion of the Phillips curve.

In sum, at least two forces for inflationary monetary policy are present: "impecuniosity" of governments, and the attempt to assure full employment by money expansion (whether through government expenditures or otherwise). The former force regards money increases as regrettable but necessary, because we just "can't" balance the budget. The latter regards them as desirable. Who can beat a combination like that?

There are other policies intended to aid high employment and rapid adaptability to changing demands and supply conditions that do not involve monetary expansion. These policies attempt to lower that natural unemployment rate by, for example, cheapening the costs of ascertaining the best unexploited opportunities or by trying to avoid downward, transient shocks in the system caused by misguided, politically motivated monetary policy keyed to interest rates, balance of payments, and fixed exchange rates.

### Irrelevancy of Monopoly

*Anyone*, unions, business firms, or a single person, can set and persist in a price too high for his full employment or output. The belief that unions or large corporations have monopoly power and thus push up prices and cause inflation is a fallacious analysis and is wrong in fact. Any union or business or seller that pushes prices above its wealth-maximizing level will lose business and reduce employment. Resources will be released for use elsewhere, and prices elsewhere will have to be lower than they otherwise would be. The price level is not changed; relative prices are changed. Once a monopoly has set its best price, it will not raise prices higher, and not even a union, which some people think wants higher wages for the fewer and fewer remaining members who retain jobs at those higher wages, would raise the price level if it raised prices higher than its best price. The unemployed in that occupation would have to work elsewhere, lowering wages. Despite this analysis and empirical studies, some people (for example, Galbraith) try to incriminate corporations for driving up prices, while others (for example, Haberler) condemn the unions. Neither accusation is correct.

What is necessary is a will by the government to increase the stock of money to assure employment to anyone who raises his wage above the market clearing wage or price. To blame unions or corporations is to misdirect attention from the critical factor at work—the will to inflate the money supply to assure employment at whatever wages or prices people may ask. Anyone who raises his prices, be he college professor, gardener, or machinist, and to whom the government responds quickly in assuring full employment, can be said to "cause" inflation. But as we said earlier, the term *cause* is so ambiguous that we should avoid putting the proposition that way. We can say that the money supply increase creates inflation—that the money supply increase occurs as the government implements its promises of full employment assurance, revising expenditures when it observes unemployment (of some degree someplace). We could say that the particular people whose unemployment is the most important to the government policy makers will be the "more important" inducers of inflation, but I don't know who they are. Nor is it conducive to clarity of analysis to try to attach the concept of "cause" to any one of those stages of the process.

The amount of verbiage in the literature arguing whether to call the inflation cost-push, demand-pull, monopoly-union, monopoly-corporate, full-employment-assurance, or money-supply-increase inflation is dismaying. One

is reminded of the scandalous literature on the equality of savings and investment by the writings on the cause of inflation. Indeed, some people have even
proposed trying to test which is the operating cause! I suppose we might interpret that to mean they are proposing to test whether the government has a full-
employment assurance policy, whether it has increased the quantity of money,
or whether anyone ever raises his wages or prices to a height which creates less
than market clearing employment or output for him. As for myself, I perhaps
foolishly was willing to take each of those factors for granted with casual
though extensive evidence. An inquiry that does appear interesting to me is
this: Given all the above, to whose unemployment is government most responsive?

We cannot wholly abandon the monopoly element in inflation. One monopoly, the government monopoly of the supply of legal base money, does indeed
permit inflation. Without that monopoly, with open competition in the creation of separate, identifiable brands of money, it can be argued very cogently
and persuasively that inflation would be avoided. Suppliers of money, each
producing a different brand of money, would compete to produce the best
money—a noninflating one. However, this possibility will remain purely hypothetical and therefore is given no attention.[2]

Money is more than a lower-cost substitute for simple barter. It also is a
store of value, a measure of debt in generalized goods. Instead of expressing
or settling all debts or expressing them in single goods, a general package in
terms of the exchange value of a medium of exchange is an economically
useful institution. But while money may perform its function as a medium of
exchange (because of easy portability, recognizability, and divisibility), its
storability, or economic value of such future claims, is more uncertain. Furthermore, variations in its rate of inflation make the value more variable.
Money loses the predictability of its value. One of our great social institutions,
money, is damaged, and our wealth is subjected to greater variations, which we
all can justifiably regard as unjustifiable.

Disposable also is the excuse that inflation is a world-wide phenomenon,
like some disease that infects us all. Such error hardly merits notice, except that

2. For the two best discussions of which I am aware, see B. Klein, "The Competitive
Supply of Money," *Journal of Money, Credit and Banking* 6, no. 4 (Nov., 1974), and E. Thompson, "The Theory of Money and Income Consistent with Orthodox Value Theory," in *Trade,
Stability and Macroeconomics: Essays in Honor of Lloyd A. Metzler* (New York: Academic Press,
1974), pp. 427–53.

sometimes we are careless and think fixed exchange rates tying all countries' monies together are a cause of inflation, a mistake that confuses covariation with inflation. The world-wide deflation of the 1930's was a result of fixed exchange rates. Fixed exchange rates imply a similarity in price level movements, not necessarily inflation or deflation. Indeed, if exchange rates are allowed to respond to free, open-market forces, I know of no basis on which to predict whether countries would inflate faster or less fast, though I would bet on less correlation and faster inflation simply because the government is released from a restraint on the rate at which it can inflate.

## A Process of Pricing in Inflation

How do expectations operate in inflation? That process is, I believe, widely misunderstood, which means that my understanding of it differs from that of most other people. I believe an analysis along the following pattern is valid. When speaking of expected price, I mean, and economic analysis refers to (or should refer to), the price (1) that a person initially (now) sets (in other words, will accept) for his services or goods, and (2) at which he believes he will sell the amount he chooses to offer at that price. For example, a producer hopes, plans, or expects to sell some amount of product at a price. He sets that price and then soon begins to learn whether he gets the amount of demand he anticipated. If he does, that price (his expectation of his market clearing price) was correct. It was the price that did permit him to sell what he offered at that price. That actual price is the one he expected to be or believed would be the market clearing price. If it is not, he will sell less than he offers or he will find more demanded than he offers. He will learn whether it is an equilibrating price. Before asking how he learns that, if he does, let me emphasize in the strongest way that I know there is reason to assume the price he asks (his "expectation") is just as solidly, firmly, or confidently held if it is a higher price than yesterday's, by, say, 10 percent, as if it were the same price. In each case, that price is an actual price *and* a prediction of what the market clearing price is. It is asked (set) and it is not withdrawn at the instant sales deviate.

As I have argued elsewhere, price inflexibility is not a silly, uneconomic thing. Nor does price firmness mean unchanged price over time. It means unchanging price in the face of only *transient* reversible deviations of sales or production around what is believed to be a market clearing rate. Noncontinuous varying sales rates are not responded to by instant changes of prices. Production and inventories are among the adjusting variables.

A price that may turn out not to be an equilibrium price is just as slow to adjust in the face of new developing information if (1) it was set higher today in response to (erroneous) beliefs that the market clearing price was higher, or (2) it is the same as yesterday's price when no inflation was (erroneously) expected. If the price is wrong, in each case correct adjustment to the new equilibrating price is equally uncertain, costly, and time-consuming and is preceded, or accompanied, by changes in output or sales. Nor is information about all other market options and opportunities provided instantly and costlessly. The new market clearing price vector can not be discovered instantly. Actual prices "lag" behind the market clearing vector. That information lag is the pertinent lag, an "error" in forecast.

A price today that is the same as a past price is no more natural than a rising sequence of prices. It all depends upon what current demands will sustain.[3] So long as demand does not sustain the price (as a market clearing price), and so long as the parties do not know the new best price vector, the search for the new best prices and best alternative activities is no simple task. Nor are the processes and implications of the search well understood. It is no less complex during stable price expectations than during rising demands with rising price expectations. (Add to this complexity the long-term commitments or arrangements emphasized by D. Gordon in explaining why wages do not fall quickly enough to permit hiring of the unemployed, even though those who retain their jobs still receive higher wages than the unemployed are asking. Gordon's analysis also is consistent with the proposition that one should not expect rising demand to be synonymous with demand rising *above* the prices people expect to be appropriate for clearing the market.)[4] Whatever people believe is today's market clearing price is asked (or bid) and persists until they are convinced of their error. Then they have to search for more appropriate price, product, rate of output, and investment. An increased nominal demand—but not sufficient to exceed or match the increased current price—is as contractionary as a falling demand with constant prices. Demand for a good is relative not only to various other goods; it is relative also to an expected market demand for the good at the currently charged prices.

3. There is no inconsistency between this analysis and the Martingale property of prices. The interest rate reflects that average belief about future price levels. Hence, the *average* equilibrating price expectation for tomorrow is today's price plus the interest rate—the usual Martingale property. See A. Alchian, "Information, Martingales and Prices," *Swedish Journal of Economics* 76 (1974): 3–11.

4. D. F. Gordon, "A Neo-Classical Theory of Keynesian Unemployment," *Economic Inquiry* 12, no. 4 (Dec., 1974): 431–59.

In the usual jargon, the preceding discussion is translated into terms of anticipations or expectations of inflation not matching "actual" inflation. I prefer to identify prices now being set as the prices that are expected to be the present market clearing prices. These prices are actual prices—not "expected" prices. What is expected is that they will be market clearing.

Can the adjustment process be reversed? Can the "latest," unknown, equilibrium price vector be revised toward actual prices? This is the reverse of the common insistence on adjusting actual prices to the new, but unknown, market clearing vector. For example, many economists in the thirties strongly recommended monetary re-expansion to restore that market clearing nominal price vector up toward actual prices, rather than await the process of search, discovery, and convergence of actual prices with the low market clearing price vector to which actual prices have to be adjusted. How can the market clearing nominal vector be inflated to match current prices?

1. New money may be sprinkled from the skies, with all demands increasing until the formerly under-priced, over-demanded goods rise in price relative to the formerly over-priced goods. This plan will increase the average price in the clearing vector, and if we assume greater upward price adjustments in response to increased demand for goods that were more fully employed at existing prices, we might ease and quicken the convergence of the clearing vector and actual prices. Old money will be taxed (or depreciated) by the price rise, and initial recipients of the new money from the skies will gain wealth. If new money is given in exact proportion to the old money holdings of each person, there is no net interpersonal wealth transfer of money.

2. New money may be initially spent directly in the excessively priced vector, increasing demand there. In this case, the tax on moneyholders finances the intentionally increased relative demand in the "depressed" sector and brings a rise in the equilibrium market clearing price for that sector, thereby bringing it closer to the actual price. The equilibrium (absolute and relative) price structure over the whole economy approaches the actual prices. Increased demand relative to newly posited prices (which are the objective aspects of "expectations") increases output and employment. Sales exceed the expected sales at the prices that are believed to be market clearing prices. No lag of any actual prices behind any other prices (no relative price change) is involved. The pertinent lag is the lag of adjustment of actual nominal prices to the market clearing vector, for which search must be made. That informational lag is critical. It creates what we call the natural rate of unemployment, it is always present— during unanticipated inflation, unanticipated deflation, anticipated inflation,

and anticipated deflation—as long as the future (that is, the market clearing vector) is not costlessly, correctly perceived by everyone.

The excessively priced sector may require a greater increase in demand relative to the rest of the economy than can be financed by the inflation tax on money—and there is a limit to how much real wealth can be taxed by an inflation. In such a case inflation simply cannot finance the required shift. It will not restore full employment in that sector if that sector insists on, and is assured of, a higher real wage relative to other sectors. Expenditures financed by a direct tax on other forms of wealth or income must be used to shift relative demands sufficiently. But if these excessive prices are "assured" in enough sectors, it will be impossible to "assure" the excessive real demands, since the price vector would more than exhaust the social product at full employment.

Political assurance of full employment has the terrible problem of ascertaining whether current prices assured politically to everyone are compatible with physical production possibilities—a problem the free enterprise price system escapes because no one can have any assurance of profits or employment at whatever real income or price he deems "right." But we have politically made that commitment—or we act as if we have made that commitment—and now we naïvely wonder why we have inflation or more and more controls by government. Whatever other reasons are increasing the role of government, that desire for full employment certainly is.

A "puzzle" disposed by the preceding analysis is the so-called paradox of inflation and unemployment, or inflation and recession. The puzzle arises only if one assumes that a zero inflation rate is the basis on which people are making price commitments. If people expect the equilibrating, market clearing prices to be higher today than in the past, and yet if today the higher actual prices are not maintainable with full employment, what is adjusted? I know of no reason to expect prices to give way under that situation any more than when market clearing prices were incorrectly expected to be the same today as yesterday (incorrect because of a deflation).

*Deflation?* Does a reduced growth of the money stock and market demand below the anticipated inflation rate produce a less severe, shorter recession than does an equal-sized difference in money growth below a formerly constant price level? If so, ability to break a recent inflation without causing a long, severe depression would be enhanced. But I have no evidence for or against that possibility.

*Irrelevancy of cost push and demand pull.* This analysis does not say that demand increases and then prices go up. Nor is it a cost-push view either. Nor is monopoly power involved. If people believe and forecast that market clearing prices will be higher, they will enter the market with higher prices which they believe are market clearing prices. If demand has increased less than that forecast, people will not instantly revise their prices downward. The erroneous belief that they will instantly bid prices down assumes costless discovery of information about the state of market demand here and about opportunities elsewhere. If prices are too high, what will happen? Unemployment and recession will be the result; indeed, they are the process of the search for the new equilibrating price vector and wealth maximizing activities (if prices were too high initially).

This analysis of the stimulation of employment does not rely on the hoary, falsified dogma that wages lag behind prices. That phenomenon *does not* occur. There is no other conclusion that can be drawn from the extensive empirical analysis or from economic analysis.[5]

## The Pace of Inflation

How fast will inflation occur? It depends upon the expectations and commitments. Whatever the forecast inflation, the government will have to validate a higher rate of inflation if it attempts to maintain employment at every price asked by a seller. Once we have embarked on the policy of validating whatever price vector exists and however rapidly anyone wants more, there is no limit to the speed of inflation.

It is commonly believed that inflation is fed by insatiable desires and attempts of people to beat each other out, and that if only we would restrain our demands or prices, inflation would not occur. That is simply wrong. (Did we all become less greedy in the Great Deflation of the thirties?) What counts are *forecasts* of the equilibrium prices. Hence, even if we all miraculously, in saintly fashion, asked for lower real incomes, but had at the same time done so on the basis of too high a forecast of the market clearing price vector, inflation would

5. M. Friedman, "The Role of Monetary Policy," *American Economic Review* 58 (Mar., 1968): 10. Even so careful an economist as Friedman slipped into the "lag of wages behind prices" error in his presidential address of December, 1967. Scores of economists, in trying to understand the relation between inflation and employment, chased him down that alley but haven't yet understood that they are as much in error in taking that path. They accept that premise and then try to find the flaw someplace else. If one accepts that error, the negative-sloped Phillips curve is hard to dismiss, but if one grasps the error, the vertical Phillips curve for correctly anticipated inflation is obvious, as is avoidance of propositions about real wage changes supposedly inherent in the process.

be induced *if the government were to stand ready to assure full employment by monetary methods.*

The motivation for resorting to an inflationary policy is the political policy of validating whatever prices the public asks in order to "assure" employment by government action. That is what is implied by a full employment assurance policy. Then in this case the public, or that portion of it that asks for the greatest increases in price, sets the rate at which inflation must be created. The governmental monetary authorities will have shirked the responsibility that belongs to a monopolist in charge of the money stock. If any monopoly is to be blamed for inflation, it is clearly the government monopoly over the money stock, not any of unions or business, that is responsible.

It does not make any difference whether only one group asks for more than is sustainable at an equilibrium price vector with existing relative demands, or whether the whole economy asks for greater real income than can be produced if full-employment promises are believed and attempted. The price level will explode at whatever rate a portion of the public asks for prices above the equilibrium. There will be an explosion, determined not by choice of some inflation rate but by how fast the public thinks the government will respond to any unemployment.

What would stop the explosion? Obviously and forlornly, we should never have started the policy of full-employment assurance by monetary expansion, however much that expansion is done in the name of "fiscal" policy. Equally forlornly, we can now stop inflating the money stock and disappoint those who seek higher employment than is maintainable at their currently requested prices. That action would, aside from resulting in transient recession, amount to reverting to price controls by market competition, not by political power, the kind of market competition that says if you raise your price above the full-employment level acceptable to buyers you will be quickly and surely punished by loss of sales or employment—a penalty imposed by consumers, not by some government agent. Or we could try to reduce the natural rate of unemployment by lowering costs of search, discovery, and transfer to new, best alternative tasks.

### The Effects of Inflation

*Wealth Redistribution Effects.* The wealth transfer effects of inflation depend on whether it was under- or over-anticipated—except for the tax on non-interest-bearing money, usually the base money of the economy. Other forms of money usually pay implicit interest (for example, bank services), and it is difficult to know whether holders of bank demand deposits lose from an inflation of, say, 10 percent a year. Services rendered as checking services are not trivial.

For under-anticipated inflation a wealth transfer from net monetary creditors to net monetary debtors is implied and well established. Usually associated with the inflation is a shift in relative demands, which the inflationary increase in money stock was created to facilitate, possibly toward the borrowing sector or any other that happens to be politically strong. (To illustrate these demands, an example of a five-person economy is given in the appendix to this chapter.) The main moral is: Distinguish between the inflation and the relative demand shifts for which the inflationary money increase may have been initiated and financed by the inflation tax on existing money.

If the inflation is anticipated correctly by every participant with complete confidence, the interest rate will have an adjustment factor and all wealth transfers from net monetary creditors or net monetary debtors will cease except for a monetary asset or liability that does not pay interest (would cash and currency be an example?). Demand deposits would pay interest explicitly or implicitly. All monetary asset claims will be indexed (though by what index, I do not know). I suspect the short-term rate will dominate most interest rate contracts. If the adjustment is made in interest rate, the term of the loan is essentially shortened, as the interest rate includes adjustment for loss of capital value due to the rising price level. Capital is repaid earlier because the constant nominal amount due always represents the falling real amount of principal still due on the longer-term loan. This means the life length or term of the loan will depend on the rate of inflation that results or is forecast during the interim. A speeding up of the rate will result in higher interest rates being placed on the loan—if it is a long-term, floating-interest-rate loan—and a shortening of the average maturity of the loan.

*Resource Use Distortions.* If *everyone* zeroed in on the forecast with no greater uncertainty in their minds than for forecasts during zero rates of inflation, the effects of error of anticipated inflation would be no different than during deviations around stable prices. But that is not our world. Not everyone will have the same forecast, though the average of their beliefs could create exactly the right market interest rate. Therefore, even if the market interest rate did correctly anticipate the inflation, two effects are significant: (1) more people are disappointed, and some are pleasantly surprised, by the wealth transfers that do or do not occur because of the incorrect forecasts by different people, and (2) the capital structure is changed.

Two extremes are instructive. One person believes that the nominal rate is the real rate, with zero expected price-level rise. He invests only up to the point at which the real and nominal return on investments equals that high real rate. He later discovers that the price level rose while the real rate was lower. He has underinvested in real capital. Another person believes the real rate is low, say 1 percent, with the rest of the nominal rate reflecting expected price-level changes. He invests heavily in real investment but suffers a loss in real terms because the real rate was higher.

The noise and random alteration of investment results imply less efficient use of investible resources and also cause disappointment and annoyance. Confidence in the economic system and the monetary system as not having an excessive incidence of socially useless, "unjustified" gains and losses provokes attempts to alter the system by giving aid to each person who believes he has been abused.

The variance of outcomes to which we are exposed increases. We are forced to play a game with a larger, more "random" variance of outcomes—one larger than with a zero price level. That is another cause for dissatisfaction. Appeals to government to compensate for the large "unjustified" changes in wealth enlarge government. Even without price controls and appeals to government to force others to compensate us for those changes, the increased insecurity and inability to know how much our wealth will be worth later tends to reduce the willingness to save and invest. The belief that price controls are then necessary (along with mandatory allocations, "compensatory" taxes, and subsidies) increases the scope of government regulation of economic action.

There is more. Normally shifting relative demands and costs cause "unemployment," a process of seeking the new best available activities (whether of employees detecting best jobs or of producers trying to detect new most profitable products, investments, or output rates). That task is hard enough during stable price levels. With a price level more subject to larger, variable rates of increase, each person now has demand for his service affected by nominal changes as well as by relative changes. A new source of noise is added. With inflation at an unpredictable rate, a new source of confusion arises. Are the shifts real (relative to others) or nominal? If all shifts that were nominal impinged on each person equally on the demand side and the cost, or input, side and were of the same proportion in each, at least the relative shifts would be less confused. But that is not the way events are understood or news is transmitted. Sales rates change, then prices change—at least in some sectors. But in others, prices change faster, with sales rates not changing (especially if buffer inventories are more expensive). Prices do not all respond at the same rate, because, for one reason at least, information about what underlying factors have changed is not freely and instantly available to everyone.

The increase in noise because of the variable and imperfectly predictable increases in rates of inflationary demand makes detection of the shifting (if it is) market clearing activity and price vector more difficult and slower. Activities are less efficiently coordinated and directed.

This inefficiency may show up as overemployment, but it may induce higher quit rates if people believe options elsewhere are increasing faster than in their present jobs. I know of no theory to rely on to derive unambiguous implications. One could get a positive-sloped Phillips curve. As an aside, I believe that a trade-off between inflation and unemployment is misinterpreted. It confuses the recovery of prices from a recession and longer-run inflation. Increased rates of inflation over the expected rate may reduce the full-employment rate of unemployment, but that is not demonstrably a desirable thing. The choices of people in jobs are distorted toward accepting less than the best available job, because they are misled into accepting jobs at lower wages than they would have obtained with more search. This stricture applies to full-employment rates of unemployment. I conjecture that inflationary increases in demand that are faster than anticipated lead to too small unemployment—too little search for the better market clearing vector of prices and activities by all people, employees, employers, equipment owners, and so on. In real terms, output value is smaller.

The higher the inflation, the greater is its component of noise—or so I believe. Please do not ask me for hard evidence or proof. I "believe" a higher inflation rate will have a higher (in basis points, at least) variance. I cannot imagine a country with a 5 percent rate experiencing the same variance around that rate, or into the near or distant future, as one now experiencing a 40 percent rate.

Implicit in the preceding argument is a presumption that beliefs of price-level stability around zero percent average change are more accurate than around high rates of inflation. A belief, faith, goal, objective, or commitment to a money that does not depreciate or appreciate relative to most other goods is a characteristic of a preferred money. I believe a zero average rate is a more clearly identified and "agreed-upon" rate than is 1 or 2 or 3 percent—any of the other infinite alternatives. But once belief in a departure from zero as a goal or criterion occurs, I know of no way to identify or produce agreement on an alternative. Do higher rates of inflation create greater interpersonal dispersions of predicted rates by different people? B. Klein seems to have demonstrated that the higher the rate, the larger the variance and the less likely are differences in successive price-level changes to be negatively correlated.[6] The variance and error for a given interval—say, a five-year span—will be larger because of the more highly positively correlated first differences. The available evidence, though it is not overpowering, is sufficiently strong to command serious consideration.

If we can identify factors that induce an inflationary monetary policy, are there reasons to conclude that when those factors make us resort to higher rates of inflation then they are also more variable? Do factors that induce inflation tend to be quickly reversing, independent, or positively correlated? We do not have sufficient evidence, but I conjecture increased variance at higher rates. My colleague E. Thompson suggested one explanation that would imply higher inflation and higher variation *across countries*. Assume, in argument, that poor countries have less efficient direct taxing systems and use inflation more as part of their general tax structure. Assume also that the poor countries have less developed, more expensive capital markets in which governments (or anyone else) can borrow funds. Then any fluctuations in government expenditures will be financed less by equivalent variations in borrowing and more by the remaining buffer source of finance: creation of new money by the government. Given those assumptions, we find that poorer countries will have higher inflation and greater variation in that rate. If that sounds like a weak proposition (and it does not sound weak to me) try conjuring up your own explanations of why higher inflations have higher temporal variance and less predictability of future price levels or rate of rise—if they do.

The problem of rising prices is not only the "random" wealth redistributions of inflation or the increased natural rate of unemployment caused by higher rates of inflation. It is, in my weighing of cultural and economic effects, the consequent increased power of government in our daily cultural, social, and economic life—an increase aided by inflation. First, inflation financing is a "convenient" form of taxation by the government—at least until the money stock is replaced with a new money that the government "promises" will be stable for who knows how long. Neat and beautiful is the inflation money tax that can be hidden from public awareness. Second, it induces more government activity. The random changes in wealth create disaffection with (or may I say "alienation" from?) the economic system. The public's attitude toward a

6. B. Klein, "The Social Costs of the Recent Inflation and Our New Monetary Standard: The Mirage of Steady 'Anticipated' Inflation," unpublished manuscript (Apr., 1974).

stable currency is not one relying on any legislative law that the money unit will be stable, but rather on a deeper, more pervasive "common law" that a stable money is a characteristic of a good economic and political system. That the instability of money values is a result of political power instead of an economic system resting on private property rights must be news to many people. Indeed, even many economists get cheap publicity by blaming unions, corporations, wars, businessmen, oil embargoes, middlemen, and greedy people (who else is there?) for inflation. The public demands correction of the random "unjust" wealth redistributions. Any ailment that befalls them during inflation is blamed on the inflation. But since the reasons for the inflation are unfathomed, they demand government correction of their idiosyncratic ills. Such demands enlarge the scope of government and are not resisted by the politically strong or aspiring. Third, direct attacks on the symptoms known to flow from inflation are politically convenient. As inflation occurs, politicians and the public blame businessmen and producers for raising prices and mulcting the public. It is even fallaciously announced by government officials that of the one-thousand-dollar rise in average annual incomes over the past year, 80 percent is eroded away by inflation. The stamp of official doctrine is established that inflation reduces real incomes, when in fact it does not. The obvious response is to call for price controls. They provoke shortages; there obviously must be government action to set matters aright. The markets have failed; the economic system has failed.

The so-called shortage of gasoline and energy in the United States was *precisely* and *only* such a political attack. It could not have been brought about more cleverly and deceitfully even if the politically ambitious had explicitly written the script. Inflate the money stock; when prices rise, impose price controls to correct the situation. These controls lead to shortages which "require" government intervention to assure appropriate use of the limited supply and to allocate it and even to control and nationalize the production of energy. The powers of political authorities are increased; the open society is suppressed.

That is, in my opinion, the problem of inflation. Those are the results of inflation that frighten me. Those are the consequences that I cannot help but attribute as a goal of those who argue that inflation is really not so serious if it is announced and anticipated and that the unemployment it "avoids" is a very small price.

In fact, there is no lasting trade-off at all. There is only a transient effect from an acceleration or deceleration, while the lasting effects are those of greater political power. Incomes policies, wage and price controls, allocations, and nationalization are politically administered, with power and wealth going to those to perform those tasks, at least until they are forced by competition into the increased costs of achieving those powers. Inflation increases government power and growth. That is the problem of rising prices. I see no escape.

## Appendix

Let us suppose that the government—which we shall arbitrarily use as our source of inflation—decides to shift its relative demands. People for whose services or goods there has been a relative increase in demand will experience an increase in income and wealth. These demand-revision effects neither cause nor are caused by the effects of inflation on net monetary status. The gross effect is a sum of both inflation and demand-shift effects, as can be illustrated by the following numerical illustration. Suppose that the government wishes to obtain wealth by printing fiat money. Assume that it creates and spends new money for services rather than for existing capital goods (although this spending does not affect the wealth transfer process). Furthermore, let the creation of money and the resulting inflation be a one-shot operation. Let the individuals in a community be typified by five individuals whose wealth and income positions are summarized in Table 1-1.

All sorts of assumptions are possible about the ratio of income from capital assets and from labor. Assume, for simplicity, that the total income flow per period from labor and capital is equal to 10 percent of the community's capital and that all income is consumed. Capital goods can be used up if consumption is to be changed. For the redistributive process, that assumption would make no difference. Only the numerical results would be modified. In equilibrium, assume that the community jointly (but not severally) holds 10 percent of the total wealth (including money) in the form of money ($6 of the money equals 10 percent of the community's wealth of $54 + $6 = $60). Let the government inflate the money supply by $1.20 of fiat money and spend $1.00 of it—all for the services of individual B.[7] When $1.00 per period of increased money de-

---

7. By the time the government has spent $1.00, prices will be 1.20 of the former level. At this price level the government, given its propensity for liquidity, will want to hold larger cash balances, because the demand for cash is in part a function of one's level of nominal wealth. If prices have risen by 20 percent, we shall suppose the government wants to hold $1.20 in money. The upshot is that only $1.00 of the new money is spent.

TABLE 1-1. *Pre-inflation wealth, debts, and incomes of individuals*

| Persons | Wealth | Cash | Goods | Interpersonal Debts (−) or Credits (+) | Income |
|---------|--------|------|-------|------------------------------------------|--------|
| A | 15.15 | 2.40 | 12.75 | 0 | 2.25 |
| B | 9.85 | .85 | 9.00 | 0 | 1.00 |
| C | 16.10 | .60 | 14.25 | 1.25 | .75 |
| D | 4.65 | .40 | 4.75 | −.50 | .25 |
| E | 4.25 | .75 | 4.25 | −.75 | .75 |
| | 50.00 | 5.00 | 45.00 | 0 | 5.00 |
| Government | 10.00 | 1.00 | 9.00 | 0 | 1.00 |
| Total | 60.00 | 6.00 | 54.00 | 0 | 6.00 |

mand impinges on B, the price of his service is assumed to double (his income was formerly $1.00 per period). The government gets only half of B's services, since the private sector was offered $1.00 for all of B's services before the government's additional demand of $1.00. None of this increased demand goes to anyone except B in the first stage. The rise in service prices is reflected in capital goods prices.

Looking at each individual, we see what this implies. A's balance sheet initially is:

A (before inflation and demand revision)

| Cash | $ 2.40 | Equity | $15.15 |
|------|--------|--------|--------|
| Goods | 12.75 | | |
| | $15.15 | | |

In the first period, his income stays at $2.25, while the price level of services rises to, say, $1.20. If he spends all his income, his consumption in real terms falls to $2.25 ($= 1.20 \times \$1.875$), a decline of $0.375 in original-price units. In the next period he receives a larger income, $2.70, as B spends part of his increased earnings. A has the choice of spending $2.70 or saving part of it to restore some of his wealth. If he spends it all in order to maintain his consumption at its original level, his balance sheet will be:

A (no saving)

| Cash | $ 2.40 | Equity | $17.70 |
|------|--------|--------|--------|
| Goods | 15.30 | | |
| | $17.70 | | |

His equity, in original-price units, would be $17.70 ÷ 1.20 = $14.75, a decline in wealth of $0.40 (from $15.15). He experienced a decline in real income in the first period of $0.375. The wealth loss, $0.40, is his wealth redistribution loss due to the inflation, and his second loss is the loss of income consequent to the *demand revision* as relative demand is shifted toward B. In fact, no matter what the demand shift, the inflationary loss is unaffected. Only if the degree of demand shift is tied to the degree of inflation are the two effects related, but this tie is a policy correlation, completely independent of the fact of inflation.

Suppose that A decides to save the increment of money income in order to increase his stock of money. His balance sheet would now appear:

A (saving all his increased money income)

| Cash | $ 2.85 | Equity | $18.15 |
|------|--------|--------|--------|
| Goods | 15.30 | | |
| | $18.15 | | |

In real terms his equity is $18.15 ÷ 1.20 = $15.125, a decline of $0.025 from the original level. He has to save still more if he wants to restore his equity to its original real level. Although he can choose any level of saving and resultant equity, he will have suffered the same loss of $0.40 in wealth because of the inflation and the reduced real income of $0.375 consequent to the demand revision. How he chooses to bear these two separate losses, that is, whether he will maintain consumption by eating up his wealth, restore his wealth by saving, or not save at all, is entirely up to his discretion. He is forced into no particular way, but he is forced into making a choice among them—a choice forced on him by both the inflationary wealth redistribution and the revised demand effect on income and asset values.

In the same manner, B's experience can be examined. Initially, his balance sheet is:

B (before inflation and before demand changes)

| Cash | $0.85 | Equity | $9.85 |
|------|-------|--------|-------|
| Goods | 9.00 | | |
| | $9.85 | | |

During the first period he has received $2.00 of income and has spent $1.00. With the higher prices, his real income is $2.00 ÷ 1.20 or $1.666, an increase of $0.666 in original-price units. He has lost wealth by being a net monetary creditor; the real value of his money stock falls to $0.85 ÷ 1.20 = $0.70833, a decline of $0.1416—exactly the same loss as if there were no demand shift. He can choose any combination of saving and consequent level of wealth that he wishes. If he saves all of his increase in real income, $0.666, this will more than offset the inflationary loss of wealth of $0.1416. He will have a net increase in wealth of $0.525. If, instead, he saves, say, only $0.20, his balance sheet will be:

B (after restoring cash ratio)

| Cash | $ 1.05 | Equity | $11.85 |
|------|--------|--------|--------|
| Goods | 10.80 | | |
| | $11.85 | | |

His equity (in original-price units) is now $11.85 ÷ 1.20 = $9.875, an increase of $0.025. This increase is the result of his voluntary decision to save $0.20. In summary, he loses $0.1416 (original-price-level units) by being a net monetary creditor during the inflation, and he gains a transitory one-period increase of $0.666 in income by the demand shift. He chose to save $0.20 of that increase in income ($0.1666 in original-price-level units), so his wealth increased by $0.1666 − $0.1416 = $0.025. The rest of the increased real income, in original-price-level units, $0.666 − $0.1666 = $0.50, is devoted to increasing his consumption. Similar analysis for C, D, and E yields the results given in the appropriate rows of Table 1-2. Columns (1) and (3), when summed, give column (4).

Table 1-2 shows that all of the income gain, $0.666, accruing to B is at the expense of the rest of the community (proportionate to their income) and not from inflation. Also, the net wealth redistribution due to inflation is independent to the degree of demand revision. With the demand revision, income revision has occurred, as shown in the second column, whereas the inflation wealth redistribution went from the moneyholders to the government and from private net creditors to private net debtors. In this particular example, the

TABLE 1-2. Summary of effects of inflation and demand shifts on income and wealth
(all in original-price-level units)

| (1) Net Wealth Redistribution from Inflation | (2) Income Change Caused by Demand Revision: One Period of Income | (3) Voluntary Savings Increments | (4) Net Changes in Wealth of Private Sector |
|---|---|---|---|
| A   −$0.4000 | −$0.3750 | $0.3750 | −$0.025 |
| B   −.1416 | .6666 | .1666 | .025 |
| C   −.3083 | −.1250 | .1250 | −.1833 |
| D   .0166 | −.0416 | .0416 | .0583 |
| E   .0000 | −.1250 | .1250 | .1250 |
| −$0.833 (to government) | 0 | $0.8333 | 0 |

amount of savings increments was simply assumed to be just sufficient to restore the private community's stock of real wealth. Under different assumptions about the desire to hold cash and to save, the numerical results would be
different. The government could get the services without at the same time inducing the rest of the community to do any saving or dissaving. Or the community could insist on maintaining its consumption rate (and consume some
wealth). In our example the community saved enough to restore its wealth to
the pre-inflation level. But in any event, the inflation effect is one thing, the
shift in relative demand another, and the resultant saving decision still another.

# 4

## EFFECTS OF INFLATION

# EFFECTS OF INFLATION

## REUBEN A. KESSEL AND ARMEN A. ALCHIAN

The object of this paper is to derive the implications of inflation, defined as rising prices. The ensuing analysis attempts to discern the consequences or implications of inflation itself—whatever may have caused it. Therefore little attention will be paid to the other effects of the events that may be regarded as causes of inflation, such as increases in the quantity of money, velocity changes, reductions in physical stocks, droughts, plagues, unemployment, wars, or other events that have produced inflation.

Inflations may be usefully classified as (a) anticipated or (b) unanticipated. Anticipated inflation is characterized by market phenomena implied by the postulate that prices are expected to rise. Unanticipated inflation is characterized by market phenomena implied by the alternative postulate, that the contemporaneous level of prices is expected to persist.[1] Inflation, of either type and regardless of cause, is defined as a rise in the general level of prices.[2]

This paper discusses the demand for money, the economics of unanticipated inflation, the transitional or intermediate stage between unanticipated and anticipated inflation, fully anticipated inflation, and deflation.

Reprinted from Armen A. Alchian, *Economic Forces at Work* (Indianapolis: Liberty Fund, 1977), 363–95. This article was previously published in *Journal of Political Economy* 70 (December 1962): 521–37.

This article is part of a larger study of inflation financed by the Merrill Foundation for the Advancement of Financial Knowledge. An earlier version of this paper was presented at the Money Workshop of the University of Chicago. The authors also benefited from the comments of Professor Karl Brunner, University of California, Los Angeles.

1. Widespread expectation that current prices will remain unchanged, when they are in fact rising, is not a necessary condition for the existence of unanticipated inflation. Some may expect prices to rise; others may expect them to fall. On balance, the anticipations of the market can be different from the anticipations of every individual in the market.

2. Problems of defining a measure of the general price level, although present, are ignored on the grounds that general agreement among observers as to when the general level of prices has or has not risen is sufficiently common to permit unambiguous identification of periods of inflation.

## 1. The Demand for Money

Inflation and the demand to hold money are intimately related. Therefore it is relevant to inquire: How is the effectiveness with which money performs its functions affected by inflation? To answer this question, it is convenient to classify the spectrum of assets into two categories, monetary and real (or non-monetary). Monetary assets are claims to fixed numbers of dollars, currency, bank deposits, bonds, notes. In contrast, real assets refer to assets whose nominal yields are affected by price-level changes. Examples are equities, real property, inventories.[3] For business firms and individuals, money is an asset, and in equilibrium the marginal net productivity of a dollar of money is equal to that of a dollar's worth of any other assets—bonds, inventories, houses.

Money, like any asset, is a store of value. Yet money appears, superficially, to be at a disadvantage because real assets yield an income stream whereas money yields "nothing." This raises the questions: What properties of money enable it to compete successfully with assets that yield an explicit income stream? What are the services that money provides that offset the absence of an explicit yield?

Two interdependent properties are relevant. First, money can be used to hedge against changes in both relative prices and interest rates. Factors that affect relative prices have comparatively little impact on the general level of prices, and conversely. As a result, the purchasing power of money is unaffected by relative price changes. In a world in which future price changes cannot be foreseen, money provides a hedge, and if prices are stable or falling, a cheap hedge, against this uncertainty.

The second distinctive attribute of money in modern societies is the zero, or near-zero, transactions cost associated with the exchange of money for other resources. Money is the most liquid of assets, if liquidity is measured by the difference between buying and selling prices at any instant of time. Because of these zero transactions costs, virtually everyone finds it optimal to hold some money. In principle, the rate of savings on transactions costs re-

---

3. Resort to the credit market is, of course, another alternative to the holding of cash balances and constitutes a substitute for money. Since repayment of debt is never certain, credit costs must reflect the existence of this risk. Therefore, for some fraction of an individual's wealth, it is cheaper to hold some cash balances than it is to hold no cash at all and utilize credit markets. This is especially true when "assets" are in human as against non-human form.

sulting from holding money equals the rate of interest. For any given rate of interest, the proportions of wealth held in money, money substitutes, and other assets will depend at any moment upon the probability of converting various amounts of wealth into other economic resources in ensuing moments. In other words, the degree to which receipts and expenditures are synchronized influences the fraction of wealth that one chooses to hold in the form of money. For example, the portion of a farmer's wealth held in the form of money will often be larger than that proportion for a civil service worker or rentier.

For performing the functions of money there exist substitutes. A portfolio of real assets could be selected so as to provide a hedge against most relative price changes. Only interest-rate changes could not be hedged thereby. Securities with low transactions costs and short maturities, such as Treasury bills, can also function as a money substitute.

An asset's substitutability for money depends upon its value as a hedge against relative price changes and its transactions costs. Government fiat or debt money is better than private debt money (demand deposits), because private money can be affected by the particular fortunes of individual banking enterprises, as has been demonstrated by the banking crises in American economic history (particularly during the Great Depression); and it often can be negotiated more cheaply. Insofar as a government insures bank deposits, savings and loan shares, or mortgages, it reduces the vulnerability of private debt to the risks of private enterprise. The value of bank deposits is affected less by imprudent lending policies of banks, embezzlements, and so on. Hence, such insurance improves the substitutability of private debts for government money. This analysis also implies that short-term securities are a better substitute for money than comparable long-term obligations, and government securities are better than privately issued securities.[4] Human resources in the form of effort and ingenuity devoted to achieving a more perfect synchronization between receipts and expenditures are also substitutes for money. This suggests that the use of money in modern societies is a result of cost advantages, and that the ratio of money to other assets held, particularly money substitutes, will change with these costs.

Some of these costs are specific to money and would not necessarily be in-

---

4. For a more detailed statement of the ideas presented here, see J. C. Gilbert, "The Demand for Money: The Development of an Economic Concept," *Journal of Political Economy* 61 (April 1953): 144–59.

curred if assets other than money are held; examples are charges for checking accounts and depreciation through inflation (appreciation in the value of money through deflation can be regarded as a negative cost).[5] As with any asset, the relevant cost and income streams are those expected or anticipated. At the margin, the difference between the capitalized value of the expenditure and receipt streams associated with holding a dollar must, of course, be equal to a dollar. Similarly at the margin, the difference in the yield between an interest-bearing security and money represents an equalizing difference that measures the difference in the money services of the two assets. A change in this difference attributable to changes in the yield of physical capital implies a change in the demand for money.

The demand for money, like the demand for any resource, is a real demand. People want to hold command in the form of money over some volume of real resources, and not just over a certain number of pieces of paper. This demand can be expressed in either nominal or real terms. To convert from one to the other, an index number of general prices is necessary. The stock of nominal balances in existence at any moment of time is independent of the real value of that stock. Price-level changes, changes in output and employment, and interest-rate changes can bring into equality desires to hold real balances with any specified stock of nominal balances in existence.

Inflation, whether or not it is anticipated, increases the cost of holding money. However, inflation will reduce the real balances a community is willing to hold only if it is anticipated. The fact that the costs of holding money have increased in the past as a consequence of unanticipated inflation has implications for the future costs of holding real balances only insofar as past inflation influences expectations about the future. It is only with respect to the future that one has alternatives with respect to the size of cash balances held; present and past costs are "sunk" costs. The same is true for deflation: unless a decrease in the cost of holding money is anticipated because falling prices are expected, the real demand for money will not be influenced.

For these reasons the state of expectations about inflation is crucial for predicting the effects of inflation. If inflation is unanticipated, that is, if the hold-

---

5. Economists have become accustomed to viewing the interest rate as the opportunity cost of holding money. This is correct only in a world of interest-bearing securities and money; it is not correct in a world that contains assets such as Van Gogh paintings, houses, and automobiles, for holding these assets also involves that interest cost.

ers of cash balances on the average expect the contemporaneous level of prices to persist, then one set of implications is generated. These are the economics of unanticipated inflation. But, if the holders of cash balances taken as a group expect the general level of prices to rise, then a second and quite different set of implications follows. These constitute the economics of anticipated inflation.

## II. Economics of Unanticipated Inflation

### A. Inaccurate Foresight and Wealth Transfers

The defining characteristic of unanticipated inflation is the expectation that the current price level will persist when prices are in fact rising. Estimates of future price-level changes are biased downward, that is, below realized price-level changes.[6] Consequently, the impact of realized but unanticipated inflation upon the actual costs of holding money fails to affect the quantity of real balances held. Yet prices, the nominal stock of wealth, and the demand for nominal money all increase.

The expectation that the current price level will persist implies that the equilibrium money rates of interest observed in capital markets are unaffected by unanticipated inflation. No changes in the relative demand and supply of bonds are implied by the observed depreciation in the purchasing power of money.[7] Consequently, interest rates fail to rise enough (real yields on bonds fall below that required) to maintain preinflation economic relations between debtors and creditors. The nominal rate of interest fails to reflect rising prices because estimates of the course of future prices are biased, not because of market imperfections. As a result there are transfers of wealth from net monetary creditors to debtors.[8] What is true of debtors and creditors linked by indebtedness in the form of bonds is equally true of all debtors and creditors, regardless of the specific security creating this relationship, which may be bonds, mort-

---

6. Expectations about the future course of prices need not be uniform. They may vary yet be so balanced that rising prices do not affect holdings of real balances.

7. There is an absolute increase in the demand for bonds because the proportion of debt to wealth has decreased. If both demand and supply increase to the same extent, there will be no change in either bond prices or interest rates.

8. This difference between the yield required to maintain pre-unanticipated inflation debtor-creditor relations and the yield realized corresponds to what I. Fisher termed the difference between the money and the real rate of interest (*The Theory of Interest* [New York: Macmillan, 1930], pp. 43–44).

gages, notes, bills, acceptances, or contingent sales contracts; relationships between debtors and creditors are systematically affected.[9] No income effects, other than those flowing from the wealth transfer, are implied.

This wealth transfer can be detected in the stock market. Prices of common stocks of net debtor companies (whose monetary liabilities exceed their monetary assets) rise relative to those of net creditor companies (whose monetary liabilities are less than their monetary assets). Similarly, individuals whose monetary liabilities exceed their monetary assets realize gains. These gains are the losses of those whose monetary assets exceed their monetary liabilities. Unanticipated inflation transfers wealth from net monetary creditors to net monetary debtors, regardless of whether the creditors and debtors are corporations, governments, widows, orphans, schoolteachers.

Taking all debts into account, public and private, the largest debtor in an economy is usually a governmental unit. Holders of government debt lose directly to the government. This gain can be used to reduce taxes or increase governmental expenditures without increasing taxes. Creditors, who lose wealth, typically react by reducing their consumption (and possibly saving). They have lost wealth because of rising prices, and this loss is the wealth gain of net monetary debtors.[10]

### B. The Inflation Tax on Money

Inflation can be deliberately utilized as a tax. A government can acquire resources by creating and spending new fiat money. This policy can cause prices to rise, and it is this rise in prices that reveals the transfer of wealth to the government from money-holders and reduces the wealth position of all (including

---

9. The rate of interest will temporarily fall in response to an increase in the nominal stock of money; with an increased stock of money (sprinkled, say, from the sky), people will increase their demand for other assets, among them bonds. Presumably this increased demand for bonds will lead to a rise in interest rates followed by an increase in the volume of bonds outstanding. The willingness to issue bonds increases as a result of the increase in wealth.

10. Conversely, private debtors increase their consumption. No one is forced to reduce consumption or engage in "forced savings" in order for inflation to transfer wealth. An entire community can, in principle, maintain its consumption standards in the face of wealth losses attributable to rising prices. The maintenance of consumption standards is not inconsistent with the use of inflation to acquire resources. What is crucial for taxation through inflation, as shall be developed, is the willingness of the community to exchange real resources for money in the face of rising prices.

government) creditors.[11] Thus it is not merely the creation of fiat money, it is the inflation that "taxes" money-holders and creditors. The gain in wealth by the government or creator of fiat money is revealed to the community when rising prices reduce the value of a nominal unit of money.[12]

This distinction may be illustrated by an analogy. If a thief steals your car (and his wealth increases), does your wealth decrease when you go out to use your car and discover it is gone, or does it decrease at the instant it is stolen, even though you don't know about it? The temptation to say it is decreased at the moment the car is stolen is strong, yet it must be remembered that behavior and expenditure patterns are unaffected until the theft of the car is discovered! For purposes of deriving implications about reactions to a reduction in wealth, it is the discovery of the theft that is crucial. For other purposes, it may be the moment that the theft occurred.

Only if the new fiat money were initially given to individuals (instead of spent by the government) in proportion to the money already held could there be no wealth transfers from fiat money-holders. The reduced value of a unit of fiat money could be offset by the new money acquired. Other interpersonal transfers would remain, because other assets and liabilities are fixed in terms of money. With respect to interest-bearing government obligations, the rise in the price level (inflation) implies a relatively lower return (or a lower "real" return) to the holders of these securities and a correspondingly lower cost of servicing this debt.

Virtually analogous reasoning applies to government-sponsored creation of money by banks for the purpose of monetizing governmental debt. When the yield on that debt is kept so low that a government cannot successfully compete

---

11. For an exposition of how a government obtains resources through inflation, see A. Alchian and R. Kessel, "How the Government Gains from Inflation," *Proceedings of the 30th Annual Meeting of the Western Economic Association* (Stanford, Calif.: Stanford University Press, 1955), pp. 13–16; also M. Friedman, *Essays in Positive Economics* (Chicago: University of Chicago Press, 1953), p. 253.

12. In a full-employment economy, an increase in the nominal monetary stock implies a tax upon creditors whether or not prices rise. The creation of fiat money implies a higher level of prices than would otherwise exist. Consequently, the welfare of creditors is adversely affected. For example, a policy designed to maintain stable prices in a progressive society characterized by an income-elastic demand for money implies a tax upon creditors. H. Simons proposed discharging governmental interest-bearing obligations by such a policy (*Economic Policy for a Free Society* [Chicago: University of Chicago Press, 1948], p. 234).

for savings in the capital markets, it sells its obligations to the banking system in exchange for newly created private debt money (demand deposits). The expenditure of these demand deposits increases the price level, and thus reduces the wealth of the holders of governmental debt. Whether unanticipated inflation is caused by the issuance of fiat money or the expansion of bank deposits in order to monetize governmental debt, it constitutes an alternative to formal taxation.

Insofar as governments employ taxation through unanticipated inflation as an alternative to formal taxation, governmental creditors replace conventional taxpayers. The losses of holders of government interest-bearing obligations (the declines in the real values of the income streams accruing to owners of these securities) constitute a reduction in the costs to taxpayers of servicing governmental obligations. The beneficiaries of taxation through inflation are those whose total taxes, conventional and inflation, are lower than they otherwise would be.[13]

Unanticipated inflation can also be used as a means of private finance. When unanticipated inflation is caused by an expansion of bank credit at the instigation of private parties, banks exchange bank demand credit (money) for the obligations of their customers. These newly created deposits are spent for real resources in commodity markets, thereby driving up prices. This produces a gain in wealth for net monetary debtors at the expense of net monetary creditors. The initiating private individuals who exchanged their debt for bank money gain when prices rise only insofar as they are *net* monetary debtors.[14] The act of borrowing increases both the monetary assets and the liabilities of bank customers. Hence the act of borrowing does not per se imply gains during inflation. Bank borrowers typically become debtors by converting their newly acquired deposits into real resources. Hence they gain through inflation as debtors and not as initiators of inflation.[15]

---

13. The transfer of wealth within the private sector of an economy as a result of the existence of private debt can be regarded as a negative or a positive "tax," as the case may be, for the purpose of evaluating the impact upon an economic unit of taxation through inflation as compared with alternative forms of taxation.

14. This refers only to direct effects. Indirectly, neutrals (neutrals are defined as economic units whose monetary assets just equal their monetary liabilities) and, possibly, some creditors gain. This indirect gain is a result of a decrease in the real costs of servicing interest-bearing governmental liabilities.

15. The losses of the holders of non-interest-bearing governmental obligations are not offset. There is, of course, a loss to the holders of cash and monetary assets generally

All of the foregoing has been an analysis of the effects of unanticipated inflation produced by an increase in the absolute stock of money. What if inflation results from a decrease in the physical stock of nonmoney resources? Suppose a community finds that its ratio of wealth in the form of money to wealth in nonmonetary forms is greater than it desires. It succeeds in reducing this ratio by increasing prices. This inflation results in transfers of wealth from net monetary creditors to net monetary debtors. Insofar as the government is a debtor, it gains, even though it had no intention of acquiring resources through inflation. Whether or not there is a transfer of resources from creditors to debtors, there is a net loss of liquidity in the community.[16] This may be seen by considering the implications of the same event, a decrease in the stock of physical wealth, in an economy whose only money is fiat money and where there are no private or public debts. The real value of the money stock declines, total liquidity in the economy falls, and there are no transfers of wealth. Inflation still taxes the holders of money, but it produces no tax receipts.[17]

--------

as a result of the creation of new money regardless of what happens to prices. If the marginal effect of the creation of new money upon prices is positive, then losses are implied.

Considering only wealth effects constitutes an incomplete analysis of the forces operating to reconcile the demands for resources with the volume of resources available for acquisition. To illustrate: consider an inflationary expansion of bank credit in an economy that uses nongovernmental money exclusively. The ensuing price increase does not reduce wealth; it does reduce the real value of liquid assets. Hence the stock of money and liquid assets falls relative to other assets and liabilities until that stock becomes an equilibrium stock. Then this inflation is brought to a halt. The effect of the expansion of bank credit is to reshuffle real resources and claims against these real resources with no decrease in the wealth position of the community as a whole.

16. An interesting question can be posed. Suppose a community has only private debt money and every person, for the sake of analysis, has a private bank debt exactly equal to his demand deposit. In this event a decrease in real resources will produce an inflation, but will the inflation (not the reduction in real resources) also change anyone's real wealth if his monetary assets just equal his monetary liabilities? No. The real value of bank money and obligations to the banks will decrease by the same amount. Hence the fall in the real value of the monetary stock will not be associated with the redistribution of wealth.

17. Objections to the use of inflation as a means of taxation have rested on equity grounds. Pesek has compared inflation, sales taxes, and income taxes and concludes, given the 1950 distribution of assets and incomes, that inflation is relatively regressive. Hence he infers that lower-income groups have an economic interest in the use of sales and income taxes, particularly income taxes, as an alternative to taxation through inflation. His conclusion follows only if a change from one tax to another affects the overall

Employment and output effects are implied by inflation if the supply of labor is a function of money wage rates and if unemployment exists. For these circumstances inflation implies falling real wage rates. Hence inflation implies increases in the quantity of labor demanded and increases in output and employment.

### C. Unanticipated Deflation

Formally, the analysis of unanticipated deflation is symmetrical to the analysis of unanticipated inflation. Wealth is redistributed from debtors to creditors. Falling prices produced a subsidy to the holders of governmental debt and a redistribution of wealth from debtors to creditors within the private sector of an economy. A subsidy to the holders of governmental debt through deflation is an alternative to other governmental expenditures just as taxation through inflation is an alternative to other taxes.

## III. Economics of Transition from Unanticipated to Anticipated Inflation

The effects of the transition from unanticipated to anticipated inflation are, by definition, results of changes in beliefs about the course of future prices.[18] When the current price level is no longer expected to persist and this expecta-

---

progressivity of a tax system, that is, of all taxes taken together. It is possible to hold constant both the progressivity of a tax system and tax receipts while varying the fraction of tax receipts attributable to a specific type of tax.

Pesek also maintains that we are continuously threatened by inflation. The evidence of the last hundred years indicates that the bulk of the inflation that has occurred in the United States is associated with wars when efficiency considerations are assigned more weight and equity considerations less weight than during peacetime.

A major difficulty with taxation through inflation as a long-run alternative is that it will become anticipated. Therefore it will have efficiency costs for an economy. For peacetime inflations that are not explained by desires to obtain resources for governmental purposes but to achieve full employment, the appropriate opportunity costs of inflation are the loss in output resulting from unemployed resources (see B. Pesek, "A Comparison of the Distributional Effects of Inflation and Taxation," *American Economic Review* 50 [March 1960]: 147).

18. The sequence in which this analysis is developed, in particular presenting the economics of unanticipated inflation before that of anticipatory inflation, corresponds to the temporal sequence of economic events during an inflation. In this light, the inflations of the United States during the last century failed to reach the anticipated stage, whereas the German inflation following World War I went through all three stages.

tion is supplanted by the anticipation of rising prices, certain adjustments that uniquely characterize this transition state are implied. These adjustments are a consequence of the expectation that the cost of holding money will increase.

The expectation that the cost of holding monetary assets will increase relative to that of real assets implies that the stock of money and other monetary assets is in excess of the desired stocks. Alternatively, the market value of the monetary assets of a community is in excess of the new present worth of the net income stream that these assets are now expected to generate. For real assets the converse is the case. Therefore, there is a communitywide attempt to shift from monetary to real assets. This attempt to substitute real assets for monetary assets produces, through a complex chain of substitutions, a rise in real asset prices, a rise in the money rate of interest, a fall in the real rate, and a decrease in bond prices.[19] The rise in prices and the decline in real rates of interest equilibrates desires to hold wealth in the form of money with the nominal balances available to be held, desires to hold wealth in the form of real assets with the real assets available to be held, and desires to hold wealth in the form of monetary assets with the monetary assets available to be held.

For any given expectation of the future course of prices, there exists some current level of prices and interest rates that reconciles the desires of a community to hold wealth in various forms with what is available to be held. (In the limiting case, this price level can be infinity and the stocks of money balances zero.) At this equilibrium price level and new rate of interest, the marginal yield derived from holding money equals the higher marginal yield on other assets, both monetary and real.

A decline in the real value of nominal balances attributable to the expectation of rising prices is implied by the recognition of a tax on money. Similar effects are produced by a tax on physical assets. For example, a tax on houses will lead to a decrease in the long-run equilibrium value of a housing stock. The key difference between the effects of these two taxes is in the time required to adjust stocks of housing and money to long-run equilibrium conditions. For a noncommodity money, short-run equilibrium conditions are nonexistent. The stock of real balances adjusts, once a tax on money is recognized, to long-run equilibrium conditions. Hence current holders of money must bear all of the tax on money.

In contrast, several years may elapse after a tax is imposed on housing be-

19. On this point, see C. Kennedy, "Inflation and the Bond Rate," *Oxford Economic Papers*, N.S. 12 (October 1960): 269–73.

fore a housing stock reaches long-run equilibrium. From the imposition of a housing tax to the moment the housing stock reaches long-run equilibrium, current users do not bear the full tax. Only after long-run equilibrium conditions are satisfied is a tax on housing borne completely by current users.

The effects of changes in expectations concerning the future course of prices are capitalized in the capital market. The prices of all debt securities fall until the gap between money and real yields reflects the current state of beliefs about the future course of prices. All assets whose explicit money yields are independent of the rate of change of prices are revaluated and converted into assets whose effective money yields are a function of the rate of change of prices. Therefore, holders of debt securities (creditors) incur capital losses. These losses represent the present worth of the future value decreases that the owners of these securities expect to bear as a result of inflation. The longer the maturity of a debt security, the greater the capital loss. Corresponding to the capital losses of creditors are the capital gains of debtors. These gains are the present worth of the future reductions in real interest and principal obligations expected to result from higher prices. The process of recognizing and compounding the capital gains and losses associated with monetary securities (other than non-interest-bearing money) converts these securities into purchasing power obligations. The extent to which the new capital values reflect the present values of losses that will, in fact, be realized depends upon the correctness of the expectations held. The change in expectations from stable to rising prices, if it is accompanied by uncertainty about the magnitude of the expected rise, usually induces the business community to incorporate price-revising procedures in its contracts. This is particularly important for long-term commitments such as mortgages and bonds. Inability to predict correctly the magnitude of an expected rise in prices may be expected to lead to a greater utilization of escalator clauses.

The revaluation of monetary assets and liabilities of enterprises causes changes in the prices of equities. In general, the prices of shares of firms whose monetary liabilities exceed their monetary assets rise relative to the price level. Conversely, the relative prices of shares of firms whose monetary assets exceed their monetary liabilities fall, and neutral firms' share prices move with the price level.[20]

20. To determine whether or not capital gains exceed capital losses as a consequence of changes in expectations from stable to rising prices, both the relative magnitudes and the average durations of monetary assets and monetary liabilities are relevant. To the

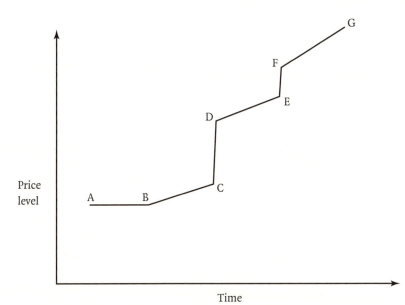

FIGURE 1. *The effect of changes in expectations upon the absolute level of prices.*

Governments, almost invariably the largest debtors in an economy, gain in wealth at the expense of the owners of their interest-bearing obligations. These gains of wealth are the capitalized values of the expected reductions in the real tax liabilities of taxpayers (governments). If the subsequent inflation is correctly anticipated during the transition, then the holders of governmental obligations (creditors) will, after the loss of wealth during the transition, incur no further losses of wealth as a result of the now correctly anticipated inflation. Only the holders of non-interest-bearing money, either government or private, will continue to incur losses attributable to inflation after the transition. The real value of fiat money balances will decrease during the transition without any counterpart gains elsewhere in an economy.

The impact on current prices of changes in expectations about future prices is shown in Figure 1. AB represents price level stability; BC denotes a period of unanticipated inflation. During both periods current prices are expected to persist, although the realized cost of holding cash balance rises during the second

———

extent that monetary assets are of shorter term than monetary liabilities, which appears to be the case for many if not most business firms, the foregoing conclusions would have to be modified.

period. There is no change (attributable to inflation) in the quantity of real cash balances demanded. CD represents an adjustment from unanticipated to anticipated inflation. The rise in prices indicated by CD is purely the result of a change in expectations and is consistent with there being no change in the nominal monetary stock. This rise in prices is associated with a rise in velocity and a fall in the real value of the nominal monetary stock of a community. It is caused by a change in the long-run equilibrium conditions for the stock of money. DE represents price rises during an inflation that was anticipated and is consistent with no further change in the real value of money-holdings. If the rate of change of prices experienced during the DE time interval is the expected rate, then the transition adjustments during CD were complete. However, if the actual rate of change of prices continues to be greater than the expected rate, another adjustment may occur. Again, real balances fall and velocity rises because of a change in long-run equilibrium conditions for the stock of money. This second round of adjustments is represented by EF and the subsequent rate of change of prices by FG. The actual realized costs of holding money are the same for both DE and FG. The jump in prices denoted by CD and EF does not reflect an increase in the actual cost of holding money. It reflects an increased awareness of the true costs.

After the transition from nonanticipated to accurately anticipated inflation (which could occur instantaneously or over a period of time), the ensuing rate of change of prices is an "equilibrium" rate of change. This rate of change of prices will not accelerate in the absence of exogenous forces. It is, of course, conceivable that expectations can be formed in such a manner that price-level increases per se will generate expectations that will lead to an acceleration of the rate of change of prices. Assuming expectations of this character, one can conceive of inflations that feed upon themselves in the absence of exogenous forces, such as those resulting from increases in the stock of nominal balances or decreases in the stock of physical wealth. Available evidence produced by the inflations the Western world has experienced, as well as existing knowledge of how expectations are formed, fails to support the belief that inflations feed upon themselves, purely by expectations feeding upon expectations.[21]

21. The seven hyperinflations studied by Cagan did not feed upon themselves (P. Cagan, "The Monetary Dynamics of Hyperinflation," in M. Friedman, ed., *Studies in the Quantity Theory of Money* [Chicago: University of Chicago Press, 1956], p. 74).

## IV. Economics of Anticipated Inflation

The previous section concentrated primarily, but not exclusively, on those economic effects that distinguished the transition stage. Here the implications of a fully anticipated inflation, and not just the transition adjustments resulting from changes in price expectations, are of paramount concern. The greater the inflation and the greater the extent to which inflation is expected, the more significant will be these effects.

### A. Tax on Money and Reduced Real Balances

Changes in expectations from stable to rising prices imply higher costs of holding money. Therefore the real value of money balances falls; this is a symptom of efforts to economize on the use of a resource expected to become dearer. Taxation of money through (partial or complete) anticipated inflation implies reductions in the real value of money balances.[22] Suppose the money in a community is inconvertible, non-interest-bearing, fiat money issued by a government. Suppose also that this government announces its intention of doubling the nominal monetary stock each year through the issuance of new money in exchange for resources. The issuance of this new money is an alternative to conventional taxes. Because of the announcement, a transition occurs during which prices rise sharply; this is followed by a steady-state rate of increase. This transition stage is a result of individuals' decisions to reduce their money-holding in view of the higher costs of holding money. The more elastic the cost elasticity of demand for money, the higher the transition increase in prices. Assume that the fraction of income (wealth) held in the form of money immediately drops by one-half to, say, 15 percent. This decline occurs by means of an immediate doubling of prices and of income velocity. If this immediate doubling of prices is followed by an annual 100 percent rate of change, then the holders of money would lose, every year thereafter, 7.5 percent of their wealth, which would represent the proceeds of the inflation tax.[23]

---

22. This is consistent with a fully and accurately anticipated inflation if the cost of holding money is not driven so high that its use is abandoned entirely.

23. This calculation is implicitly based on the assumption that there are no welfare or efficiency costs associated with this tax, so that postinflation and preinflation real incomes are equal. This assumption does not change the analysis in any essential way. The use of a more appropriate assumption would reduce the estimated tax receipts.

It is incorrect to infer from this example that higher rates of inflation will necessarily produce larger tax receipts for a government. A higher rate of anticipated inflation will produce larger tax proceeds per unit of real value of money balances held by a community, but it also reduces stocks of money balances in real terms. What is relevant for calculating the proceeds of an inflation tax is the elasticity of demand for money in real terms with respect to the rate of change of prices. The principles of optimal pricing for monopolists are relevant for determining the rate of anticipated inflation that maximizes the proceeds of an inflation tax for a government.[24]

### B. Money Substitution

Given the expectation of an increase in the costs of holding money, the preexisting marginal rate of substitution of money for real resources becomes nonoptimal. At first blush, this suggests that fewer resources will go into the production of money and more into the production of all other output than would be true under a regime of stable prices. However, in a fiat or noncommodity money economy, only a negligible volume of resources goes into the production of money. Therefore, virtually no resources are released if less money, in real terms, is used as a result of inflation. An increase in the cost of holding money induces a community to divert some resources to the production of money substitutes. Consequently, a good that is nearly costless to society is in part supplanted by goods that have greater costs. These costs constitute the efficiency losses, or the welfare effects, of anticipated inflation.[25] Both the duration of an inflation and the rate of change of prices affect the costs of holding money. Hence both play a role in determining the volume of resources that goes into economizing on cash balances. The expectation of rising prices leads to a revaluation of securities, both debt and equity, so that their effective yields are consistent with the real rate of interest.

Since assets differ in their capacities as money substitutes, the anticipation of rising prices produces relative price changes among assets. In general, this

---

24. An application of these principles to an inflation tax may be found in M. Bailey, "The Welfare Cost of Inflationary Finance," *Journal of Political Economy* 64 (April 1956): 105.

25. Bailey (ibid., p. 95) has estimated the welfare costs of anticipated inflation to be a function of the size of the reduction in the real value of the nominal monetary stock. For comparing inflation with other tax alternatives, a relevant criterion is the relative size of these efficiency losses.

implies that long-lived assets, such as land, and purchasing-power securities will rise in value relative to wealth in human form. The use of money substitutes that are infinitely elastic in supply in the short run, such as foreign currencies, increases very rapidly.[26] For assets whose supply is less elastic in the short run, and which are good money substitutes, the revaluation produces rents and quasi-rents for their owners, with subsequent effects on production. This increased demand is spread out generally over the entire range of highly marketable assets. In the long run, the pattern of output in an inflationary economy changes toward the production of more money substitutes. Human capital is a poorer money substitute than nonhuman capital. Therefore the output of capital in nonhuman form rises, and the output of capital in human form falls, relative to what it would be in the absence of inflation.[27]

The substitution of real resources for money, and the corresponding welfare loss caused by any given rate of change of prices, is greater in the long run than in the short run. In the long run, by definition, the supply conditions of money substitutes are more elastic. Hence more resources will flow into the production of money substitutes in the long run than in the short run. The more a community shifts from money to money substitutes, the greater the welfare loss and the smaller the real tax receipts attributable to any given rate of change of prices.[28] The difference between the income yielded by the allocation of resources under a regime of stable prices and the income yielded during inflation, both measured using the relative prices that exist during price-level

26. A country whose currency is relatively stable in purchasing power has a comparative advantage in producing money, and as a result its money is held by foreign nationals. Therefore, in a world of currencies whose purchasing power is unstable, a stable currency can be a valuable national asset.

27. This assumes that inflation replaces an income or generalized sales tax as a source of governmental revenues. Taxes on other classes of nonhuman wealth or an explicit excise tax on money of the type that was proposed in the 1930s as an antidepression measure could produce effects similar to those of inflation. These taxes are capable of producing the relative price effects of anticipated inflation with stable prices.

28. Insofar as the supply of money substitutes is completely inelastic, there can be no reallocation of resources to the production of them. Hence there can be no change in the way a society uses its resources and no welfare losses resulting from inflation. The more elastic the supply of money substitutes, the smaller the stock of real balances a community will want to maintain for any given rate of change of prices. Therefore, the tax potential of inflation is inversely related to its effect on efficiency.

stability, constitutes a measure of the cost to a community of using real resources as money substitutes.[29]

A recognized increase in the cost of holding cash balances can lead to decreases in the currency-deposit ratio. Rising prices imply, in the absence of controls, that interest rates on demand deposits will rise. Hence the advantage of holding non-interest-bearing currency relative to demand deposits changes in favor of deposits, and the currency-deposit ratio decreases.

Barter increases during anticipated inflation. No economy, even during stable prices, negotiates all of its output through its market sector; every economy contains a barter sector. Anticipated inflation raises the costs of using money in exchanges as compared with "do-it-yourself" activities or barter. Therefore, some of the economic values that are normally created through money exchange will, in the presence of anticipated inflation, pass from the market to the barter sector. The greater the expected rate of change of prices, the greater will be the relative advantage of barter vis-à-vis using money exchange markets, and the greater will be the bias in the usual measurements of national income. At some rate of change of prices, the costs of holding money become so high that barter replaces money exchange entirely.

Money economizing, somewhat related to barter, is achieved through vertical integration, so that transactions formerly involving the use of money can be consummated without it. The internal bookkeeping and transfer pricing arrangements of a firm, which may be thought of as a form of private money, replace higher-cost money during anticipated inflation. Consequently, anticipatory inflation implies the existence of incentives to form more highly integrated firms.[30]

### C. Product Shifting

The relative profitability, in the short run, of producing particular products is affected by an increase in the costs of holding money. Since money, like inventory, plant and equipment, and labor, is an agent of production, a rise in the

---

29. This measure, as well as that used by Bailey, should not be interpreted as an answer to the question: How much larger would income be if inflation did not occur? If inflation did not occur, then governmental tax receipts would be smaller. What is being measured is the welfare costs of inflation, holding constant the volume of real resources going to the government, and assuming inflation is replaced by a tax completely free of efficiency losses!

30. Shortening of pay periods, which appears to be a uniform feature of hyperinflations, represents a substitution of bookkeeping services for money. During the height of

costs of using money is a change in the relative prices of inputs. Just as production techniques vary in their mixes of capital and labor, so also do they differ in the extent to which they use money. For industries that employ relatively money-intensive methods of production, anticipated inflation implies that their product costs rise and their profitability falls relative to industry generally. In the long run, this difference in profitability implies a reallocation of resources toward less money-intensive products and techniques.

A money-intensive production process employs a large volume of money services relative to the services of other human and nonhuman capital. This suggests that the ratio of average cash balances to sales represents a criterion by which the money intensiveness of a production process can be evaluated.[31] The long-run impact of an inflation tax upon the relative prices of products is greater, the greater the dispersion of the cash to sales ratio.[32] The short-run effects on profits are a function of the size of cash balances relative to the investment of equity holders. The larger this ratio, the greater the adverse effects on profits, and presumably stock prices, of a tax on money.[33]

In general, holdings of money are related to the future outlay and receipt streams of an enterprise. The greater the outlays and receipts per dollar of share capital, the higher the ratio of money to equity. Firms with relatively low outlays and receipts per dollar of share capital usually employ capital-intensive methods of production that involve the use of long-lived capital. At the other

---

the post–World War I German inflation, some workers were paid as often as three times a day. This made it possible to reduce the volume of real balances held.

Similarly, banks find it profitable to expand their banking services to include deposits of stable foreign currencies. During the height of the German inflation, a large fraction of the deposits of German banks consisted of foreign currencies.

31. The market price of a product represents a fuller accounting of its economic costs of production than do accounting costs. Since the ratio of costs to sales varies from product to product, the former is a better criterion. The size of a cash balance is by definition perfectly correlated with the size of the service stream rendered by that cash balance. Consequently, no useful purpose is served by computing the service stream of a stock of money. The ratio of cash balances to total assets of an enterprise would be an indicator of the money intensiveness of its products if all of the resources employed were the property of that enterprise.

32. The substitutability of other resources for money by business firms and their demand elasticities are both assumed to be randomly and independently distributed with respect to this ratio.

33. This abstracts from differences in the length of the short run for various enterprises.

extreme, firms with relatively high outlays and receipts per dollar of share capital are usually labor-intensive enterprises such as retailing and service trades. Consequently, an increase in the cost of holding money implies increased output and employment in the long run, and profits in the short run, for capital-intensive economic activities; conversely for labor-intensive activities.

If the use of long-lived assets economizes on money balances through the reduction in the size of receipt and expenditure streams during anticipated inflation, a community is induced to use longer-lived assets than it otherwise would. To illustrate, consider a firm that is indifferent between investing in two wooden buildings or one steel building during price-level stability. Either alternative involves the same capital costs and the same present worth of the difference between the expected cost and income streams. The steel building, however, has a lower annual rate of receipts and outlays per dollar of invested capital. Consequently, smaller cash balances are held on the average as a result of investing in the steel building. Therefore, a rise in the cost of holding money, aside from any interest-rate changes, increases the relative value of the more durable asset.

### D. Factor Price Effects

In factor markets, anticipated inflation leads to a fall in wages and other factor prices relative to consumer prices. This fall is not a manifestation of market imperfections. It results from an increase in business costs produced by a tax on money. Such an increase in business costs implies a decline in the returns to the cooperating agents of production relative to prices. The effects of anticipated inflation are similar to the effects of excise taxes upon wage-price relationships. A decline in wage and other costs relative to final prices is a result of the imposition of any form of indirect taxes that affects business costs and is not specific to money.[34] The fall in real wage rates attributable to an increase in

34. For a discussion of the effects of indirect taxes on wage-price relationships, see R. Kessel, "The Measurement and Economic Implications of the Inclusion of Indirect Taxes in the Consumers' Price Index," in G. Stigler, ed., *The Price Statistics of the Federal Government* (New York: National Bureau of Economic Research, 1961), p. 517. Per dollar of tax receipts, indirect taxes produce a greater fall in measured real wages than an inflation tax. Wage-price relationships are affected by an inflation tax only insofar as the money-holdings of enterprises, but not of private individuals, are taxed. In contrast, all excises are business taxes and therefore affect wage-price ratios. At the other extreme are personal income taxes which are not business taxes and do not affect wage-price ratios.

business costs reinforces the other, already mentioned, effect on real wages. This is the decline in the profitability of labor-intensive business enterprises.[35] The withdrawal of labor from the market into barter partially mitigates these forces. With respect to capital, the rise in the profitability of capital-intensive enterprises constitutes a force operating to counter the effects of an inflation tax on the return to capital. Consequently, rents rise relative to wages.

Anticipated inflation affects the real rate of interest. An increase in the demand for money substitutes implies the replacement of money with physical assets as a means of holding wealth. Hence an increase in the savings function is implied. The improvement in the profitability of enterprises producing goods with capital-intensive production techniques implies the substitution of capital for labor-intensive methods of production. Hence the investment function increases. The increases in the investment and savings functions produce higher rates of capital formation and conflicting forces acting upon the real rate of interest.[36]

### v. Deflation

For deflation, many of the foregoing conclusions are reversed. During the transition, real money balances are increased. Associated with a rise in the equilibrium size of real money balances is a fall in the quantity of real assets demanded. Hence interest rates rise, and the prices of real assets fall.

During anticipated deflation, the output of nonhuman capital falls and that of human capital rises. This is caused by the replacement of capital-intensive by labor-intensive methods of production and the substitution of money for physical assets as a means of holding wealth.[37] Hence the fraction of national

35. This does not necessarily imply that all wage rates will decline. Anticipated inflation probably leads to an increase in the real demand for accountants, bookkeepers, and brokers; hence their wages will rise relative to wages generally.

36. This argument is capable of explaining the observation of Bresciani-Turroni: "Germany offered the grotesque, and at the same time the tragic spectacle of a people which, rather than produce food, clothes, shoes and milk for its own babies, was exhausting its energies in the manufacture of machines or the building of factories" (as quoted by D. Robertson, *Essays in Monetary Theory* [London: P. S. King, 1940], p. 183).

37. If a policy of falling prices is an alternative to one of stable or rising prices, then alternative monetary-fiscal policies are also being compared. To achieve falling prices, either higher interest rates or greater budgetary surpluses or some combination of the two is required. In any case, the holders of money are subsidized by taxpayers.

income devoted to capital formation falls, and both investment and savings functions decrease. What happens to the real rate of interest depends upon the relative strength of these conflicting forces.

The economic costs of holding non-interest-bearing money when prices are not falling are less than the private costs. Additional real balances can be obtained, if prices are stable, only by surrendering the income from other assets. If prices are rising, there are, of course, additional costs. Because falling prices imply an appreciation in the value of money, it is possible to lower the cost of holding real balances relative to the cost of holding other forms of wealth. In principle, there exists a negative rate of change of prices that will make the private and economic costs of holding money equal; this rate of fall will make the marginal costs of holding real balances zero. This rate of change of prices will satisfy the Pareto optimality condition that the marginal rate of substitution of money in consumption and production be equal, and will induce a community to hold what can be regarded as an optimal stock of real balances.

Insofar as a society moves in the direction of Pareto optimality with respect to its money-holdings, resources are liberated from activities associated with the use of money for other economic activities.[38] The specific activities from which these resources are liberated depend upon whether a community is holding too much or too little money. In the case of too little money, which is the usual situation, resources are devoted to the production of assets because of their money substitute properties. Resources in the form of bookkeeping and clearing services are taken from other activities. For the case of too much money, which is rare in nature, resources are devoted to safeguarding and maintaining cash balances that have a negative marginal social product.

A deliberate policy of anticipated deflation to achieve "optimal" utilization of society's cost-free ability to create money involves two problems. One is an equity problem. An anticipated deflation produced by reducing the absolute money stock constitutes a subsidy to money-holders from taxpayers and, in the absence of compensating changes in the tax structure, will affect the tax system. To offset such changes may involve the creation of new inefficiencies. If anticipated deflation is achieved with a stable nominal monetary stock through

38. See W. Vickrey, "Stability through Inflation," in K. Kurihara, ed., *Post-Keynesian Economics* (New Brunswick, N.J.: Rutgers University Press, 1954), pp. 89 ff.; and G. Tolley, "Providing for Growth of the Money Supply," *Journal of Political Economy* 65 (December 1957): 477.

increases in desired real cash balances resulting from growth in real per capita income, then an explicit subsidy from taxpayers is not required.

The other problem is the historical association of deflation and unemployment. This association has been explained by ad hoc assumptions about the supply conditions of labor. These assumptions are ad hoc because supply conditions usually are specified in real terms independently of the absolute level of prices. When the price level is relevant for specifying the supply conditions of labor, then it is the current, not any, price level that is pertinent. For such supply conditions, it can be demonstrated that deflation causes unemployment. Since this is a widely accepted explanation of unemployment, it must be regarded as a strong indictment of anticipated deflation as a means for achieving optimal real balances.[39]

## VI. Conclusions

Inflations, or types of inflations, should be distinguished according to prevailing anticipations about the future course of prices, a distinction essential for analyzing the economic consequences of rising prices. They should also be regarded as a tax on money and hence an alternative to conventional explicit taxes. When rising prices are not anticipated, but nevertheless occur:

1. Net monetary debtors gain at the expense of net monetary creditors.
2. Governments, that is, taxpayers, gain at the expense of the holders of governmental obligations, both interest-bearing and non-interest-bearing.

During the transition to a correctly anticipated inflation:

1. The quantity of real balances demanded decreases, the real value of the nominal stock of money falls, and prices rise. The rise in prices, unlike the rise in prices during unanticipated inflation, represents an adjust-

---

39. Often it is asserted that the distribution of productivity gains is affected by the course of prices. If price-level changes are anticipated, and the supply of labor is a function of real wage rates, then the distribution of productivity gains is determined by real forces and is independent of both the absolute level of prices and the rate of change of prices. If price-level changes are not anticipated, then debtor-creditor relationships affect the personal but not the functional distribution of income. There seems to be virtually no evidence that real wages, interpreted as either functional or personal income, are affected (see R. Kessel and A. Alchian, "The Meaning and Validity of the Inflation-Induced Lag of Wages Behind Prices," *American Economic Review* 50 [March 1960]: 43).

ment by money-holders to the increased costs of holding money. This implies a decrease in the efficiency with which a community utilizes its resources and, of course, a loss to money-holders.

2. All existing interest-bearing securities are revalued so that their yields will reflect an unbiased estimate of the future course of prices. Consequently, the holders of all debt, both governmental and private, incur capital losses.

And during a correctly anticipated inflation:

1. Prices can rise at a constant rate.
2. The continuing depreciation in the purchasing power of a unit of money induces a series of substitutions for money. In particular, real assets are substituted for money as a means of holding wealth, except for interest-bearing money.
3. The tax on money bears most onerously upon economic activities that are relatively labor-intensive. Converse implications hold for economic activities characterized by low cash-to-equity ratios. Consequently, the demand for labor falls and real wages decline. The demand for capital rises, and rents rise relative to wages. The fraction of national income devoted to capital formation increases.

# REDISTRIBUTION OF WEALTH
# THROUGH INFLATION

## ARMEN A. ALCHIAN AND REUBEN A. KESSEL

Economists have long speculated about the effects of inflation upon the economic welfare of the owners of business enterprises. This speculation has almost invariably led to the conclusion that business firms gain through inflation. This conclusion has been reached through two independent arguments. One, enunciated by both J. M. Keynes and I. Fisher, is that inflation enables business firms to discharge their debts with depreciated money, the creditors' losses being the debtors' gains.[1] Strictly speaking, the validity of this conclusion depends upon two propositions: (i) that business firms are debtors, and (ii) that interest rates reflect biased estimates of the future course of prices when prices are rising. The other argument, advanced by E. J. Hamilton and W. C. Mitchell, is that inflation causes prices to rise faster than wage rates.[2] Consequently, workers are systematically underpaid during inflation, this loss by the working class being a gain for the entrepreneurs.[3] This explanation rests upon special assumptions about the character of labor markets that are generally regarded as invalid in other markets.

Practical men of affairs, in particular investment advisers, have been much

Reprinted from Armen A. Alchian, *Economic Forces at Work* (Indianapolis: Liberty Fund, 1977), 397–411. This article was previously published in *Science* 130, no. 3375 (Sept. 4, 1959): 535–39.

1. J. M. Keynes, *Tract on Monetary Reform* (London, 1923), p. 18; I. Fisher, *The Purchasing Power of Money* (New York, 1920), pp. 58–73, 190–91.

2. E. J. Hamilton, *J. Econ. Hist.* 12 (1952): 325; W. C. Mitchell, *A History of the Greenbacks* (Chicago, 1903), pp. 347–48, and *Gold, Prices, and Wages Under the Greenback Standard* (Berkeley, 1908), pp. 275–76.

3. Some economists and noneconomists also contend that anyone who holds inventories gains through inflation. Since the price of inventories rises above their cost, this difference is regarded as a real gain in economic welfare. But holders of inventories cannot acquire with their inventories any more of the world's goods and services than they could in the absence of inflation.

less confident than professional economists that the owners of business enterprises gain through inflation. They have generally concluded that investors can maintain their capital intact during inflation by investing in common stocks, such an investment being roughly equivalent to an investment in inventories. (Common stocks are ownership or equity shares in a corporation, while bonds represent debt obligations of the corporation.) In other words, an investor in common stock could expect neither to increase nor to decrease his wealth, whereas an investor in bonds and other cash-type investments would suffer a real loss.

This cautiousness of investment counselors is traceable to the experience of investors in equities during the great inflations that have occurred in countries with organized stock markets. It was found during the German runaway inflation following World War I, during the Austrian and French inflations of the 1920s, and more recently during the inflation in Chile that the owners of business firms did not obtain the gains that might have been expected on the basis of the hypotheses set forth by Keynes and Fisher, on the one hand, and Hamilton and Mitchell on the other. These observations are also consistent with the behavior of stock price indexes in the United States during the inflations associated with World Wars I and II.

What was especially puzzling was the fate of the owners of banks. Banks are typically enormous debtors, larger debtors, in fact, than most business firms by an order of magnitude. Furthermore, banks employ relatively more labor per dollar of invested capital than is characteristic of business firms generally. Consequently, it is an implication of both hypotheses that banks ought to be enormous gainers through inflation. Yet the available evidence suggests that one of the regular results of inflation is that the owners of bank shares suffer. The experience of the owners of bank shares in the United States, Germany, Austria, Chile, and France suggests that the real value of bank shares declines during inflation. (Real value is simply price divided by an index number reflecting changes in the price level. Consequently, if the price of an asset rises more than the price level, then its real value has increased, and conversely.)

### Reconciling Hypotheses with Experience

How can this evidence be reconciled with either of these hypotheses? A step toward reconciling the Keynes-Fisher reasoning with the lessons of experience as revealed by the stock market was taken by Kessel when he showed that, despite the enormous debts owed by banks to depositors, there exist offsetting credits that are even larger than these debts.[4] These credits are bank assets which are almost entirely (with the exception of bank buildings and business machines) either money or money-type assets such as notes and other obligations payable to banks by either private customers or the government. The existence of these credits led Kessel to argue that one should do more than merely look at the credit that business firms have extended to their customers. What business firms gain from bondholders may be lost to those to whom these firms have extended credit and may never redound to the interests of the owners.

From his analysis emerged a classification for determining whether or not a business firm is, on *net* balance, a debtor or creditor. Kessel classified assets and liabilities into categories, monetary and real. A monetary asset was defined as an asset whose market value is independent of changes in the price level. These would include money, accounts and notes receivable, government and corporate bonds, life insurance, prepaid taxes, and so on. A monetary liability was defined as a liability whose amount is independent of changes in the price level; these would include accounts payable, notes payable, mortgages, bonds, preferred stock, and so on. Preferred stock, although called a stock, is typically corporate debt rather than equity. A net monetary debtor was then defined as a firm whose monetary liabilities exceeded its monetary assets; and conversely for a net monetary creditor. The net monetary status would indicate the magnitude of the gain or loss a firm would incur from a given amount of inflation. However, firms with the same amount of indebtedness but of unequal size, where size is measured by the aggregate value of the equity of the owners, would have unequal movements in absolute stock prices. Therefore, in order to compare corporations of unequal size, the ratio of net monetary debt to equity, as measured by the market price of shares times the number of shares outstanding, is used as the measure of net monetary debtor or creditor status.[5] The effects of stock dividends, stock splits, and rights offerings were held constant and did not affect measurements of changes in stock prices. "Stock dividends" and "splits" increase the number of shares of common stock without chang-

---

4. R. A. Kessel, *Am. Econ. Rev.* 46 (1956): 130.

5. This is one of the respects in which the present study is an advance over Kessel's early work. While his concept of net debtor or net creditor was correct, his criterion of intensity of debtor or creditor status was wrong, and consequently the measurements based upon his criterion were also wrong.

ing the total investment, whereas "rights" entitle existing stockholders to increase the investment in the corporation by purchasing new shares at a price below existing market prices, thereby also involving some dilution in per-share value. And it was assumed that dividends were continuously reinvested in the shares of the companies that issued them, because this would eliminate variations caused by differences in the extent to which profits were reinvested.

For the United States, Kessel found in his preliminary study that banks were typically net monetary creditors, and that the real value of their shares actually did decline during the World War II inflation, in accordance with the Keynes-Fisher hypothesis. Furthermore, the real value of bank shares seems to have gone down during inflation for every country for which data are available.

Kessel also examined the balance sheets of a small random sample of industrial firms whose stock is traded on the New York Stock Exchange. (Railroads, utilities, and investment companies were omitted. Railroads and utilities were not included, because it was supposed that their very close regulation might conceal the effects of inflation upon their stock prices. Investment companies were omitted because of the magnitude of the problems encountered in evaluating the debtor-creditor status of their assets.) In 1939, about 40 percent of the observed firms were creditors and could be expected to lose through inflation, according to the Keynes-Fisher reasoning. After the firms had been divided into the two categories, debtor and creditor, and after the changes in share prices between 1939 and 1946 had been examined, a significant difference was detected between the rise of share prices in the two categories. The share prices of net monetary debtor firms rose significantly more than the prices of net monetary creditor firms. For a period of deflation, 1929–33, the reverse was found to be true. The share prices of net monetary creditors fell significantly less than the share prices of net monetary debtors.

The behavior of the stock prices of bank shares during the inflation associated with World War II was indistinguishable from the behavior of the shares of equivalent industrial creditors. Other evidence indicates that banks were characterized by large amounts of labor per dollar of invested capital as compared with enterprises generally. This evidence casts doubt upon the validity of the Hamilton-Mitchell reasoning, that inflation causes real wages to fall. If the wage lag had been operative, the value of bank shares would have risen more than the value of the shares of equivalent industrial creditors.

This evidence validated the proposition that during inflation interest rates are systematically lower than they ought to be if inflation is not to transfer wealth from creditor to debtors, but it also challenged the assumption that business firms are, in large part, debtors. The mechanism for redistribution that Keynes and Fisher envisaged was correct, but their assumption that business firms were generally debtors was wrong, and it was this that led them to the erroneous conclusion that business firms gain through inflation. This evidence also explains the behavior of stock-price indexes during inflation. If a substantial fraction of all business firms were net monetary creditors, then an index number of stock prices that was composed of both net monetary debtors and net monetary creditors would not necessarily rise in real value during inflation. Indeed, if the debtors just balance out the creditors, one would expect stock prices generally to keep pace pretty closely with the general price level. These results led to a much larger-scale investigation, designed both to provide stronger evidence of the validity of the mechanism for redistribution envisaged by Keynes and Fisher and to enlarge our empirical knowledge of stock prices.[6]

### New Evidence for Mechanism of Redistribution

The population of firms investigated includes all of the industrials whose common stock was traded on the New York Stock Exchange at any time between 1914 and 1952. For 1933–52, the American Stock Exchange was also included. Furthermore, four separate industries were studied for the period 1940–52—chemicals, steels, retailing, and textiles—in order to hold constant any industry differences. The period of the study, 1915–52, includes two inflations (World Wars I and II), two deflations (1921–22 and 1928–33), and two periods of relative price stability (1923–30 and 1933–40). The number of firms observed in a year ranged from a minimum of 71 to a maximum of 885. In all, nearly 14,000 firm-years of data were observed and analyzed.

What do these data show? The distribution of firms by net monetary debtor and net monetary creditor status has changed spectacularly since 1914. The percentage of firms in each category is shown in Figure 1. These data are based on the New York and the American Stock Exchange samples. The shift from predominantly net monetary debtor status, around the time of World War I, to a ratio of approximately 50:50 in 1952 may explain why Keynes and Fisher made the assumption they did about business firms being debtors.

Apparently, individual firms usually did not shift their net monetary status

6. This study was undertaken with the aid of a research grant from the Merrill Foundation for the Advancement of Financial Knowledge. The article, from this point on, constitutes the first statement of some of the results of this study.

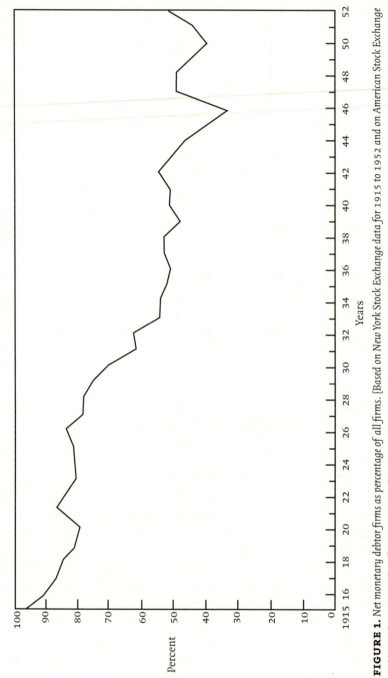

**FIGURE 1.** Net monetary debtor firms as percentage of all firms. [Based on New York Stock Exchange data for 1915 to 1952 and on American Stock Exchange and "over-the-counter" data for 1940 to 1952]

frequently. A firm that was a net monetary debtor in one year was very likely to be one in the next year, despite a gradual shift of the population as a whole. A classification of firms during the 1915–20 inflation according to net monetary status shows that 78 of the firms were net monetary creditors during at least four years of the six-year span, while 22 were net monetary debtors during at least four of the six years. A few did not retain their status for as long as four years. According to Keynes and Fisher the net monetary debtors should have had an increase in the values of their stocks relative to the net monetary creditors. The observed data show that $1.00 of equity of the net monetary debtors increased to $2.66, while the net monetary creditors' dollar increased to only $1.60; the superiority is 57 percent and one which would have less than one chance in 1,000 of occurring by an unusually favorable random selection of firms if there really were no transfers of wealth from creditors to debtors.

Table 1 contains more details, as well as the results for the inflation of 1940–52, for each of the populations of firms studied. In every instance the net monetary debtors did better. In Figure 2 these results are given in the form of a graph. The probability sampling levels are sufficiently small to make it extraordinarily difficult to attribute such results to random sampling. And when the probability levels are combined by the Fisher chi-square method, the sampling probability falls to below one chance in 10,000.

To test whether the results are attributable to inflation rather than to a hidden factor which makes the better firms become net monetary debtors, the deflationary episodes were also considered. In the two deflations of 1921–22 and 1928–33, the firms were again classified according to whether they were persistently net monetary debtors or creditors. In the short deflation of 1921–22, each firm in the sample maintained its monetary status during the entire period. In the 1928–33 episode, one deviation was permitted. In both deflations the net monetary creditors did better than the net monetary debtors—just the opposite of the finding for inflations and in conformance with the predictions of the Keynes-Fisher model. The sampling probability levels are small, being less than 5 percent for the shorter deflation of 1920–22 and less than 0.1 percent for 1929–32. The combined sampling probability is less than 0.01. Finally, for the periods of price stability of 1923–30 and 1933–40, a similar classification of firms revealed no difference in performance between the net monetary creditors and the net monetary debtors, again in conformance with the Keynes-Fisher hypothesis as modified here. These results are also given in Table 1.

TABLE 1. Observed stock prices values (with reinvested dividends) for episodes of inflations, deflations, and stable prices, by exchanges and industries. [From Moody's Industrials (1914–53); Commercial and Financial Chronicles (1921–53); Bank and Quotation Journals (1928–53); and New York Times (1915–53)]

| Population sampled | Kind and no. of firms* | | Mean resulting equity value† ($) | Mean of debtor minus creditor‡ ($) | t§ | p¶ |
|---|---|---|---|---|---|---|
| *Inflations* | | | | | | |
| 1915–1920 | | | | | | |
| New York Stock Exchange | Debtors | 78 | 2.66 | +1.06 | 3.27 | .001 |
| New York Stock Exchange | Creditors | 22 | 1.60 | | | |
| 1940–1952 | | | | | | |
| New York Stock Exchange | Debtors | 29 | 5.93 | +1.47 | 1.80 | .05 |
| New York Stock Exchange | Creditors | 35 | 4.46 | | | |
| American Stock Exchange | Debtors | 57 | 11.30 | +3.25 | 1.65 | .05 |
| American Stock Exchange | Creditors | 70 | 8.05 | | | |
| Over-the-counter | Debtors | 22 | 9.38 | +2.93 | 1.19 | .12 |
| Over-the-counter | Creditors | 45 | 6.45 | | | |
| Steel industry | Debtors | 29 | 6.92 | +0.25 | .15 | .44 |
| Steel industry | Creditors | 27 | 6.67 | | | |
| Chemical industry | Debtors | 19 | 7.17 | +2.53 | 1.24 | .12 |

| | | | | | | |
|---|---|---|---|---|---|---|
| Chemical industry | Creditors | 19 | 4.54 | | 1.45 | .07 |
| Textile industry | Debtors | 29 | 16.33 | +6.67 | | |
| Textile industry | Creditors | 22 | 9.66 | | | |
| Department stores | Debtors | 29 | 8.96 | +4.81 | 2.64 | .007 |
| Department stores | Creditors | 22 | 4.15 | | | |
| New York Stock Exchange wage firms | Debtors | 50 | 7.85 | +2.07 | 1.76 | .04 |
| New York Stock Exchange wage firms | Creditors | 32 | 5.78 | | | |
| *Deflations* | | | | | | |
| 1921–1922 | | | | | | |
| New York Stock Exchange | Debtors | 118 | 1.48 | −0.30 | −1.73 | .045 |
| New York Stock Exchange | Creditors | 24 | 1.78 | | | |
| 1928–1933 | | | | | | |
| New York Stock Exchange | Debtors | 63 | .49 | −0.60 | −3.17 | .001 |
| New York Stock Exchange | Creditors | 35 | 1.09 | | | |
| *Stable prices* | | | | | | |
| 1923–1930 | | | | | | |
| New York Stock Exchange | Debtors | 50 | 2.78 | +0.45 | 1.08 | .14 |
| New York Stock Exchange | Creditors | 15 | 2.33 | | | |
| 1933–1940 | | | | | | |
| New York Stock Exchange | Debtors | 56 | 4.31 | −0.80 | −.89 | .81 |

*(continued)*

TABLE 1. (continued)

| Population sampled | Kind and no. of firms[*] | | Mean resulting equity value[†] ($) | Mean of debtor minus creditor[‡] ($) | t[§] | p[¶] |
|---|---|---|---|---|---|---|
| New York Stock Exchange | Creditors | 54 | 5.11 | | | |
| American Stock Exchange (curb) | Debtors | 17 | 6.44 | +1.72 | +.71 | .52 |
| American Stock Exchange (curb) | Creditors | 20 | 4.72 | | | |

[*] Number of firms that maintained debtor (or creditor) monetary status during at least 2/3 of the episode.
[†] Mean price plus reinvested dividends at the end of the episode, per dollar of 1940 stock prices.
[‡] Mean equity value for net monetary debtors minus mean value for net monetary creditors.
[§] Student's t test coefficient:

$$t = d \left/ \left( \frac{s_1^2}{N_1} + \frac{s_2^2}{N_2} \right)^{1/2} \right.$$

[¶] Sampling probability of t (one-tailed) based on Welch approximation. [B. L. Welch, "The generalization of student's problem when several different population variances are involved," *Biometrika* 34 (1947): 28. Two-tailed test is used for periods of price stability.]

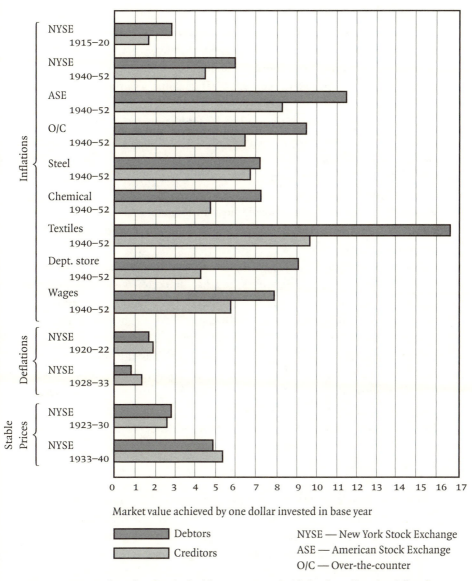

**FIGURE 2.** *Market value of equity for debtors as compared with that for creditors (per dollar of base-year common stock value).*

But what about the Mitchell-Hamilton wage-lag hypothesis and its implications for business profits? Possibly labor intensiveness is correlated with net monetary status. Under these circumstances, the wage lag, while unrevealed, might yet be operative. To explore this possibility as well as the possibility that growth might be correlated with debtor-creditor status, a sample of 113 firms listed on the New York Stock Exchange was obtained. These firms were the entire population of industrials that reported wage bills sometime during the interval 1940–52. Three variables—(i) net monetary debtor or creditor status per dollar of equity, (ii) wages paid per year per dollar of equity, and (iii) yearly sales per dollar of equity—were evaluated for potential predictive content by means of partial correlation analysis. (Equity values were determined by the market price of shares.) And in order to avoid violating assumptions underlying probability tests of significance for correlation analysis, ranks for the three independent variables were used.

The results of this analysis revealed that only net monetary status was correlated with relative stock price changes, and that this correlation was in the predicted direction. Moreover, the chance that this observation would be produced by random sampling from a population characterized by an absence of this correlation is less than 1 in 1,000. This evidence is completely consistent with the hypothesis that the wage lag is inoperative—that is, that the imperfection of the labor market postulated by the wage-lag theorists is nonexistent. Consequently, these results must be regarded as evidence against the hypothesis that a wage lag increases business profits during inflation. However, one must not lose sight of the fact that this is only partial evidence, from a nonrandom sample consisting of 113 firms.

## Conclusion

These results, reported here for the first time, while constituting overwhelming evidence in support of the Keynes-Fisher reasoning about the bias in interest rates during inflation, fail to support their conclusion that business firms gain through inflation. The frequency of debtors in the business population is not great enough to justify Keynes and Fisher's sweeping statements about the gains of business enterprise through inflation. This evidence also suggests that the Keynes-Fisher theorizing about the effects of inflation is not specific to business enterprises; it is a general theory of wealth transfers caused by inflation and is equally applicable to individuals. What count are monetary asset and monetary liability positions and not the type of economic activity in which one engages.

Especially pertinent to much of the current discussion of the consequences of inflation is that the present evidence, by validating the wealth-transfer effect from monetary creditors to monetary debtors (and rejecting the wage-lag hypothesis), verifies the implication that inflation is basically a "tax" on creditors in favor of debtors. Inflation constitutes a tax on the wealth of individuals to the extent that they are holders of money-type assets rather than savers, wage earners, businessmen, widows, orphans, or retired schoolteachers.

These results have implications for the adjustment of personal investment and wealth portfolios (including not only stocks, but bonds, life insurance, mortgages, charge accounts, cash holdings, and so on) in order to hedge against inflation or to profit if inflation comes. Similar reasoning applies to the management of investment, pension, and trust funds.

# MORE EVIDENCE ON INFLATION-CAUSED
# WEALTH REDISTRIBUTION

## ARMEN A. ALCHIAN AND REUBEN A. KESSEL

In an earlier article, the reader was promised the results of a large-scale empirical test of the wealth redistribution effect of inflation implied by economic theory. In that paper the small-scale test supported the theory.[1] Now we present the results of a study covering the American industrial corporate population from 1915 through 1952, a period marked by two inflations (1915–20; 1940–52), two deflations (1920–22; 1929–32), and two periods of price stability (1921–29; 1933–40).

As remarked in the earlier paper, the belief that business firms gain through inflation is common among both economists and the lay public. Some believe that business firms are debtors and gain from inflation just as does any other debtor. Underlying this belief is the hypothesis that the inflation was unanticipated and that, therefore, the interest rate did not reflect completely the price-level changes that occurred. This is to be contrasted with an anticipated inflation, in which price-level changes were correctly anticipated so that the market produced a rate of interest sufficiently high to compensate for the rise in the price level. Therefore, to assert that debtors gain from inflation is to assert that the inflation was not completely anticipated. This implies also that it is not true that debtors must gain from inflation—they gain only from unanticipated inflation. The test of whether debtors do or do not, in fact, gain is a test of whether the inflation was or was not anticipated.

A second rationale for the conclusion that business firms gain from inflation rests on the assumption that wages lag during inflation, producing a rise in profits at the expense of wage earners. A third argument that is more common in the lay literature than in the economic periodicals is that business firms gain because they carry inventories. Clearly, in real terms this is no source of

This previously unpublished 1961 article appears here by permission of the author.

1. Reuben A. Kessel, "Inflation-Caused Wealth Redistribution: A Test of a Hypothesis," *American Economic Review* 46 (March 1956): 128–41.

gain to business firms and constitutes a source of nominal increase in wealth no greater and no less than the rise in the price level, in either unanticipated or anticipated inflation.

The first and second rationales are independent. The third, insofar as it uses economic analysis, does not imply gains in wealth relative to the price level. Therefore, it is the first two that are interesting. The test of the first rationale involves two stages. First, is it true that business firms are debtors? If not, then the rationale is irrelevant, for the premise is wrong. It may, of course, still be true that business firms gain because they employ labor—even if they are not debtors.

Both of these questions have been investigated, and on the basis of the evidence reported herein, the conclusions that are overwhelmingly dictated are:

1. Business firms are not typically debtors.
2. Those firms that are debtors gain at the expense of the creditors; this suggests the generalization that debtors gain (business firms or not) from creditors (business firms or not) because the inflations experienced in the United States since 1915 have been unanticipated.
3. During deflations, the opposite effects occur, again indicating that the deflations were also unanticipated.
4. Business firms do not obtain profits from any lag in wages, probably because there is no wage lag. This conclusion is taken from a study reported in detail elsewhere.

### Populations Sampled

A test can be made with those American business corporations that publish balance sheets annually. The corporations whose common stocks are traded on the major exchanges have measures of their equity provided by the prices of their stocks. Since the United States has experienced inflations and deflations since 1915, the stock prices of American business corporations from 1915 through the early 1950s should provide a test of the implied wealth-transfer effects of inflation and deflation.

Inflation characterized the periods 1915–20 and 1940–50. Deflations occurred in 1920–22 and 1929–33, with relatively stable prices in 1923–29 and only a very slight rise in the price level from 1933 to 1940. A more precise picture can be obtained from figure 1 and table 1, which present a measure of the price level, the Bureau of Labor Statistics Consumer Price Index (for December 15 of each year) from 1914 through 1952. In essence, there are two periods each of inflation, deflation, and stable prices.

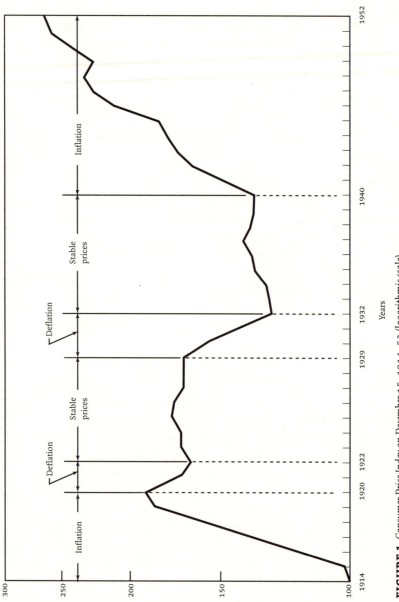

**FIGURE 1.** *Consumer Price Index on December 15, 1914–52 (logarithmic scale)*

TABLE 1. *Consumer price index\* (as of December 15 annually, December 15, 1914 = 100)*

| Year | Index | Year | Index |
|------|-------|------|-------|
| 1914 | 100   | 1934 | 132.5 |
| 1915 | 101.9 | 1935 | 136.0 |
| 1916 | 113.4 | 1936 | 137.4 |
| 1917 | 134.6 | 1937 | 141.8 |
| 1918 | 162.5 | 1938 | 138.0 |
| 1919 | 186.3 | 1939 | 137.1 |
| 1920 | 190.4 | 1940 | 138.7 |
| 1921 | 170.2 | 1941 | 152.2 |
| 1922 | 165.8 | 1942 | 167.4 |
| 1923 | 170.0 | 1943 | 175.3 |
| 1924 | 169.6 | 1944 | 180.9 |
| 1925 | 176.5 | 1945 | 185.9 |
| 1926 | 173.6 | 1946 | 214.9 |
| 1927 | 170.5 | 1947 | 230.9 |
| 1928 | 168.5 | 1948 | 237.1 |
| 1929 | 169.1 | 1949 | 232.4 |
| 1930 | 158.8 | 1950 | 246.2 |
| 1931 | 143.5 | 1951 | 260.4 |
| 1932 | 128.7 | 1952 | 262.6 |
| 1933 | 129.3 |      |       |

*Source:* "Changes in Cost of Living in Large Cities in the U.S. 1913–1942," *Bulletin,* no. 699, U.S. Department of Labor, 1941, p. 43, Table I; and "Interim Adjustment of Consumers' Price Index," *Bulletin,* no. 1039, U.S. Department of Labor, 1951, Appendix A, Table A-1, p. 21; and *Monthly Labor Review,* 1951, 1952, 1953, Table D-1 in each January issue.
\*Indexes of the cost of living of wage earners and lower salaried workers in large cities.

That business corporations could provide a test of wealth transfer among net monetary debtors and creditors may be somewhat surprising. Contrary to widely held beliefs and to the case in some other countries, the set of industrial corporations in the United States is almost evenly divided into net monetary debtors and creditors. It has not always been so in the United States. Figure 2 shows the percentage of the sampled industrial firms that were net monetary

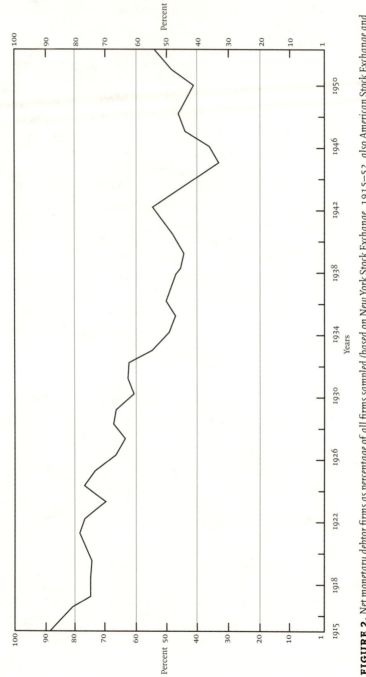

**FIGURE 2.** Net monetary debtor firms as percentage of all firms sampled (based on New York Stock Exchange, 1915–52, also American Stock Exchange and selected over-the-counter firms for 1940–52)

debtors.[2] From a high of almost 90 percent in 1915, the percentage declined to about 50 percent in 1952. This suggests that a test of the wealth transfer from creditors to debtors should be possible with American industrial corporations.

One source of possible misunderstanding should be removed. The theory does not say that every net monetary debtor will, in fact, be observed to have experienced an increase in equity greater than that experienced by every net monetary creditor, including all other possible factors that may have occurred. What it does say is that for each firm there are a myriad of factors, some of which will increase equity and some not. For example, one can be lucky or unlucky, with respect to the quality of the management, the results of sales program, the incidence of fashion or demand shifts among products, the occurrence of strikes, fires, lawsuits, deaths of key employees, etc., etc. All of these will vary so that whatever the host of such factors impinging on any firm, one thing is predicted—a net monetary debtor during inflation will experience a greater increase in equity than a net monetary creditor or a firm whose net monetary debtor status is smaller. Just as people differ in their weights for various reasons, it can still be said that those who eat more will weigh more—reference being made to the effect of that *one* factor, whatever the variety of other factors that increase or decrease the predicted variable, in our case equity, rather than weight.

The simplest (and sometimes best) way to allow for the various factors is to randomize the selection of firms from the pertinent population. These various factors are not kept, or even assumed, constant. Instead, they are allowed to vary. Random-sampling theory provides an estimate of how much of the observed changes in equities can be attributed to these other factors. However, sometimes these other specified factors can be controlled, or their effects eliminated, without too great a cost.

One way is to study industries separately so as to eliminate sources of difference arising from industry idiosyncracies. And this we shall do. But this is expensive, and sometimes there are not enough firms in one industry to yield adequately discriminating evidence. A disadvantage of exclusive reliance on special industries is that generalizations derived from the analysis will be strictly applicable only to those industries. Therefore, a more broadly based sample is desirable.

But aside from these considerations, some factors can be identified in advance and their effects eliminated by excluding those firms heavily subject to

2. The populations from which the samples were taken and the method of measuring net monetary debtor or creditor status are given below.

the effects of these factors, for example, price or profit controls by state authorities. We have therefore excluded from the population under study all public utilities or businesses that were conventionally subject to profit regulation. But during World War II, the general prevalence of wage and price controls was not taken as a basis for excluding firms. Instead, variations in the impact of such regulations entered into the sample results for all firms, and we hope that despite this extra source of variation among firms, the wealth transfer effect will be strong enough to be noticed—even over that background "noise."

Financial institutions have been excluded because, in part, their operations are rigorously controlled by various regulatory authorities, and also because almost all financial institutions are net monetary creditors. The difficulty of finding net monetary debtors with which to make comparisons raises the costs of relying on such firms to prohibitive heights.

Foreign corporations were excluded to reduce the effects of asset holdings in countries having different degrees of inflation. Furthermore, their balance sheet data could not be accurately interpreted.

Any firm whose balance sheets or common stock prices were unavailable had to be omitted. Therefore, the population of acceptable firms was restricted at most to that set whose balance sheets were reported in either Moody's *Industrials* or Standard *Corporation Records*.[3]

The sampled populations can be described as follows:

1. The New York Stock Exchange was sampled over the period 1915 to 1922, inclusive.[4] This sample of 1915–22 spans one inflation and one deflation.

2. A new sample was drawn from the New York Stock Exchange list of firms of 1922.[5] This sample was used for the period 1922–30, a period of essentially stable prices.

3. A third sample from the New York Stock Exchange was taken as of the be-

---

3. John Moody, *Moody's Industrials, American and Foreign*, Industrial Securities, Moody's Investor Service, New York, vols. for 1914 through 1953; *Standard Corporation Descriptions*, vols. 10 through 15, Standard and Poor's Corporation, New York.

4. The sample was a gradually increasing sample. In 1915, all 87 eligible firms that had their common stock traded on the Exchange, according to the *Commercial and Financial Chronicle*, Jan. 2, 1915, pp. 39–43, vol. 100, are included in the sample. In 1916 the number in the population grew to 98. In 1917 and 1918, the entire population of eligible firms was included in the sample. Thereafter and through 1922, a sample of the new firms was included.

5. *Ibid.*, Jan. 15, 1921, pp. 143–45, vol. 112, part I. This sample was not completely independent of the former sample, there being some firms that were in both samples.

ginning of 1928, and its experience was traced through 1933, a period of deflation.[6] The major price decline occurred during 1930–32, but to avoid defining the deflation period too narrowly, the sample was started as of the beginning of 1928, when the Consumer Price Index seems to have started down. Identifying a real peak is difficult because the Consumer Price Index, being a sample of prices, is subject to random-sampling fluctuations. Whether an observed peak should be regarded as the true maximum, or merely a sampling fluctuation, can't be resolved with existing data. To avoid these problems, we sampled early enough to avoid criticism for not having looked at the whole episode.

4. A fourth sample of firms was taken from the New York Stock Exchange at the beginning of 1933 and traced through 1940.[7] This is considered to be a period of essentially stable prices, although there was a slight upward movement during the period.

5. For the same episode, a sample was also taken from the Curb Exchange (now the American Stock Exchange).[8] The sampling was curtailed shortly after it was started so that only one-fifth of the intended sample was collected. Costs of continuing the sample were becoming too high in view of the information to be gained. Since sampling was done from an alphabetic listing, the sample stopped when the J's were reached.

6–12. Seven more samples were taken from seven populations as of January 1, 1960: (6) The New York Stock Exchange,[9] (7) Curb (American Stock Exchange),[10] and (8) over-the-counter firms.[11] Four industry samples were taken from firms classified as (9) steels,[12] (10) retail department stores,[13] (11) chemicals,[14] and (12) textiles.[15]

---

6. *Ibid.*, Jan. 7, 1928, pp. 79–84, vol. 126, part I.

7. *Ibid.*, Jan. 2, 1932, pp. 99–106, vol. 134, part I.

8. The population sampled was that listed in "New York Curb Exchange," *Bank and Quotation Record*, Feb. 5, 1932, pp. 39–56 (Wm. B. Dana, New York).

9. Defined by the listing in *Bank and Quotation Record*.

10. Defined by the listing in *Bank and Quotation Record*.

11. Defined by "Over-the-Counter Securities," *Commercial and Financial Chronicle*, Jan. 6, 1940, pp. 118–19, vol. 150, part I; "Over-the-Counter Securities," E. F. Hutton *Pocket Manual*, Nov. 1939, p. 320; "Unlisted Securities—Industrial," *The Annalist*, Jan. 4, 1940; and "Over-the-Counter (Industrial)," *New York Times*, Jan. 2, 1940.

12. Moody's *Industrials*, 1941, p. 134.

13. *Ibid.*, p. 133.

14. *Ibid.*, pp. 126–27.

15. *Ibid.*, pp. 134–35.

These seven samples were traced through 1952. The industry samples are not confined to firms whose shares were traded only on national or regional stock exchanges. A very few firms (5–10) in the industry samples were also in the New York, or American, or over-the-counter samples. Deletion of these common firms did not change any sample results to any significant extent. Therefore, they have been kept in each sample.

13. A "wage bill" sample was taken from the New York Stock Exchange as of 1952, and the experience of these firms was traced from 1940 to 1952. This sample consists of all firms that reported their total annual wages costs, for ten years, and a sample of those firms that reported for at least 1952, 1951, and 1950. The end-date selection basis was necessary because the source of information for total annual wages bills was available only for those firms that were in existence in 1952 and were, in fact, reporting such data. These firms were found by examining annual reports of all firms on the New York Stock Exchange in 1952.[16]

14. In all, 13 samples were taken—all nearly independent in the statistical sense. One of these samples, that for 1915–22, will hereafter be considered as two samples, in the sense that it covers an inflation (1915–20) and a deflation (1920–22). Its experience over the inflation should differ from its experience over the deflation, and therefore we shall usually refer to the 1915–20 and the 1920–22 samples as if they were two separate samples. And in a pertinent sense they are, because they are samples of different episodes. Under this arrangement we count a total of 14 samples:

    a. One for the inflation of 1915–20, and eight for the inflation of 1940–52.

    b. One each for the deflations of 1920–22 and 1928–32.

    c. One for the stable price period of 1923–29 and two for 1933–40.

Each firm included in a sample was traced throughout the episode of that sample. In relatively rare instances, a firm did not survive the episode; short-lived firms fall in the following categories:

(1) Cessation of business by liquidation or bankruptcy. In every instance, the value of the liquidated assets received by the shareholders was counted as the last recorded value of equity. For bankruptcy cases, equity was counted as zero, or whatever small liquidation value the stock had as of the last known date of trading.

(2) Mergers. The value received by stockholders of the purchased or

---

16. Corporation Annual Reports, Godfrey Memorial Library (Yale University), 1952 and 1953.

merged firm, either as cash or as new securities, was recorded as the last equity value for the firm, and the analysis of that firm brought to an end as of the end of the year of the merger. This was the most common reason for short-lived firms. In the textile industry sample for 1940–52, 38 percent of sampled firms in 1940 were short-lived from this cause, far above any other sample.

(3) Lack of public interest. Extremely few firms, primarily among the over-the-counter firms that were in the industry samples, became so closely held that public interest disappeared as sales became rare.

## Data Required

Since the implication to be tested is that net monetary debtors experience an increase in equity relative to net monetary creditors during inflation, and the opposite during deflation, the data collected have to enable classification of each firm by its net monetary status and also to reveal its change in equity, for each year.[17] To classify each firm, knowledge of its monetary assets and liabilities is required. This balance sheet information was obtained for the beginning of each calendar or fiscal year. (Fiscal year data were interpolated linearly to obtain estimates of calendar year-end values.) In a later section we identify the various balance sheet accounts according to whether they were regarded as monetary or non-monetary accounts. For the moment we turn to the equity measure.

### Equity Data

The change in the market price of one share of stock, including dividends, during the year was the basic measure of equity change. Price was obtained for the trading day nearest to December 31 of each year. The change in the price of one share of stock was used rather than the change in the total equity of all shares of stock, because it was assumed that new issues of stock for assets or mergers, as well as stock options to employees, resulted in increased investment equivalent to the market value of the new shares. Therefore, these were regarded as identifiable factors whose effects could be controlled or eliminated.

Changes in formal capital structures also were controlled or corrected. A stock split of, say, two to one was interpreted as a purely formal accounting

---

17. For all the sampled firms, basic sources of data were primarily Moody's *Manual of Investments* for balance-sheet and equity-structure data. Occasionally, resort was had to Standard and Poor's *Statistical Reports*. For common stock prices, the *Commercial and Financial Chronicle*, the *New York Times*, and *Bank and Quotation Record* were the main sources. In rare instances the National Quotation Bureau *Reports* were used for some over-the-counter issues.

arrangement wherein each old share was equivalent to two new shares. The same logic was applied to stock dividends. A change in value of one share of original stock is defined to be the difference between the market price of the adjusted number of shares and the price of a pre-split share. The formula for the adjusted number of shares also covers issuance of stock rights to new shares.[18]

If the company had conversions of convertible bonds or preferred stocks into common stocks, no adjustment was made for the effect this might have on the value of one share of stock. We have let such effects be included in the many factors that are uncontrolled and contained in the measurable random-sampling error. But the conversion of bonds and preferred stocks, where convertible, introduces more than a random-sampling error. It also introduces a bias. A firm with convertible bonds has part of the equity value residing in the bonds. And therefore the value of the common stock understates the equity. As the common stock rises in value and conversions are made, the rise of the value of the common stock is reduced by the amount of equity value accruing to the convertible issues. Therefore, the rise in the value of one share understates the rise in equity.

The direction of this bias understates the rise in large net monetary debtors (and possibly creditors). It does so because the *measure* of large or small net monetary debtor or creditor is the ratio of net monetary debts to equity. If the equity is initially understated for firms with convertible securities, this ratio will be overstated. But the effect is most serious for the debtor firms because the convertible issues are treated as monetary debts. Therefore a firm with a convertible issue is very likely to be classified a net monetary debtor rather than a creditor. In net, the effect of this bias is to make it more difficult for the sample to show a net wealth gain to net monetary debtors during inflation. During deflations, the equity fall of net monetary debtors will be understated (because convertible issue values are ignored); so here too the sample observations will be biased against the effect we are testing—that net monetary debtor firms should experience a greater fall in equity relative to that of creditors. We could only hope that this bias is not so great as to more than offset the inflation-deflation wealth transfer, and thereby result in sample results that show no wealth transfer. As will be seen, that hope was fulfilled.

---

18. The factor used for adjusting the prices of the new shares to comparability with the old shares is $(1 + \alpha\beta)/(1 + \alpha)$, where $\alpha$ = ratio of number of newly issued shares to formerly outstanding number of shares, and $\beta$ is the ratio of offering prices of new issues to prior price of old issues. If stock is split or stock dividends declared, $\beta$ is zero. If the new rights price is zero, this is equivalent to a stock dividend or split.

Dividend payments during any calendar year were added to the end-of-the-year price of the share to which the dividends were paid during the year. The total was regarded as the end-of-the-year equity, which in comparison with the beginning-of-the-year equity gave the change in equity.

### Monetary Asset and Liability Data

The net monetary debtor or creditor position of a firm is defined as the total monetary assets minus the total monetary debts. This difference was, in part, a function of the size of a firm, although some large firms had nearly zero differences. To compare wealth transfers in different-sized firms, the net monetary position was measured as per dollar of equity. Then the change in wealth for each firm was measured as a ratio of beginning-of-the-year equity. In this way, a large change in wealth for a large firm could be compared with a small increase in wealth for a small firm, where size of firm is the total equity, here defined as number of shares times market price.[19]

The following classification (table 2) of balance sheet accounts covers over 95 percent of all accounts.[20] Three accounts, in particular, were most difficult to classify. "Advances" (both on the liability and on the asset side) could represent loans repayable or advance payments on items being produced for the firm. In the latter case they represented real assets. Even questioning the accountant of the firm was not always helpful. In the motion picture industry, for example,

---

19. This can be treated as an index of equity that is proportional to whatever one means by the total market equity value of a firm. The number of shares was the number of outstanding common shares, despite any convertible issues. Treasury shares were subtracted. Shares that were called by other names but which were in fact common stock were included; for example, some firms had Class A and Class B shares. Usually the former were simply preferred stock, but occasionally both were common shares, differing in voting rights but not in other rights. Similarly, some "preferred" shares were non-callable and were fully participating; if so, they were treated as part of equity. Since the prices of these paired classes of stock moved almost exactly together—as would be expected from the fact that they were titles to essentially identical rights—the price of the "common" share was used in recording market values.

20. Very rare (and almost always trivial) accounts are not included. For example, items like "employee agreement obligation" and "termination claim advances" (both called monetary liabilities, but with no great confidence) and "Red Cross dividends," "transit items," and "copper warrants" (all called non-monetary assets) occur once or twice at most. Classification is in some of these cases impossible, but in almost every case the amounts were so small that it made less than 1 percent difference in the net monetary status.

**TABLE 2.**

Asset classification (M = monetary; R = non-monetary)

| | |
|---|---|
| Accounts receivable (M) | Inventories (R) |
| Accrued interest (M) | Investments (R unless details show monetary |
| Advances (M) | items) |
| Advances to affiliated companies (M) | Investments in subsidiary (R) |
| Bills (M) | Leasehold improvements (R) |
| Bonds (M) | Life insurance cash value (M) |
| Bond discount (M) | Marketable securities (M) |
| Call loans (M) | Merchandise (R) |
| Cash (M) | Notes receivable (M) |
| Certificates of deposit (M) | Officers accounts (M) |
| Claims (M) | Organization expense (R) |
| Compensation fund (M) | Other current assets (R) |
| Contract work (R) | |
| Contract work in process (R) | Patents (R) |
| Contracts (R) | Patent rights (R) |
| Customers accounts (M) | Plant and buildings (R) |
| | Prepaid rentals (R) |
| Debenture bonds owned (M) | |
| Deferred assets and accounts (R) | Real estate (R) |
| Deferred charges (R) | Restricted deposit (M) |
| Deferred claims (M if current, | |
| otherwise R) | Sinking fund (M) |
| Deferred debts ($^{1}/_{2}$M) | Special deposits (M) |
| Deferred expenses (R) | Securities pledged (M) |
| Deferred interest receivable (M) | Stocks pledged (R) |
| Deferred taxes (M) | Sundry debtors (M) |
| Deficit (R) | Sundry investments and receivables (M) |
| Deposits on purchases (R) | Suspended debit items (R) |
| Development expense (R) | |
| | Tax refund claims (M) |
| Employees accounts (M) | Treasury bonds (M) |
| Employees pension fund (M) | Treasury stock, common (R) |
| Employee stock notes (M) | Treasury stock, preferred (M) |
| Employee stock subscriptions (M) | Trustee account (M) |
| Employer stock allotment (M) | Trustees insurance fund (M) |
| Gold, silver (M) | Unamortized discount on debt (M) |
| Goodwill (R) | U.S. securities (M) |
| | Water and power rights (R) |

Liability classification (M = monetary; R = non-monetary)

Acceptances (M)
Accounts payable (M)
Accrued items (M)
Advances (M)

Bills payable (M)
Bonds (M)
Bond interest (M)

Common dividends (M)
Common stock (R)
Coupon notes (M)
Customers unfilled orders (R)

Debentures (M)
Deferred credits (R)
Deferred foreign exchange credits (M)
Deferred income (R)
Deferred interest receivable (R)
Deferred liabilities (R)
Deferred mortgage interest (M)
Deferred revenues (R)
Deposits (M)
Dividends payable (M)
Drafts in transit (M)
Due customers (M)
Due officers and employees (M)

Employees liability insurance (M)
Employees stock subscriptions (R)
Equipment trust notes (M)

Federal tax reserve (M)
Funded debt (M)

Income bonds (M)
Insurance fund reserve (R)
Insurance reserve (R)

Minority interest (R)
Mortgages (M)

Notes (M)

Participating preferred
  Callable (M)
  Non-callable (R)
Pension fund (M)
Premiums of stock (R)
Preferred sinking fund (M)
Preferred stock (M)
Prepaid on sales (R)
Profit and loss (R)
Purchase money obligations (M)
Purchase obligations (M)

Replacement (R)
Reserve for accruals (M)
Reserve for bond redemption (R)
Reserve for completion of accounts (M)
Reserve for contingencies (R)
Reserve for depreciation (R)
Reserve for doubtful accounts (M)
Reserve for preferred dividend (M)
Reserve for taxes (M)
Reserve for unemployment benefit (M)

Serial notes (M)
Stock dividends declared (R)
Subordinated notes (M)
Surplus, capital (R)
Surplus, earned (R)

Unclaimed wages (M)
U.S. government advances (M)

Workman's insurance reserve (M)

"advances to producers" could represent advance payments for a film, owner-ship of which would vest in the company, or loans to producers. Our usual in-formation was that they represented monetary claims, rather than claims to goods in kind. These were especially prevalent during the war of 1940–46 in the aircraft industry and in other industries producing single large orders.

Another large and "ambiguous" item was "investments," or some variant thereof. If the securities were stocks, the account was called real, but if they were bonds it was called monetary. Unfortunately, when data were available about the composition, both monetary and non-monetary items were present in quite varying proportions among firms. Our procedure was to classify ac-cording to the revealed proportions, when possible; otherwise, the account was arbitrarily called real.

A third account of substantial magnitude is "marketable securities." Details were occasionally given of the portfolio, and these were used to classify the ac-count when available. The general information available from these suggested the following rule for cases where no details were given: treat the account as all real before 1934, and one-half monetary from 1934 on.

Incomplete reporting of items caused a problem of undetermined signifi-cance. Accounting conventions do not require that all monetary claims be re-ported. For example, long-term leases are monetary obligations and are offset by long-term claims to real services. Similarly, backlogs of orders are not usu-ally reported.[21]

The data collected for each firm in each year can conveniently be indicated with a firm in the New York Stock Exchange sample for 1940–52. Table 3 shows the data collected for the Coca-Cola Company for a few years.[22]

21. Personal conversations with corporation accountants reveal many cases of this kind of non-reporting. To the extent that these exist, the measure of net monetary status is incorrect.

22. Fiscal year data for balance sheet accounts were converted to calendar year data by linear interpolation—except for number of shares of common stock, because the calen-dar year-end data could be measured by inspection of amounts reported outstanding and dates of splits and new issues. Approximately 20–25 percent of the firms had fiscal years differing from calendar years, although this varied among industries. For example, al-most all retail department stores had fiscal years ending on January 31. Two of the items of information collected have not been used; these are total assets and annual earnings. Neither figure is a market-revealed figure. Each relies on accounting conventions and per-sonal estimates of company officials. All other data are essentially market revealed or objectively measurable.

TABLE 3. Data collected for each firm, illustrated by the Coca-Cola Company, for years 1940–43 only

|  | 1940 | 1941 | 1942 | 1943 |
|---|---|---|---|---|
| 1. Common stock shares, calendar year end | 4,000,000 | 4,000,000 | 3,995,200 | 3,995,200 |
| 2. Common stock shares, fiscal year end | 4,000,000 | 4,000,000 | 3,995,200 | 3,995,200 |
| 3. Dividends paid per share, calendar year ($) | 5.00 | 5.00 | 4.00 | 4.00 |
| 4. Stock split factor, calendar year | 1.00 | 1.00 | 1.00 | 1.00 |
| 5. Stock split factor, fiscal year | 1.00 | 1.00 | 1.00 | 1.00 |
| 6. Earnings per share, fiscal year ($) | 6.77 | 6.78 | 5.37 | 5.93 |
| 7. Total assets, fiscal year ($000) | 107,763 | 133,574 | 140,523 | 133,638 |
| 8. Market price of common, end of calendar year ($) | 105.75 | 78.00 | 87.50 | 113.50 |
| 9. Type of preferred stock outstanding |  |  |  |  |
| 10. Last month of fiscal year | December | December | December | December |
| 11. Total monetary assets end of calendar year ($000) | 22,834 | 19,514 | 19,889 | 41,884 |
| 12. Current monetary liabilities end of calendar year ($000) |  |  |  |  |
| 13. Total monetary liabilities end of calendar year ($000) | 11,534 | 17,182 | 34,396 | 37,172 |

From these basic data all derived statistics used in testing for the wealth transfer effect, in subsequent sections, were computed by IBM electronic computing machines.[23] All the basic data (some 13,000 firm-years) are stored on two reels of IBM tape. Derived statistical analysis data used in the subsequent sections are on one other tape.[24]

## Statistical Analysis of Data and Tests of Economic Analysis

In all, this amounts to almost 12,000 firm-years of data. Several alternative ways exist to distill the pertinent evidence. As will be seen, the first and simplest way to analyze the data, the "cohort" test, is sufficient to reveal the presence of the wealth transfer. Had this simplest test failed to detect the wealth transfer, a more sensitive (and more expensive) statistical procedure would be desirable. However, since the second test, called the "portfolio" test, indicates the usefulness of knowledge of the wealth-transfer effect, it too was used. The

23. The first ten items in that table were originally collected on one piece of paper, on which was also recorded information about new issues of stocks for mergers, splits, dividends, rights, etc. With this information, adjustments were made in dividends, earning, and stock-split factors, which were then entered in the appropriate column. All the data were transferred to punch cards and ultimately to computing-machine tape. The last three items were recorded separately, so that all the data for each firm-year were ultimately collated on tape. Incidentally, all items were checked by a second clerical worker against the sources.

The incidence of error was high enough only to be annoying, but absolutely rare. The most common detected error was in stock prices—because of picking up numbers from the wrong line in lists of prices. Another detected error arose from occasions in which we had failed to note that balance sheet valuations of outstanding preferred stock differed from the callable value—sometimes by a factor of ten to one (where a legal "par" value had no implications as to "callable" value or value derivable by discounting "dividend" obligations at anything like a reasonable rate of interest). If the call price was within 10 percent of the par value or stated value, the stated or par value was used. Special efforts were made to avoid this error; given the nature of data collecting, we can only hope—and sincerely believe—that the incidence of such error is insignificant.

24. Data collection (from source to tape) costs are estimated at about $25,000. Fortunately, after the expenditure of an initial $1,000 for machine processing costs for commercial computing service indicating that at least $10,000 would be required for subsequent computations, the Western Data Processing Center, established at the University of California, Los Angeles, by a gift from the International Business Machine Corporation, provided all subsequent computing services on an IBM 709 at no further machine cost.

Individuals or organizations interested in obtaining the collected data for their own use may do so if they pay the costs of tapes, duplicating, and attendant services.

results, accordingly, are presented after the cohort data. A third and still more expensive technique, multiple regression analysis, is the most sensitive, but most delicate, of all. If certain statistical conditions are not fulfilled, it will fail. Because an IBM 709 computer was available, the cost of the correlation analysis was not prohibitive. Given free time on the new computer, all three analyses were made, and their results are reported.

### The Cohort Test

The cohort test compares the average growth of equity for cohorts of net monetary debtors and of net monetary creditors during inflation, deflation, and stable price periods. For example, for each firm in the 99-firm sample from the New York Stock Exchange for 1940–52, net monetary status was computed as of January 1 of each year. A firm that was a net monetary debtor on every January 1 over the whole episode was placed in the debtor cohort, and similarly for the creditor cohort. The ratio of the price on January 1, 1941 (after adding in the dividends distributed during the year on one share of stock), to the January 1, 1940, price was computed. Dividends during 1941 were included in order to adjust for different earnings-payout policies. In the same way, for each of the ·subsequent years in the episode, the equity growth ratio was computed. These ratios were then multiplied together to give the equity growth ratio over the entire episode for each firm.

For example, the Coca-Cola Company was in this sample from the New York Stock Exchange for 1940–52. Its pertinent balance sheet and equity data are given in table 4. The "net monetary status" column shows this firm was a net monetary creditor during each year.[25] On January 1, 1940, its net monetary assets equalled 1 percent of its equity (common shares times market price), and by January 1, 1941, the net monetary status had increased to .13. Coca-Cola was a net monetary creditor through the whole episode and was therefore placed in the creditor cohort.

The price of one share of its common stock fell in 1940 from \$117.00 to \$105.75, but \$5.00 of dividends were paid out during the year. Its equity

---

25. Precisely, the average net monetary status was equal to:

$$\frac{M_0 + M_1}{E_0 + E_1}$$

where $M_0$ and $M_1$ are the net monetary assets at the beginning and end of the year, and $E_0$ and $E_1$ are equity at the beginning and end of the year.

TABLE 4. Equity growth, and net monetary status of the Coca-Cola Company, 1940–52

| Year | Price of common stock, Jan. 1 | Dividend during year | M, net monetary status | G, wealth growth ratio during year | E = ΠG cumulated growth ratio |
|---|---|---|---|---|---|
| | | | | | 1.00 |
| 1940 | 117.00 | 5.00 | .01 | .95 | .95 |
| 1941 | 105.75 | 5.00 | .13 | .78 | .74 |
| 1942 | 78.00 | 4.00 | .24 | 1.17 | .87 |
| 1943 | 87.50 | 4.00 | .39 | 1.34 | 1.17 |
| 1944 | 113.50 | 4.00 | .35 | 1.24 | 1.45 |
| 1945 | 137.00 | 4.00 | .32 | 1.35 | 1.97 |
| 1946 | 181.25 | 4.00 | .25 | .79 | 1.56 |
| 1947 | 140.00 | 5.00 | .24 | 1.34 | 2.09 |
| 1948 | 182.00 | 5.00 | .22 | .77 | 1.60 |
| 1949 | 134.25 | 6.00 | .20 | 1.28 | 2.05 |
| 1950 | 166.00 | 5.00 | .31 | .73 | 1.50 |
| 1951 | 117.00 | 5.00 | .36 | .92 | 1.38 |
| 1952 | 102.50 | 5.00 | .15 | 1.12 | 1.55 |
| 1953 | 109.75 | — | — | — | — |

growth ratio is therefore (105.75 + 5.00)/117 = .95. In 1941 its equity (plus dividends) fell to .78 of the value at the beginning of 1941. In 1942 it grew to 1.17 of its value at the beginning of 1942. Multiplying these ratios gives .87, the value to which one dollar of equity on January 1, 1940, had fallen by the end of 1942. In table 4, the column "cumulated growth ratio" gives the ratios of equity, at the end of each year, to the base date of January 1, 1940. By the end of 1952 the equity growth ratio was 1.55. In all, 14 of the 99 firms were monetary debtors during the whole episode of 1940–52, and 21 were monetary creditors.

The arithmetic average of these final compounded growth ratios for the 22 firms in the net monetary creditor cohort is 4.08, and for the 14 net monetary debtor cohort is 5.15. This agrees with the wealth transfer implication except for two considerations. First, even if there were no wealth effect, the two cohorts would not have exactly the same growth, simply because of the many other factors impinging on a firm's growth. Second, we have merely sampled from the whole potential population of debtors and creditors. The question to be faced is, How much difference could be expected from these other factors if, in truth, there were *no* wealth transfer? The answer is that a small difference is almost inevitable, and half of the differences would be in favor of debtors, and the other half against them. The size of the observed difference that can probably be observed, because of these various factors, when there is, in truth, *no* wealth transfer among debtors and creditors, can be measured by modern statistical tests of significance and inference.

For the present rather small cohort, consisting of 14 debtors and 21 creditors, a difference at least as large as that which was observed in favor of debtors could be produced by these various factors with a probability of only about .15. Although the difference is economically large and in the right direction, the contention is not unreasonable that this is a result of good luck in sampling rather than of a wealth transfer effect. To detect the wealth transfer over the background of other factors, a larger sample could be taken, or a more severe inflation should be studied. The former will reduce the size or probability of accidental agreement effects so that if there really is a wealth transfer effect, it will have greater assurance of being detected above and beyond the many fortuitous background factors, commonly called "random-sampling variation." A more severe inflation would increase the size of the wealth transfer so that it would more surely be observable against the background effects of random-sampling variation.

Larger cohorts were formed by including among the debtors those firms that were creditors for only one year, while debtors for all the other years. Although this would reduce the wealth transfer effect, it was believed that the increase in sample size would reduce even more the background effects, hereafter called random-sampling error. This modification increased the cohort to 20 debtors and 27 creditors. Further modification by admitting firms with 2 and 3 years of exception (out of a total of 13 years) increased the cohort of debtors to 26 and to 29; the sample size of creditors was increased to 32 and to 35. Thus the sample size was almost doubled at the cost of some reduction of the absolute size of the wealth transfer. The random-sampling error was decreased, while the observed difference between means remained sufficiently large so that the probability the observed difference could have arisen from sampling error fell to .03 for the one exception cohort, to .06 for the two, and .05 for the three exception cohorts, if in truth there were no wealth transfer effect.

Each of the samples was analyzed and the results tested in the same way. The results are given in table 5. Figure 3 shows the equity growths for the largest

TABLE 5. *Average equity growth of cohorts of net monetary debtors compared with net monetary creditors with statistical significance levels*

| Net monetary condition | All years in same net monetary condition | | | | At least 2/3 of years in same net monetary condition | | | | Variant firms | |
|---|---|---|---|---|---|---|---|---|---|---|
| | No. of firms | $x^\star$ | $s^\dagger$ | $p^\ddagger$ | No. of firms | $x^\star$ | $s^\dagger$ | $p^\ddagger$ | No. of firms | $x^\star$ |
| **A. Inflation** | | | | | | | | | | |
| **New York S.E.** | | | | | | | | | | |
| **1915–20** | | | | | | | | | | |
| **(6 years)** | | | | | | | | | | |
| Debtors | 70 | 2.72 | 2.39 | | 77 | 2.68 | 2.33 | | | |
| Creditors | 5 | 1.53 | .79 | .03 | 17 | 1.77 | .92 | .006 | 2 | 8.68 |
| Mean diff. | | $\overline{+1.19}$ | | | | $\overline{+.91}$ | | | | |
| **New York S.E.** | | | | | | | | | | |
| **1940–52** | | | | | | | | | | |
| **(13 years)** | | | | | | | | | | |
| Debtors | 14 | 5.15 | 3.18 | | 29 | 5.93 | 3.60 | | | |
| Creditors | 21 | 4.08 | 2.20 | .15 | 35 | 4.46 | 2.76 | .045 | 21 | 5.39 |
| Mean diff. | | $\overline{+1.07}$ | | | | $\overline{+1.47}$ | | | | |
| **American S.E.** | | | | | | | | | | |
| **1940–52** | | | | | | | | | | |
| **(13 years)** | | | | | | | | | | |
| Debtors | 32 | 9.02 | 12.73 | | 58 | 11.18 | 14.60 | | | |
| Creditors | 39 | 8.87 | 8.25 | .43 | 69 | 8.11 | 7.30 | .06 | 44 | 7.70 |
| Mean diff. | | $\overline{+.15}$ | | | | $\overline{+3.07}$ | | | | |
| **Over-the-counter** | | | | | | | | | | |
| **1940–52** | | | | | | | | | | |
| **(13 years)** | | | | | | | | | | |
| Debtors | 15 | 9.17 | 9.41 | | 21 | 9.59 | 10.52 | | | |
| Creditors | 23 | 5.20 | 6.08 | .08 | 44 | 6.30 | 6.93 | .10 | 13 | 7.95 |
| Mean diff. | | $\overline{+3.97}$ | | | | $\overline{+3.29}$ | | | | |
| **Steel industry** | | | | | | | | | | |
| **1940–52** | | | | | | | | | | |
| **(13 years)** | | | | | | | | | | |
| Debtors | 16 | 5.08 | 7.37 | | 29 | 6.77 | 6.52 | | | |
| Creditors | 12 | 5.00 | 3.28 | .48 | 26 | 6.18 | 5.70 | .36 | 18 | 8.29 |
| Mean diff. | | $\overline{+.08}$ | | | | $\overline{+.59}$ | | | | |

| | | | | | | | | | | |
|---|---|---|---|---|---|---|---|---|---|---|
| **Chemical industry** | | | | | | | | | | |
| 1940–52 | Debtors | 14 | 8.94 | 9.49 | | 19 | 7.17 | 8.62 | | 12 | 6.87 |
| (13 years) | Creditors | 11 | 4.62 | 2.81 | | 19 | 4.54 | 3.27 | | |
| | Mean diff. | | +4.32 | | .07 | | +2.53 | | .12 | |
| **Textile industry** | | | | | | | | | | |
| 1940–52 | Debtors | 17 | 9.50 | 11.65 | | 29 | 16.33 | 23.58 | | 7 | 8.07 |
| (13 years) | Creditors | 13 | 9.21 | 6.72 | | 21 | 9.67 | 6.53 | | |
| | Mean diff. | | +.29 | | .45 | | +6.66 | | .08 | |
| **Department stores** | | | | | | | | | | |
| 1940–52 | Debtors | 19 | 10.77 | 7.52 | | 29 | 8.67 | 9.60 | | 15 | 33.05 |
| (13 years) | Creditors | 12 | 4.02 | 1.84 | | 21 | 4.23 | 1.80 | | |
| | Mean diff. | | +6.75 | | .002 | | +4.44 | | .012 | |
| **Wages bill** | | | | | | | | | | |
| **Sample of NYSE** | Debtors | 31 | 8.50 | 6.73 | | 50 | 7.85 | 6.38 | | 20 | 6.04 |
| 1940–52 | Creditors | 15 | 4.65 | 2.48 | | 32 | 5.78 | 4.29 | | |
| (13 years) | Mean diff. | | +3.85 | | .005 | | +2.07 | | .04 | |
| **B. Deflation** | | | | | | | | | | |
| **New York S.E.** | Debtors | 118 | 1.48 | 1.00 | | | | | | 6 | 1.64 |
| 1921–22 | Creditors | 24 | 1.78 | .72 | | | | | | |
| (2 years) | Mean diff. | | −.30 | | .045 | | | | | |
| **New York S.E.** | Debtors | 54 | .42 | .47 | | 63 | .49 | .56 | | 3 | .28 |
| 1928–33 | Creditors | 19 | 1.05 | 1.01 | | 35 | 1.09 | 1.04 | | |
| (6 years) | Mean diff. | | −.63 | | .006 | | −.60 | | .001 | |

(continued)

TABLE 5. (continued)

| Net monetary condition | All years in same net monetary condition | | | | At least 2/3 of years in same net monetary condition | | | | Variant firms | |
|---|---|---|---|---|---|---|---|---|---|---|
| | No. of firms | $x^\star$ | $s^\dagger$ | $p^\ddagger$ | No. of firms | $x^\star$ | $s^\dagger$ | $p^\ddagger$ | No. of firms | $x^\star$ |
| **C. Price stability** | | | | | | | | | | |
| **New York S.E.** | | | | | | | | | | |
| **1922–30** | | | | | | | | | | |
| **(9 years)** | | | | | | | | | | |
| Debtors | 45 | 2.76 | 4.40 | | 51 | 2.75 | 4.30 | | 6 | 2.78 |
| Creditors | 11 | 1.89 | 1.78 | | 15 | 1.98 | 1.62 | | | |
| Mean diff. | | +.87 | | .32 | | +.77 | | .30 | | |
| **New York S.E.** | | | | | | | | | | |
| **1933–40** | | | | | | | | | | |
| **(8 years)** | | | | | | | | | | |
| Debtors | 47 | 4.75 | 4.55 | | 55 | 4.38 | 4.39 | | 1 | .73 |
| Creditors | 40 | 4.46 | 5.16 | | 54 | 5.11 | 5.02 | | | |
| Mean diff. | | +.29 | | .76 | | −.73 | | .43 | | |
| **American S.E.** | | | | | | | | | | |
| **1933–39** | | | | | | | | | | |
| **(7 years)** | | | | | | | | | | |
| Debtors | 11 | 8.61 | 10.06 | | 17 | 6.44 | 8.95 | | 4 | 3.70 |
| Creditors | 15 | 3.33 | 3.20 | | 20 | 4.72 | 4.93 | | | |
| Mean diff. | | +5.28 | | .12 | | +1.72 | | .52 | | |

$\star$ x = mean price plus reinvested dividends at end of episode, per dollar of January 1940 stock prices (adjusted for dilutions)

$\dagger$ s = standard deviation of December 1952 stock values with reinvested dividends, per dollar of January 1940 stock prices

$\ddagger$ Based on Student's t-test coefficient;

$$t = d \Big/ \sqrt{\frac{S_1^2}{N_1} + \frac{S_2^2}{N_2}} \quad \text{and,}$$

one-tailed probability with Welch approximation, but two tails for "price stability" periods

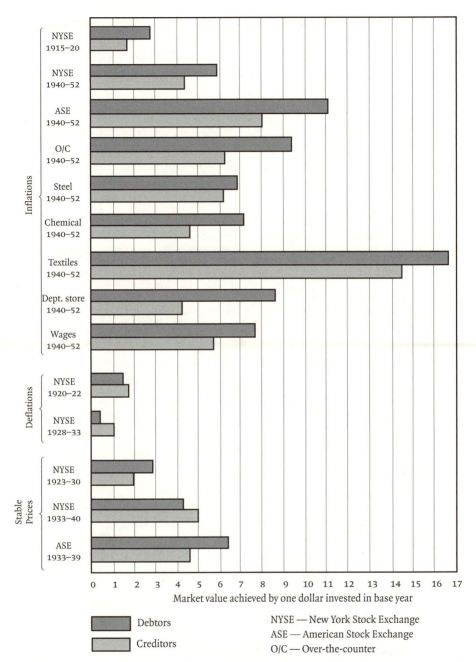

**FIGURE 3.** *Market value of equity for debtors compared with creditors (per dollar of base year common stock value)*

pair of cohorts in each population. All samples from inflation periods should show superiority for net monetary debtors, those from deflations should show superiority for net monetary creditors, while those from periods of no general price movements should show no difference other than within the realm of sampling variation.

This is, in fact, what is observed. It is significant that in every sample from the two inflation episodes the net monetary debtors' average equity grows more than that of the net monetary creditors—as predicted by the theory. And, furthermore, these observed differences are statistically significant in all except two samples (steel and textile), and even there moderately small probabilities are obtained.

In deflations, net monetary creditors do better than net monetary debtors. In the deflation of 1920–22 the respective growth ratios are 1.78 and 1.48, a superiority attributable to random sampling with a probability of only .05. For the deflation from 1928 to 1933, net monetary creditors (including firms with at most two years of opposite status) did better than net monetary debtors— the respective equity growth ratios being 1.09 and .49. This degree of superiority could occur by random-sampling variation with probability .001, if in fact there were no wealth transfer.

During stable price periods the observed differences between debtor and creditor growth ratios should not be different beyond the differences attributable to random-sampling variation. For the episode 1922–30 the equity growth ratio for the cohort of net monetary creditors was 1.98 compared with 2.75 for the debtors. Such a difference could be produced by random-sampling sources of variation with probability in excess of .3. For the stable price period from 1933 to 1940, the New York Stock Exchange sample cohort of net monetary debtors had a growth ratio of 4.38 compared with 5.11 for creditors, a difference that can be exceeded purely by random-sampling variation with probability of over .4. Similarly, the sample from the American Stock Exchange (then known as the Curb) showed a growth ratio of 6.44 for debtors and 4.72 for creditors, for which the probability is over .5 that a difference of at least this magnitude can be produced by random-sampling variation, if there is no wealth transfer.

### Significance of Evidence

In assessing the significance of sample results, the question arises as to whether the samples are large enough to carry much conviction. More precisely, are the samples large enough to give a sufficiently high probability of (1) getting results that are consistent with the wealth transfer if it is present, or (2) if the transfer really is absent, getting results consistent *only* with the absence of wealth transfer effect? The answer should be yes to both questions, if much weight is to be attached to the results. Other forms of these same questions are, If there really is a wealth transfer during price level changes, is there a high probability (and what is it?) that our sample results will lead us correctly to the conclusion that there *is* a wealth transfer force? and, Is there a high probability (and what is it?) that our sample will give us differences so small as to correctly suggest there is no wealth transfer, when in truth there is not?

These questions are basic to the interpretation of all empirical evidence. The answer, in the present case, to the second question is that the probability is .95 that, if there truly is *not* a wealth transfer, the observed difference will be so small as to lead to the conclusion of no redistribution. For the first question, calculations indicate that the probability, for *each* sample, is around .7–.9 that the observed difference will be large enough to correctly conclude that the wealth transfer is present during inflation and deflation. Since we have 11 independent samples, each with that high a probability, we are almost surely to be led to the correct conclusion. In other words, the sample sizes are adequate to provide decisive evidence.

### Significance of Combined Evidence of All Samples

All nine samples from the two inflations show a superiority for the net monetary debtors. There is only 1 chance in 512 that such favorable agreement could have been the result of random-sampling differences, if no wealth transfer really were operating. And when the two samples from deflations are also considered—both showing differences in favor of creditors—the probability of such agreement in 11 samples being the result of lucky observations is 1 in 2,048. And given that the wealth transfer really is operating according to theory, the probability of getting favorable differences in *every* sample is about one-half. In other words, such unanimous agreement is not "too good" to be true.

A more sensitive and powerful method of consolidating the results of the various samples is the chi-square compounding of probabilities from independent samples, a procedure developed by R. A. Fisher.[26] This method

26. The Fisher chi-square combination technique is presented in L. H. C. Tippett, *The Method of Statistics*, 4th rev. ed., William and Norgate, London, 1952, pp. 159–62. See also E. Pearson, "The Probability Integral Transformation for Testing Goodness of Fit and Combining Independent Tests of Significance," *Biometrika* 30, p. 134.

avoids the bias that may result when all the data are pooled in one large sample; any correlation between the extent to which a population is composed of debtors and the rise in stock prices for reasons other than debtor status would introduce (for whatever reason it may have arisen) a bias. And a correlation does in fact exist; from 1915 to 1920 the New York Stock Exchange was predominantly composed of debtors, and stock prices rose less than in 1940–52, when the population was composed of about equal fractions of debtors and creditors. Combining these two sets of data would overweight the debtor cohort with World War I experience, while the creditors would be overweighted with World War II data. A comparison between debtors and creditors would, in part, really compare World Wars I and II. The Fisher method of compounding probabilities avoids this bias.

There are four stock exchange and one over-the-counter samples from two inflations. Compounding their probabilities indicates less than 1 chance in 500 of obtaining such agreement as these five samples give if, in fact, there were no wealth transfer during inflation. Considering just the four industry samples from the inflation of 1940–52, the Fisher chi-square compounding yields a probability of less than 1 in 100,000 of getting such agreement by accident of sampling. And if all nine inflation episode samples are compounded, the probability of such agreement is less than 1 in 1,000 or less than 1 in 10,000, depending upon how broadly the cohorts of debtors and creditors are defined.

For the two deflation samples, the probability produced by compounding the sample probabilities is less than .01. And if these two sample probabilities are compounded with those of the inflation samples, the probability is less than 1 in 1,000 or, having such agreement with the hypothesis both in inflation and in deflation (when creditors gain), produced by mere random-sampling factors.

Also in complete agreement with the theory is the experience during stable prices. In the three samples, two differences were in favor of debtors, and one in favor of creditors; the results were consistent with absence of any wealth transfer effect.

### Evidence from Cohort of "Variants"

Many firms did not qualify for the cohorts of debtors or creditors, because they did not maintain a creditor (or debtor) status for at least two-thirds of the time. These "variant" firms are more nearly neutral and should experience smaller wealth transfer than the persistent debtors or creditors. If they were exactly neutral they would experience no transfer of wealth according to the theory. Their mean growth should therefore be between that of the cohort of debtors and creditors. In a small sample, however, there is a substantial chance that the recorded mean growth will lie above the debtors' or below the creditors' during inflation (and conversely during deflation). Furthermore, the predicted difference between mean growth of extensive debtors and creditors was large enough to be readily detectable, whereas the difference between debtors and variants (or between variants and creditors) is only about half that amount. Therefore, for these reasons, one would expect a greater disparity from the predicted outcome.

Table 5, which lists the mean growth ratios of the "debtors" and "creditors" for each sample, gives the mean growth of the long-lived variant firms. Usually the "variant" means lie between. We attribute the exceptions to sampling fluctuations—since such deviations are well within the range of sampling fluctuation for such small samples.

### Short-Lived Firms

All the preceding cohorts contain a small bias, because if a firm was merged into some other firm, the equity growth of the firm was recorded only up to the date of the merger. For example, if a firm was merged at the end of 1940, its equity growth for that one year was treated as if it were the total growth over the whole episode. In a rising stock market, this would understate the true growth of the sampled population. Omission of such firms would produce an opposite bias. To detect the possible effect of this bias, the samples were analyzed with all such firms omitted. (Bankrupt firms were, of course, not omitted.) The results are only trivially different, because there were so few such firms. As expected, the equity growth is smaller when these firms are included in the sample, but the differences between debtor and creditor cohorts remain highly significant.

In summary, differences between the averages of net monetary debtors and creditors provide overwhelming evidence in support of the validity of a wealth transfer from net monetary creditors to debtors during inflation (and the converse during deflation) in the episodes and populations covered by the study.[27]

27. *Logarithmic Transformation.* The assumption of normality of the distribution of changes of equity for each firm is certainly not satisfied. Yet the preceding statistical tests were derived on the basis of that assumption. Departures from normality in the underlying distribution will not substantially affect the distribution of the differences of means of random samples of the size of the samples available here. For many non-normal distributions, a fairly accurate calculation of probabilities can be computed.

To obtain some idea of the effects in the present situation, the data for ratio increases in equity were converted to logarithms, since the distribution of growth ratios is nearly

## Portfolio Test

The preceding "cohort" test relies on the persistence of a firm's net monetary status over several years. As a result, some firms (earlier called the "variants") are excluded from the main comparison. An alternative test—a portfolio test—can include every firm in every year and, in addition, compare the year-by-year wealth transfer effect.

The portfolio test compares the annual growth in equity (including reinvested dividends) of a portfolio of the stocks of firms that are net monetary debtors with that of a portfolio of stocks of net monetary creditors. In a year of inflation the equity growth rate of the net monetary debtor portfolio should exceed that of the net monetary creditors, and conversely for deflation. At the beginning of each year the portfolios must be reconstituted by trading stocks of firms that change status. The growth of a debtor portfolio during an inflationary episode of several years can be computed by multiplying together the average annual growth factor of each year's debtor portfolio. In this way, the growth rate resulting from debtor status can be measured over several years even though many firms do not stay net monetary debtors (or creditors) over the entire episode. If many firms changed status frequently within a year, even this annual revision would be inadequate. However, few firms switch status so rapidly as to cause any difficulty, so for present purposes a yearly revision is adequate. A firm was deemed to be a debtor if the average of its net monetary status at the beginning and end of the year was debtor. Since this is used to test for *presence* of wealth transfer, and not the ability to forecast, the average is permissible.

For the period 1915 through 1951 the samples from the New York Stock Exchange (1915–51), the American Stock Exchange (1933–51), and over-the-counter (1940–51) are assembled into one larger supersample for the first portfolio. Industry and wage samples are omitted to prevent industry correlated

———

log-normal. Thus if equity per share of stock doubled, the ratio was converted to .301, the logarithm of 2.00. If a stock price fell to zero, it would be impossible to assign a logarithmic value, since the logarithm of zero is minus infinity. To avoid this, an arbitrary small constant (1.00) was added to all the ratios of price rises.

An analysis similar to that presented in table 5 was performed on the logarithms. The results are essentially the same as in the preceding tests. The probabilities are about the same order of magnitude and, for all practical purposes, are identical in their implications.

effects from weakening the effectiveness of this test. (Later we analyze samples separately, and it will be seen that the results are fundamentally similar.)

During 1915, 77 firms were net monetary debtors of one degree or another, while only 10 were net monetary creditors. The average growth ratio for the 77 debtors was 2.30; if one dollar were invested in the common stock of each company on January 1, 1915, the total value of the investment a year later, *including dividends received*, would have been 2.30 as large. This is the average for one dollar's worth of stock in each firm. (The average over one share of stock in each firm would be affected by the absolute price of a share.) The creditor portfolio rose to $1.59. From January 1, 1916, to 1917, the growth factor of the portfolio of firms that were net monetary debtors in 1916 was 1.06; 81 firms were in this status. There were 16 creditor firms, and their equity rose by a factor of 1.19.[28] Multiplying the debtor portfolio growth factors of 1915 and 1916 gives a cumulated growth of $2.43, compared to $1.90 for the creditor portfolio. Continuing year by year in this way produced the results given in table 6, column 2, up to 1920. But 1921 was a year of deflation (the Consumer Price Index ended the year at a level lower than at the start). Therefore, we shall, at first, skip to the next year of inflation, 1923. And if we consider only those years in which the price index rose, the value of the net monetary debtor portfolio should increase more than that of the net monetary creditor portfolio. If only the years of deflation are considered, the net monetary debtor portfolio should grow less than the net monetary creditor portfolio. Again, as can be seen in table 7, this is exactly what happens.

Alternatively, the two sets of years can be combined chronologically by comparing (1) a portfolio composed of net monetary debtors during years of inflation and creditors during deflations with (2) a portfolio composed of the net monetary creditors during inflations and debtors during deflations. A portfolio consisting of debtors during inflation and creditors during deflation should grow in wealth at the expense of creditors during inflation and debtors during deflation. Therefore, the pertinent comparison is between an *optimal* portfolio (net monetary debtors during inflation and net monetary creditors during deflation) and a *"pessimal"* portfolio (net monetary debtors during deflation and net monetary creditors during inflation). The compounded growths of such optimal and pessimal portfolios are given in the right-hand "optimal" and

28. The number of firms whose stock was traded on the New York Stock Exchange increased; these were included.

TABLE 6. *Values of portfolios of net monetary debtor stocks and of net monetary creditor stocks during years of inflation in period 1915–51, exchange and over-the-counter data (end of 1914 = $1.00)*

| Years of inflation | Compounded growth in equity of portfolios of net monetary | | Ratio of equity growth of net monetary debtors to creditors |
|---|---|---|---|
| | Debtors | Creditors | |
| 1914 | 1.00 | 1.00 | 1.00 |
| 1915 | 2.30 | 1.59 | 1.45 |
| 1916 | 2.43 | 1.90 | 1.28 |
| 1917 | 2.18 | 1.76 | 1.24 |
| 1918 | 2.97 | 2.33 | 1.27 |
| 1919 | 4.81 | 3.55 | 1.35 |
| 1920 | 3.10 | 2.41 | 1.29 |
| 1923 | 3.42 | 2.38 | 1.44 |
| 1925 | 4.61 | 3.15 | 1.46 |
| 1929 | 2.86 | 2.24 | 1.27 |
| 1933 | 6.60 | 4.87 | 1.35 |
| 1934 | 8.77 | 6.66 | 1.32 |
| 1935 | 14.61 | 11.83 | 1.23 |
| 1936 | 23.35 | 17.04 | 1.37 |
| 1937 | 13.40 | 10.47 | 1.28 |
| 1940 | 13.15 | 11.21 | 1.17 |
| 1941 | 13.17 | 11.19 | 1.18 |
| 1942 | 16.71 | 13.65 | 1.22 |
| 1943 | 31.36 | 21.23 | 1.48 |
| 1944 | 51.43 | 30.85 | 1.67 |
| 1945 | 95.65 | 50.99 | 1.88 |
| 1946 | 87.80 | 47.22 | 1.86 |
| 1947 | 87.10 | 49.58 | 1.76 |
| 1948 | 79.44 | 48.09 | 1.65 |
| 1950 | 112.09 | 65.74 | 1.71 |
| 1951 | 134.96 | 79.61 | 1.70 |

TABLE 7. *Values of portfolios of net monetary debtor stocks and of net monetary creditor stocks during years of deflation in period 1921–49, exchange and over-the-counter data (end of 1920 = $1.00)*

| Years of deflation | Compounded growth in equity of portfolios of net monetary | | Ratio of equity growth of net monetary debtors to creditors |
|---|---|---|---|
| | Debtors | Creditors | |
| 1920 | 1.00 | 1.00 | 1.00 |
| 1921 | 1.14 | 1.30 | .88 |
| 1922 | 1.45 | 1.82 | .80 |
| 1924 | 1.83 | 2.47 | .74 |
| 1926 | 1.82 | 2.66 | .69 |
| 1927 | 2.40 | 3.24 | .74 |
| 1928 | 3.80 | 4.43 | .86 |
| 1930 | 2.22 | 2.65 | .84 |
| 1931 | 1.33 | 1.70 | .78 |
| 1932 | 1.25 | 1.72 | .73 |
| 1938 | 1.67 | 2.07 | .81 |
| 1939 | 1.67 | 2.11 | .79 |
| 1949 | 1.94 | 2.44 | 1.92 |

"pessimal" columns of table 8 and are graphed in figure 4. The optimal is based on debtors during 1915–20, on creditors during 1921 and 1922, as can be seen in the table from the column of pluses and minuses, indicating whether the Consumer Price Index ended the year higher or lower than it was at the beginning of the year. By the end of 1920 the optimal portfolio growth ratio had compounded to $3.10. For 1921 this is multiplied by the growth of the creditor portfolio (this being a year of deflation); the 1921 creditor portfolio rose by a ratio of 1.30. This multiplied by $3.10 produces the 1921 value ($4.03) for the optimal portfolio. Since 1922 also was a deflationary year, the creditor portfolio value is again used and compounded to the optimal portfolio, giving $5.65 as the end of 1922 equity value for the optimal portfolio. By 1952 the value of the optimal portfolio had risen to $327, compared with only $152 for the pessimal portfolio.

The ratio of the optimal portfolio equity relative to the pessimal portfolio equity values should grow during periods of price-level changes (both inflation

TABLE 8. Equity growth of optimal and pessimal portfolios for exchanges plus "over-the-counter" sample, 1915–51 (end of 1914 = $1.00)

| Year | Direction of CPI[a] | Number of firms in portfolio | | Annual equity growth factor of portfolio | | Equity compounded growth | | Ratio of compounded growth of optimal to pessimal portfolios | Year |
|---|---|---|---|---|---|---|---|---|---|
| | | Net monetary debtors | Net monetary creditors | Debtors | Creditors | Optimal portfolio[b] | Pessimal portfolio[b] | | |
| 1915 | + | 77 | 10 | 2.297 | 1.595 | 2.30 | 1.59 | 1.44 | 1915 |
| 1916 | + | 81 | 16 | 1.058 | 1.193 | 2.43 | 1.90 | 1.28 | 1916 |
| 1917 | + | 82 | 28 | 0.897 | 0.925 | 2.18 | 1.76 | 1.24 | 1917 |
| 1918 | + | 94 | 32 | 1.363 | 1.322 | 2.97 | 2.33 | 1.28 | 1918 |
| 1919 | + | 98 | 34 | 1.617 | 1.524 | 4.81 | 3.55 | 1.36 | 1919 |
| 1920 | + | 111 | 32 | 0.645 | 0.679 | 3.10 | 2.41 | 1.29 | 1920 |
| 1921 | − | 116 | 31 | 1.138 | 1.300 | 4.03 | 2.74 | 1.47 | 1921 |
| 1922 | − | 68 | 20 | 1.275 | 1.402 | 5.65 | 3.49 | 1.62 | 1922 |
| 1923 | + | 57 | 24 | 1.102 | 0.986 | 6.23 | 3.45 | 1.81 | 1923 |
| 1924 | − | 59 | 17 | 1.261 | 1.354 | 8.44 | 4.34 | 1.94 | 1924 |
| 1925 | + | 54 | 20 | 1.348 | 1.327 | 11.37 | 5.76 | 1.97 | 1925 |
| 1926 | − | 48 | 23 | 0.994 | 1.079 | 12.26 | 5.73 | 2.14 | 1926 |
| 1927 | − | 45 | 25 | 1.319 | 1.215 | 14.20 | 7.55 | 1.97 | 1927 |
| 1928 | − | 114 | 56 | 1.580 | 1.368 | 20.40 | 11.94 | 1.71 | 1928 |
| 1929 | + | 111 | 53 | 0.621 | 0.709 | 12.67 | 8.47 | 1.50 | 1929 |
| 1930 | − | 56 | 35 | 0.585 | 0.599 | 7.58 | 4.95 | 1.53 | 1930 |
| 1931 | − | 56 | 32 | 0.601 | 0.641 | 4.86 | 2.98 | 1.63 | 1931 |
| 1932 | − | 54 | 31 | 0.936 | 1.010 | 4.91 | 2.79 | 1.76 | 1932 |

| 1933 | + | 133 | 111 | 2.307 | 2.178 | 11.32 | 6.07 | 1.87 | 1933 |
|---|---|---|---|---|---|---|---|---|---|
| 1934 | + | 80 | 79 | 1.330 | 1.367 | 15.06 | 8.30 | 1.81 | 1934 |
| 1935 | + | 77 | 80 | 1.665 | 1.777 | 25.08 | 14.75 | 1.70 | 1935 |
| 1936 | + | 76 | 81 | 1.598 | 1.441 | 40.07 | 21.25 | 1.89 | 1936 |
| 1937 | + | 81 | 76 | 0.574 | 0.614 | 23.00 | 13.05 | 1.76 | 1937 |
| 1938 | − | 78 | 78 | 1.340 | 1.204 | 27.68 | 17.48 | 1.58 | 1938 |
| 1939 | − | 72 | 83 | 0.997 | 1.019 | 28.22 | 17.43 | 1.62 | 1939 |
| 1940 | + | 182 | 194 | 0.981 | 1.071 | 27.68 | 18.67 | 1.48 | 1940 |
| 1941 | + | 194 | 178 | 1.002 | 0.998 | 27.74 | 18.64 | 1.49 | 1941 |
| 1942 | + | 205 | 167 | 1.269 | 1.220 | 35.20 | 22.73 | 1.55 | 1942 |
| 1943 | + | 179 | 191 | 1.876 | 1.555 | 66.03 | 35.35 | 1.87 | 1943 |
| 1944 | + | 150 | 218 | 1.640 | 1.453 | 108.29 | 51.37 | 2.11 | 1944 |
| 1945 | + | 127 | 238 | 1.860 | 1.653 | 201.43 | 84.91 | 2.37 | 1945 |
| 1946 | + | 134 | 225 | 0.918 | 0.926 | 184.91 | 78.63 | 2.35 | 1946 |
| 1947 | + | 162 | 192 | 0.992 | 1.050 | 183.43 | 82.56 | 2.22 | 1947 |
| 1948 | + | 168 | 183 | 0.912 | 0.970 | 167.29 | 80.08 | 2.09 | 1948 |
| 1949 | − | 153 | 194 | 1.147 | 1.152 | 192.72 | 91.85 | 2.10 | 1949 |
| 1950 | + | 148 | 197 | 1.411 | 1.367 | 271.92 | 125.56 | 2.17 | 1950 |
| 1951 | + | 171 | 172 | 1.204 | 1.211 | 327.39 | 152.06 | 2.15 | 1951 |

[a]Plus sign (+) if Consumer Price Index rose from January to December; minus sign (−) if it fell.

[b]Optimal portfolio is based on net monetary debtors in years of positive CPI change and net monetary creditors in years of negative change.

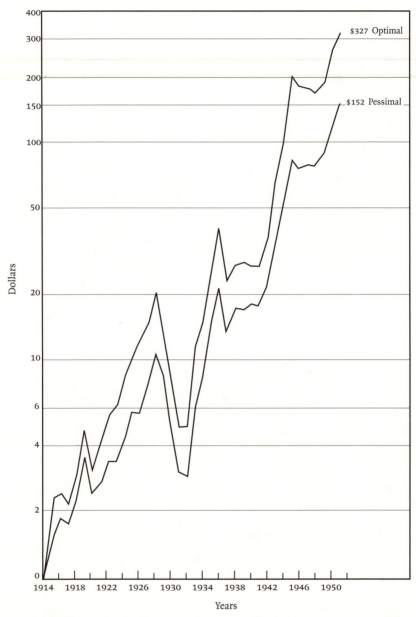

**FIGURE 4.** *Growth of equity of optimal and pessimal portfolios (exchange and over-the-counter)* (1914 = $1.00)

and deflation). But it should stay constant during periods of stable prices. Any observed computed value will fluctuate because of sampling variations in selecting firms which are subject to a myriad of various other influences all impinging on the many firms in different degrees. Nevertheless, if our samples are large enough and randomly drawn from the pertinent population, the wealth transfer effect should produce an observable growth in the *ratio* during episodes of inflations and deflations—a growth that should be large enough to be detected against the background "noise" of the many other idiosyncratic factors contributing to the growth of the various firms.

Figure 5 is a graph of the *ratios* of optimal to pessimal portfolio equity values. It shows an upward movement from 1915 through 1951. Of particular importance is the fact that the trend is noticeable in each period of inflation and of deflation, while it is absent during periods of stable prices, as can be seen in figure 6, which shows the behavior of the ratio by inflation, deflation, and stable prices. Each episode of inflation and deflation ends with a higher value of the ratio, even after the random variations, whereas periods of stable prices show fluctuations but neither an upward nor downward trend. Thus, note the rises in 1914–20, 1921–22, 1930–32, and 1941–47. All other intervals are periods of essentially steady price levels, and they show no trend in the ratios.

To test whether this upward trend over the whole interval from 1915 through 1952 in the combined exchanges and over-the-counter sample (excluding the special industry and wage sample) could have resulted from random-sampling fluctuation even if there really were no wealth transfer, the weighted regression coefficient of the logarithms of the growth of the ratio of the optimal to the pessimal portfolio values (column on the right in table 8) against time was computed and found to be larger than that to be expected from random sampling alone.[29]

Table 9 shows that the equity of the optimal portfolio grew relative to the

---

29. The intercept of the regression line is constrained to go through zero (or through 1.00 in arithmetic measure) because the ratio between the equity of the two portfolios is set at 1.00 in the first year of each episode. If logarithms of the ratios of the growth of equity of optimal and pessimal portfolios are used, the regression coefficient of these logarithms will be the logarithm of the annual ratio by which the optimal portfolio equity outgrows the pessimal.

The number of independent observations in a time series cannot be assumed to the actual number of observations. However, measures of the correlation of first differences of the observations give a small correlation, +.15. Even if the number of observations were cut by one-fourth as an extreme, the significance of the regression coefficients would remain.

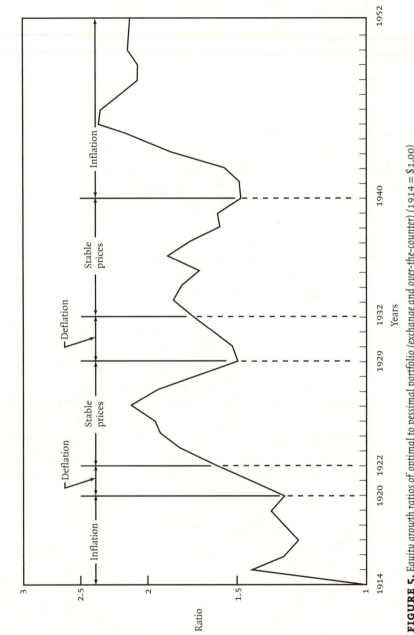

**FIGURE 5.** Equity growth ratios of optimal to pessimal portfolio (exchange and over-the-counter) (1914 = $1.00)

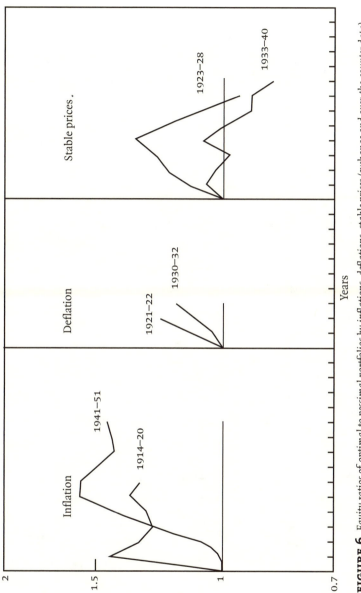

**FIGURE 6.** Equity ratios of optimal to pessimal portfolios by inflations, deflations, stable prices (exchange and over-the-counter data)

TABLE 9. *Measures of growths of equity of optimal and pessimal portfolios, exchanges plus over-the-counter samples, and for all data, 1915–52*

| Exchanges plus over-the-counter samples | | Weighted[a] | Unweighted |
|---|---|---|---|
| Annual percentage growth of optimal in excess of pessimal portfolio equity (based on regression coefficient of logarithm of ratios of optimal to pessimal portfolio)[b] | | 2.0%[c] (p < .01)[d] | 2.5%[c] (p < .001)[d] |
| Regression coefficients of logarithms of annual equity growths[e] | Optimal | 16.1% | 16.2% |
| | Pessimal | 13.7% | 14.1% |
| | | (p < .001) | (p < .01) |
| Geometric means of annual growth rates | | | |
| 1915–52 | Optimal | 22.0% | 17.0% |
| | Pessimal | 19.6% | 14.3% |
| | | (p < .07) | (p < .05) |
| Years with price level change > 3%[f] | Optimal | 18.0% | 9.3% |
| | Pessimal | 13.8% | 6.2% |
| | | (p < .025) | (p < .05) |

| Entire sample | | Weighted | Unweighted |
|---|---|---|---|
| Annual percentage growth of optimal in excess of pessimal portfolio equity (based on regression coefficient of logarithm of ratios of optimal to pessimal portfolio) | | 2.1% ($p < .01$) | 2.5% ($p < .001$) |
| Regression coefficients based on logarithms of equity growth | Optimal | 16.1% | 16.0% |
| | Pessimal | 13.7% ($p < .001$) | 13.3% ($p < .001$) |
| Geometric means of annual growth rates | | | |
| 1915–51 | Optimal | 21.7% | 17.0% |
| | Pessimal | 19.5% ($p = .05$) | 13.3% ($p < .05$) |
| Years with price level change > 3% | Optimal | 20.4% | 8.9% |
| | Pessimal | 16.9% ($p < .02$) | 6.2% ($p < .05$) |

[a] Weighted by number of firms in smaller portfolio of each year.

[b] $\log R_t = a + bt$, where $R$ is ratio of optimal to pessimal portfolio value of equity at end of year $t$, and $a = 0$, by definition.

[c] Antilog of $b$, converted to percentage annual rate by which optimal equity grows faster than pessimal, thus $10^{.0107} = 1.025$, which is converted to 2.5%. This applies to all regression coefficients reported in this table.

[d] One-tailed statistical significance levels of difference between optimal and pessimal portfolio in parentheses.

[e] $\log G_t = a + bt$, where $G_t$ is equity value of a portfolio at end of year $t$; $a = 0$, weighted by number of firms in each year in each portfolio.

[f] Includes 1916–19, 1921, 1925, 1930–32, 1941–44, 1946–47, 1950–51.

pessimal by 2.5 percent per year for the unweighted series, and 2.0 percent for the weighted.[30]

The weighted coefficient is more meaningful as a measure of difference, because the weights, based on the size of the sample in each year, give to each year a weight proportional to the accuracy of measurement for that year.[31] However, since the degree of inflation varies from year to year, a year of little price-level change, but big sample, would give lots of weight to observations with little wealth redistribution and, hence, would bias the measurement against detecting the wealth transfer—with opposite bias if large samples are correlated with years of big price-level change.[32] Therefore, both weighted and unweighted regression coefficients have been computed.

These coefficients tell us only that the optimal portfolio grew in equity relative to the pessimal—that there was a wealth transfer. However, it is interesting to know the annual percentage rate of growth for each portfolio. This can be estimated for each portfolio separately with the regression coefficient of the logarithms against time over the interval 1915–51 (with weights according to the size of the sample in that year, and also without weights). The antilog of the regression coefficient can be converted to the annual percentage rate of growth (by simply subtracting 1.00 from the antilog).

The coefficients reported in table 9 are, 16.1 percent per year for the optimal portfolio and 13.7 percent per year for the pessimal. The difference is statistically significant, in exceeding zero, beyond the .01 probability level.

According to these measures, the optimal outgrew the pessimal by 18 percent. The unweighted coefficients (antilogs) show 16.2 percent for the optimal and 14.1 percent for the pessimal, a superiority of 15 percent. Incidentally, if the two portfolios are combined into one, as a sample of the exchanges and over-the-counter stocks, the average annual growth rate is 15 percent for the weighted as well as for the unweighted.

Another kind of measure of annual growth can be made by computing the geometric average of the *annually* observed growth rates. As reported in table 9, the unweighted averages for the optimal and pessimal portfolios are 17 percent

---

30. These exceed zero by a margin beyond the .01 level of statistical significance.

31. Technically, the variance of each year's mean is adjusted so as to give equal variances. In doing this the smaller N of the two portfolios in any particular year is used as a measure of the reciprocal of the variance.

32. In fact, there is no correlation between sample size and degree of price-level change.

and 14.3 percent respectively, a superiority of 19 percent. The weighted averages give 22 percent and 19.6 percent respectively, a relative superiority of 12 percent. On this basis of averaging annual growth rates, the average of the combined portfolios grew (weighted) 21 percent and (unweighted) 16 percent per year.

A more sensitive test can be made by using only the 18 years in which the price level changed by at least 3 percent (1916–19, 1921, 1925, 1930–32, 1937, 1941–44, 1946–47, 1950–51). For these years the optimal portfolio average annual rate of growth was 18 percent compared with 13.8 percent for the pessimal, or 30 percent greater.[33]

All the preceding results are based on the exchanges plus over-the-counter samples combined. If all the data, including the industry and the "wages" samples are added in to form one supersample, the resulting regression coefficients are almost identical. The lower half of table 9 presents the data, calculated similarly to that in the upper half for the exchanges and over-the-counter sample.

All the figures given so far are in nominal—not adjusted for price level—terms. Since the price level rose about 2.5 percent per year on the average over the interval 1915–52, the above-reported figures should all be reduced by subtracting 2.5 percent (not by dividing by 1.025).[34] When this is done, the difference between the various rates of growths are left unchanged, but the relative difference, expressed relative to the pessimal portfolio's growth is increased. Whereas in nominal units the relative superiority was between 12 and 18 percent, in price-level-adjusted units (or in real units) the relative superiority is between 15 and 25 percent, depending upon which measure is used.

In our opinion the weighted regression coefficients for the exchanges and over-the-counter sample are the most reliable and unbiased estimate of the differences between the growth rates of the two portfolios. (This happens to be identical with the results from portfolios based on all the samples—a coincidence.) In nominal units the relative superiority was 18 percent, and in real units it was 21 percent. However, the purpose of deriving these estimates was to test that net monetary debtors did, in fact, grow in equity relative to the net

---

33. The reason this growth rate is smaller for the 18-year episode of "severe" price level change than for the whole episode is that it includes the depression of 1930–32 and excludes the recovery years of 1933–36 and 1938–39.

34. Subtraction rather than division is appropriate because we are comparing *exponents* that are additive; that is, the nominal growth rate of each portfolio is in exponential terms the sum of the price-level rate of rise and the wealth transfer effect.

monetary creditors during inflation and conversely during deflations. This is amply verified. But the superiority of about 20 percent is simply a consequence of the extent of the difference between the two portfolios and of the changes in the general price level that occurred during the years 1915–51. The superiority would undoubtedly have been quite different for some other population or historical episode, depending upon the degree of net monetary status and price-level changes. But one thing would remain—if these statistical results are believed and the conclusions generalized—the difference between the optimal and pessimal portfolios will be positive, not negative.

### Individual Sample Analysis

To see if the results are consistent within each sample episode and are not produced by unusual events in one or two years or samples, the equity growth of each sample was subjected separately to regression analysis. The equity growth of each sample's pair of portfolios—the optimal and the pessimal—was measured by estimating the regression coefficient, $b$, in the regression equation:

$$\log E_t = a + bt$$

where $E_t$ is the equity value to which one dollar in a portfolio at the beginning of the episode grows by the end of year $t$ (and $a = 0$ because the regression line must equal 1.00 in the first year). The regression coefficient for the optimal portfolio should be larger than that for the pessimal portfolio, unless the period is characterized by a constant price level. These coefficients and their antilogs are in table 10. For example, the antilog of $b$ for the New York Stock Exchange sample of 1915–20 is 1.30 for the optimal portfolio; this is approximately equivalent to an annual rate of growth of 30 percent, or an annual ratio of growth of 1.30. The pessimal portfolio gives 1.23 for its annual growth ratio. This means the optimal growth rate exceeded the pessimal rate by about 30 percent, $((.30 - .23)/.23)$. Although the margin of superiority in this sample is in the right direction, because of the small sample size, it is not large enough to fall beyond the realm of superiority attributable to random samples from populations in which the growth rates are the same. This is indicated by the sampling probability figure of .015 given in the last column of table 10.[35]

---

35. This is the probability from the test of the difference between the two regression coefficients, $b_o$ and $b_p$, the optimal and the pessimal portfolio coefficients.

TABLE 10. *Separate sample regression coefficients of logarithms of equity growth optimal and pessimal portfolios**

| Samples | | Regression coefficients | | % excess of optimal over pessimal portfolio[b] | Probability significance levels[c] |
|---|---|---|---|---|---|
| | | Optimal portfolio[a] | Pessimal portfolio[a] | | |
| *Inflations* | | | | | |
| New York Stock Exchange | 1915–20 | 1.30 | 1.23 | +6.1 | .015 |
| New York Stock Exchange | 1940–51 | 1.17 | 1.17 | −.2 | .63 |
| American Stock Exchange | 1940–51 | 1.26 | 1.23 | +.8 | .06 |
| Over-the-counter | 1940–51 | 1.29 | 1.19 | +8.5 | <.001 |
| Steel industry | 1940–51 | 1.18 | 1.21 | −2.5 | .95 |
| Chemical industry | 1940–51 | 1.16 | 1.13 | +3.2 | .02 |
| Textile industry | 1940–51 | 1.23 | 1.20 | +1.8 | .15 |
| Retail department stores | 1940–51 | 1.46 | 1.30 | +1.3 | <.001 |
| Wages sample | 1940–51 | 1.19 | 1.15 | +3.2 | .05 |
| *Deflations* | | | | | |
| New York Stock Exchange | 1921–22 | 1.34 | 1.19 | +12.4 | .28 |
| New York Stock Exchange | 1930–33 | .69 | .64 | +6.8 | .28 |
| *Stable Prices* | | | | | |
| New York Stock Exchange | 1922–29 | 1.17 | 1.19 | −1.9 | .60 |
| New York + American[d] | 1933–40 | 1.24 | 1.26 | −1.6 | .60 |

*Note:* Fisher's $\chi^2$ compounded sampling probability for inflations and deflations is less than .001; for deflations only, it is .30. For inflation and deflation together $p$ is still less than .001.

* Regression coefficients are antilogs of $b$ in equation $\log E = a + bt$, where E is compounded equity value; $t$ is time in years; $a$ is set at zero, because E is 1.00 for first year. Data are rounded to second decimal.

[a] Antilogs of $b$ (regression coefficient).

[b] Ratio of antilogs, minus 1.00.

[c] One-tailed sampling probabilities, except in stable price periods when two-tailed distribution is used.

[d] Samples combined because American Stock Exchange sampling not completed.

Examination of the rest of the samples shows that 2 of the 11 samples do not have superiority for the optimal portfolios. However, the probability of getting as many as 9 out of 11 samples showing superiority for the optimal samples, if there were really no wealth transfer, is .03. A more powerful way of combining the sample results so as to give some heed to the size of the differences rather than just to the direction of difference is provided by Fisher's chi-square combination of independent sample probabilities. This test yields probabilities of less than .001 of observing such favorable results by random sampling in the absence of a wealth transfer.

The individual samples can be analyzed in still another, slightly different, way by regressing the *ratio* of the equity value of the optimal portfolio to the pessimal portfolios against time. If at the end of each year the value of the optimal portfolio is divided by the value of the pessimal portfolio (with dividends counted in), the ratio will start at one and should steadily increase, depending upon the extent of change in the price level in ensuing years. Table 11 gives the rate by which R, the ratio of $E_t^o$, equity of optimal to $E_t^p$, the equity of the pessimal portfolios, grew. These are the regression coefficients, $b$, in the equation:

$$R_t = a + bt$$

where $R_t = \dfrac{E_t^o}{E_t^p}$

Again, since the same data underlie the analysis, the regression coefficients are positive for 9 of the 11 samples from price-level-change episodes. Ideally, they should have been positive for all periods of price-change inflation or deflation. The random-sampling probabilities for statistical significance tests are given in parentheses. These results cannot be regarded as *more* evidence in support of the preceding regression analysis. Instead they are merely alternative ways of analyzing essentially the same data. The reason for having used this alternative method is primarily to avoid the possibility that one particular method of testing may fail because some necessary assumptions were not satisfied.

*"Year-by-Year within Sample" Regression Analysis*

A regression analysis was made by studying each firm in each year for each sample. The following prediction equation is implied by the theory, if we use a discrete period analysis of one year, and if inflation in each year is unanticipated.

$$G_{ti} = a_t P_t + \beta_t [(1 - P_t)M_{ti}] + \varepsilon$$

where

TABLE 11. *Separate sample regressions of ratio of growth of optimal to pessimal portfolio equity*

| Samples | | Regression coefficient of ratios of equity growth | Probability significance levels[a] |
|---|---|---|---|
| *Inflations* | | | |
| New York Stock Exchange | 1915–20 | +.025 | .16 |
| New York Stock Exchange | 1940–51 | −.0036 | .65 |
| American Stock Exchange | 1940–51 | +.036 | .01 |
| Over-the-counter | 1940–51 | +.13 | <.001 |
| Steel industry | 1940–51 | −.011 | .95 |
| Chemical industry | 1940–51 | +.034 | <.001 |
| Textile industry | 1940–51 | +.015 | .02 |
| Retail department stores | 1940–51 | +.27 | <.001 |
| Wages firms | 1940–51 | +.04 | <.001 |
| *Deflations* | | | |
| New York Stock Exchange | 1921–22 | +.13 | .05 |
| New York Stock Exchange | 1930–33 | +.06 | .01 |
| *Stable Prices* | | | |
| New York Stock Exchange | 1923–29 | −.011 | .67[a] |
| New York + American[b] | 1933–39 | +.071 | .32[a] |

Fisher's $\chi^2$ compounded sampling probability for inflations and deflations is less than .001.
[a] One-tailed for inflations and deflations, and two-tailed for stable price periods.
[b] Combined because American Exchange sample not complete.

$G_{ti}$ is the ratio of equity plus dividend at the end of the year t to the beginning of the year for the ith firm;[36]

$P_t$ is the ratio of the price level at the end of year to the beginning of the year;

$M_{ti}$ is the ratio of *average* (over the year) net monetary assets to equity of the ith firm during the year t, being positive for net monetary creditors and negative for net monetary debtors;

$\varepsilon$ is the error term.

According to the theory, $\beta_t$ should be positive and equal to 1.00 in the completely unanticipated deflation or inflation. If the price level rises, P will be bigger than 1.00, so that $1 - P_t$ will be negative. If the firm is a net monetary

36. The relationship between $E_t$ and $G_t$ is: $E_t = \prod_0^t G_t$

debtor, $M_i$ will be negative, so the bracketed term will be positive. The firm should experience an increase in wealth, meaning that β should be positive. If P were less than 1.00 and if the firm were a net monetary creditor, again the firm should experience a net wealth transfer in its favor, meaning that β should be positive. And if the two terms in the bracketed expression have opposite signs, the firm should lose from the net wealth transfer. Since the bracketed expression will be negative, $β_t$ should again be positive. Thus, in general, if a wealth transfer is present as predicted by the theory, β should be positive. All other factors affecting the firm's equity will operate through $a_t$, insofar as they are common to all firms. To the extent they are unique with each firm, they will have to be included in the host of random factors—and if they are sufficiently varied and offsetting, the persistent effect of the net monetary status should be noticed via a positive regression coefficient.

Two methods are available for testing the regression coefficient $β_t$ with the data. First, for each year $β_t$ could be estimated on the basis of all the firms' paired values of $G_t$ and $M_t$. Unfortunately, the power of this test is very small for inflations of the magnitude that occurs in any one year. For example, if the inflation is 5 percent in one year, the probability of getting a value of b (in samples of size 100) beyond the .05 random-sampling level of significance (under the hypothesis that there is no wealth redistribution) is about .07–.10. One might as well toss a coin as a basis for testing whether β is positive or negative. But if the inflation is as great as 100 percent in one year, the probability of getting a b that rejects a zero value for β is about .99 (for samples of size 100).[37] Because of this extremely low power for the test in one year, the following alternative method was used.

The equity growth ratio $G_{ti}$ was predicted in each year t for each firm i with the equation:

$$G_{ti} = P_t + β_t [(1 - P_t) M_{ti}]$$

setting $β_t$ equal to 1.00 and using the actually observed $P_t$ and $M_t$ in each year for each firm. The implied growth ratios for a firm, one for each year, are multiplied together to get the predicted cumulated growth ratio for each firm over the years of the *episode*. If there is a wealth transfer, as implied by this analysis, a correlation between the unpredicted and the actual cumulated growth ratios

37. These calculations are based on the following estimates:

$$σ_{y \cdot x} \cong .25, \qquad σ_x \cong .2, \qquad P = 1.05$$

in the equity should be observed. The advantages of this method of compounding predicted growths of equity over *episodes* is that the price level change is greater.

The episodes of 1915–20 and 1940–52 experienced inflations of over 90 percent. The episodes of 1921–22 and 1928–33 showed deflations of 15 percent and 30 percent, respectively; these are equivalent to inflations of about 18 percent and 42 percent. From 1933 through 1939 the *net* rise in prices was slightly under 8 percent, but the fluctuations from year to year over the episode were equivalent to a one-directional price rise of 17 percent.[38] Similarly, the episode of 1923–29 was equivalent to a one-directional rise of 12 percent, even though the price level at the end of the episode was almost precisely the same as at the beginning.

All the samples for all the episodes should therefore show a positive correlation between predicted and observed equity growth. For every sample in every episode, there is a positive relationship between net monetary status and observed growth in equity. Table 12 presents for each sample three estimated probabilities of observing such close relationship as was observed, and in the right direction, between net monetary status and growth in equity—if in fact there were *no* wealth redistribution at all.[39] The small probabilities serve to deny

38. A fall from 110 to 100 in the price level is a fall of 9.1 percent. This is equivalent in wealth redistributing effect to a rise of 10 percent. An episode in which prices in four successive years were alternately up 10 percent and down 9.1 percent would, over a four-year period, be equivalent to a one-directional price rise of about 46 percent insofar as wealth redistributive effects are concerned. $(1.10)^4 = 1.46$. If a firm were to switch monetary status in perfect accord, it would gain just as if there were a continued rise in prices instead of an up-and-down movement. To our knowledge no firm switched as if it had perfect foresight and wanted to gain from the price-level changes that were unanticipated by the market.

39. The best measure of the positive correlation between predicted and observed values depends upon several factors. The usual Pearson linear regression coefficient test based on normality in the residuals of the predicted variable is very sensitive to departures from the assumptions underlying its sampling distribution. In the present case, the residuals are not normally distributed. A logarithmic transformation would destroy the theory underlying the derivation of the regression equation. Also, the linearity assumption is suspect when several years are compounded. For example, if in some year the firm did not increase its equity as predicted, the next year's net monetary status will again be large (because the equity is in the denominator). Another big increase will be predicted for the next year if the two years are successive years of inflation. When these successive predicted growths are compounded, any firm that did not grow will have the next year's growth predicted as being larger than if the equity had increased (which would have reduced the

that the observed relationship is merely the result of fortuitous random sampling instead of a real wealth transfer during inflation and deflation.[40]

---

firm's monetary status). Chaining the annual predictions cumulates earlier excesses in prediction, in the direction of overpredicting the change in equity.

Tests that are relatively insensitive to these factors and which still can utilize much of the information are the Kendall tau-rank correlation test and the Mann-Whitney test for association. These tests rank the predicted growths for firms and rank the observed growths. Absolute values are replaced by order data. Assumptions about normality, about linearity of the regression, and about homoscedasticity are eliminated. Of these two tests, the Mann-Whitney is probably the most reliable. For details, see, for example, S. Siegel, *Nonparametric Statistics for the Behavioral Sciences*, McGraw-Hill, N.Y., 1956, pp. 116–23, 156–58, 213–23, 238–39.

If all firms are included, *even those that were short-lived*, the results will be biased toward agreement with the hypothesis because of a joint correlated growth over time. But if they are omitted (a firm might have a short life because of bankruptcy or some factor related to its monetary status or to inflation), the analysis could be criticized because of potential, even if unspecifiable, non-random-sampling bias; in other words, randomness of the selection process is destroyed. To avoid either error, the samples were analyzed in two ways—including all firms *and* also excluding them. The results are essentially identical but, as expected, with *stronger* correlation in the samples with short-lived firms included. Table 12 gives the result for the samples with the short-lived firms *excluded*.

40. To assess the weight of this evidence, some measure of the power of these tests is necessary—that is, the probability of getting significant sample results if the wealth effect is present to the degree implied by a completely unanticipated price level change. The power cannot be computed for the Mann-Whitney or the Kendall rank correlation tests, but calculation for the Pearson regression coefficient may be suggestive. Since the Mann-Whitney test is roughly 90 percent efficient (meaning that it is equivalent to the conventional regression coefficient test if it had roughly 10 percent more observations), the power of the Pearson regression coefficient test should suggest something about orders of magnitude. Estimating the standard deviation of the predicting term to be .3, and .25 for the standard error of the predicted term, with a regression coefficient of 1.00, the following estimates of power (from the conventional formula for the standard error of the regression coefficient) are derived.

The period from 1923 to 1929 is equivalent to a 12 percent one-directional price change. The probability of getting *positive* (but not necessarily significant) coefficients is roughly .7 (as compared with .5, if there were no wealth transfer associated with price-level changes). The probability of getting such large correlations as to be regarded as significant (at the 5 percent significance level) is estimated to be about .2 to .4. Slightly better chances hold for the period 1933–39 because of the larger samples at that time and the greater "one-directional equivalent" price-level change of 17 percent. Probability of *significant* correlations showing up (if the wealth effect really is present) is estimated to be

Fisher's chi-square statistic provides a test of whether such good agreement with the wealth transfer implication could have arisen in this set of samples from fortuitous random sampling in the absence of a wealth transfer effect. The probability that it could be so explained is less than .001.

Again we repeat that these results cannot be regarded as *more* independent evidence in support of the preceding analyses. Instead they are alternative ways of examining the same evidence, primarily to avoid the possibility that one particular method of testing may give deviant results because some necessary assumptions were not satisfied. That all three methods give the same conclusion is to be regarded as evidence that the statistical analyses have been correctly performed.

### Test Conclusions

The three preceding classes of statistical analyses (cohort, portfolio, and firm-year prediction) of the approximately 12,000 firm-years of data provide what appears to be overwhelming evidence that the inflations and deflations have been at least partly unanticipated, with a consequent transfer of wealth from net monetary debtors to creditors. The *extent* of the net wealth transfer depends upon the extent of the price-level changes, the extent to which they are unanticipated, and the extent of net monetary debtor or creditor status. How serious or economically important the net wealth transfer is can be predicted only after those factors are known. Nevertheless, for the population of business firms from which our samples have been taken, it appears that the net monetary debtors have, during inflations, extracted a not insignificant amount from net monetary creditors, and conversely during deflations.

### Extent of Wealth Transfer

What is the extent of the wealth transfer? The answer will tell us whether we should then ask, Can one successfully use a policy deliberately designed to make himself a net monetary debtor or creditor at the appropriate times so as to capture the wealth transfers during periods of price-level changes?

The observed difference between the optimal and pessimal portfolio equity values is not a direct measure of the wealth transfer, because that difference involves double counting. It is the absolute sum of the gains and losses. If the

---

somewhat over .5, with a probability of approximately .9 of at least *positive* association being observed in the sample.

Samples from the periods of major inflations and deflations have an even greater power.

TABLE 12. *Sampling probabilities of statistical tests of association between predicted and observed equity changes during episodes of price-level changes from 1915 through 1952: computed by Mann-Whitney, Kendall, and Pearson tests of associations[a] (short-lived firms excluded)*

| Episode, gross price-level change,[b] and sample size | Random-sampling probabilities[c] of observed degree of association— if wealth transfer were absent | | |
|---|---|---|---|
| | Mann-Whitney | Kendall | Pearson |
| 1915–20: 90% | | | |
| New York Stock Exchange (85) | .27 | .16 | .80* |
| 1940–52: 96% | | | |
| New York Stock Exchange (99) | .02 | .07 | .28 |
| American Stock Exchange (177) | .17 | .10 | .48 |
| Over-the-counter (88) | .06 | .05 | .26 |
| Steel industry (75) | .02 | .58* | .001 |
| Chemical industry (48) | .12 | .07 | .44 |
| Textile industry (78) | .01 | .001 | .025 |
| Retail department stores (56) | .005 | .001 | .16 |
| "Wages" sample firms (113) | .015 | .02 | .29 |
| 1921–22: 18% | | | |
| New York Stock Exchange (146) | .001 | .001 | .03 |
| 1928–33: 42% | | | |
| New York Stock Exchange (88) | .01 | .01 | .27 |
| 1923–29: 12% | | | |
| New York Stock Exchange (72) | .01 | .01 | .08 |
| 1933–39: 17% | | | |
| New York Stock Exchange (120) | .025 | .07 | .37 |
| American Stock Exchange (38) | .03 | .03 | .31 |
| Fisher's $\chi^2$ compound sampling probability | <.0001 | <.0001 | <.001 |

[a] S. Siegel, *Nonparametric Statistics for the Behavioral Sciences* (New York: McGraw-Hill, 1956).

[b] All price-level changes expressed as equivalent percentage rise in price level over entire episode.

[c] All probabilities are one-tailed probabilities because only positive and zero associations are admissible under hypotheses.

*Probability over .5 indicates association in subject test was negative instead of positive. In this case very large probabilities would be an indication of absence of wealth transfer.

optimal and the pessimal portfolios were always of the same numerical net monetary status—but with opposite signs—the amount of wealth transfer would be *half* the difference between the two portfolios' equity value growths. However, if the pessimal portfolio were always exactly a neutral portfolio, the entire difference would be the net wealth transfer to the optimal portfolio.[41]

In our *total* set of data, the average net monetary debtor status was usually between two and five times as great as the average net monetary status of the creditors. The ratio was largest during the early part of the period 1915–52, and it gradually decreased thereafter. Hence, roughly two-thirds to four-fifths of the difference between the two portfolios' equity growth is probably a fair measure of the extent of wealth transfer during inflations. During deflations, when the net monetary creditors should gain wealth, only a small fraction of the difference between the equity growth of the two portfolios is a measure of the net gain in wealth. But over the whole period, since inflation was much more prevalent, roughly .7–.8 of the difference between the growth of the equity in the optimal and the pessimal portfolios is a measure of the net gain in wealth to the optimal portfolio. On this basis it is possible to make a rough estimate of the total annual growth of the optimal portfolio that is attributable to the wealth transfer effect of price-level changes. Table 13 presents the equity values of an optimal and a pessimal portfolio composed of all the firms in the study (including the industry and wage samples as well as the exchange and over-the-counter samples).

Since the optimal portfolio based on all the sample populations grew about 16.1 percent per year, compared with 13.7 percent for the pessimal portfolio, the difference of 2.4 percent, when multiplied by about .7 or .8 gives 1.7–1.9 percentage points as the net annual growth in the optimal portfolio attributable to the wealth transfer caused by non-neutral monetary status during price-level changes. This amounts to about 10–15 percent of the total growth of the optimal portfolio, which grew 16.1 percent per year in nominal and 13.6 percent per year in "real" units. In sum, the optimal portfolio grew during 1915–51 at a (relative) rate of about 10–15 percent more than it would have had there been no changes in the level of prices or if the optimal portfolio had always

41. If the net monetary debtors are debtors to the extent of $-.50$, while the creditor portfolio averages $+.25$, the difference is composed of a gain that is twice the loss. The net gain is then two-thirds of the total difference in growth of wealth between the debtor and the creditor portfolio. If the net monetary status of one portfolio is $-1.00$, while the other is $+.20$, then of the difference, five-sixths is a gain, and one-sixth is a loss.

TABLE 13. Equity growth of optimal and of pessimal portfolios based on all firms in all samples combined, 1915–51 (for average-over-year criterion of net monetary status) (end of 1914 = $1.00)

| Year | Direction of CPI[a] | Number of firms in portfolio | | Annual equity growth factor of portfolio | | Equity compounded growth | | Ratio of compounded growth of optimal to pessimal portfolios | Year |
|---|---|---|---|---|---|---|---|---|---|
| | | Net monetary debtors | Net monetary creditors | Debtors | Creditors | Optimal portfolio[b] | Pessimal portfolio[b] | | |
| 1915 | + | 77 | 10 | 2.297 | 1.595 | 2.30 | 1.59 | 1.44 | 1915 |
| 1916 | + | 81 | 16 | 1.058 | 1.193 | 2.43 | 1.90 | 1.28 | 1916 |
| 1917 | + | 82 | 28 | 0.897 | 0.925 | 2.18 | 1.76 | 1.24 | 1917 |
| 1918 | + | 94 | 32 | 1.363 | 1.322 | 2.97 | 2.33 | 1.28 | 1918 |
| 1919 | + | 98 | 34 | 1.617 | 1.524 | 4.81 | 3.55 | 1.36 | 1919 |
| 1920 | + | 111 | 32 | 0.645 | 0.679 | 3.10 | 2.41 | 1.29 | 1920 |
| 1921 | − | 116 | 31 | 1.138 | 1.300 | 4.03 | 2.74 | 1.47 | 1921 |
| 1922 | − | 68 | 20 | 1.275 | 1.402 | 5.65 | 3.49 | 1.62 | 1922 |
| 1923 | + | 57 | 24 | 1.102 | 0.986 | 6.23 | 3.45 | 1.81 | 1923 |
| 1924 | − | 59 | 17 | 1.261 | 1.354 | 8.44 | 4.34 | 1.94 | 1924 |
| 1925 | + | 54 | 20 | 1.348 | 1.327 | 11.37 | 5.76 | 1.97 | 1925 |
| 1926 | − | 48 | 23 | 0.994 | 1.079 | 12.26 | 5.73 | 2.14 | 1926 |
| 1927 | − | 45 | 25 | 1.319 | 1.215 | 14.90 | 7.55 | 1.97 | 1927 |
| 1928 | − | 114 | 56 | 1.580 | 1.368 | 20.40 | 11.94 | 1.71 | 1928 |
| 1929 | + | 111 | 53 | 0.621 | 0.709 | 12.67 | 8.47 | 1.50 | 1929 |
| 1930 | − | 56 | 35 | 0.585 | 0.599 | 7.58 | 4.95 | 1.53 | 1930 |
| 1931 | − | 56 | 32 | 0.601 | 0.641 | 4.86 | 2.98 | 1.63 | 1931 |

| | | | | | | | | |
|---|---|---|---|---|---|---|---|---|
| 1932 | − | 54 | 31 | 0.936 | 1.010 | 4.91 | 2.79 | 1.76 | 1932 |
| 1933 | + | 133 | 111 | 2.307 | 2.178 | 11.32 | 6.07 | 1.87 | 1933 |
| 1934 | + | 80 | 79 | 1.330 | 1.367 | 15.06 | 14.75 | 1.70 | 1934 |
| 1935 | + | 77 | 80 | 1.665 | 1.777 | 25.08 | 14.75 | 1.70 | 1935 |
| 1936 | + | 76 | 81 | 1.598 | 1.441 | 40.07 | 21.25 | 1.89 | 1936 |
| 1937 | + | 81 | 76 | 0.574 | 0.614 | 23.00 | 13.05 | 1.76 | 1937 |
| 1938 | − | 78 | 78 | 1.340 | 1.204 | 27.68 | 17.48 | 1.58 | 1938 |
| 1939 | − | 72 | 83 | .997 | 1.019 | 28.22 | 17.43 | 1.62 | 1939 |
| 1940 | + | 428 | 350 | 1.035 | 1.070 | 29.21 | 18.65 | 1.57 | 1940 |
| 1941 | + | 453 | 321 | 1.025 | 1.006 | 29.94 | 18.76 | 1.60 | 1941 |
| 1942 | + | 461 | 309 | 1.223 | 1.202 | 36.61 | 22.55 | 1.62 | 1942 |
| 1943 | + | 408 | 354 | 1.711 | 1.498 | 62.64 | 33.79 | 1.85 | 1943 |
| 1944 | + | 341 | 410 | 1.544 | 1.426 | 96.72 | 48.18 | 2.01 | 1944 |
| 1945 | + | 299 | 437 | 1.837 | 1.613 | 177.67 | 77.71 | 2.29 | 1945 |
| 1946 | + | 300 | 427 | 0.995 | 0.967 | 176.79 | 75.15 | 2.35 | 1946 |
| 1947 | + | 345 | 373 | 1.030 | 1.077 | 182.09 | 80.93 | 2.25 | 1947 |
| 1948 | + | 362 | 348 | 0.964 | 0.996 | 175.53 | 80.61 | 2.18 | 1948 |
| 1949 | − | 333 | 368 | 1.165 | 1.159 | 203.44 | 993.91 | 2.17 | 1949 |
| 1950 | + | 324 | 373 | 1.427 | 1.405 | 290.31 | 131.94 | 2.20 | 1950 |
| 1951 | + | 372 | 318 | 1.175 | 1.190 | 341.12 | 157.01 | 2.17 | 1951 |

[a]Plus sign (+) if Consumer Price Index rose from January to December; minus sign (−) if it fell.

[b]Optimal portfolio is based on net monetary debtors in years of positive CPI change and net monetary creditors in years of negative change.

been neutral during the price-level changes that did occur. And the pessimal portfolio, being closer to neutral status, lost through wealth transfers about 5 percent of its earned growth.

The same kind of calculations for the 18 years during which the price level changed by at least 3 percent in each year, suggests a growth for the optimal portfolio of about 20–25 percent greater than it would have been in the absence of the wealth transfer, and about 20 percent slower growth for the pessimal portfolio.[42]

## What Is the Practical Applicability of Knowledge of Wealth Transfer?

The prospect of capturing the wealth transfers arising from inflation immediately suggests itself. Could one gain wealth from inflation by holding net monetary debtor stocks during price-level rises and net monetary creditor stocks during deflations?[43] (It would make no difference what was done during periods when the price level did not change.)

A measure of the extent to which a person can deliberately capture wealth transfers caused by price-level changes can be obtained by comparing the results of this deliberate policy with some "other" investment policy. The "other" investment policy may capture wealth gains—though not by design. Therefore, the answer to the question which is asked here—How much can be captured by deliberate design?—depends upon what would have been captured with some other policy. In order to answer this question, "other" policy is defined to be that of simply holding a portfolio that is the average of all the stocks in our study. (Each person is entitled to define his "other" policy as he wishes.) To capture the wealth transfers, one would have to predict inflation or deflation, and he would also have to predict the net monetary status of any firm whose common stock he might hold in his portfolio. In our case the net monetary status of each firm for the ensuing year was assumed to be predicted by

42. These results are virtually unchanged if the analysis is confined to the "exchange and over-the-counter" samples.

43. A discerning person might suggest that the predicted optimal portfolio should switch into bonds during years for which the price level is predicted to fall. A quick test of that has been made, assuming a 5 percent return on bonds. Not so surprising—for those who are experienced in the stock market—is that this is worse than holding creditor common stocks. Vivid memories of the spectacular stock market decline in 1929–32 blot out memories of many years in which the prices of common stocks rose despite declines in the general price level.

TABLE 14. *Net monetary status at beginning of year compared with average over year, all firms and all years (plus is net monetary creditor)*

| Net monetary status at beginning of year | Average net monetary status over year | | | | | |
|---|---|---|---|---|---|---|
| | Creditors | | | Debtors | | |
| | Over .50 | .50 to .10 | .10 to −.10 | −.10 to −.50 | Under −.50 | Totals |
| Over .50 | 769 | 217 | 3 | 2 | 4 | 995 |
| 50 to .10 | 96 | 2,531 | 366 | 27 | 1 | 3,021 |
| .10 to −.10 | 7 | 275 | 1,907 | 258 | 14 | 2,461 |
| −.10 to −.50 | 2 | 29 | 307 | 1,618 | 192 | 2,148 |
| Under −.50 | 4 | 5 | 17 | 290 | 2,837 | 3,153 |
| Totals | 878 | 3,057 | 2,600 | 2,195 | 3,048 | 11,778 |

Total of 11,778 omits firms in the last year of each sample. The average over last year is not computable, because net monetary status at *end* of last year was not obtained.

its net monetary status at the beginning of the year. The prediction about the price-level changes was made as follows: the coming year would be inflationary or deflationary according to the sign of the change in the Consumer Price Index between the preceding July and December. For example, if the index was higher in December 1959 than in July 1959, predict that December 1960 will be higher than December 1959. (Other devices can be suggested, but we have tried only this one.) For the period 1915–52, errors were made when predicting for 1924, 1926, 1933, 1938, and 1950.

How accurately can net monetary status be predicted? Table 14 gives an idea. However, the real test of goodness of any prediction is in the extent to which a predicted optimal portfolio does in fact do better than a pessimal portfolio, or a neutral portfolio.[44] Table 15 and figure 7 show that this prediction portfolio barely surpassed the average of all stocks. In fact, the difference is too small for statistical significance.

However, there is a bolder policy; hold only the more extreme debtor or

---

44. One important problem of practical application must be mentioned. Costs of collecting data, selling and buying stocks, and taxes should be included. This has not been done, because the present test is to see if there is any possibility of capturing the wealth in the first place. Secondly, the other costs will vary with institutions applying the method. All of which says that the costs of trying all these variant measures were beyond our budget.

TABLE 15. *Observed equity rise of predicted optimal and pessimal portfolios, using net monetary status at beginning of year as prediction of net monetary status, all firms, 1915–52 (end of 1914 = $1.00)*

| Year | Direction of CPI[a] | Number of firms in portfolio | | Annual equity growth factor of portfolio | | Equity, compounded growth | | Ratio of compounded growth of optimal to pessimal portfolios | Year |
|------|------|------|------|------|------|------|------|------|------|
| | | Net monetary debtors | Net monetary creditors | Debtors | Creditors | Optimal portfolio[b] | Pessimal portfolio[b] | | |
| 1915 | + | 82 | 5 | 2.260 | 1.491 | 2.26 | 1.49 | 1.52 | 1915 |
| 1916 | + | 82 | 16 | 1.050 | 1.187 | 2.37 | 1.77 | 1.34 | 1916 |
| 1917 | + | 84 | 26 | 0.916 | 0.867 | 2.17 | 1.53 | 1.42 | 1917 |
| 1918 | + | 95 | 31 | 1.365 | 1.315 | 2.97 | 2.02 | 1.47 | 1918 |
| 1919 | + | 98 | 34 | 1.620 | 1.516 | 4.80 | 3.06 | 1.57 | 1919 |
| 1920 | + | 106 | 39 | 0.648 | 0.688 | 3.11 | 2.10 | 1.48 | 1920 |
| 1921 | − | 125 | 28 | 1.126 | 1.295 | 4.03 | 2.37 | 1.70 | 1921 |
| 1922 | − | 182 | 53 | 1.318 | 1.376 | 5.55 | 3.12 | 1.78 | 1922 |
| 1923 | + | 64 | 19 | 1.089 | 0.972 | 6.04 | 3.03 | 1.99 | 1923 |
| 1924 | − | 60 | 21 | 1.168 | 1.412 | 7.06 | 4.29 | 1.65 | 1924 |
| 1925 | + | 56 | 20 | 1.390 | 1.194 | 9.81 | 5.12 | 1.92 | 1925 |
| 1926 | − | 52 | 22 | 0.985 | 1.118 | 9.67 | 5.72 | 1.69 | 1926 |
| 1927 | − | 48 | 23 | 1.323 | 1.178 | 11.39 | 7.57 | 1.50 | 1927 |
| 1928 | − | 118 | 53 | 1.603 | 1.296 | 14.76 | 12.14 | 1.22 | 1928 |
| 1929 | + | 113 | 55 | 0.604 | 0.733 | 8.91 | 8.90 | 1.00 | 1929 |
| 1930 | − | 108 | 56 | 0.595 | 0.669 | 5.96 | 5.29 | 1.13 | 1930 |
| 1931 | − | 57 | 34 | 0.629 | 0.598 | 3.57 | 3.33 | 1.07 | 1931 |

| 1932 | − | 58 | 30 | 0.916 | 1.006 | 3.59 | 3.05 | 1.18 | 1932 |
| 1933 | + | 133 | 113 | 2.309 | 2.137 | 7.67 | 7.04 | 1.09 | 1933 |
| 1934 | + | 134 | 110 | 1.260 | 1.316 | 9.66 | 9.27 | 1.04 | 1934 |
| 1935 | + | 81 | 78 | 1.665 | 1.765 | 16.08 | 16.35 | .98 | 1935 |
| 1936 | + | 76 | 81 | 1.603 | 1.436 | 25.78 | 23.48 | 1.10 | 1936 |
| 1937 | + | 74 | 83 | 0.577 | 0.608 | 14.87 | 14.28 | 1.04 | 1937 |
| 1938 | − | 83 | 74 | 1.311 | 1.221 | 19.50 | 17.43 | 1.12 | 1938 |
| 1939 | + | 76 | 80 | 1.030 | 1.015 | 19.79 | 17.96 | 1.10 | 1939 |
| 1940 | + | 441 | 371 | 1.025 | 1.070 | 20.29 | 19.21 | 1.06 | 1940 |
| 1941 | + | 436 | 340 | 1.044 | 0.981 | 21.18 | 18.85 | 1.12 | 1941 |
| 1942 | + | 482 | 292 | 1.220 | 1.211 | 25.84 | 22.83 | 1.13 | 1942 |
| 1943 | + | 444 | 326 | 1.720 | 1.466 | 44.44 | 33.46 | 1.33 | 1943 |
| 1944 | + | 386 | 376 | 1.547 | 1.420 | 68.75 | 47.52 | 1.45 | 1944 |
| 1945 | + | 319 | 432 | 1.809 | 1.616 | 124.38 | 76.79 | 1.62 | 1945 |
| 1946 | + | 275 | 461 | 1.004 | 0.971 | 124.87 | 74.56 | 1.67 | 1946 |
| 1947 | + | 332 | 395 | 1.031 | 1.080 | 128.74 | 80.53 | 1.60 | 1947 |
| 1948 | + | 355 | 363 | 0.953 | 1.002 | 122.69 | 80.69 | 1.52 | 1948 |
| 1949 | − | 363 | 347 | 1.163 | 1.157 | 141.96 | 93.84 | 1.51 | 1949 |
| 1950 | + | 302 | 399 | 1.431 | 1.402 | 199.02 | 134.29 | 1.48 | 1950 |
| 1951 | + | 339 | 358 | 1.177 | 1.194 | 234.25 | 160.34 | 1.46 | 1951 |
| 1952 | + | 394 | 296 | 1.050 | 1.045 | 245.96 | 167.55 | 1.47 | 1952 |

[a]Plus sign (+) if Consumer Price Index rose from January to December; minus sign (−) if it fell.

[b]Optimal portfolio is based on net monetary debtors in years of positive CPI change and net monetary creditors in years of negative change.

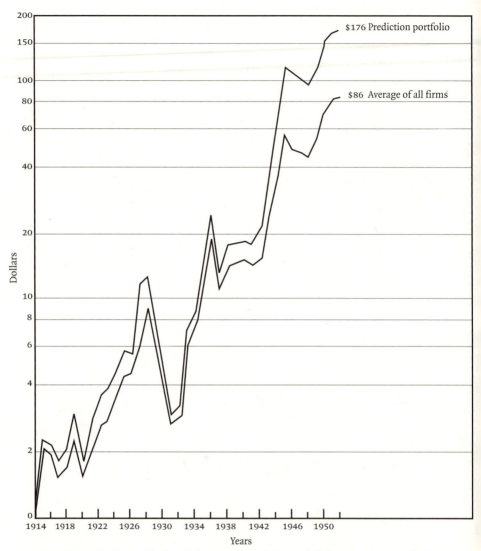

**FIGURE 7.** *Equity growth of prediction portfolio and average of all firms in constant purchasing power dollars (1914 = 1.00) (deflated by Consumer Price Index) (logarithmic scale)*

creditor firms and ignore the near-neutral firms. In this way one should get both a more reliable predictor of monetary status and a bigger wealth transfer. Omitting all firms with net monetary status between plus and minus 10 percent monetary status or between plus and minus 25 percent or even between plus and minus 40 percent gives the results shown in table 16. The data for the portfolio exceeding 0.25 is shown with the average of all firms in figure 8 (logarithmic scale) and figure 9 (arithmetic scale). The results border on the spectacular, even when allowance is made for the fact that sample sizes get smaller as only the more extreme firms are admitted. The small sample sizes occur before 1935; therefore, the results after that period should be given most weight. Even then, the more extreme portfolio increases by a factor of almost 24 during 1935–52, while the portfolio above the 10 percent range increases by 18—all these are to be compared with the average rise of 12.7. Only during the years 1928–33 do the optimal prediction portfolios fail to advance relative to the average. The only consistent explanation is the relatively small sample sizes for 1928, 1930, and 1931. Incidentally, during the deflation of 1920–22, the relative growths were as expected—even with very small samples. The difference between the growth of the two more extreme portfolios, on the one hand, and the average portfolio growth is statistically significant.[45]

Because of the rise in the price level, the increase of the equity values of the various portfolios overstates the rise as compared with "constant purchasing power dollars." This has been eliminated by use of the Consumer Price Index. The results are presented in table 17 and graphed in figure 9. The prediction portfolio, using firms of over .25 net monetary status, grows in "constant dollars" at about 14 percent per year—to $176—compared to 12 percent per year—to $85—for the average of all the stocks in the present study. This

45. As a *curiosum*, the growth of these more extreme portfolios—*if foresight with respect to inflation were perfect*—is even greater, as it should be. The portfolio of stocks in excess of .40 net monetary status grew by a factor of 1,222 from 1915 to 1952. The portfolio with stocks only in excess of .25 net monetary status grew by 985, while the portfolio with only those in excess of .10 grew by 346. The difference between these figures and those presented for 1952 in table 16 is the result of errors in prediction of year of inflation or deflation for the years 1924, 1926, 1933, 1938, and 1950. It is surprising that errors for 5 years out of 39 would cause so much difference. Undoubtedly the small sample sizes for 1924, 1926, and 1933 contribute to a relatively large error difference between the various portfolios. How much of this loss is the result of the inability to predict inflations accurately and how much is sampling variation cannot be determined. It is apparent that sampling error has worked in the direction of making the difference larger rather than smaller.

TABLE 16. *Observed equity rise in three alternative portfolios designed to capture wealth transfers during price-level changes, compared with average of stocks of all firms in study, 1915–52*

| | | ±0 (average of all stocks) | | Portfolios with net monetary status beyond | | | | | |
| | | | | ±.10 | | ±.25 | | ±.40 | |
| Year | Predicted change in CPI | N | Equity | N | Equity | N | Equity | N | Equity |
|---|---|---|---|---|---|---|---|---|---|
| 1914 | | | $1.00 | | $1.00 | | $1.00 | | $1.00 |
| 1915 | + | 87 | 2.21 | 77 | 2.30 | 67 | 2.34 | 61 | 2.48 |
| 1916 | + | 98 | 2.26 | 77 | 2.45 | 65 | 2.46 | 58 | 2.63 |
| 1917 | + | 110 | 2.04 | 79 | 2.24 | 71 | 2.43 | 64 | 2.66 |
| 1918 | + | 126 | 2.76 | 89 | 3.10 | 80 | 3.36 | 76 | 3.69 |
| 1919 | + | 132 | 4.40 | 89 | 5.07 | 80 | 5.64 | 76 | 6.13 |
| 1920 | + | 145 | 2.90 | 95 | 3.25 | 77 | 3.44 | 68 | 3.74 |
| 1921 | − | 153 | 3.36 | 18 | 4.38 | 9 | 4.99 | 7 | 5.05 |
| 1922 | − | 235 | 4.47 | 33 | 5.97 | 10 | 6.09 | 4 | 6.56 |
| 1923 | + | 83 | 4.75 | 56 | 6.49 | 50 | 6.57 | 48 | 7.08 |
| 1924 | + | 81 | 5.84 | 55 | 7.63 | 49 | 7.56 | 45 | 8.14 |
| 1925 | + | 76 | 7.82 | 50 | 10.62 | 42 | 10.28 | 37 | 11.40 |
| 1926 | + | 74 | 8.01 | 43 | 10.34 | 38 | 9.76 | 29 | 10.71 |
| 1927 | − | 71 | 10.22 | 12 | 12.69 | 2 | 20.21 | 2 | 22.18 |
| 1928 | − | 171 | 15.41 | 26 | 15.76 | 5 | 21.42 | 3 | 23.95 |
| 1929 | + | 168 | 9.95 | 91 | 9.13 | 68 | 12.42 | 56 | 14.13 |
| 1930 | − | 164 | 6.17 | 39 | 6.00 | 16 | 7.21 | 8 | 5.79 |

| Year | | | | | | | | | |
|------|---|-----|-----|------|-----|-----|--------|-----|--------|
| 1931 | − | 91  | 3.81  | 29  | 3.54   | 21  | 4.18   | 17  | 3.42   |
| 1932 | − | 88  | 3.61  | 30  | 3.57   | 22  | 4.14   | 20  | 3.42   |
| 1933 | − | 246 | 8.04  | 105 | 7.70   | 91  | 9.07   | 80  | 7.41   |
| 1934 | + | 244 | 10.33 | 116 | 9.94   | 104 | 11.70  | 98  | 9.64   |
| 1935 | + | 159 | 17.71 | 67  | 16.56  | 58  | 19.88  | 54  | 16.58  |
| 1936 | + | 157 | 26.87 | 58  | 27.75  | 49  | 33.80  | 42  | 29.02  |
| 1937 | + | 157 | 15.93 | 59  | 16.09  | 41  | 18.59  | 32  | 15.67  |
| 1938 | + | 157 | 20.22 | 69  | 21.52  | 56  | 24.54  | 45  | 19.89  |
| 1939 | − | 156 | 20.66 | 67  | 21.84  | 38  | 25.03  | 26  | 19.70  |
| 1940 | + | 812 | 21.61 | 379 | 22.56  | 314 | 25.78  | 271 | 20.09  |
| 1941 | + | 776 | 21.96 | 372 | 24.05  | 284 | 27.84  | 246 | 21.90  |
| 1942 | + | 774 | 26.70 | 418 | 29.85  | 319 | 36.48  | 284 | 29.13  |
| 1943 | + | 770 | 43.40 | 388 | 52.14  | 293 | 69.67  | 259 | 56.81  |
| 1944 | + | 762 | 63.87 | 320 | 81.55  | 232 | 114.26 | 196 | 94.86  |
| 1945 | + | 751 | 108.5 | 268 | 150.79 | 168 | 222.80 | 133 | 187.83 |
| 1946 | + | 736 | 106.6 | 196 | 155.16 | 106 | 230.17 | 80  | 202.86 |
| 1947 | + | 727 | 112.7 | 261 | 159.35 | 153 | 243.25 | 119 | 206.92 |
| 1948 | + | 718 | 110.2 | 287 | 151.54 | 187 | 233.52 | 142 | 194.50 |
| 1949 | − | 710 | 127.8 | 273 | 175.64 | 160 | 268.55 | 106 | 227.57 |
| 1950 | − | 701 | 180.8 | 320 | 246.25 | 182 | 384.03 | 119 | 334.52 |
| 1951 | + | 697 | 214.4 | 263 | 286.63 | 162 | 445.47 | 117 | 388.04 |
| 1952 | + | 690 | 224.7 | 313 | 298.38 | 196 | 463.29 | 136 | 395.81 |

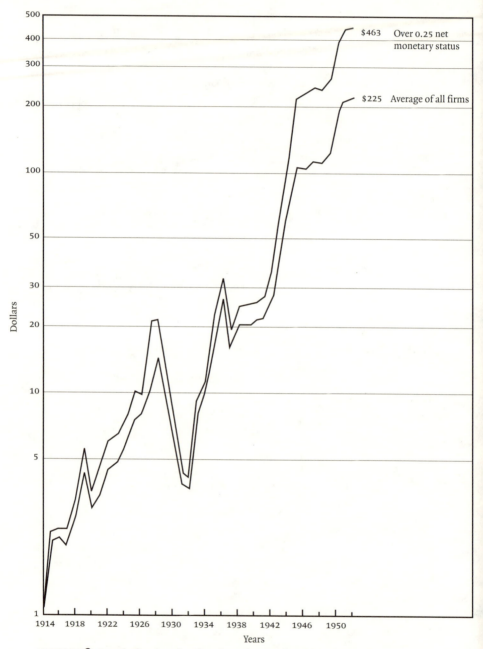

**FIGURE 8.** Growth of equity values from $1.00 in 1914 for prediction (over 0.25 net monetary status) portfolio compared with average of all firms

TABLE 17. *Observed equity rise, in constant purchasing power dollars for prediction portfolio and for average of all stocks, entire sample, 1915–52*

| | | | Portfolios with net monetary status beyond | | | |
|---|---|---|---|---|---|---|
| | Actual CPI | Predicted direction | ± (average of all stocks) | | ±.25[a] | |
| Year | Dec. 15 | change in CPI | N | Equity | N | Equity |
| 1914 | 100. | | | $1.00 | | $1.00 |
| 1915 | 101.9 | + | 87 | 2.17 | 67 | 2.30 |
| 1916 | 113.4 | + | 98 | 1.99 | 65 | 2.17 |
| 1917 | 134.6 | + | 110 | 1.52 | 71 | 1.81 |
| 1918 | 162.5 | + | 126 | 1.70 | 80 | 2.07 |
| 1919 | 186.3 | + | 132 | 2.36 | 80 | 3.03 |
| 1920 | 190.4 | + | 145 | 1.52 | 77 | 1.81 |
| 1921 | 170.2 | − | 153 | 1.97 | 9 | 2.93 |
| 1922 | 165.8 | − | 235 | 2.70 | 10 | 3.67 |
| 1923 | 170.0 | + | 83 | 2.79 | 50 | 3.86 |
| 1924 | 169.6 | + | 81 | 3.44 | 49 | 4.46 |
| 1925 | 176.5 | + | 76 | 4.43 | 42 | 5.82 |
| 1926 | 173.6 | + | 74 | 4.61 | 38 | 5.62 |
| 1927 | 170.5 | − | 71 | 5.99 | 2 | 11.85 |
| 1928 | 168.5 | − | 171 | 9.14 | 5 | 12.71 |
| 1929 | 169.1 | + | 168 | 5.88 | 68 | 7.34 |
| 1930 | 158.8 | − | 164 | 3.89 | 16 | 4.54 |
| 1931 | 143.5 | − | 91 | 2.65 | 21 | 2.91 |
| 1932 | 128.7 | − | 88 | 2.80 | 22 | 3.22 |
| 1933 | 129.3 | − | 246 | 6.22 | 91 | 7.01 |
| 1934 | 132.5 | + | 244 | 7.80 | 104 | 8.83 |
| 1935 | 136.0 | + | 159 | 13.02 | 58 | 14.61 |
| 1936 | 137.4 | + | 157 | 19.56 | 49 | 24.59 |
| 1937 | 141.8 | + | 157 | 11.23 | 41 | 13.11 |
| 1938 | 138.0 | + | 157 | 14.65 | 56 | 17.78 |
| 1939 | 137.1 | − | 156 | 15.06 | 38 | 18.25 |
| 1940 | 138.7 | + | 812 | 15.58 | 314 | 18.59 |
| 1941 | 152.2 | + | 776 | 14.43 | 284 | 18.29 |

(continued)

TABLE 17. (continued)

| Year | Actual CPI Dec. 15 | Predicted direction change in CPI | Portfolios with net monetary status beyond | | | |
|---|---|---|---|---|---|---|
| | | | ± (average of all stocks) | | ±.25[a] | |
| | | | N | Equity | N | Equity |
| 1942 | 167.4 | + | 774 | $15.95 | 319 | $21.79 |
| 1943 | 175.3 | + | 770 | 24.76 | 293 | 39.74 |
| 1944 | 180.9 | + | 762 | 35.31 | 232 | 63.01 |
| 1945 | 185.9 | + | 751 | 58.36 | 168 | 119.84 |
| 1946 | 214.9 | + | 736 | 49.60 | 106 | 109.90 |
| 1947 | 230.9 | + | 727 | 48.81 | 153 | 105.34 |
| 1948 | 237.1 | + | 718 | 46.47 | 187 | 98.49 |
| 1949 | 232.4 | − | 710 | 55.90 | 160 | 115.55 |
| 1950 | 246.2 | − | 701 | 73.40 | 182 | 155.98 |
| 1951 | 260.4 | + | 697 | 82.33 | 162 | 171.15 |
| 1952 | 262.6 | + | 690 | 85.56 | 196 | 176.31 |

[a]Composed of net monetary debtors in years when CPI was predicted to rise and net monetary creditors in years when decline was predicted for CPI.

2 percent higher growth rate is about 16 percent per year higher (2/12 = .16) than for the average of all stocks. When assessing the significance of this, it is important to note that this 16 percent relatively (or 2 percent absolutely) higher growth rate is an *average* of years of both substantial price-level changes and years of essentially *no* price-level change. It is not the measure of results during inflationary or deflationary periods only.

There still remains a conservative policy of investment. Instead of trying to capture the wealth transfers resulting from price-level changes, one can instead insulate himself from these transfers. This is much easier to do. Simply maintain a portfolio that on net balance over all holdings is a net monetary neutral. This does not require that every stock held be exactly a neutral. It suffices that the extent of the net monetary debtor holdings is balanced by net monetary asset holdings. In this way one can proceed to make investments in an attempt to realize gains from normal growth and investment acuity without any fear that inflation or deflation will affect one's fortunes through wealth trans-

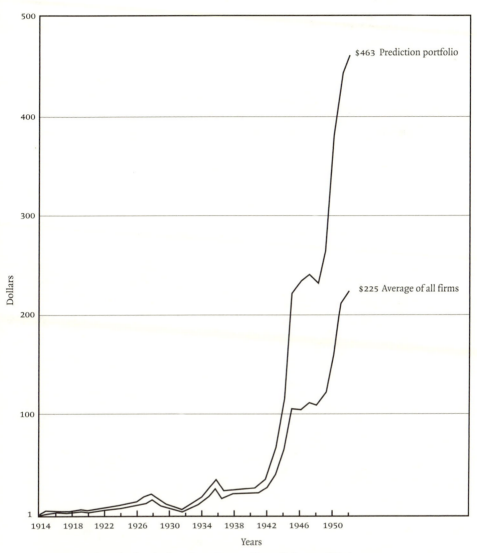

**FIGURE 9.** *Growth of equity from $1.00 in 1914 for prediction portfolio (over 0.25 net monetary status) compared with average of all firms (arithmetic scale)*

fers. If inflation or deflation have other defects, say those producing business depressions or prosperity, the neutral net monetary status will not protect from those effects.[46]

Finally, a repeated warning—the extent of the superior performance of the prediction portfolio depends upon the extent to which inflations and deflations do in fact occur. If the future should bring relatively slight changes in the price level, the advantages of a successful prediction portfolio would be trivial.

46. As matters stand now, there is no evidence that price-level changes such as have been experienced in the United States have any other effects. The depression- and prosperity-inducing effects may flow from changes in the quantity of money—but these are not the effects of inflations—that is, price-level changes. Further, if it happens that certain other events are characteristically correlated with inflations, such as wars, droughts, plagues, and expanded government activity, action to protect one's self from these events is quite independent of action required to protect one's wealth from the effects of inflation.

# INFLATION AND DISTRIBUTION
# OF INCOME AND WEALTH

## Introductory

Inquiries into the income distributive effects of inflation have been performed in several ways. Easiest is a count of assertions and allegations in the fashion of a public opinion poll. Obviously our task is not to conduct such a survey of opinion, for then we could dispense with the science of economics. Instead we take it to be that of reviewing briefly what presently validated economic theory implies about the wealth and income distributive effects, only, of inflation and to what extent we have empirical evidence supporting those implications.

Wealth and income effects are the same thing. Wealth is a present value measure of income, and conversely. But for people whose wealth is essentially human talents, a marketplace for observing changes in their wealth is not readily available. As a surrogate variable, current rates of wage receipts are often used to detect wealth changes.

## 1. Inflation and Concurrent Events

In investigating the effects we had best be certain that it is an inflation whose effects we are investigating, and not the effects of other events which also cause or are concurrent with an inflation. Therefore we should separate the side (non-inflationary) effects of such things as increases in the quantity of money, war damages, blockades, droughts, plagues, unemployment, or any events that can instigate a *policy* of inflation. For example, we should not jump to the conclusion that an increase in the quantity of money affects employment and output only by raising the general level of prices. Nor should one blame inflation for the effects of a war that initiates an inflationary finance policy. Yet that is exactly what has been said for every war episode by many responsible writers on economic affairs. The fall in real income in the South during the Civil War, the rise in the real wages during the early plagues, the shifts in demands from peacetime-type jobs and goods to munitions-type goods with the resultant

Reprinted from The Distribution of National Income, ed. Jean Marchal and Bernard Ducros (London: Macmillan, 1968), 618–32, by permission of Palgrave Macmillan.

shift in relative prices and wages have also been blamed on the inflation rather than on losses of wealth and resources and on the demand shifts. Our first conclusion must be that by utilizing this distinction we can separate confusion and myth from verifiable and verified analysis.

Let us see what validated economic theory has to say. We have been warned that this is a dangerous approach—apparently because there is presumed to be no body of valid, useful economic theory—a false judgment which one sometimes is tempted to accept when surveying the assertions about inflation. It is because that core of theory is not consistently applied that disparate and inconsistent analyses of inflation can result. Of course, each person is free to set up his own special assumptions and grind out the implications. After all, anything is conceivable and so anything must be possible.[1] But we are here bound by a more severe constraint—that of using valid economic theory and its verified implications. We must recognize and accept that constraint, for it is the economist's source of comparative advantage in analysing this question.

## II. Unanticipated and Anticipated Inflation

By inflation we mean a rise in the general level of prices. We can agree also on certain episodes as having been inflations, even if this is not possible for all episodes.[2]

We hope it will be agreed there is no point to having different techniques of analyses of inflations according to the rate of inflation (e.g., creeping, chronic, galloping, hyper). In Fisherian and Keynesian fashion (provided we confine ourselves to the Keynes of the *Tract on Monetary Reform*), we classify inflations

---

1. For excellent illustrations, see the survey called a "Survey of Inflation Theory" (M. Bronfenbrenner and F. Holzman, *American Economic Review*, September 1963, pp. 593–661). A more accurate title would have been a "Survey of Inflation Literature," for it is an excellent survey of opinions, assertions, and models, many inconsistent with each other as well as with what we had thought were well-validated economic theorems. One can hardly conceal dismay at what that survey has so ably exposed. Mistake us not; this is no criticism of the authors. Anyone should have been delighted to have discharged a duty so well.

2. For example, has there been any inflation in the United States from 1952 through 1963? Despite a rise in the official price index, its margin of error or confidence interval, and its biases are sufficiently large that it would take a rise in the various respected indices of at least 3 per cent a year to provide persuasive evidence of inflation. But for present purposes, surely, we can all agree there are lots of episodes that we would all quickly agree to classify as inflations.

into unanticipated and anticipated.[3] Anticipated inflations are characterized by market phenomena implied by the postulate that prices are expected to rise. Unanticipated inflation, as you can guess, is characterized by market phenomena implied by the postulate that the contemporaneous level of prices is "expected" to persist.

### (1) Net Monetary Status Effects

The economic analysis of the effects of inflation is simple. Since inflation is a rise of prices in terms of money units it follows, by definition, that monetary assets (claims to fixed amounts of money) fall in relative value. In contrast, non-money (real) assets rise in value with the price level. The nominal yields of real assets rise along with the price level, whereas those of monetary assets do not. Examples of real assets are common stock, real estate, buildings, inventories. Monetary assets are exampled by money, bonds, and accounts receivable, to name a few.[4]

Since the price rise is unanticipated, the increased cost of holding money fails to affect the quantity of money people want to hold, in real terms (i.e., relative to nominal wealth and income). Because of the imperfect foresight, interest rates on monetary assets do not reflect the change in the price level so as to maintain pre-inflation economic relations between net monetary debtors and creditors (monetary assets minus monetary liabilities). As a result there are

3. I. Fisher, *The Purchasing Power of Money*, rev. ed., New York, 1926; J. M. Keynes, *A Tract on Monetary Reform*, London, 1923, p. 18.

4. Let R and M be net real and net monetary assets, respectively, and E, the initial equity. Thus:

$$E = R + M.$$

If $E^1$ is the new equity when prices rise by proportion, P, then:

$$E^1 = PR + M.$$

Finally, let Q be the proportionate increase in the money value of the equity:

$$Q = E^1/E.$$

Now, substituting and rearranging:

$$Q = \frac{PR + M}{E} = P - (P - 1)\frac{M}{E}.$$

Whether Q is larger than, equal to, or smaller than P (assumed larger than 1) depends on whether M is negative, zero, or positive.

transfers of wealth from net monetary creditors to net monetary debtors. What is true of debtors and creditors linked by interpersonal monetary claims in the form of bonds is equally true of monetary debtor-creditor relationships created by mortgages, notes, bills, leases, demand deposits, prepayments, and fiat money.

A rise in the price level—whatever its cause—reduces, by definition and in fact, the value of the non-interest-bearing money, in units of which prices are expressed. Those whose debts form the money, if it be debt money, gain real wealth because of their reduced real liabilities.[5] If the inflation was induced by an increase in printed fiat government money, the government gains wealth and then exchanges one form of wealth for another when the money is spent—with the gain being at the expense of those who held money at the time the price level rose.[6]

### (2) Other Presumed Effects of Inflation

No income effects other than those flowing from the wealth transfer among net monetary creditors-debtors are implied. There are implied no wage lags, no forced saving, no suffering by widows, orphans, and old people, no profits to businessmen and speculators, and no price distortions. Then so much the worse for the validity of economic theory—unless these phenomena are illusions, as we are convinced they are. The available evidence and data simply do not support the presumption of the presence of those alleged phenomena. The reconciliation of observation and analysis lies, we are convinced, in avoiding a prevalent, earlier-mentioned confusion between the effects of events initiating an inflation and the effects of the inflation itself. Let us look into these briefly.

There is nothing in economic analysis that says an inflation must first occur with a more rapid rise in consumer goods prices. Yet this preconception underlies many of the statements of the wage-lag doctrine.[7] Another preconception is that wages are naturally sticky, rigid, and immobile relative to consumer-goods prices. Finally, another preconception is that during an inflation, with

---

5. We note that if the money were bank debt money, it does not follow that banks will gain wealth on *net*, because every bank is a net monetary *creditor* and loses more than it gains from the inflation. R. Kessel, "Inflation-Caused Wealth Redistribution: A Test of a Hypothesis," *American Economic Review*, March 1956, pp. 128–41.

6. See Appendix.

7. A. Alchian and R. Kessel, "The Meaning and Validity of the Inflation-Induced Lag of Wages Behind Prices," *American Economic Review*, March 1960, pp. 43–66.

the increase in wealth to those who gain from the inflation, there must be a reduced income left to the rest of the community. If, for example, the government gains from an inflation by printing new money and taking some of the wealth and income from the community, the smaller remaining income must imply a reduction in real wages. Given the preconceptions, one hardly needs to look at evidence, for if he does he can certainly find support for his belief if he is a little careless in his evaluation of the evidence or use of statistical principles.

(a) *Wage Lags.* As every economist understands, real wages can be affected by real forces like changes in the relative supplies of labour and capital, changes in the quality of the labour force, changes in the pattern of consumer demand, and changes in the state of the arts. Only if one abstracts from the effects of known real forces can one determine the effects of inflation upon an observed time series of real wages. To illustrate, real wages and money prices since 1889 show a very high positive (not negative) correlation. Is this evidence against the wage lag? Certainly not. Real wages rose during this time according to informed observers, because of *per capita* increases in skill, capital, technology, etc. Those who believed in the wage lag would not have denied this. Their position would have been that real wages rose despite inflation and that if the effects of real forces upon real wages were accounted for properly, one would observe a fall in real wages attributable to inflation.[8]

No amount of examination of time series will convince some people of the absence of a wage lag. The theory they have adopted simply requires its presence, and if the data do not show it, so much the worse for the statistical data. But once the implications of economic theory are pointed out and once it is shown that a wage lag is not implied, even with a decrease in real income or wealth for the rest of the community during an inflationary expropriation of wealth by, say, the government, everything falls into place. What, as we now know, happens is that the wealth transfer is accomplished via a tax on money— a transfer of wealth from net monetary creditors to net monetary debtors (and

8. Note momentarily a common and humorous error of statistical interpretation and evaluation of evidence. Given the presence of a myriad of "random" forces on wages and prices, one would expect that during inflation, deflation, or price stability there would be observed a negative relationship between changes in prices and real wages half the time, and a positive correlation half the time. It is no inaccuracy to say that some observers cite the negative relationships as evidence, while ignoring the positive relationships— exclaiming that the wage lag operates for about half of the cases, just as a gambler could claim that a roulette wheel is biased toward red half the time!

money is an important form of monetary credits). The lower income to the rest of the community is borne by those who have lost that claim to wealth. There is no implied real wage-rate decline. Instead there is a lower share of wealth and income to net monetary creditors. Wage-earners have the same income as formerly. A failure to recognize the process as a specific form of *wealth* transfer rather than a kind of *generalized income* transfer was, we believe, the responsible culprit in causing so much confusion of analysis.

A careful review of all the available evidence simply does not support the wage-lag contention, even if one goes back as far as 1350! On the other hand, the available evidence of a wealth transfer according to net monetary status is overwhelming.[9]

(b) *Forced Savings.* Associated with the wage-lag contention is the well-known, but still mysterious, forced savings doctrine—a doctrine as vulnerable as it is ambiguous. At least three versions exist.[10] One identifies it with the wage lag, often with the explicit addendum that wealth so saved is necessarily or usually devoted to investment. A second contention is that those who first spend new money get wealth by driving up prices and depriving those who held the prior existing money. Finally there is the argument that since the government gets wealth, or more income, by inflation, all the rest of the community *must* have less income, and this smaller income therefore must result in a rise in consumer-goods prices relative to factor prices. Now the fact is that none of

9. A. Alchian and R. Kessel, "Redistribution of Wealth through Inflation," *Science*, 4 September 1959, pp. 535–39; G. L. Bach and A. Ando, "The Redistributional Effects of Inflation," *Review of Economics and Statistics*, February 1957, pp. 1–13; D. Felix, "Profit Inflation and Industrial Growth: The Historic Record and Contemporary Analogies," *Quarterly Journal of Economics*, August 1956, pp. 441–63; B. Pesek, "Distribution Effects of Inflation and Taxation," *American Economic Review*, March 1960, pp. 147–53.

10. Jacob Viner, *Studies in the Theory of International Trade*, Harpers, New York, 1937, pp. 187–97, finds two versions. The first citation of the wage lag is to Henry Thornton, while a quote from T. Joplin contains a nearly correct version of the money tax, which Viner calls forced saving, despite the fact that he later implicitly denies it when saying Ricardo did not have a "forced savings" thesis. Gottfried Haberler, *Prosperity and Depression*, United Nations, Lake Success, 1946, pp. 42, 43, 138, and 310, has all three versions. J. M. Keynes, in *The General Theory of Employment, Interest and Money*, Macmillan, London, 1936, pp. 79–81, 123–24, contains a well-directed and potentially effective attack on the idea that savings in any of the three above versions are forced in any sense different from that which results from a change in circumstance like a loss of wealth, whatever the cause; but he blunted his attack by his simultaneous acceptance of the wage-lag doctrine, which to many economists (e.g., Robertson, Haberler, Viner) is the forced savings doctrine.

these will stand up either to theoretical analysis or to empirical evidence. As we have indicated, the wage-lag assertion is neither theoretically nor empirically sound. The second version, implying a forced saving on those who do not get the new money, comes close but is fundamentally wrong. The interpretation simply fails to distinguish between the fact of a wealth transfer and the way in which it is achieved. A change in consumer-goods prices relative to factor prices simply is not implied by a loss of wealth.[11]

(c) *Losses by Economic Classes.* Although our interest in the net monetary status of business firms was based on a desire to obtain economic ownership units of different net monetary status in order to test the wealth redistribution effect, there is interest also in relating net monetary status to other personal or occupational characteristics. In other words, who are the net monetary debtors and the creditors? Their incidence in various occupations and wealth levels is still unknown. Some attempts have been made in this direction, but these have relied on aggregative data for a class as a whole. They tell us nothing about the proportions within the class. Furthermore, the data so far available by groups or classes involve much ambiguity in assigning assets and liabilities to monetary or non-monetary status. Even if data were available accurately and for individuals, there is a disturbing element in the attempt to classify occupational or wealth *groups* on this basis.

In the first place, it invites attention to superficial characteristics, especially if not everyone in that class or category is of the same net monetary status. Second, it suggests policy action toward one class, as if everyone were of the same net monetary status within that class. For example, comparisons of the progressivity of the inflation tax on monetary assets with the progressivity of the graduated income tax leads precisely to that policy.

And again, the impression that widows, orphans, and retired people suffer from inflation is also wrong, even if more of the widows, orphans, and retired people are net monetary creditors than debtors. We think it is clearer, and more relevant to say simply that net monetary debtors gain at the expense of net monetary creditors, whatever their other attributes, and that if one wishes to take action to "correct" that, attention should be directed to the net monetary status, not some other superficial classification criterion. However, this is a matter of conjecture as to what the consequences and general interpretation of

11. Despite the logical vacuity and empirical falsity of all versions of the forced savings doctrine, we predict a continued vigorous and long life. Its emotional appeal and obviousness is too strong to kill with reason and evidence.

such studies will be and, of course, does not mean that it is wrong to make such studies nor that they are useless. We merely wish to emphasize and warn of a source of potentially dangerous misinterpretation.

Disclaiming any implication that inflation-induced gains to those of a net monetary debtor status justify a special tax on net monetary debtors, we can nevertheless inquire whether businessmen as a class typically are net monetary debtors or creditors. In general, the evidence is that it varies in time and by countries. In the United States, the proportion of firms that are net monetary debtors has varied from a high of close to 90 per cent down to about 50 per cent, from 1915 to 1946.[12] Most recent data for 1956 indicate the proportion is about 60 per cent.[13] These data refer to firms whose stock is traded on the organized security exchanges. In England in the post-war period, the fraction has run higher, running at about three-fourths of all firms (although the type of business seems to be a determining factor).[14] In Japan, for the post-war period the proportion runs close to 90 per cent.[15]

An amusing example of reliance on casual empiricism and abandonment of analysis is provided by Keynes's discussion of the "gains" to businessmen from inflation. In his *Tract*, he had the analysis straight.[16] There he had no wage lag, no inventory gains, just debtor status—but no supporting statistical data. Yet within ten years Keynes had abandoned the analysis and was asserting that businessmen gained from inventories and from wage lags. At some place between the *Tract* and the *Treatise* he had been induced to change his mind (we believe by Professor E. Hamilton's persuasive publications as evidenced by the extensive reference to his work in Keynes's *Treatise*).[17] It is hard to believe that Keynes could have thrown aside all his theoretical rigour and seized upon the wage-lag hypothesis—especially in view of the inadequacies of the data and the more consistent alternative interpretations of which Keynes showed appreciation in his *Tract*. But he did. In any event, in the *Treatise*, he defended and interpreted the excess profits tax during World War I as a means of appropriating inflation-induced "gains" of businessmen resulting from the wage lag. In

---

12  Alchian and Kessel, *Science, loc. cit.*

13.  Unpublished doctoral dissertation of V. Boursalian at UCLA.

14.  L. De Alessi, "The Redistribution of Wealth by Inflation: An Empirical Test with United Kingdom Data," *Southern Economic Journal*, October 1963, pp. 113–27.

15.  Unpublished doctoral dissertation of J. Kuratani at UCLA.

16.  J. M. Keynes, *loc. cit.*

17.  J. M. Keynes, *A Treatise on Money*, II, Macmillan, London, 1930, pp. 148–81.

a sense, his behaviour is more a tribute to his open-mindedness than to his confidence in economic theory.

(d) *Price Distortions.* Price distortions are commonly alleged to be results of inflation. Sticky, inflexible customary prices are the usual basis of the alleged distortion of prices. If we recognize that inflations often are the result of changes in factor supplies or are policy responses to desires to revise relative demands (e.g., armaments versus retail clerks), we should not be surprised to see changes in relative demands at times of inflation. Again, it is said that government employees have fixed wages. Even though this may be true it does not indicate that job reclassification or job shifting is not equally efficient as a wage-rate reviser. Sticky, inflexible customary or rigid prices are easy to talk about but harder to substantiate. We suspect the illusion arises partly from a comparison of the price of a single good with an index of many prices. If all prices are equally flexible and responsive, each single price will appear to lag (or lead!) the smoother-changing average of all other prices.

The only available evidence germane to the presumption of increased dispersion of prices during inflation is that presented by Wesley Mitchell.[18] And that evidence does not show any increase in relative price or wage dispersions in inflation as compared with non-inflations. We would have expected an increase at the onset and termination of an inflation—in response to changes in relative demands—not because of relative price stickiness. Suffice it to say that here is an unexplored, but we think, tractable and useful area of empirical research. And while performing that research, it will be desirable to see if there are any relative price effects arising from relative demand shifts associated with changes in real value of money stocks.

### III. Losses of Interest Receivers

Income data can be used to supplement wealth statistics. Here, too, the evidence about shares going to various factors shows no wage lag nor, for that matter, any substantial changes in factor incomes systematically related to inflation, except for *explicit contractual* interest receipts.[19] But notice that we have emphasized the *explicit contractual* interest. We emphasize that because the share going to interest is *measured* with a serious bias.

We are accustomed to measuring the interest rate as a form of payment for

18. W. Mitchell, *The Making and Using of Index Numbers*, U.S. Department of Labor, Bulletin No. 656, 1938.

19. Bach and Ando, *op. cit.*

loans. It is, of course, a payment or reflection of differences in present prices of present consumption rights and future consumption rights—a payment for deferral of consumption. But not all such deferrals are in the form of contractual loans in monetary amounts. Consumption rights can be deferred in many ways; one need not lend money in return for a monetary asset claim; he can invest in long-lived assets to put the matter allegorically. These investors receive interest, not in the form of pre-assigned monetary amounts but in real terms, and also stand to receive profits or losses. Therefore it is not entirely correct to say that interest receivers lose from unanticipated inflation. It is only those interest receivers who take their interest claims in monetary forms rather than in non-monetary forms; they lose because they have chosen to express their interest claims in monetary units and have underestimated the extent of future price rise.

We are forced to return to our initial implication of economic analysis for unanticipated inflations. It is the net monetary status that is the source of income and wealth redistributions—not even the interest receiver can, in strict accuracy, be claimed to be a loser from even unanticipated inflation. It is his tie to fixed monetary contracts for the interest that is the source of the redistribution. All other contentions have as yet failed to be supported by the available empirical evidence. We must exclude from this generalization the effects of price control and tax policies adopted by governments (e.g., the effect of a graduated income tax in the face of rising prices). We make this exclusion not because they could not be considered effects of inflation, but because they represent effects of discretionary actions and laws. Rather than associate them with the inflation *per se* we have chosen to separate them as policy variables. However, if you wish, you may put them wherever you wish and modify the conclusion in a consistent fashion, without, we think, changing one's understanding.

## IV. Anticipated Inflation

A fully anticipated, in contrast to unanticipated, inflation implies interest rates that do accurately allow for the inflation that will occur. As a result net monetary assets bearing explicit interest do not impose a loss on the creditor. It is difficult to imagine an economy without some non-interest-bearing monetary assets. But, only difficult, not impossible. Some major banks would find it profitable to issue purchasing-power or interest-bearing securities or monies —unless prohibited by government edict. The switch to such money would, of course, mean the inflation would come to an end—since there would be no inflation in terms of this money. What is difficult to imagine is any government permitting that kind of competition in issue of money. Implicitly, we are assuming that anticipated inflations are results of government policy—an *ad hoc* presumption, but one which we think is justified by historical fact. Therefore we say that we cannot imagine interest-bearing or purchasing-power money really being issued by any non-government agency, and we cannot bring ourselves to imagine a government willing to cut off its power to claim a share of the community's wealth and income by inflation, and that is what a really effective purchasing-power money would do.

In the absence of perfect purchasing-power or interest-bearing money the inflation, anticipated or not, will continue to impose a loss of wealth on money holders. Also imposed is a general loss of efficiency and, consequently, of wealth on the community at large as a result of its resort to less efficient means of exchange and specialization in production. This revision in exchange procedures will, of course, imply a gain in wealth (and hence income) for people who provide services that facilitate economizing on money. But this is essentially identical to the analysis of the effects of a tax on any resource. In this case the resource is money. We conjecture that non-human capital is a better money substitute than human labour. If so, there is a shift in relative demand from labour to non-labour wealth as a money substitute, with a consequent fall in real wage rates.

Again we have come full circle. The decrease in real wages is now not a result of a wage lag but of a shift in relative demand for money substitutes—if it is correct that non-human goods are a better money substitute than labour. Unfortunately empirical evidence on these implications for anticipated inflations is sparse, and we can only wish for more evidence, while waiting for others to obtain it.

### Appendix

This appendix presents a simple numerical illustration of a wealth transfer via net monetary status in the context of a simultaneous revision of relative demands. We emphasize that this is an illustration of the process implied by economic analysis; it is not evidence in support of that theory. Because it helps clarify the meaning of some of the implications contained in the text, we have taken the liberty of including it as an appendix.

Let us suppose that the government—which we shall arbitrarily use as our

TABLE 1. *Pre-inflation wealth, debts, and incomes of individuals*

| Persons | Wealth | Cash | Goods | Interpersonal Debts (−) or Credits (+) | Income |
|---------|--------|------|-------|----------------------------------------|--------|
| A | 15.15 | 2.40 | 12.75 | 0 | 2.25 |
| B | 9.85 | .85 | 9.00 | 0 | 1.00 |
| C | 16.10 | .60 | 14.25 | 1.25 | .75 |
| D | 4.65 | .40 | 4.75 | −.50 | .25 |
| E | 4.25 | .75 | 4.25 | −.75 | .75 |
| | 50.00 | 5.00 | 45.00 | 0 | 5.00 |
| Govt. | 10.00 | 1.00 | 9.00 | 0 | 1.00 |
| Total | 60.00 | 6.00 | 54.00 | 0 | 6.00 |

source of inflation—decides to shift its relative demands. People for whose services or goods there has been a relative increase in demand will experience an increase in income and wealth. These demand-revision effects neither cause nor are caused by the net monetary status inflation effects. The gross effect is a sum of both inflation and demand-shift effects. This can be illustrated by the following numerical illustration: Suppose that the government wishes to obtain wealth by printing fiat money. Assume that it creates and spends new money for services, rather than for the purpose of existing capital goods (although this does not affect the wealth transfer process). Furthermore, let the money creation and resulting inflation be a one-shot operation. Let the individuals in a community be typified by five individuals whose wealth and income positions are summarized in Table 1.

All sorts of assumptions are possible about the ratio of income from capital assets and from labour. Assume, for simplicity, that the total income flow per period from labour and capital is equal to 10 per cent of the community's capital and that all income is consumed. Capital goods can be used up if consumption is to be changed. For the redistributive process that assumption would make no difference. Only the numerical results would be modified. In equilibrium, assume the community jointly (but not severally) holds 10 per cent of the total wealth (including money) in the form of money ($6 of money equals 10 per cent of the community's wealth of $54 + $6 = $60). Let the government inflate the money supply by $1.20 of fiat money and spend $1.00 of it—all for the services of individual B.[20] When $1.00 per period increased-money demand impinges on B, the price of his service is assumed to double (his income was formerly $1.00 per period). The government gets only half of B's services, since the private sector was offering $1.00 for all of B's services prior to the government's additional demand of $1.00. None of this increased demand goes to anyone except B in the first stage. The rise in service prices is reflected in capital-goods prices.

Looking at each individual we see what this implies. A's balance sheet initially is:

A (*before inflation and demand revision*)

| Cash  | $ 2.40  | Equity | $15.15 |
|-------|---------|--------|--------|
| Goods | 12.75   |        |        |
|       | $15.15  |        |        |

In the first period, his income stays at $2.25, while the price level of services rises to, say, $1.20. If he spends all his income, his consumption in real terms falls to $2.25/1.20 = $1.875, a decline of $.375 in original price units. In the next period, he receives a larger income, $2.70, as B spends part of his increased earnings. A has the choice of spending $2.70 or saving part of it to restore some of his wealth. If he spends it all in order to maintain his consumption at its original level, his balance sheet position will be:

A (*no saving*)

| Cash  | $ 2.40  | Equity | $17.70 |
|-------|---------|--------|--------|
| Goods | 15.30   |        |        |
|       | $17.70  |        |        |

His equity, in original price level units, would be $17.70/1.20 = $14.75, a decline in wealth of $.40 (from $15.15). He experienced a decline in real income in the first period of $.375. The wealth loss, $.40, is his wealth redistribution

20. By the time the government has spent $1.00, prices will be 1.20 of the former level. At this price-level the government, given its propensity for liquidity, like everyone else, will want to hold larger cash balances—because the demand for cash is in part a function of one's level of nominal wealth. If prices have risen by 20 per cent, we shall suppose the government wants to hold $1.20 in money. The upshot is that only $1.00 of the new money is spent.

loss due to the *inflation*, and the second is the loss of income consequent to the *demand revision* as relative demand is shifted toward B. In fact, no matter what the demand shift, the inflationary loss is unaffected. Only if the degree of demand shift is tied to the degree of inflation are the two effects related, but this tie is a policy correlation, completely independent of the fact of inflation.

Suppose that A decides to save the increment of money income in order to increase his stock of money. His balance sheet would now appear:

A (*saving all his increased money income*)

| | | | |
|---|---|---|---|
| Cash | $ 2.85 | Equity | $18.15 |
| Goods | 15.30 | | |
| | $18.15 | | |

In real terms his equity is $18.15/1.20 = $15.125, a decline of $.25 from the original level. He has to save still more if he wants to restore his equity to its original real level. Although he can choose any level of saving and resultant equity, he will have suffered the same loss of $.40 in wealth because of the *inflation* and the reduced real income of $.375 consequent to the *demand revision*. How he chooses to bear these two separate losses—that is, whether to maintain consumption by eating up his wealth, or to restore his wealth by saving, or to not save at all—is entirely up to his discretion. He is forced into no particular way, but he is forced into making a choice among them—a choice forced on him by both the inflationary wealth redistribution and the revised demand effect on income and asset values.

In the same manner B's experience can be examined. Initially, his balance sheet is:

B (*before inflation and before demand changes*)

| | | | |
|---|---|---|---|
| Cash | $ .85 | Equity | $9.85 |
| Goods | 9.00 | | |
| | $9.85 | | |

During the first period he has received $2.00 of income and has spent $1.00. With the higher prices, his real income is $2.00/1.20, or $1.666, an increase of $.666 in original price units. He has lost wealth by being a net monetary creditor; the real value of his money stock falls to $.85/1.20 = $.70833, a decline of $.1416—exactly the same loss as if there were no demand shift. He can choose any combination of saving and consequent level of wealth that he wishes. If he saves all of his increase in real income, $.666, this will more than offset the inflationary loss of wealth of $.1416. He will have a net increase in wealth of $.525. If, instead, he saves, say, only $.20, his balance sheet will be:

B (after restoring cash ratio)

| Cash | $ 1.05 | Equity | $11.85 |
|------|--------|--------|--------|
| Goods | 10.80 | | |
| | $11.85 | | |

His equity (in original price-level units) is now $11.85/1.20 = $9.875, an increase of .025. This increase is the result of his voluntary decision to save $.20. In summary, he loses $.1416 (original price-level units) by being a net monetary creditor during the inflation, and he gains a transitory one-period increase of $.666 in income by the demand shift. He chose to save $.20 of that increase in income ($.1666 in original price-level units), so his wealth increased by $.1666 − $.1416 = $.025. The rest of the increased real income, in original price-level units, $.666 − $.1666 = $.50, is devoted to increasing his consumption. Similar analysis for C, D, and E yields the results given in the appropriate rows of Table 2. Columns (1) and (3), when summed, give Column (4).

This table shows that all of the income gain, $.666, accruing to B is at the expense of the rest of the community (proportionate to their income) and not

TABLE 2. Summary of effects of inflation and demand shifts on income and wealth (all in original price-level units)

| | (1) Net Wealth Redistribution from Inflation | (2) Income Change Caused by Demand Revision: One Period of Income | (3) Voluntary Savings Increments | (4) Net Changes in Wealth of Private Sector |
|---|---|---|---|---|
| A | −$.4000 | −$.3750 | $.3750 | −.025 |
| B | −.1416 | .6666 | .1666 | .025 |
| C | −.3083 | −.1250 | .1250 | −.1833 |
| D | .0166 | −.0416 | .0416 | .0583 |
| E | .0000 | −.1250 | .1250 | .1250 |
| | −$.833 (to Govt.) | 0 | $.8333 | 0 |

from inflation. Also the net wealth redistribution due to inflation is independent of the degree of demand revision. With the demand revision, income revision has occurred, as shown in the second column, whereas the inflation wealth redistribution went from the money holders to the government, and from private net creditors to private net debtors. In this particular example, the amount of savings increments was simply assumed to be just sufficient to restore the private community's stock of real wealth. Under different assumptions about the desire to hold cash and to save, the numerical results would be different. The government could get the services without at the same time inducing the rest of the community to do any saving or dissaving. Or the community could insist on maintaining its consumption rate (and consume some wealth). In our example, the community saved enough to restore its wealth to the pre-inflation level. But in any event, the inflation effect is one thing, and the shift in relative demand another, and the resultant saving decision still another thing.

# EFFECTS OF INFLATION UPON STOCK PRICES

## ARMEN A. ALCHIAN AND REUBEN A. KESSEL

Both the subject of stock prices as well as the subject of inflation has been of very great interest to economists and, as you might expect, has led to a lot of speculation about the effects of inflation on stock prices.

Probably the most important ideas on the subject have been enunciated by Keynes and Fisher. Both John Maynard Keynes and Irving Fisher concluded that inflation enables business firms to discharge their debts with depreciated money, and, hence, they view inflation as being of considerable advantage to business enterprises.

Their reasoning depends upon two premises: One is that business firms are debtors; the second is that interest rates somehow don't properly reflect expectations of future price changes; i.e., interest rates are really biased estimates of the future course of prices.

There is also a second line of argument which has led to the same conclusion—but by quite a different route—that has been advanced by Earl J. Hamilton and Wesley C. Mitchell. They reason that inflation causes prices to rise faster than wages. Consequently, when prices are rising, workers are systematically underpaid. These losses of the working class are the gains of business enterprises. This explanation doesn't depend upon assumptions about debtors or interest rates. It rests on very special kinds of assumptions about the character of labor markets.

## Investment Counselors' View

In contrast to these views, practical men of affairs such as investment counselors have been much less confident than professional economists that the owners of business enterprise have gained through inflation. In general, they have concluded that investors can maintain their capital intact during inflation by investing in common stocks, but they have viewed such an investment as

Reprinted, by permission of the author, from *Commercial and Financial Chronicle* 202 (November 18, 1965): 10–11.

being roughly equivalent to an investment in inventories. In other words, an investor in common stock could expect to approximately break even with respect to the changes in price level. But this was a lot better than he would do, say, if he invested in bonds or other cash-type investments, where the real value of assets would decline.

The cautiousness of investment counselors is traceable, we think, to the fact that they are willing to go out and examine some evidence as to what happened during inflations. In particular, when you look at what happened during the German runaway inflation following World War I, during the Austrian and French inflations of the 1920's, and even more recently, if you look closer to home at Chile and the United States, it wasn't unambiguous that the owners of business firms gained in a way which you might expect if you read either Fisher and Keynes on the one hand, or Hamilton and Mitchell on the other. This, of course, leads to the question, how do you reconcile this theorizing with what, in fact, was observed during these famous inflations?

### Bank Equities

A striking piece of evidence that we think enables us to reconcile these views is provided by what happens to owners of bank equities. Banks, in the Keynes-Fisher sense, are extremely large debtors. When you look at the ratio of debt to equity for a bank, they are in a completely different league than ordinary industrial enterprises. And banks have in the past been relatively laboristic-type enterprises, too. They hire, or used to hire, a lot of clerical work and have large wage-bills so that on the Hamilton and Fisher argument, they should also gain. Yet, when you look at what does happen to banks, and particularly if you looked at what happened to bank equities in the United States during World War II and also in these other countries, they didn't do well. In fact, they did poorly; bank equities did not rise with the general level of prices.

Well, what's wrong? We think the analysis of Keynes and Fisher is in part correct. The real problem is that it doesn't go far enough. And the banks really illustrate what's wrong with the Keynes-Fisher reasoning. If you look at banks, it's absolutely true that they have a large volume of debt. But if you look at what their money is invested in, by and large, it's invested in money-type assets. And if you look more closely, you will see that despite their enormous debts, typically their money-type assets exceed their debts. In other words, the equity of the bank owners is, in fact, invested in money-type assets. So, while superficially banks appear to be enormous debtors, if you take both sides of the balance sheet into account, you don't come up with the conclusion that they are debtors. They are, in fact, creditors. That is, if you compare their money-type assets with their money-type liabilities, you will see that their monetary assets really exceed their monetary liabilities and that they are really, in fact, creditors—and should lose during inflation.

## Business Firms

What about business firms generally? To our great surprise, when we started looking at balance sheets of business firms (and the balance sheets we looked at are primarily those of so-called industrials as contrasted with utilities and rails), the frequency of creditors in the business population is extremely high.

Now, when we say creditors or debtors, we are taking a somewhat unorthodox view, or using a somewhat unorthodox definition, because in terms of this frame of reference, a creditor is a firm whose monetary assets—money-type assets, say, cash, accounts receivable, bonds, and so on—exceed monetary liabilities. And the converse, of course, is true for a debtor. Our studies show that there is a high frequency of creditors among the business population. The distribution of creditors and debtors in the business population as reflected in our samples indicates it's a little reckless to think of business firms as being generally debtors.

## Lagging-Wage Theory

We won't spend much time discussing the Hamilton-Mitchell hypothesis about the effects of lag of wages behind prices. Let me just briefly explain how we tried to get at that, and then I'll dismiss it for the time being, and we'll go on to the main body of thought.

What we did was get the names of all the firms listed on the New York Stock Exchange between 1940 and 1950. Then we looked at all of those that published their wage bill, and we said, OK, if workers are being milked by inflation, then the firms with relatively high wage-bills will do relatively well, will profit, and those with relatively low wage-bills will do relatively poorly. And so we somehow ranked firms by how labor intensive their production processes are. I shouldn't say "labor intensive their production processes" but really how labor intensive their activity is. The criterion we used to measure labor intensiveness is the ratio of wages, measured annually, to market value of equity. The larger the wage bill, the better off these firms should be as a result of inflation.

## Negative Wage Association

We could find no association between firms that had relatively large increases in their stock prices and firms with relatively large wage-bills, and conversely. This led us to conclude that the hypothesis was not supported by the evidence. It may be important to note that we did devote the bulk of our efforts to testing the Keynes-Fisher hypothesis. What we did was go through, year by year, balance sheets and classify them in terms of monetary assets and monetary liabilities. As you can well imagine, this was quite a job. And it was not always clear whether an asset was a monetary asset or a real asset or whether it was a monetary liability or a real liability. Fortunately, all the important items were relatively easy to classify. The ones that gave us some problems were relatively unimportant in terms of magnitude. And what we then did was say, Well, let's compare the behavior of debtors' stocks with those of creditors. If there is anything to the idea that inflation redistributes wealth from creditors to debtors, then we should be able to observe that the stock prices of debtors rise more than those of creditors during inflation.

So we started putting together this data, which went back to 1950. We examined the behavior of stock prices and balance sheets continuously from 1915 to about 1950. In 1915, the listing of industrials on the New York Stock Exchange was a lot smaller, as you can well imagine, than it is now. And, hence, our sample, which was then the universe, was smaller than the samples for more recent times.

The virtue of looking at this long time span is that it includes periods of inflation, periods of deflation, and periods of stable prices. By prices we, of course, mean the general price level. This will enable us to see if debtors gain at the expense of creditors during inflation, or if the creditors gain at the expense of debtors during deflation, and whether or not there is any relative advantage to being a debtor or creditor when prices are stable.

We had some problems when we examined a period of inflation about firms changing their status; i.e., the firm in a particular year might be a debtor and in the following year might be a creditor. To cope with this problem, we classified firms every year and then defined a firm as a creditor if two-thirds of the time during an inflationary episode it was a creditor. This definition was adopted in order to cut down on data losses. If we said a firm had to be a creditor all the time during an inflation, we would lose too much of our data. Similarly, two-thirds represented a compromise between conflicting desires. If a firm was a debtor two-thirds of the time, we defined it to be a debtor. And if it wasn't in one class or another two-thirds of the time, it didn't show up in the sample.

For inflations, we worked up nine samples. There are two inflations—1915–20 and 1940–50. There are nine virtually independent samples there. If debtors gain at the expense of creditors during inflation, we should expect to see that a dollar invested of invested capital in debtors' stocks should do better than a dollar invested capital in creditor stocks.

### Debtor Corporations' Stocks Gain

Let's turn to the evidence. During the period from 1915 to 1920, the mean for debtors was greater than the mean for creditors. In all the other samples, that's the case for both inflations. For all nine samples, debtors do better than the creditors. The probability of this occurring by chance is relatively small; it's two to the ninth power. It's the same question as, what's the probability of throwing nine heads in a row by chance? Because the probability of obtaining these results by chance is so low, these results constitute powerful evidence in support of the theory presented.

Let's turn to deflation and see if converse results are obtained. There are two periods of deflation during this time period—1921–22, 1928–33. The mean values obtained gave us the converse results; namely, that the creditors did better here than the debtors. Again we have results consistent with the theory.

Turning to the period of stable prices, during two periods, the debtors did better, and during one period, the creditors did better. What's more important, the difference between the performance of the debtors and creditors was not significant. In contrast with the other periods, the difference between performance of debtors and creditors was not, in fact, significant in a statistical sense.

### Portfolio Test

This evidence led us to have a fair degree of confidence in the theory under investigation. Nevertheless we undertook another kind of test that was somewhat different than the foregoing, because it has the virtue of utilizing a larger fraction of data that we have collected. Instead of examining cohorts of debtor firms and creditor firms over periods of inflation, deflation, and stable prices, we examined portfolios of debtors and creditors over time. The firm composition of these portfolios is free to vary from year to year.

In other words, a firm that might be in a debtor portfolio one year might be in the creditor portfolio in the next year, and the debtor portfolio the following. We didn't care how often debtor-creditor status changed. This enabled us to use all the data. And we asked ourselves, how does the behavior of a debtor portfolio differ from the creditor portfolio?

But, then, if we are going to look at a time span like this that encompasses periods of inflation and deflation, we've got another problem. We don't want to see how the debtors and creditors fare for the entire period, because the debtors would gain from 1915 to 1920, but lose from '20 to '23 or whatever it was when we had deflation. Hence, some of the gains of the debtor would be offset by this deflation and by the deflation from '29 to '33. To meet this problem, we compared the results obtained by holding an optimal and a pessimal portfolio. What do we mean by an optimal portfolio? An optimal portfolio is defined to be a debtor portfolio when we have inflation, when prices generally are rising. But if prices are falling, an optimal portfolio is defined to be creditors' stocks. In contrast, the pessimal portfolio is defined to be debtors' stocks when prices are falling and creditors' stocks when prices are rising.

And then we said to ourselves, Let's take a look at the question, what difference will it make? Or, how much redistribution would take place if we had portfolios so defined and we looked at a span from 1915 to 1952?

## Optimal Portfolio Results

Utilizing all of our data we found that, in general, the rate of growth of the optimal portfolio was significantly higher than the debtor portfolio. As a rough rule of thumb, the optimal grew by twice as much as the pessimal portfolio. That is, roughly speaking, it did twice as well. Both portfolios had positive growth rates, but the growth rate of the optimal portfolio was significantly greater than the pessimal portfolio. But the thing that's really significant about it is that the optimal portfolio gained relative to the pessimal portfolio only when we had instability in prices, i.e., when the general price level was either rising or falling. When the general price level was stable, the ratio of the values of these two portfolios was also stable. All the gain of one relative to the other can be accounted for by the years when prices were either rising or falling.

Now, let me give you some feel for what these numbers look like. In general, the rate of growth of the optimal portfolio was something on the order of 16 per cent a year, and about 13 per cent for the pessimal portfolio. This is per year from 1915 to 1951. That's a long period of time. Or to put matters another way, the optimal portfolio outgrew the pessimal one by 18 per cent.

## Rising and Falling Price Years

A more sensitive test of the same point just uses the years when you had rising or falling prices. It throws away the years when prices are relatively stable. And for our purposes, we define rising and falling prices when you have greater than a 3 per cent change of prices. The years that were included in this period would be 1916–19, 1921–25, 1930–32, 1941–44, 1946–47, and 1950–51.

For these more volatile years, the optimal portfolio annual growth rate was 18 per cent, compared with about 14 per cent for the pessimal portfolio. As one would expect, the differential growth rate for the optimal portfolio increased. The advantage became 30 per cent if you looked at just those select years.

These figures we have given you are in nominal terms; i.e., they are not adjusted for changes in the price level. And, roughly speaking, during this period you had about a $2^1/_2$ per cent—for the whole period—rate of growth in prices—average rate of growth.

Adjustment for price level changes doesn't change the relative differences between the optimal and pessimal portfolios. Adjustment for changes in price level, i.e., putting things in real terms, simply increases the comparative advantage of the optimal over the pessimal portfolio. In nominal units, the relative superiority is between 12 and 18 per cent, depending on how you want to measure it; if you adjust for changes in price level, the superiority of the optimal portfolio is roughly between 15 and 25 per cent.

Subsequently, we pushed our research a little further along another line. Many firms have their monetary assets approximately equal to their monetary liabilities. Our procedure forces us to classify these firms as either debtors or creditors. Nevertheless they are essentially neutral with respect to price level changes. If these firms are dropped, will a wider disparity between the optimal and pessimal portfolios be produced?

For this purpose, we had to get in the question of how you define an extreme debtor or an extreme creditor. What we did was look at the difference between monetary assets and monetary liabilities and take that as a ratio to equity, so that we essentially said when you go out and buy a stock of XYZ company, how much debt, negative or positive, do you buy? The more debt, negative or positive, that you buy, the more extreme this firm is. Well, we looked at three classes, firms where this ratio was above .10, that is either plus or minus; about .25; and above, plus or minus again, .40. And we asked ourselves, does the difference between the optimal and the pessimal portfolios widen out if we just look at the extremes? The answer turns out to be yes. When you get to .25 and

.40, the ratio of the performance of the optimal and the pessimal runs in terms of 4 to 1. This is against 2 to 1 when we included all firms and did not just look at the extremes. And this is another piece of evidence that lent support to the view that debtors gain and creditors lose because of inflation. Because we look at the more extreme debtors and the more extreme creditors, we should get more extreme variations in their performance. And that is, in fact, what does occur—that we observe these greater extremes.

## Stock Split and Stock Dividend Problem

We have skipped over a number of problems. For example, how should one measure equity, and why did we use market prices? One of the problems of using market price as a measure of equity is that the rate of growth of equity from year to year must be adjusted for stock splits, stock dividends, and differences in corporation payout policy. There are many problems associated with using equity. We tried to adjust our figures to take account of stock splits and stock dividends, and in our calculations, we assumed that cash dividends would be reinvested. By this process we abstracted from the factors that affect stock prices that are the result of technical details of corporate financial policy.

It is also very clear that in investigation of this sort there are other things going on in the world besides inflation and deflation. And these also affect stock prices. And we tried to handle that problem by random sampling. We also looked at specific samples of industries in an effort to hold that problem constant, and, in general, we got the same kinds of results when we looked at samples of industries that we got when we used random samples. There was a great deal of consistency.

We did run into other kinds of problems of firms merging, the stock of a firm being closely held, and inability to obtain quotations. This proved to be a terrible nuisance for over-the-counter firms. Mergers also proved to be something of a nuisance when we dealt with textiles, because textiles were merged a lot during the period when this industry was studied. In general, we came away with the impression that pushing studies of over-the-counter firms was a very expensive procedure. Once we saw we had consistency between our results for over-the-counter firms, industry studies, textiles, chemicals, steel, department stores, and firms that reported their wage bills, we became very confident that the forces that are postulated by the Keynes-Fisher reasoning are, in fact, correct and are operative and have been at work during this time.

# HOW THE GOVERNMENT GAINS FROM INFLATION

## ARMEN A. ALCHIAN AND REUBEN KESSEL

How does inflation redistribute income and wealth? What redistributions does it cause? To these questions, economists have said:

Almost no one gains from inflation.
Inflation destroys savings.
The rich get richer.
Business firms' stockholders profit from inflation.
Holding inventories produces a gain during inflation.
Inflation leads to speculation in the promise of increased profits.
Income is redistributed in favor of profits and away from labor income.
Widows, orphans and, of course, college professors suffer.
Inefficient firms are subsidized by inflation.
Speculators merge businesses to reap capital gains as prices rise.
Real wages decline during inflation.
Debtors gain at the expense of creditors.

The statements are taken from first-rate economists like Keynes, Millikan, Chandler, Hart, Hamilton, Marshall, Friedman, Fisher. That many, many others hold the same views need not delay us here. But, as distinct from economists, what does economics tell us?

In the first place, it tells us not to confuse nominal, with real, value. From this we can see that holding inventories is not a source of real gains or profits during inflation any more than during deflations. Yet this error in reasoning will probably survive as long as inflation does.

Another thing that economics tells us is to distinguish between inflation and concomitant factors, such as war, famine, plagues and similar events which change the available supply of productive factors. For example, in the South during our Civil War, the blockade and loss of capital equipment reduced the wealth of the South. Inflation or no inflation, that would have been a big

Reprinted from *Proceedings of the Thirtieth Annual Conference of the Western Economic Association* (1955) (Salt Lake City, 1956), 13–16.

decline in real income to labor. But should one attribute this decline in real wages to the inflation? Not necessarily. Similarly in England during the two wars, at first her real wages declined, but this effect must not therefore be attributed to the concurrent inflation, since she suffered a tight blockade and loss of wealth from non-monetary causes. Similarly the Black Death and similar plagues were accompanied by rising real wages rates, and also by inflation. But is it not sensible to reason that the rise was caused by the changed ratio of labor to capital, and not by any concurrent inflation? Our moral, obvious but frequently forgotten, is "look behind the veil."

But economics does not say that changes in the money supply are merely ways to make the veil less transparent. Changes in money stocks that yield inflation do have real effects on the distribution of wealth.

Now this takes us a long way toward revealing the errors in some of the statements quoted earlier. But not all of the statements have been disposed of. If the government takes services in exchange for new money, the community is left with a smaller flow of income and with more money. Real wages must decline. At least, this is what Keynes and everyone else we have seen, who have been explicit on this point, say occurs with inflation. They say there is a lag in money wage rates behind advancing prices; this increases the profits of businessmen; this excess profit is then taxed by the government; thus the government uses businessmen as their taxing agencies, taking from them what the inflation took from wage earners. E. J. Hamilton says that the major source of capital accumulation during the industrial revolution was precisely this wage lag which increased capitalists' profits which were used to finance new investment.

But is this what economic analysis tells us? It does tell us that with rising prices, claims to fixed sums of money represent reduced real wealth. If the interest rate anticipated the future price level rise, it could compensate for the loss in real value of the fixed monetary claims. To do this would require market foresight; failure to do this means lack of market foresight—not merely a lag in response to current market factors. Thus, this interest rate maladjustment is not similar to the usually talked about stickiness or inertia.

If we postulate that foresight is imperfect and that the usual market forecast is to underestimate the future price swings, the implication is that debtors will gain and creditors will lose during inflation.

What are the implications of this? First, when prices rise, net debtors—that is, those whose monetary debts exceed their monetary claims (cash, bonds, accounts receivable) and, hence, who are called net monetary debtors—will gain while net monetary creditors will lose in real terms. Incidentally, this implication has been verified by a study of business firms listed on the New York Stock Exchange from 1928 through 1952. That study, reported at the Western Econometric meetings in the summer of 1953, indicated that approximately half of the business firms are net monetary debtors and half are net monetary creditors—thus nullifying the very widely held presumption that business firms are debtors. That study showed that the creditor firms, in fact, suffered a loss in real wealth, while the net debtors were the gainers. A striking feature is, of course, that half of the business firms were net creditors. That they should therefore lose and that the debtors should gain may not be so surprising; although it is worth noting that Alfred Marshall testified that debtors and creditors did not experience this gain and loss because they had foresight.

A second implication of the net monetary-status hypothesis is that it is capable all by itself of explaining how the government via inflation extracts services or resources from the rest of the community. "All by itself," means that no wage lag phenomenon is required to enable the government to get the resources. The lost services need not be reflected in lower real wage rates. But before exploring more deeply the further consequences of this implication, let us see in detail just how the government extracts services or resources from the community, and exactly who it is that suffers the loss.

The questions which we will answer now are, How does a government extract real income and resources from the community by inflation? And from whom? The answer, subsequently to be developed at some length, is, in one sentence, this: The government exchanges money for real resources or real income, and the net monetary creditors in the community are the ones who lose resources. That simple answer is the obvious implication of the net-debtor-status hypothesis. Yet apparently it is neither widely understood nor accepted.

The question just stated will be noted to consist of two parts; first, how does the government get the resources and, second, who suffers the loss? The government gets the services or resources by exchanging new money for them (and the fact that this money may be obtained by exchanging debt with the Federal Reserve System is irrelevant) with private persons for services or resources. In other words, the government gets resources by inducing the private sector of the economy to exchange services or resources for money. It is this simple—if we don't ask how much money will have to be printed, or how many resources the government will get for a given dose of money creation, or how much prices will rise or who loses. And we aren't asking all those questions just yet.

Whatever the pre-existing situation may have been with respect to money and prices, the new, larger supply of money will induce individuals to revise their asset holdings. The larger amount of money available would be an equilibrium amount only if the total nominal value of other forms of wealth were higher, something that will occur only through a price rise as individuals try to reduce their balance between cash and other forms of wealth. The real value of money stocks falls as prices rise, reducing the real wealth of new money-asset holders. Conversely, the price rise lowers the real value of monetary debts and increases the real wealth position of net debtors. The price rise brings about a redistribution of real wealth in favor of net monetary debtors at the expense of net monetary creditors.

We shall explain the process in greater detail by reference to Table 1. For the moment it is emphasized that the examples will show that the process by which inflation redistributes resources need not depend in any way, shape or form upon a lagging sub-set of prices, e.g., wage rates behind consumption of goods prices. To isolate the effects of inflation, we assume the government spends the new money proportionate to current demands; in this way we do not introduce relative demand and relative price shifts. It can be shown that shifts in relative demand are additive to the effects of inflation and that each is a different phenomenon.

The operation of inflation as a means whereby the government is able to take resources from the private economy can be summarized as follows: The government creates new cash; it exchanges the new money for services or capital resources. The increased amount of money relative to the existing stock of real goods and services induces the members of the community to reduce their relative cash holdings. This bids up prices of capital goods and services. There need be no lag in this process of bidding up prices—prices could rise at the moment the government begins to spend its money. The rise in prices reduces the real value of monetary assets and of monetary debts. The fall in real value of cash holdings reduces the net real wealth of cash holders—who thus discover they are the ones who have lost wealth or income equivalent to that taken by the government. The inflation ends up as a tax on monetary asset holders and a gain to monetary debtors: (1) The tax on cash holdings matches the transfer of resources or services to the government. And, like any other government operation, the persons who benefit from this transfer of resources from cash holders to the government are those for whom the transferred resources are used. It may be the community as a whole, certain politically powerful groups or particular subsidized groups.

TABLE 1. *Illustrative data for wealth redistribution to government*

Initial Conditions

| Persons | Wealth | | Cash | | Goods | | Interpersonal Debts (−) or Creditors (+) | Income |
|---------|--------|---|------|---|-------|---|------------------------------------------|--------|
| A | 15.15 | = | 2.40 | + | 12.75 | + | 0 | 2.25 |
| B | 9.85 | | .85 | | 9.00 | | 0 | 1.00 |
| C | 16.10 | | .60 | | 14.25 | | 1.25 | .75 |
| D | 4.65 | | .40 | | 4.75 | | −.50 | .25 |
| E | 4.25 | | .75 | | 4.25 | | −.75 | .75 |
| | 50.00 | | 5.00 | | 45.00 | | 0 | 5.00 |

A (Before)

| Cash | 2.40 | Equity | $15.15 |
|------|------|--------|--------|
| Goods | 12.75 | | |
| | $15.15 | | |

A (After)

| Cash | 2.85 | Equity | $18.15 |
|------|------|--------|--------|
| Goods | 15.30 | | (15.125) |
| | $18.15 | | |

B (Before)

| Cash | .85 | Equity | $9.85 |
|------|-----|--------|-------|
| Goods | 9.00 | | |
| | $9.85 | | |

B (After)

| Cash | $1.05 | Equity | $11.85 |
|------|-------|--------|--------|
| Goods | 10.80 | | (9.875) |
| | $11.85 | | |

C (Before)

| Cash | .60 | Equity | $16.10 |
|------|-----|--------|--------|
| Goods | 14.25 | | |
| Credits | 1.25 | | |
| | $16.10 | | |

C (After)

| Cash | .75 | Equity | $19.10 |
|------|-----|--------|--------|
| Goods | 17.10 | | (15.9166) |
| Credits | 1.25 | | |
| | $19.10 | | |

D (Before)

| Cash | .40 | Debt | .50 |
|------|-----|------|-----|
| Goods | 4.75 | Equity | 4.65 |
| | $5.15 | | $5.15 |

D (After)

| Cash | .45 | Debt | .50 |
|------|-----|------|-----|
| Goods | 5.70 | Equity | 5.65 |
| | $6.15 | | (4.7083) |

E (Before)

| Cash | .75 | Debt | .75 |
|------|-----|------|-----|
| Goods | 4.25 | Equity | 4.25 |
| | $5.00 | | $5.00 |

E (After)

| Cash | .90 | Debt | .75 |
|------|-----|------|-----|
| Goods | 5.10 | Equity | 5.25 |
| | $6.00 | | (4.375) |

(continued)

TABLE 1. (continued)

Final Result

| Person | Net Monetary Status | Real Wealth Change from Inflation | Changes in Wealth from Voluntary Savings (Reductions in Consumption) | | Net Change in Real Wealth (Old Prices) |
|--------|--------|--------|--------|--------|--------|
| | | | New Prices | Old Prices | |
| A | +2.40 | −.4000 | .45 | .3750 | −.025 (−.4000 + .3750) |
| B | +.85 | −.1416 | .20 | .1667 | +.025 |
| C | +1.85 | −.3083 | .15 | .1250 | −.1833 |
| D | −.10 | +.0167 | .05 | .0416 | +.0583 |
| E | .00 | .0000 | .15 | .1250 | +.125 |
| | 5.00 | −.8333 | 1.00 | .8333 | 0 |

(2) A side effect redistribution of wealth occurs through the existence of the interpersonal debt structure. (3) And, finally, the existence of government debt constitutes another side effect transfer from government debt holders to taxpayers liable for the interest and principal payments, which are not always in proportion to their government debt holdings.

The principle is clear: if one is a debtor on net status, it pays, on that count at least, to have inflation. And if one can go into debt and have new money created, it will pay him to do it if he is a debtor on net status. If he is a creditor on net status, then inflation is bad for him. Thus it is no different whether the government or private individuals are in the first instance the ones who are getting the new bank credit by borrowing. In fact, it makes no difference whether or not one is the initial borrower who gets the new money. All members of the community gain or lose exactly in the same way and solely on the basis of their net monetary status. For example, you may be the one who borrows from the bank and first gets the new credit. At the same time, I borrow existing cash from a friend. I gain and you gain, in exactly the same way and in the same amount if our net monetary status is the same and the borrowing rates of interest are the same.

Thus, if I were a net monetary debtor who wanted to borrow some more money, I would, other things being equal, prefer to borrow in such a way, e.g., from banks, so as to increase the total money supply. This would be inflationary, and being a net monetary debtor, I would gain. But few people, if any, are able to affect the total money supply in sufficient amount to give this a thought—except possibly the minister of public finance in a Machiavellian state. It is the property of being a net monetary debtor, not that of being one of the persons who first had access to new money, that gives one a gain from inflation. If the initial borrowers—those who first get the new money—are on net status monetary creditors, they will lose in this inflationary situation.

What do these examples show? They show the operation of the wealth redistribution mechanism of an inflation as implied by the postulate that the market fails to foresee the course of future prices and hence operates with an interest rate structure that produces wealth shifts from creditors to debtors. These examples show that *income* changes are not implied by this inflation mechanism. Income changes are implied by demand or supply shifts which need have no relationship to inflation per se. Prices are perfectly flexible and in constant equilibrium. Not implied by this analysis is a wage-rate lag, or a decline in the share of labor's income as a consequence of inflation. If, in fact, there is such a lag or decline it must be rationalized or explained by factors not presently contained in economic analysis. All of which may be so much the worse for current theory, or else it may be so much the worse for our beliefs and prejudices about the world of reality. It may be that allegations about such lags and leads were once believed to be necessary in order to explain gains from inflation; it may be that concomitant with inflation, but not consequent to it, there were certain other observed changes, such as declines in real income to labor, or to capital, or growth of capital, and these were as a result erroneously attributed to inflation instead of to contemporary factors, such as war damages, blockades, population changes, etc.

Repeatedly we have said that this process of wealth or service transference to the government does not involve a wage lag or a real wage rate decline. And we hope it should now be clear that it does not. However, if the government extracts resources from the community, in particular capital goods, and destroys them, the ratio of capital to labor will decrease, and the total national income will also decrease. And this is probably what happens in wartime and possibly even in peacetime. In this event, there will be a decrease in real wage rates resulting from the changed marginal productivity of labor. But notice— this is a consequence not of the inflation, but rather of the mode of use of the wealth taken from the community through the inflationary process. Such a decline in real wages would have occurred even if there had been a deflation and if the government had taken the capital by a capital levy, for example. Or if there had been an inflation, not brought about by the government, but instead by private monetary expansion through privately induced monetary expansion, there would be no decline in real wages, either during or after the inflation, because there is no extraction of resources *from* the community. Instead there would only be a transfer of wealth from net monetary creditors to debtors.

Time forces us to skip a discussion of the implications of this analysis for government debt structure effects, purchasing power bonds, hyper-inflation, effects on the real value of the nominal money stock, effects on the banking system, the forced saving concept, the inflationary gap concept, the Gibson paradox and investment portfolio policy.

But we will take time to point out that not implied by this analysis is the implication that the individuals who gain from inflation are those who first get their hands on the money or those first to sell to the government at higher prices than the costs of what they sold. Excluded is the implication that profit receivers gain and do so at the expense of non-profit receivers. This analysis states that *only* net monetary debtors gain from inflation. If others gain during a particular inflation they must do so only by fortuitous random accidental factors unrelated to the force of inflation. We do not deny that such exogenous factors operate, but they are not to be attributed to inflation. Nor is there any implication that wage earners suffer during inflation. The facts may be that they do, but the present analysis does not imply that—all of which may be so much the worse for the present analysis—or for the allegation about the facts. Nor does the present analysis imply that the government should tax profits in order to confiscate the unjustified increments accruing to profit receivers during an inflation at the expense of the laborers. This last policy recommended by Keynes for war finance during inflation rests on a hypothesis about leads and lags among prices and labor costs during inflation. That same hypothesis was used by Hamilton in his explanation of how the inflations beginning in the sixteenth century are supposed to have contributed to the capital growth which produced the industrial revolution. Nor does this analysis imply that widows and orphans and college professors suffer from inflation—unless they are net monetary creditors, and there is no necessity for that. Nor does this analysis imply that common-stock holders will gain from inflation, unless common stock represents equity in a net monetary debtor institution—and the facts, as we shall perhaps surprisingly discover, do not support that generalization. None of these things is implied by the present analysis. Yet every treatise on economics and inflation asserts at least one of the implications—which the present analysis does not imply.

Certainly there is nothing in economics that justifies any of them except one. And our conscientious search of the evidence in the economic literature suggests that they may well be false. Only the creditor-debtor hypothesis has evidence in its favor. The rest are denied or still await verification.

# THE MEANING AND VALIDITY OF THE INFLATION-INDUCED LAG OF WAGES BEHIND PRICES

REUBEN A. KESSEL AND ARMEN A. ALCHIAN

Many economists write as if the proposition that inflation causes prices to rise faster than wages were well established. From this proposition at least two important classes of inferences have been derived.

1. A lag of wages behind prices as a result of inflation produces extraordinarily large business profits. These swollen profits generate a high rate of capital formation. In this role, the wage-lag axiom constitutes the foundation of a theory of industrial development.

2. The lag of wages behind prices caused by inflation accentuates oscillations in the general level of economic activity. The failure of wages to keep pace with prices reinforces disequilibrating movements in the general level of economic activity. In this capacity, the wage-lag axiom functions as an integral part of both overinvestment and underconsumption business cycle theories.[1]

The contention that inflation causes real wages to fall appears frequently in the literature of economics. Those who make this contention argue, in effect, that inflation produces a negative correlation between real wages on the one hand and money wages and prices on the other. As a practical matter, it is extremely difficult to employ this idea as a tool of analysis for understanding ob-

Reprinted from Armen A. Alchian, *Economic Forces at Work* (Indianapolis: Liberty Fund, 1977), 413–50. This article was previously published in *American Economic Review* 50 (March 1960): 43–66.

This paper is one of a series reporting the results of a study of inflation made possible by a grant from the Merrill Foundation for the Advancement of Financial Knowledge. The authors are indebted to Karl Brunner, Gregg Lewis, William Meckling, Albert Rees, and William Taylor for improvement in analysis and exposition.

1. G. Haberler, *Prosperity and Depression*, 3d ed. (New York: United Nations, 1946), 137ff.

served movements of time series of wages and prices. This difficulty stems from the fact that, as almost everyone would agree, the level of real wages can be affected by such real forces as the relative supplies of labor and capital, the quality of the labor force, the pattern of final demands in the economy, and the state of the arts. Furthermore, increases in the general price level can be produced by changes in the real stock of goods, e.g., by droughts, plagues, wars, etc., even with a fixed money stock. For any time series of real wages, there exists a fantastically difficult problem of imputing changes in the level of real wages to one or the other of two classes of variables, i.e., real or monetary forces. Only if one is able to abstract from the effects of real forces can one determine the effect of inflation upon an observed time series of real wages.

To illustrate this problem, consider the data showing real wages, money wages, and prices in the United States since 1889.[2] These data indicate a high positive correlation between real wages on the one hand and money wages and prices on the other. Are these positive correlations to be interpreted as evidence against the proposition that inflation causes real wages to fall? Surely not. Real wages rose during this time, according to most observers, because of the per capita increase in capital, improvements in technology, and improvements in the skills of the labor force. Those who believe that inflation causes real wages to fall would not deny this. Their position would be that real wages rose despite inflation and that if the effects of real forces upon real wages were properly abstracted, one could observe a fall in real wages attributable to inflation.[3]

## I. Some Alternative Wage-Lag Hypotheses

What, then, is the wage-lag hypothesis? To answer this question, we have turned to the works of those economists who have used this idea. The most important "explanation," importance being measured by either the extent to which it has been used or its deviation from the way economists explain behavior in nonlabor markets, is the belief that wages have more "inertia" or "sluggishness" than other prices because of custom, weak bargaining power of labor, or lack of foresight of workers. For example, Hamilton states: "The

2. A. Rees, "Patterns of Wages, Prices and Productivity," in *Wages, Prices, Profits and Productivity*, Fifteenth American Assembly (New York, 1959), 15–16.

3. Or for a less recent inflation, consider the Black Death period. During this time prices rose and real wages rose. Clearly, what explains this phenomenon is the decrease in the stock of labor which also produced a fall in rents. See E. Lipson, *The Economic History of England*, vol. 1, 4th ed. (London, 1926), 93ff.

chief factor in the failure of wages to keep pace with soaring prices in the second half of the eighteenth century was the 'natural' inertia of wage movements in both directions. History records few instances of wage movements in unison with rapidly changing commodity prices."[4] And:

> There have been no such offsets to the strong tendency during most of the last four hundred years for wages to lag behind prices whenever they were rising. This lag has benefited capitalists as a class at the expense of laborers as a class and awarded gains that dwarf into insignificance the profits from inventory appreciation and from declines in the real value of debts. A tendency for wages to lag behind falling prices has inflicted losses on businessmen, discouraged saving and investment, and aggravated commercial crises.[5]

Mitchell also contended that an imperfection exists in the labor market. He wrote:

> In the 60's and, though in somewhat less degree, in the 70's, the labor market of the United States was one in which individual bargaining prevailed. Now the individual laborer is a poor bargainer. He is ignorant of the possibilities of his situation, exposed to the competition of others with the same disabilities, more anxious to sell than the employer to buy. Moreover, custom in the form of rooted ideas about what is a "fair wage" has a peculiarly tenacious hold upon the minds of both parties in the labor market, weakening the wage-earner's aggression and strengthening the employer's resistance.[6]

In his study of the Civil War, Mitchell concluded: "All of the statistical evidence that has been presented in the preceding pages supports unequivocally the common theory that persons whose incomes are derived from wages suffer seriously from a depreciation of the currency."[7] Basically, the rationale for this position is that there exists a flaw in the labor market which, during times of inflation, lowers the wage rate below the marginal product of workers. In effect Mitchell and Hamilton are saying that the same principles economists use in

---

4. E. J. Hamilton, "Profit Inflation and the Industrial Revolution, 1751–1800," *Quart. Jour. Econ.* 56 (February 1942): 259; reprinted in *Enterprise and Secular Change*, ed. F. C. Lane and J. C. Riemersma (Homewood, Ill., 1953).

5. E. J. Hamilton, "Prices as a Factor in Business Growth," *Jour. Econ. Hist.* 12 (Fall 1952): 327.

6. W. C. Mitchell, *Gold, Prices, and Wages under the Greenback Standard* (Berkeley, 1908), 275–76.

7. W. C. Mitchell, *A History of the Greenbacks* (Chicago, 1903), 347.

explaining what happens in other markets are invalid for explaining what happens in labor markets during inflation.[8]

Bresciani-Turroni enunciated, in his famous study of German inflation, a hypothesis that could explain declines in real wages during inflation and be consistent with a perfectly functioning labor market.[9] This hypothesis rests on the postulate that employees, as a condition of employment, are almost invariably creditors of their employers. And as creditors, employees lose to their employers for the same reason that creditors generally lose to debtors as a result of inflation. Therefore, even if wage rates correctly represented the marginal product of workers, the fact that wages accrue, i.e., that wages are paid after they are earned, implies that workers extend credit to their employers and incur a loss on this account.

There exists strong prima facie evidence for accepting the wage-accrual hypothesis of Bresciani-Turroni. This explanation rests upon a debtor-creditor relationship that is essentially similar to debtor-creditor relationships between, say, department stores and their charge customers, finance companies and the credit purchasers of automobiles and other appliances, corporations and their bondholders, etc. Since there already exists evidence that supports the belief that interest rates are biased downward during inflation, because of the public's lack of knowledge of the course of future prices, there appears to be a reasonable basis for accepting the proposition that wealth is transferred from employees to employers when inflation occurs.[10]

8. Explanations of this type may be found in A. Marshall, "Answers to Questions on the Subject of Currency and Prices Circulated by Royal Commission on the Depression of Trade and Industry (1886)," *Official Papers by Alfred Marshall* (London, 1926), 7ff.; H. P. Willis and J. M. Chapman, *The Economics of Inflation* (New York, 1935), 213; E. M. Bernstein and I. G. Patel, "Inflation in Relation to Economic Development," *Internal. Mon. Fund Staff Papers* 2 (November 1952): 380; W. A. Lewis, *The Theory of Economic Growth* (Homewood, Ill., 1955), 222; and G. M. Meier and R. Baldwin, *Economic Development: Theory, History, Policy* (New York, 1957), 88.

9. "In fact, wages were fixed on the basis of an index number of prices which, at the time of payment, no longer represented actual conditions" (C. Bresciani-Turroni, *The Economics of Inflation* [London, 1937], 310). It failed to represent actual conditions because of the bias in interest rates. Also he argued that wage earners lost because they held cash during inflation (302). Both of these are, of course, special cases of the proposition that creditors lose during inflation.

10. This, of course, does not imply that business firms gain through inflation. Such a statement would be correct only if an examination of all of their debtor-creditor relations, of which relations with employees are only a part, revealed that business firms are, on bal-

As a practical matter, it does not appear that this relationship between employees and employers, at least in modern times, has the potential for transferring a great deal of wealth from employee to employer. Consider a case that is most favorable for sustaining the proposition that accrued wages constitute an important source of business profits during inflation. Assume that cash is acquired for wage payments at the very instant these payments are made by a business firm. Therefore this firm may be regarded as a consistent net debtor with respect to its employees.

What can be said about the magnitude of such profits under these assumptions? Of all industrial firms listed on the New York Stock Exchange in 1952, approximately 200 reported the size of their aggregate wage bills, or more properly the size of their aggregate wage and salary bills, for at least one year between 1939 and 1952. Among these 200 firms, the ratio of total annual wages to equity (equity being measured by the market value of outstanding shares) ranged from a low of .1 to a high of about 4, depending upon firm and industry. If it is assumed that wages are paid biweekly, then the average amount of wages and salaries accrued is 1/52 of the annual wage bill. Consequently it follows that accrued wages range from a low of about .2 percent to 8 percent of equity. This analysis implies that if the price level doubled in any given year, the real value of stock prices would rise from a minimum of .1 percent to a maximum of 4 percent.[11]

Using this same debtor-creditor relationship, Fisher had earlier set forth still another explanation of why real wages would fall during inflation. Like the Bresciani-Turroni explanation, Fisher's was consistent with a perfectly functioning labor market. Fisher contended that relations between employer and employee can be viewed as being contractual, just as are economic relations between, say, bondholders and those who incur bonded debt.[12] The same lack of

---

ance, debtors. On this point, as well as for evidence that interest rates are biased during inflation, see R. A. Kessel, "Inflation-Caused Wealth Redistribution: A Test of a Hypothesis," *Am. Econ. Rev.* 46 (March 1956): 128. Nor does the "bias" of interest rates imply any defect in the capital market; instead it reflects people's inability to predict future prices.

11. The Bresciani-Turroni hypothesis also appears in F. V. Meyer, *Inflation and Capital* (Cambridge, Eng., 1954), 17: "Creditors lost in inflation. Wage-earners and salary-earners normally work before they are paid. They lend their labour until pay day; their work is work given on credit." Meyer also asserts that wages lag because of contractual arrangements between employers and employees.

12. I. Fisher, *The Purchasing Power of Money*, rev. ed. (New York, 1926), 185ff.

foresight that would lead to too low an interest rate to permit debtor-creditor relations to be unaffected by inflation would lead to an effective wage below the marginal product of labor when prices are rising. Only at the time wage contracts are signed would wages be equal to the marginal product of labor. Between contract negotiations, real wages would fall as a result of rising prices.

Prima facie evidence does not support this hypothesis. Wage contracts are typically nonenforceable when broken by employees. Consequently, the legal reasons for arguing that contracts between employers and employees are on a par with contracts between creditors and debtors are of dubious validity. As far as employees are concerned, wage contracts have generally been continuously renegotiable, at least until relatively modern times. Employees can almost always leave their current jobs in favor of alternative employment possibilities in complete freedom from legal sanction by employers. Consequently, in the absence of other evidence there is very little basis for accepting Fisher's hypothesis.

However, there is more to a substantive hypothesis than its logical structure. In its broader aspects, the Fisher hypothesis implies that during inflation there exists a differential in the movements of wage rates of workers under contract as compared with workers employed without contract. It also implies that the longer the life of a contract, the greater the differential in the movements of real wages during inflation. No evidence is contained in this paper for evaluating these two implications.

If one abandons a legalistic frame of reference and argues, as Fisher has, that custom plays a great role independent of contractual arrangements, then this hypothesis becomes indistinguishable from the argument of Hamilton and Mitchell, namely, that a flaw exists in the labor market which manifests itself during times of inflation by a fall in real wages.

The use of inflation as a means of taxation appears to have created a belief that inflation causes real wages to fall. Inflation is a means of taxation, and has been used by those who control the stock of money as an alternative to explicit forms of taxation, such as income taxes, excises, tariffs, etc. Using their power to create money, governments have exchanged money for real resources. Such an exchange reduces the volume of real resources available to the private sector of the economy. The mere existence of an exchange of this character has led many observers to conclude that a fall in real wages is necessarily implied.[13] Yet

13. J. M. Keynes, A Treatise on Money, vol. 2 (New York, 1930), 171–74.

it can and has been shown that taxation through inflation is consistent with no reduction in real wage rates.[14]

Inflation constitutes a tax upon monetary wealth and not upon wages or other factor incomes. This tax affects the real functional returns of the cooperating agents of production if inflation is anticipated, i.e., when the increased cost of holding money caused by rising prices is recognized and enters into the calculations of the community. Under these circumstances, both velocity and the nominal or money rate of interest rise. These higher costs of using money are ultimately reflected in a rise in product prices relative to the sum of the returns to the cooperating agents' production. Whether or not real wages fall depends upon the cross-elasticity between the price or cost of holding money and the quantity of labor demanded. If one is prepared to argue that capital is a better substitute for money than labor, and to assume that the alternative to inflation as a means of taxation is no tax or a wealth or income tax, then the argument that anticipatory inflation can cause real wages to fall can be sustained.

However if inflation is not anticipated, then the losses of the money holders are on a par with an *ex post facto* penalty or Knightian profits and do not affect resource allocation. In general, it appears that the inflations associated with our Civil War in the North and our two world wars were unanticipated. If excise taxes or turnover taxes are regarded as the alternative to taxation through an unanticipated inflation, then inflation implies a higher level of real wages than would otherwise be true.

## II. The Empirical Evidence

The remainder of this paper falls into two parts: (1) a review of the statistical evidence that has been used to support the Mitchell-Hamilton hypothesis and (2) a new test of this hypothesis based on differences in the labor intensiveness of business firms and the performances of their stock prices during inflation.[15]

14. A discussion of the mechanism by which the government acquires resources from the rest of the community through inflation has been presented in A. Alchian and R. Kessel, "How the Government Gains from Inflation," *Proceedings of the Thirtieth Annual Conference of the Western Economics Association (1955)* (Salt Lake City, 1956), 13–16. For the first published analysis of the mechanism that the authors have encountered, see the revised portion of M. Friedman, "Discussion of the Inflationary Gap," in *Essays in Positive Economics* (Chicago, 1953). See also P. Cagan, "The Monetary Dynamics of Hyperinflation," in *Studies in the Quantity Theory of Money*, ed. M. Friedman (Chicago, 1956), 25–117.

15. The field of income and employment theory contains still another hypothesis that implies the existence of a lag of wages behind prices when prices are rising. It stems from

What is the empirical evidence used to support the hypothesis that inflation, independent of real forces, causes real wages to fall when prices are rising? Major data used to support this hypothesis have been collected for six inflationary episodes: (1) the period from 1350 to 1800 in Spain, (2) the early days of the industrial revolution in England, (3) the U.S. Civil War in the North, (4) the U.S. Civil War in the South, (5) the German inflation following World War I, and (6) the inflation in the United States associated with World War I.

### A. Spanish Data

E. J. Hamilton probably has contributed more to the acceptance of the hypothesis that inflation causes real wages to fall than has any other single economist.[16] His evidence consists almost entirely of time series of wages and prices. In order to use such data as evidence of a wage lag, the impact of real forces must be distinguished from that of inflation. Hamilton is not unaware of this difficult problem of imputation. Throughout his monumental three-volume work on Spanish wages and prices, which covers the interval from 1350 to 1800, are references to real forces and their impact upon the price level and

---

the observation that less than full employment, where full employment is defined as a labor market in which everyone who wants a job at the prevailing wage rate can find one, implies nonprice rationing of employment opportunities. This is consistent with an infinitely elastic supply function of labor that relates the quantity of labor offered with money wages if rising prices will restore full employment. Under these assumptions, increases in prices at times of less-than-full employment imply a fall in real wages.

This hypothesis is clearly relevant to the present discussion, if it is relevant at all, only for inflations or portions of inflations associated with less-than-full employment. Since the authors cited believe that inflation causes wages to lag behind prices independently of whether full or less-than-full employment exists, this is not a hypothesis they considered extensively although it appears in the work of Mitchell and Bresciani-Turroni.

This model leads to difficult questions. One is: Shouldn't the wages of unemployed workers be considered in the wage index? If they are included in the wage index, then it is not clear that real wages decline under these circumstances. Another difficulty is that we do not know enough about how an economy returns to full employment to impute to inflation a fall in real wages of those continuously employed. Possibly real supply conditions have not changed but demand conditions have changed. Real aggregate demand could increase, through an increase in the nominal monetary stock, and with an infinitely elastic aggregate supply function, full employment would be restored with no fall in real wages.

16. This view runs through most of his works. See, particularly, "Profit Inflation," 256, and "Prices as a Factor," 335–36.

real income.[17] Yet, as far as we can discover, he consistently forgets about real forces when using his time series to test the hypothesis; any fall in real wages when prices are rising he interprets as evidence supporting the wage-lag hypothesis.

Yet even with this implicit assumption that real forces are constant during inflation and that consequently any change in real wages is attributable to inflation, Hamilton's data in his study of Spanish wages and prices fail in large part to support his thesis.[18] Of the three areas studied in the first episode from 1350 to 1500, Valencia, Aragon, and Navarre, only Navarre incurred inflation during this time. He concludes: "The greatest anomaly disclosed by the present study is the complete failure of wages to lag behind prices in any of the kingdoms during a single period of upheaval. In fact, Navarrese wages advanced much faster than prices in the last decade of the fourteenth century."[19]

For the second period, 1501 to 1650, he concludes: "With few interruptions, the trend [in real wages] was downward from 1520 to 1600."[20] And, "The calamitous depreciation of the inflated Castilian vellon and debased Valencian silver coinage in 1623–1650 impaired the economic welfare of workers no less catastrophically than had the influx of American gold and silver in the last eight decades of the sixteenth century."[21] However, again, and once more holding real forces constant, Hamilton's conclusion is not supported by his data. While it is strictly true that real wages as reported by Hamilton were lower in 1600 than they were in 1520, the trend he reports is absent from his data. The reason he gets the results that he does is that 1520 is a year when real wages were exceptionally high when compared with the years immediately preceding and succeeding 1520. On the other hand, 1600 appears to be a year when real wages were exceptionally low when compared with the years immediately preceding and succeeding 1600. If real wages in 1522 are compared with real wages in 1602, then one can conclude that real wages rose. The results Hamilton obtained can be obtained from random series. There is no downward trend in real

17. E. J. Hamilton, *Money, Prices, and Wages in Valencia, Aragon, and Navarre, 1351–1500* (Cambridge, Mass., 1936), 100–104.

18. In the ensuing examination of his statistical results, the reported data will be taken at face value. However, the statistical procedures employed merit more extended critical examination than is possible here.

19. Hamilton, *Money, Prices, and Wages*, 203.

20. E. J. Hamilton, *American Treasure and the Price Revolution in Spain, 1501–1650* (Cambridge, Mass., 1934), 280.

21. Ibid., 282.

wages nor any coincidence of wages lagging with inflation.[22] Hamilton's data for the episode are reproduced in Table 1.

In his third volume, Hamilton covers the time interval from 1651 to 1800, and he finds that real wages declined in the urban areas, Madrid and Valencia, in the second half of the eighteenth century. What happened to real wages for the country as a whole is unclear since real wages rose in some rural areas and presumably the country as a whole was predominantly rural.[23] The second half of the eighteenth century was characterized by rising prices. However, it was also a time when the Spanish population was increasing sharply; it doubled during this century, and was associated with migration from rural to urban areas.[24] Consequently, one would expect, in the absence of any imperfections in the labor market, that such a population increase would lower real wages. Yet Hamilton did not disentangle the effects of this population increase from the effects of inflation upon real wages, and he concluded in the final sentence of his last volume:

> By involuntarily sacrificing real income through the price-wage squeeze, the laboring class bore the burden that implemented material progress, just as laborers and peasants in Soviet Russia, sacrificing through governmental directives, have largely financed the mechanization of industry that was instrumental in the recent expulsion of German invaders.[25]

### B. English and French Data

Hamilton buttresses his conclusions about the effect of inflation upon industrial development by citing similar effects for England and France during inflations that occurred in these countries. Specifically, in his third volume he says:

> The concurrence of profit inflation and of rapid economic development in England and France tends to confirm the thesis that the lag of wages behind prices was an important factor in the great material progress in Spain during the second half of the eighteenth century.[26]

22. Alternatively one might say that the base year for Hamilton's observations had a strong plus random factor, and the final year a strong minus random factor, and what he attributes to inflation can be attributed very easily to sampling error. In statistical jargon, he commits the regression fallacy.

23. E. J. Hamilton, *War and Prices in Spain, 1651–1800* (Cambridge, Mass., 1947), 210.

24. Hamilton, *War and Prices in Spain*, 216.

25. Ibid., 225.

26. Ibid., 224.

TABLE 1. Composite index of real wages base 1571–1580, period 1501–1650

| Year | | Year | | Year | | Year | | Year | | Year | |
|---|---|---|---|---|---|---|---|---|---|---|---|
| 1501 | 112.78 | 1526 | 105.66 | 1551 | 100.27 | 1576 | 103.47 | 1601 | 100.88 | 1626 | 101.15 |
| 1502 | 115.55 | 1527 | 102.26 | 1552 | 98.64 | 1577 | 106.52 | 1602 | 108.68 | 1627 | 97.82 |
| 1503 | 118.96 | 1528 | 106.62 | 1553 | 102.76 | 1578 | 102.95 | 1603 | 112.80 | 1628 | 102.44 |
| 1504 | 111.56 | 1529 | 100.15 | 1554 | 108.40 | 1579 | 97.81 | 1604 | 111.94 | 1629 | 104.22 |
| 1505 | 108.62 | 1530 | 91.35 | 1555 | 110.41 | 1580 | 102.86 | 1605 | 112.10 | 1630 | 109.31 |
| 1506 | 92.47 | 1531 | 94.39 | 1556 | 109.60 | 1581 | 104.43 | 1606 | 116.80 | 1631 | 110.89 |
| 1507 | 99.68 | 1532 | 99.40 | 1557 | 100.66 | 1582 | 101.12 | 1607 | 119.60 | 1632 | 107.79 |
| 1508 | 102.75 | 1533 | 106.25 | 1558 | 101.75 | 1583 | 100.09 | 1608 | 121.35 | 1633 | 111.11 |
| 1509 | 117.06 | 1534 | 102.43 | 1559 | 111.05 | 1584 | 102.48 | 1609 | 127.83 | 1634 | 113.47 |
| 1510 | 127.84 | 1535 | 114.03 | 1560 | 110.75 | 1585 | 102.22 | 1610 | 125.49 | 1635 | 114.60 |
| 1511 | 120.80 | 1536 | 104.49 | 1561 | 102.02 | 1586 | 106.01 | 1611 | 130.56 | 1636 | 111.63 |
| 1512 | 126.85 | 1357 | 108.19 | 1562 | 96.50 | 1587 | 103.14 | 1612 | 127.96 | 1637 | 105.83 |
| 1513 | 125.48 | 1538 | 99.82 | 1563 | 100.96 | 1588 | 111.63 | 1613 | 128.09 | 1638 | 105.86 |
| 1514 | 122.04 | 1539 | 104.06 | 1564 | 102.12 | 1589 | 107.31 | 1614 | 122.85 | 1639 | 110.81 |
| 1515 | 118.56 | 1540 | 102.30 | 1565 | 101.27 | 1590 | 105.85 | 1615 | 126.57 | 1640 | 111.59 |
| 1516 | 120.62 | 1541 | 103.73 | 1566 | 99.22 | 1591 | 107.70 | 1616 | 121.45 | 1641 | 106.13 |
| 1517 | 123.87 | 1542 | 98.23 | 1567 | 103.37 | 1592 | 104.12 | 1617 | 119.81 | 1642 | 98.07 |
| 1518 | 118.36 | 1543 | 97.24 | 1568 | 105.80 | 1593 | 107.07 | 1618 | 122.90 | 1643 | 101.30 |
| 1519 | 119.77 | 1544 | 101.45 | 1569 | 108.14 | 1594 | 106.47 | 1619 | 127.08 | 1644 | 102.45 |

| Year | Value | Year | Value | Year | Value | Year | Value | Year | Value | Year | Value |
|------|-------|------|-------|------|-------|------|-------|------|-------|------|-------|
| 1520 | 125.56 | 1545 | 105.14 | 1570 | 105.56 | 1595 | 106.29 | 1620 | 121.61 | 1645 | 105.91 |
| 1521 | 112.61 | 1546 | 98.36 | 1571 | 99.58 | 1596 | 103.84 | 1621 | 112.11 | 1646 | 102.07 |
| 1522 | 104.81 | 1547 | 99.28 | 1572 | 100.02 | 1597 | 99.00 | 1622 | 121.85 | 1647 | 103.10 |
| 1523 | 109.89 | 1548 | 95.54 | 1573 | 97.40 | 1598 | 93.02 | 1623 | 120.16 | 1648 | 98.20 |
| 1524 | 109.36 | 1549 | 93.61 | 1574 | 100.11 | 1599 | 91.40 | 1624 | 114.64 | 1649 | 97.53 |
| 1525 | 106.87 | 1550 | 97.61 | 1575 | 94.18 | 1600 | 91.31 | 1625 | 113.82 | 1650 | 93.30 |

Reproduced from E. J. Hamilton, War and Prices in Spain, 1651–1800 (Cambridge, Mass., 1947), 278, with permission of Harvard University Press.

Again, even if the potential impact of real forces upon wage-price relationships is ignored, can it be said that wages fell during the inflation in England?

Hamilton's study of the movement of prices and wages in London between 1729 and 1800 indicates that real wages fell.[27] Mrs. Gilboy, however, who also studied prices and wages in England at this time, supports Hamilton's findings of fact but not his conclusions. She found that real wages fell in London and rose in the north of England.[28] Therefore she concluded: "Generalizations as to what happened to English wages as a whole must at present meet no little skepticism."[29] Her findings were particularly damaging to Hamilton's interpretation of the implications of a fall in real wages during inflation. Capital formation in the north of England was especially high, whereas Hamilton's hypothesis implies that capital formation ought to have been particularly low in this area.[30]

Hamilton has also examined data for an earlier period of English history, 1500 to 1702.[31] Will these data support the hypothesis that inflation causes wages to lag behind prices if one abstracts from the effects of real forces? (See Table 2.) Taking the period as a whole, Hamilton is right. Real wages declined. However, virtually all of the decline occurred during the first 50 years of this period, and it is unclear whether this shorter time interval ought to be regarded as being on net balance inflationary or deflationary. Prices were about 17 percent lower at the end of these 50 years than they were for the base observation.

27. Hamilton, "Profit Inflation," 259. One of the relevant problems for analyzing Hamilton's data, which he fails to discuss, is the fact that he has more observations, typically, in his price than in his wage index. Consequently, if the price and wage observations change with the same degree of frequency, say once a year, it will appear, falsely, as if wages were lagging behind prices. This error accounts for much of the intuitive appeal of the wage-lag hypothesis. If during inflation one sees prices moving up day by day whereas one's own wage rate changes once a year, the conclusion that wages lag behind prices during inflation is difficult to resist.

28. E. Gilboy, *Wages in Eighteenth Century England* (Cambridge, Mass., 1934), 191–215.

29. Ibid., 227. In a paper dealing with this same issue, Mrs. Gilboy puts the case even more forcefully. "Sufficient data are not at present available to make any statements concerning the movement of real wages in England as a whole for this period" ("The Cost of Living and Real Wages in Eighteenth Century England," *Rev. Econ. Stat.* 18 [1936]: 141).

30. For a partially overlapping time period, 1790–1830, T. S. Ashton does not believe that real wages declined ("The Standard of Life of the Workers in England, 1790–1830," in *Capitalism and Historians*, ed. F. A. Hayek [Chicago, 1954], 158).

31. E. J. Hamilton, "American Treasure and the Rise of Capitalism (1500–1700)," *Economica* 9 (November 1929): 3351, chart 1.

TABLE 2. *Index numbers of prices and wages in England, 1500–1702 (index for 1451–1500 = 100)*

| Period | Prices | Wages |
|---|---|---|
| 1501–1510 | 95 | 95 |
| 1511–1520 | 101 | 93 |
| 1521–1530 | 113 | 93 |
| 1531–1540 | 105 | 90 |
| 1541–1550 | 79 | 57 |
| 1551–1560 | 132 | 88 |
| 1561–1570 | 155 | 109 |
| 1571–1582 | 171 | 113 |
| 1583–1592 | 198 | 125 |
| 1593–1602 | 243 | 124 |
| 1603–1612 | 251 | 124.5 |
| 1613–1622 | 257 | 134 |
| 1623–1632 | 282 | 138.5 |
| 1633–1642 | 291 | 152.5 |
| 1643–1652 | 331 | 175 |
| 1653–1662 | 308 | 187 |
| 1663–1672 | 324 | 190 |
| 1673–1682 | 348 | 205.5 |
| 1683–1692 | 319 | 216 |
| 1693–1702 | 339 | 233 |

Reproduced from E. J. Hamilton, "American Treasure and the Rise of Capitalism (1500–1700)," *Economica* 9 (November 1929): 352, with permission of London School of Economics and the author.

The first 40 years were inflationary, and real wages fell. However, the next 10 were deflationary, and real wages fell even more. Again these data will not support even this very simple conception of the wage-lag hypothesis.[32]

Tucker studied real wages in London during the latter half of the eighteenth

32. Using time series of wages and prices as Hamilton does involves the vexing question of how to choose one's starting point or base observation. Presumably one wants to start observations when prices start to rise. But the trough of a price series is usually determined by random components. This produces a transitory peak in the real wage series; the subsequent decrease, if interpreted as a lag, provides an example of the regression

century but has no data for the country as a whole.[33] In view of Gilboy's findings, his data are not of great relevance for England as a whole. Tucker, for reasons quite different from Hamilton's, was interested in testing the hypothesis that real wages fall as a result of rising prices. However, every time he observes a fall in real wages, he is able to explain this fall by real factors such as poor crops, resources consumed by wars, etc. (p. 82, for example). Yet he ignores these explanations when drawing his conclusions.

For France, Hamilton does have data that unambiguously show that real wages fell.[34] (See Table 3.) However, his explanation of why they fell is not supported by related evidence. His hypothesis implies that the larger the fall in real wages, the greater the rate of industrial development. Differences in the rates of capital formation between England and France ought, therefore, to be related to differences in either the observed fall in real wages or the rates of change of prices. Nef was unable to explain differences between the rates of capital formation in France and England with Hamilton's hypothesis.[35] Similarly, the failure to find "correlation between inflation, or its absence, and variations in the rate of economic growth" has led another student of industrial development, Felix, to reject Hamilton's theory of development.[36]

---

fallacy. Only by averaging out transitory or random variations about some turning point can one avoid part of this problem.

Only after acceptance of this paper for publication did we discover the following corroboratory conclusion, "It follows that Keynes was misled when he argued in the *Treatise* that the general rise in prices had stimulated industrial growth by widening profit margins," in E. H. Phelps Brown and S. V. Hopkins, "Wage-rates and Prices: Evidence for Population Pressure in the Sixteenth Century," *Economica*, N.S. 24 (November 1957): 299.

33. R. S. Tucker, "Real Wages of Artisans in London, 1729–1935," *Jour. Am. Stat. Assoc.* 31 (1936): 73–84.

34. *American Treasure*, 353.

35. J. Nef has collected evidence that fails to show a relationship between the magnitude of the lag and the rate of industrial development. He also has evidence that Hamilton's data exaggerate the magnitude of the fall in real wages ("Prices and Industrial Capitalism in France and England, 1540–1640," *Econ. Hist. Rev.* 7 [May 1937]: 155–85; reprinted in Lane and Riemersma, *Enterprise and Secular Change*, 292–321).

36. See also D. Felix's discussion, "Hamilton's *Tour d'Horizon*," part 3 of "Profit Inflation and Industrial Growth: The Historic Record and Contemporary Analogies," *Quart. Jour. Econ.* 70 (August 1956): 457–59.

TABLE 3. *Index numbers of prices and wages in France, 1500–1700 (index from 1451–1500 = 100)*

| Period | Prices | Wages |
|--------|--------|-------|
| 1501–1525 | 113 | 92 |
| 1526–1550 | 136 | 104 |
| 1551–1575 | 174 | 103 |
| 1576–1600 | 248 | 113 |
| 1601–1625 | 189 | 113 |
| 1626–1650 | 243 | 127 |
| 1651–1675 | 227 | 127 |
| 1676–1700 | 229 | 125 |

Reproduced from E. J. Hamilton, "American Treasure and the Rise of Capitalism (1500–1700)," *Economica* 9 (November 1929): 353, with permission of London School of Economics and the author.

### C. The Civil War in the North

Mitchell's basic time series of wages and prices for the North during the Civil War are substantially better than the data for the early days of the industrial revolution.[37] And there is little doubt that real wages truly fell during the Civil War; most of Mitchell's results cannot be rationalized as an artifact resulting from the choice of the time period said to be inflationary. Moreover, these data indicate that a substantial fall in real wages occurred.[38]

One might quarrel with Mitchell's use of a wholesale price index as a deflator of real wages. This index was in large part composed of commodities like opium, mercury, zinc, soda ash, tin plate, blue vitriol, etc. A mere count of such items indicates that an unweighted index overrepresents their effect on the cost-of-living index. Rent, as is typically the case for wholesale price indexes, was absent. But it is easy to make too much of this point. Mitchell also computed a cost-of-living index for this period, and when either this index or one computed by Ethel Hoover, who used the same source material, is used as a deflator, the results still indicate a substantial fall in real wages, although smaller than when wholesale prices are used.[39]

37. Mitchell, *A History of the Greenbacks.*

38. Ibid., 343.

39. Ethel Hoover's index (*Prices in the United States in the 19th Century* [presented at a National Bureau Conference on Research in Income and Wealth, September 4–5, 1957,

These results led Mitchell to conclude that: "All of the statistical evidence that has been presented in the preceding pages supports unequivocally the common theory that persons whose incomes are derived from wages suffer seriously from a depreciation of the currency."[40] They also led Mitchell to embrace the hypothesis that the labor market in the 1860s and 1870s was imperfect and that this imperfection was of a kind that virtually no serious student of industrial organization asserts exists in any other factor or product market.[41] However, there is an alternative explanation of the fall in real wages in the North during the Civil War that is consistent with the way economists explain changes in price relationships in markets other than labor and it explains more of the relative price movements that occurred. Indeed, this explanation is consistent with the postulate that the labor market was operating perfectly during the inflation associated with the Civil War. Because it has none of the ad hoc character of the explanation employed by Mitchell and Hamilton, it is to be preferred.[42]

The outbreak of the Civil War substantially destroyed a triangular trading relationship between the North, the South, and England. The South earned foreign exchange through its exports of cotton, which accounted for roughly two-thirds of all U.S. exports. It, in effect, traded these foreign exchange earnings for Northern goods and services, and the North, in turn, used this foreign exchange to purchase imports. The outbreak of hostilities, in addition to destroying a mutually profitable trading relationship between the North and the South, presented the North with what would be regarded today as an extremely difficult balance-of-payments problem. This problem was aggravated by a capital flight of foreign investments during the early years of the war.

That this important problem confronting the North has been largely unrecognized is in large part to be explained by the fact that it was solved unobtrusively and successfully by a measure designed for a largely unrelated function. During the war, the North engaged in the printing of greenbacks, and the re-

-----

mimeographed], 40, table 1) is better than Mitchell's CIP because it uses more of the available data and better techniques for accounting for gaps in the data. Mitchell's data are reproduced in R. A. Kessel and A. A. Alchian, "Real Wages in the North during the Civil War: Mitchell's Data Reinterpreted," *Jour. Law and Econ.* 2 (October 1959): 102.

40. Mitchell, *A History of the Greenbacks*, 347.

41. Mitchell, *Gold, Prices, and Wages*, 276.

42. The analysis which follows is more fully developed in a paper which appears elsewhere. See Kessel and Alchian, "Real Wages in the North."

sulting inflation and the maintenance of convertibility at the prewar exchange rate were incompatible. In consequence, the North abandoned the gold standard in favor of an inconvertible paper standard and a freely fluctuating exchange rate which inadvertently solved the balance-of-payments problem.

The rise in the prices of imports relative to the rise in domestic prices and wages inevitably produced a fall in real factor incomes of all types. Insofar as money wages are deflated by a price index that includes international goods, particularly imports, real wages decline. Since Mitchell's wholesale price index was more heavily weighted by imports than his consumer price index, the use of the former as a deflator produces a greater fall in real wages than does the latter. And, of course, if imports are excluded from his consumer price index and what remains is used as a deflator of money wages, a still smaller fall in real wages is measured.

However, this is only part of the explanation of the fall in real wages that Mitchell observed. The North, in addition to taxing through inflation, employed turnover taxes and tariffs as means of war finance. The severity of these taxes increased during the course of the war. These taxes produced a divergence between the sum of the payments to agents of production and final product prices, because unlike retail sales taxes today, they became a part of final product prices. One would also expect for this reason to find that real wages, as measured by Mitchell, declined during the course of the Civil War.

Both the balance-of-payments problem and the turnover taxes would have produced a fall in real wages whether or not inflation had occurred. If the government's increased expenditures had not been financed by inflationary methods, some other means of taxation would have been required. Had tariffs or turnover taxes in any part replaced the inflation tax, an even greater fall in real wages would have occurred. The inflation tax implies that real wages were higher than they otherwise would have been.

### D. The Civil War in the South

In a number of respects, Eugene Lerner's study of the Confederacy is parallel to Mitchell's work.[43] In particular, both found that real wages declined. In neither case can most of the decline be attributed to the special characteristics of the base or terminal years for the time period defined as inflationary. Like

---

43. E. M. Lerner, "The Monetary and Fiscal Programs of the Confederate Government, 1861–65," *Jour. Pol. Econ.* 62 (December 1954): 506–22, and "Money, Prices, and Wages in the Confederacy, 1861–65," *Jour. Pol. Econ.* 63 (February 1955): 20–40.

Mitchell, Lerner attributes the fall in real wages to the lag of wages behind prices and accepts the extraordinary profitability implication of the wage-lag argument. "Prices rose much faster than wages in the Confederacy, and southern businessmen made large profits."[44] His paper contains virtually no evidence on profits.

The acceptance by Lerner of the wage-lag explanation of the fall in real wages is inconsistent with another interpretation of the events of the time that may be found in his own papers. He indicates that much of Southern capital was highly specialized to the production of cotton for an international market and that the Northern blockade sharply reduced the productivity of this capital. Lerner also reports that excises, either in the form of taxes or payments in kind, constituted an important means of war finance. In fact, Lerner implicitly presents a hypothesis that explains the fall in real wages by nonmonetary phenomena, but he explicitly accepts the thesis that the fall in real wages is attributable to inflation.

### E. World War I

Hansen's study is concerned with real wages and price changes in the United States from 1820 to 1923 and thus includes the inflation associated with World War I. His position is much like that of Mitchell and Hamilton. "Rising prices cause a gap between the marginal productivity of the various factors employed by the entrepreneur and the return that each receives. Indeed in such periods it is literally true that 'labor does not receive the full value of its product.'"[45]

However, even if real forces are assumed to be constant, as Hansen presumably assumed, the data do not support the wage-lag hypothesis. Indeed, they can be just as easily construed as undermining the hypothesis. Only if one chooses the year 1916 as a base and compares it with 1919 or 1917, can one show that real wages fell.[46] (See Table 4.) If one uses 1913 as a base, and every succeeding year through 1920 as a terminal point, there is nothing to indicate a fall in real wages. In fact, Hansen's data show that real wages were almost 10 percent greater in 1920 than in 1917.

These data of Hansen's contain an unfortunate bias in favor of the wage-lag

---

44. Lerner, "Money, Prices, and Wages," 31.

45. A. H. Hansen, "Factors Affecting Trend of Real Wages," *Am. Econ. Rev.* 15 (1925): 40.

46. Hamilton, in a parenthetical remark, selects 1916 as a base year and observes that ". . . American profiteers reaped [income] from a similar divergence between prices and wages from 1916 to 1919" (*American Treasure*, 355). Hansen's data, reproduced as Table 4, show a less than one percent fall in real wages for this period.

TABLE 4. *Hansen's series of money wages, cost of living, and real wages (1913 = 100)*

| Year | Index of money wages | Index of cost of living | Index of real wages |
|------|------|------|------|
| 1910 | 94 | 94 | 100 |
| 1911 | 95 | 92 | 103 |
| 1912 | 98 | 96 | 102 |
| 1913 | 100 | 100 | 100 |
| 1914 | 102 | 102 | 100 |
| 1915 | 104 | 104 | 100 |
| 1916 | 118 | 111 | 106 |
| 1917 | 134 | 131 | 102 |
| 1918 | 168 | 159 | 106 |
| 1919 | 193 | 183 | 105 |
| 1920 | 232 | 208 | 112 |
| 1921 | 207 | 182 | 114 |
| 1922 | 201 | 168 | 120 |
| 1923 | 220 | 171 | 129 |

Reproduced from A. H. Hansen, "Factors Affecting Trend of Real Wages," *Am. Econ. Rev.* 15 (1925): 32.

hypothesis for the entire time interval with which he was concerned. Starting with 1890, Hansen uses weekly earnings rather than hourly earnings. If leisure is a superior good, and if real hourly earnings per capita rise, then weekly earnings understate real wages because of the substitution of leisure for income from work. Consequently, evidence collected to reveal a fall in real wages can be explained, at least in part, by the hypothesis that they were in fact rising. This bias is particularly unfortunate in a study of secular inflations, because the longer the time period considered, the greater the error it introduces into the calculations.

### F. The German Inflation

Bresciani-Turroni contends that real wages declined as a result of the inflation in Germany following World War I.[47] For the entire inflationary episode, he concluded: "But it may be said that on the whole the inflation generally favored

47. Bresciani-Turroni, *The Economics of Inflation.* "The increase in nominal wage rates was slower than the increase in prices caused by monetary inflation. In other words, real

the entrepreneurs and the owners of material means of production, especially strengthening the positions of industrial capitalists; that it caused a lowering of the real wages of workmen . . ." (286). However, leaving aside questions of the impact of real forces upon real wages, Bresciani-Turroni's wage data, which consist almost exclusively of miners' wages, show that real wages sometimes declined and sometimes rose during the course of the inflation. Over the period as a whole, real wages did not fall (307, 309).

During the later stages of the inflation, when the real value of the nominal stock of money declined sharply, or during the time that velocity increased at a rate more rapid than the rate of increase of the monetary stock, Bresciani-Turroni found that real wages fell. This rise in velocity was attributable to the recognition by the community of the increased cost of holding cash balances caused by rising prices. In this respect the German hyperinflation was unlike the inflations examined by Mitchell, Hansen, Hamilton, Gilboy, and Tucker, and it led to a marked reduction in the effective stock of capital in money form. Under these circumstances, the higher marginal cost of using money is an additional cost of doing business, and this implies that the share of the final output of the economy going to the other cooperating agents of production has decreased. Consequently, a fall in real wages during an inflation that is generally anticipated is consistent with a perfectly functioning labor market and does not imply an increase in business profits. In fact, this analysis is consistent with Bresciani-Turroni's data on share prices, which do not support the thesis that business firms are extraordinarily profitable as a consequence of inflation (253).

In general, it appears that a highly selective sampling from the population of all inflations has produced two important unambiguous cases of a fall in real wages for individual economies, those of the North and the South during the Civil War. For these cases, the wage-lag hypothesis has to compete with price theory. For the one case that has been studied in great detail, that of the North during the Civil War, price theory offers a more satisfactory explanation.

Whether or not available data indicate that real wages fell during inflation for some particular economy does not in itself establish or disprove the existence of an inflation-induced wage lag unless one assumes real forces to be inoperative. A time series of wages and prices can be made relevant evidence for testing the wage-lag hypothesis only after the effects of real forces are

---

wages" (305; see also 186–88). This fall in real wages, according to Bresciani-Turroni, continued until the summer of 1922.

controlled. Unfortunately, the wage-lag theorists have generally ignored real forces. In the case of the North during the Civil War, the real forces ignored are substantial in magnitude and capable of producing the effects upon real wages imputed to the wage-lag hypothesis. When one considers the implications of this hypothesis, as the wage-lag theorists have not, the differences between industrial development in the North and South of England during the early days of the industrial revolutions, along with the Nef findings, must be regarded as still more evidence against this hypothesis.

### III. New Evidence

In an effort to bring some new evidence to bear on the validity of wage-lag hypothesis, the annual wage bills for 56 industrial corporations listed on the New York Stock Exchange during the time interval 1940 to 1952 have been collected. These were all the industrial firms listed that reported their wage bills during this entire period.

The proposition tested was that the firms with large annual wage bills would experience an increase in profits (and wealth) relative to firms with smaller annual wage bills. That is, for any given rise in prices, sales and costs other than wages rise by the same proportion, whereas total wages [W] rise by less, e.g., by only some fraction, $\alpha$, of the general price rise. Thus, $W(1 - \alpha)$ constitutes the size of the gain in profits for any firm. The relative magnitude of the gain is a function of the size of a firm's wage bill relative to its equity, as measured by its market value. In other words, the ratio of wages to equity is an indicator of the relative rise in stock prices attributable to a lag of wages behind prices.[48]

The ratio of wages to equity was obtained for each of the years from 1940 to 1952 through the use of the annual wage bill and the market value of stock outstanding at the end of the year. Unfortunately, testing for a relationship between the relative change in market value and the wage-to-equity ratio produces a bias in favor of finding a positive correlation because ratios with the same denominator are being correlated. To reduce this bias, the annual wage-to-equity ratios, one for each year in the 1940 to 1952 period, were averaged for

---

48. Hamilton evidently regards the ratio of wages to total costs as the correct indicator of the size of the gain attributable to the lag of wages behind prices ("Profit Inflation," 262). However, two firms with identical equity values and identical ratios of wages to total costs might have different markups and consequently different aggregate wage bills. (For example, consider a jewelry store and a supermarket grocery.) What is relevant is the size of the wage bill. And for interfirm comparisons, the relationship of the wage bill to total equity is the appropriate one.

each corporation and then used as a predictor of relative changes in equity values.[49]

The use of this average seemed reasonable because the differences between firms with respect to this average were significantly greater than the variations of any given year from the average for any firm. (The wage-to-equity ratios exhibited no trend over time.) The standard deviation of the ratio of wages to equity for any given year was about 20 percent of the average for any firm. On the other hand, the average ratio varied, from firm to firm, from a low of 1 to a high of 7.[50] And because the interfirm variation was so much greater than the intrafirm variation, it seemed sensible to enlarge the size of the sample by using data for firms that reported annual wage bills for as little as two years of the time span studied. This brought the sample to 113 firms. (A listing of the firms and other relevant data may be obtained through personal communication with the authors. Unfortunately, space constraints do not permit us to publish them here.)

By trying to detect a correlation between wage-to-equity ratios and changes in stock prices, the effects of a lag of wages behind prices caused by inflation can be disentangled from the effects of real forces upon real wages. After all, if one believes that real and monetary forces can operate independently and concurrently, the wage lag should be operative regardless of whether time series of wages and prices during inflation show that real wages fell, rose, or were constant. Given independence between real forces and the wage-to-equity ratio of a firm, this test ought to reveal the presence of the effects of inflation upon real wages.

According to the wage-lag hypothesis, the greater the wage-to-equity ratio, the larger should be the rise in equity values as a result of inflation.[51] To test whether or not this implication is in fact correct, firms were ranked according to their average ratio of wages to equity. The percentage increase in equity for firms with an average ratio of annual wages to equity below .5 were compared

49. This also buys some insurance against committing the regression fallacy. If the wage-to-equity ratio at the beginning of the time period were used, firms with large wage-to-equity ratios might be those with transitorily small equity valuations, and conversely.

50. This ratio is affected by the financial structure. A firm with large debts and small equity financing will have a high wage-to-equity ratio and conversely.

51. For example, if a firm's stock sold for $4 at the end of 1939 and for $40 at the end of 1952, the equity increase is shown as a ratio, 10. Dividends paid are assumed to be reinvested into more shares of the same firm, and thus their growth was compounded. In this way, differences in dividend payout policy were held constant.

TABLE 5. *Mean equity increases of firms classified by wage-to-equity ratio*

| Ratio of wages-to-equity | Average increase in equity (1939–52) | Number of firms | Variance |
|---|---|---|---|
| Under .5 | 8.41 | 34 | 48.4 |
| .5 to .99 | 7.40 | 30 | 39.1 |
| 1. and over | 6.19 | 49 | 26.5 |
| "t" for $8.41 - 6.19 = +1.58$ | | | |
| $P(t \geq 1.26) = .12$ | | | |

Sources: Moody's Manual of Investments, American and Foreign, Industrial Securities, Moody's Investor's Service, New York, annually, 1939–53; Corporation Annual Reports, Godfrey Memorial Library, Yale University, New Haven, 1939–52; New York Times, daily edition, 1939–52.

with those above 1. The results of this comparison are presented in summary form in Table 5. The average equity rise was greater, the lower the wages-to-equity ratio. Such a difference in the wrong direction clearly does not support the wage-lag hypothesis. Dividing the sample into two equal parts, one consisting of firms with the larger wage-to-equity ratios and the other of firms with the smaller wage-to-equity ratios, yields similar results.

In any attempt to impute the absence of causality to the absence of correlation between two variables, there always exists the danger that still another variable is so correlated with what is regarded as the independent variable that the effects of the independent variable upon the dependent variable are concealed. Relevant to this problem is the fact that a relationship is known to exist between the net monetary status of a firm and the relative change in its stock prices during inflation.[52] The increase in the equity of the 43 firms in the sample that were net monetary debtors at least two-thirds of the time from 1940 to 1952 was greater than that experienced by the 29 firms in the sample that were net monetary creditors at least two-thirds of the time.[53] These results

52. Kessel, "Inflation-Caused Wealth Redistribution," 28.

53. There were 43 debtor and 29 creditor firms. The mean rise for the debtor firms was 8.25 with a variance of 39.67; for the creditor firms, the mean was 5.94 and the variance 19.20. $\bar{x}_d - \bar{x}_o = 2.31$, $t = 1.82$, $P(t \geq +1.82) \approx .04$. Sources: Corporation Annual Reports, Godfrey Memorial Library, Yale University, New Haven, 1939–52; Moody's Manual of Investments, American and Foreign, Industrial Securities, Moody's Investor's Service, New York, annually, 1939–53; New York Times, daily edition, 1939–52.

are consistent with known effects of debtor-creditor status upon stock price changes during inflation.[54] Consequently, if firms that were large net debtors were also firms that had large wage-to-equity ratios, debtor status would counteract the effect of the wage lag upon stock prices, and the consequences of inflation-induced lags of wages behind prices would go undetected.

In order to determine whether or not debtor-creditor effects were masking the effects of inflation upon business profits, the relationships among (1) changes in equity values, (2) annual wage-to-equity ratios, (3) debtor-creditor status, and (4) annual sales-to-equity ratio (for those who think that sales are correlated with wage-to-equity ratios) were explored by means of a multiple correlation analysis. As a measure of a firm's net monetary creditor or debtor status over the interval 1940 to 1952, the average of debtor-creditor status in each year was weighted by the price rise for the year as measured by the change in the consumer price index of the Bureau of Labor Statistics.[55] For each of 113 firms, there are observations with respect to four variables. The simple correlation coefficients among these four variables are presented in Table 6 along with the partial correlation coefficients of each predictive variable, with the other two predictive variables held statistically constant. Results of this partial correlation analysis do not support the wage lag.[56] However, these correlation coefficients are difficult to interpret because the necessary conditions for computing their sampling distribution are not satisfied. In particular, the predicted

54. Possibly this is too strong a statement. G. L. Bach and A. Ando ("The Redistributional Effects of Inflation," Rev. Econ. and Stat. 39 [February 1957]: 1–13) report that they were unable to detect the debtor-creditor effect. There seem to be two reasons for the apparent difference between the outcome of Kessel's early work and the results reported here on the one hand, and the results reported by Bach and Ando on the other. Bach and Ando used several criteria for determining whether or not the debtor-creditor effect existed. Only one of these criteria was implied by the hypothesis being tested. On that one pertinent criterion their results do verify the debtor-creditor wealth transfer. But they relied on the rule of the majority rather than on the rule of a decisive test. This error was compounded by their erroneous use of a "two-tailed" probability calculation instead of a one-tailed calculation. For additional evidence, published subsequent to the Bach and Ando paper, see A. Alchian and R. Kessel, "Redistribution of Wealth through Inflation," Science 130 (September 4, 1959): 537.

55. Subsequent examination indicates that an unweighted average, which is cheaper to compute, would have given essentially similar, but not quite as effective, results.

56. Since these are the same data used in the previous test, these results cannot be construed as new independent evidence against the wage-lag hypothesis.

TABLE 6. *Matrix of simple and rank correlation coefficients among equity rise, wage-to-equity ratio, net monetary status, and sales-to-equity ratio**

|  |  | (1) | (2) | (3) | (4) |
|---|---|---|---|---|---|
| Equity rise, 1952/1939 | (1) | 1. | .04 (−.09) | .01 (.24) | .10 (.02) |
| Ratio of wage-to-equity | (2) |  | 1. | .33 (.15) | .51 (.83) |
| Net monetary status | (3) |  |  | 1. | .10 (.36) |
| Ratio of sales-to-equity | (4) |  |  |  | 1. |
| Partial correlation coefficients $r_{12.34} = -.09 \, (-.11)$ |  |  |  |  |  |
| $r_{13.24} = .04 \, (.36)$ |  |  |  |  |  |
| $r_{14.23} = .16 \, (.08)$ |  |  |  |  |  |

*The rank correlation coefficients are in parentheses. For the ranks, the one-tailed 5 percent probability value is .16, the two-tailed probability value is .22, $P(r > .36) < .001$.

or dependent variable is not normally distributed.[57] Therefore, no reliable probability tests of significance can be applied.

To obtain a probability test, the values associated with each of the variables were converted to ranks, and rank correlation coefficients were computed. These are reported in Table 6. These calculations indicate a positive partial correlation between net monetary status and increases in equity values. And there is only one chance in 1,000 that such a result could be obtained by randomly sampling from a population characterized by an absence of this relationship. The negative partial correlation of wage-to-equity ratios and changes in stock prices still persists; however, this correlation can be easily rationalized as the result of random sampling from a population characterized by an absence of this relationship. Again the wage-lag hypothesis is not supported after the potential masking effects of two variables are specifically eliminated. The absence of a relationship between sales and changes in equity values is probably the result of using the level of sales rather than the rate of change of sales as an independent variable.

57. One objection to this procedure that does not seem warranted is the objection that correlations among ratios, such as these are, must be invalid because they are subject to biases. But it is the ratios themselves that are interesting in an economic sense. Secondly, even if one thinks in absolute terms, the weighting of observations by the inverse of their standard deviation eliminates the bias. Moreover, the bias of ratios, if present, would work in favor of the wage-lag hypothesis, not against it.

If neither a regression phenomenon nor a masking effect from monetary status is operating, can the results obtained be attributed to a correlation among specific industries? Relative price changes have possibly favored industries consisting of low wage-to-equity firms. Eight of the 34 firms in the low wage-to-equity class are oil firms. The removal of these firms from the sample failed to alter significantly the results obtained. The average equity rise, with the oil firms removed, of the low wage-to-equity firms was still greater than for the other class by a 6.76 to 6.19 margin. Needless to say, there exists an indefinitely large number of variables that might be so correlated with wage-to-equity ratios that the effects of the wage lag upon changes in equity values would be concealed. All any investigator can do is to eliminate only the most promising candidates in the light of his knowledge of the economics of the problem.

## IV. Conclusions

One of the important advances in economic analysis in the postwar period has been the formal incorporation into theory of the effects of wealth upon consumption expenditures. Previously it seemed reasonable to argue that wages must lag behind prices during inflation if the government acquired resources through inflation. The logic of this argument has been shown to be false.

Another independent line of argument for the proposition that inflation causes real wages to fall is based on sluggishness or flaws in the labor market whereby wage earners receive less than their marginal product when prices are rising. But much of the data which investigators have collected to show a fall in real wages during the course of selected inflations simply fail to support the hypothesis. By one selection of beginning and terminal points for an inflation it can be shown real wages fell; by another selection it can be shown that real wages rose. The fall in real wages reported by these observers is a product of the arbitrary way the time period during which inflation occurred was defined.

However, data do exist, particularly in Mitchell's work, that unambiguously indicate a fall in real wages. But before such data can be seriously considered as supporting the wage-lag hypothesis, one must first show that even after price theory has done all it can to explain the altered price-wage relationship, there is still something left to explain. The advocates or investigators of the wage-lag hypothesis have never shown this. As for the time period studied by Mitchell, it appears that known and measurable real forces can and do explain the fall in real wages that he has observed.

Efforts to detect the existence of the wage lag during inflation through the examination of stock prices of firms that differed with respect to the volume of labor hired per dollar of invested capital by owners have also failed. This evidence contradicts the wage-lag hypothesis. Still, it is easy to make too much of this evidence, since it was based on a nonrandom sample and was obtained for only one inflation.

In general, it appears that unwarranted validity has been assigned to the wage-lag hypothesis, given the character of the evidence that has been used to support it. A rereading of this evidence suggests that the wage-lag hypothesis ought to be regarded as essentially untested.

# REAL WAGES IN THE NORTH
# DURING THE CIVIL WAR
# MITCHELL'S DATA REINTERPRETED

## REUBEN A. KESSEL AND ARMEN A. ALCHIAN

The hypothesis that inflation causes real wages to decline has won wide acceptance among economists.[1] Probably the strongest piece of empirical evidence that has been mustered in its support is the data on wages and prices contained in Mitchell's famous study of inflation in the North during the Civil War. It is the thesis of this essay that there exists an alternative explanation that Mitchell failed to consider which constitutes a more satisfactory explanation of the phenomena he observed. The purpose of this essay is to present this alternative explanation.

In his study of inflation in the North during the Civil War, Mitchell, after examining the evidence for the period, concluded:

> All of the statistical evidence that has been presented in the preceding pages supports unequivocally the common theory that persons whose incomes are derived from wages suffer seriously from a depreciation of the currency. The confirmation seems particularly striking when the conditions other than monetary affecting the labor market are taken into considera-

Reprinted from Armen A. Alchian, *Economic Forces at Work* (Indianapolis: Liberty Fund, 1977), 451–79. This article was previously published in *Journal of Law and Economics* 2 (October 1959): 95–113.

The authors benefited from the comments of Professor Cagan of Brown University, Professors Hamilton, Lewis, Rees, and Stigler of the University of Chicago, and Professor Evans of the Massachusetts Institute of Technology.

1. This is the subject of another paper entitled "The Meaning and Validity of the Inflation-Induced Lag of Wages Behind Prices," which appeared in *Am. Econ. Rev.* 50 (March 1960). Both of these papers are part of a larger study of the redistributive effects of inflation sponsored by the Merrill Foundation for the Advancement of Financial Knowledge.

tion. American workingmen are intelligent and keenly alive to their interests.[2]

The evidence that led Mitchell to this conclusion consists primarily of the time
series of real wages shown in Table 1.[3]

Mitchell also arrived at the conclusion that "real profits were unusually large
during the Civil War, therefore, but large because real wages, rent and interest
were low," with virtually no direct evidence on real returns to profit receivers.[4]
In reaching this conclusion that real profits increased because real wages and
real returns to rent and interest receivers declined, Mitchell postulated, and this
is not explicit, that the rate of return to all agents of production taken jointly
was constant between 1860 and 1865.[5]

The price index for Mitchell's real wage calculations is based on the median
observation of ninety wholesale prices using 1860 as a base. Observations
(January, April, July, and October) were recorded for every year studied. The observations for the wage index are weighted. Mitchell, in his chapter on prices,
argues that a wholesale-price index ought to be satisfactory for detecting the
effect of the issuance of greenbacks upon prices, but he revealed some reservations about the suitability of this index for cost-of-living calculations.[6] Despite these reservations, Mitchell used this wholesale-price index for measuring real wages.

The representativeness of the ninety commodities in Mitchell's wholesale-
price index of wage goods (or, for that matter, prices generally) is highly ques-
tionable. His index, like most wholesale-price indexes, contains no rent component. Internationally traded goods are strongly represented, and this, as will
be developed, gives the index a strong upward bias for most of the time period
with which Mitchell was concerned. (Almost two-thirds of the commodities
that could be unambiguously classified as either domestic or international were

2. W. C. Mitchell, A History of the Greenbacks (1903), pp. 347–48.

3. Ibid., p. 342. This is one-half of Table 46. It is the half computed with variable
weights for the wage index. Since Mitchell regarded variable weights as better than constant weights, the index with variable weights will be used as Mitchell's wage index
throughout this paper.

4. Ibid., p. 382.

5. Ibid., chaps. 6, 7 (Part II), which contain direct evidence on the real returns to interest and rent receivers. Almost no evidence on profits appears in this volume.

6. Ibid., p. 244. Even for this limited purpose of detecting the effect upon prices, it appears that this index overstated the extent of inflation, particularly from 1860 through
1864.

TABLE 1. *Average change in real wages of over 5,000 wage earners*

| Date | Index of real wages | Date | Index of real wages |
|------|---------------------|------|---------------------|
| Jan. 1860 | 100 | Jan. 1863 | 89 |
| July 1860 | 100 | July 1863 | 86 |
| Jan. 1861 | 102 | Jan. 1864 | 81 |
| July 1861 | 104 | July 1864 | 71 |
| Jan. 1862 | 102 | Jan. 1865 | 67 |
| July 1862 | 101 | July 1865 | 97 |

found to be international [see the Appendix].) Furthermore, many of the commodities in the index—opium, copper, linseed oil, soda ash, quinine, oxide of zinc, sulfuric acid, turpentine, rubber, copperas, lead, tin plate, and alum—should be regarded as of little direct significance for measuring prices of wage goods.

Yet it is easy to make too much of the fact that Mitchell employed a wholesale-price index as a deflator. In his subsequent work on the Civil War, Mitchell computed a consumers' price index for this same period with an independent set of data.[7] These data (reproduced as part of Table 2)[8] also reveal a substantial fall in real wages, although neither as large a fall as observed when the wholesale-price index is used nor as sharp a recovery in 1865. They buttress Mitchell's conclusion that real wages fell during the Civil War. Incidentally, this later study seems to have shaken Mitchell's earlier confidence in the alertness of American workmen to their interests; and he observes in this later work:

7. W. C. Mitchell, *Gold, Prices, and Wages Under the Greenback Standard* (1908). This is the data contained in the so-called Weeks report. They were collected in 1890 by questionnaires sent to businessmen. The data used for Mitchell's wholesale-price index are contained in the Aldrich report, also collected in 1890 but by government agents from actual records rather than from questionnaires. Consequently, it appears that Mitchell chose the wholesale-price index because it contained what most observers would regard as "better data."

8. The semiannual wage data are reported for January and July of each year. The July observations are used on the grounds that they are a better match for the annual price data than either the January figures or an average of January and July. See ibid., p. 91, Table 30, for the price data. The wage data are from Mitchell, *A History of the Greenbacks*, p. 310, Table 30.

TABLE 2. *Consumers' prices, money wages, and real wages*

| Year | Prices | Wages | Real Wages |
| --- | --- | --- | --- |
| 1860 | 100 | 100 | 100 |
| 1861 | 104 | 99 | 95 |
| 1862 | 117 | 104 | 89 |
| 1863 | 140 | 119 | 85 |
| 1864 | 170 | 142 | 83 |
| 1865 | 179 | 155 | 87 |

In the 60's and, though in somewhat less degree, in the 70's, the labor market of the United States was one in which individual bargaining prevailed. Now the individual laborer is a poor bargainer. He is ignorant of the possibilities of his situation, exposed to the competition of others with the same disabilities, more anxious to sell than the employer to buy. Moreover, custom in the form of rooted ideas about what is a "fair wage" has a peculiarly tenacious hold upon the minds of both parties in the labor market, weakening the wage earner's aggression and strengthening the employer's resistance.[9]

Mitchell readily accepted the hypothesis that inflation accounted for the observed fall in real wages, with substantially no consideration of conditions other than monetary despite his protestation to the contrary.[10] Because of his failure to consider conditions other than monetary (i.e., "real forces"), Mitchell accepted an explanation of his observations that is inconsistent with the way economists explain changes in price ratios in markets other than labor. He rejected a standard explanation with a wide range of applicability in favor of an ad hoc explanation, without first showing the inapplicability of the standard explanation. It is the thesis of this paper that, if Mitchell had considered nonmonetary conditions more extensively, he would not have regarded his observations as unequivocally supporting the hypothesis that the observed fall was attributable to inflation. Indeed, there are grounds for inferring that the infla-

9. Mitchell, *Gold, Prices, and Wages Under the Greenback Standard*, pp. 275–76.

10. The factors other than monetary that Mitchell considered are: (1) the withdrawal of one-seventh of the labor force for war services; (2) more fully employed workers during the war than before the war started; and (3) a decline in the average quality of the labor force. Mitchell, *A History of the Greenbacks*, pp. 348, 350, 383, respectively.

tion resulting from the issuance of greenbacks led to a higher level of real wages than Mitchell would have observed in the absence of inflation.

Mitchell's real wage data and the observed fall in real rates of return to other agents of production can be explained as a consequence of three nonmonetary phenomena. These phenomena can be regarded as "real" forces, in the sense that the implications of their existence for real wages can be analyzed by the theory of relative prices as distinguished from monetary theory. These three forces are (1) the outbreak of warfare between the North and the South, which curtailed, if it did not eliminate, previous trading relationships; (2) the special economic characteristics of the base year, 1860; and (3) the tax system used to divert resources from the community to the government. All three of these phenomena operated jointly and independently of inflation to drive up the prices of goods and services relative to wages and other factor incomes generally during the Civil War. The remainder of this paper is concerned with the economic implications of these events.

## I. The Outbreak of Warfare

The outbreak of the Civil War almost completely destroyed the triangular trade relationship between the North, the South, and England. Before the war the North had an export surplus on current account in its trade with the South and a deficit with England, while the South had a surplus with England. Hostilities and the ensuing blockade forced all three parties into what must be presumed inferior trade relations, with a consequent loss in real income for all. In particular, the North was left with inferior markets for its exports and inferior sources for many commodities such as cotton and turpentine formerly imported from the South. Similarly, the South had to find new markets for its cotton and new sources for the manufactured goods and foodstuffs previously obtained from the North.

An examination of the relevant trade statistics leads to the conclusion that the outbreak of hostilities presented the North with what would be regarded, by modern standards, as an incredibly difficult balance-of-payments problem. Before the war, roughly two-thirds of all exports of goods and services for the entire country consisted of cotton.[11] This source of foreign exchange was, for all practical purposes, completely lost to the South and, hence, to the North. Moreover, Southern sources of cotton were in part replaced by imports of cotton from abroad. This implies not only that the North lost much of its power to earn for-

---

11. U.S. Dept. of Commerce, *Historical Statistics of the United States, 1789–1945*, p. 247, series M56-67 (1949); and Secretary of the Treasury, *Commerce and Navigation of the U.S.* (1859), and (1860).

eign exchange at the prewar exchange rate but also that its foreign-exchange "requirements" increased because foreign cotton in part replaced Southern cotton.

During the early years of the war the loss of foreign-exchange earnings resulting from decreased cotton exports was partly offset by extraordinarily large Northern wheat crops at a time when crops were short elsewhere in the world. Consequently, exports of wheat, particularly to England, increased sharply.[12] Wheat exports, as compared with prewar, increased by a factor of between four and five during the fiscal years 1861, 1862, and 1863.[13] Nevertheless, total wheat exports in each year represented less than one-fourth of the decline in the yearly value of cotton exports caused by the Northern blockade. Consequently, one would expect enormous deficits on current account for this reason and large exports of gold as a result.

The difficulties of the North with respect to its trade balance on current account were aggravated by capital flights during the early part of the war. Before the war the United States was normally a net importer of capital. This source of foreign exchange was lost during the early years of the war, and, in addition, many foreign investors converted their American securities into gold.[14] Net interest payments to foreigners declined by one-third between 1860 and the wartime low point (1863).[15] In part, these capital movements out of the country were offset by the sale of American-owned ships abroad.[16] Nevertheless, for the early years of the war, international capital movements intensified the North's balance-of-payments problems.

The problem of reconciling the reduction in the North's ability to pay for imports with its desires for imports was resolved by a measure undertaken to achieve quite another purpose. The suspension of specie payments was the consequence of the incompatibility between the issuance of greenbacks and the maintenance of convertibility of notes into gold at prewar exchange rates.

---

12. C. W. Wright, *Economic History of the United States* (1941), p. 530; and Mitchell, *A History of the Greenbacks*, p. 530. Fite says: "The largest increase in demand came from foreign countries, for in the three years 1860, 1861 and 1862 the harvests of Great Britain were a failure, and in one of the years those of all Europe" (E. D. Fite, *Social and Industrial Conditions in the North During the Civil War* [1930], pp. 17 et seq.).

13. U.S. Dept. of Commerce, *Historical Statistics*, p. 247. These are fiscal years ending on the last day of June.

14. D. R. Dewey, *Financial History of the United States* (12th ed., 1934), pp. 294–95.

15. F. D. Graham, "International Trade Under Depreciated Paper: The United States, 1862–79," *Q. J. Econ.* 36 (1922): 220, 231.

16. Ibid.

As a result, the North abandoned the gold standard at the end of 1861.[17] Gold became a commodity that was freely bought and sold without the government's taking a position in the gold market. Consequently, gold was released from some of its monetary functions, and the hoarding which had begun as a result of gold's undervaluation at the old exchange rate was reversed.

Abandonment of the gold standard, while the major trading countries of the world remained on this standard, made the price of foreign exchange a function of the price of gold, or, to use the language of the times, the premium on gold. Inconvertible fiat money, referred to popularly as "greenbacks" and officially as "United States notes," was issued as a means of war finance and became the currency of the times (except in California and Oregon). As a result, the price of gold as measured in greenbacks determined the cost of foreign exchange. The free exchange rate eliminated the development of foreign-exchange "shortages," and the magnitude of the foreign-exchange problem of the North was largely unrecognized both then and now.

After the abandonment of the gold standard, the price of gold rose relative to prices generally. This change in the real cost of gold (i.e., the increase in the cost of gold as measured by the exchange value of gold for goods and services generally) is crucial for sustaining two related propositions: (1) that Mitchell's wholesale-price index overstated the rise in prices because of the strong representation of internationally traded goods in the index, and (2) that nonmonetary forces played a role in reducing real wages as measured by Mitchell.

A rise in the price of gold relative to prices generally implies that the real costs of imports rose. Or, to put the matter another way, the amount of a typical export the North exchanged for a pound of pepper increased. This is equivalent to saying that the terms of trade turned against the North. However, inflation should not cause the terms of trade to change. Inflation, according to purchasing-power-parity theory, causes the money cost of foreign exchange to rise as the price level of domestic goods and services within a country rises relative to comparable price levels abroad. Consequently, the domestic prices of imports should increase *pari passu* with the general price level as a result of inflation.[18]

---

17. The departure from gold was precipitated by the so-called Trent affair. However, the run on the banks would not have been as severe as it was if notes had not been created as a means of war finance. And, in any case, suspension was inevitable if greenbacks were to be issued as they, in fact, were. See Mitchell, A History of the Greenbacks, pp. 37 et seq.

18. During an inflation that was generally anticipated, i.e., one in which the real value of the nominal stock of money fell and velocity rose, and the interest rate reflected the

Any increase in the domestic price of imports beyond what is implied by purchasing-power-parity theory reflects the operation of nonmonetary forces. Changes in the prices of domestic goods vis-à-vis corresponding foreign price levels reflect the increase in the greenback cost of gold attributable to inflation. The rise in the price of gold beyond that attributable to the inflation is to be ascribed to nonmonetary or "real" forces.

As a practical matter, foreign price levels can in this instance be represented by English prices, since most of American foreign trade was with England. Therefore, the ratio of United States to English domestic prices can be used as an indicator of how much the exchange rate (i.e., the price of gold) should have risen as a result of the issuance of greenbacks. And the difference between the rise in the price of gold predicted by purchasing-power parity and the actual price of gold is imputable to noninflationary forces.

Fortunately, at that time English prices and price ratios were relatively stable. Therefore it is of little consequence whether a wholesale or a consumers' price index is used. This is borne out by calculations of purchasing-power parity based on the Wood (consumers') and Sauerbeck (wholesale) price index.[19] If there had been less stability, then the Wood index would be better. It

---

future course of prices, there are reasons for expecting the exchange rate to increase more than the price level. The evidence presented by Mitchell on the behavior of interest rates during the Civil War suggests this inflation was largely unanticipated. See Mitchell, A History of the Greenbacks, pp. 367–68.

19. Cotton and wheat prices are exceptions and did change substantially. Wheat was relatively expensive around 1860 and 1861, and cotton rose dramatically in price during the latter years of the war. In large part the differences in weighting of these commodities account for the differences in the movements of the two indexes. This leads one to suspect that the Wood index overstates the fall in English domestic prices and that the Sauerbeck index overstates the rise in prices and that, on the whole, English domestic prices were stable. See G. H. Wood, "Real Wages and the Standard of Comfort since 1850," J. Royal Stat. Soc. 72 (1909): 91; and Sauerbeck, "Prices of Commodities and the Precious Metals," J. Royal Stat. Soc. 49 (1886): 581.

| | Sauerbeck | Wood | | Sauerbeck | Wood |
|---|---|---|---|---|---|
| 1857 | 105 | 119 | 1863 | 103 | 107 |
| 1858 | 91 | 109 | 1864 | 105 | 106 |
| 1859 | 94 | 107 | 1865 | 101 | 107 |
| 1860 | 99 | 111 | 1866 | 102 | 114 |
| 1861 | 98 | 114 | 1867 | 100 | 121 |
| 1862 | 101 | 111 | | | |

is strongly weighted by rents and includes marketing costs in bringing goods from the wholesale to the retail level. Both classes of services are unambiguously noninternational. The results of these calculations are summarized in Table 3. For the United States the consumers' price index computed by Ethel Hoover with the Weeks data is used in preference to Mitchell's consumers' price index.[20] It is decomposed to show the relative price movements of imports, international goods, and domestic goods. (See Figure 1.)

The greatest discrepancy between purchasing-power-parity exchange rates and actual exchange rates occurred in 1864, when real wages were at their lowest (see Table 3). And this was the time when grumbling about the cost of living was loudest:

> There was indeed much grumbling over high prices, especially toward the end of the period, which must not be mistaken for direct dissatisfaction with government exactions. The spirit was most pronounced when the premium on gold was highest, in the summer of 1864, and when, consequently, the war was coming home to the people every day through high prices.[21]

Similarly, the second largest discrepancy occurred in 1863, when the fall in real wages ranked second in severity. And, of course, the differences between purchasing-power parity and actual exchange rates are in the right direction. The exclusions of internationally traded goods from the Hoover index suggest that a rise in the prices of internationally traded goods, imports in particular, which was not compensated for by a decline in other prices accounted for most of the observed fall in real wages during these two years. This is precisely what

---

20. A mimeographed and unpublished manuscript by E. D. Hoover, "Prices in the United States in the 19th Century," Conference on Research in Income and Wealth, National Bureau for Economic Research, Sept. 4, 5, 1957, is the source of this index. In principle it is better than Mitchell's CPI because it uses more of the available data and better techniques for accounting for lapses in the data. Actually there is very little difference in the final result:

|  | Mitchell | Hoover |  | Mitchell | Hoover |
|---|---|---|---|---|---|
| 1860 | 100 | 100 | 1863 | 140 | 140 |
| 1861 | 104 | 101 | 1864 | 170 | 177 |
| 1862 | 117 | 114 | 1865 | 179 | 176 |

21. Fite, op. cit., p. 136.

TABLE 3. Exchange rates implied by purchasing-power parity compared with actual exchange rates and real wages

| | (1) | (2) | (3) | (4) | (5) | (6) | (7) | (8) | (9) | (10) |
|---|---|---|---|---|---|---|---|---|---|---|
| Year | Actual exchange[a] | Real wages[b] | England consumers' price index (Wood)[c] | England wholesale prices Sauerbeck index[d] | U.S. consumers' price index (Hoover)[e] | (5) ÷ (3) | (5) ÷ (4) | (5) ÷ (3)[f] | (5) ÷ (3)[g] | (5) ÷ (4)[h] |
| 1860 | Parity | 100 | 100 | 100 | 100 | 100 | 100 | 100 | 100 | 100 |
| 1861 | Parity | 98 | 103 | 99 | 101 | 98 | 102 | 98 | 97 | 99 |
| 1862 | 113 | 91 | 100 | 102 | 114 | 114 | 112 | 107 | 107 | 104 |
| 1863 | 145 | 85 | 96 | 104 | 140 | 146 | 135 | 128 | 126 | 119 |
| 1864 | 203 | 80 | 96 | 106 | 177 | 184 | 167 | 163 | 152 | 142 |
| 1865 | 157 | 88 | 96 | 102 | 176 | 183 | 172 | 167 | 157 | 153 |

[a] Mitchell, Gold, Prices, and Wages Under the Greenback Standard, p. 4.

[b] These are the July wage data taken from variable weight column of Mitchell, A History of the Greenbacks, p. 310, Table 30, and the Hoover price data, Hoover, op. cit.

[c] Wood, op. cit., p. 91.

[d] Sauerbeck, op. cit., p. 581.

[e] Hoover, note 20, infra.

[f] Imports are excluded from the Hoover index.

[g] Internationally traded goods are excluded from the Hoover index.

[h] Internationally traded goods are excluded from the Hoover index.

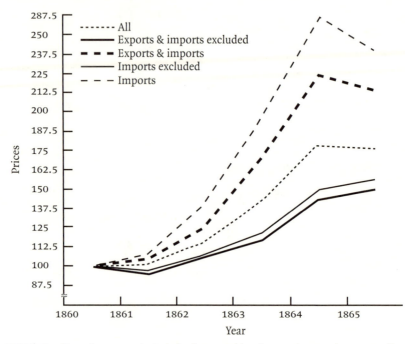

**FIGURE 1.** Hoover's consumers' price index decomposed into imports, imports plus exports, all except imports, and all except imports and exports.

would be expected if one argued that adverse movements in trade terms lowered real incomes.

The change in the relative prices of internationally traded goods may be seen more clearly by examining the relative movements of the import and domestic goods components of Mitchell's wholesale price index (see Figures 2 and 3). Imports at wholesale are "purer" international goods than the same commodities at retail, because of differences in domestic marketing costs. Consequently, these relative price movements are more pronounced if wholesale rather than retail prices are observed. If Mitchell's wholesale-price index is divided into four categories—exports, imports, domestic goods, and unclassified goods—it is very clear that the prices of internationally traded goods rose relative to domestic goods when the gap between the purchasing-power-parity exchange rate and the actual exchange rate was widening. Conversely, when the gap between the two exchange rates narrowed, the spread between domestic and import prices narrowed.

Mitchell's observations, however, are far from fully explained. In 1865 real

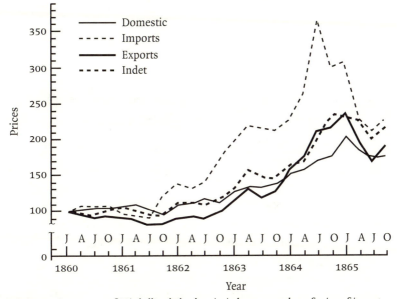

**FIGURE 2.** Components of Mitchell's wholesale-price index: mean values of prices of imports, exports, and domestic and indeterminate goods.

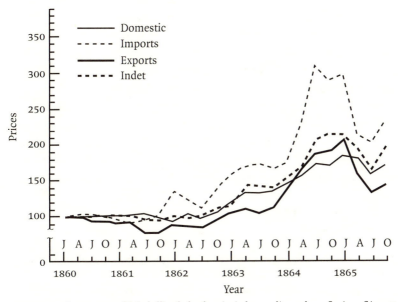

**FIGURE 3.** Components of Mitchell's wholesale-price index: median values of prices of imports, exports, and domestic and indeterminate goods.

wages were lower than they were in 1860, although, with the given premium on gold, purchasing-power-parity theory implies that they should have been roughly identical. Similarly, the prices of imports should have been lower in 1865 in order to reflect the absence of a discrepancy between purchasing-power parity and actual exchange rates. The answer to these problems turns on two independent phenomena, the special characteristics of the base year, 1860, and the tax system used for financing the war.

## II. The Base Year for Mitchell's Calculations

The fiscal year that started in July 1860 was a very remarkable one in many respects. It was the only such year between 1850 and 1877 that the United States was a net importer of gold. Mitchell observed that sterling was selling at a discount in New York during part of this year, which is what one would expect if gold were being imported.[22] An inflow of gold, for a country on a gold standard, can be rationalized as the result of a fall in internal prices relative to the rest of the world. This implies an increase in exports and a fall in imports. An alternative to this explanation was used by Mitchell. He argued that the inflow of gold was a consequence of a depression at home which reduced the flow of imports with little effect on exports.[23] Part of Mitchell's explanation of this depression was the failure of Southerners to pay Northern creditors, which caused some business failures and a worsening in general business conditions.[24]

Neither of these interpretations of events can be justified by the movements of the well-known price indexes of the time or by data reflecting the international trade of the time.[25] The deficit on current account for fiscal 1860–61 increased by a factor of three over the previous year.[26] Moreover, the widening of the trade gap on current account is primarily, although not wholly, attributable to a decline in reported exports. Clearly, part of the reason these gold imports are not explained by either of these hypotheses is that the trade data are internally consistent only if one assumes that there was an extraordinarily large inflow of capital during this year. Simon and Graham both estimate international

22. Mitchell, *A History of the Greenbacks*, p. 22.

23. Ibid., pp. 21–22.

24. Mitchell seems to have overestimated the importance of the recession in explaining the inflow of gold and underestimated the role of the special conditions in the wheat market. According to Thorp, business conditions were much worse in 1858, and yet there was a substantial gold outflow that year. See W. L. Thorp, *Business Annals* (1926): 127.

25. U.S. Dept. of Commerce, *Historical Statistics*, pp. 232, 234–35.

26. Ibid., p. 244.

capital movements from the balance-of-payment statistics for the time. For fiscal 1860–61 Graham simply has an unexplained excess of debits over credits of about $90 million, which represents about one-third of total credits.[27] Simon obtained capital flows as a residual after estimating gold flows and trade of all kinds on current account. His estimate of a $100 million capital inflow for the year exceeds the inflow for the peacetime years of 1865 and 1866.[28]

However, it is difficult to accept such estimates for the year in which the Civil War began. This year can be characterized as one in which it was widely recognized that the country was at the brink of war. This circumstance would hardly appeal to English and Continental investors. A rereading of the available evidence suggests, if anything, that there was a net outflow of capital during this year. Fiscal 1861 ended about two and a half months after the firing on Fort Sumter. The blockade of Southern ports was proclaimed on April 19, 1861. Southern states were seceding from the Union during the preceding winter. With the secession of these states, in particular Louisiana, reports of what was going into and coming out of Southern ports were no longer sent to Washington. As a result, Southern exports, which for all practical purposes may be regarded as cotton, were grossly understated in the Commerce and Navigation publications issued by the government in Washington. These official trade statistics report exports of about $40 million of cotton.[29] Yet available evidence suggests that about $190 million of cotton was in fact exported. Since cotton is harvested in the fall, there was plenty of time to ship the cotton crop of 1860 before the blockade of 1861. Hunt reported that cotton exports in physical terms for 1861 had declined only 20 percent from the previous year.[30] When price differences are taken into account, there was almost no fall in value. This interpretation is supported by data reflecting imports and stocks of cotton in England, which at the time was receiving over 80 percent of her cotton from the United States.[31] These cotton exports, combined with an increase in the exports

27. Graham, op. cit., p. 231.

28. M. Simon, "Statistical Estimates of the Balance of International Payments and the International Capital Movements of the United States, 1861–1900," Conference on Research in Income and Wealth, 1957, p. 116, Table 27.

29. Secretary of the Treasury, *Commerce and Navigation of the U.S.* (1863): 6.

30. *Merchant's Magazine & Comm. Rev.* (Hunt's) 45 (1861): 498. See also J. L. Watkins, *Production and Price of Cotton for One Hundred Years*, United States Department of Agriculture (1895), p. 11.

31. *Merchant's Magazine & Comm. Rev.* 45 (1861): 10, reports that stocks in Liverpool were about 10 percent smaller in April 1861 than in April of the preceding year. The pre-

of grain of about $40 million, resulting from our abundant crops and unusually small crops abroad, explain the bulk of the gold inflow. It is true that imports into Northern ports decreased somewhat during this fiscal year, but this decrease may have been more than offset by unreported increases in imports into Southern ports. Some imports that normally were shipped into the North were instead shipped directly to the South. And the South probably imported larger quantities than usual in anticipation of hostilities and the blockade.

The calendar year 1860 is labeled by Thorp as "Prosperity: Recession," with the "slackening" coming late in the year. This recession continued into the fall of the following year and gave way to a rapid revival of business activity.[32] The recession in 1861 was associated with a large number of business failures resulting from the unwillingness of Southerners to remit to Northern creditors.[33] Thorp also characterizes 1860 as a foreign-trade boom year. Given the high world prices for wheat that prevailed at this time, this evidence, considered in conjunction with the extraordinary gold inflows, implies that 1860 was a year when the terms of trade were relatively favorable for the country.[34] This favor-

------

ceding year's crop was the largest pre–Civil War cotton crop on record. This report is confirmed by English sources. Arnold wrote: "There was a larger supply of cotton in England, than there had been for years previous to this time. The increasing probability of hostilities in America had induced the shippers of the Southern states to bring forward the crop of 1860 with unusual haste; and before the end of May 1861 the imports from America for the five months of the year amounted to 1,650,000 bales—a supply largely exceeding the total importation from the same source during the whole year of 1857." R. A. Arnold, *The History of the Cotton Famine* (1864), p. 43.

32. Thorp, op. cit., p. 127.

33. See Mitchell, *A History of the Greenbacks*, p. 21, especially note 5. The evidence on this point is not unambiguous. McCulloch, who was president of the Bank of Indiana and subsequently Secretary of the Treasury, reports: ". . . I cannot forbear to refer to the action of the New Orleans banks towards their Northern correspondents at the outbreak of the civil war. The Southern branches had large dealings with men who were engaged in the Southern (Mississippi) trade, and when measures were being instituted for the secession of Louisiana from the Union, and, indeed, after the ordinance of secession had been adopted, these branches had large cash balances and large amounts of commercial paper in the New Orleans banks. Against the remonstrances of the secession leaders, and in disregard of threatened violence, these cash balances and the proceeds of the commercial paper as it matured were remitted for according to directions—not a dollar was withheld." H. McCulloch, *Men and Measures of Half a Century* (1888), pp. 138–39.

34. For the prices of wheat in England, see Fite, op. cit., p. 18; and Wood, op. cit., p. 91.

able development is by and large attributable to the extraordinary output and prices of wheat that occurred and should not normally be expected to recur. Consequently, real wages as measured by Mitchell, particularly with respect to imports, were abnormally high during this year. These considerations suggest that the real wage level measured by Mitchell in 1860 was higher than the level that normally could be sustained.[35]

### III. The Tax System Used to Finance the Civil War

Three means of war finance, important because of their implications for real wages during the Civil War, are the use of excises, import duties, and the tax on money imposed by inflation. Excises and import duties grew in importance during the war years, with extension of coverage and increases in rates. In 1861 the Morrill tariff (under consideration in the House of Representatives before the war) was enacted. This tariff increased the cost of many imports, particularly iron and wool.[36] While this tariff was announced as a revenue measure, the heaviest duties were imposed on commodities produced in the United States, and revenue was in part sacrificed for protection.[37]

In 1862 a comprehensive system of excise taxation was enacted. Specific taxes were imposed on the production of iron, steel, coal, oil, paper, leather, and several other goods. A general ad valorem tax was imposed on manufacturing output. Import duties were also increased.[38] In 1864 all these taxes were once more increased and enlarged in scope.

> Every ton of pig-iron produced was charged two dollars; every ton of railroad iron three dollars; sugar paid two cents a pound; salt, six cents a hundred weight. The general tax on all manufactures was five percent. But this tax was repeated on almost every article in different stages of produc-

---

35. This suggests that time series of real wages from 1858 or 1859 ought to be rising at an abnormal rate. This can or cannot be shown, depending upon which time series one chooses to employ. For a time series favorable to this interpretation, see Hansen, "Factors Affecting the Trend of Real Wages," *Am. Econ. Rev.* 15 (1925): 27, 32. The Federal Reserve Bank of New York and the Burgess cost-of-living indexes (*Historical Statistics*, p. 235, series L36–39) will also support such an interpretation. On the other hand, the Hoover index will not.

36. F. W. Taussig, *The Tariff History of the United States* (1923), p. 160.

37. Mitchell, *A History of the Greenbacks*, p. 9.

38. Taussig, op. cit., p. 163.

tion. Raw cotton, for instance, was taxed two cents a pound; as cloth it again paid five cents.[39]

Wells observed that, under the impact of these turnover taxes, "the government actually levied and collected from eight to fifteen and in some instances as much as twenty percent on every finished product."[40] The average rate on dutiable commodities, which had been 37 percent under the act of 1862, became 47 percent under that of 1864.[41] Indeed, import duties became so high in 1864 that collections from this source decreased relative to the preceding year as a result of smuggling.[42] The 5 percent tax on manufacturing imposed in 1864 was increased to 6 percent in 1865.[43] Needless to say, as a result of the imposition of these taxes, revenues from customs and internal revenue increased enormously over their prewar level (see Table 4).[44]

39. Ibid., p. 164. Taussig argues that increases in internal taxes were used to justify prohibitive tariffs. As a consequence, tariffs increased more than excises on internally produced goods.

40. D. A. Wells, *The Recent Financial, Industrial, and Commercial Experiences of the United States* (2d ed., 1872), p. 18. Another source reports: "Every product of the mill or factory was taxed at each turn of its manufacture, so that not infrequently an article bore a duty imposed twice, thrice, and even four times, before it reached the market. The system operated like a series of barriers, across which passage could be secured only by the payment of toll, which was re-enacted at every phase of the process of manufacture" (F. C. Howe, *Taxation and Taxes in the United States Under the Internal Revenue System, 1791–1865* [1896], pp. 155–56).

41. Taussig, op. cit., p. 167.

42. Mitchell, *A History of the Greenbacks*, p. 130.

43. Ibid., p. 268. By 1865, the tax system had broadened considerably. Gross receipts taxes of $2^1/2$ percent were imposed upon railroads, steamboats, canals, ships, barges, stage coaches, and canal boats. Ferryboats, toll bridges and roads, advertisements, telegraphs, and express companies paid 3 percent. Insurance companies paid $1^1/2$ and lotteries 5 percent. The deposits and capital of banks were taxed. Federal stamps were required for a wide variety of transactions involving legal instruments and the sale of proprietary articles. Sales of goods at auctions and sales of stocks and bonds and foreign exchange were taxed. Licenses were required to enter many trades and professions as well as certain types of business enterprises. For a description of these taxes and a statement of the receipts derived from each tax category, see H. E. Smith, *The United States Federal Internal Tax History from 1861 to 1871* (1914), especially his tables in the appendix.

44. Mitchell, *A History of the Greenbacks*, p. 129. Total receipts include the issuance of greenbacks. It must be remembered that not all internal revenue came from excises. A

TABLE 4. *Receipts from custom duties and internal revenue (in millions of dollars and as a percentage of all receipts)*

|                   | 1861        | 1862        | 1863       | 1864         | 1865         |
|-------------------|-------------|-------------|------------|--------------|--------------|
| Customs           | $39.6       | $49.1       | $69.1      | $102.3       | $84.9        |
|                   | (61.4%)     | (10.1%)     | (9.8%)     | (10.9%)      | (7.1%)       |
| Internal revenue  | 0           | 0           | $37.6      | $109.7       | $209.5       |
|                   |             |             | (5.3%)     | (11.7%)      | (17.5%)      |

It is evident that these excises and import duties diverted resources from consumers to the government and raised the prices of all goods and services relative to factor incomes. These excises were to a great extent turnover taxes and as such became imbedded in the prices observed by Mitchell in the latter years of the war. As a consequence, taxation operated to widen whatever divergence existed between the value of final output and the sum of the payments to the cooperating agents of production. This means that some of the fall in real wages Mitchell observed resulted from custom duties and excises and would have taken place whether or not inflation occurred during the Civil War.

As a result of the extensive use of turnover taxes, real wages as measured by Mitchell ought to have fallen, even if the foreign-exchange rate were equal to the rate implied by purchasing-power parity. Consequently, the level of real wages observed in 1865 ought to be below that of 1860, by an amount greater than the differential attributable to the abnormally high real wages in 1860. This comprehensive system of excise taxation taxed imports much more heavily than it taxed goods produced in the United States, and imports as a class were therefore forced up in price relative to domestically produced goods and services. The fall in real wages attributable to taxation should be concentrated upon internationally traded goods, and this appears to be the case. Or this is why, at the end of the war, the prices of imports were high relative to domestic goods, despite equality between the exchange rate implied by purchasing-power parity and the actual rate.

---

general income tax was imposed in 1862 and was raised in 1864 to 5 percent on moderate incomes and 10 percent on incomes of more than $10,000. See Taussig, op. cit., p. 164. About 20 percent of all internal revenue receipts were from income taxes in 1864 and about 15 percent in 1865. See E. Young, *Special Report on the Customs-Tariff Legislation of the United States* (1874), p. 136.

The inflation associated with the Civil War in the North was caused by a government-imposed tax on cash balances. Through the exchange of greenbacks for real resources, the government progressively reduced the real value of a unit of currency, and the rising prices that resulted imposed economic losses upon money holders. But if inflation had not occurred, and if real expenditures by the government had not been reduced, then alternative taxes would have had to be employed. If the inflation tax on cash balances were replaced by a tax on income or wealth, then Mitchell's real wage measurements would be unaffected. On the other hand, if the alternative tax were higher tariffs or turnover taxes, then a greater fall than Mitchell measured is implied.[45] If turnover taxes or higher tariffs are regarded as the alternatives to taxing through inflation, the Civil War inflation kept the real wages measured by Mitchell from falling more than they in fact did. Therefore, a rationale exists for a conclusion that is the converse of Mitchell's—were it not for the inflation, he would have found that real wages would have fallen more than they did.

The analysis contained in this paper constitutes an alternative explanation that is better than Mitchell's interpretation of these data in at least two senses: (1) It explains why the fall in real wages was greater with respect to internationally traded goods than it was with respect to domestic goods. The wage-lag hypothesis implies that there ought to be no difference between the fall in real wages with respect to the two classes of goods. Consequently, the interpretation of events presented here constitutes, at least in this respect, a fuller explanation of Mitchell's observations. (2) The interpretation presented in this paper is consistent with the analysis used by economists to explain similar changes in price relationships in markets other than labor. And, in general, the hypothesis which explains a wider range of phenomena is to be preferred.

However, a word of caution is in order. It is possible that the destruction of prewar trading relationships, the rise in the premium on gold relative to prices, and the excises and import duties could have so affected factor incomes that the returns to labor did not decrease *pari passu* with the fall in the sum of all factor

---

45. This analysis is based on the premise that the inflation associated with the Civil War was largely unanticipated. This seems to have been the case, judging by the behavior of interest rates. Consequently, the losses of the money holders were negative profits in the Knightian sense and never became part of the cost of doing business during this time. In the case of an inflation such as the one following World War I in Germany, these costs do become anticipated, and both excises and taxing through inflation will lower Mitchell-type measurements of real wages.

incomes.[46] All the preceding analysis has assumed that what happened to real factor incomes also happened to real wages. The analysis presented here has not included the effects of the change in the composition of the final output of the economy on the real demand for labor. Nor have we considered the impact of the mobilization of manpower for the armed forces, the influx of new migrants into the United States during the concluding years of the war, or the damage to Northern resources imposed by Southern armed forces, upon the supply of labor.[47] A more complete analysis might still find that there was some lag of wages behind prices to be explained by monetary forces. Alternatively, it might reinforce the argument presented here, or indicate that both explanations have a role to play in interpreting Mitchell's data. However, in the absence of such a demonstration, and in view of the preceding evidence, it appears that Mitchell's conclusion—that "all of the statistical evidence that has been presented in the preceding pages supports unequivocally the common theory that persons whose incomes are derived from wages suffer seriously from a depreciation of the currency"[48]—cannot be sustained.

In summary, the fall in real wages observed by Mitchell can be explained by the kind of analysis appropriate to the analysis of changing price relationships in other markets. An ad hoc theory is unnecessary. This fall in real wages can be rationalized as a consequence of the extraordinary level of real wages in the base year, 1860, the rise in the price of foreign exchange relative to domestic prices and wages, and the tax system used to finance the war.[49] Most of the fall in 1865 relative to 1860 is attributable to the tax policy used to finance the war.

46. The principles affecting the real returns to labor as a result of changes in import duties may be found in Stolper and Samuelson, "Protection and Real Wages," *Rev. of Econ. Studies* 9 (1941): 58.

47. Migration into the United States seems to have been at a low ebb during the early years of the war and increased toward its end. In this respect, the movements of human and nonhuman capital seem to be alike. In *Historical Statistics*, p. 34, immigration, by fiscal year, is shown as:

| Year | Immigrants | Year | Immigrants |
|------|-----------|------|-----------|
| 1859 | 121,282 | 1863 | 176,282 |
| 1860 | 153,640 | 1864 | 193,418 |
| 1861 | 91,918 | 1865 | 248,120 |
| 1862 | 91,985 | 1866 | 318,568 |

48. Mitchell, *A History of the Greenbacks*, p. 347.

49. The recognition of the implications of excise taxes for the relationship of wages and other factor incomes to prices is of some contemporary interest. Our present con-

The extraordinary characteristics of the 1860 base ought to be assigned minor responsibility. In the year 1864 the fall in real wages was greatest, and so, too, was the discrepancy between purchasing-power-parity exchange rates and the actual rate. This analysis suggests that at least half of the fall in that year was attributable to the relative rise in the foreign-exchange rate and that taxes and the properties of the 1860 base account for the remainder.

## Appendix

The practical problem of determining which of the 90 commodities in Mitchell's wholesale-price index ought to be regarded as internationally traded involved a number of arbitrary decisions. Graham, working with a series composed of 92 commodities taken from Mitchell's *Gold, Prices, and Wages Under the Greenback Standard* and in large part the same as the series used for Mitchell's real wage computations, classified 14 of the 92 as import, 18 as export, 42 as purely domestic, and 18 as indeterminate.[50] Graham, incidentally, was also concerned with the movements in the prices of internationally traded goods relative to all prices. The time period of concern to Graham began in 1866. The series used in *A History of the Greenbacks* contained several commodities which did not enter into Graham's series, and conversely.

Using the information provided by Graham, who unfortunately failed to list specifically the commodities in each of his categories, and (1) allowing for the differences between the series used in *A History of the Greenbacks* and by Graham, (2) taking account of the differences in time periods which would change the classification of some commodities such as cotton and turpentine, (3) using whatever clues provided by Graham as to his classification procedure, and (4) employing the Commerce and Navigation reports of the time, the classification of export, import, domestic, and indeterminate shown in Table A was obtained.[51]

Mitchell, to obtain his 90 commodity series, started out with a list of 135 and winnowed them down to 90 by averaging closely related commodities in

---

sumers' price index reflects state sales taxes, import duties, manufacturers' excises, and property taxes upon dwellings. Insofar as these taxes rise in real terms, as a result of our desire to allocate more resources to governmental activities, real wages, as measured by the ratio of wages to the consumers' price index, will fall. If instead income taxes are increased and these taxes correspondingly decreased, real wages will rise.

50  Graham, op. cit., p. 250.

51.  Graham regarded cotton, textiles, furniture, glass, metals, paper, pottery, tanneries, and wool textiles as export industries. Lumber and hides, fish, flesh, and fowl were in the indeterminate category. Ibid., pp. 249–50, 268.

TABLE A

| Export | Import | Domestic | Indeterminate |
| --- | --- | --- | --- |
| 1. Wheat | 1. Coffee | 1. Beef | 1. Flaxseed |
| 2. Tobacco | 2. Nutmeg | 2. Mutton | 2. Rye flour |
| 3. Ship biscuit | 3. Pepper | 3. Pork | 3. Salt |
| 4. Alcohol | 4. Cotton | 4. Eggs | 4. Bichrom of potash |
| 5. Dried apples | 5. Jute | 5. Bread | 5. Brimstone |
| 6. Butter | 6. Quinine | 6. Cement | 6. Blue vitriol |
| 7. Lard | 7. Silk | 7. Chestnut lumber | 7. Castor oil |
| 8. Glass | 8. Zinc spelter | 8. Hemlock | 8. Linseed oil |
| 9. Tables | 9. Opium | 9. Pine lumber and boards | 9. Muriatic acid |
| 10. Cheese | 10. Sugar | 10. Starch | 10. Oxide of zinc |
| 11. Corn | 11. Turpentine | 11. Brick | 11. Sugar of lead |
| 12. Mercury | 12. Currants | 12. Corn starch | 12. Sulfuric acid |
| (quicksilver) | 13. Tinplate | 13. Codfish | 13. Coal: anthracite |
| 13. Rye | 14. Raisins | 14. Vegetables | 14. Coal: bituminous |
| 14. Barley | 15. Rubber | 15. Pails | 15. Matches |
| 15. Oats | 16. Lead | 16. Tubs | 16. Lime |
| 16. Chairs | 17. Alum | 17. Harness leather | 17. Spruce |
| 17. Corn meal | 18. Soda ash | 18. Timothy seed | 18. Butts |
| 18. Tallow | 19. Copperas | 19. Hides | 19. Copper |
| 19. Candles | 20. Carpets | 20. Putty | 20. Iron wire |
| | 21. Molasses | 21. Rifle powder | 21. Shovels |
| | | 22. Beans | 22. Wood screws |
| | | 23. Clover seed | 23. Rope |
| | | 24. Soap | |

order to avoid duplication. These 90 were not specifically listed as such. By following Mitchell's directions, this same base of 135 was reduced to 87 here.[52]

In Hoover's consumers' price index, the commodities classified as import were rice, tea, coffee, sugar, molasses, and all cotton and wool materials. These constituted 22.6 percent by weight of all commodities in the index. The exports were wheat flour, rye flour, corn meal, butter, cheese, and lard and constituted, again by weight, 16.6 percent.

52. For Mitchell's directions for winnowing, see *A History of the Greenbacks*, pp. 248–57. The difference between these results and Mitchell's, and this is only a guess, is attributable to two series for beef and one each for zinc spelter and mercury (quicksilver). These are represented by three commodities in the series presented here.

# 5

## PRICE CONTROLS

# REVIEW OF THE COUNCIL OF ECONOMIC
# ADVISERS' 1972 REPORT
## A COMMENT

*The freeze slowed down the rate of inflation dramatically. . . . More than a
decade of balance-of-payments deficits had built up an overhang of obligations and
distrust which no longer left time for the gradual methods of correction which had been
tried earlier. . . . The freeze was a great testimonial to the public spirit of the American
people. . . . The operation of the new control system of an economy without inflationary
pressure of demand holds out great promise of sharply reducing the inflation rate. . . .
We have imposed price and wage controls to assure that the expansion of demand does
not run to waste in more inflation but generates real output and real employment. . . .
We will persevere until the goal is reached, but we will not keep the controls
one day longer than necessary.*

These "thoughts of Nixon" (in the *Economic Report of the President* to the Congress) presage the analytic quality of the 1972 *Annual Report of the Council of Economic Advisers.*

The report, revealing little about analyses or advice to political authorities, however much that advice may have been ignored, is largely a self-serving recital, with assurance that anything is possible, or might have been responsible for this or that event, or might be useful. The scientific and analytic content (except for 15 pages in chapter 4) is dismal.

I could find not a single hint that any member of the council (past or present) opposed wage and price controls, nor that any proposed them. Instead, controls just became "necessary" in August, if we take the President literally. No one resigned in the face of that gigantic policy change; the rewards of office must be great indeed.

What made controls "necessary"? Unemployment had not fallen in the first half of 1971 as much as the council had expected. The rate of inflation, though decreasing, had not decreased with enough regularity to be "assuring" that it

Reprinted from *Journal of Money, Credit, and Banking* 4 (August 1972): 704–12, and is
reprinted by permission of Ohio State University Press.

was still declining. Yet this information was certainly available by July, when the administration troika, via Secretary Connally, assured us that wage and price controls would not be instituted. So, now the status of wage and price controls matches the currency devaluation credibility gap—the stronger and more frequent the official denials, the surer and quicker the event.

The council asserts that the controls will reduce—and have reduced—expectations of inflation. "The price-wage controls were meant to be emergency expedients required in a particular historical context but expected to fade away, leaving no permanent change in the system except the eradication of inflationary expectations."[1] What is "expected" to fade away—the historical context, the controls, or inflationary expectations? Other felicitous convenient ambiguities will plague the careful reader. (I cannot resist quoting the next sentence—"The suspension of convertibility, on the other hand, signalled the determination of the United States to achieve a permanent reform of the international monetary system." Is a new set of pegged exchange rates a reform? Does anyone want a small bet the reform will be less permanent than wage-price controls?)

But three pages later, from the necessity of wage-price controls, the argument moves to doubts. "And although the character and operation of the price-wage control system give grounds for confidence, it must be recognized that there is little relevant precedent for predicting its effects." (As a matter of fact there is plentiful relevant precedent for predicting many, if not all, of its effects.) Once the doubts are admitted, they flood the discussion. "The possibility that the rise of the economy and the decline of unemployment might lag behind the estimates made today calls for readiness to take additional steps if this should turn out to be the case." (Such as not engaging in the greater expansive fiscal actions recently announced?) "If excess demand is avoided, the control system can help to break the habitual or contractual repetition of large price and wage increases that keeps inflation going." (If one doesn't cut off his leg, the doctor can help stop the bleeding that causes death.) "It can generate the *expectation* of reasonable price stability that is essential to the *achievement* of reasonable price stability. And as that happens it will be possible to eliminate the controls." Not even a mediocre editor would permit such a change of mode of verbs from possibility to actuality. (But will it happen—"it" meaning both the expectation of price stability and the abandonment of the controls?) "How

---

1. *Economic Report of the President together with the Annual Report of the Council of Economic Advisers*, Washington, 1972, p. 24.

soon that can be done will have to be determined in the light of experience." (In light or in darkness, it's all the same if one has no theory or if he has several inconsistent ones.) Continuing, "One of the most common causes of the breakdown of price-wage control systems has been excess demand for goods and labor, which places upon the control system the burden of resisting market forces." (What else is a control system for? Isn't excessive demand also the reason for inflation?) "The control system which has been established is meant to assist market forces that would be working to hold down inflation; it is not meant to resist market forces working to accelerate inflation." (Political forces to monetary expansion are, of course, irrelevant.)

All this is topped off by the suggestion that when the inflation and its consequences are finally eradicated, questions will remain of whether there are persistent structural characteristics of the American economy that make inflation inevitable—a question to which the council promises to turn next. Would it not be better to ask if there are persistent characteristics of *every political* system that make a policy of inflation inevitable? Of course, I have been pedantic in taking the President's letter literally when it says controls will not be kept one day longer than *necessary*. If that were true, the controls never need have been instituted. Would it not be better to ask if there are persistent characteristics of every political system such that, having created inflation, it solemnly pronounces the necessity of wage and price controls to prevent inflation?

Why then, really, were they instituted? What does the council say? The council asserts, in presenting the case against wage and price controls, that, first, they would not work with much effect or very long because their "success would require that powerful groups suspend the effort to reap the full advantage of their power." In any event, I don't understand that. Why should they not reap full advantage of their power? That power is not illegal or immoral. If it were, the administration should strike at that power, for those reasons rather conjure some presumed side effects of otherwise valid activity. Inflation is not the result of powerful economic groups reaping full advantage of their *market* power. Inflation is the result of an expansion in the money supply relative to demand. Did the council mean that *political* power was responsible, in that survival of politicians in office depended upon expansion of the money supply? Does the evidence support that contention? Did the council mean that unions asking for higher wages would induce political authorities to expand the money supply to prevent unemployment at those new wages? If so, is the council assuming that fiscal policy without money expansion would be effective in expanding general demand? In either case, did the council decide that unemployment in response to such increases was political suicide, i.e., worse than open inflation as a means of reducing the real wages of those who had been able to obtain the higher money wages initially?

The second argument against controls adduced by the council is that they would interfere, at least if continued for very long, with "the efficiency of the economic system and might create an undesirable increase in the power of the government over its citizens." Might?

Against these two reasons, the council asserted five arguments for controls:

1. "Progress against inflation was disappointingly slow and the possibility of some kind of assistance from controls, even if temporary, could not be ruled out or discounted." "Disappointingly" is purely a function of one's own prior expectations. Does this really mean that if the council had earlier foreseen more accurately that the decrease in inflation would have taken two years rather than one year, it would have not opposed controls? Furthermore, was the council really as desperate as is suggested by the hope of "the *possibility* of *some* assistance from controls, even if temporary?" A national policy that relies on reeds like that is reassuring to no one, not even the Democrats.

2. "There *seemed* to be a large and growing sentiment in the country for *some* kind of incomes policy, and steps in that direction *might* relieve anxiety, strengthen confidence, and improve the economy. This sentiment also increased the *chance* of getting the kind of voluntary self-restraint required for success." What "voluntary self-restraint" does the "Council of Psychiatric Advisors" have in mind? This neurotic theory of inflation is a new one. It "might possibly," "temporarily" give "some assistance." It might, indeed, if one ignores the empirical evidence on inflations.

3. And to calm our nerves, the council assures us: "The Administration's *acute* consciousness of the pitfalls encountered in previous attempts *might* enable it to avoid, on the one hand, *premature* collapse of the control system, and on the other hand, its *unnecessary* prolongation." (The italics are mine and should speak for themselves.) May I not characterize that as hopeful psychiatric arrogance?

4. A fourth reason, though not listed as such, is the belief that the international situation required convincing action on the domestic front, presumably to reduce inflation. The experience of foreign countries with incomes policies makes it hard to see that wage-price controls would be interpreted as anything other than inability to control inflation.

5. The council alleged "a powerful, but temporary, price-wage control system" would permit "more expansive fiscal policy." The council report does not

explain the logic of that, probably because it would be difficult to find one. If a more expansive fiscal policy can be instituted without inflationary effects (no money supply increase?), why was it not done earlier to combat unemployment? If it does involve money supply expansion, then no room for such expansion was provided by wage-price controls—unless the council proposes to force people to hold more money by controlling expenditure via rationing. The council's assertion that there "could be no doubt that the tolerable rate of expansion had been increased" is doubtful. Is it hard to suppress as suspicion that a 5 to 2 dominance of arguments dictated controls?

"The basic premise of the . . . control system is that the inflation of 1970 and 1971 was the result of expectations, contracts, and patterns of behavior built up during the earlier period, beginning in 1965, when there was an inflationary excess of demand." Passing over those ambiguities, we find the next sentence. "Since there is no longer an excess of demand, the rate of inflation will subside permanently when this residue of the previous excess is removed." What is the "residue"? Try the next sentence. "The purpose of the control system is to give the country a period of enforced stability in which expectations, contracts, and behavior will become adapted to the fact that rapid inflation is no longer the prospective condition of American life. When that happens controls can be eliminated." The council really is a council of psychiatrists!

When will controls end? "The conditions now existing and the policies in operation are unprecedented. The only sensible course is to observe the behavior of the economy closely and to avoid commitment to either a minimum or maximum duration of controls." Of course! The goal is a "condition of the economy in which we can have a significantly lower rate of inflation without controls than we were experiencing in the first part of 1971. Speculation that the administration will abandon the controls prematurely out of fatigue, ideological aversion, or other causes is groundless. Having embarked upon this course, the administration has no intention of departing from it in circumstances where it would risk . . . resumption of inflation." Which means they would never be abandoned, for the risk of inflation is always present.

The preceding remarks reveal a basic difference between the understanding of economic processes and analysis by this reviewer and the propositions in the report. There is also room for dispute over statistical procedures and inferences. The council expressed alarm because it believed the indices in mid-1971 reflected a change in the rate of decrease of inflation and even a "possible" upturn in the rate. Yet, given the period-to-period variation and the quantity of alternative indices, one should not impute a trend or a change in trend to a couple of sequential observations, which is what the council did. My reading of the charts and data cited by the council (pages 42–47) does not and should not have heightened concern about inflation, unless one adopts a psychiatric theory of statistical inference. The rate of inflation had decreased since mid-1970, and it continued to decrease through August, 1971. The rate, given any extrapolation, would have fallen to below 3 percent by the end of 1972. What was there to suggest the decrease was not going to continue bringing the rate down from about 4 percent to 3 percent? Nothing, except that the monetary base and money stock was increasing at an abnormally high rate again! But the council makes no reference to that—to which there was a clear solution other than irresponsible advocacy of wage-price review boards and incomes policy by the Federal Reserve Board chairman, which smells of wage-price controls no matter how much it is spiced with words about "abuses of private power in our labor and product markets."

Controls are supposed to break inflation anticipations. How? By the firm pledge of the administration to prevent wage and price increases that would have required money supply expansion and consequent inflation if those initial higher wages were to be consistent with high employment? Or by suppressing prices when the money stock is increased while people remain in total ignorance of the cumulating money supply and shortages and non-price rationing? Is there any evidence that this has ever stopped inflation, or even the anticipation of inflation? That rhetorical question has a clear negative answer. Meanwhile, the money stock lurches upward at a rate consistent with continuing inflation.

The council has accepted both the excess demand from money supply expansion and the Galbraithian administered-price allegations as possible causes of inflation. Thus, the report asserts exclusions of small firms from price controls will enable the administration to concentrate attention on a few key sectors. "[The exclusions] may, in fact, make the system stronger and more durable by permitting the administrative effort to be concentrated on the sectors most significant for inflation. This is especially true when, as is often the case, price increases in the excluded sector would be effectively limited by competition from the parts of the economy that remain under legal control." These sentences provide a fine example of frequent careless transitions of passage from subjunctive to the indicative verbal mood. Perhaps it is churlish, though fun, to note that this passage is taken from the same page as the statement that the basic premise of the controls is the inflationary excess demand. There is also a suggestion that unions cause inflation, but there is nothing yet about middlemen causing inflation. (I'll offer a small wager that time will correct that last omission.)

Even if one believed the wage-price controls would restrain inflation, one has to suppress shock that in the face of a decreasing rate of inflation from 6 percent to no more than 4 percent in 1971, the administration imposed controls with the objective of getting the rate down to 3 percent by the end of 1972! All that for what would have happened anyway if the clear trend could be extrapolated? And if the rate would not have fallen below 4 percent, is the price-wage control cost worth a 1 percent reduction in the rate of inflation? In the kind of words of the council report, it "seems" to me that it "may, in fact" "possibly" not be worth that. In my words, "It is not," even, if for argument's purpose, we beg the question of whether it really would have any effect on the rate of inflation.

It might be countered that the unemployment rate was staying too high for too long and therefore motivated the decision to use wage-price controls in order to permit an expansionary fiscal policy. (With no money supply expansion?) The report states on page 69 the controls permitted a greater expansionary program without increasing the rate of inflation. I could find no explanation of just how that was supposed to happen. (Perhaps the author of p. 69 should talk to the authors of p. 108 and p. 27.) In any event, price data subsequently reported do not support the contention that controls have affected the rate of inflation, nor employment, except possibly for second-class economists.

Why is it desirable to reduce or change the *anticipated* rate of inflation? The well-established wealth transfers from net monetary creditors to net monetary debtors are those of incorrect (low) anticipations about rates of inflation. The evidence is strong that there is no wage lag. There is evidence that the rate of unemployment is independent of the correctly anticipated rate of inflation and dependent on incorrect anticipations. What then is the point of trying to reduce the anticipated rate? Was it an incorrect anticipation? Was it to prevent loss to net money creditors—those who formed their credit contracts prior to the onset of currently (Aug. 14) held anticipation—or was it to give a gain to those who formed contracts after those new anticipations? Which? It can't be both; there is no way to unscramble the eggs. Equity considerations do not tell what to do. The rationale has to rest on the desirability of some uniquely appropriate predictable rate—and presumably zero (or is it 2.5 percent?) is the best predictable rate, though, to the best of my knowledge, that has not yet been established.

Two arguments against a predictably positive rate of inflation are (1) the costs of making allowances for present versus future values (though such allowances are made even with a zero rate of inflation because interest is positive) and (2) the progressive income, or wealth, tax increases real tax collections and enhances increased government activity and wealth redistribution. These, so far as I know, are the principal (only?) significant arguments against correctly anticipated inflation—and the *second* is the only one worth trying to avoid by controls, *if* controls really had that effect, which they don't. Still, the administration apparently believes that something of importance will be achieved by reducing the actual (anticipated?) inflation from 4 percent to 2–3 percent per year. I wonder what?

To compound my misgivings, the "tocsin" index of prices is the wrong one for the value of nominal units of money. Current services predominate in the CPI, with only minor weight attached to durables. But asset prices are significant components of the value of money. The CPI, designed for wage earners and clerks, is insufficiently weighted with durable assets, like land, houses, commercial and industrial machines and buildings, which are purchased with money. If one includes an appropriately weighted set of durable goods prices, he will in fact be recognizing, as he should, that higher real interest rates mean lower current prices, for the higher real rate (not in anticipation of inflation) is a fall of the rate of inflation! Yet in fact, the exact opposite and erroneous interpretation is adapted by the people who stare at the CPI data. The value of money which is used for goods as well as for current services must, and does, depend upon asset prices and hence upon the interest rate in a way *reversed* from that usually and erroneously publicized. A higher real rate of interest is a reduction in the cost of life, or the purchasing power of nominal money. During the past year or two, with all the alarm about higher interest rates, has anyone determined whether house and durable goods prices were falling relative to current service prices? If they were, the value of the dollar was rising, and failure to adequately include such assets is to look at the wrong index—and if administration counsellors are thrown into panic by fractions of 1 percent gyrations in the rate of change of that index they are trying to read "noise" and in the *wrong* series! The council is not alone in this respect, but that is no consolation to all of us plagued with the consequences. Today we are amused at the Delphic oracles, followers of eagles' flights, and astrological diviners. Tomorrow, our descendents will do the same for us, but, I hope, with forgiveness.

Why are dividends restricted? Is the transfer of wealth or money from one pocket to another inflationary? Dividends are not prices, nor are they inflationary. Should restriction of dividends not be interpreted as a sop to what the administration "may" be inclined to regard as public opinion and understanding of inflation? The extent to which the report suggests that much of the price-wage control program is a sop to public opinion raises a conjecture the administration is confusing democracy with representative government. Are overriding regulatory agencies like the FDA and SEC and ICC and FCC and CAB to be regarded as experts, whereas the CEA and FRB assume that expert economic analysis is unavailable, irrelevant, or common knowledge to everyone?

The report sermonizes that the greatest contribution to the avoidance in the future of the kind of inflationary surge of demand that occurred after 1965 is to "keep alive the memory of our recent experience." What should be remembered in order to avoid the inflation? Memory of its consequences will not avoid the event. For inflation is not a cost to all people!

Chapter 4, "Effective Use of Resources," a refreshing contrast to the rest of the report, displays excellent analysis, frankness, and attempts to clarify issues without debilitating ambiguities. Energy, environmental quality research and development, transportation, and medical care are discussed. This chapter seems to be the product of the research staff of the council, while the other chapters resemble a political platform to extenuate whatever the administration does. The revealed willingness in this chapter to use a given theory as the basis for the analysis is the basic contrast with the preceding chapters. The not-so-veiled criticism of the Interstate Commerce Commission and the Federal Power Commission will not pass unnoticed. Since those two commissions are operated, like all other institutions, in no small accord with the interests of the commissioners, it is interesting to wonder why there seems to be a presumption that the other great "institution" underlying much of the first three chapters of the Report—the Federal Reserve Board of Governors—should be expected to operate differently than other governmental commissions. If the SEC, FCC, FPC, ICC, CAB, and FDA are interpreted as responsive to the industries they are designed to regulate (albeit insofar as that serves the interests of the commissioners), why exclude the FRB?

The fifth, and last, chapter is below the quality of the fourth chapter and is far superior to the first three in analytical content. But even here there are some puzzling features. In trying to explain the decline in the U.S. trade surplus, blame is placed on the poor relative price-cost performance of the U.S. But comparisons of unit labor cost in manufacturing between countries are beside the point. Even ignoring that labor costs are not the only cost components, the more rapid rate of inflation *coupled with fixed exchange rates* was the culprit. Yet the council report asserts the wage-price controls and the revaluation of foreign exchange rates relative to the dollar will increase the competitive position of the U.S. Why not add factors like the amount of snowfall in Vail, Colo., and the golf score of my next round, both of which are just as pertinent as the wage-price control program will prove to be?

"The basic goals of the founders of the Bretton Woods system were achieved to a high degree." That does not mean the Bretton Woods agreement contributed to that achievement of goals, though the council also elsewhere asserts that it does. Considering the number of "crises," emergency meetings, exchange rate changes, it is hard to know why the consequences were any better than if there had been no Bretton Woods and, instead, market-determined exchange rates. "The unprecedented progress for the world economy" instead of being an "impressive tribute" to the Bretton Woods agreement is an impressive tribute to ability of business people and individuals to progress despite the Bretton Woods agreement. If that remark seems churlish, so be it; but it serves to emphasize that "post hoc, ergo propter hoc" propositions are not substitutes for evidence.

"A secure payments position would require that this estimated $6 billion capital outflow be covered by a surplus on current account." Is security or profitability the relevant criterion? Does a commercial bank become more insecure the larger its demand deposits, or is it a better bank in providing better money? The so-called secure position turnaround of $13 billion is a delusion, pure and simple. Let the foreigners own as many American dollars as they want to; the more, the better. Except, of course, for the Federal Reserve Board of Governors, which then has to work a little more perceptively and responsibly.

If the council reports are to be reviews of the year, they should be so in a more objective and analytical fashion; they "should," for my preferences. But that, of course, is ridiculous. We have newspapers and journals doing it better. What the report does is comment on a few of the year's events, defend administration intentions and "will" to cure problems, curable or not, and, in the realm of employment and inflation, promise to look at future events "closely" with every theory or policy from which some possibility of assistance cannot be ruled out.

One last bark. Criticism of the report is not criticism of the council's work, which must be a very different thing, fortunately.

# AN INTRODUCTION TO CONFUSION

*A Time to Choose*—better titled *A Time to Confuse*—regrettably confuses energy and environmental issues, enters the *Guinness Book of World Records* for most errors of economic analysis and fact in one book, is arrogant in assertions of waste and inefficiency, is paternalist in its conception of energy consumption management, is politically naive, and uses demagoguery. That is a shocking indictment of a final Report of a $4 million project financed by the Ford Foundation. Let us see why it is deserved.

## Scenarios: Crystal-Ball Visions

What problems, according to the Report, call for political control? As a sample: "widening gap between energy consumption and domestic production," "growing dependence on foreign supplies," "energy shortages," "energy budget out of balance," "abrupt withdrawal of foreign supplies," "energy-environment crisis," "inefficient use of energy," "saving energy," "soaring prices," "ensure adequate supply," "independence of U.S. foreign policy" (pp. 2, 4, 8, 11)—enough? Cutting through the morass, we detected four events about which it is argued some political action presumably can or should be taken:

1. Increased imports of foreign energy.
2. Rising costs of energy.
3. Environmental effects not fully counted in market-revealed costs of energy.
4. Political miscontrol of energy.

The Report proposes three "scenarios" of 1975–2000; one, the first ("historical growth") assumes continued growth of energy use at the historical rate; the second ("technical fix") assumes energy use at about half the past rate, with adjustments in use responsive to higher price and value of energy with

Reprinted, by permission, from Morris Albert Adelman et al., *No Time to Confuse: A Critique of the Final Report of the Energy Policy Project of the Ford Foundation, A Time to Choose* (San Francisco: Institute for Contemporary Studies, 1975), 1–25.

presently known technologies for substitution of other materials and less energy-using activity; the third ("zero energy growth") projects a zero increase in energy use after 1985. All scenarios terminate at the century's end—a remarkably short horizon. The thesis is that once "we" understand the implications of these scenarios, "we" can better choose upon which to embark.

The Report commends the technical fix future, but recommends a zero energy growth because it is "desirable, technically feasible, and economical to reduce the rate of energy growth [to] 2 percent annually," and "provides benefits in every major area of concern, avoiding shortages, protecting the environment, avoiding problems with other nations, and keeping the real social costs as low as possible" (p. 325). In fact, it does none of those, as should have been evident to the authors.

The Report recommends a great debate to determine the future: "legal maneuvers, lobbying, propaganda and conflict of regional interests, public referenda, writing to Congressmen, making political contributions, writing letters to newspapers, attending meetings and generally raising their voices" (pp. 9, 11). In a word, as the authors themselves observe, politics.

The scenarios are, *at best*, worthless for identifying or understanding energy issues. Instead, they present some facts about energy uses and possibilities for adjusting to higher cost energy supplies—issues better understood outside the context of *any* presumed future path. The scenarios are neither predictions of the future nor accurate guidelines for achieving future goals. They are *imagined* future itineraries. In fact, of course, whether we experience faster, lower, or possibly negative energy growth depends upon yet-to-be-revealed costs and values of energy uses.

### Economic Analytic Errors

Unfortunately, the Report is inexcusably ignorant of economics—indeed, it is so fatally dosed with economic error, fallacy, and confusion at critical stages as to border on dishonesty.[1]

1. That so many distinguished economists, acknowledged as having served as advisers or as early members of the staff, would have so little effect on the final Report suggests refusal to have paid attention to them. They were reported to be Kenneth Boulding, Hendrik Houthakker, William Iulo, Walter Mead, Marc Roberts—a really excellent group of economists (plus, apparently, aid from the Brookings Institution). Economists of that calibre simply would not make the errors in the Report. Somebody else must have been responsible. It is professionally gratifying to a fellow economist that none are listed as members of the staff responsible for the final Report.

1. Needs: Singular or Plural?

A serious, fatal analytic error is the Report's too-frequent refusal to use the fact that the amount of energy demanded can, has been, and will be reduced by a higher price to match the supplies that are available at that price. A famous economic principle of demand is ignored in the Report: the principle that the amount of petroleum demanded depends on the *price* of petroleum. The lower that price, the more we "need," require, or demand. That the Report of a $4 million project would ignore such a well-established, powerful fact of life would be incredible were it not that so many politicians, bureaucrats, and even oil industry people also ignore or ignorantly deny it. A similarly powerful general proposition is that the amount supplied will be larger, the higher the price offered to sellers or producers.

These fundamental, inescapable propositions are shown graphically in the elementary demand diagram in Figure 1. As curve D (for *demand*) plainly shows, the amount of a good that is consumed, needed, required, or demanded depends on the price of the good. That "demand" curve slopes from the upper left to the lower right, suggesting a whole *series of alternative* amounts we "need," "require," or "demand," depending on the price. We have needs, requirements, demands—depending on the price. Anyone who ignores these facts of life is irresponsibly playing a dangerous and expensive game. He is increasing society's problems. The way he conceals those facts of life is to talk of a need or requirement as if it were a natural, unique, given quantity—independent of the cost or price of getting more. Such an intellectually bankrupt—though commonly held—conception is shown in Figure 2; "need-requirement-demand" is expressed as a vertical line, with price having no effect. The counterpart to this error is the notion of supply as a fixed amount, regardless of price. Then the difference between the two is, naturally, called a shortage or gap. And anyone who swallows that propaganda probably deserves the consequence: the espousal of political control over the consumer's use of the available supply by allocations, rationing, or political pressures in order to divert that supply to politically approved "needs."

In fact, the diagnosis is simply wrong, no matter how often it is repeated in the media by political aspirants, bureaucrats, and even some energy industry officials—who, of all people, should know better. The actual reason, as shown in Figure 3, surprisingly, that supply does not approach what people want to consume at the "market price" is that the price is kept too *low*. This is shown in Figure 3. If you think the price is too high at $10 a barrel, why did you not think it was too high at $3 a barrel? After all, $1 a barrel or even $.20 a barrel would

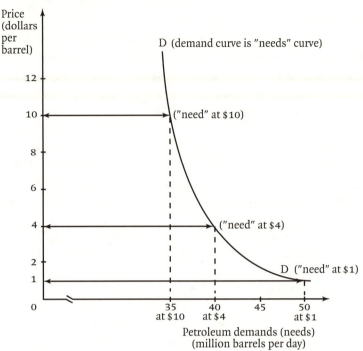

**FIGURE 1.** *Needs are variable, depending on price*

*Needs are really a range of petroleum uses not all equally valuable. The lower the price, the more petroleum we will put to our lower-valued uses. At a higher price, we will deem those lower-valued uses not worth achieving. They will no longer be in our "needs." Failure to understand that the variety of petroleum uses have different values leads some people to argue fallaciously that existing supplies will not cover our needs. They are saying all our current uses are of equal importance or value, that we do not regard some uses as more valuable than others; this is an incorrect conception, as illustrated by the simplistic fantasy theory graphed in Figure 2.*

be better and feasible—if there were so much oil that we could put it to such low-valued uses as would be worth only $.20 a barrel.

Today, like it or not, and whatever the reason—embargo, fewer resources, increased population, you name it—the amount of petroleum available to us is such that, as we progress down to its lower-valued uses, we still have unsatisfied uses worth on the margin as much as $10 a barrel. That is why the price of available petroleum is now $10 on the world markets. The issue of why we have only as much petroleum available to us as we do is another thing entirely. To fail to separate the two issues—how much oil is available and how much each extra barrel of petroleum is worth to us—is to lead the nation into confusion, not toward

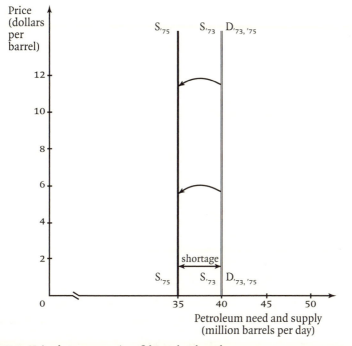

**FIGURE 2.** Naive, but common, view of demand and supply

*The vertical line of Demand, or Need, portrays the false conception that there is no ranking of alternative uses with some having lower values than others and that regardless of how costly it is to get petroleum we are incapable of deciding that some uses are less valuable than that cost and hence we will not curtail our demand or "need" for so much petroleum. This is the absurd model of human behavior and valuation of petroleum uses employed by people who talk about our "needs," "requirements," and basic necessities and wish us to believe that an increased market price will not bring about a voluntary revision in our uses to match the available supply at the higher equilibrating price, as portrayed in Figure 3.*

rational choice. And it is the demand curve that reflects the use value of extra barrels of petroleum. The less we have, the greater the value of a barrel of petroleum; the more that is supplied, the lower the value of the uses to which the extra oil is put.

Irresponsible talk about an oil or energy shortage leads the nation to confuse (1) the fact of a reduced supply of oil with (2) the fact of people using oil in some low-valued uses while other higher-valued uses are unfulfilled. Thus, the unfulfilled higher-valued uses provoke talk of shortages with regard to those uses. Why *do* we use some petroleum in the less valuable ways? The answer is clear and simple. We are told the "price" should be low; therefore, at that price,

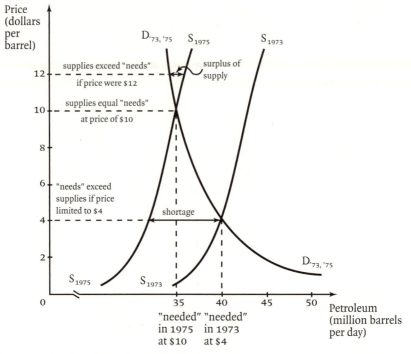

**FIGURE 3.** *Price rations out lower-valued uses*

At an open-market price, the amount "needed" or demanded is restrained along the demand curve to match available supply. Suppose marketed supplies were reduced—shown by the leftward-shifted supply line. If price within the U.S. is held below the $10 equilibrating price, shortages occur as people seek to satisfy lower-valued uses requiring more petroleum than is available. With a curtailed price, competition by queueing, political and arbitrary allocations, favoritism, and side payments will determine which claims will be denied. If price is allowed to rise to $10, individuals themselves decide which lower-valued uses are to be eliminated, so only higher-valued uses are satisfied by supplies. (The leftward shift in the supply line only crudely depicts the effect of an oil cartel's output restriction from existing sources by existing producers from existing fields. Also, the effects of higher price on discovery of new fields by other producers should be considered. Therefore, this diagram shows no more than the effect of an open-market price in changing our "needs" to match whatever supplies are available.)

we try to use the petroleum in ways that have use values as low as that artificially low price. In exactly the same way, too-low privately perceived energy costs (that do not include environmental effects) mislead us to abuse the environment—a factor rightly to be deplored.

Those low prices restrained (by domestic price controls) literally mislead us into trying to achieve such low-valued uses of oil, rather than restricting it to our higher-valued uses. Each of us is led to think, as if by a malicious devil, that oil is plentiful enough to satisfy those lower-valued uses. None of us is effectively impressed with the fact that the oil we use in those low-valued ways is of greater value to other people in other uses. Prices, as measures and signals that restrain and control the way we use petroleum or energy, are destroyed by such politically imposed price controls.

Seeing the damage wreaked by our attempts to use available petroleum wastefully, politicians complain that the market system of prices and free enterprise won't work—that it must be replaced by political controls. Indeed it must; break the horse's leg and then say it can't gallop. It is no accident that the strongest appeals for political action in the present situation are made by the strongest opponents of free-enterprise activity: those who would prefer to cripple the process of voluntary exchange through market prices, which might otherwise help us reserve petroleum for its highest-value uses.

The failure to perceive the fundamental distinction between (1) *schedules* of associated alternative possible amounts demanded or supplied at *alternative* prices, and (2) *a* particular amount demanded and *a* particular amount supplied at some one price leads the Report to other confusions. The word "shortage" is used to mean situations where prices rise because of increased demand *schedules* relative to a supply *schedule*. But it is also used to refer to a very different situation created by political controls on permissible price: where the amount *demanded* at that price exceeds the amount *supplied* at that price, because price is politically fixed below the open-market price. This *undervalued* price is the energy adjustment obstacle. That is a crucial part of our energy problem.

The battle lines are now drawn between politically ambitious people and those who would rely on a liberal society in which individuals can express, compare, and be guided by their individual use values relative to those of other people—the condition fulfilled by market exchange prices! The energy situation is one of the critical battlefields. The issues of the appropriate degree of environmental protection, Arab wealth, and foreign dependence have been transformed—wittingly or unwittingly—into smoke screens to hide the real field of battle.

### 2. Contrived vs. Natural Supply Change

A reduction in petroleum availability can result from either a naturally decreasing supply relative to demands or a government cartel or both. Each situation commands a different response. Unfortunately, though the Report discusses both, its recommended responses do not account for the differences involved. To recommend higher use taxes to *suppress energy uses*, where prices are rising in response to natural forces that reduce available supply, is to overkill. The higher market price *alone* is sufficient to restrict use and channel available energy to the highest-valued uses. To impose, in addition, taxes or mandatory controls over uses is to arrogantly assume that people *over*-value energy uses (as we are prone to assume they do for smoking, drinking, pornography, and gambling) and should be restrained even more than justified by the *true* costs of energy. This is the implication of conservation proposals directed to situations in which energy costs are rising because of decreasing relative supplies.

But if the price rise is caused by a *cartel* of producers who have banded together to restrict available petroleum, then sale by us to foreign governments of rights to sell oil in the U.S. market (not imposition of tariffs) would make more sense in liberal free society—as a means of taxing the monopoly rents of the cartel without raising domestic prices. This is a subtle issue, apparently too subtle for the Report. Indeed, it may be too subtle for political application, because it is too easily diverted to other objectives. Nevertheless, the Report should have considered the import quota sale tactic.

### 3. Efficiency: Technical or Social Cost?

The Report, incorrectly, focuses on technical instead of economic or social cost efficiency. Technical efficiency simply means minimizing the amount of *one* input per unit of output—number of towels used in the washroom per unit of gasoline produced in a refinery, or pounds of steel per automobile produced, or "this" input per unit of "that" output. But total *costs of all* inputs are pertinent, not just one component. No engineer or economist worth his salt seeks to minimize gasoline used per mile driven, or electricity or fuel oil per cubic foot of house kept warm—criteria which the Report repeatedly *does* employ in bewailing alleged inefficiency and waste of energy in the past. On the contrary, to use *less* energy in the past would have been wasteful; it would have meant sacrificing more of other useful and desirable things than the energy was worth. This broad, inclusive view of costs and values escaped the attention of the authors of the Report, despite correct statements in Appendix F, "Economic Analysis of Alternative Energy Growth Patterns, 1975–2000."

Ironically, this disastrous failure to acknowledge the totality of inputs and their costs rather than the physical amounts of one input (whose costs can always be reduced by increasing other costs) is cited in the Report as a criticism of *other* people's behavior. The Report *accurately* expresses the well-known fact that not all consequences are contained or reflected in market prices—in particular some (not all!) sacrificed values of the environment. The environment is a re-source (air, water, land), and the costs of using it should be known by or im-posed on users. Why are they not? Because *no one owns* those resources; no one can control their use, as one can control the use of one's own labor or one's own goods. Otherwise, the abuse would be avoided, as with my labor for which I am paid more by its "abusers" than I would be for any other alternative use. In the same fashion, water or air would be used in some particular way only if that use or abuse were of greater value than the best alternative use. That selectivity is what ownership and marketability of a resource at open-market prices induces.

And so it might be with water and air, if only we knew how to enforce prop-erty rights in those fleeting, unappropriable assets. But those goods are not yet appropriable as marketable property; everyone uses them as if they were cost-less. No one has to compensate others for their use and thereby heed the costs that do, in fact, exist. Prices do not reflect *those* costs—abuses of non-owned re-sources. That is why the environment is abused—exactly as my labor would be abused if I did not have rights to myself, or as my car would be abused if I had no marketable, defined property rights to the car. *That* is the problem of envi-ronmental control. Yet, we repeat, it is precisely this *same error of excluding* some components of cost that the Report commits in persistently advocating *techni-cal efficiency*. No useful analysis can be derived by using "technical efficiency" as the criterion.

### 4. Present Value of Costs or Present Outlays?

The Report asserts that buyers of homes and automobiles pay inadequate attention to future expenses that these items entail and are guided only by the current purchase price; therefore, auto producers or house builders have no in-centive to economize on energy by using higher initial outlay means of im-proved mileage or insulation (pp. 54ff). Are these dumb, shortsighted con-sumers the ones the Report proposes make a "choice"? And add the frothy topping that capital markets are "imperfect" in not permitting as low a rate of interest in housing as in other markets, so future savings are not capitalized into greater present values. Well, what is the evidence? The Report offers none. Are houses in the cold Northeast built the same as those in Florida or Califor-nia? Are picture windows in California homes used just because the views are better? Are brick two-story houses with storm windows more common in cold areas because bricks are handier and storm windows more fashionable in the East? Are eastern homes more draft-proof than California homes because westerners love fresh air? A realistic interpretation, of course, is that the present costs of avoiding those future costs *exceed* the future costs. It is efficient *not* to *over*-spend for insulation or for low-energy-use heating equipment that costs much more to produce initially than the value of the energy later saved.

In concluding, the Report makes this profound recommendation: "All possible measures should be taken to encourage the most efficient production and use of energy" (p. 329). If the authors seek technical efficiency in minimizing energy use, the best "possible" route to their objective would be for all of us to commit suicide. But if they are talking about economic efficiency, then those measures are already being taken—in that all of us are interested in reducing costs and balancing more of one use against more of another. The authors appear to think either that developers, builders, and middlemen are insensitive to the sale value of what they produce, or that consumer buyers are too ignorant to anticipate future outlays. But they have no evidence to support that charge, and there is much evidence to refute it.

### 5. Waste or Paternalism?

The Report flies in the face of analysis and evidence in alleging energy waste in automobiles or inefficiently insulated buildings. True, many air-conditioned buildings have big windows that lose heat and use heating and cooling equipment that use up lots of energy. Indeed they do, but that was *not* wasteful when the costs of energy use *were* lower than the value of window views and comfortable temperatures. Big cars, with powerful motors, air conditioning, and power steering, were *not* inefficient or wasteful. The energy used provided more valuable services than any other use to which that energy could have been put. If that were not true, *no* one would have obtained gasoline for those end services. After all, no one was compelled to buy those cars; those were all options. As prices of energy are bid up, reflecting the higher values of available energy, people use less energy for those particular end results. Those options are still worth as much as before but are now too costly to indulge in to the same extent. Higher prices induce us to curtail our amounts demanded (needs?) to the amounts available and to use what little is available in ways that give us the highest personal values. With *higher prices* to inform and impress us about the higher value of a gallon of the reduced supply of gasoline, we will foresake the least valuable marginal uses. We will drive smaller cars with greater (not maximum!) mileage per gallon, drive less often, drive slower, all *without* rationing or reduced speed limits or weekend closing of service stations.

Such paternalist political controls *are wasteful*, because they divert some energy from higher- to lower-valued uses. If $.60 a gallon for gasoline permits each user to buy as much as he demands (needs?) *at that price,* he will use it in the ways that are of most value to him. If quick starts and faster trips at 70 mph are worth more to him than more miles slowly, he will get more value from the gasoline through 70 mph speeds than if he, *or anyone else,* used that gasoline or petroleum in some other way. Shouldn't he? Are we to become paternalist life arrangers under the guise of "conserving" energy?

To say that no one could or should value driving 70 mph more than any other use he or anyone else might have for the gasoline, or any other good he could have had if he did not use that gasoline, is to say paternalistically that "we" know what is best for everyone else. To advocate a reduced speed limit to conserve energy is to commit an arrogant intellectual error. It does *not* conserve energy. Instead, it *diverts* some of the available supply to less valuable uses. Whatever is made available will be used in one way or another. Petroleum prohibited from use for high-speed driving is diverted in part to fuel oil. The reduced speed limit can hardly be viewed as anything but a political power play to divert petroleum to people with political influence who want fuel oil for their own lower-valued uses.

Political controls on our use of energy—whether for outdoor lighting, household heating, or swimming pool heating—means simply that an elite group is undertaking to limit the options of other people. Has the lesson of Nixon's administration been ignored? The Report recommends a higher gasoline tax and mandatory gasoline mileage standards to conserve gasoline—even beyond the amount available at costs that match the price people are willing to pay to get the gasoline (the value they place on it). Such *over*conservation, making the costs of energy use appear higher than they really are, is a kind of masochism.

### 6. "Lot's Wife" Fallacy

Even the hoary sunk-cost fallacy is resurrected. "High cash bonus bids for oil lands tend to motivate the lessee to get back his bonus payment through early production. This is, of course, less true when bonuses are low" (p. 290). Of course, except that the rate of extraction is not affected by the bonus. It is affected by the profitability of extracting the oil, regardless of the size of the payment. The authors forget that large bonuses reflect large future profitability of extraction, and so confuse bonus with future productivity as the reason for earlier extraction.

Other related errors are a source of fallacious deductions regarding advisable policy. For example, "Once the resource development rights are sold, the public, as consumer, has an interest in the development of those resources for its use at an early date and at a fair price. Assuming that energy prices are on the rise, if the lessee is allowed to sit on his lease without developing it, it will be costly to the public in two ways. The lessee will have purchased the development rights—with a lower payment to the treasury than at future prices; and by not producing his lease until some future time, he can sell the resource back to the public at a higher price than if he develops it immediately. The legal system is designed to encourage early production of the leased resources and thus discourage private speculation" (p. 289). That is an elementary (and hence inexcusable) error. If prices are on the rise (rising now, or expected—by whom?—to rise in the future) it is desirable to defer use of the resources until they attain higher use value later. Here the conservationist is 180° off course. The role of capital values in preventing abuse and premature use is ignored in the Report.

The authors offer the premise that only political authorities can determine and control the appropriate exploration and exploitation rate. The knowledge and incentive with which these activities will be carried out is left to the presumed "good intentions" of political administrators, despite the Report's own emphasis on their dismal past performance. The Report contends that although past performance was bad, *more* political control will improve, not worsen, the situation. Ever the theme—We'll be better. The future always lies ahead!

### 7. Leisure Is Unemployment

The Report repeatedly calms fears of unemployment with remarkable assurances that reduced use of energy, whether by deliberate policy or natural reduction of available supply, will not create long-term unemployment. Indeed, it would increase employment—it could even bring back the man-drawn plough. If cheaper and more plentiful supplies of energy tend, happily, to reduce voluntary employment by increasing the supply of other goods relative to leisure, then surely less nonhuman energy will induce us to work harder. One cent would be too high a price to pay for the revelation that long-term employment could be increased by reducing the supply of nonhuman power—let alone $4 million. Yet the Report treats reduced nonhuman power and the consequent inducement to work more (i.e., more employment) as an *advantage* of zero energy growth. Less is more!

### 8. Marginal Cost Pricing, Price Discrimination, and Subsidies

Promotional pricing by utilities is misinterpreted when the Report confuses (1) block pricing with lower prices for large quantities, (2) marginal prices that differ for consumers, and (3) prices below marginal costs. Different *marginal prices* for customers are usually considered to be price discrimination. At worst, they lead to inefficient allocation. At best, they will increase output and avoid the loss of the extra use value (measured by price) over marginal costs. And if marginal prices are equal, then even with lower prices for larger amounts, the effect is to prevent underusage and wasteful failure to produce electricity when price exceeds marginal cost. But the Report thinks promotional pricing means (subsidized) production at marginal costs greater than the value of the extra output, just because some can purchase at a lower price than others, or at lower prices for more goods. That is an error.

### 9. Summary

This list does not cover all the economic fallacies and errors in the Report, but it should suffice to illustrate the Report's inadequacy as an instrument for *understanding* and *informed* action. Its main policy recommendations, based on analytic errors, could not achieve the stated objectives: efficiency in energy use, an increase in reliable energy supplies, more accurate reflection of true environmental costs in costs of energy supply and use. What these policies would do is place more control over consumers in the hands of political energy czars. In this sense, the Report may be viewed as a demagogic appeal for greater political power.

## Energy-Related Issues

Throughout the Report, the authors refer to "policy" without defining it or as though none existed. But the absence of a national political energy policy does not mean the absence of extensive, continuous, private economywide planning of energy uses and production for both present and future. The lack of political management on a national level is not "drift." The Report fails to comprehend economic markets and property rights as controlling and coordinating devices that enable us to anticipate future possibilities and respond promptly to information on current issues.

### 1. Foreign Supply

The Report provides no careful discussion or exposition of problems possibly caused by reliance on foreign supplies. If foreign *governments* (not private concerns!) can interrupt energy supplies, what do we do? The Report presents a knee-jerk response. Go independent by using less energy, at least to the extent of what would have been imported, and find new domestic sources of energy.[2] To treat the events of Fall 1973 (the so-called Arab boycott) as identical to the cartel policy of restricting output is to generate more confusion. The interruption effects of the Arab actions were not serious enough to change any country's foreign policy toward Arab interests. And *cartel pricing* is not an *interruption* threat. It is a device to increase Arab wealth. To confuse cartel pricing with interruptions is a disservice to economic understanding and efficient response. But the Report is not alone in this error; it is by no means uncommon.

The use of foreign supplies over the long pull (by importing, say, 20 percent of our petroleum) will affect our foreign policy. But *how*, and what will these effects be? And if we are energy independent, but Europe and other western nations depend on imports, are we asked to be so naive as not to revise our foreign actions? The Report would have been of some value had it more carefully analyzed the potential gains from *our* energy independence, instead of naively referring to "independence," "cooperation," "shared interests." The Report suggests "no artificial barriers to . . . trade" (p. 175) while proposing to limit our oil imports.

### 2. Rising Energy Costs

Energy prices rise because the demand *schedule* expands more than the supply *schedule* does. That implies that higher prices will be needed to equalize the amount demanded and the amount supplied. As we observed earlier, the Report confuses *an* amount demanded at *a* price with "needs," as if the current demand did not depend on price or costs. This failure to distinguish between (a) "shortages" (resulting from price controls), (b) reduced supply resulting in higher prices, and (c) costs of environmental use not reflected in existing market prices is pervasive. We adapt to reduced supply (relative to demand) by private actions in response to higher market prices; this process is the economic market in action, doing its job as it always has except when disrupted by government controls on use and price. Unless one understands this operation, one tends to assume that any economic upheaval demands a purposive political response—while in actuality, such intervention works to destroy the effective national energy policy *already* in existence.

After World War II, the government—wisely—refrained from adopting a political policy in response to falling energy costs (due to more plentiful sup-

---

2. More enlightening is *Energy Self-Sufficiency*, by the M.I.T. Energy Laboratory Policy Study Group (Washington, D.C.: American Enterprise Institute for Public Policy Research).

plies). Market prices and the economic system induced adaptation, exactly as they will today if current higher energy costs continue. No one has to use political power to enforce a pattern of decreed behavior intended to shape the future; the authors of the Report should heed the principles of substitution and pricing described in Appendix F. The market's pricing system *works*, as long as we do not disable it with political controls and allocations (ordered by officials who, unlike private energy providers, are relatively immune to the consequences of such actions).

The Report contends that energy adjustments can be achieved without resorting to government compulsion or force, and then blithely recommends mandatory controls and taxes (p. 68)—not to mention such deceptively authoritarian recommendations as, "It is important that Congress debate *and enact* legislation which declares that energy conservation is a matter of *highest* national priority and which establishes energy conservation goals for the nation" (p. 329, italics added).

Appendix F of the Report, "Economic Analysis of Alternative Energy Growth Patterns, 1975–2000," by respected Harvard economists E. A. Hudson and D. W. Jorgensen, predicts substitution of other resources for energy *consequent to higher prices* (reflecting the more valuable uses to which relatively reduced supplies of energy can be put), with an apparently small loss of output consequent to hypothesized lower energy supply. If one believes that Appendix, why fuss about this being a time to choose? One debilitating and disquieting feature of Appendix F's zero economic growth projection is the imposition of a heavy tax on energy use, with the proceeds used by political authority to divert production toward services that use less energy. Compulsory shifts do not correspond to users' valuations. Even if so-called real output, with zero energy growth, were to be only 3–4 percent less in 2000 than predicted from historical growth, that is an underestimate of the costs of the proposed energy tax, because the output conforms less to consumer valuations. Appendix F gives no indication of the magnitude of that bias, nor any test of the sensitivity of the projection to changes in the assumed operative parameters.

### 3. Environment

The Report also clouds the problem of environmental use values that are not captured or reflected in market prices. We need an accurate technique for evaluating environmental use, and we must be able to use that measurement to ensure that users will balance environmental considerations against other priorities. Preventing *all* deterioration of environment is not the object, as even the

Report (at one point) concedes: ". . . there is a limit to what clean air is worth" (p. 201). Close, but not close enough. It is not a question of *clean* air, but *cleaner* or *less* clean; the problem is how to ascertain the values of changes in the environment relative to consequent value changes in other goals and goods. What is the cost (value sacrificed) of more pollution relative to the value of other benefits thereby attainable? Most of us work—we pollute our leisure and our lives with sweat, tedium, and occupational hazards because we think the gains outweigh the value of our unpolluted leisure. Should any man who is not now working be forbidden to work, to avoid polluting his leisure? Should *any* deterioration in the environment be intolerable, regardless of values thereby achieved?

Reduced energy use does not necessarily improve the environment. On the contrary, greater use of a greater supply of energy could be an effective means of *improving* (not just preserving) our surroundings. While energy production may injure the quality of some natural resources in some areas, cheaper, more plentiful energy permits improvements in other areas (possibly even the energy production locale). Air-conditioning improves our environment (in a sense); more gasoline for engines with lower mileage but greater effectiveness in curtailing pollutants would also help; pumping water to arid areas (by means of energy) makes the desert bloom. The correct issue is the optimal degree and type of pollution, the optimal mix of environmental effects, the optimal degree of personal abuse via work or loss of leisure. Despite the Report's seeming bias in favor of energy reduction, nowhere does it actually demonstrate that decreased energy growth or a return to our original environment is the ideal objective.

The Report is not alone in the belief that an all-out rescue plan for the environment is indicated. Some of our laws and judicial decisions prohibit *any* air pollution, regardless of subsequent benefits. But this approach imposes waste on society and requires belated correction after the damages are incurred and revealed. We do not live in an all-or-nothing world, the Report's authors notwithstanding: "Some pollution is unavoidable—either because we don't know how to control it, or because it is inherently uncontrollable" (p. 224). But pollution is inherently *controllable*; the point is, we do not *want* to avoid all of it. The authors oversimplify a complex problem by reducing it to meaningless alternatives: "Ultimately, it comes down to a fundamental value judgement of which is the worse: the risks of nuclear power; or air pollution and the destruction of recreational areas and the fragile coastal environment from oil drilling; or air pollution and disruptive changes in the way of life in the Rocky Mountain region from coal and shale production" (p. 225). As a matter of simple fact and logic, those are *not* the choices facing society. The correct problem is that the optimal degree of pollution is not ascertainable, because we do not yet know how to determine the values of relative amounts of pollution—and persuade the public to heed those values.[3]

Despite its concern for our environment, the Report does not consider how the benefits of reduced pollution might be distributed. For example, how much of the benefit of smog abatement would redound to landowners in central Los Angeles, Chicago, and New York? Would all the benefits accrue to them, while nonlandowners paid higher rents and consumed less of other goods? This issue is not mentioned, yet a report that expresses concern about the distributive impact of higher energy prices should at least hint at the distributive effects of pollution reduction.

There is a role for government action: to help ensure that the cost of resources used in producing and consuming energy are accurately and effectively revealed in market prices or user fees. Given that some of those resources are unowned, they cannot be accurately priced, nor can users be effectively charged for them. Yet it appears sensible and desirable that people who use those resources should be made to heed those costs by compensating the owners. Three tasks are involved: (1) assessing the value of the abuse, (2) making that cost impinge on the user, and (3) identifying the resource owners. Those *may* be roles for governmental personnel, *if* we believe that gains from government participation would outweigh gains from continued abuse of the resource— which is not a foregone conclusion. Politicians and bureaucrats (as recent legislation controlling any new use of the California coastline suggests) tend to be overly protective. Why assume that *new* uses are less valuable than old ones? What do political controllers gain or lose by seeking to under- or overvalue alternative uses of a resource? These problems are germane to a discussion of *any* scarce resource—natural or not.

An acknowledgement that the market system has not worked and will not work in these areas is no more earthshaking than the fact that past political actions have opposed clear, secure, and transferrable property rights that enable us to possess and exchange goods. The question is, what is the best way to help

---

3. Worthy of attention are W. F. Baxter, *People or Penguins: The Case for Optimal Pollution* (New York: Columbia University Press, 1974), and E. W. Erickson and L. Waverman, *The Energy Question* (Toronto: University of Toronto Press, 1974), especially vol. 1, parts 2 and 3.

both open market *and* government fulfill their proper roles—and why have they sometimes performed unsatisfactorily in the past?

### 4. Control of Energy Industry and Energy Users

Since no government agency overtly controls the energy industry, some political action is needed—in the Report's view—to make private producers responsive and answerable to the public. But the absence of political control by a public *group* does not mean the absence of public control. Consumer decisions on the value of various kinds of energy control the actions of major corporations. General Motors could not make us all buy Cadillacs, or even 1975 models; nor could Ford make us all buy Pintos. Private producers offer, at their risk, the kind of cars they *predict* we will prefer, as evidenced by our willingness to pay the costs. Control is exercised by the people through market-revealed willingness to work at various wages in light of their range of work opportunities, and by their willingness to buy the offered cars in the open market. Producers propose, consumers dispose.

But the authors of the Report, seeing that a few auto company managers are sensitive and responsive to this public control by consumers and workers, confuse response with control, and proposers with disposers. Even U.S. senators must consider the wishes of their constituents; in formulating policies, they are trying to forecast what the public will accept. The same holds true for the private sector. But very important differences lie in the speed and accuracy with which true desires are revealed, compared, and enforced and the performers rewarded, punished, or displaced.

If this review seems tart, sample the comments of individual members of the project's Board of Advisory at the end of the Report. Many are in sharp disagreement with its conclusions, particularly industry members (energy users and producers); their observations should be carefully scrutinized as a balance for the Report's excessive errors. Comments by most of the academic advisors are superficially less critical, though just as devastating in a few instances. (Some of the academics, however, apparently regret that the Report did not err even more extensively on the side of the environment.) Conservationist advisors, predictably, held that environmental preservation should be the dominant factor in determining energy (or any other) policies.

# ABBOTT AND COSTELLO IN WASHINGTON

The university classroom is confining. The dominance of theoretical and empirical integrity is overwhelming—indeed sometimes stifling. The teacher must be extremely wary of teaching or indoctrinating ethical and normative judgments about social matters. Yet economics is a social science, and people will ask, perhaps a little thoughtlessly, for opinions of what ought to be—as if we could affect that. And the temptation to yield to that query is impossible to resist always.

Now, here in this public lecture, I offer some observations in the spirit of the Peterkin professorship which is to promote teaching and scholarship in economic analysis that is in the tradition of the leading ideas associated with Adam Smith. The fact is that Adam Smith was not only an analyst, he was a moralist and expressed his conception of the good world very forcibly, elegantly and persuasively. I happen, for reasons I have not been able to articulate with sufficient rigor and persuasion, to agree with the moral sentiments or cultural traits which Smith implicitly and, at times, explicitly avows. So let me today, here in this room, escape from the confines of the classroom insistence on only objective scientific analysis. Let me review with what I believe to be intellectual integrity and empirical accuracy a recent event, and at the same time, let me relax and give vent to my unscientific impressions as to what has happened and why I don't like it. And let me do so without making you believe that in my regular classroom I engage in these moralistic, ethical revelations.

When searching for a cast to act in the film, of which this talk is the scenario, I considered first the team of Laurel and Hardy. It was initially proposed that I make a documentary with the real characters. But the real lead characters, Jimmy Carter and James Schlesinger, or Gerald Ford and Frank Zarb, are amateur actors. A cardinal rule of film casting is never use amateur comedians if professional comedians are available. So my first thought was Laurel and Hardy—bless their souls.

You remember Hardy, the fat one (if I discriminate on that basis), was the

Peterkin professorship lecture, March 23, 1978. Reprinted by permission of the author.

bumbling fool who got the pair of them in trouble and who would then complain to his innocent partner Laurel, "Well, here's another nice mess you've gotten us into." That line is, of course, exactly the punch line for the energy situation—the politicians turn to us innocent bystanders and say, "Now, look at the mess you've got us into." And like innocent Laurel we whimper, cry and feel guilt-ridden, ready to accept their alleged solution. But the Hardy character had a fatal failing. He was merely a bumbling fool—in contrast to the politicians who have generated our energy situation. (And if that last sounds pejorative, it is the theme of the movie and an accurate one.) Hardy does not portray a scheming devious plotter seeking to enhance his wealth, power and status at the expense of his innocent partner while veiling his intentions with pious phrases about helping his innocent partner. No, that character is better portrayed by Abbott of Abbott and Costello. Abbott was always scheming to advance his interests at the expense of Costello, the gullible confused fall guy. Contrary to Hardy, who usually ended up in the same disastrous predicament as his partner Laurel, Abbott, on the other hand, usually achieved his objective while Costello suffered.

So Abbott will play the politicians, and Costello, us ordinary working people. The casting is, I think, perfect.

An Abbott and Costello or a Laurel and Hardy film makes us laugh at the disasters that befall the actors. Why we should laugh at their troubles is hard to understand. Perhaps, because it is they rather than we who are suffering. If I relied on that principle for making my viewers laugh I would be guilty of deception. For when you see the film and laugh at the hilarious antics portrayed, Costello, at whom you are laughing, is portraying you. Then, you may not laugh. But what difference does it make who it is that provides the laughs? When Costello takes a pratfall or a pie in the face or is hilariously embarrassed we laugh. So if you are broadminded and find yourself in his place, be detached. Look at the humor of the situation—however costly the comedy may have been to construct.

When you see my film, you will enter at the middle. You'll want to know what has happened. Let me tell you what has happened up to here, so you'll understand what happens next.

About 50 years ago, oil sources became more plentiful. The world price of oil fell. American oil producers in California, and Texas especially, reacted. To keep up prices, the Texas Railroad Commission—the euphemism for the Texas oil cartel agency—acted as OPEC, the Arab cartel, is acting today. Only the Texans were smarter—naturally. They asserted they were cutting the production of

oil to conserve for the future, not to get higher prices or to punish people helping the Jews.

Incidentally, it is an interesting, but apparently secret, fact that it really
didn't pay to conserve so much oil. To use the oil at that time was more valuable
than the uses for which it was being saved at a later time—as some economists
at Texas A&M have verified in a study of conservation. But in any event, the
Texas cartel certainly did raise the domestic price of oil. But not without
difficulty. Just as modern-day Mexicans, Canadians or Americans are not part
of the OPEC cartel, the oil producers of Louisiana in those days were not
part of the Texas oil cartel that was restricting Texas output. Under the incentive of a higher price, maintained by the reduced Texas output, Louisiana producers expanded like mad and made a killing.

Who gained? The Texas producers, exactly like the modern Saudi Arabians
who had to reduce output to get higher prices, gained, while the smaller producers got the advantage of the higher price without cutting their output, and
indeed were even able to expand their output.

When the U.S. price was raised above the prices in world markets, foreigners tried to ship oil to the U.S. But we kept out that foreign oil—as one always
should "Buy American" though travel abroad!—otherwise disloyal Americans
would buy lower-priced foreign oil instead of good old U.S.—i.e., Texas—oil.
At first, that foreign oil was kept out by tariffs—taxes on imports of oil. Then,
later, import quotas were placed on foreign oil to prevent the imports of foreign oil from driving down the U.S. price, which would harm American producers and benefit American consumers.

The federal politicians, even Eisenhower, supported that policy. That tended
to make America independent and strong—or so they said, whereas it actually
made us weaker at the present. Had the foreign oil been allowed to enter we'd
have had more oil and at a lower cost.

What has all that got to do with Abbott and Costello? Well, Abbott, our
scheming character, plays the politician. The excess of the domestic price over
the world price did not all go to American producers of oil. Part was taken as a
tax on foreign imports—a tax available to the politician, Abbott, a tax paid by
foreign producers and by domestic consumers, the Costellos. American producers did *not* keep all the advantage of the higher price. They had to transfer
some (most?) to the government as political contributions to maintain the restriction on foreign imports. We should not be surprised that the oil producers
had to contribute to *both* parties, nor that the oil interests were *believed* to be politically powerful. Were they not the dupes of the politician Abbott, who used

the oil producers essentially as tax collectors—collecting higher revenues from oil prices and then handing a part of the revenue on to the politicians as profits, taxes or political contributions, in precisely the way the oil companies in Arabia are collectors of revenue for Arabian and Iranian politicians? If that's having political power, I fail to see the difference between it and being a slave who, by the threat to stop work, forces his master to feed him.

Incidentally those domestic refineries to whom import quota rights were assigned were thereby able to get cheaper foreign oil and increase their profits. How did they get the quotas? And which foreigners got the right to sell oil to the U.S.? Those who bid the most in the way of political favors to politicians. Oh, I've already explained that, haven't I?

In the intervening years, the U.S. Abbott resorted to printing more money to finance government deficits and did so faster than the growth in real output. With disproportionally more money chasing goods, prices began to rise—known as inflation. The politicians, refusing to acknowledge this cause of higher prices, like Abbott, blamed Costello. The political Abbotts—or political Nixon—imposed wage and price controls on the Costellos—instead of money-creating controls on themselves. As any economist deserving the name will tell you, shortages were not far behind. And they came quickly in gasoline with outages, queues, Sunday closings and unscrupulous, devious political demagoguery attributing blame to sellers or profligate consumers—the Costellos. In fact the control that prices exert over the amounts we demand of any good was destroyed. Absent that self-control decision to buy less at higher prices, because these higher prices weren't legal, the political Abbotts seized the excuse to step in where the economic system was said to have failed—or, to put it accurately, where they had prevented its working. Having prevented market prices from controlling demands, they announced that since that device was ineffective (they asserted that the oil companies were holding back oil or that we Costellos wanted too much); they stepped in with political allocation and controls, which are manna to politicians. And befuddled Costellos gullibly accepted their announcements and actions as patriotic and helpful. Their calls for us to "sacrifice" to stop inflation, more accurately, were calls for us to sacrifice for their benefit. But we Costellos believed our Abbotts.

And when the Saudi Arabians compounded matters by restricting output to get higher prices, the politician's insistence of price controls on gasoline and domestic oil brought our economy to its figurative knees—as we Costellos soon were on our knees begging the political Abbotts for favors—for allocations of oil. We Costellos pleaded for oil and gasoline we would have otherwise been able to buy in the smaller amounts we would have chosen to buy if prices had been higher. Those higher prices are simply ways of telling us Costellos and Abbotts that some of the old uses, those that aren't as valuable as the new higher prices, could not be achieved. And each of us could decide which of those old uses were the less valuable ones to give up in order to have the uses that were still worthwhile. Price controls prevent individuals from choosing which of available alternative uses are most worthwhile. Price controls permit politicians to make more of those decisions.

I am not overstating the situation. Let me recount some examples. In California, it is illegal to use natural gas for what the public-utility politicians call *unessential* uses. And unessential uses are declared to be heating swimming pools, lighting fireplaces and outdoor lighting. But to me, heating a pool 5 degrees higher is more valuable than heating the bedroom an additional 10 degrees. Sweaters and warmer nightclothes are less undesirable than colder swimming—except to those who don't have pools and would like to switch gas from my pool to making beer for them in some brewery or to make more aluminum to can beer or to decorate their offices. Lifestyles are now judged by politicians. The Abbotts decide what are the less valuable or the more valuable uses of more or of less gas for us Costellos.

But there is more. We Costellos are told we cannot legally travel faster than 55 mph. As a result I am a chronic law breaker who now has less regard for the sanctity and propriety of our legal system. I drove at 70 miles per hour crossing West Texas—to avoid being run over by smart Texans going 80 mph with CB radios. But even before coming here, I drove my car faster than 55 mph because I wanted to *not* be a law breaker. Consider, if I drive 55 instead of 65, I save about 4 gallons per hour of driving time, and thereby earn the equivalent of about $2.50 an hour; that means I am working and earning less than the minimum legal wage. With a passenger, we're earning only half the legal rate. Now what shall I do? Break the speed limit or the minimum wage law—it's one or the other. Since I dislike both laws I wish I could break both—but I can't; it's one or the other—and it's the speed limit that I choose to break because my time is valuable.

In the city I can't find places to exceed 55, so I start and stop like a jackrabbit in a powerful car with power windows, air-conditioning, automatic transmission and quietness. Wasteful? Not at all. Indeed, it contributes to social welfare. How?

Social welfare is increased when resources are put to more valuable rather than less valuable uses. Using gasoline for fast starts and stops is more valuable to me than any other use of that gasoline to anyone else. What I pay for a gallon of gasoline exceeds what it is worth to some other person in his most valuable forgone use. Since I pay more than that to other people to get the gallon, the total social value is higher than if I could not use gasoline that way. If you think that strange, you are simply saying that you believe my valuation of uses of gasoline is wrong. But who do you think you are? You are not the judge of what I think most valuable for myself. The real rub comes because the Abbotts think they know better than the Costellos what is good for the Costellos.

We are told by that we cannot have cars that provide less than 14 miles per gallon. I simply don't accept that standard of control.

In California, a state energy board must approve all commercial building plans to see that no excessive energy is used to warm or cool the building. If too much window space is used requiring more heating or cooling, the plans will not be approved. I do not accept that standard of control. If I want rooms with high ceilings (to swing a golf club) and with large windows that take up a lot of energy, then so long as I deem that use of the energy more valuable to me than the required energy would be worth to anyone else—and that is measured by the price in the open market, I should be allowed to live the kind of life I am willing to pay for—i.e., not make other people worse off, because I pay them more for the energy than it is worth to them. But the law now prevents that.

Another law says the California Apparel Approval Board must approve any new cloth made for clothing to ensure that commercial firms do not waste energy on high-energy-using cloth production. Since cotton denim for blue jeans requires a lot more energy per yard produced than other equally durable and equally warm cloth, blue jeans for Levi's are now illegal. The public who prefer blue jeans, which are energy guzzlers, merely to look more stylish and popular, are no longer permitted. I'm serious. That is, I am serious in asserting that is exactly equivalent to the energy-use regulations now imposed on us. How do politicians decide which restrictions to place on us? I don't know. I remind you there are no restrictions on how far you can drive, nor on gas consumption in private airplanes or power boats. I recall recently when Frank Sinatra was on the Johnny Carson show as a substitute host, he allowed as how the speed limits and mileage restrictions were desirable means of conserving gasoline. Sinatra didn't say that he had flown in from Palm Springs at 400 mph in his jet plane using gasoline at the rate of 5 miles per gallon. But still Sinatra is my favorite singer.

The plot of my film is more complicated. Meanwhile, with price controls on crude oil produced domestically, every refiner would love more domestic crude at the bargain price, but everyone wants more at that bargain price than is available. So who is going to get the oil at that bargain price of about $8 a barrel compared with its true market value of $14. Whoever does, will reap a quick $6 profit by getting for $8 oil whose refined value (net of refining and distribution costs) is $14. The crude producers who have to sell to some refinery at that low price futilely scream "expropriation and theft of property values." Similarly, where there are rent controls on apartments, the apartment owners are expropriated of the value of their apartments.

Why are crude oil prices kept down? Abbott says and Costello believes that gasoline prices will be kept down. Not so.

Price controls on gasoline are not effective. The legal limit on gasoline prices is above the current market price, which clears the market so that the amount that people want just equals the amount that is available, no more, no less. The current price of gasoline is consistent with the world price of crude oil, $14 a barrel, and that means the value of a barrel of oil used to make gasoline is about $14 a barrel—not $8. If the price of domestically produced *crude* were allowed to rise to its true value of $14—the way the prices of houses, shoes, leather, meat, labor and coal are allowed to be determined—the price of *gasoline* will *not* rise. The rise in the crude oil price would merely *absorb* the full market price value of the end products refined from a barrel of oil. The value of $14 imputed to the barrel of oil is now being kept by the refiners lucky enough to get claims to the arbitrarily low-priced $8 oil which producers must transfer to refiners at that low price on pain of being criminals.

I repeat, "the price of gasoline or refined products is not lower because of price controls on the crude oil produced in the U.S." The effect, instead, is to transfer that $6 excess of the market value of the crude oil above the arbitrary low price from crude producers to whom it would normally have gone—to refineries with enough political clout to get claims to buy that low-priced oil.

You can well understand why those refiners are willing to pay off politicians to continue that price control while crude producers are willing to pay off politicians to be rid of the controls. Heads Abbott wins, tails Costello loses.

And President Carter has the composure to say that the crude oil prices, if allowed to rise, would constitute a rip-off of the public—who already are paying prices as high as they would be paying without price controls on crude. In fact, Carter wants to get that difference between the $14 market value and the restricted $8 price for the political boys—some $14 billion annually. That proposed tax is euphemistically called a crude equalization tax. Carter has even had the astuteness to allege that the crude equalization tax—which will *not* raise the price of gasoline—would raise the price of gasoline and that the price should rise in order to persuade us to consume less oil and conserve more. In fact, that tax would not raise the price of gasoline. It would only absorb the excess of the true value of the crude over the arbitrary low price permitted to crude producers.

And more, they will, like Abbott, throw more oil in your eye by alleging that we are importing too much oil and should be less dependent on foreigners. Well, to that there are two devastating responses. First, the energy laws actually encourage and induce the import of more oil than would be imported if the energy laws were repealed. Why? Do you remember that difference between the $14 value of oil and $8 domestic price? Every refiner wants to get more of that. How does he get a claim to more of that undervalued oil? He gets to claim more if he runs more oil through his refinery. And how does he run more through his refinery? He buys crude from abroad, and for every barrel he buys abroad at $14, to increase his refinery output, he gets a claim (and entitlement) to appropriate about a quarter of a barrel of that underpriced domestic oil from a domestic crude producer. As a result, every imported barrel that costs him $14 really gives him, in addition, a claim (an entitlement) to a part of that $6 domestic crude oil undervaluation. When taking this into account, the *net* cost of buying foreign crude is only about $12. So refineries import more crude whose refined product *value* is $14. No wonder every refinery is buying foreign oil. It's an automatic profit-making deal. And we are importing oil to the tune of about $13 billion *more* annually because of that import subsidy feature of our entitlements program being financed out of the wealth—or what would have been the wealth—of domestic crude producers, probably some of you sitting here today.

The consumer of refined product is getting lower prices because of the greater imports, not because of price control on crude oil. We could just as well have encouraged the import of more foreign crude by taxing all people over 6 feet tall and using the proceeds to subsidize the import of oil rather than by taxing the producers of crude. But we all know that crude producers are undeserving of higher prices, since Abbott says so. Carter says the crude producers don't deserve to get those higher prices. The price didn't rise because of anything they did except, of course, that the oil is available because of something they did.

What does it add up to? We import an extra $13 billion from foreigners, giving them $13 billion of extra income and taking it from domestic crude producers. The extra imports lower the price of gasoline to consumers by about at most 2¢ a gallon. So to raise gasoline prices to reflect their true value, instead of ending the subsidy inducement to import more oil, Carter and Schlesinger propose to tax that difference away from crude producers. With that extra tax income, the politicians can go far. Second, the belief that we can be independent from foreign power over oil by being more self-sufficient is fallacious. Being self-sufficient will make us weaker in using up more of our oil earlier, so we will have to rely on more imports later. But more to the point, we are tied to Europe, and there is no possibility that we would treat an oil threat to Europe as anything other than a threat to ourselves. Europe and we are tied together. There is no independence from Europe, however inspiring the word "independence" may appear.

And that's what has been happening. This is where you came in. What happens next? Will Abbott succeed in getting that tax or will the Costellos have enough clout to avoid it and let the value of oil accrue to those who thought they owned the oil. Will the northeast retain the expropriatively low price on natural gas, thereby extracting wealth from Texans? Will the War between the States be settled by a victory for the South or will the North continue with its current punitive wealth redistribution tax on Texas, Oklahoma and Louisiana?

Why should I tell you how my film ends? No director gives away the ending of his plot. If you want to know what happens, watch your local TV news or newspaper, but don't believe the interpretations given there. Remember they are, or represent, Abbott. You are Costello.

# THERE'S GAS IN YOUR FUTURE

"Fuel is scarcer: use it wastefully!" Those who propose governmental allocations and rationing of fuel and energy are saying, in effect, precisely that. Surely fuel should be assigned to its most beneficial uses; every gallon of fuel should be employed where the benefits of using it exceed those of all other possible uses. It would hardly seem necessary to state so basic a principle. Yet the most beneficial use of fuel is exactly what rationing, allocations, and price controls prevent.

It is remarkable that many people do not understand this. They are usually ignorant of two crucial facts about the market economy: (1) free market prices direct fuel to more important, higher valued uses; (2) free markets compensate people who transfer fuel from less important to more important uses.

How would rationing and price controls defeat both of these desired effects? When all men receive equal amounts of fuel, their needs remain unequal (N.B.: there is no necessary relation between need and wealth; a poor man may need his quota of a given good either more or less than a rich man). Peter's last gallon, useful as it may be for his own purposes, may be worth still more to Paul. But if they can neither measure the relative values of the fuel nor transfer it, the misallocation will remain undetected and uncorrected. If, however, the market price is allowed to serve as a measure of that fuel's value to Paul as against its value to Peter, the appropriate allocation can be made by simple exchange: Peter can sell to Paul. The buyer finds the fuel more useful than the goods he forsook to get it; the seller finds the goods he received more useful than the fuel. The public generally ignores this effective direction of fuel and goods toward their most valued uses, since the whole process occurs dispersedly, in thousands of independent market transactions, rather than as the result of deliberate government actions or conscious social control, which, if less efficient, are at least more obvious.

Both effects—allocation to better uses, and compensation for forsaking inferior ones—are achieved by permitting sale at free market prices. Both are

From *National Review* (January 4, 1974), 22–23. Copyright 1974 by National Review, Inc., 215 Lexington Avenue, New York, NY 10016. Reprinted by permission.

prevented by price controls, rationing, and governmental allocations. And so strong is the desire for better allocation (and for its concomitant compensations) that all such controls will be violated at every chance, as each man sees that it is sensible—even if illegal—to violate them. Bad laws make for bad citizens as well as for poor production. (If you think market values are not good or appropriate measures of value of uses, read on—we shall come to that problem later.)

The damage done by rations and allocations—their stifling of the efficient distribution of available fuel—can be somewhat reduced if recipients are permitted to sell and transfer them at free market prices. But the sad irony is that proponents of rationing rarely provide for that critical transferability. Why not? Some conjectures are possible.

## Is It a Rip-off?

One cynical conjecture is that advocates of rationing want to disrupt our economic system, gain control over our lifestyles, and destroy our free, liberal society. A more respectful conjecture is that they don't comprehend the real consequences of their schemes. Why should they? Economic wisdom is not instinctive or inherited. You pay taxes to hire economists to teach these simple principles to college students. If they were all that obvious, why pay to have them taught? The second conjecture is both more charitable and more probable.

There is, however, a third: that proponents of quotas expect allocations of fuel to conform to their own priorities, without the burdensome conditions of adjustment to the values of others, conditions inherent in the free market. To put it bluntly, they see political power as a means of confiscating fuel without compensation—a neat rip-off. Of whom? Of U.S. fuel producers (not, of course, of the Arab producers, whose oil we have to buy at world prices whether or not we ration it here). You may say, "So what? Oil companies don't deserve higher prices." But that answer, however phrased, is not only destructive but immoral. The mechanic, the soybean farmer, the teacher, and the truck driver get higher incomes when demand for their services increases in relation to supply. Can we seriously (and morally) propose that their services be rationed and assigned in the manner being proposed for fuel? Not if we want our society to be efficient—or free.

But let us face up to the confiscation issue, and to the argument that higher prices could hurt the poor disproportionately. Honesty compels us to acknowledge that stockholders of U.S. fuel companies are people like everyone else, poor, middle class, and rich: they are taxpayers, your neighbors and friends. If their wealth is confiscated and given to others, why are the recipients more deserving of it? That is a question for the conscience.

But moral considerations aside, permitting the sale and transfer of quotas would dispose of the objection that higher market prices for fuel would hurt the poor most. The freedom to sell one's rations would be an *advantage*—to everyone, rich and poor. Instead of being stuck with an assigned amount of fuel, unalterable regardless of its value to him, the poor man would be free to exchange as much of his quota as he saw fit for other more desirable goods, thereby releasing so much fuel to higher valued uses. He would in fact be better off than he had been without transferable rations at free market prices. Since transferability, as against nontransferability, is a boon to everyone, the poor would be disproportionately *helped*.

Again, to summarize, if quotas, rationing, and controls are imposed, it would at least help minimize the harm they do to permit quotas to be purchasable or divisible and transferable at free market prices. For fuel would then tend to go to its highest valued uses; nobody would willingly put fuel to uses worth less than either any other use to which it could be put, or the goods that could be had in exchange for it. So if we must restrict oil stockholders' wealth, at least let us transfer the wealth to poorer ration recipients without preventing the available fuel from finding its most valuable uses. Taxing oil companies for the sake of the poor need not, after all, condemn what fuel is available to bad or wasteful uses.

Even if we have the minimal wisdom to allow the sale of whatever rations we adopt, increased production of fuel will still not be properly encouraged. We shall have reduced people's incentive to direct their wealth and efforts toward finding and producing the fuels we most desire. In trying to effect the "equitable" distribution of a scarce commodity, we will condemn ourselves to a longer period of greater scarcity. Why handicap our efforts to get more fuel with a scheme that doesn't really protect the poor, but does discourage production?

A better, simpler, proven method exists which not only helps the poor, but also fosters the production (and productive use) of more fuel: higher market prices. If, for example, we insist that poorer gasoline-users must not be required to pay what the fuel is worth in the free market, it is still better to permit prices to rise to whatever heights they will, and *then* take supplementary government action: subsidize the "poor," who are most heavily dependent on purchasing fuel for their livelihood, perhaps by giving them fuel stamps (like food stamps) which they can either use to defray part of the higher price of fuel or sell as they please. The cost of such supplements should be covered out of general tax revenues (as is done with food stamps).

And if we fear that these supplements would permit stockholders to gain "unjustly," we can still impose a percentage-of-excess-profits tax on the oil companies. This would restrict output less than an excise tax of so much per gallon of gasoline. An excise tax levied on each unit of fuel would not encourage increased productivity; but the percentage-of-excess-profits tax would, by increasing the after-tax profits of those who expand fuel production.

## Rich v. Poor

The question remains: is market value an appropriate value? Some will object to our proposition that fuel, on the open market, will be transferred to its "best" uses; a rich man, they will argue, would use fuel for a faster drive or a pleasure trip, while the poor man who gives up some fuel to the rich man would suffer by having to find other means of getting to work. And surely (and here's the clincher) the rich man's whims are not as important as a poor man's transportation to work!

But this does not affect our argument, for two reasons: (1) We did not say they *were* as important. What we did say was that both the rich man and the poor man would agree that it is better to be free to transfer their rationed amounts than to be forbidden to do so. Again: if the available gallon of gasoline is worth more to Peter than the goods he must give up to get it, he will want to exchange; and if Paul wants to gain possession of those goods more than he wants to keep the gallon, he will agree to the exchange. The prohibition of that exchange by a third party—the state—would prevent that direction of the fuel and other goods to the highest valued uses as judged by the parties to the exchange themselves. And since society is made up of just such parties, society at large suffers under such prohibitions.

(2) It is true that a poor man's consumption values, as expressed in the market, do reflect his poverty. Having said this, we must distinguish between the interpersonal distribution of general wealth (*how much* men have) and the interpersonal mixture of goods (*what* they have). We may think the present distribution of general wealth is unjust by this or that criterion, and that a fuel scarcity will exacerbate the injustice. Even so, forbidding the transfer of rations would diminish the freedom (and, concretely, the wealth) of all, including the poor, by preventing each person from using his available wealth to secure the particular mixture of goods that suits him best according to his personal pref-

erence and lifestyle. Rationing, allocations, and price controls would freeze some goods in uses worth less to the recipient than (a) what he could get for them and (b) their value to another consumer. Who profits by this? Only an authoritarian controller.

To prevent free market prices from allocating goods (whether or not some redistributionist supplement like fuel stamps is used) is to prevent fuel from finding its more important and beneficial uses. To deny this, is to contend that political authorities should decide what uses are "more important and beneficial"; a contention which, for consistency's sake, requires the further contention that political authorities should also decide which TV news programs are "beneficial and important" enough to merit allocation of energy, or which newspapers and magazines deserve the allocation of paper. The scarcity of fuel (or any other good) relative to demand is not a valid reason for imposing government controls. We have used for centuries a method consistent with—indeed a foundation for—a free society. It is both more effective in adapting to changes in supply, and more consistent with the rights we treasure. Why abandon that method at exactly the moment when it is most useful?

# OIL DECONTROL WINDFALL
## MAGICAL OR REAL?

Much of what seems to be happening isn't! Indeed, the same illusions occur over and over. An especially neat example is the current illusion or deception in President Carter's oil decontrol arguments. The deception is in reversing the true direction of determination of values: the value of a resource is derived *from* the ultimate consumer value of its services. The error is the common one of believing the reverse—the values to consumers depend on the costs of productive resources. Let me explain.

President Carter wants to decontrol the price of old crude oil and impose a tax on what he claims will be a resultant profit. He proposes to permit owners of wells that began producing crude oil before 1973 to now get the current world market price of about $15–$20, rather than continuing to be required to give their oil to refineries at the currently artificially low controlled $7 price.

That control was imposed when the Arabs reduced their petroleum output, which thereby caused the world crude price to increase to about $15. As a result *all* domestic crude oil, *no matter whether new or old*, also became worth $15. But, under the price control on domestic crude oil, well owners had to transfer their more valuable oil to refiners for the controlled low price of $7 even though *when refined into consumers' products it was worth* $15 (after allowing for refining and distribution and taxes). Do not miss that point! Those refiners who are lucky enough to get that crude oil for only $7 are getting something worth $15—a gift of $8. That gain now occurring is what Carter mistakenly asserts will occur if prices at which that oil from old domestic wells were allowed to rise to about $15. In fact, that difference *already* is being captured by those lucky enough to get the crude oil actually worth $15 from current producers at only $7. Decontrol would merely shift that gain, or difference between $15 and $7, back to crude producers and away from those who *now* get the gain. That gain will not be created by allowing the controlled price on old crude oil to rise. It will merely be transferred from one group to a different group.

This is true because the market value of the end products of the refining of

Reprinted, by permission of the author, from *Los Angeles Times*, 1979.

a barrel of oil are high enough to make it worthwhile paying as much as $15 for a barrel of crude oil to refine into those end products—even after refining, distribution, and tax costs. For example, the crude oil is refined into gasoline, asphalt, heating oil, kerosene, synthetic fibers, paints, drugs, etc., all of which are worth about $15 per barrel *more* than the refining, processing, distribution, and tax costs. In other words, after all those costs, the remainder is $15. That's what a barrel of old oil is actually worth. That is why refiners are willing to bid as much as $15 to get a barrel of oil. At any price of old crude oil lower than $15, they are getting the profits. The profits are there—going to the refiners.

Had the Arabs supplied more crude, the greater supply of end products to consumers would have commanded a lower price, and the value of crude oil would have been lower because the residual left to apply to the purchase of oil would have been lower. Then the world price of all crude would be lower, say $8. But by restricting the world supply of crude oil and hence restricting the supply of final consumer products, the value imputed to the crude oil (old, new, foreign, or domestic), and derived from the ultimate consumers of the end products, was raised to about $15 a barrel. It is absolutely essential that one understand this if one is to avoid the confusion or deception in the Carter magic show.

Note carefully that there are at least two stages in the process. The first is extraction of crude oil by the oil well owner, and the second is the refining and distribution of the refined consumer products. The crude oil producer is not necessarily the same firm as the refiner and distributor. If he was, the crude oil price control would be irrelevant, since the control would merely be a transfer from one pocket to another of the same person. If the crude oil well owner is not a refiner, the crude oil producer gets only $7 for a barrel of oil that is already worth $15 to the refiner. The $8 difference is being kept by the lucky refiner who sells the end product at the open market, uncontrolled price of end products, rather than being paid to the crude oil well owner.

Though crude oil from 1973 wells (which are still producing) can be sold legally to refiners for only $7, despite the barrel's true value of $15, it is important to recognize that the prices received by the refiners of the end products have been open market prices which fully reflect the end product's values to consumers. Hence, those crude oil price controls do *not* keep down the prices paid by consumers for the refined end products. (At least there were no effective controls on gasoline prices until about a month ago—which has caused the recent gasoline shortages—but that doesn't alter the present analysis.) In effect, price controls on *crude* oil were merely a method for *transferring* the higher value of the crude (after the Arab cutback) to refiners and not allowing it to go to the crude oil investors.

The so-called windfall, which Carter says will be magically created by de-control of domestic crude oil prices, will not (repeat, *not*) create or cause any profit or windfall. The increase or profit occurred back in 1973, and it has been acquired by refiners who were lucky enough to get that crude oil at the under-valued price of $7. They are among the beneficiaries of the crude oil price con-trol. You can now see, I trust, why decontrol now would permit that full value of crude oil to go to the investors who discovered that crude oil before 1973, rather than to politically favored refiners. I add that last clause about "politically favored refiners" because it helps understand the forces at work.

They were, in part, people who agreed to build new refineries. Integrated oil companies that pumped up more crude than they refined had to sell that higher valued crude at the artificially undervalued price to other companies which were primarily refiners. What has been going on is a gigantic distribution of about $10 billion annually of crude oil from some crude producers to other oil refining companies. No wonder some oil companies (primarily crude produc-ers) are seeking decontrol and others (primarily refiners) are not. And you can readily see how the politicians gain power and wealth as the people who decide to whom the undervalued oil is assigned—or "entitled" as the political euphe-mism puts it.

You can also see why Carter's proposal to decontrol the old crude oil price will not magically create any profit at all, nor will it raise the price of gasoline. It will not create what he perceives to be a windfall. What it will do is reallocate the difference in value between the open market price and the lower controlled price from political favorites back to domestic crude oil investors. But no politi-cian who is worth his salt—or knows his peanuts—will ignore an opportunity to acquire control of economic wealth. So Carter (and Senator Jackson), either deceived or deceiving, seek to *continue* use of that wealth difference for political purposes. But it is now obvious that decontrol would remove that power to con-trol that wealth. It would remove the difference by restoring it to the crude oil producer. It will not create any increased profit or windfall, because it will not affect prices of gasoline or of refined products, all of which are already at the market clearing price based on world supplies of oil. It will not reduce the supply of crude oil available to the U.S. and, hence, will not reduce the supply of final refined products, and it will not affect consumer prices—regardless of how often Carter or Senator Jackson says "abracadabra." In fact, it will merely transfer wealth from refiners to crude oil investors, where some old-fashioned people believe it should go.

A more detailed analysis, going beyond the preceding story, would reveal that, indeed, the refiners are not the only ones now sharing that excess value of the real market value of the crude over the controlled price. The favored refiners have to compete politically to get those entitlements to buy undervalued oil for $7, which is really worth $15 in final market value of end products to consumers. The politicians tell the refiners that whoever imports more from the Arabs will get more of the bonanza of American undervalued oil, which the refiners can resell for its true market value of $15 in finished products. Under that system it will pay the refiners to import more oil. As a result the Arabs sell more oil to the U.S. for more money—wealth that would have gone to American crude oil investors—some $10 billion annually. Not a bad way to subsidize Arab friendship, if not reliability.

Finally, it might be thought that if refiners compete to import more oil we would have more oil in the U.S., with lower prices of refined products. Some people think this subsidy to importers of more oil lowers the price of gasoline about two to three cents a gallon. However, this overlooks the fact that Arabs are not fools. They simply have been enabled to get a higher price. Without the subsidy that increases our demand for imports from the Arabs, they would charge a lower price for their oil. And when that fact is taken into account, it is not clear that the subsidy has any detectable effect on gasoline prices.

But to come back to the basic issue. The decontrol of domestic crude will not create a wealth gain for the oil industry. It will only alter the way in which the true market value of the domestic crude is being currently distributed to politically favored oil companies and Arabs, depending on which are the domestic crude producers and which are the favored refiners. Any tax to prevent an alleged windfall gain is clearly a deceiving or deceived proposal.

The magic is gone. The illusion is shattered. That is why politicians fear economic analysis—and hide it when they understand it.

# ENERGY ECONOMICS

The energy crisis reflects one simple fact. The old reliable market price rationing system is being destroyed by price controls. Free market prices are powerfully effective means of (1) comparing different use values so as to (2) reveal wasteful use while (3) making amounts demanded equal the available supply (4) without having to know what aggregate supplies are, and (5) compensating people for diverting it from the low value to the more high value uses. But with price controls all of that is prevented and confusion reigns. It is as simple as that.

Why then do we have price controls? Not insufficient energy, for there never has been enough, never will be enough. Not the actual or threatened Arab oil embargo; the crisis, so-called, began before that. Not the oil companies who responded sensibly by trying to stockpile oil for later periods of threatened smaller supplies; not environmentalists who restricted the production of energy; and not the pollution controls on cars that increased the amount of gasoline demanded for transportation. Some of those things make us poorer in energy and give us a more primeval environment. Some increase our demands for gasoline. But none caused the crisis or so-called crisis.

The crisis and shortage—that is, the allocative confusion caused by the destruction of the price system—is caused by price controls imposed by political authority.

It started with natural gas price controls in an ill-conceived attempt to protect consumers. What made these price controls so quickly and extremely destructive for energy was the rapid monetary inflation and the increased demands and reduced supplies caused by the environmental factors I have just mentioned. Without price controls there would have been no shortages, no "outages," no distorted uses of natural gas, no frustration in trying to get it, no non-price rationing or reduced real income.

More recently, during the past two years, the present administration, in its predictably foolish and futile attempt to restrain monetary inflation, imposed

Reprinted, by permission of the author, from *Conservative Digest Special Report* (1975): 5–6.

general price controls. Now why restrain inflation? Presumably to preserve the dollar market price system. If that sounds like destroying a village to save it, you get the message.

The political powers made the irresponsible response to monetary inflation. They directed their political fire not at the real culprit—themselves, in their money-creating means of financing greater governmental expenditures—but at the greedy businessmen and union leaders. Actually, you know, the rest of us are not greedy!

The predictable shortages and confusion appeared right on schedule. Seizing on the self-created shortages and the competition for available fuel at excessively low legal prices, the nimble politicians, your bosses, using freely available newsprint and television news time, demagogically again accused— you guessed it—greedy businessmen for the shortages.

To solve the problem of shortages, politicians propose rationing. They even are investigating oil companies to see if there really is a shortage. As foolish an inquiry as one can imagine—except that it will enhance the power of politicians.

Now the administration, in its zeal to protect us, hopes to win the war on inflation with "peace with honor." We have the honor; they have a piece of our wealth. They now control by political direction what will be done with fuel. And who do you think gets first priority? Why, federal government agencies, of course—then local political authorities, and last comes private consumption. And even that is assigned and rationed to uses they deem best—so much to heating, so much to aviation, and so much to private cars in a process that defies their own comprehension: ten gallon purchase limits, reduced speed limits, Sunday closing, daylight saving, no outdoor lighting, no ornamental lighting. How do they know the most valuable uses? How do they know outdoor lighting is less valuable to me than a well-lighted house, or another ounce of electrically produced aluminum? They do not.

So to conceal their errors, the police power of the state is imposed so that we do not upset their ideas of what we should do. State and national energy boards and policies are proposed. The purpose is not hard to see, if only we will look. The crisis is the loss of our right to express and enforce our values as free men in a liberal society. Our values are being replaced by the values of political authority.

Now what about those oil company profits? I wish they were larger. I don't understand why the Exxon people are apologizing. I would like to see profits twice as large. I foolishly believe oil stockholders are people, too, real honest-to-God people like you and me. Some are rich, most are poor, many are beneficiaries through retirement fund systems that hold Exxon stock. Before I decide their profit is a uniquely undeserved gain, consider! If I tax it away with special taxes am I more deserving when I get those tax proceeds? It is no less a windfall to me. Is "taxation might" really "right"? Did we impose special taxes on the gains to doctors when Medicare was installed, or on professors when the student population explosion increased our wages far beyond what I worked for initially, or on farms whose land value increases during the past year were gigantic, or on the increased city center land values from subsidized rapid transit, or on gains to lawyers when the government expanded its legal actions against the private sector and raised lawyers' fees, or on Heller and Samuelson when their texts and speeches commanded enormous royalties and fees as large windfalls? No. They, like oil producers, undertook risky investment in their textbooks and government service. But they certainly have received windfalls, and I am glad they did. I don't want that system destroyed.

Though most economists agree on the urgency and desirability of abandoning price controls immediately, why does the public seem to opt for mandatory allocations and strict rationing and price controls? The public knows that demands have risen; everyone wants more at current prices. They then conclude that if somehow people could be controlled to not buy more than their existing amount, no one would have to pay higher prices to the producers. Consumers simply collude to restrict prices and make that collusion effective by rationing and legally punishing any buyer who tries to cheat on that arrangement by proferring a higher price. Of course, this kind of activity is illegal or immoral when tried by businesses or sellers, but it's okay for consumers to do so. But this reasoning fails to recognize that everyone can't do this because each consumer is in fact some sort of producer. It is only if you have a small number of producers as your victims that this will work. And furthermore, the collusion reduces total real income—with disruptions, frustrations, and disrespect for the law and the weakening of our fabric of social and cultural relations.

Why do the politicians who condemn the Nixon administration as corrupt, devious, morally bankrupt, untrustworthy, imperialist, disregardful of the basic rights of other people, and grasping for power to maintain itself in office—and you could add more—urge more power for that same administration to exercise greater control over our basic rights and lifestyles, controls that are far more damaging to our liberties, rights, and culture than the Watergate tragedy? The administration's Watergate abuse of political power was directed at his opposing politicians. But economic controls and suppression of the economic liberties and rights of individuals are but a mild threat to those now in the political arena. All presently politically powerful people—not only those in elected or appointive offices—gain from greater political control over economic resources. The greater will be the value of political office and power inherited by successor political groups; Republicans now, Democrats later. This shift of power is at the expense of the private sector and is shared by those presently in power with political opponents. Their national anthem is: "Greedy businessmen and unions with their insatiable lust for wealth must be restrained, and the obvious way to do it is by political controls over the economy."

And that is a sickness of our society—the fantasy that greater political control will set aright those defects. Are these politically powerful people fools, dissimulating, or ignorant? Not at all. They are as sincere and as greedy in seeking wealth and power as you and I. But their comparative competitive talents are in political, rather than market, economic activities. Hence they benefit from greater political controls over the economy. Their condemnation of Nixon is consistent with their thrust on him—no, on the presidency—of greater power against his professed wishes. But he, like anyone else, is too weak to resist using that power once he gets it. But some day a president will not be too weak to use it against his political opponents.

But whatever the explanation, political power over prices reduces our basic freedoms and culture. It is the culture and wealth so characteristic of liberal society that I am urging you to protect by the immediate abandonment of wage and price controls and without resorting to special discriminatory taxes. A free democratic political system cannot survive without private property rights in free open markets. Show me a society without private property and free prices, and I'll show you a totalitarian state.

# IT'S EASY TO END GAS SHORTAGE

The current calamitous, unnecessary gasoline shortage is caused by the recent effectiveness of legal ceilings on the price of gasoline. And the shortage would be eliminated overnight if those price controls were removed. Let me explain why that statement is not foolish.

Controls on retail prices of gasoline were imposed several years ago, but up until about a month ago the ceiling permissible price—about 90 cents a gallon—was far above the market-clearing price, about 70 cents.

In the past few months the Iranian cutback, with continued inflation of prices in general, and now the government-mandated reduction in production of gasoline to stockpile more heating oil for the winter, has reduced the supply of gasoline so much that the market-clearing price has risen far above the currently permissible ceiling of about 90 cents. The current market-clearing price is probably about $1 to $1.25 a gallon.

But whether that guess is correct or not would quickly be verified by removal of the legal ceiling on gasoline prices. Then prices would rise enough to eliminate the shortage, and, furthermore, that would not raise everyone's cost of getting and using gasoline. If all that weren't true, all economists paid by your taxes at the state universities should be fired, since that is an important implication of what they are paid to teach.

To see why, the first thing is to realize that the amount of gasoline demanded, like any good, depends not only on its usefulness, and one's income, family size, type of job, age, etc., but also upon the market price. But only price can adjust quickly to avoid imbalances between amount available and amount demanded. If supply falls, whether of meat, shoes, or gasoline, remaining use values and hence its market price rises. How high? To whatever height will do what the old price did, and that is to make the amount people want to buy not exceed the amount available. Always there is some higher price that will do that, whether you like it or not. By rising that high, "shortages" are avoided, even if it doesn't reduce "scarcity." And it is the crucial, but ignored, distinction between "increased scarcity" and "shortage" that helps understanding of the present events.

Reprinted, by permission of the author, from *Los Angeles Times*, 1979.

1. Scarcity always exists for all goods: meat, shoes, clothing, cars, housing, pencils, and Rolls-Royces, yet for none of these is there a shortage. Anyone can buy whatever amounts of those goods his income and personal circumstances and market price induce him to try to buy. Scarcity of a good means it is not so plentiful as to make one more unit worthless. It isn't free. It is valuable.

Increased scarcity is a reduced supply relative to demand, so that each unit is more valuable. Even then, a shortage will not occur unless the price is not allowed to rise to match the new higher value of each remaining unit.

2. Any good whose price is restrained below a market-clearing level will experience a "shortage." People want to buy more than is available. Queues, outages, and waiting lists develop as people find that at the price being asked sellers don't have as much as buyers demand. That "excessive amount demanded" relative to supply is what we see as a "shortage."

But when not held down by law, the price will be bid up to whatever height will make the good so costly as to restrain people from trying to buy more than is available. Before deciding that is cruel, unfair, and undesirable, it must be admitted it would, in any event, eliminate the excessive demands—even though it may not necessarily increase the supply.

A higher price of gasoline will, and does, in fact, make people consume less. Though most people do not talk that way, they act that way. They say, "I must have gasoline to drive to work." But when faced by higher prices and a higher cost of getting and using gasoline, those who drive to work do act differently, or at least some of them do—with sharing, less frequent shopping, smaller cars, slower speeds, less acceleration, and more bus riding. They forsake less valuable uses so as to continue the more valuable uses, like driving to work.

No escape is possible from these facts and behavior. When prices are released, as they someday certainly will be, they will rise to where we will pay a money price exactly as high as the now higher valued use of a gallon of scarcer gasoline. And that will mean we will pay the cost by exchanging useful goods rather than by wasting time waiting in line at less convenient times—activities with no socially redeeming merit.

When exchanges via prices are used to get gasoline, the buyer is giving to the rest of society something useful in exchange for the gasoline that he, rather than the rest of society, gets to use.

Failure to perceive the difference between (a) increased scarcity caused by a reduced supply and (b) a shortage (excessive demand) caused by an insufficiently high price is the source of our current calamity. Most people, including

President Carter, Energy Secretary James Schlesinger, and Sen. Henry Jackson (to name but three), do not recognize the differences. Since both are now happening, they confuse those two as if they were one and the same thing.

Because there is truly no cure for the reduced supply, they talk as if there must be no cure for "shortage." Not so. There is.

They probably believe that the "shortage" of gasoline in 1974 during the first Arab cutback, which reduced supply, ultimately disappeared as more gasoline was later produced. Not so. More gasoline was not produced. Increased scarcity remained. Instead, the shortage disappeared only because the ceiling prices were raised. The market price was permitted to rise high enough to restrain the amounts demanded by the public to the smaller supply. The shortage disappeared in 1975 only because prices were allowed to rise; the supply of gasoline did not increase.

It is important to see also that the cost of getting and using scarcer gasoline will increase with or without price controls, even if perfectly enforced. Why? When less is available, the pertinent issues are: Who is going to use less? For what uses? And who will make those decisions?

No matter why the amount of gasoline is reduced, the fact that less is available forces some answer to each of those questions. "What uses shall we forsake?" I assume we want to forsake only the less valuable uses, as we judge them, in order to continue with the more valuable. Those remaining higher valued continuing uses to which gasoline can be put are higher valued whether or not government limits the legal price. Do not confuse the legal price with the use value.

An obstinate belief of some people that the value of having gasoline can be kept low by limiting the price to be as low as when there was more gasoline is just plain wrong. The quicker that obstinate error is understood by politicians and the public, the better. Yet Carter and his politicians refuse to either understand or admit they understand that pervasive, inescapable, overwhelming fact of life. As a result we are suffering the consequences of these price controls. We are not allowed in a civilized fashion to offer money to sellers of gasoline. Instead we now compete like barbarians in wasteful forms—standing in lines, inconvenient service hours—a gigantic social waste in a futile, ignorant, deceptive effort to keep values and costs low.

Why not issue ration coupons? Someone must then decide who is going to get some more and who is going to have less, since gasoline is obviously more valuable in some uses than in others. So, certainly, coupons should be and would be marketable, once issued to the initial recipient.

Users will have to pay a money price (below the market-clearing price, else there would be no shortage), plus give up the value of the coupon. Consumers will pay the full price for gasoline in the form of too low a money price to the gasoline supplier plus either some payment for purchase of extra coupons or some amount of wealth forsaken if people use their own coupons instead of selling them.

# TO BE FAIR, LET EACH SOLVE
# HIS OWN FUEL CRISIS

When President Carter, Energy Secretary James R. Schlesinger, and other politicians urge us to conserve oil by calls for factories and offices to lower their thermostat settings, for state legislators to maintain the 55 m.p.h. speed limit, and for service stations to shorten their hours, they are being foolish. What would be more appropriate is to urge us to use oil for its more valuable purposes.

What the United States should be doing today, to cope with the reduced supplies of Iranian oil, is what it should do at all times and with all goods and resources: namely, direct whatever the total supply may be toward its more valuable uses.

But we have substituted another method of control in the last several years for oil and natural gas. As a result we have created many unanticipated problems, but we seem unable to appreciate what caused those problems. Currently, the legal prices of some domestic oil and natural gas are controlled below the market value of the available supplies. This induces us not only to demand more than is available but also to use what we do get in ways that are only as valuable as that artificially low price.

As a result, shortages develop, and some of what we do manage to get is used in excessively low-valued, wasteful ways.

Politicians contend the only way to avoid that vicious effect of price controls is to institute political controls on the public use of the energy to prevent us from wasting it. That is why Energy Department employees are authorized to decide who are the appropriate people to make what uses of how much oil and natural gas. They pretend to be able to compare our values of different uses. For example, they say gas and oil are more valuable for heating homes on the East Coast than for manufacturing or transportation.

They assert reductions in use of natural gas for manufacturing is preferred to reductions for home heating, when supplies decrease.

How do they decide that some oil is more valuable for extra heat for a home

Reprinted, by permission of the author, from *Los Angeles Times*, March 11, 1979, 74a.

than for the manufacture of more steel or plastics, or for travel in private automobiles? I conjecture votes are counted to enhance the political authorities' probability of staying in office—and the relative value of oil and gas to the users ignored as pawns in the fight for political power.

How much simpler this process would be if the nation relied on price to reconcile supply and demand for oil.

The value of any use of oil to you is easily assessed. You consider what next best uses you are willing to give up for more of "this" use. You decide yourself your most valuable uses of whatever amount of oil you choose to buy.

For example, if using gasoline for weekend travel to a ski resort is more valuable to you than its next best use—say, going to work by car rather than by jogging or riding the bus—then you should, and would decide to drive to the resort and take the bus to work. You don't need a dictator of life styles to make that decision by prohibiting Sunday sales of gasoline.

If driving to the resort at 65 m.p.h. to save time to ski more is of greater value to you than driving an hour longer at 55 m.p.h. to save $2.50 worth of gas for some other use, then you'll drive faster and save time, and not use the saved gasoline for some other less valuable trips. Indeed, if you use an extra hour driving slower you will earn in reduced gasoline costs about $2.50—not even the legal minimum wage. Should you break the minimum wage law by driving as slow as 55, or should you be allowed to drive 65 in order to at least earn the minimum wage in wasted time?

And if an extra gallon for a powerful, quiet gas-guzzler is worth more to you than for several longer trips in smaller cars, why can't you decide that—as you do everything else?

But though each of us can compare values of different uses of oil for the same person, how can values of uses to different people be compared?

Again, the answer is easy. If your best use of another gallon of oil is worth more to you than its most valuable use to me, we will quickly discover that, because it means you would offer more for the gallon than I would. That comparability isn't denied even if one person be rich or one be poor, or both be of the same wealth.

No matter how disparate our wealths, if a gallon is more valuable to you than to me, it means that you prefer to give up more to the seller for that gallon than I would. The gallon will be put to its highest valued use—highest of all the perceived of my and your, or anyone else's, possible uses. The rest of society is better off letting you use the oil if its use is more valuable to you, because the rest of society, in exchange for giving up that oil, gets more from you than it would from me.

The market price forces all us consumers to compare our valuations of a given good or service. And we, as a group, influence the market price by refusing to buy as much as is offered if the price is too high. When that happens, the unsold supply forces down price to the value of the remaining best fulfillable uses for the extra oil. On the other hand, if we have unsatisfied uses worth more to us than the price being asked, the competition to get more to satisfy those highly valued uses at that bargain price will push the price to the value of the fulfillable uses with the existing supply. That is what happens for oil, as well as for shoes, paper, pencils, and soap, etc. That is how a private property, free market exchange system operates, if there are no price controls that restrict our right to make offers and to decide how much to buy and consume and in what ways.

It may be objected that we consumers don't buy and sell oil to each other. We buy it from foreign or domestic producers. Why should we pay foreigners that high price? We would rather pay than not have the oil, that's why. But under the present system of price controls on oil and natural gas, we can take it from domestic producers without paying its full value.

Some people assert the domestic producers don't deserve the higher market price because they didn't do anything to make the value that high. However, we should remember a few things. No matter what the reason, the value is higher and therefore someone is going to enjoy the higher value. It may be the politician who takes command over the oil and distributes it at low prices as largesse to political favorites, as happens under the entitlements program to some favored refiners. Rather than letting the investors in discovering crude oil have that increased value, the politicians, under price controls, take it from them and distribute it by a political program.

The politicians, ever pretending to save us from the troubles they impose on us with those price controls, are now grasping for even more power over our lives and wealth. The ability to choose our life styles consistently with whatever amount of resources and goods are available is being attacked by politicians who, under the veil of price controls, acquire power to control our lives to their benefit.

Those who are strongest in bending political power to their interest will be benefited by that political power. But the conflict between a more free society and a more politically directed one is the fundamental issue being masqueraded as an energy crisis.

# 6

## SEMANTICS AND METHODS

# THE ECONOMICS OF POWER

What economics has to say about power and the way it's used won't be found in any book on the principles of economics. Yet I believe there is a set of valid theorems of economics ready to be set down in one small volume. And I believe they are applicable to almost every bit of human history. Until that volume is actually written, I shall have to use my personal estimates of its contents. For present purposes I shall cite those theorems which appear to be pertinent. But I advise you to discriminate carefully between what I or any other *economist* may say and what *economic theory* says. I have much more confidence in the latter.

One of the propositions is that man is a choosing animal, who chooses to have more goods rather than less. Thus food, shelter, wealth, beauty, friends, respect, leisure, and political power are "goods" or attributes he would welcome.

It is not only pecuniary wealth that counts, but leisure, prestige, your wife's behavior, your colleagues' looks and attitudes, relief from anxiety and stress, etc. Businessmen do not ignore these other attributes any more than anyone else. Furthermore, economics does not make any assumptions about *why* man wants these various things. He may want them so that he can give them to other people as gifts out of the pure goodness of his heart. His ultimate ends or purposes in wanting these various things and attributes are unknown and irrelevant. What economics says is that businessmen, laborers, and housewives do *not* devote all their effort and skill to getting profits, wages, or shopping bargains. Other things count too. And their reason for wanting more of various things is not necessarily that they want them for their own self-benefit, however narrowly one may define self-benefit. What economics *does* assume is merely that a person chooses his actions in the light of the gains and costs as *he* sees them and as he weighs them. The *choice* is his—not necessarily the end benefit sought by the choice. The chooser may seek to benefit other people. Whom he may seek to benefit is irrelevant. He may be charitable; he may work for the good of others. Notice—this does not deny that most people, or even all people, act primarily for their own benefit.

Speech given at the University of Chicago Law School Dedicatory Conference, November 18, 1957. Reprinted by permission of the author.

Nor can economics classify people according to their preferences for wealth, relative to political power or to leisure. People certainly differ in these respects. Economics does not assert that no differences exist among people in their preference patterns for wealth, power, leisure, or prestige. It merely cannot in this respect classify the preference patterns of women and men, young and old, or Occidental and Oriental.

I presume we all know what we mean by wealth, friends, prestige, leisure. But what about power? It connotes physical power—the movement of foot-pounds per second. But it also connotes the ability to affect the behavior of people. The sources of physical power are obvious, for example, heat, magnetism, and gravity. Of course, I do not intend to apply the laws of physics to human behavior.

Yet physical power is indeed important in economic problems. Our material wealth and standard of living come in part from our control of physical power. This form of power is, at least in a free, individualistic society, typically applied against nature and not against other men. I say typically, because we do apply it to people when we imprison adults or spank children. But such application of physical power to people is so generally despised that it is severely restricted by "constitutions, checks and balances, divisions of authority, and short tenure of office." It is reserved primarily for use against individuals who have themselves applied power (coercion, theft) to other individuals—something that is not sanctioned in a capitalistic private property society.

But it is not this political or police power that concerns us today. Rather it is another form of power—the power to affect the behavior, actions, or choices of people *without* resort to physical violence. This other form of power is non-violent, in that actions are affected through voluntarism, persuasion, and bribery. I induce you to give me your attention by the bribe of giving you some pearls of wisdom in exchange. I bribe you into giving me your automobile in exchange for four cases of champagne, a refrigerator, and an automatic dishwasher, or any other combination of goods that you can bribe from others with the money I paid for your car. I allow that calling this bribery is provoking, but I do not mind provoking you into thinking about what kinds of trades are bad and, hence, called bribery and which kinds are good and, hence, called exchanges.

Exchanges among people involve choices among all kinds of things and attributes, whether they be meat, shoes, leisure, peace of mind, play, prestige, friends, love, children, freedom of thought, political power, and so on. Extra hours of leisure cost me sacrifices of earnings (i.e., what I could have bought).

Prestige may have to be sacrificed in order to obtain love, political power, or wealth. To be nice to others is not costless. Everything has its costs.

And by the way, this suggests that the way to have a happy marriage is never to refuse your wife anything. Let her have everything she wants. When she asks for a fur coat, a trip to Europe, or a new rug, say, "Why, of course you may have it if you wish. What do you wish to sacrifice for those things?" Let *her* choose what she wants in the face of the costs. Don't choose for her.

You may note that I separate forces of rewards and costs. This is an economics distinction, and a crucial one, that helps us distinguish between power (ability to meet costs) and incentives for doing so. For example, we refer to the power of General Motors, or the power of rich men, or the power of the President or of a senator's vote. But what power—in the sense of changing someone else's behavior—does a senator *use* if his vote on some issue may cost him votes? A rich man has the power to affect my behavior if he is prepared to give up some wealth to induce me to change my behavior. He gives up wealth, and he presumably gets something desirable in return. If *he* believes that the gain is less desirable, as he values it, than the cost, as he values it, then no matter how rich he is, he is constrained by his own decision to not act. He lacks the power to evade the costs. While he is potentially capable of applying much force or persuasion to affect my behavior, he is at the same time under the force of considering the *cost* to him of applying such force in comparison to the gain to him of doing so.

The temptation to conclude that the rich really have lower costs because extra dollars don't mean as much to them must be resisted by the thought that if the rich also have so much in the world, extra gains to them don't mean so much either. The so-called trivial importance of a dollar is matched by the trivial importance to them of what they can get with a dollar. If the psychological costs are low, so are the gains, for costs are nothing but forsaken gains.

We hear a lot about the power of giant corporations. GM has great political influence. It can affect wage rates by withdrawing from the market. It can drive small businessmen out of business by threats of withholding business. It can affect the prices at which it sells cars depending upon how many cars it produces.

Right off, I should admit I don't know what to make of all that. What is General Motors, other than a group of individuals? The stockholders are constantly changing. The directors change, and the employees change—at a rate no different from any small furniture store or drug store. To say it has great political influence leaves me mystified. Its many employees and stockholders constitute a large bulk of people, but do they have any more power than any other similar bulk of people? It could certainly drive out of business many firms if it wanted to. But to do this would cost GM a large amount of wealth. We could all do lots of things, but when the costs are considered, we don't. In the same sense, the people in GM could do lots of things, but the sheer economic costs are such that they don't. They may have the power but they haven't the power to ignore the costs. In other words, it's not some social responsibility or business statesmanship that is needed to explain why GM stockholders, directors, or employees are unwilling to use power in so-called irresponsible ways. Concern with their own wealth restrains them—wealth that would be lost by the economic costs of such "irresponsible" action. At least, and this is the point I would emphasize, this is what economic theory says.

One also hears that GM could drive down wages by withdrawing its labor demand from the market. What this means is that by having entered the market, it has driven up wages. And the question to consider is, "even if it has the power to withdraw and let wages fall to what they would have been in the absence of General Motors, what incentive would GM have to do this?" They would only suffer a loss of wealth. The stockholders of GM surely have this power, but they haven't the power to ignore these costs—they haven't the incentive to lose wealth.

You know, I could have come here dressed in California sports clothes. That would have been much more comfortable—at least in this room. There is no law that prevents me from doing this. It's just that the costs to me would be too high. I suspect I wouldn't be invited again to any other meeting. And in the same way, the reason that clerks in stores are polite to me, rather than rude when I take up their time, is that they don't want to pay the cost of sacrificed income. And the same applies to illegal acts. A reason that contracts are usually fulfilled is not that legal action would be taken but rather that future contracts would be hard to find. Honesty is the best policy because it is the least costly or most profitable in terms of all the things a person wants.

Take, for example, the newspapers. Why do they have an editorial page separate from their news pages? Because news reporting must be honest and as free from opinion as possible. Let any newspaper report false news, say about the outcome of a baseball game, or about a corporation's earnings, or about what some person says, and any other competing newspaper would be delighted to catch a falsehood and reveal it—not because the paper loves the truth or because it is subject to some self-policing code of ethics imposed by a council of its own industry—rather it does so in the interest of increasing its wealth by getting customers from other papers. It is this dog-eat-dog competition that keeps the news pages of the newspapers on the straight and narrow track. The test of the truth is ultimately with the public, and it is they who make or break a newspaper according to whether it reports truthfully or falsely. The only way the owner or editor can present biased stories or opinions or distortions is to label them plainly as such—which is what it does when it confines such things to its editorial pages.

The power of the public through its dollar votes is what imposes the costs of dishonesty on a dishonest newspaper. And in this connection I cannot restrain from two side remarks. First, the *New York Times* prides itself on printing all the news that's fit to print. Actually, the *Times* merely has broader coverage of some topics. The fact is that they present less truth than the so-called scandal sheets that do tell the *whole* truth, about who slept with whom at what time and place. And second, television and radio are not "free." Despite the name "free" radio and television, the public has to pay for them by putting up with programs poorer than they want or would buy. "Free" radio and TV are really costly radio and TV. The costs or sacrifices in wealth that the public can impose on the newspapers for bad reporting, or on the theaters for unwanted movies or plays, cannot be so directly imposed on radio and TV stations for bad programming, since we don't reward them or punish them with our purchases of radio and TV programs. They survive because they are protected from competitors by federal laws and because the public cannot reward good programming and punish bad programming with "pay" TV and radio.

In summary of this first point—it is the costs that one bears consequent to his actions—or the rewards that he gets—that determine how he shall use his wealth and power. And these costs and rewards are not merely those imposed by our legal system: our economic system of exchange provides an extremely effective control to use of power if competition and exchange are not made illegal.

The main point of all this is that an *exchange* is involved. I apply some "force" to you; i.e., I have some power over you as a result of offering you something, and you have power over me by offering me something. If the gain in my opinion of what I get is greater than the costs in my opinion, the exchange is consummated—behavior is affected.

This is what economic theory says, as I read it. Is it correct? All the evidence I've seen in my myopic way is consistent with economic theory. But I don't wish to debate this point. I merely wish to reveal what economics appears to say.

Let me now introduce the second fundamental theorem. The amount of anything a person chooses to earn or strive for depends upon *how much* of other goods he must sacrifice, just as my wife's purchases of new dresses depend upon how much of other things she must sacrifice in that purchase. What does a businessman sacrifice when he strives to increase his pecuniary wealth? He sacrifices leisure, tranquility, family life, and even some pleasantness with employees. The second fundamental theorem of economics says that the more of these things he must sacrifice to increase his pecuniary wealth, the less wealth he will seek. Conversely, the less wealth he must sacrifice to obtain an increase of leisure, tranquility, etc., the more of these attributes he will choose to have. In sum, the lower the cost of any good, the more he will take, where cost means not merely pecuniary cost, but also sacrifices of all or any other attributes or goods.

We are all familiar with some examples. The man who burns trash in his yard and thereby dumps the smoke and airborne ashes onto his neighbor is violating property rights in the same way he would if he were dumping garbage on his neighbor's property. A classic example is the dog owner who imposes the costs of dog care on his neighbors when he takes the dog for his nightly walk. If the costs were kept on the dog owner, we would have cleaner sidewalks as well as fewer dogs. Our tax laws give another example. Taxes on profits mean that increased business costs do not reduce after-tax profits an equivalent amount. Thus, an extra dollar spent on thicker rugs, while reducing pre-tax profits one dollar, reduces the after-tax profits by a smaller amount. This means that an extra dollar spent in the business costs less than a dollar to the owner; it costs him only the after-tax profits.

These are all obvious enough. But there is a special class of situations to which I would like to direct your attention, one in which the presence of monopoly produces what I think can justifiably be called irresponsible uses of power, irresponsible in that the costs are being borne by other people. By monopoly I mean restraints on entry. Precisely I mean either there are laws prohibiting competitors from entering or else there is a threat of physical harm to potential new competitors. I do *not* mean that potential entrants are dissuaded by the economic costs of setting up a competing business—I mean legal barriers and threat of physical harm. Consider our public utilities, such as gas, electricity, and telephone service. Public utilities are guaranteed protection from anyone who attempts to compete in the service. Lest any of you contemplate buying a diesel motor to generate electricity to sell to your neighbors, I warn you that the electric company merely has to pick up the telephone and you are stuck in jail. In return for this monopoly protection by the state police force, the monopolist agrees not to take a profit in excess of some standard, say 6 percent. Now, and this is essential for what follows, if the monopolist public utility is earning profits at the allowable rate, as the railroads are not, what will the owners gain from further increases in profits? Bigger wealth and profits involve more work, less leisure, less tranquility, more attention to business problems, less generous attitudes toward employees, and less to community activity. But worst of all, if profits *were* increased, regulatory commission converts them into lower prices for consumers.

Directors, managers, and employees of a public utility learn that a more leisurely pace, greater attention to community prestige, and charitable activities are tolerated by stockholders because the profits that are lost by such behavior could not have been captured by the owners. Had these profits been earned by greater business efficiency, utility rates could be reduced. But they are not, and the consumers' utility bills include the costs of this new kind of business statesmanship or social responsibility or inefficiency. And I suspect the public's only conscious awareness of this kind of inefficiency is based on observations of lagging expansion of services.

Economic theory, then, tells us that among the class of businessmen a larger proportion of the executives of public utilities (now earning near their profit limit) will be found using their business hours in non-business activities—like attending this meeting or giving funds of the company to charities or to schools. Not only that, they will direct more of their action to making their working conditions more pleasant—all of which really costs more to the consumer. This should be noticeable even in such simple things as prettier secretaries, thicker rugs, larger offices, more expensive furniture, and other obvious comforts in public utilities as compared with private competitive business. In a non-regulated private business more of the costs would be borne by the owners.

Please don't misunderstand me. I am not attacking or criticizing the morals or ethics of public utility officials. They are honest, moral, and virtuous, like me and thee. You and I would behave in the same way if put in their place, although we wouldn't be nearly as effective as they are. Nor am I here suggesting that we should change our laws.

Non-profit enterprises, and public-owned enterprises are subject to the same complications. It is no accident that this discussion is being presented by an employee of a non-profit public-owned institution, a state university. It was only when I began to wonder why professors behaved so differently from ordinary businessmen that the light dawned. Only self-protection prevents me from having used a state university or a heavily endowed non-profit university, instead of the public utility, as my example of irresponsible use of power resulting from the ability to thrust costs on to other people.

Before you lose patience, let me outline one other example of how irresponsible response to power arises from monopoly situations.

The bedrock foundation for the economic power of a labor union is its monopoly position. Without that it could not enforce wages above a free entry competitive level, for if it tried to do so, non-union workers would offer to work at competitive wages, thus destroying the union scale. To enforce its higher wage rates, it must keep out the wage-cutting competitors—it must be a monopoly. How does it get to be a monopoly and how does it remain one? First you induce the rest of society to accept your goals of being a monopolist. In the case of public utilities, this has been easy. In the case of unions, this was much harder, although it seems now to be widely enough accepted for all practical purposes. But when it comes to enforcing the monopoly right, i.e., keeping out competitors, the public is not willing to help the union be a monopolist in the way it will help a public utility. The union cannot telephone the police and have non-union competitors put in jail. Although the public attitude toward labor monopoly seems favorable, the public is not willing to let its police power be used to enforce it, nor, and this is most important, is it willing to use its police power to prevent it by protecting "strike breakers."

Instead, our police power is used neutrally; that is, it is not used to protect labor rights of non-union workers. How then does the union enforce its monopoly? It resorts to private threats and applications of violence rather than enforcement through publicly operated agencies. Private police forces are called "goons and gangsters," presumably because their actions are reprehensible or illegal. These special employees are specialists in private applications of force and violence and compulsion, although literally they are in the same class as police or military action. One is state owned; the other is privately owned. One is socially acceptable; the other is not, although its purposes are. Thus, if striking is done peacefully—that is, if potential strike breakers are kept out with no *overt* violence—no legal sanctions are available. Mind you, I do not decry this. I merely recite it as a fact of life which our society accepts and encourages—as, for example, when we urge collective bargaining between owner and union without non-union workers being allowed. Public utility officials can act in a civilized, socially acceptable way, but union officials cannot. Until the union is granted the aid of the police force, as utilities are, or until the picket is recognized as the equivalent of a policeman, union officials must retain specialists

in violence, if not themselves be such people. We have come close to this position in many unions, where the picket line or mere strike call is accepted by all
people as equivalent to the force of law. And just as overt violence is unnecessary to make you and me obey most laws, so *overt* violence is absent in these
unions. But the fact remains that so long as the law is not available to them in
the same way it is to utilities, they must at least have a standby army ready for
action. I illustrate this by noting that one labor union already has the power of
the police behind it, and the union officers do not need specialists in violence—
thugs—and the union officers and members are recognized as among the most
respected members of our society. I mean, of course, the American Medical
Association.

But it is not only this feature of irresponsible use of power, the presence of
gangsters and thugs, that is implied in the effort to obtain monopoly power.
There is also the *use* that is made of this monopoly power, the power to keep out
competitors by threat of violence. In some instances the power to create this
kind of monopoly is used to raise wages of the union members to the full monopoly height, with the benefits going to the members who are employed. In
other instances the employed must share part of their gains with the unemployed members of the union, but not with those workers who are unable to
work because union membership is denied them. Part of the unemployment is
disguised by non-union members being forced to work at wages, in other
areas, even lower than the competitive wage would have been in this industry
had it not been monopolized. It is the sharing of these monopoly gains and the
fight for them that is characteristic of much of the labor union behavior that
seem to us to be so reprehensible.

One can imagine what would happen if our public utilities, say our electric
company, were to seek to exploit its monopoly position to the hilt. It could enter into agreements with certain companies to not provide power to competitors, if in return a part of the resulting profits was shared with the utility. The
electric power company could easily shut off the power and keep out competitors. It is to avoid exactly this kind of action that we try to make utilities provide
services to all competitors on essentially equal terms. The union is not compelled by law to provide equal service to all competitors—the ease with which
special strike causes can be conjured up would frustrate such an attempt—
hence the incentive to engage in sweetheart contracts.

I need not detail this to any extent in Chicago, for the point I seek to develop
is that monopoly power, whether bestowed legally or obtained by threat of violence, results in displays and use of power that seem to fall in the irresponsible

category. The union, in achieving effective monopoly and then in dividing the monopoly surplus, displays its irresponsible use of power. The public utility displays what I would say is irresponsible use of power, not in the continuance of its monopoly position, but rather in the ways in which the monopoly surplus is utilized. I do not derive from economics any implication that this is bad or should be stopped. On this, economics is neutral. It merely implies certain forms of behavior, given certain standards of property rights.

If you wonder why I have talked so long, you have missed the whole point of my main theme. This lecture is free. I do not obtain a portion of any admission price—else I should be more careful to not abuse your patience with boredom. To continue even longer means that in the future my competitors would displace me from similar enjoyable opportunities of trying to stimulate your appreciation of economic theory. And so only because of that competitive threat, I stop and thank you.

# SUMMARY NOTES ON MISLEADING
# ECONOMIC JARGON

The terms *market power, monopoly, monopoly rent, Ricardian rent, collusion, cartel, output distortion, predatory pricing, exclusion,* and *anticompetitive* are widely used in economic and legal literature. Some have a precise, unambiguous meaning; others are ambiguous to the point of being useful as emotional, pejorative expressions which often confuse the reader and the writer. We shall use terms according to the following definitions:

## 1. Market Power

The power to affect one's selling price by the amount offered. This requires that a seller have a negatively sloped demand for his product such that the marginal revenue is sufficiently below the price to make the seller heed marginal revenue rather than price. Of course, *any* negative slope of a demand function means the marginal revenue is less than price, but the slope and quantities involved may be sufficiently small that marginal revenue is virtually equal to price. One possible source of market power is monopoly. (See figures 1 and 2.)

## 2. Monopoly

Initially this meant a seller protected by some legal or political restriction from competition of some other actual or potential sellers whose entry to the market would reduce the first seller's demand. The protection usually was in the form of politically imposed restrictions (laws, fines, taxes, franchises, or quotas on other sellers—as examples).

It is common, but not universal, that protected sellers thereby face demand curves that are less elastic (more negatively sloped) at any particular output and price combination; that is, he has market power.

This previously unpublished October 1977 article appears here by permission of the author.

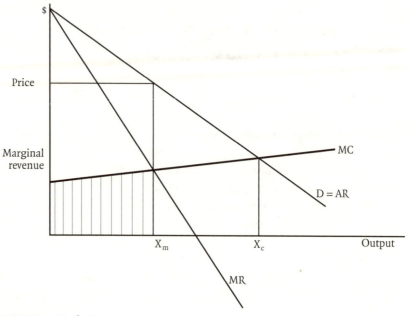

**FIGURE 1.** *Market Power*

### 3. Monopoly Rent

Usually, but not always, the protected seller (monopolist) can get a price for any output that is higher than he would receive without the restriction on other sellers. In other words, this means that usually the result is greater net income for the protected seller, greater than he would have obtained without the restriction. That *increase* of net income is called *monopoly rent*. (But beware, often a protected seller gets no advantage, because the demand for his product may be sufficiently small to not cover costs of production.) A law prohibiting anyone else from making sketches of my golf swing wouldn't do me any good, since my own sketches are so lousy. Still, it might be that some people would buy my sketches at a sufficiently low price—one so low that I would not produce any. Of course, if I did produce some and could affect their price by the quantity I produced, I would have market power, but no power to get any monopoly rents—let alone any net income. In sum, neither monopoly nor market power *guarantees* a gain.

Market power and monopoly tend to be confused with each other. Indeed, in some economic texts the two terms are synonymous. But they are different.

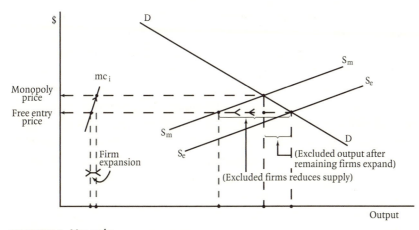

**FIGURE 2.** *Monopoly*

A person can have market power but no monopoly. Nothing restricts other people from offering lectures. Nevertheless, by charging a higher fee, I would sell fewer lectures—or putting it in reverse, by offering fewer lectures, I would get a higher price for those few I gave. Thus market power (i.e., marginal revenue less than price) can exist with or without monopoly (i.e., legal restrictions on competitors).

### 4. Ricardian Rent

Monopoly rent, the gain because of protection from other potential sellers, should not be confused with Ricardian rent, the higher income attributable to superior productivity. For example, I have the talent to write especially good books or to give especially good lectures, or I may have some especially fertile land. In all three cases I could get a higher price than could those selling poorer substitutes. I may also be able to affect the selling price of my services or of the rent I get for the land by the amount I offer to provide. That is, I may also have market power—or I may not. In any event, I have no legal monopoly position; I just have superior abilities that are *naturally rare or scarce.* For example, fine musicians command a higher fee than do the less talented. No contrived restrictions restrain others from trying to do as well, yet even without contrived restrictions, the superior resources or people get higher prices for their services. Their higher income is called a differential return of superiority, or Ricardian rent in honor of the person who first effectively explained the difference between (a) higher incomes to superior resources (Ricardian rent) and (b) higher incomes to those protected by contrived restrictions on other possible sellers (monopoly rent).

Economists long ago began indiscriminately to use a measure of market power (the extent to which price exceeds marginal revenue) as a measure of monopoly. This ensured persisting confusion and opportunity to hoodwink the general public and lawyers into bringing all kinds of antitrust or monopoly suits (for which economists are then hired to testify to either muddy issues or clarify the source of the confusion). How would I have measured monopoly? By the extent to which one's demand for his service or product is *shifted upward* as a result of the monopoly restriction on other sellers to yield a higher price than if the restriction were not imposed.

We can summarize as follows:

Market power (i.e., negatively sloped demand curve) holds in two different situations: (1) contrived restrictions on other sellers—which we here denote as monopoly; (2) natural limitations on amount and number of feasible suppliers, thereby implying that anyone can affect price by the amount he offers. Some, like Samuelson, avoid confusion by referring to natural versus contrived monopoly. We prefer to avoid the dangerous connotations of monopoly by restricting the term *monopoly* entirely to situations of political (or contrived) restrictions. But in any event, if the different *concepts* are understood and kept separate, then no matter what terminology is used the speaker or listener may avoid confusing one situation with the other.

Are contrived restrictions exclusively the result of political or legislated action? I believe that the overwhelming majority of cases of what is meant by contrived are in fact imposed by political, legislative action. There may be instances where other potential sellers are excluded by concerted private action. If so, then they, too, would be in the class of contrived monopoly. For example, it may be that the economically workable ores often are so limited that only three producers exist. They are not preventing others from entering the market. The value of their tin represents its superiority over other metals. This implies both (a) Ricardian rent of superiority and (b) a larger income from exercise of market power by producing less at a higher price than if they had no market power—but no monopoly rent occurs. There simply are no other sources. Do these three have market power?

Indeed they may not even have market power. Suppose, for example, that tin were exactly twice as good as steel—in whatever task was considered. Then tin would sell for exactly twice the price of steel, and if the price were raised ever so slightly above twice the price of steel, users would switch to steel. The three tin producers would have no market power—no negatively sloped demand for tin. But they would still be getting a Ricardian rent because of the superiority of tin over steel, just as land that is twice as productive will get twice the rent. Even if the three producers were divided into 1,000 small producers, no change would occur in price. The issue hinges on the elasticity of demand as seen by sellers. In this example, the elasticity of demand for this tin is so high—even for the industry demand—that the marginal revenue and price are virtually the same. No market power could exist regardless of fewness of sellers.

Recognizing that superior resources can produce higher incomes (called Ricardian rent) and that monopoly may, but not necessarily, result in higher incomes (called monopoly rent), one can ask if an increase in income necessarily will accrue to those who have market power, compared with what they would have earned without market power. There is no implication that market power yields larger incomes. Remember, market power refers only to elasticity of demand (i.e., the relation of price to marginal revenue). Sellers can have market power for any of several reasons. (They may also be monopolists by contrived restrictions against other sellers and get monopoly rent because of monopoly, not market power.) By superiority, they may have so large an output that the demand for their product is sufficiently reduced in elasticity to make the marginal revenue significantly lower than the price (i.e., give them market power). This may induce the firm to produce less than otherwise. But the question is, what would be the position of the demand or market price for such a seller? We don't have any way of knowing whether it would be lower or higher than if he had a small share, because we don't know why his share is large or small. The product could be different. Or identical to others, for if he could imitate the product of others, he might command a higher price. And they would then get a lower price. It's not possible to deduce on the basis of elasticity of demand what the effect of whatever made him have that kind of demand would be on the income of the firm or its market price. Furthermore, firms with market power but without monopoly protection may in fact be producing at a rate of output at which marginal cost equals price, and not some lower marginal revenue, because the marginal revenue under some very common selling arrangements could be virtually identical to price. We do not here go into that, except to note that it does not follow automatically that existence of market power implies a higher price or higher income or smaller output.

## 5. Collusion, or Cartel

Suppose many producers, say of wheat or steel, were to agree to restrict output to equate the *group's* marginal revenue to its marginal cost, thereby avoiding each firm's getting revenue at the expense of others. This joint action to maximize the group's income could be achieved by a merger or by a formal agreement or by all joining some association or cooperative-action group which would guide each firm's actions. This is an attempt to raise the price and lower the output below what it would be without the agreement. We use the term *collusion* or *cartel* for any joint action taken to raise price or lower output, even though demand and costs have not changed, so that the buyers are worse off than if the joint action were not taken. The concept of collusion hinges on the purpose and effect, not on coordinated joint action per se. Coordinated joint action could reduce price or increase output or reduce costs. For example, two lawyers may form a partnership to provide better service at a lower cost. Indeed, that is why firms exist. Yet firms are *coalitions* (not collusions). It is not joint action or coalitions that are objectionable. It is the intended or *realized* effect that distinguishes the concept of a coalition from that of a cartel or collusion.

*Conjectural Remarks.* OPEC is not a cartel in the strict sense of the term. A cartel requires a joint restriction of output; some method must exist for each member's output to be restricted below what the member would prefer to sell *at the cartel price*, because the marginal revenue of each exceeds its individual marginal costs. No central control of a member's output exists. Each produces whatever amounts it likes. Only one member, Saudi Arabia, has reduced its output below what it would like to sell *at the existing price*. And it is Saudi Arabia which sets the price, while the other members produce as much as they wish, leaving Saudi Arabia with the remainder. It is the largest producer; its perceived marginal revenue at any given price is less than the perceived marginal revenue of any other producer. This more appropriate model is the dominant firm model. This survives because the nondominant firms can rapidly expand capacity to produce. For oil, this is not true. Oil is not produceable as readily as most other goods.

The preceding paragraph assumed that the non-Saudi oil producers were at liberty to sell whatever amount of oil they had, at whatever price they could get. Another producer could not get more than Saudi Arabia's price, because of the Saudi ability and willingness to produce whatever oil would prevent the price from being higher. That some producer might want to lower the price below the Saudi price was assumed unreal. But if some other producer did want to lower its price (because it had not been able to sell all it had at the existing Saudi price, and it believed it could make greater income by selling more at a lower price), Saudi Arabia would have to take preventive action—possibly an extreme transient price cut to teach the price-cutter, and other possible cutters, a transient lesson of long-lasting value. Then the preventive action or punishment imposed on potential price-cutters would mean a cartel was at work, as defined earlier, because now some restrictive action was taken to reduce the output of other members of the group. In fact, insofar as I can ascertain, the OPEC group does *not* face this problem. The other smaller-supply countries apparently want a higher price—obviously—because Saudi Arabia would have to be the country that cut back output while the remaining smaller members continued to operate at full blast at a higher price—at Saudi Arabia's expense.

OPEC is not a cartel in strict technical terms. That Saudi Arabia is a dominant firm raising prices, with the rest unable to destroy that situation by increasing their capacity, is a better interpretation, though it, too, may be inferior to the conjectured view that the current price now more correctly anticipates the future value of oil and is correctly inducing a lower consumption rate.

If I may go further, it is not out of the realm of plausibility that the current price is the competitive price. The projected demand and supply of oil in the future implies a price that is much higher than it was a few years ago. As demand increased and oil supplies did not at the same rate, sudden perception of the future higher value of oil led to a higher present value and reduced rate of present consumption. It makes no difference who reduces his sale of oil or who decides to hold the oil. The gains to the holder of oil match those he would get if he were to sell his oil and invest the proceeds in any other venture. That is, wealth grows at the rate of interest. Saudi Arabia is the principal party holding back its sale of oil. So long as someone does it, no matter. And if no one else does, it will pay anyone to hold his oil awaiting the future higher price—higher than that implied by the rate of interest as other current suppliers foolishly sell off their oil.

## 6. Monopoly Output Distortion versus Monopoly Inefficiency

To be distinguished from output distortion caused by the difference between price and marginal revenue—often called *monopoly output distortion*—is *monopoly inefficiency*. This latter is the effect on productiveness when a person is protected from potential rivals. The denial of the right to experiment or try alternative techniques or methods of production or organization reduces the range of alternatives that society can appraise. As a result, less growth in productive ability is said to occur. Notice that we are not asserting that a monopolist has less incentive to search and to experiment to increase his wealth by selective improved ways of production or better goods. He has just as much to gain as if there were scores of others competing for that business; indeed, he may gain more because others cannot imitate him so quickly. With competition, more of the gain will go to consumers and less will remain with the innovator. What we are asserting is that, given the incentives in either case, *more* experimentation can occur because more people can try their hand in more activities. That wider span of aspirants trying a wider range of alternatives permits selection from a wider range of new ideas and techniques. Insofar as a wider range implies discovery of better methods than a smaller range of restricted experiments, one can argue that monopoly which prevents others from attempting to outperform existing sellers in some area will reduce the pace of progress. We should not confuse these two different forms of advance: degree of individual effort and degree of new methods from which society can select superior techniques.

### 7. Predatory Pricing

Again, as with collusion, the intent is crucial. If I succeed in making something at lower cost and sell more of it at a lower price, others are forced to switch to other kinds of work. I have excluded them from this market. My intent was to benefit myself and my customers, not to harm other sellers. That behavior is socially commended. Socially approved behavior does not occur only if no one is made worse off. It is approved because it provides more output or reduced costs, and those who can not do as well must switch to other activities at which they can produce at lower costs than those of competitors (and there always are such other activities—though we shall not demonstrate that elementary fact here). Such displacement and switching means a larger, more valuable social total.

The common objection is that after I have eliminated some other sellers I will later try to reduce output or raise prices and capture from the consumers a monopoly rent during the interval before new suppliers can enter. I have heard this allegation often, but I have yet to see evidence of it. What I have not seen may nevertheless exist. I believe this is a tactic not worth trying to restrain by legislative or administrative action. First, it has not been demonstrated to be an occurrence of any significance. Second, the frequency of "false arrests" is costly. Confusion arises because price-cutting to meet changing market demand and supply is often misconceived as predatory pricing.

False appearances of predatory pricing:

(a) Often in charges of predatory pricing, in which the price is said to be below the costs of production, the costs are misinterpreted as being higher than they really are. The true cost is the marginal cost of the extra output being sold at the "low" price. This can be far below or above the irrelevant average cost.

(b) Another confusion is thinking that the current price or sales value is the total price obtained by the sale of a good. Free samples and introductory offers often bring in revenue *later* in excess of the cost of the item being given away now. Most prepurchase information is provided to *prospective* buyers free (i.e., at the risk of the supplier). When, and if, someone makes a purchase, that buyer pays in the price enough to help cover the cost of the earlier information provision.

(c) The price at which an item is sold could be below its cost if the sale of the item is tied to another good whose price is sufficient to cover the cost of both the tied item and the one being given away, or sold at a "low price." For example, a free ride to the hotel from the airport is not given free to the traveler. He gets the ride only if he stays at the hotel. What is happening is that he is being given a discount or lower price on the hotel room (equal to cost of the taxi) and is being charged the normal price of the room. The purpose of the "free" taxi ride is to enable the hotel operator to cut the price of his rooms to some occupants who would not otherwise come to the hotel, while not cutting the price to patrons who come anyway. This is exemplified also by so-called loss leaders.

In none of these three cases is there predatory pricing intent or pricing below cost. The costs are misunderstood or the price is not correctly perceived by the critic charging predatory pricing.

## 8. Exclusion

Clearly something undesirable is meant, similar to that in the concept of collusion. What must be meant is that duties, costs, or actions are forced upon others which are not the consequences of having to match my offerings to the public. These costs are a result of one party's actions designed to reduce someone else's competitive ability without in any way having reduced the first party's costs or increased the attractiveness of his products.

Exclusionary tactics are those that do not improve one's productive abilities or product offerings *and* which do reduce someone else's by imposing new duties or costs on others. Were I to get a law passed prohibiting others from giving lectures in economics, that would be exclusionary. Improving my teaching talents and techniques and developing a superior reputation by excellent performance make it more difficult for others to get business, but that is not an exclusionary (i.e., undesirable) tactic, nor is extensive advertising that informs more people of my offerings and attributes. That advertising cost is one I bear, and a newcomer bears similar advertising costs.

Prohibiting downline retailers (who retail my product) from selling products other than those manufactured by me is not exclusionary, *if* that enhances the consumers' knowledge of the availability of my offerings or increases the reliability of the quality of my product, which knowledge and reliability are often affected by what retailers do. Exclusive selling arrangements can be a means of improving service and quality of product to consumers. They cannot be considered exclusionary in causing undesirable exclusion or in being undesirable means of competition.

The term *barrier to entry* is a synonym for *exclusionary device.*

Ultimately what is considered desirable competition comes down to defining what kinds of actions to advance one's interest are considered socially acceptable and which are not. Those that are, are often called *competitive,* and those that are not, are often called *anticompetitive.* In strict language all are competitive. Two quarterbacks on a football team can compete for that position either by outperforming or by maiming each other. Both are competitive. The question is, "which methods are acceptable and which are not?" That is to be answered after discerning their effects. And that is what economics is all about—the discerning of the effects of alternative social arrangements or rules.

### 9. Anticompetitive

The word *anticompetitive* is widely used in legal arguments, resulting in confusion. The word has at least five meanings because there are at least five types of competitive action.

1. *Striving to overcome nature.* One sense of the term is that of struggling to overcome natural forces, such as discovering new knowledge or techniques for coaxing more from the nonhuman environment. Call this *working.* The only anticompetitive action in this sense is simply a prevention of work or learning by others or by oneself.

2. *Rivalry against second parties for approval by third parties.* A second sense is striving to offer better terms than second parties for contracts with third parties. The contracts may be informal, such as friendship, marriage, and games, or they may be formal exchange contracts. This behavior relies on making more

appealing offers to third parties than are offered by rival second parties. Call this *rivalry*.

3. Two parties to a contract may haggle over the division of gains of trade exceeding those over the next best offers. They are attempting to reach an acceptable division of the excess gains. Call this *haggling*.

4. Killing, maiming, or otherwise reducing the ability of others to make acceptable offers to third parties is a kind of behavior that is called competitive, though regarded as undesirable. Aside from the moral disapproval, third parties (as well as the second) are deprived of offers with no countervailing gain. Call this *interference*.

5. Another sense, possibly a subcase of interference, is the taking of wealth from another person for one's own benefit. Interference means only the reduction of some other person's wealth or ability without adding to one's own. But this fifth sense, *predation*, is one in which the predator gets what the prey lost. Call this, in accord with conventional legal language, *theft*.

Obviously, if someone is accused of anticompetitive behavior, we must be told exactly what type of competition he is using to restrain what other type. If he is restraining type 1, 2, or 3, objections might be raised. If the so-called anticompetitive action is designed to prevent type 4 or 5, should we object? If what is meant by an anticompetitive action is type 1, 2, or 3 competition, should it be called anticompetitive?

*Concluding notes on Anticompetitive Behavior*

(a) We can now see that a first party who outperforms a second party by superior offers to a third party, who thereby reduces what the wealth of the second party would otherwise have been, is not engaged in type 5 competition—predation. He is engaged in type 2 competition—rivalry—and possibly in type 1—work.

(b) If two people join into one firm and the second party no longer makes separate offers to third parties, the action is not anticompetitive in the sense of type 2, rivalry—if it results in improved offers by the pair over what would otherwise have been available to third parties. No member of the pair is restrained from making better offers to consumers than formerly. (They now make them jointly *and make better offers*.) If, however, the parties jointly restrict their offers and thereby give third parties *poorer* offers (poorer quality or higher prices) than had they not joined together, they would be anticompetitive of type 2, in that they have restrained the rivalrous actions. The method of restraining the sets of offers or their quality is not crucial. Any restraint that leads to reduced quality of offers is pertinent in being undesirably anticompetitive of type 2 competition. Or it could be considered a form of type 4 or 5 competition, and hence undesirable.

(c) Competition in *all* forms is never reduced due to anticompetitive action. It is *diverted* to more of some other form, from, say, type 2 to 3, or the reverse. Hence, one should refrain from "anticompetitive" terminology and think, instead, of type 1, 2, 3, 4, or 5 competition—or of working, rivalry, haggling, interference, or theft.

# WORDS:

## MUSICAL OR MEANINGFUL?

Melody: Traditional    Arranged by Armen A. Alchian

The terminology of economics (and of the law) encourages romance, emotion, confusion, and lawsuits. Words like *efficiency, monopoly, collusion, anticompetitive, freight absorption,* and *cartel* are only a few. Herein, as a means of future recall, is a brief summary of the meanings of some commonly used words.

### A. Efficiency

In a situation characterized by at least two controllable variables, one cannot generally maximize nor minimize both. For example, if I could grow wheat and soybeans, it would be senseless to speak of maximizing the amounts of both wheat and soybeans, because the more soybeans I produce, the less wheat I can produce. What is logical is a *constrained maximum*—that is, the maximum feasible amount of one for a specified amount of the other. Almost all economic analysis involves a constrained maximum (or minimum) of this kind.

A graph illustrates how the concept of efficiency differs from a simple maximum (figure 1). All points on the curved line are efficient combinations of outputs of soybeans and wheat, because for any specified amount of the variable on the horizontal axis (soybeans), the maximum possible quantity of the other variable (wheat) is indicated by the vertical height of the curved line. Each point on that line represents "efficiency," because each is the maximum amount of wheat feasible, given the constraint of a specified amount of the other variable, soybeans. In general, one must first identify the desired entities (or variables, goods, services, amenities, features, or whatever), and second, ascertain all achievable different combinations of amounts of these entities. Of all these, the efficient combinations are those for which an increased amount of one entity necessitates a reduction in some others. To agree with (indeed, even

This previously unpublished 1979 article appears here by permission of the author.

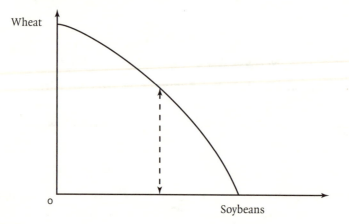

**FIGURE 1.**

to understand) someone else as to whether or not efficiency is desirable requires agreement about the variables included in a set of relevant entities.

However, can any actual situation fail to already be efficient? After all, if there is a more desirable, feasible situation, why has it not been achieved? Perhaps people have not perceived it. Maybe the costs of communication, negotiation, enforcing a contract, or the fear that some would cheat on a contract prevents it. However, these obstacles are as real as the lack of knowledge of electrical theory two hundred years ago. To say man, therefore, was inefficient two hundred years ago would empty the concept of any usefulness. Nevertheless, unless we do say that man was inefficient in the past because he did not know as much as we do now, we must say that every *existing* situation is efficient. Otherwise, why is the improvement not already realized? Because of these considerations I prefer to use the word *efficiency* only when dealing with the implications of some hypothetical *model*. In other words, it is a property of the implication of a theory or model, not of reality.

### B. Pareto Efficient

"Pareto efficient" is the description given to any situation with respect to welfare of different people—that is, in which there is no known feasible means for any persons to achieve more preferred situations without necessarily making some other people worse off. (The name Pareto is for Vilfredo Pareto [1883–1923], who first formally used this criterion analytically.) If a better situation for some person could be achieved without making any others worse off, the existing situation is, by definition, not yet Pareto efficient—or *Pareto optimal*, as it is sometimes called. For a private property, market and exchange situation this idea is usually expressed as, "The parties maximize the sum of the total personal values of the buyers (consumers) and sellers (producers) relative to their initial situation."

Underlying the apparently innocuous, widely averred Pareto efficient criterion is the assumption that each person's opinion of what is most desirable for himself is what counts. But this self-appraising assumption is not generally accepted—for my children, senile people, and mental incompetents (which, of course, means everyone who behaves in ways I disapprove). The choices made by other people which I (and some other people) regard as "intolerable," "inappropriate," "immoral" are so common that Pareto optimality is not robust and universally accepted, however much lip service is paid it. "The" conception of the good life need not utilize the self-appraisal preference norm. And if it doesn't, the Pareto optimal criterion is inappropriate.

The classical economic method of *analysis* is accused (validly) of being individualist. But in economic analysis, individual choice is an *analytic* foundation, not a *normative* standard or justification of an individual's behavior nor of the propriety of the implied or observed events.

Incidentally, it is incorrect to say that mutually agreed-upon exchanges of private property rights never hurt other people. I may offer a third party better terms of trade than you can. In that event you do not get as much from trade as you would if I were not making the better offer. My superior competitive offer hurts those from whom customers are diverted. These effects on *exchange rates*, or prices, are unavoidable. One's offer is someone else's competition. To prevent better offers is to make buyers captives of their *current* sellers. The right to buy or sell from new, better competitors is permitted, I conjecture, because the gains exceed the loss to suppliers whose customers are bid away by better offers.

### c. Monopoly and Monopoly Rent

The word *monopoly* has been used in so many different ways that it is impossible to find a generally accepted meaning for the term. The term appears in the Sherman Antitrust Act without either a denotative or a connotative definition. Interpretations have varied wildly and inconsistently in the judicial records. Nevertheless, some analytically useful meanings remain. One historical usage applied to a seller, the demand for whose services is increased by "inessential" restrictions imposed on uses of resources by other actual or potential sellers.

A monopolistic—or "inessential, unnecessary"—restriction on the choice of uses of one's resources is one which denies or erases rights which could be exercised without restricting other people's rights to use of their resources. Such a restriction is not one imposed by Nature. It is not one caused by necessary, inescapable physical incompatibility between uses of resources. As a result, it reduces the scope of one's rights to use resources without enhancing the scope of rights of other people to use other goods. For example, a denial of the right of a person other than person A to operate a flower shop is inessential, because A could operate the flower shop in any event without reducing the rights of others to use their resources. An inessential restriction denies or removes a right to use resources even in ways that would not affect or alter the physical use potential of other resources by other people. It is not a restriction resulting from any incompatibility in alternative physical uses.

An essential restriction is one imposed by natural incompatibility of physical uses. In this case, "rights" state who has the authority to decide which of the physically incompatible uses is to be chosen for a resource—say, some acre of land. It does restrict others from the choice among the physically conflicting uses of that acre of land. Such rights are assignments of rights to choose among the inevitably or inescapably incompatible uses, since it is impossible for one party to have rights to choose uses of that land without denying rights to others to choose the uses of that land. Rights identify who has authority to choose uses. Rights do not impose restrictions that would not otherwise have existed. Incompatibility of some simultaneous uses of a resource is an inescapable natural fact, not one arbitrarily added as some contrived restraint. It assigns decision rights over that set of alternative uses to that resource.

Restrictions that prevent A from growing tobacco on some land are not necessary to permit others to exercise control of physical uses of other land. Note the term "physical"; in contrast, the exchange value of rights to resources is affected by what other people do with their resources when they compete for the patronage of buyers or sellers. Therefore exchange value interdependence is not avoided in the exercise of private property rights.

A zoning law may state that B has no right to open a restaurant at some particular site if the odors are thrust on the neighbors' properties is an essential restriction. The zoning law is a clarification, identification, allocation, or assignment of property rights to physical uses of goods. It states that B cannot thrust noise or odors on the neighbors' land without the approval or permission of the neighboring landowners. This kind of law clarifies who has what rights to physical conditions or uses of land. However, some zoning ordinances transfer or eliminate (rather than clarify or reduce ambiguities of) rights to uses of land; such restrictions are not necessary to protect rights to use of neighboring land. For example, a zoning ordinance that would permit an apartment building on Blackacre for rental, but not for condominiums, imposes "inessential" restrictions.

Inessential ("contrived, artificial, monopolistic") restraints against potential suppliers reduce customers' opportunities to be served by those suppliers. The resulting increased income to the protected supplier, called a monopolist, is called *monopoly rent*. Typically, a measure of the monopoly rent is difficult or impossible, though often tangential evidence reveals its presence. For example, liquor stores in California are limited in number by legislation. The license to operate a liquor store has a value to the license owner—the monopoly rent. Similarly, some members of some unions which restrict membership will get a higher wage because of their monopoly position—restricting other people's use of their labor services. Or farmers may get a higher income in the form of monopoly rent because the quantity of tobacco or peanuts that may be grown legally by other farmers is restricted. In all these cases monopoly rent (not the same as profit) is created—a higher income transferred to the monopolist by the added restriction on other people's use of their resources. The monopolists' higher income is not an increase on social product. It is merely a transfer of income from consumers. Such monopolists have to compete in seeking those political favors and protection. We call that competition for monopoly status *monopoly-rent seeking* competition—that is, competition to *get* protected monopoly status. Often that costs as much as—or more than—it is worth.

### D. Market Power

*Market power* and *monopoly* power (in the preceding sense) are often confused with each other. Sometimes, unfortunately, the two terms are even used as synonyms. But a person can have market power without monopoly and monopoly without market power. Market power is the power to raise one's price without losing all customers. For example, nothing is imposed as a restriction restraining other people from offering to give lectures to compete with me, so I am not a monopolist in the sense of being protected by restraints on others' use of their resources. Nevertheless, by charging a higher fee, I would sell fewer lectures; that is, I have market power. Or by offering fewer lectures, I would get a higher price for each of those I do give. The same is true for almost every retailer, with respect to the prices and the quantity. They have market power.

Economists long ago (1936) began to use and identify market power as a criterion or measure of the price increasing effect of monopoly. Market power was defined and *measured* by the extent to which price exceeds marginal revenue and marginal cost. If a seller with market power produces less, the resources released to other producers elsewhere produce other goods. The output of *other* goods will be larger. What, if anything, is bad about that? The answer proferred by economists is that the potential but forsaken output *here* is worth more to consumers than what is produced elsewhere instead.

How is that deduced? By the meaning of the demand curve. The seller seeks to produce a rate of output beyond which the cost of producing more would exceed the increased sales receipts (marginal revenue) of a greater output. To produce more, the extra costs would exceed the extra sales receipts (marginal revenue) and would create losses on the increased output. But we know that the value *to customers* of the potential *extra* output exceeds the marginal revenue to the seller. The seller looks at *the marginal revenue* of the output and adjusts output so as to equate that with marginal cost. Remember, marginal revenue is not the same as its value to consumers, which is measured by the *price* which that extra output would command in the market. The seller's marginal revenue is *less* than the selling price, and that disparity, wherein the seller heeds his increment in sales revenue (i.e., marginal revenue) rather than the larger true value (price) to the customer, is a measure of forsaken potential consumption value.

The value to consumers of what could have been produced here—measured by the price—exceeds the value of what could be produced elsewhere (measured by the marginal cost of this product). That excess of the value (price) to the consumer of more goods here over the value of the other goods that could be produced instead (measured by the marginal cost of goods here) is the sacrificed potential gain in consumption value. Resources that could produce more-valuable goods for the customers of this seller with market power are not used to do so and instead are left to producing other goods that are worth less. That is the so-called potential *distortion of output* (or inefficiency) that may result from market power. It may occur if the marginal revenue is significantly less than price. Ironically, the seller would be better off if he could find a way to sell more goods, or to some additional customers, without lowering price on all his current sales. But we do not here review some means by which this can be done.

It is important to distinguish between contractual restraints mutually agreed to by the parties to a contract. The latter are *ancillary* contractual restraints (e.g., the Addyston Pipe suit in the Supreme Court). Thus, though two independent lawyers form a partnership and restrain each other, they are able to offer consumers better service. *Better* situations for consumers do not require more suppliers. In the present example the number of independent competitors is reduced, but consumers have better (lower-cost or higher-valued) options. The Addyston Pipe decision clearly laid down these conditions, but several subsequent decisions have ignored that clarification and have ensured persisting confusion between ancillary contractual restraints and monopoly restrictions and also between market power and monopoly; the result has been that economists are then paid handsomely either to testify to muddy issues even more or to clarify the source of the confusion. If the concepts are understood and kept separate, confusion will be reduced.

The preceding exposition of the terms *monopoly* and *market power* should clarify a serious confusion in recent discussions of "competition for monopoly status." It has been argued that a bad feature of monopoly, in addition to the worsening opportunities for consumers, is the expenditure of resources to obtain the restrictions that create monopoly. That argument is correct if it is confined to a monopoly constraint on competitors. However, just because *market power*, meaning a negatively sloped demand for a seller's services, is often also called *monopoly*, it cannot be argued that competition that results in having a negatively sloped demand curve (market power) is wasteful. That non sequitur arises because of confusing monopoly and market power. Market power can be the result of providing a preferred, better product.

Will an increase in income accrue to those who have either monopoly power or market power? Yes, for monopoly, but there is *no* implication that market power yields larger incomes. Remember, market power refers only to degree of elasticity of demand. It is not possible to deduce from the elasticity of demand what gave the producer that kind of demand, nor what that means for the income of a firm or its market price, nor the effects on consumers. Furthermore, firms with market power, but without contrived monopoly, may be producing an output at which price does equal marginal cost, that is, without market power distortion of output. The reason is that under some very common selling arrangements marginal revenue can be made virtually identical to price of the extra units sold. Several pricing and selling tactics are available to avoid market power distortion.

### E. Ricardian Rent

Ricardian rent is the name of the higher income of a resource attributable to *superior* productivity or lower costs. For example, suppose I have the talent to write unusually good books or am unusually beautiful or own some superior located or fertile land. I have superior natural abilities that are better *and* sufficiently scarce that I can get a higher price for my services or do the same task at lower cost. More-talented musicians command higher fees. Better programmers for computers do also. No contrived, inessential restrictions restrain other musicians. The higher differential return is due to superiority.

### F. Basing Point Pricing

One important example of the serious errors from failure to recognize Ricardian rent of superior resources is the alleged phenomenon called *phantom freight*. For example, in 1978 a federal court jury in New Orleans declared the southeastern producers of plywood were collecting phantom freight on shipments to Florida by charging a price equal to "the Seattle price of plywood plus freight" without actually shipping the plywood from Seattle. The error is in neglecting to notice that the plywood produced in the Southeast is produced with superior resources (land closer to the Florida market). That land, being nearer the consumer, is worth a higher rent as a source of plywood nearer to Florida. And the larger rental value of the nearer land is equal to, and captures, the transport savings to Florida. The owners of the land where the trees grow for making plywood in the Southeast get a higher rent or payment because of that superior location nearer consumers (lower cost of supply). That difference *absorbs* the freight saving and is due to the superior location of southeastern lumber growth. To confuse that higher value of the superior land with phantom freight is to misunderstand that the higher rent is received by the superior land because it *is able to eliminate* that transport cost.

Under the confused phantom freight allegation, an auto mechanic who diagnoses and repairs a car faster than a poorer mechanic "should not" get a higher wage. The extra wage he earns would, under that phantom freight analogy, be payment for the phantom hours he didn't use to repair the car. Because he provides the service at a lower cost than the mass of average mechanics, he keeps the difference between their competitive price and his costs.

To allege phantom freight in shipping plywood to Florida is to say Floridians should have rights to that value of the superior land, not the landowners. With that kind of argument, *all* landowners, no matter whether the land is located in the center of the city or in the extreme margin distant from the city, would be paid the same rent (presumably zero)—with the higher value of the superior land being given to the lucky renters or buyers of the services and taken from the owners of that land which is located closer to the consuming population. (How will it be decided who are to be the lucky renters to get the superior land at that price below the competitive price?) Those who allege phantom freight are implicitly contending that all resources, no matter how different their value or productivity, should get the same reward, with the gains of value of superior, cost-saving resources going to buyers—which buyers and at what noncompetitive price?

Such are the consequences of failing to recognize differences in productivity of resources and the associated differences in rent, or price, received—an amount that lawyers would like to collect in costs of misguided overpricing or price-fixing cases rather than permit the owners of the more productive resources to have it. Basically the phantom freight contention says that the price to customers should be below the price that equates amount demanded to the amount supplied.

*Freight absorption* is a difference between the prices in two places that is less than the transport cost. For example, if the price at the production site is $1 and is $1.50 at a distant site, when transport costs are $.75, freight costs of $.25 are absorbed by the shipper. The reason for such an apparently anomalous situation is that marginal revenue, not price, is the supplier's basis for comparison. The difference in marginal revenues will match the transport cost. No cartel or monopoly restraint on competition is required for freight absorption to be present. It is consistent with independent competition.

*Cross hauling.* The same kind of goods are transported past each other in opposite directions. Cross hauling can typically be explained by the presence of multiple source supply to ensure against supply interruption, high planning costs, nonlinear costs of transport, or nonhomogenous goods that are erroneously thought to be homogenous.

*Basing points.* Prices are quoted as the sum of a price at some geographic base plus transport, even though the supplier is not located at the base site. This is consistent with independent competition when the price-setting dominant supply to other areas comes from the basing point, while other producers nearer the market do not supply enough to affect the price.

A cartel would not engage in marginal revenue equalization, cross hauling, freight absorption, or basing points, since it heeds different marginal revenues than do independent competitors.

## G. Competition

*Competition* is here defined as any activity which is intended to improve one's situation relative to another person. It is difficult, indeed impossible, to imagine a world of scarcity in which competition—a striving to improve one's circumstances—does not occur.

*Working to overcome nature.* One sense is that of working to overcome natural forces, such as discovering new knowledge or techniques for coaxing more from the nonhuman environment.

*Rivalry against second parties for approval by third parties.* Another sense is rivalry in striving to offer better terms than second parties for contracts with third parties. The contract may be informal, such as friendship, marriage, or games, or it may be a formal exchange contract. This behavior relies on making more appealing offers to third parties than are offered by rival second parties.

*Bargaining.* A proposed trade will benefit both parties if the buyer's value exceeds the seller's. The division of that difference between the two parties is the object of bargaining. The form is varied, ranging from standing pat, bluffing, and threatening to not trade, to whatever else may be persuasive, short of threatening to take the item by theft.

*Theft,* or violent taking of resources from another party, is a common form of competition, usually undesirable, illegal, and socially condemned. Similarly, violence, killing, and maiming or a threat to do so are forms of competition, usually considered illegal except in some international disputes.

This question of allowable forms of competition is an exquisitely crucial issue in every society. The members of the society must be inculcated with the recognition of which forms of competition are the "right," "legitimate," and "honorable" forms. If the overwhelming majority of the society does not agree, it will not manifest cohesion or viability. But not any type of competition is equally good as a viable basis. It makes a difference if the rules are those of honesty, contract fulfillment, and exchangeable private property rights in controlling resources or are, instead, say, political control of resources backed by potential military force and dictation as to what goods to produce and how to distribute the results. We all have our convictions about the answers.

But whatever the case, the only economic analysis which has passed the test of scientific validity is that which analyzes a society whose dominant institution for controlling people and for selections of uses of resources is that of private property rights, with people competing by striving to produce more and by using offers of exchange. Unfortunately the analytic laws of other systems still escape us.

## h. Coalition, Collusion, Cartel

If a group of producers, say, of wheat or of steel, were somehow able to agree and could enforce a restriction of their aggregate output to equate the group's marginal revenue to its marginal costs, they would each avoid getting revenue at the expense of other firms. This joint action to maximize the group's income by restricting output might be achieved by a merger or by a formal agreement or by all joining some association or cooperative-action group. This would result in a higher price and lower output—assuming no effect on costs. We use the term *collusion* or *cartel* for any joint action taken to (a) raise price or lower output and where (b) demand is not increased and (c) costs are not reduced. That attitude toward joint action depends not on the fact of coordinated action but on the effects. Thus, two lawyers who form a partnership may provide better service at a lower cost. Firms are *coalitions* and are not called cartels, because it is assumed the coalition is beneficial to consumers and producers. The effects, not the form of organization, distinguish the concept of the (good) coalition from the (bad) collusive cartel.

### 1. Intra-brand Competition

Few expressions generate more error than *intra-brand competition*, which conjures sales agents striving to provide a branded product more successfully than other sellers of the same brand. Such competition is alleged to be reduced when several retailers of a branded good are not allowed to sell for less than a price set by the manufacturer or have exclusive territories or areas of primary responsibility. But it should be observed that a manufacturer wants his downstream retailers to compete prices down to the lowest level, since the manufacturer is already charging his best wholesale price to the retailers. For example, Campbell Soup's manufacturer has no interest in permitting retailers to overcharge customers and reduce the manufacturer's sales.

Under some circumstances the appearance of restraints on intra-brand competition among retailers can be beneficial to consumers and producers alike. The critical circumstances are these: (a) a branded product's quality or characteristics are affected significantly by *both* the downstream retailer and the manufacturer, (b) the consumer cannot tell easily who is to blame for defective products, and (c) the retailer performs these services at his own investment expense and (d) expects to be rewarded in the purchase price of those who do buy the goods *from him*. These conditions make what is misleadingly called "intra-brand" competition degenerate into "contra-brand" competition among the retailers, unless each retailer and the manufacturer are protected from free riding by other retailers.

For example, a discount-house–type retailer might let other retailers provide inventory for display, demonstration, selection, and warranty service, while it sells at a price that does not cover the costs of those activities on which the customers rely. Such discount houses cheat (i.e., free ride) by reaping the harvest of the retailer who provides those services at a cost which the retailer is not enabled to recover when losing sales to the discounter. Customers who rely on these retailers for prepurchase information while buying from discount houses are free riders also. Since discounting by selling at a price that does not cover the costs of services provided by some *other* retailer will destroy the incentive of other retailers to provide these services so essential to the acceptability of the product, the product will not be born or survive in the market. Such stealing, or cherry picking, is reduced by use of exclusive territories for retailers, by retail price maintenance, and by areas of primary responsibility. Clearly such practices do not restrict intra-brand competition. Instead they restrain contra-brand activities, which are socially *undesirable* forms of competition, just as stealing is an undesirable form of competition. A restraint on undesirable forms of competition is not usefully called anticompetitive.

### J. Predatory Activity

*Predatory activity* usually is an undefined activity. If I succeed in making something better or at lower cost and selling it at a lower price, other producers will be forced by consumers to switch to other kinds of work. Other producers are excluded from this market—by *consumers* who refuse to buy from them. My intent was to benefit myself by benefitting customers. That intended behavior is socially commended. I did not intend to affect the wealth or income of other sellers in such a way as to *improperly* alter their decisions to produce. Socially approved behavior does *not* mean competitors are not hurt or that they are not excluded by better competitors. It is approved because it provides either more-valuable or lower-priced output. Those who cannot do as well will have to switch to other activities at which they can produce at lower costs than those of competitors (and there always are such other activities—though we shall not demonstrate that elementary fact here).

But suppose that instead of really being a low-cost producer, I sell at a price below true cost (mine and yours), with the result that you switch to other work. Why is that condemned? Because, since my costs really are not lower, total social value of output is decreased, not increased. In other words, productive resources that could be used in other more valuable ways (*which is what costs measure*) are used instead to produce something worth less to buyers.

But, then, if I price below cost, what is the objection to my own acceptance of that loss? I bear that social loss. No one else does. Is that not a form of charity? One possible objection is that at the same cost (sacrifice of other goods) I could simply give money to my customers, and they would be better off than if I gave them only the right to buy some particular good below cost.

The usual objection is that after eliminating other—and all future—sellers, I will, it is argued, reduce output and raise price higher than if they were still a threat. This allegation is common, has no logical flaws, but seems very unlikely to succeed. In any event, I have yet to see good evidence of it. (What I have not seen may nevertheless exist. I *believe*, but cannot prove, that this tactic is not worth trying to forestall by legislative or administrative action.) It has not yet been demonstrated to be an occurrence of sufficient significance to warrant the apparently high costs of trying to deter it. The frequency of "false arrests" is costly, because desirable price-cutting to discover and respond to nontransient changes in market demand and supply is often misconceived as predatory pricing or price discrimination.

In some cases in which the price is said to be below the costs of production, the costs are misinterpreted as being higher than they really are. The true cost is the incremental cost of the extra output (the marginal cost). This can be lower than average cost (total costs divided by units of output), and it can be less than the so-called average variable costs. One reason is that often the output is not unambiguously identified and adequately measured. (This will be explained in Section P.)

A particularly important confusion is in interpreting or identifying the price received. Free samples, introductory offers, and the like can be expected to bring revenue later (i.e., have a higher present capital value of future revenue), far in excess of the price for the current item. Most information about the quality or availability of a good is provided to prospective buyers without charge *before* they decide to purchase. That is not free; it is costly to the seller. When, and if, a consumer later makes a purchase, then the price of those purchased goods covers the cost of the earlier prepurchase information. That information was provided to *prospective* customers at a *zero price*, which is certainly below the costs of producing that information, but it is paid for by those who, after getting the information, deem the product worth purchasing.

A price is not necessarily below the cost if the provision of an item accompanies another good whose price is sufficient to cover the cost of both. Paper bags at the supermarket are an example. A more sophisticated example is that of a free ride to a hotel from an airport. It is not given free to the traveller if the ride is tied to the rental of a room. What is happening is that the nominal price paid for the room includes the normal taxi fee plus a *lower*, discounted, price for the *room* (i.e., a discount equal to the cost of the taxi). What appears to be a "free" (i.e., at no extra cost) taxi ride is really a cut in the price of the rooms to those people who presumably would not otherwise have come to the hotel. At the same time, the price is not cut to patrons who would have come anyway. This is exemplified also by so-called loss leaders. Actually, there is no loss on even the loss leaders. This, by the way, also helps to avoid market power output distortions.

In none of these examples is there predatory intent or pricing below cost. The costs are misunderstood, or the price is not correctly perceived by the critic alleging predatory pricing.

### ᴋ. Bargaining Power

Economists often use names as definitions. Do not confuse a name with a meaningful, analytically useful definition of what is meant. After all, we all have heard of cowboys, who are neither cows nor boys. *Bargaining power* is an especially common example.

If the highest price a person would be willing to pay for some item exceeds the price he is asked to pay by a large amount, one can choose to say he has great bargaining power. Thus, one could define bargaining power as the ratio of (a) the value of good to some person to (b) what he must pay to get it. If (a) does not exceed (b), he has zero bargaining power. This definition has the virtue of being definite and devoid of implications of proper or improper activity by the person. It does not say what circumstances enable a large or small difference. If the buyer's personal valuation was barely higher than the seller's, there would be no bargaining power. And even if there were two or more suppliers bidding to sell their goods, the bargaining power of the single buyer would be small, if each of the sellers' own reservation value on the good was close to the highest price the buyer was willing to pay. Clearly, the number of bidding buyers or asking sellers does not necessarily tell whether or not there is substantial bargaining power for any of the parties, as defined here.

Now consider what appears, at first sight, to be a different interpretation. Driving on a desert road, you suffer a broken water pump. The sole repair station, 10 miles away, asks a price higher than if there were two repair shops competing for your business. Assume, further, that the price asked is in excess of the amount that would keep the person in business in that area. If the value to you of getting the car towed to that shop and repaired is, say, $300, and his costs of doing so (full costs of such repairs adjusted for the frequency of occurrence) is $50, you would contend he has strong bargaining power—a big difference between his costs and what you are at most willing to pay him under your unfortunate position. He has high bargaining power as defined here. This is precisely the same interpretation as given in the preceding paragraph; merely the setting is changed.

What bothers travellers about the repairman's bargaining power is that they are surprised. Had they anticipated he would ask so much more than $50, they would have taken costly alternative, anticipatory precautionary actions, or other suppliers would have developed to undercut him. But the moral is clear. High bargaining power, as defined here, implies nothing about size, wealth, or number of bidders or sellers.

If you think some other conception is meant by bargaining power, state it. If you search economics textbooks for a meaning, you will search in vain.

## L. Leverage of Monopoly by Tie-ins?

A *tie-in* is the sale of one good on the condition some other specified good is also purchased at a price covering both of them. It is always possible to set a lower price for one of the goods and then charge a correspondingly high price for the other good in the package. If that is what is meant by "leverage," so be it. But to call that leverage is to add nothing to the statement that the price of a package of A and B is simply the sum of the price for A and the price for B, which under no circumstances can exceed the sum of the value of A plus the value of B to the buyer. And if they are worth more as packages, then the package will always be offered, as with the wheels, seats, and body when selling cars. The seller isn't able to get a *higher* price for the wheels just because the body is desirable—unless the seller lowers the price of the body as much as he raises the price of the wheels. Indeed, he could sell the body at a zero price on the condition that the buyer buys the wheels at a price correspondingly higher. This is merely saying that if the total value, C, is separated into two components, A and B, where A + B equals C, then any arbitrary price for A will be matched by a corresponding change in the price of B. Calling that leverage adds nothing to understanding and, more likely, creates confusion.

The motivation for the term *leverage* probably arises in cases in which some observer doesn't understand why a seller insists that a buyer of A also buy B. The confused interpreter asserts the seller must be somehow extending his power in the sale of A to get more income by selling B, too. The above discussion shows that is fallacious.

Instead, what may be happening is that the seller is trying to get more of the value of the tying good, A, from that buyer than he gets from *other* buyers who value A less. At the same price to all buyers of A, the seller does less well than if he could separate the buyers and charge more for A to the higher-valuing buyers. If a buyer's valuation of A is correlated with the quantity of B that he also wants to have with that A, then the seller, by insisting the buyer buy all the B from him, is able to use the *quantity* of B demanded as a measure of how much the A is valued by that buyer. What is happening is that the seller is using the quantity of B demanded to measure that buyer's value of A and is also using the quantity of B as a means of collecting the higher value of A from that buyer— more than he collects from other buyers of A who buy less B. The higher value of A is being collected in the higher price and larger amount of B. This works only if buyers differ in their valuations of A *and* if the quantity of B they want to buy is correlated with their valuation of A. Calling this leverage or extension of monopoly misses the point and leads to erroneous understanding. Of course, what it is called is really irrelevant for understanding, except that names often are treated as explanations, and they certainly are not in this case.

Finally, despite the repetitions of the judicial assertion in *Standard Oil Co. of California v. United States*, 337 U.S. 293 (1949), that "tying agreements serve hardly any purpose beyond the suppression of competition," many tying agreements have socially beneficial effects fully consistent with open market competition. Furthermore, the hallowed judicial assertions that tie-ins necessarily or typically "deny competitors free access to the market for the tied product," or that "buyers are forced to forego their free choice between competing products" are incorrect (if indeed those denied statements make any sense in the first place).

## M. Relevant Markets

This is an expression in search of economic meaning. An examination of economic textbooks will reveal no use of the concept *relevant market* until one comes to discussions of legal terms of art in cases involving *concentration*, itself a loose conception.

Defining a relevant market for some seller is, at best, a way of suggesting the scope of significant alternatives facing potential customers of that seller. Clearer understanding would result if one stated the criteria for determining the set of sellers and buyers to be dubbed the "relevant market." That requires knowing or estimating the elasticities of demands of the current and potential buyers for this seller's products. That also depends on the prices and qualities of other goods provided by other present or potential suppliers. Even if one asserts some relevant market in the above sense, one seller's current *share* of the current sales in that market does not enable any inferences as to the shape or elasticities of demand facing that seller. The reasons are that "share" tells *nothing* about the potential sellers who will spring up if price becomes more attractive; it tells *nothing* about the elasticities of demand, and it tells *nothing* about which customers have the less elastic response to price or product-service quality; it implies *nothing* about a seller's influence over his or other sellers' prices, qualities, or quantities of output.

### 1. Elasticity of demand facing a seller

(a) Back in the 1930s and earlier, some firms were analytically treated as essentially *individually* ineffective in altering prices. None was big enough to significantly affect the supply conditions and, hence, could not affect the price of industry output.

(b) Yet it was recognized that a second type of situation also existed. There were sellers of some goods for which the customers could not turn to other equally good suppliers at the same price. More significantly, a supplier could raise his price without losing *all* his sales. Some customers would continue to buy, though less, at the higher price. Some sellers were protected by legislation (e.g., public utilities). Analytically, all this can be characterized by the demand curve facing the firm. If the seller supplied more, the price would have to be lowered, or the price could be raised if he were to supply less.

On the assumption that these situations should be separated analytically—economists gave each a name. The former, (a) above, was called "pure competitor" or "price taker," and the latter, (b), was called "monopolist" (also "monopolistic competitor," "price setter," "price searcher," "price administrator," or "imperfect competitor"). Going further, a name of (and a measure of) a *difference* was proposed: "monopoly degree" was measured by the price elasticity of demand for a seller's product. If the elasticity was infinitely large (i.e., if his supply had no effect on his price), the seller was called a "pure competitor." He had zero degree of monopoly. (Or as we prefer to call it, zero market power.) If the elasticity was finite so that he could force up his or others' prices by offering a smaller supply, he was called a "monopolist" or a seller with "market power." But names, with all their connotations, however suggestive, are not definitions. The Sherman Act says it is illegal to monopolize, but "monopolize" is left undefined.

*2. Is concentration a good surrogate for elasticity of demand?*

The fact is that the overwhelming majority of sellers face less than infinite elasticities of demand for their services. They have market power. But, as yet, economists have no validated analysis or theorem of how much effect on output and prices occurs when elasticities are not infinitely large. Scores of scenarios and conjectures are available, but their empirical relevance is still unestablished—though widely assumed. Since direct measures of demand elasticities facing sellers are prohibitively difficult to measure, surrogate measures are proposed which are *presumed* to be reliable indices of the elasticities of demand facing a seller. One of these is the concentration measure.

Unfortunately, accumulated evidence does not suggest it is related to that elasticity. The concentration index rests on guesses as to which other sellers the potential customers would turn to if one seller raised his prices. And those to which the potential customers would turn are assumed to be suppliers to the same market—suppliers to the *relevant market*—to the relevant set of potential customers. So the concentration index requires two presumptions—a set of potential customers somehow to be identified and a set of actual or potential sellers to whom those customers would turn if the price of the first seller were to be increased. But how much of an increase in price is not specified.

The difficulties and confusions become apparent once the problem is stated. In defining the set of *potential* customers, *how much difference in price* is to be the standard? And how can one determine the other sellers or product to whom the customers could and would turn in response to some higher price? Nor does the existence of only a few other suppliers of the same or similar goods make the demand for the first seller's less elastic. What counts are the elasticities of supply of each of the other actual and potential suppliers in response to a higher price. And that can be very large with only a few other existing suppliers. And it depends on how long a time one is considering.

*3. Concentration, mergers, and collusion*

One other argument for worrying about concentration is the probability of an effective collusion among sellers. The presumption is that if the set of sellers is smaller, the ability to collude effectively is stronger. Mergers, in contrast to internal growth, are sometimes regarded as means of enabling merged firms to heed their group, instead of their individual, marginal revenue more accurately. When separate, the firms ignore the effects of their own price cuts on the reduced revenues of other firms. But when firms are merged, those revenue effects are perceived and heeded by the *combined* firm. So, the argument goes, merging two or more firms into one tends to raise price. However, the other nonmerged firms will have greater opportunity to expand if price is raised (and output restrained) by this larger firm. The number of firms that have merged, or the number that are small and unmerged, is not important; it is the ability of the outside (actual or potential) firms to increase supply if the merged firm raises prices. It comes down to elasticities of demand and supply.

So long as any other productive resources can be purchased to produce more of the good, the merging firms will not find their long-run elasticities of demand for their product decreased by merging, since the elasticity of demand for their output depends on the cross-price elasticity of supply from other firms. It does not follow that if two or more firms merge, they will, as a new entity, have a less elastic demand and can therefore raise price profitably. What is crucial is the ability and inducement of other firms to expand output or enter into production if some firm raises its own price. Internal growth, presumably exempted from this type of consideration, is no different. It has the same effects. Why the firm becomes larger, whether because of lower costs of production or merger, does not tell us anything about the elasticity of demand and of supply by other actual or potential producers.

In principle the market or source of supply is the whole world of potential consumers and suppliers. What restricts the set of customers is the cost of finding, communicating, and transporting the exchanged goods. For example, the relevant (achieved) market for American land is worldwide, since knowledge of the land and ownership of it can be cheaply transferred to distant foreigners. In contrast, the potential set of customers for my textbook is somewhat smaller, because of language difficulties and transport costs of the book. The higher those costs, the smaller the number of buyers I can have at any given price, and the lower or smaller will be the market demand for my product. The variety and quality of other economics texts in English or any other language affect the demand for my text. And beyond books there are lectures that can be obtained. And at sufficiently higher prices, I will lose customers not only to other books in English or Spanish and even to oral lectures, but also to books in psychology or biology as people decide to learn something instead of economics.

A seller who is said to have 80 percent of some designated "relevant market" may have a very elastic demand, or he may have a very inelastic demand. And whether the share be 10 percent or 90 percent does not permit any inferences as to the elasticity of demand facing the seller. General Motors may have 55 percent of the automobile market, while Mercedes has 2 percent. Yet the latter may (probably does) have a less elastic demand than the former. But whether or not that guess is correct, that guess cannot be correlated with an *independent* determination of some so-called market share. Only if one first knows the elasticity and then defines the relevant market so that his market share is large when his elasticity is small can he correlate the two measures. But that procedure is viciously circular, since the answer is assumed in order to construct the appropriate share, which is then alleged to be evidence of the initial assumption. No correlation between reported shares of market and elasticity of demand has been established.

A second contention on which the concentration or market share doctrine is supposed to stand is that concentration is correlated with effective collusion among firms. This presumption has been upset, though the Supreme Court and the FTC and the Antitrust Division of the Justice Department and several senators are slow to heed the implications. The earlier reported data and analysis purporting to be evidence supporting the assumption have been thoroughly discredited. The best available evidence is that the observed pattern of events is consistent with the alternative explanation of the more efficient firms growing, and, hence, serving a large number of buyers. But whether the alternative is overwhelmingly supported and the collusion interpretation thoroughly disproven is less significant than the fact that the collusion presumption now stands without evidence to support it.

### 4. Racial discrimination and relevant markets

Finally, the expression "relevant market" has also appeared in legal issues of employment discrimination. If the ratio of employees hired does not correspond sufficiently to the ratio of specified types in the same relevant labor market, a *prima facie* assumption of discrimination is often presumed. But by "labor market" what should be meant is the *labor supply* facing the firm. Since the labor supplied to a firm depends on the wages and working conditions offered, the relevant market will be smaller, the lower the wage the firm chooses to offer, and larger, the higher the wage it offers. At one extreme the relevant market supply to the firm may be one mile in radius—and at the other extreme, it comprises the whole world. The labor supply is not an independent entity but a large range of potential suppliers from various areas depending on the wage offered. Perhaps the question to be answered could be phrased as follows: At the wages offered, who applies for a job? No matter where the applicants come from, does the firm select from them in a manner that indicates differential illegal criteria of preferences? Does the firm use tactics designed to discourage differential supply of labor by particular racial types? The relevant market approach won't answer those questions.

### N. Horizontal vs. Vertical Integration

Horizontal vs. vertical integration is misleading, as displayed in many opinions or decisions on franchise territorial allocation and merger issues. Though the horizontal-vertical distinction may be clear for some problems or issues, it is not for many others. Horizontal originally referred to the same stage of activity, such as retailing, wholesaling, manufacturing. A vertical agreement involves successive stages of production, distribution, and retailing. The Supreme Court declared that the form of agreement—called horizontal—to alter competition could serve no other purpose than to restrict competition (i.e., alter it undesirably). So the Court has tended, not entirely consistently, to declare any horizontal form of agreement illegal. But it has, at times, backed off from that position when it saw vaguely and with some confusion what benefits some such agreements achieve (e.g., the White Motor, Sandura, and Snap-on decisions). To escape that dilemma it has sometimes argued that the arrangements in those cases were really vertical agreements, not horizontal, and, therefore, not per se illegal. So, up to the present, the term horizontal tends to become attached to an agreement if the Supreme Court finds it illegal, but if an agreement is found not illegal, it may be called vertical. Thus, to call something horizontal or vertical (at the present time) is merely to express an opinion or forecast what the Supreme Court would say about legality.

Consider agreements between a franchiser of fast foods and the local franchised retail outlets, each selling the same branded product. This case is similar to a manufacturer and his salesmen with territories, or a department store with clerks assigned to certain departments or areas in the store, or to a houseseller who gives an exclusive to one real estate agent with several offices. Whether they are employees, agents, or franchisees does not change the purpose, though that may affect the usefulness of such agreements. And trying to decide first if they are vertical or horizontal is to be playing with words, not analyzing substance.

### O. Costs

#### 1. Definition

The cost of any act is always the best (i.e., most valuable) alternative action necessarily forsaken. Ambiguity arises if the act is not precisely specified. Since variants can have different costs, there is room for confusion as to what it is that is being costed. For example, consider the cost of producing a house. Even assuming that the house is itself unambiguously specified, is the house to be produced in three months or six? Is it to be produced with several other houses simultaneously or alone? The cost of *producing* the house (often called cost of the house) will depend on which of those "*producings*" is meant.

Another, and surprising, attribute of the definition is that cost is not the work, sweat, hours of labor, toil, or effort involved in an activity. The cost of an act is the *best* of the desirable alternative acts necessarily forsaken when this act is performed. For example, the cost of my writing this exposition of costs between the hours of 2 and 5 P.M. on February 12, 1982, is playing a round of golf. That is the best thing I could have done had I not written this section on costs at that time. And so the cost of my writing this section is that round of golf.

### 2. Measures for comparability: dollars

Why and how, then, can we speak of the dollar measure of a cost? We do it as follows: Since the round of golf is the best (i.e., most preferred) alternative, what other actions could be just as desirable to me as the round of golf? More specifically, what is the minimum amount of money that would have enabled me to purchase any other set of goods and services that are just as desirable (valuable) to me as the forsaken round of golf? The market value of the least expensive other equally desirable set of goods and services is a *measure* of the cost.

In this way, different acts, each with its different cost, can have the different costs expressed and measured in a common denominator, or measure, of value—a marketable value. But beware. That does not mean that the costs *are* those marketable goods. For example, the cost of my crossing a park at night will include the sacrifice of a healthy body for a couple of days—because I'll surely get mugged. The cost of crossing the park is the loss of the desirable healthiness I otherwise would have had. Now someone could then ask me, "How much of some marketable goods and services would have to be presented to me to exactly offset that temporary sacrifice of health?" If $500 would enable me to be exactly compensated for the sacrificed health, we can say the cost of crossing the park is measured at $500 (not is the cost). Hence we are able to assign dollars-and-cents values as common denominators to such things as risk of life, limb, health, degrees of honesty, speedier trials, and, indeed, *any* desirable activity in which we might engage, since each act necessarily requires forsaking a next best alternative. MORAL: We *can* and do assign dollar-and-cents market values to risk of life, health, and safety.

### 3. Implicit and explicit

Costs occur every time we have a choice, not only *when we buy something*. If I use my garage as a woodworking shop, I sacrifice its use as a shelter for my car or for that of my neighbor, who might have rented the garage. I'll use my garage as a shop only if its use as a shop is more desirable to me than as a garage or whatever I could buy with the receivable rental. (Economic translation: I'll use my garage as a shop only if its value as a shop exceeds its costs, i.e., the highest valued forsaken use.) That cost is just as real as if I had to rent some building for a shop. I would be forsaking some marketable goods I could have purchased. And in the case where I use my garage instead of, say, renting to a neighbor, I am sacrificing some purchasable goods I could have bought with the rent proceeds. Costs occur not merely when we pay money, but whenever we make a choice—which necessarily implies not being able to do something else we could have done. We use the term *implicit cost* to remind ourselves that the cost is a sacrificed use of *something already owned*. We use the term *explicit cost* in those cases in which a payment of money occurs.

### 4. Variable and constant

Some costs are constant despite changes in rates of output. They are costs that continue at some rate that does not change even though the output may change over the range listed here. For example, if the garage rental for a taxi were *constant per month regardless of how many miles of service* were obtained from the taxi, it would be called a *constant cost*. But the cost of gasoline, repairs, or anything else that depend on mileage is called *variable*.

Table 1 is an example of the arithmetic division of costs into the constant costs and the other costs that vary with the output—usually called constant and variable costs.

### 5. Acquisition costs and sunk costs

We can introduce more realism by considering an often ill-defined act. Suppose a car is bought to serve as a taxi, at a price of $10,000. Suppose also, for exposition, that once the car is produced and purchased for $10,000, its highest value to any other person for any other purpose is less than $10,000, say $8,000. That is, if sold to someone else immediately after it was purchased, it would fetch $8,000—even though it is still unused and worth $10,000 as a taxi for me. Only $8,000 is recoverable from *other* uses or users. This is expressed by saying that $2,000 of the initial price is sunk once the car is purchased. That is the cost of my *acquiring title* to the car. That cost may, of course, be more than

TABLE 1. *Output and Cost*

| Output | Total | | Constant | | Variable | Marginal | Average constant | | Variable | | Average total |
|--------|-------|---|---------|---|----------|----------|------------------|---|----------|---|--------------|
| 0 | 5 | = | 5 | + | 0 | — | | | | | |
| 1 | 15 | = | 5 | + | 10 | 10 | 5.00 | + | 10 | = | 15 |
| 2 | 24 | = | 5 | + | 19 | 9 | 2.5 | + | 9.5 | = | 12 |
| 3 | 32 | = | 5 | + | 27 | 8 | 1.67 | + | 9 | = | 10.67 |
| 4 | 41 | = | 5 | + | 36 | 9 | 1.25 | + | 9 | = | 10.25 |
| 5 | 51 | = | 5 | + | 46 | 10 | 1.00 | + | 9.20 | = | 10.20 |
| 6 | 62 | = | 5 | + | 57 | 11 | .833 | + | 9.50 | = | 10.33 |
| 7 | 73 | = | 5 | + | 68 | 11 | .714 | + | 9.71 | = | 10.42 |
| 8 | 84 | = | 5 | + | 79 | 11 | .625 | + | 9.88 | = | 10.505 |
| 9 | 96 | = | 5 | + | 91 | 12 | .555 | + | 10.11 | = | 10.66 |

covered by the value of my owning the taxi. That $2,000 difference is the cost of a past action—acquisition of title—and might as well be forgotten insofar as subsequent use of the car is concerned.

It is not a measure of the cost of subsequently using the car. The cost of subsequent use must come out of only the $8,000. This is often expressed by saying that the *sunk* or *fixed* cost of the taxi is $2,000. A *sunk* cost is a cost of past action and not a cost of any present or contemplated action. It was incurred in the past, as the acquisition cost.

Of course, it is hoped that the future proceeds of the taxi service will cover that initial $10,000 cost (of which $2,000 is now sunk), else it will not have been profitable to have entered the business. But once I am in the business (i.e., having acquired the taxi), the costs of subsequent service *do not* include any of that $2,000 sunk past acquisition cost.

So long as I continue to own the car, I incur more costs, because the $8,000 value could have earned interest elsewhere at the rate of, say, 1 percent per month. That ownership-holding cost accrues at the constant rate (not affected by extent of output) of $80 a month ($=.01 \times \$8,000$).

### 6. Depreciation cost

We add more realism. Suppose the car, now worth $8,000, will depreciate in salvageable value, whether or not it is used, by $1,000 annually. We assume for expositional simplicity that this depreciation in value of the car, whether or not the car is used, continues at a *uniform amount per year*. We call it part of the constant costs because it does not vary with the amount of use of the taxi. Like the interest cost, it is a cost of continuing to own the car. (It is also called an implicit cost.) However, any depreciation that depends on the rate of use of the car will be counted in the variable cost.

### 7. Marginal cost

Long-run *marginal cost* has no relevance for output and pricing decisions by a firm. It merely states the amount of revenue which, if received, would cover the costs of the extra output, where the extra (marginal) output is either (a) an output produced using all the time desired to make adjustments in the production facilities and processes, or (b) a long-lasting marginally increased rate of output. In either case, the price that can be obtained will not depend on that calculation, since once the investment is made, the state of demand, the available production facilities, and future uncommitted costs will determine the optimal output and price. If that optimal price for the extra output does not yield a revenue flow sufficient to cover the long-run incremental cost, the investment for that contemplated output program will simply not have been profitable. The costs that do count in affecting output and, hence, price are only the uncommitted costs. (These may include some depreciation of the investment, since current use can imply a future replacement cost—if replacement is to occur.) In any event, the long-run cost is irrelevant for any pricing decision or input decision once the investment is made.

In other words, for a particular output, there are not two marginal costs— a long-run and a short-run cost. Instead, these refer to two different actions— a long-run output action, presumably lasting for a long time, or else an output of some particular duration but starting at a later time after all desired adjustments are made in productive facilities. Notice how time enters in two ways— length of the output program, and the date (after adjustment of facilities) at which it is to start. This ambiguity has caused excessive confusion and error. There is also a short-run output, again ambiguous because it begins immediately or is short-lived. One should unambiguously define the output at issue.

Another confusion exists. It is not true that short-run marginal cost is less than long-run marginal cost, in the sense of the effect on costs of an increase in output with existing facilities compared with an increased output achieved by allowing all desired adjustments in the production process (long-run marginal cost). The slope of a long-run total cost curve (LRTC) is the long-run marginal cost. For any output X, there is a short-run total cost curve (SRTC) for the facility that is optimal for output rate X. It lies below the long-run total cost curve because of sunk costs of investments. But its slope at X equals that of LRTC, so the long-run and short-run marginal costs are of equal magnitude at X. But at larger outputs than X, the slope is steeper on the short-run total cost curve; that is, the short-run act's marginal cost is greater than the marginal cost of the long-run marginal increase in output. Beware! The two output actions being compared are different. And it is not surprising that their marginal costs would be different, or that the short-run act's cost (the so-called short-run marginal cost) would be higher at larger outputs than the marginal cost of an output increase achieved with a long-run type of output adjustment. The cost of an increase in output is different in each case, because acts called "the increase in output" are different.

### P. Common Costs of Joint Output

*1. Nonsense of fully distributed overhead costs*

Overhead costs usually are common to several operating divisions or types of customers served by a firm. For example, the management and office staff of an airline provide services common to freight and passengers. A power-generating utility serves many classes of customers. Can the overhead cost be divided and distributed to the divisions or customers? The answer is no for all the overhead costs that do not vary with the scale of operations of each division or type of service. Any allocation or distribution of the constant overhead costs is arbitrary and without economic significance for output rates or prices. Only costs that vary or depend on the rate of operations, whether or not they are counted in overhead, are pertinent to pricing and output decisions. Sunk costs of capital equipment are past costs and should never be counted as costs nor distributed among outputs. Attempts to fully distribute overhead costs are illogical and pointless. See table 2.

No matter how the constant overhead cost of $10 may be divided and allocated to X and Y, the profit-maximizing outputs are unaffected. Any computation of profit for X and for Y on the basis of an allocation of the $10 of constant overhead costs serves no purpose. For example, if $P_x = \$12$ and $P_y = \$19$, the profit-maximizing output of X and Y are 4 and 6 units, respectively. Revenue equals $(4 \times \$11) + (6 \times \$19) = \$44 + \$114 = \$158$. Costs are $\$10 + 4 + 7 + 36 + 100 = \$157$; profit is $1. No matter how arbitrarily the $10 constant overhead cost is distributed, each division's output and contribution to the firm's profits is unaffected. (If demand curves for X and Y were used, instead of given set prices, the irrelevance of allocating any of the $10 of constant overhead costs would still hold.)

TABLE 2. *Common Costs*

| Outputs | | Overhead costs ($) | | | Total variable operating costs ($) | | Marginal costs ($) | | $D_Y$ ($) | |
|---|---|---|---|---|---|---|---|---|---|---|
| X | Y | Total = Constant | + Varies with X | + Varies with Y | of X | of Y | of X | of Y | $P_Y$ | $MR_Y$ |
| 0 | 0 | 10   10 | 0 | 0 | 0 | 0 | — | — | — | — |
| 1 | 1 | 12   10 | 1 | 1 | 6 | 11 | 7 | 12 | 19 | 19 |
| 2 | 2 | 15   10 | 2 | 3 | 16 | 24 | 11 | 15 | 18.5 | 18 |
| 3 | 3 | 17   10 | 3 | 4 | 26 | 39 | 11 | 16 | 18 | 17 |
| 4 | 4 | 19   10 | 4 | 5 | 36 | 55 | 11 | 17 | 17.5 | 16 |
| 5 | 5 | 21   10 | 5 | 6 | 48 | 72 | 13 | 18 | 17 | 15 |
| 6 | 6 | 34   10 | 6 | 7 | 61 | 100 | 14 | 19 | 16.5 | 14 |

Only costs in overhead that do vary with output should be allocated, but the costs that are fixed, in the sense of being independent of the output of some division, cannot be allocated. Any imposed allocation would be purely cosmetic for some arbitrary pricing patterns.

*2. What is the output whose cost is to be determined?*

Another especially disturbing confusion arises when a seller uses some common resources to make more than one good or sells to more than one buyer. The impression seems to exist that the cost of each good or the cost to each buyer ought to be unambiguously definable. In fact, it is often not definable. For example, consider a wholesale baker who provides bread to some retailer, A. Along comes a second retailer, B, who orders for the next week a few loaves of bread. At this point an inspection of the numbers in table 3 will guide you through the following analysis. Assume that the ovens and equipment will be used and subjected to normal wear and tear in producing the output for A or for B. How much *more* expense will be incurred by producing for the second retailer for, say, the next week? Since the baker is going to heat the ovens and incur start-up costs whether or not he produces a few extra loaves for a week or so, the costs of the extra output are just the extra costs that may not involve any extra overhead or depreciation costs whatever. In that case, the costs are very low for the new retailer's bread. But if we turn the story around and assume that the baker regarded the second retailer's bread as the output to which he attributes all the initial start-up and depreciation costs, and counted only the

TABLE 3. *Joint Cost Calculation and Pricing Example*

|  | Costs |
|---|---|
| A and B produced together | 140 |
| A produced alone | 90 |
| B produced alone | 60 |
| Costs of A, if B produced in any event | 80 ($10 costs avoided) |
| Costs of B, if A produced in any event | 50 ($10 costs avoided) |
| Minimum price to induce production of B | |
|     if produced alone, | = $60 |
|     if produced in addition to A. | = $50 |
| Minimum price to induce production of A | |
|     if produced alone, | = $90 |
|     if produced in addition to B. | = $60 |

Note that joint production prices are $60 + $50, which does not cover costs of either separate production or joint production.

extra costs of servicing the first retailer, then the first retailer's bread costs less than before.

However, there is no unique conception of costs separately for the output for the first retailer and for the second retailer. This is simply the consequence of common costs of joint outputs. But people persist in asking about *fully allocated common costs* of each buyer's portion. The question is ambiguous. "Fully allocated" sounds neat but is without unique meaning. Instead, a useful query is, what price must the baker receive (*given the initial continuing situation*) if he is to be induced to produce more bread? Clearly, if he was going to produce for the first retailer—whether or not he produces for the second—then the cost of the second retailer's bread is whatever extra costs are incurred. If, on the other hand, the baker did not intend to produce for the first retailer unless he also got an order from the second retailer, then all we can ask is whether the amount received from each buyer is at least equal to the extra costs of producing for that buyer—*assuming the other output was going to be produced anyway*. The cost of a loaf for A on that calculation would have been $80, and for B, $50, and if priced that way, that would not cover the total costs, $140, of both outputs. In this case the baker would not produce for either.

There is no principle on the basis of which it can be determined what the price to each buyer must be. All that can be obtained are lower bounds below which the output would not be produced, even under the most favorable circumstances to that buyer (the circumstances being that the output for the other buyer will be produced anyway because it is worth doing). Which buyer will be paying more than this lower conditional bound—the condition being that the other party's production will occur in any event? At least one or both may be paying more. But who *should* pay how much is unanswerable because the question is ambiguous or incomplete. It does not state on what criterion the "should" is to be determined.

For this reason, laws, judicial decisions, and contentions that buyers should pay at least the costs of their output are not separable from what is assumed about the remaining output. If the costs of joint products are interdependent, there is *no* uniquely determinable or defined cost.

Many people are disturbed by this because they think it poses some problem in what to produce and problems of *equity*. Each person is entitled to his own conception of what is equitable. But no place in economic analysis can any such conception be found, let alone be used as a criterion for proper pricing. More significantly, it doesn't make any difference anyway. This absence of a unique cost of components of joint outputs creates no problems in actual pricing and determination of viable outputs. So long as the total proceeds from the set of joint outputs cover the total costs of the entire operation, operation will continue. If any portion of output fails to earn a sales value that at least equals the costs of continuing to provide that output—*assuming the other outputs continue*—the considered output will not continue. But if it cannot be assumed that the other output will continue in any event, because the other output's proceeds will be insufficient to sustain that other output alone, more must be received, or both outputs will be terminated.

What all this says is that if one believes that the price charged for each of several joint outputs should equal only the costs of producing that output, assuming other outputs will continue to be produced with some common inputs, the believer is confused about the relevant issues and problems. That is an incomplete criterion because it assumes that all components of costs vary proportionally with every attribute of output when, in fact, they do not.

### Q. Quasi-Rent, Asset Revaluing, and Price Competition

A *quasi-rent* is the portion of the revenue from the use of some equipment in *excess* of current operating cost and which covers at least some of the *initial, past* investment cost of having produced that equipment. Since the equipment has already been produced, it will be worth using to render services so long as its services will be worth more than enough to cover the current operating costs, without regard to the initial cost of its having been created. If, however, the revenue does not prove large enough to cover that past sunk cost also, the producer will have lost money in entering the business. But he'll continue operating, once he's in business, if the revenue from services is more than enough to cover operating. If the revenue also covers the sunk costs, the producer will be earning a profit on his current and entry costs.

But, and this is the important fact here, once a resource exists, it will continue to be used so long as its service or rental value exceeds current operating costs (*not* also the initial sunk costs of creating the equipment). If the current services are not worth even as much as the current operating costs, the resource will not be used. (If the prospective value of *future* services appears even larger, it will be conserved for future use.)

All this is implied by the somewhat cryptic definition that a quasi-rent is any revenue accruing from the current services of an asset in *excess* of that necessary for its current use (but not in excess of that which is necessary *if* it is to be replaced in the future). If the revenue exceeds even this latter cost also, profits are being earned.

To illustrate, consider the simple example of a telephone wire line installed in a city and capable of carrying 50 messages (channels) simultaneously. The investment cost of installing the wire system was $1,000,000, and it will last 20 years, so each of the 50 channels initially costs $20,000. This is equivalent to $1,000 a year per channel (if we ignore interest and discounting to present values in order to keep the arithmetic simple). Suppose that to operate the wire service it costs $100 a year per channel in electricity, labor, etc. The total of the (amortized) initial investment plus operating cost is then $1,100 annually.

It follows that if the wire line service can be rented to customers for $1,100 a channel per year, the investor will just break even. He will cover his operating costs and his initial investment. But if the best price he can get per channel turns out to be less than $1,100, he will not recover his initial sunk investment plus the current operating costs. However, he will continue to operate so long as he can get at least $100 per channel annually—the operating costs (or the direct or variable costs). Any rental value he can get in excess of the $100 per channel per year cost would be a gain compared with shutting down and would go toward recovering at least part of his initial sunk investment of $1,000,000. This means all the rental income *over* the $100 per year operating cost per channel is unnecessary to get that wire service to operate *once it has been set up* at the $1,000,000 cost. Hence, any revenue in excess of $100 per channel per year (and not over $1,100) is a quasi-rent. If the rental does not also cover the $1,000 initial cost, he'll be a sadder and poorer man with losses. If it exceeds $1,100, he would be happier and richer with profits, and he might even be induced to replace the wires with new ones after 20 years if prospects later look as good.

Now we come to the "so what?" about quasi-rents. Suppose that after installation of the wire system, say a few years later, someone invents a microwave system capable of the same service at a lower total cost per channel. Suppose the initial investment cost per channel for a microwave is only $300 per year. And suppose its operating cost, once it is set up, is $50 a year per channel, or $350, including initial investment costs. If the microwave system were installed, what would the existing wire system operator do? He might have tried to compete *politically* to close entry to newcomers. But to compete in the *market* against the lower costs of the microwave he would have to lower his rates. And he could! He could cut his price as low as his wire system operating costs of $100 to keep customers and still provide service. That would be better than shutting down. So the wire system would compete by cutting its annual channel rates down to at least $350 in order to keep customers and operate.

Even worse, if the new microwave were installed, there would be twice as much capacity for communication and no greater demand than before. The price per channel if *both* systems are to operate might have to fall to, say, $200 as both services compete for customers. Both would continue to operate, but neither would be earning enough to recover investment costs. That would be a social waste, because the second system, the microwave, *should not* have been installed until the wire system wore out, or until the total costs of installing a better microwave system and operating it fell to $100 a channel per year, or until demand increased enough to utilize all 100 channels at a rental of $350.

Before the occurrence of any of those events, it would be wasteful to install more capacity at a cost of $350. That cost would exceed the value of the service and be greater than the operating costs of obtaining the service via the old system. Not until the existing wire system wears out (i.e., until its *operating* costs exceed the *full* costs of the new microwave) will the microwave be socially efficient.

What could be done to avoid the waste of introducing the microwave system too early? If the investor in the new system realizes that the existing equipment operator can cut prices down to at least its own operating costs (and not necessarily recover his initial investment), the new promoter will hesitate until he believes that the rental prices for his system, once his system is in existence, will cover his contemplated initial investment and operating costs. He will be kept out of business by the threatened price cuts to the low continued operating costs of the old equipment. He will not invest in new equipment until the prospective returns are high enough to cover all his costs. If he invests earlier, he will be creating new capacity at a cost that exceeds the costs of service from the old, and he will therefore be wastefully introducing new techniques too early. The initial wire service owner who cuts his price when faced with the threat of a challenger informs the challenger that the latter must have costs at least as low as those of the incumbent's *operating* costs or else the challenger will lose money. And society, incidentally, would be worse off by having its resources put to use in the new microwave system at a cost that exceeds the cost of getting services via the existing wire service.

Another example of the same principle is the use of piston engine DC-3 aircraft despite the introduction of new jet engine planes. While it wouldn't pay to manufacture more DC-3 planes, it does pay to operate them so long as they earn a quasi-rent, that is, so long as they earn anything over the remaining operating costs, with the initial investment cost of production being sunk and hence irrelevant for future use of existing planes.

Some people (e.g., the Department of Justice, the Federal Communications Commission, the Federal Trade Commission, and many businessmen) chronically misinterpret these events. When they see the initial wire service cutting prices in the face of the threat of new competitors and cutting prices below what would have covered the old investment costs (which, *we* now know, are sunk and irrelevant), they say it is engaging in undesirable (i.e., predatory), below-cost pricing to keep out competitors. In truth it is keeping out competitors, *fortunately*, because it is preventing wasteful premature investment in new equipment. It is not pricing below cost, because the only true costs are costs yet to be incurred. Its past initial investment, sunk costs, are bygones. They are not costs of what is done now or hereafter. The competitive pricing response is neither below cost nor undesirable. It is socially desirable because it forestalls waste of premature investment and use of economic resources.

### R. Derived Demand Value of Production Assets

Underlying the preceding analysis is the fundamental and widely unappreciated principle that all resources derive their values from their future service values to consumers, not from the costs of producing the resources. Resource values are *derived* from consumer demand for the services. No matter what was paid for a good, its current market value is its value in its best uses. The cost of using it up is, by definition, the reduction in its value—not some portion of its past cost of production.

If someone else comes along unexpectedly with a lower-cost method of producing what a particular machine produces, or a better product than this machine yields, as explained earlier, the marketable value of the old machine will fall by exactly the amount of the new machine's lower cost or superior quality. This means that the value of an asset is made equal to the perceived value of its future services to consumers. And since the wear and tear of using a machine reduces its future serviceability, that reduction in future service value is the cost of using the machine.

### s. Economic Rent

A *pure economic rent* is any revenue or value to the owner of a resource in excess of the costs of *permanent* use of the item. "A diamond is forever." Hence all the revenue paid for its purchase or use is an economic rent, since that diamond and its beauty would exist even if nothing were ever paid—after the diamond is cut. Similarly, insofar as land is permanent, the rent received for land use is unnecessary for the continued permanent existence and availability of the land. But some parcels of land are subject to natural erosion; some revenue must be in prospect if that land is to be maintained as arable land. (Note: in economics it is customary to use the term "land" to mean anything that is indestructible and maintenance free in all its relevant characteristics.)

Though pure economic rent (also sometimes called simply *pure rent*) is unnecessary for the continued permanent existence of the land, it determines who gets to use it. The highest-valuing bidder pays (determines) the pure rent for land, and though that pure rent is not necessary for the continued existence of the land, it does affect who gets to use the land. Thus, the value of pure economic rent for any permanent, indestructible asset has a rationing function of directing land to its highest-valued uses.

### t. Goodwill

Goodwill is derived from at least two features. One is the savings to the public resulting from the less costly provision of information about product availability, performance, and prospective price. For example, suppose that prior to purchase it would cost you $70 to get some information about the features, expected performance, and prices of various suppliers of some kind of good you desired. Alternatively, suppose you know of a supplier who gives that same assurance and predictability without that $70 of search costs, but charges $40 extra, which is what it cost him earlier to establish that reputation. You have a net benefit of $30 (spending only $40 rather than $70). The brand name reputation as an identifier of a predictably reliable supplier provides the customer a net gain of $30.

Competition among suppliers in providing assurance will be attracted by the $15 value above the costs of producing that assurance. The price paid by the consumer for assurance will be competed down to the costs of producing it, say $35.

However, it would appear to pay some supplier to cheat in the future by delivering a lower quality (lower cost) service and make a short-lived gain.

What could restrain that deception? He would be restrained if cheating meant that he would be discovered and relegated to some other activity in which he could earn less. For example, he would no longer be a car repairman earning $100 for his services, but would become a parts clerk earning only $70 or he would continue as a repairman but be regarded as a lower-quality provider and earn only $70. If that loss of future income has a present value exceeding the gain from short-run cheating, he will not cheat, for he would lose his Ricardian rent or his quasi-rent of his past investment in being a superior mechanic. The same principle holds for the goodwill of the name GM, GE, or McDonalds, and every person known by a name of repute.

A second part of the value in what is called the *goodwill* of a firm is its team discovery assembly value. A successful firm is a collection of inputs, successfully working as a team with specially interrelated inputs and producing more value than the assembled inputs could otherwise produce. One cannot copy a successful team of inputs by costlessly finding and buying and organizing similar separate components, as one might assemble a house, hi-fi, or microcomputer system. A successful firm is a tested combination of inputs that have been proved especially appropriate to each other and to the task for which they were assembled. That cost must be incurred by a newcomer as an initial investment in search, discovery, trial, error, and revision—all reflected in the value of an already successfully assembled profitable team. The cost of actually replicating a successful team must be covered by the anticipated future revenue of the new successful strivers. The revenue, above the salaries, rentals, and prices of the inputs actually used, must be expected to cover the total search and assembly costs. Once achieved, that may appear to be a surplus, but only if one ignores that prior investment in search and assembly in creating a successful team. Therefore, the price of buying an already successful firm will exceed its continuing costs of presently hired inputs or resources. The value of a successful firm exceeds the value of the future net revenues above its future outlays by the average of those expected search and assembly costs. That higher value is in goodwill as part of the value of the firm.

### u. So-Called Barriers to Entry?

To what extent does a firm that has successfully catered to customers' preferences and become large and that provides a large fraction of the services to the customers (however one may define the market so served) thereby create obstacles or higher costs to new potential entrants who would strive for the business of the existing firm's customers? Do the incumbent firms pose obstacles or difficulties or *barriers to entry* for new entrant firms? The answer is yes and no.

Successful firms raise the costs or reduce the demands facing new entrants seeking to get customers successfully (i.e., profitably). But "raise" costs over what? And reduce demands below what? Cost to newcomers may be high because the incumbent is so superior in his services. The challengers' less desirable product will not sell unless it incurs more costs. To call that an obstacle is to call one person's superior talents an obstacle to a less able person. From the consumer's point of view, it is desirable that the superior options exist. The advantage for the consumer is a "barrier" one would *not* want to eliminate by penalizing or restraining superior producers.

Another barrier is the necessity of making a large initial investment in equipment. Unquestionably if we could discover a way to do things just as well with less initial investment to be risked, it would be desirable. But that hope is no different than the wish that petroleum were not so rare or so expensive to find. The fact is that producing some goods with techniques involving bigger initial investment is less expensive and hence preferred by consumers. It would be easier to enter the medical profession if highly trained, more effective surgeons were not preferred by the public. That desired initially high investment in medical education is therefore misnamed "barrier to entry," as if to suggest it was undesirable—even though the public prefers the expensively educated surgeons. That kind of "barrier" is really a "filter" and is to be desired if one is interested in the well-being of mankind. To decry that barrier would be sensible only if somehow one could educate doctors without the initial investment.

A similar kind of differential between a large successful incumbent firm and a potential newcomer exists where the successful incumbent has established a strong reputation for the product and service. The consumers reliably know what they are getting when buying from the established incumbent, whereas purchases from a newcomer are riskier or require expensive experimentation to reveal to consumers whether or not the new challenger is as reliable as or better than the incumbent. This advantage to firms that have successfully proven their reliability is a source of savings to customers. Customers are relieved of the costs of constantly discovering which of potential suppliers are the more reliable. The reputation of successful—and only of the successful—caterers to consumer preferences is valuable to consumers, and that value is reflected in the value of the successful incumbent firm's trade name or brand. That asset which the newcomer does not yet have is often called a barrier to the newcomer. Yet, if an incumbent firm has created a building or equipment or resource, it hardly advances understanding to say that is a barrier to entry for new potential competitors who also must increase that cost.

Another phenomenon called a barrier is the inability of newcomers to borrow money for investment at the same interest cost as established firms. But again, this reflects lenders' lack of confidence in the new challengers' prospects or ability—or the lenders' confidence that the newcomers are riskier borrowers. That belief is well-founded, for it is a fact that newcomers *are* riskier than those who have proved to be superior and successful.

Another phenomenon dubbed a barrier to entry is product differentiation. This is said to arise when consumers have strong preferences for an incumbent's products or brands. Challengers must then offset or defeat those preferences by lower prices or large advertising or even superior products. But why do consumers have these preferences? The *successful* incumbent is a reliable supplier with known qualities. Differences in products or qualities are features that consumers prefer. Newcomers could provide an improved product or service, which is to say that they can take advantage of the ability to differentiate (i.e., improve their product or cater to the variety of tastes of customers). Indeed, if all suppliers had to provide identical goods, the only way a newcomer could attract customers would be by price, as for example, if all soap had to be the same shape, smell, and density, or if all breakfast foods had to be corn flakes or oatmeal (and if customers could tell at a mere glance how good each supplier's wares really were). The potential for product and service variations increases the ability of newcomers to capture a niche of the market of varied preferences. Indeed, product differentiation is nothing more than product superiority, already discussed above.

Superior ability, proven talents, large initial investments in equipment, and consumer knowledge of reliable suppliers are created or paid for by incumbent successful firms. To call these "barriers" rather than "filters" is to suggest that they are undesirable and should be reduced. They can be reduced, but only at the cost of destroying valuable assets of the incumbents, assets whose values reflect their value to consumers in permitting lower costs of production and greater confidence and reliability of service without expensive repetitive search and experimentation. Surely it would be wonderful if that information or ability could be achieved without those initial costs, but so would it be desirable if refined copper sprung from the ground without refining.

"Rent" is the payment for use of a resource, whether it be land, labor, equipment, ideas, or even money. Typically the rent for labor is called "wages," the payment for land and equipment is often called "rent," the payment for use of an idea is called a "royalty," and the payment for use of money is called "interest." In economic theory, the payment for a resource where the availability of the resource is insensitive to the size of the payment received for its use is named "economic rent" or "quasi-rent," depending on whether the insensitivity to price is permanent or temporary.

To early economists, "rent" meant payments for use of land; Ricardo, in particular, called it the payment for the "uses of the original and indestructible powers of the soil."[1] Subsequently, in recognition that a distinctive feature of what was called "land" was its presumed indestructibility (i.e., insensitivity of amount supplied to its price), the adjective "economic" was applied to the word "rent" for any resource the supply of which is indestructible (maintainable forever at no cost) and non-augmentable, and hence invariant to its price. In the jargon of economics, the quantity of present and future available supply is completely inelastic with respect to price, a situation graphically represented by a vertical supply line in the usual "Marshallian" price-quantity graphs.

### Economic Rent

The concept of "economic rent" is graphically depicted by the standard demand and supply lines in Figure 1 with a vertical supply curve (quantity supplied invariant to price) at the amount $X_f$. At all prices the supply is constant. The entire return to the resource is an "economic rent." If the aggregate quantity of such resources may in the future be increased by production of more indestructible units of the resource in response to a higher price (but the amount available at any moment is fixed regardless of the rent for its services), the

This previously unpublished August 1, 1985, paper appears here by permission of the author.

1. David Ricardo, *Principles of Political Economy and Taxation* (1821; 3rd ed., London: Dent Dutton, 1965), 33.

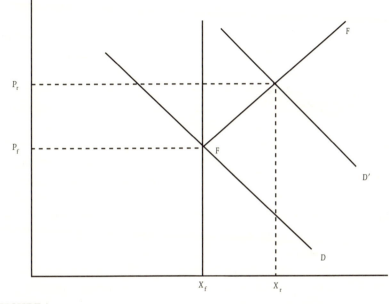

**FIGURE 1.**

supply line at the current moment is vertical. The supply curve for future amounts slopes upward from the existing amount, as depicted by the line FF in Figure 1. The long-run price would be $P_r$, and the equilibrium stock would be $X_r$; at that equilibrium stock the "market supply" (in Marshall's terminology) would be a vertical line. Thus, the supply of indestructible units would have depended on past anticipated prices about the present prices, but the supply of current units would be insensitive to the current price or rent. The return could be called "economic rent," except that no convention has developed with respect to the terminology for this situation of indestructible but augmentable resources.

## Quasi-Rent

Closely related to "economic rent" is "quasi-rent," a term apparently initiated by Alfred Marshall.[2] Because virtually every existing resource is unresponsive to a change in price for at least some very small length of time, the return

2. Alfred Marshall, *Principles of Economics* (1890; 8th ed., London: Macmillan, 1920), bk. 2, chap. 2, par. 12.

to every resource is like an "economic rent" for at least a short interval of time. In time, the supplied amount will be altered, either by production or by non-replacement of current items. Yet the fact that the amount available is not instantly affected by price led to the term "quasi-rent," which denotes a return, variations in which do not affect the current amount supplied to the demander but do affect the supply in the future.

If a rental (payments) stream to an existing resource is not sufficient to recover the costs incurred in its production, the durability of that existing resource will nevertheless enable the resource to continue to provide services, at least for some limited time. In other words, because of the resource's durability, it will continue for some interval to yield services even at a rent insufficient to recover its cost of production, but sufficient for current costs of use including interest on its salvage value (which is its highest value in some other use). Any excess over those current costs is a "quasi-rent."

Quasi-rent resembles an "economic rent" in that it exceeds the amount required for its current use, albeit temporarily, except that a flow of rents that did not cover all "quasi-rent" would preserve it for only a finite future interval, after which the resource would be diminished until not worth more than its salvage value. If the resource received a payment exceeding all the initially anticipated costs and the realized costs of production and operation, it will have achieved a profit, i.e., more than pure interest on the resource's investment cost. The question exists as to whether "quasi-rent" means just that portion of the rent in excess of the minimum operating costs over the remaining life of the asset, or all the excess, including profits, if any. Convention seems still to be missing. Marshall seems to have excluded interest on the investment as well as any profits from what he called quasi-rents, so that any excess over variable costs of operation were partitioned into quasi-rents, interest on investment, and profits.[3]

## Composite Quasi-rent

"Composite quasi-rent" was another important, but subsequently ignored, concept coined by Marshall.[4] When two separately owned resources are so specific to each other that their joint rent exceeds the sum of what each could receive if not used together, then that joint rent to the pair was called "composite quasi-rent." The two resources presumably already had been made specific to each other (worth more together than separately) by some specializ-

---

3. Ibid., bk. 5, chap. 9, par. 21.
4. Ibid., bk. 6, chap. 8, par. 35.

ing interrelated investments. Marshall cited the example of a mill and water-power site, presumably a mill built next to a dam to serve the mill, each possibly separately owned. One or both of the parties could attempt to hold up or extract a portion of the other party's expropriable quasi-rent. It is interesting to quote Marshall about this situation.

> The mill would probably not be put up till an agreement had been made for the supply of water power for a term of years; but at the end of that term similar difficulties would arise as to the division of the aggregate producer's surplus afforded by the water power and the site with the mill on it. . . . For instance, at Pittsburgh when manufacturers had just put up furnaces to be worked by natural gas instead of coal, the price of the gas was suddenly doubled. And the history of mines affords many instances of difficulties of this kind with neighbouring landowners as to rights of way, etc., and with the owners of neighbouring cottages, railways and docks.[5]

A reason for attributing importance to the concept of "composite quasi-rent" is now apparent. If it arises with resources that have been made specific to each other in the sense that the service value of each depends on the other's presence, the joint value or composite quasi-rent might become the object of attempted expropriation by one of the parties, especially by the one owning the resource with controllable flow of high alternative-use value. To avoid or re-duce the possibility of this behavior, a variety of preventative arrangements, contractual or otherwise, can be used prior to making the investments in re-sources of which at least one will become specific to the other. These include, among a host of possibilities, joint ownership, creation of a firm to own both, hostages and bonding, reciprocal dealing, governmental regulation, and use of insurers to monitor uses of interspecific assets. This is not a place to discuss these arrangements, beyond asserting that without the concept of "quasi-rent" and especially "expropriable quasi-rent"—which Marshall called "composite quasi-rent"—a vast variety of institutional arrangements would otherwise be inexplicable as means of increasing the effectiveness of economic activity.

Though Marshall briefly mentioned similar problems between employers and employees, I have not found any subsequent exposition by him about the precautionary contractual arrangements and institutions that attempt to avoid this problem, which has become a focus of substantial important research on what is called, variously, "opportunism," "shirking," "expropriable quasi-rents,"

5. Ibid., bk. 5, chap. 11, par. 32, 33.

"principal-agent conflicts," "monitoring," "problems of measuring performance," "asymmetric information," etc.

### Ricardian Rent

The rents accruing to different units of some otherwise homogeneous resource may differ and result in differences of rent over the next most valued use, differences that are called "Ricardian rents." This occurs where the individual units, all regarded as of the same "type" in other uses, are actually different with respect to some significant factor for its use here, though this factor, which is pertinent here, is irrelevant in any other uses. Examples of such factors can be location, special fertility, or talent that is disregarded in the other potential uses. For some questions, the inaccurate "homogenization" can be a convenient simplification, but for explaining each unit's actual rents, it can lead to confusion and misunderstanding. The service value, hence rents, for the use of the services here may differ, though equal in every relevant respect elsewhere. Whether the specific use uniqueness is created by natural talent or sheer accident, the special differences in use value here imply differences in payments, often called "Ricardian rents" to distinguish them from differences in rents (prices) obtained because of monopolizing or unnatural restrictions on any potential competitors, which may lead to higher rents, called "monopoly rents" for the protected resources.

### Differential Rents

"Differential rents" are another category representing rent differences in a sort of reverse homogeneity. Units of resource that are equal with respect to their value in use here differ among themselves in their values of use elsewhere. This can be represented graphically as in Figure 2. The differential rents of successive units are represented by the differences between the price line and the curve RR, which arrays the units from those with the lowest alternative use values to the highest, a curve labeled RR. The arrayed units are not homogeneous for uses elsewhere, so even if identical for use here, calling them successive units of the same good is misleading. They are not totally homogeneous; if they were, each unit would have the same as any other unit's use value and rent elsewhere. A curve like RR is equivalent to Marshall's particular expenses curve which arrayed units according to each individual unit's cost of production, or use value elsewhere, from lowest to highest.[6] The difference between price or

6. Ibid., app. H, n. 86.

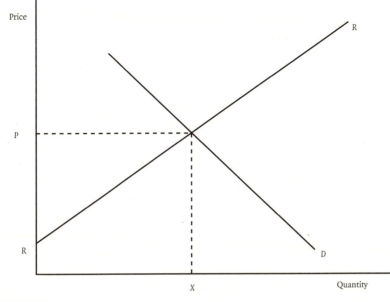

**FIGURE 2.**

rent here and the value on the RR curve is called "producers' surplus," or "differential rent." In sum, "Ricardian rents" indicate differences in rents to units that are equal in their best alternative use values, but different in their rent value here, while "differential rents" are the premia to units that are the same value here but different in their best alternative use values.

It is worth digressing to note that an upward rising true supply curve, which reflects increasing marginal costs of production, is different from the RR curve. In the true supply curve the area between the supply curve and the price line does not represent any of the above-mentioned rents nor "producers' surplus" (as it does with the RR curve). It is the portion of earnings of the supplier that exceed the variable costs and are applicable to cover the costs (possibly past investment costs) that are invariant to the rate of output. That area does not represent any excess of rental or sale value of units produced over their full costs, since only the variable costs are under the marginal cost curve. It represents the classic distribution of income to capital, if, for example, labor is presumed to be a variable input and capital a fixed input.

### High Rents a Result, Not Cause, of High Prices

An earlier, unfortunate analytic confusion occurred in the common misimpression that high rents of land made its products more expensive. Thus the high rent of land in New York was and is still often believed to make the cost of living, or the cost of doing business, higher in New York. Or higher rent for some agricultural land is believed to increase the cost of growing corn on that land. Proper attention to the meaning of "demand" and "costs" would have helped avoid that confusion. Demand here for some unit of resource is the highest value use of that resource if used here. The cost of using it here is the highest-valued forsaken alternative act elsewhere. For any resource, the cost of its use here is its best value elsewhere, i.e., its demand elsewhere. Land rent is high for "this" use because the land's value in some other use is high. The reason the rent is high here and can be paid is that its use value here is bid by competitors for its use here into the offered rent and exceeds the value in some other use. The product of the land can get a higher price here; that is why the rent is bid up so high, even though the particular winning bidder then believes a high price of the products must be obtained because the rent was high, rather than the reverse. As with every marketable resource, its highest value use here determines its rent, rather than the reverse. It was the implication of this kind of analysis that Marshall attempted to summarize in the famous aphorism, which he attributed to Ricardo (1817): "Rent does not enter into the cost of production."[7]

Probably the source of the confusion in believing that high rents of land caused high prices for products produced on expensive land is that an individual user of that expensive resource has to be able to charge a higher price for the product if the rent is to be covered. Bidders for that land compete for the right to the land that can yield a service worth so much—though to any individual successful bidder that rent has to be paid regardless of how well the successful bidder may be at actually achieving the high valued use of the land. Hence it may appear to an individual bidder that the rent determines the price that must be charged, rather than, as is the correct interpretation, the achievable high valued use enables the high bid for the land for the person best able to detect and achieve that highest valued use.

---

7. Ibid., bk. 5, chap. 10, n. 95.

## Function of Rent

Indeed, some people were aware of this bidding for the "land" and concluded that the receipt rent served no social purpose, since the land would exist anyway. But the high rent resulting from competitive bidding for its uses serves a useful purpose. It reveals which uses are the highest valued and directs the land to that use. In principle, a 100% tax on the land rent would not alter its supply (assuming initially that "land" is the name of whatever has a fixed indestructible supply). It could be correct if in this case the "owner" of the land had any incentive left to heed the highest bidder where the highest bid determines the rent. The assertion assumes that somehow the highest valued use can be known and that amount of tax be levied without genuine bona fide competitive bids for its use, a dubious, if not plainly false, proposition.

## Monopoly Rent

Let the word "monopoly" denote any seller whose wealth potential is increased by restrictions on other potential competitors, restrictions that are artificial or contrived in not being naturally inevitable. Laws prohibiting others from selling white wine or opening restaurants or engaging in legal practice are examples. It should be immediately emphasized that this does not imply nor is it to be inferred that all such restrictions are demonstrably undesirable.

Nevertheless, the increased wealth potential is a "monopoly rent." Whether it is realized by the monopolist as an increase in wealth depends upon the costs of competing for the imposition of such restrictions. Competition for "monopoly rents" may transfer them to, for example, politicians who impose the restrictions, and in turn may be dissipated by competition among politicians seeking to be in a position to grant such favours.

The "monopoly rents" may be dissipated (by what is often called "rent-seeking" competition for such monopoly status or rights to grant it) into competitive payments for resources that enable people to achieve status to grant such restrictions. Those who initially successfully and cheaply obtained such "monopoly" status may obtain a wealth increase, just as successful innovators obtain a profit stream before it is eliminated by competition from would-be imitators.

# ALLOCATIVE EFFICIENCY WITH
# EDGEWORTH-BOWLEY BOXES

### I

*Production possibility.* Let A and B be two people, able to produce commodities x and y. Postulate independent preference maps, described by isoutility lines. *Initially* assume independent production possibility functions for A and for B, each denoting the maximum daily *rates* of production of y admissible for specified *rates* of x.[1] Any point of production inside this maximum output line is called inefficient, and inadmissible if it is outside. Hereafter we shall assume each person's output is an efficient one; that is, his output mix is always a point on his production possibility curve, called PPC. Figure 1 presents the PPC of A and B. With two dimensions available, the output *rates* of x and y are shown on the appropriate x and y axes. According to the diagram the production possibility curve is not a straight line; that is, constant costs are excluded. The slope of the production possibility curve expresses the marginal rate of substitution or transformation in production between y and x. As one increases x, the slope becomes steeper, indicating that larger amounts of y must be sacrificed for unit increments in x. Marginal costs of x increase with larger *rates* of output of x— also for y.

The derivation of the PPC for A is shown in Figure 2. Let the rates of input of factor 1 and factor 2 be given for A. That is, A is to produce x and y efficiently, given that he has fixed rates of inputs 1 and 2; he cannot, yet, buy and sell inputs. (Later we shall relax this assumption.) Each point inside the Edgeworth-Bowley *input-production* box of Figure 2 denotes some allocation of rates of inputs 1 and 2 to x and y. The tangencies of the production isoquants define the efficient input allocations, and if the output rates of the tangent isoquants are read off in numerical magnitude, and plotted against each other, we will obtain the PPC of Figure 1 for person A. Under no circumstances should person A select an allocation of inputs 1 and 2 that does not give a point on the "contract

---

This previously unpublished, undated article appears here by permission of the author.

1. This is relaxed in section IV below.

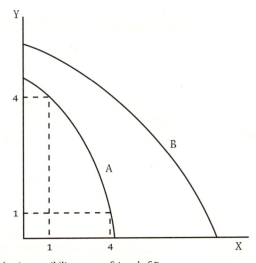

**FIGURE 1.** Production possibility curves of A and of B

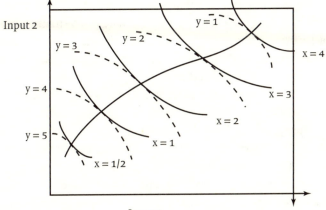

**FIGURE 2.** A's efficient production path for outputs of x and y, given the available amounts of inputs 1 and 2

curve" in Figure 2. Clearly, if he picked an allocation of inputs 1 and 2 off that line he could reallocate and move to the contract curve and obtain more of both x and y than he had before. *A test of efficiency is that the ratio of the marginal productivities of input rates for 1 and 2 in the production of output x be the same as in the production of output y.* It is worth emphasizing that this is a purely technical efficiency concept. No values or prices for x and y are required; no way for comparing the worth of x against y is needed to establish that one is inefficient in the sense of being able to produce more and not doing so. (But values of 1 relative to 2 are involved.) In the same way, the production possibility curve could be derived for B. Convex-shaped PPCs for A and for B mean (is tautological with) decreasing returns for x and for y as in Figure 1.

Given the inputs or resources available to A, if A cannot trade inputs with B, the production possibility curve of A indicates the maximal (efficient) output mixes he can produce with the resources (inputs) given to him. The output possibility curve, PPC, of A is independent of what B does. For the moment let us continue with this assumption that they cannot trade productive resources.

Rotate through exactly 180 degrees the PPC of B and place it tangent to the PPC of A (keeping the axes of B parallel to the axes of A's PPC) as shown in Figure 3. Then by sliding B's PPC along A's PPC, there will be traced out a path of points of B's origin, in the northeast (upper right-hand) part of the diagram. This is the additive or *total* PPC of A and B. B's origin is located on the total PPC, and we must read downward and to the left to measure B's output mix. And further, the tangency of the PPCs of A and B for any specified efficient total output is now made obvious. What this method emphasizes is that for any given efficient output point, the necessary output of A and of B is a pair of outputs, one on the PPC at which the Marginal Rate of Substitution (MRS) on A's and MRS on B's PPC are equated. Arrows connect one particular total output point to the particular outputs required of A and B. One could draw an arrow from each point on the total PPC curve to the associated point on A's PPC, thus linking the output of A (and also of B) required for any specified total output point. It should also be noticed that the MRS (slope) of the total PPC is numerically equal to MRS for A and for B. This is nothing more than geometric representation of the well-known marginal equality condition that *for an efficient total output point, the MRS in production between all pairs of commodities must be equal for all producers.*

If A and B are producing outputs at which their MRSs are not equal, the output is smaller than it could be. This can be seen by arbitrarily picking an output point for A, then picking an output for B, other than the one whose MRS is equal

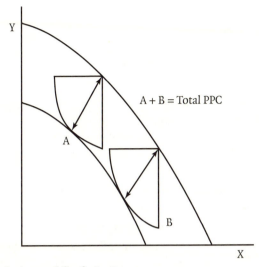

**FIGURE 3.** *Production possibility for A + B*

to that for the output mix of A. Superimposing the two PPCs of A and of B, these two points, the PPCs of A and B, instead of being tangent, will intersect each other. The total output falls inside the total output production possibility achieved by apportioning a specified output between A and B so as to equate their MRSs.

If both A and B see the same numerical value for the ratio of prices of outputs x and y, and if each is interested in maximizing his income, then each will produce at that point on his own PPC where its slope equals the ratio of the price of y to the price of x. This is the well-known proposition that A and B, by looking at the same price and at their own marginal costs of production (the slopes of their PPCs), will produce jointly a total output of y and x that is on the PPC. This simply means that *equality between ratios of marginal costs and the ratio of output prices is a necessary condition for efficient production*, that is, for achieving a point on the total PPC.[2] (We shall later see the reason for each marginal cost to equal the price of each good. Here we have only equality of ratios—i.e., $MC_1/MC_2 = P_1/P_2$; later we shall use $MC_1 = P_1$ and $MC_2 = P_2$.)

2. Actually, while all we appear to have employed is equality between the *ratios* of price and marginal costs, absolute equality between marginal costs and prices is really implied in this case. Why? Because the equality can be shown to be necessary for efficiency if any self-owned items are used both in production and directly in household consumption.

## II

*Utility maps.* The questions now are: (1) what total output mix is to be produced and (2) how is its consumption to be divided among A and B? We separate these two questions as best we can in exposition, even though they are analytically inseparable. Our procedure will be to test each possible output point on the total PPC to see if this output is desired over some other point by A and B, as consumers. We already have the total production possibilities; we need the consumption preferences. For this we resort to the isoutility, or indifference preference maps of A and B.

Postulated properties of the utility map are: The isoutility lines are continuous; points with more of x and y are preferred to points with less of each; the indifference lines are negative in slope and convex.

With these two indifference maps, we can again form an *output-consumption* Edgeworth-Bowley box by rotating B's indifference map through 180 degrees and placing its origin in the upper right-hand side at a distance from the origin of A's indifference map equivalent to the total of x (measured on the horizontal axis) and to the total amount of y (measured on the vertical axis). Figure 4 is the result. A contract curve is drawn through the indifference curve tangencies. Given the totals of x and y and an initial division of the stock of x and y between A and B (that which they produce), there will be a mutually beneficial movement available toward the contract curve, from the initial point, if exchange is permitted. The mode of approach to the contract curve will depend upon the initial prices at which exchange occurs, and upon each person's behavior as a price taker or price searcher. We shall assume each to act as a price taker; that is, he assumes the price is independent of his purchases or sales. In any event, the well-known property of a final equilibrium position *on the contract curve* is: the MRS in consumption (and in production, from preceding section) are equal to the market exchange ratio of x and y. With price searchers, this contract curve will not be reached, unless there is price discrimination or fixed fee pricing.

## III

*Full exchange and production equilibrium.* We can combine the consumer goods exchange equilibrium (Figure 4) with consumer goods production equilibrium, Figure 3, by combining the Edgeworth box of Figure 4 with the production possibility curve of Figure 3. Placing the lower left-hand corner of Figure 4 over the same corner (the origin) of Figure 3 yields Figure 5. The upper right-

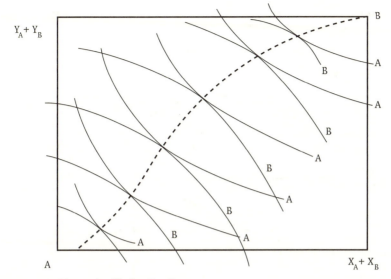

$Y_A + Y_B$

$X_A + X_B$

**FIGURE 4.** *Edgeworth utility box* $X_A + X_B$

hand corner of the Edgeworth-Bowley box of Figure 4 will be on some point of the total PPC curve of Figure 3. It cannot be outside the total PPC, for this would indicate the impossible situation of more goods available for distribution than can be produced, and to be inside the total PPC would indicate inefficient production. We are assuming efficient production allocation; that is, the total output is the total PPC. Each person is producing at the appropriate point on his own PPC—each person is producing at a point at which the MRS between x and y in production for A are equal to those for B.

A moment's thought will reveal that while any point on the total PPC (combination of outputs) can be selected for the upper right-hand corner of the box, it might not be compatible with consumer demands.

In full equilibrium each person must be unable to produce y at less cost than he can buy y, and he must also be unable to produce x at less cost than he can buy x. Furthermore each person must be unable to produce or buy one more x for smaller losses of y than his consumption MRS (personal valuation) between y and x, else it would pay him to give up some y for more x. In other words, in full equilibrium for each person, the MRS between x and y in consumption and in production must equal the interpersonal (market) exchange rate between x and y.

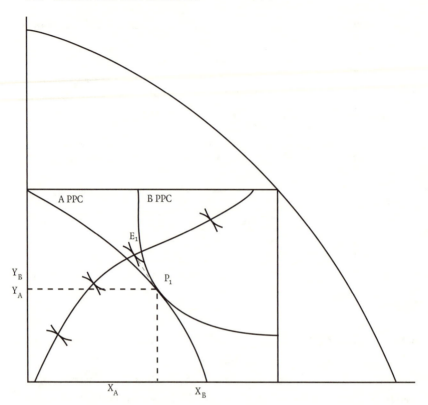

**FIGURE 5.** *Edgeworth-Bowley consumption box plus total PPC equilibrium conditions*

Not *every* point on the total PPC is a full competitive equilibrium point. See Figure 5. The total output point $P_1$ in Figure 5 is a full equilibrium point. A produces $x_a$ and $y_a$, while B produces $x_b$ and $y_b$. A sells some x to B and receives y in return. The price-takers market rate of exchange is given by the slope of the line from $P_1$ to $E_1$. The slope of this line also equals the production MRS between y and x for both A and B (slopes of their PPC), and it is equal also to the MRS in consumption for both A and B (slopes of indifference curves).

If we tested some other output point, say $P_2$ (Figure 6), we would see that it is not a full equilibrium point. This total output is obtained by A and B producing at the point $P_2$ (where A's output is read from the lower left-hand origin and B's from his origin at the upper right-hand corner at point $P_2$). For this output to be a full equilibrium, the market exchange ratio should be the same as the MRS in production for both A and B; else A and B would be induced to change their outputs. But if a tangent line is drawn from point $P_2$ (with a slope equal to

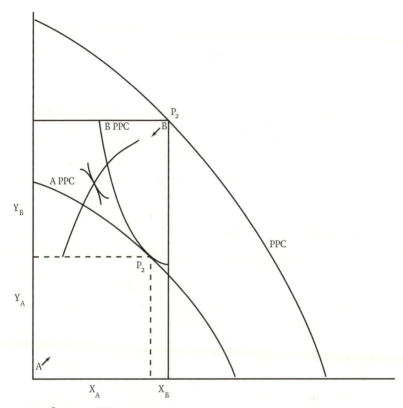

**FIGURE 6.** Non-equilibrium output, $P_2$

the production MRS slopes of the two production functions of A and B at their tangency), it will cut the contract at point $E_2$, where the tangent indifference curves have a common slope different from the common slope of the production possibility curves. This discrepancy between the production tangency slope and the utility curves' tangency slope means that the consumption-dictated market exchange trading ratios differ from the production exchange ratios at point P. There would be incentive for both A and B to change their output mixes to move to higher utility. This would move the total output point away from $P_2$ on the total PPC.

Graphically, a point on the total PPC will be a full equilibrium output, if, and only if, a straight line drawn from the tangency point of the two individual PPCs (associated with the specified total output), with a slope equal to the common tangency slope of those two PPCs, intersects the contract curve where the slope of the tangent utility curves is equal to the slope of that straight line extended from the two individual PPCs.[3] (This slope is also the slope of the total PPC at the output point.) In other words, only if there is equality among the MRSs in production for A and for B at their production points and the MRSs in consumption for A and B at their final consumption points can there be a full equilibrium.[4]

A compatible, or full, equilibrium output point is one for which neither A nor B can improve his utility by (i) modifying his output mix (by moving along his PPC) or by (ii) changing his sales or purchases (by offering different sales or purchases *prices* which are acceptable to the other person) or by (iii) varying his consumption pattern (by changing his actual purchases or sales at *existing* market exchange ratios). When each person finds himself in this situation, the situation is a "full equilibrium." Each person is maximizing his utility subject to his production function and voluntary exchanges with the other person at freely negotiable, mutually acceptable market exchange rates.

### IV

The preceding discussion is based on trading of *consumers* output x and y only, with a ban on the trading of *productive* resources. Up to this point, we can refer to the outcome as an equilibrium for a *fixed* distribution of productive resources (i.e., there is no trade in productive resources). If trading in productive resources is permitted, the PPC of A is not independent of the output that B happens to produce. Suppose that under a resource trading ban, A and B are producing some total output. A and B both are efficient, given their non-exchangeable productive resources. This means that each input available to A is being used in producing x and y so that the marginal value of output of any one resource is the same in producing x as it is in producing y for A. Also for B, the marginal output value of any available resource is the same in x as it is in y. But there is no assurance that the marginal value productivities of the input in

---

3. By using four plastic sheets, the operation of Figure 5 can be made more lucid. On one sheet, draw A's utility map with isoutility lines. On a second, draw B's. On a third, draw A's PPC (from Figure 4), and on the fourth sheet draw B's PPC. By proper superimposition the equilibrium output, consumption, and prices can be readily obtained. By changing one of the charts, the effects of postulated types of events can be discerned.

4. Except for our assumption of price-takers—i.e., where each person takes the price as given—the line drawn from the production point of A and B could be a curved line and then the MRS in production and consumption need not be equal for equilibrium to exist. Also the relevant slope seen by each party may differ from price if marginal revenue differs from price.

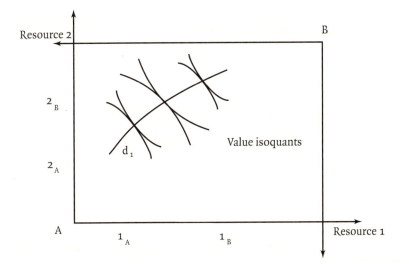

**FIGURE 7.** *Resource trading contract curve*

producing x and y are the same for A as for B. In the absence of such equality, it is possible for A and B to trade productive resources with each other and thereby increase the total output of both x and y. And this will be induced by the desire of A and of B to increase their separate net incomes.

This can be illustrated by Figure 7. The horizontal length of the box measures the total of resource 1, and the vertical scale the total of resource 2. An allocation of resources 1 and 2 between A and B is indicated by a point in the box. For example, point $d_1$ is one division of the total resources—A has $1_A$ of resource 1 and $2_A$ of resource 2, with the remaining distance on each axis indicating the amounts going to B. The curved lines, with pattern similar to production isoquants, are *value of output* isoquants. They represent input combinations of 1 and 2 that A can use to produce output mixes of x and y that yield him a constant total value of output. For example, from the point $d_1$, if A gave up some of resource 1, reducing his output of x and y and reducing the total value of his output, he could, by increasing the amount of resource 2 available to him, revise and increase his output of x and y in order to increase the total value of the output back to its original amount. Implicit in the value of output isoquant for A, with the resources as substitutable inputs, is the internal optimizing by A of the output mix of products x and y on the basis of their *given* selling prices (as covered in preceding sections).

A similar mix of value isoquants can be drawn for B. Then another

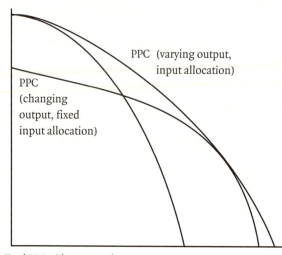

PPC (varying output,
input allocation)

PPC
(changing
output, fixed
input allocation)

**FIGURE 8.** *Total PPC with resource sales*

Edgeworth-Bowley box can be formed with the upper right-hand corner of the
box as B's point of origin. Then the path of tangencies of the value isoquants
for A and for B is a contract curve. Here we have replaced consumers by producers, utility by value of output, and consumers goods by productive resources on the axes of the box. The contract curve is the path of efficient and
distributive allocations of productive resources between A and B. But there is
one difference. We can now identify an "optimal" point on the contract curve,
whereas it will be recalled that in the consumers Edgeworth-Bowley box, no
comparison could be made among alternative points on the contract curve.

Each point on this contract curve in Figure 7 denotes a distribution of resources 1 and 2 between A and B. And each alternative possible distribution implies a whole PPC for A and a whole PPC for B, of which examples were given in
Figure 1. Each adjunct pair of PPC for A and PPC for B can be added into a total
PPC. As *resource* allocation moves along the contract curve in Figure 7, we are
necessarily changing the total PPC by changing the individual PPC. If we plotted all these different total PPC, one for each point on the contract curve of Figure 7, we would have some outer boundary or envelope of PPC. See Figure 8.
This outer boundary is the total PPC with no restraints on resource trading.
Clearly it is made up of the outermost sections of the PPC, each for a particular
resource distribution of inputs 1 and 2 between A and B. By moving along the
outer *envelope* boundary we assume different resource allocations of inputs 1
and 2 between A and B. If we hold resource allocations fixed, we shall move

along some restricted PPC inside the outer boundary (unless we insist on producing that combination of x and y for which we accidentally happen to have the right distribution of resources 1 and 2 between A and B). To each point on the contract curve in Figure 7, there corresponds a total PPC curve, some of which are shown in Figure 8. Which of the points on the contract curve of Figure 7 is "best"? Which point yields the total PPC that forms part of the outer envelope of PPCs in Figure 8? If some point on the super envelope curve of Figure 8 is optimal in a utility sense to each person (given his endowment), which point is it? And which point on the contract curve of Figure 7 gives the PPC that forms that portion of the super PPC envelope?

In the producers' resources Edgeworth-Bowley box (Figure 7), we can identify this optimal point on the contract curve. This follows from the fact that here we are using comparable values of output isoquants. Each isoquant has a market value. The point with the largest sum of values of two tangent isoquants is the optimal. It maximizes national income. For whatever point on the contract curve that may be initially considered, A can ask, "If I bought more of resources 1 and 2 from B—i.e., if I pushed him back up the contract curve—could I go to higher-value isoquants which are higher by an amount in excess of the cost of buying the extra amounts of resources 1 and 2 from B?" If so, it will be in A's interest to do so.

If A and B are seeking wealth, they will move each other along the contract curve. A will buy resources away from B if he can move to higher-value isoquants which are higher by more than the cost of buying resources from B. And B will be agreeable. And when A can no longer buy resources from B, at costs less than increment of value, he can no longer increase his net income. This will happen when (1) for A the marginal values produced by a resource are the same in the production of x as in the production of y, (2) these are also equal for B, (3) the values in (1) equal those in (2), and finally (4) these conditions hold for every input. The output of x and y will then be at a point on the total PPC curve identified with that particular distribution of resources. Will this point on this particular PPC also be a point on the outer boundary—the super PPC envelope—in Figure 8? The answer is yes. Here is where equality of $MC_A = P_A$ enters. This now replaces equality of ratios $MC_A/MC_B = P_A/P_B$. So we see equality of $MC_A$ and $P_A$ is a result of resource trading, an outcome that occurs if the outputs of x and y are sold in consumers markets at prices that are equal to the marginal costs, and if these are the prices which A and B use in valuing their outputs, and if resources 1 and 2 are exchanged at prices that equal their marginal value productivities. In other words, given consumers preference patterns, production functions, and the total stock of resources, a full production equilibrium is that allocation of resources with an output mix on the super production possibility curve. Full technological efficiency is obtained, even for allocation of resources.

A next step would be to remove the restriction on fixed totals of resources or, in other words, to explain the initial availability and ownership of resources. This we cannot do.

## V

Is there any process which we can postulate for this model that would lead it to a full equilibrium point (i.e., to a vector of prices, outputs, and input allocations) having all the information collected in one place and having every possible output point tested or without having a computer solve for that solution vector? All we need to do to answer this is see what would happen under a "self-seeking, individualistic price-takers' free price" postulate. At a non-equilibrium point (e.g., $P_2$, Figure 6), if the available inputs are being traded between A and B along the line whose slope equals the production MRS, the market will not be cleared. (The meaning of an uncleared market is not explained here.) Assume that market prices rise with excess demand and fall with excess supply as consumers reveal their preferences by bidding; this changed slope of the market exchange line through point $P_2$ will induce each individual, who is seeking greater income, to shift his production toward the commodity whose price (in terms of the other) has risen. The result will be a movement along each individual's production possibility curve, each person shifting to the new higher priced commodity. This will appear on the total PPC as a shift along it to a new total output point, geometrically shown by sliding the individual PPCs of A and B along their surfaces while maintaining tangencies (as in Figure 3). The increasing output of the formerly under-produced commodity will lower its price (and also change the MRS in consumption as consumers adjust their consumption rates) until the price is brought to equality with the production MRS which is rising as the production mix is revised.

The changes in prices of x and y will change the values on the output isoquants of Figure 7. This will also change the marginal value productivities of inputs 1 and 2 in the production of x and y, leading to a change in allocation of inputs to outputs of x and y. The output will shift toward the output whose price has risen; the prices of inputs will be altered, raising those whose marginal productivity in the output of the increased consumption goods falls relatively slowly (i.e., whose elasticity of substitution is lower in the production of this product).

## VI

We can digress momentarily to relate these diagrams to the Pareto optimal-ity idea—the kernel of modern welfare theory. For each point on the total PPC, we superimposed an Edgeworth-Bowley consumption box with its contract curve running from the upper right corner down to the lower left-hand origin. We know that the utility efficient allocations of consumers goods between A and B all lie on the contract curve. If total production were for the moment somehow fixed by fiat at the point P, and if output were then traded between A and B, some point on the contract curve would be achieved. If we now could move A and B down that contract curve, A's utility would decrease and B's would increase, and conversely for movements toward the upper right corner. We can plot the utility to A and to B on a new graph, A's utility on the horizontal axis and B's on the vertical axis. See Figure 9. This resulting *utility possibility curve*, asso-ciated with the consumer trading contract curve in the box associated with the particular total output point P, shows the maximum utility to A for given utility to B, and conversely.

To each *point* P on the total production possibility curve there is a consumers trading contract *curve*, and each of these contract curves gives a *utility possibility curve*. Thus to each *point* P on the PPC, there is a utility possibility *curve*. For ex-ample the utility possibility curves for two points in Figure 8 are shown in Fig-ure 9. If all of these utility possibility curves are drawn for all points on PPC they will have an outer envelope. Being on the envelope is better than being inside it.

But we know from the earlier analysis that there is an equilibrium point on the total PPC, for given consumer utility functions, production functions, en-

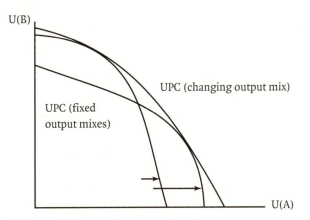

**FIGURE 9.** *Utility possibility curves fixed resource allocation*

dowments, and price-takers markets. And this equilibrium point P is unique and tied to an exchange equilibrium point E (on a consumers goods contract curve) which in turn is associated with a unique point U on the envelope of the utility possibility curve graph. If, and only if, the final equilibrium is a "competitive" (price-takers) price equilibrium in the consumers and in the producers resources markets—that is, price equals marginal costs both in factor and in production markets—will the equilibrium point U be on the envelope of the utility possibility curve.

All points on the utility possibility envelope are Pareto optimal points; that is, it is impossible to increase anyone's utility without reducing someone else's. This could be called a utility efficiency frontier. It can be shown under certain postulates about production function conditions and utility patterns that every Pareto optimum point (points on the utility envelope) is a competitive equilibrium point on the total PPC curve. And the converse is also true—every full competitive equilibrium point (prices equal marginal cost in both consumers and producers goods) is a Pareto optimum.

To be on the envelope PPC, it is sufficient to have a production equilibrium (prices equal to marginal cost in production), but to be on the utility possibility frontier, competitive equilibrium in consumers goods markets is also necessary. Not every point on this total PPC need be a potential competitive equilibrium point. For example, some of them may not be achieved through competition, because, given the utility functions, the required consumer price ratio cannot be realized; but then, it can be shown that those points are not Pareto optimal.

### VII

We can now make some supplementary remarks. (1) With trading, and given technology and preference maps, no matter what the initial distribution of resources, the end distribution will depend upon the consumers product demands and the imputed demand for production resources which depend also upon technological skills of each person. A person rich in one kind of resource will find himself fortunate to live in a community that imputes a high demand for that kind of resource. Thus the expression "given the initial distribution of physical resources" is not equivalent to the expression "given the distribution of wealth."

(2) If input prices did not equal their marginal costs to buyers (price-searchers) in the factor markets, because some producers do not regard price as independent of their behavior, the achievable total PPC curve is smaller than

when marginal costs equal prices. And, in any event, if marginal costs to consumers of consumers goods do not equal price of consumers goods in the *consumers* markets, the actual output point on the total PPC (assuming price did equal marginal costs in the factor markets) would be different from the output point where prices of consumers goods did equal marginal cost. The actual output point, although on the PPC, is not a Pareto optimum, because it would be possible, in principle, to change to a new point on the PPC and redivide this new product so as to increase everyone's utility via a system of transfer payments.

(3) How can there be *many* points of Pareto optimality, if each is uniquely tied to an exchange and production equilibrium, when there is only *one* competitive equilibrium? Actually there is a competitive equilibrium for each initial distribution of resources. If the initial distribution of resources among the people were different, there would be a different final output point, someplace on the super PPC. To this there corresponds a point on the superutility possibility curve.

(4) If once-and-for-all lump-sum transfer payments were made among the individuals, there would still, aside from these imposed income transfers, be competition in consumption and production. Once-and-for-all revisions in resource ownership, or transfer of payments of a fixed lump-sum type (but not continuing excise taxes, or proportional taxes), are consistent with optimality in the Pareto sense. These would affect only the point achieved on the superutility possibility curve. Therefore by appropriate combinations of once-and-for-all fixed total taxes, various points on the superutility possibility surface can be achieved with their associated points on the total PPC and on the contract curves. The particular set that is achieved depends, then, upon the initial distribution of resources and set of transfer payments.

(5) Beware. Lump-sum once-and-for-all transfers of wealth are not so efficacious in a deeper sense. Presumably they are lump-sum once-and-for-all in order to not "distort" prices. But consider the following possibility. A lump-sum once-and-for-all tax is levied on Mr. A, an industrious pinchpenny, and the proceeds given to Mr. B, who, though a spendthrift, is now as rich as Mr. A. Where will they be in five years? Probably Mr. A will be rich and Mr. B poor. Has the *final full* equilibrium been changed? No. Do we therefore have another lump-sum once-and-for-all tax? Not if "once-and-for-all" means *once*. All this suggests that the given initial situation might be characterized in terms of a person's personality traits and talents rather than in terms of some initial stock of marketable goods. The moral is that once-and-for-all wealth transfers may be transitory in their effects.

## VIII

We may summarize by noting at least five kinds of inefficiency: (1) Everyone says "idle" resources is an obvious one. (2) Another is misused production resources, in the sense that a reallocation of the resources *to different products within* a firm could increase the output of everything, despite full employment. This is a kind of efficiency the economist usually takes for granted (although he is likely assuming too much). (3) Inequalities between price and marginal costs in resource trading among firms is another source of production inefficiency. (4) Inefficiency of *utility* results from an inappropriate basket of final products. The output basket, although an efficient production one, could be revised to everyone's benefit by making prices equal marginal revenue for consumers goods, and also prices of inputs equal to marginal factor costs, i.e., no monopoly and no monopsony. (5) There is the utility inefficiency that results despite efficient and even appropriate production, because consumers goods are allotted to each individual and then consumers trading is restricted and held short of full mutual benefit.

A Pareto optimal implies production and utility efficiency in all five senses, and conversely. Failure of prices to clear the factor market upsets efficiency in sense 1. Failure of a firm's ratios of marginal products to be proportional to prices of outputs upsets efficiency in sense 2. Failure of prices of factors in the factor markets to equal marginal value products upsets efficiency in sense 3. Failure of prices in consumers markets to equal marginal costs in production markets will upset efficiency in sense 4. Failure of prices to be the same to all consumers (restricted trading) upsets efficiency in sense 5.

Excise taxes on consumers goods, some kinds of price discrimination among consumers, and price controls are examples of causes of inefficiency of type 5—price control because some who would like to buy at the prices others can buy at are unable to do so. Production inefficiency in sense 3 is also caused by factor price controls (e.g., rates set by law, convention, agreement, or union pressure).

## IX

Crucial but common assumptions that we have tacitly employed are that utility of any person depends only upon the commodities which he has for consumption purposes, and not on the kind of work he does, where he sells his resources, the utility of other persons, and the process of resolving interpersonal conflict. These are strong assumptions, but all except the last can be relaxed.

If, however, the process of resolving conflict is changed, trouble arises. Trade involves property rights in goods. If these rights are removed, we enter a new area of study. Candidly, we don't know very much. But we do know that with weakened private property rights and/or with significant transactors and market exchange opportunity search costs, many situations that appear non-optimal may in fact be optimal in the Paretian sense, once the costs of property rights, information, and exchange are recognized. For example many alleged externalities become not "failure" but high-cost activities—such as producing steel. To complain of failures to achieve Pareto optimality as achieved with zero costs of information, exchange, and property rights is to complain of the failure of nature to make goods free.

# THE RATE OF INTEREST, FISHER'S RATE OF RETURN OVER COSTS AND KEYNES' INTERNAL RATE OF RETURN

Republication of Irving Fisher's *The Theory of Interest*[1] will enable economists to correct an error propagated by a careless statement in Keynes' *General Theory*. Keynes erroneously alleged that his marginal efficiency of capital is identical with Fisher's marginal rate of return over cost, and that it is used for exactly the same purpose. Unfortunately Keynes was wrong; they are not the same, and they were not used for the same purpose.

1. *Keynes' Marginal Efficiency of Capital.* Keynes' marginal efficiency of capital is the rate of discount which equates the present worth of the receipt stream to the present worth of the expense stream.[2] If $R(t)$ denotes the receipt stream and $E(t)$ denotes the outlay stream, both as functions of time, and if $e^{-rt}$ be the discount factor for $t$, then $\int_0^t [R(t) - E(t)]\, e^{-rt}dt$ is the net present worth of an investment option. The rate $r$ which sets this present worth equal to zero is the marginal efficiency of capital, or the internal rate of return, but it is not Fisher's rate of return over cost.[3]

However, it is interesting to note that Keynes did believe he was really following Fisher, for he wrote, "Professor Fisher uses his 'rate of return over cost' in the same sense and for precisely the same purposes as I employ the 'marginal efficiency of capital.'"[4]

2. *Fisher's Rate of Return over Cost.* Fisher's rate of return over cost concept, de-

---

Reprinted from *American Economic Review* 45 (December 1955): 938–43.

1. Irving Fisher, *The Theory of Interest* (New York, 1930), and reissued by Kelley and Millman, New York, 1954.

2. J. M. Keynes, *The General Theory of Employment Interest and Money* (New York, 1936), p. 140. The distinction between the marginal internal rate of return and the average internal rate of return, provided that the reader thinks in terms of either an incremental unit or a lump-sum nondivisible investment, while important for some problems, is not critical for the present discussion.

3. Fisher, op. cit., pp. 151–55.

4. Keynes, op. cit., p. 141.

veloped in order to rank investment alternatives by the universally correct criterion of maximum present value, can be defined only by reference to at least two alternative investment options. Letting subscripts denote investment options,

$$\int_0^t ([R_1(t) - E_1(t)] - [R_2(t) - E_2(t)])e^{-rt}dt$$

is the difference in present worths of the two investment options when each is discounted at the rate r. The rate r which sets this *difference* equal to zero is Fisher's marginal rate of return over cost.[5] Fisher always meant by the expression "opportunity" a choice between two alternative investments.[6] Therefore he could say that for this opportunity (between the two options) the advantage of 1 over 2 at any moment t, is $(R_1 - E_1) - (R_2 - E_2)$, or upon rearranging terms, is $(R_1 - R_2) - (E_1 - E_2)$. Fisher called this latter expression the surplus of advantages over disadvantages.[7] The rate of discount which equates the present worth of the advantages, $(R_1 - R_2)$, to the present worth of the disadvantages, $(E_1 - E_2)$, is the rate of return over cost.[8] If one makes the careless step of thinking of the advantages as a simple receipt stream and the disadvantage as a simple cost stream for a *single* investment, he will then be able to think that the internal rate of return is the rate of return over cost. Fisher's rate of return over cost *always* involved a comparison of two options, not a discounting of merely one option.

A numerical example might sharpen the difference. Suppose that each of two alternative investment options requires an immediate outlay of $25. Suppose that one, A, yields a receipt stream of $5 per year for ten years, and the other, B, yields $1 in the first year, $2 in the second, etc., up to ten years. The internal rate of return of A is about 17 per cent, while B's is about 12.5 per cent. Yet the Fisherian rate of return over cost of B compared with that of A is 6 per cent. Figure 1 shows the present value of the net receipt streams of A and of B for different discount rates. The discount rate at which line AA cuts the horizontal line for $25 is 17 per cent. Line BB cuts the $25 line at 12.5 per cent. But notice that BB intersects AA at 6 per cent; under 6 per cent B is superior because it has the larger present value, while at rates over 6 per cent A is superior. The distance between the line AA (or BB) and the $25 cost line, at any rate of interest, measures the net present worth of opportunity A (or B).

5. Fisher, op. cit., p. 155.
6. Ibid., p. 151.
7. Ibid., p. 153.
8. Ibid., p. 155.

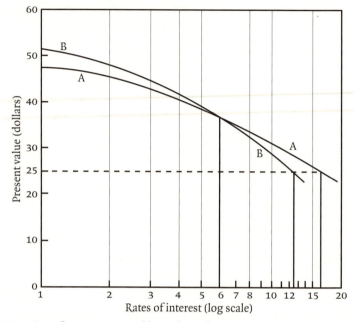

**FIGURE 1.** *Rate of return over cost and internal rate of return*

According to their internal rates of return, A would be preferred to B (17 per cent as compared to 12.5 per cent); yet B will be the preferred investment at interest rates below 6 per cent according to the maximum present wealth criterion. Before the reader interjects that both investments will be profitable and hence both will be undertaken, let him assume that the two investments, A and B, are mutually exclusive alternatives, e.g., a wood bridge or a steel bridge, an electric bus system vs. a gasoline one, a brick house vs. a wood house. Hence both cannot be undertaken. A ranking of substitutable investments by the Keynesian internal rate of return is not consistent with the maximizing of net present wealth.

Fisher wanted to show that the ranking of alternatives according to the maximum wealth criterion would depend upon the market rate of interest. To emphasize this, he developed the rate of return over cost concept as a means of determining at what rate of interest the reversal of preference would occur.[9]

9. "To induce him to make a change, the *rate of return over cost must exceed the rate of interest.*" But Fisher attaches the following generalizing footnote to this sentence: "In case the advantages (returns) precede the disadvantages (costs), . . . the proposition must be reversed, as follows: The earlier advantage will be chosen only in case the rate of future costs over present returns is *less* than the rate of interest." Ibid., p. 159.

Fisher's rate of return over cost serves merely as a device to determine all the rates of interest at which investment 1 would be preferred to 2. It does not give a rate of return over cost with which to rank investments once and for all, for the simple reason that the rankings change as the rate of interest changes. Now, ranking on the basis of internal rates of return is correlated with present-worth rankings if the only investment options compared are a particular investment and an option to invest at the market rate. But if there are two investment options alternative to market lending, the internal rates of return of the two options will *not* rank them consistently with their present values.

3. *Sources of Confusion.* A plausible source of the confusion is Fisher's sentence which Keynes quoted in his *General Theory.* "The rate of return over cost is that rate which, employed in computing the present worth of all the costs and the present worth of all the returns, will make these two equal."[10] But Keynes did not quote the next sentence which reads, "Or, as a mathematician would prefer to put it, the rate which, employed in computing the present worth of the whole series of differences between the two income streams (some differences being positive and others negative) will make the total zero."[11] And the next sentence, "If the rate, so computed, were taken for every possible pair of income streams compared as to their advantages and disadvantages, it would authentically decide in each case which of the pair is to be preferred."

Or possibly Keynes had read the section in Fisher's book just preceding the quoted sentence—a section titled "The Case of Perpetual Returns," which discusses investment options that generate constant net receipt streams to perpetuity. In that case, the ranking provided by Keynes' internal rate of return will conform to Fisher's ranking by the present value at the market rate. This means that Keynes' and Fisher's rankings will agree in the event that two special conditions (which are not usually fulfilled) are fulfilled: (1) the net receipt stream generated by the nonconstant nonperpetual investment option can immediately upon its generation be reinvested in new investment options with the same Keynesian internal rate of return, and that (2) this reinvestment of the generated net receipts can be continued in this way at this same internal rate *forever.* Any net receipt stream can be converted in the market to a constant net receipt stream to perpetuity, but this does not mean that the Keynesian internal

10. Keynes, op. cit., p. 140. This sentence quoted by Keynes is the only one I can find in Fisher's *Theory of Interest* which referred to equating costs and returns, without also referring to *two* investment options.

11. Fisher, op. cit., pp. 168–69.

rate of return for the nonconstant nonperpetuity investment prior to conversion to a constant income perpetuity will be the same as the internal rate of return on the purchase after conversion to a constant perpetuity in the market; this latter rate will equal the market rate.[12]

If the time paths of the net receipts of the compared options are identical (except for a proportionality factor), the Keynesian internal rate of return ranking will agree with the Fisherian maximum wealth criterion. In other words, in order to have the Keynesian ranking agree with Fisher's either we must assume exactly similar time paths, or we must assume the net receipts from the two alternatives can be *immediately* and perpetually reinvested at their own internal rates of return.

4. *Significance of Confusion.* Many economists agree with Keynes in attributing the internal rate of return to Fisher, but they seem to have overlooked the fact that Keynes' internal rate of return did not give an investment demand function according to the maximum present wealth criterion of choice by investors.[13] Consequently their rationale for explaining why the rate of investment increases as the rate of interest falls has been logically defective (inconsistent with wealth maximizing) and may be empirically inconsistent.

12. For example in the earlier examples, investment option B had an internal rate of return of 12.5 per cent. If it were sold in the market at $42 (with the market rate at 4 per cent), the $42 would buy a constant 4 per cent perpetuity of $1.68 per year, equivalent to 6.7 per cent of $25. If the market rate had been 2 per cent—i.e., if the present value of option B turned out to be $48—it could have been converted into an annual perpetuity of 2 per cent on the $48, equivalent to 3.87 per cent on the $25 cost. Of course, the ratio of the converted perpetuity rate of return on the cost to the market rate, 3.87/2.00, always equals the ratio of present value to cost $48/$25.

13. See, as typical examples, D. Dillard, *The Economics of John Maynard Keynes* (New York, 1948), pp. 135–42; S. Enke, *Intermediate Economic Theory* (New York, 1948), pp. 141–48 (e.g., compare the statements on p. 141 with those on pp. 146–47); A. Hart, *Money, Debt and Economic Activity* (New York, 1948), p. 180; A. Hansen, *Monetary Theory and Fiscal Policy* (New York, 1949), pp. 57–58; R. Ruggles, *National Income and Income Analysis* (New York, 1949), pp. 262–65; E. Schneider, *Pricing and Equilibrium* (London, 1952), p. 166; T. Scitovsky, *Welfare and Competition* (Chicago, 1951), p. 210.

Many others without using the concept of the marginal efficiency of capital (the internal rate of return) reach essentially correct formulations, although they do not indicate that there is a conflict in the literature. J. Bain, *Pricing, Distribution and Employment*, rev. ed. (New York, 1953), pp. 695–96; P. A. Samuelson, *Economics*, 3rd ed. (New York, 1955), but see his footnote 1, p. 578.

In so far as Keynes' *General Theory* is concerned, the error is completely harmless. Keynes sought a proposition about the slope of the aggregate investment function. Whether one uses the internal rate of return or the Fisherian rate of return over cost to rank investment options according to present net wealth, lower market rates of interest imply larger rates of investment. The fact that his derivation of the negative slope did not correspond to Fisher's led to no difficulty in Keynes' *General Theory*. How one derives a proposition is irrelevant if one is interested only in the empirical validity of the proposition. Keynes might aptly have said, "Merely another example of the advantage of practical knowledge over logical analysis."

Fisher's theory is a model for deriving propositions about how the economic system operates and how it reacts to changed circumstances. He asserted that the kinds of investment that will be characteristic of a low-interest-rate economy are so-and-so as compared with those in a high-interest-rate economy. Or that certain kinds of cultural attitudes or technological changes will lead to lower interest rates, etc. And these theorems are valid even when uncertainty prevails for the individual economic participants—uncertainty which destroys the prescriptive and descriptive content of the postulates of individual behavior which Fisher used to derive his economy-wide theorems.

From the methodological point of view, the interesting feature is the way in which Fisher derived his theorems. He assumed certainty, and he built up the investment demand schedule by changing the rate of interest and for each rate computing the implied present value of different actions. This opens him to a charge of logical inconsistency—one that can be levied against the internal rate of return also. The internal rate of return depends upon present and future prices; present prices reflect future use values through the marketplace's discounting process, which depends upon the rate of interest. As the interest rate changes, the structure of prices changes, especially the ratio of present prices to future prices. This in turn will affect the internal rate of return. Thus the internal rate of return cannot be measured independently of the existing rate of interest, and therefore a schedule of investment demand at different market rates of interest requires that one compute the internal rates of return in terms of the prices that would prevail at each potential market rate of interest. Hence, in addition to its inconsistency with wealth maximizing, it has an inherent logical inconsistency as a basis for deriving the demand curve of investment; i.e., it is dependent upon the rate of interest.

In a nutshell, we cannot in full logical consistency draw up a demand curve for investment by varying only the rate of interest (holding all other prices in the impound of *ceteris paribus*).[14] Fisher, despite his exposition which is based on the supposition that one merely changes the rate of interest and holds other prices fixed, understood this. He said that interest rate changes were part and parcel of changes in the structure of price ratios.[15] For example, he discussed how low rates of interest mean that steel bridges, which have relatively higher present worths than at higher rates, will be able to bid away land sites.[16] He could have gone even farther and indicated that changed tastes, new inventions, increased supplies of resources (discovery of new ores, etc.) all lead to revised demand and supply relations among present resources as well as between present and future resource availabilities. A discussion of the effects of changes in the rate of interest in the context of a given price structure is likely to be misleading.[17] Fisher illustrated the process of change via changes in the price structure. The proximate Fisherian analysis of interest rate effects via a fixed price structure is not adequate for deeper understanding of the significance of interest rate changes. However, these logical inconsistencies or shortcuts enable a simpler analysis which has led to valid theorems about observable investment events and characteristics.

14. This is exactly analogous to the distinction between the Marshallian partial equilibrium demand and the Walrasian general equilibrium demand discussed by Milton Friedman, "The Marshallian Demand Curve," *Jour. Pol. Econ.*, Dec. 1949, 57, 463–95. In the present context the partial analysis curve misses the essence of capital theory, the relationship between interest rates and the price structure.

15. Fisher, op. cit., footnote, p. 131.

16. Ibid., pp. 178–205.

17. It might be that standard textbook discussions are vulnerable on this count. See, for example, J. Bain, op. cit., pp. 695–96; A. Hansen, *Business Cycles and National Income* (New York, 1951), pp. 133–35.

# LINEAR PROGRESS CURVES ARE ILLUSIONS

The following is presented for criticism and the possible inclusion of its essential ideas in a report on the general rationale, validity and usefulness of the "learning curve" or "progress curve."

1. In the statistical analysis of the reliability of the learning curve, the assumption that the learning curve is a straight line on double log paper was accepted, but the identity of slopes and positions among various model facility combinations (MFC) was tested. The conclusion was that the learning curves were different for the various MFC; that is, they differed in their slopes and in their heights.

2. An attempt to assess the validity of the assumption of linearity failed because no adequate test could be made of that hypothesis against some alternative hypothesis. One important reason for this was that no reasonable alternative hypothesis could be suggested without at the same time biasing the tests (because the data had already been observed). Another reason was that even if a test could have been devised the available amount of carefully observed data seemed inadequate for this degree of discrimination.

3. Yet inspection, with intuitive applications of probabilities as well as rigorous probability tests, indicated that the slopes (on the assumption of linearity) were certainly negative. There simply can't be any denial of the progress or learning phenomenon. Now, it is the purpose of this note not to review the many reasons for the existence of this phenomenon but to examine the validity of the assumption of linearity. It seems to be a very simple matter to produce logical evidence to indicate that the hypothesis of linearity as the fundamental law of progress is consistent only in very strange cases.

4. We must examine the situation very carefully before accepting even the linearity *approximation*. If linearity is really not valid, why do the data *appear* to satisfy the linearity hypothesis even as an approximation? This appearance of linearity can be explained in a very simple fashion; in fact, it is an elementary explanation but one which we are prone to ignore. It rests essentially on the

This previously unpublished January 1, 1950, manuscript appears here by permission of the author.

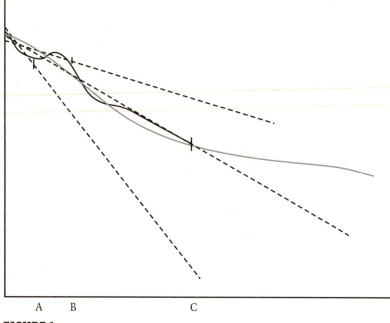

A    B                    C

**FIGURE 1.**

ease of describing the true path of a non-linear curve that is masked with random deviations so that a fitted straight line appears to represent the truth. When the straight line extension begins to break down, a new one is drawn from that point on, with the explanation that conditions changed.

5. The dangers of this proneness to "linearity" are increased by the prevalent confusion between prediction and description. This is best illustrated graphically. In figure 1 there is drawn a "true" curve shown as a light gray solid line. The solid black line is the true curve with some superposed random deviations. The upper dashed line is the straight line "fitted" to the observed black line. At point B the straight gray line begins to depart from the black line. If on the evidence up to B, a prediction by a straight line were to be made of the future, the middle dashed line would soon get one into trouble, even though it seems to fit well, up to point B. If instead more evidence were available to point C a new gray line would fit to that point, but it too would soon get one in trouble. No matter how much evidence is observed in the form of the solid black line, it can after the fact be described by some dashed line. But this is far different from knowing which dashed line one should have started with. Consequently merely because one can, after the fact, draw a straight line to

some series (which straight line is different from the one that would have been fitted had a shorter series been drawn) is no evidence whatever that linearity is a good basis for prediction. (Indeed, if evidence were available only up to point A, the bottom dashed line would have resulted.)

6. Furthermore it is not evidence that a straight line is sufficient even for description of the fundamental law underlying the process. By looking at figures 2 and 3, where the underlying facts are different, it can be seen that the same straight dashed line comes out of all of them. Beyond the point B (end of available observations) the underlying true gray curve becomes noticeably different.

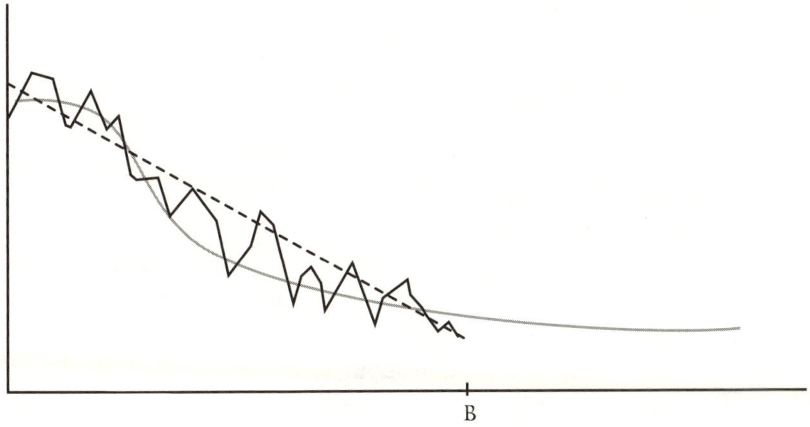

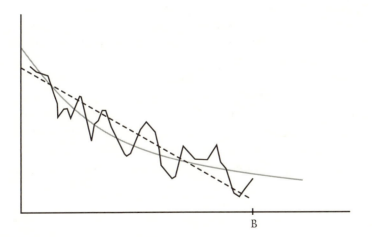

FIGURE 2.

FIGURE 3.

How is this accounted for? One might say that there has been a change in the underlying process. But what has really changed is not the underlying process but the appropriateness of the linearity assumption. Since it is well known that a wide variety of curves can be approximated with two joined straight lines, it is not surprising that linearity all the way, or semi-linearity in two joined sections, becomes a very plausible "hypothesis."

7. In the previous discussion the usefulness of this linearity hypothesis was implicitly questioned. Is it of value for predictive extrapolation? The mere fact that the total range of experience turns out to be describable by a straight line does not mean that the line fitted to an earlier portion of that experience would have predicted the later experience. The only way to test the validity of such prediction is by trying it and seeing what the error amounts to.

8. Is the hypothesis of value for historical description purposes? If this means that one wants to describe a path historically, why bother with a fitted line? The line of actual observations is even better. If one replies that he wants a simple description he must state a description of what and for what purpose. If he is trying to describe a general relationship free of the detailed erratic variations, he is seeking the underlying solid gray line; and the ease and dangers of "discovering" or using "linearity" have been revealed in figures 2 and 3. The only other reason seems to be that he may want to carry this experience over to some other problem or production situation. But this brings us back to the prediction problem of paragraphs 5–7, completing the closed vicious circle. We are in a circle because one must justify this transference of linearity as a valid interpretation of the nature of the underlying phenomenon.

9. A final incidental point is worth emphasizing. Linearity of the progress curve of some final product is impossible if there are spare parts or suppliers who are serving others also and if the learning curves for the component parts have different slopes. The existence of spare part production is an indisputable fact. Nevertheless, if it weren't, one could not argue that observed experience indicates a common slope for all learning curves. The temptation to so argue is suggested by references to the "minus one-third curve" or the 80% progress curve. These are merely average quantities and are not typical. Any set of numbers has an average no matter how much the numbers vary. And the inappropriateness of considering the average as typical of the various observed slopes is well known.

# LINEAR PROGRESS CURVES ARE NOT ILLUSIONS

1. Assume that the cost of the nth item produced, $C_n$, is equal to $\rho^{1/n} C_{n-1}$, where $\rho$ is a random variable. The distribution function of this random variable is such that it has a mean between zero and one. Whatever its other characteristics, e.g., higher moments, the variable $\rho^{1/n}$ has a distribution whose mean converges to 1 as $n$ increases and whose higher moments, e.g., variance, become smaller.

2. Economically, this is a way of saying that as $n$ increases, the chances of making substantial reductions in costs decreases. More particularly the average rate of improvement declines as $n$ increases, and also the variability or erraticness of magnitudes of improvements decreases.

Graphically, the probability (shown on vertical scale) of reduction in cost (shown on horizontal scale) is portrayed in figure 1. As $n$ increases the distribution of cost ratios, $C_n/C_{n-1}$ moves toward 1 and concentrates around it.

3. What sort of learning curve would this produce? The answer is "a straight line on double log paper," and the linearity is independent of the spread of the distribution. Furthermore $\rho^{k/n}$ could be used instead of $\rho^{1/n}$ without changing the conclusion.

In other words if the first item cost \$1, the second one would cost $\rho^{1/2} \cdot \$1$ where $\rho^{1/2}$ is obtained by selecting at random a value out of the $\rho$ distribution and taking its square root. Then for the cost of the third item, $C_3$, we would draw another value and take its 3rd root and multiply it by $C_2 = \rho^{1/2} C_1$ getting $\rho^{1/3} \rho^{1/2} C_1$.

In general the nth item would cost, $C_n = \rho^{1/n} \rho^{1/n-1} \rho^{1/n-2} \ldots \rho^{1/2} C_1$. Treating $C_1$ as an arbitrary constant, we take logs and get

$$\log C_n = \sum_{i=2}^{n} \frac{\log \rho_i}{i} + \log C_1.$$

Now it can be shown (see any mathematician) on the basis of some theorem on the convergence of series and *via* a Euler constant that

This previously unpublished January 1, 1950, manuscript appears here by permission of the author.

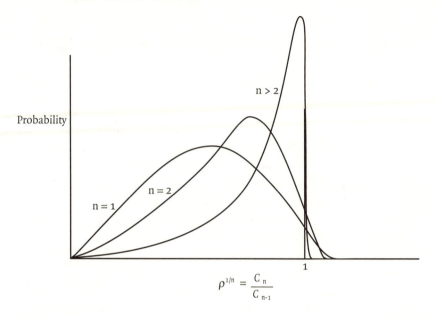

FIGURE 1.

$$\log C_n \cong \log N + K.$$

Other models can be constructed in which linearity will *not* result. If the expectation of $\rho$ on any trial is a constant the curve will fall faster than a straight line on double log paper.

I am approaching the stage of thought where I am about ready to believe that there is a learning curve (unknown in exact shape and unpredictable in the sense of extrapolation) that falls at *least* as fast as a straight line. But to see why this is a perfectly safe thing to believe, see the note on induced linearity. More meaningful is the proposition that the learning curve *really never* becomes horizontal, which I am prepared to defend as follows:

1. On double log scale the increase in absolute $n$ on the horizontal scale becomes of *gigantic* amounts. Thus a 5% drop in costs between the 10th and 100th items seems *less* plausible than a 5% drop between the 10,000th and 100,000th items.

2. Related to above the masking of time (by $n$) is such that to go from 10,000 to 100,000 requires a *long* time compared with 10–100. There "ought"

to be lots of time for new ideas on technology and inventories, even after all coordinating and learning on a *given* method has occurred.

3. The compression of time on the horizontal becomes perfectly fantastic as *n* gets large, and it appears incredible that mere progress in related technologies will not be available. (These are the exogenous, external economics.) See "Why the Learning Curve Is Convex on Double Log Scale."

# WHY THE LEARNING CURVE IS CONVEX
## ON DOUBLE LOG SCALE

The learning curve can be made convex (see figure 1; the second derivative is negative) by the following simple assumption. Assume that the process under consideration is subject to increased productivity (reduced cost) per unit of output at the rate of 3 percent per annum. This increase is due to external factors and in general to any and all factors except those dependent upon the total number of items produced. For example, for reasons which need not be labored here, productivity of labor will increase with time, even if no output occurs.

This means that the cost of an item if produced one year later is 3 percent less, aside from any increase in number produced. Now let the rate of output be a given function of the growth curve type, so that the rate of output reaches its maximum in about a year or two. Suppose (to make the case as unfavorable as possible for what I am arguing) that there is *no* learning at all that is a function of the number of items produced. This means that if the 3 percent productivity assumption here used were made zero, the learning curve would be a horizontal line.

However because of this 3 percent increase in productivity (a function of factors other than number of items produced), the learning curve will fall; i.e., we have a negative slope. Now if one expresses the cost per unit of output as a function of the number of items produced (which can be done since the rate of output is given as a function of time), it will be seen that the resulting function, if plotted on double log scale with cost on the ordinate and number of items produced on the abscissa, falls at a *steeper and steeper* rate as n increases.

Graphically, figure 2 shows the assumed relationship between rate of output and time. Figure 3 shows the decline in costs per unit of output solely as a function of time. Thus, regardless of the n of the item produced, the cost would be lower if it were produced later. Cost is assumed here not to fall as a result of more items being produced, but only with the passage of time.

This previously unpublished January 1, 1950, manuscript appears here by permission of the author.

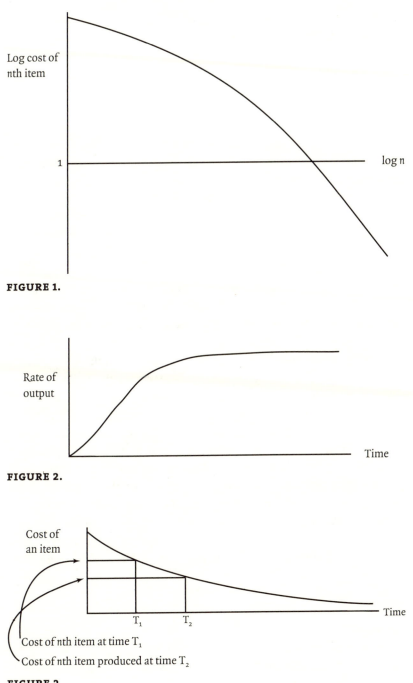

**FIGURE 1.**

**FIGURE 2.**

**FIGURE 3.**

A mathematical statement of some conditions under which this is true is presented in the appendix (by T. Youngs).

If it is plausible to believe that the costs (in this case direct labor costs) are affected by the general advance in technology and arts, and if it also is assumed that this advance occurs at a constant rate, then the learning curve on double log paper will be falling at a faster and faster slope over those periods in which the rate of output is constant.

A subsidiary conclusion to be drawn from this is that charting on a double log scale is extremely dangerous and misleading. The log scale for cumulated output is the mischievous element. For example, consider a case in which the rate of output is constant at 100 per month. Let the first inch on the horizontal scale show the output from 1 to 10 and the second inch from 10 to 100. Now the first two inches show the first one month's production. How long will it take to span the second two inches? At the end of that two-inch span will appear an $n$ of 10,000. Thus the second two-inch span will require 99 months, or over 8 years. The third two-inch span will require over 800 years. How will one ever be able to tell what the curve really looks like? All this merely illustrates the tremendous compression in time that can be so innocently portrayed on a log scale.

Another way to express this compression is to say that the first 3/4 of the horizontal distance is based on about only 10 percent of the production experience. If the tendency toward linearity is visually impressed by the first 3/4 of a line, then in reality the impression is based on only 10 percent of the production experience. To make matters worse, if the early production occurs during a production build-up period, when the peak rate of output is being reached, essentially the entire impression of linearity is based on the experience of building up to capacity. If the first portion of the $n$ scale is obtained from a build-up period, the effect is to modify the above conclusions about the fraction of the production experience portrayed in the first 3/4 of the horizontal scale; instead of 10 percent it will be somewhat larger (maybe 15 percent), thus weakening the effect of the preceding argument, but only to a very slight extent.

## Appendix (by T. Youngs)

ASSUMPTIONS

1. Factory producing uniform items.
2. Cost of producing the $n$th item at time $(t + k)$ is $p_k$ times the cost of producing the $n$th item at time t. $(k > 0)$

CONSEQUENCES

Cost of producing the $n$th item at time $t_o$ = cost of producing the $m$th item at time $t_o$.

Suppose cost of producing the $n$th item at time o is given as $C_o$. This is independent of n by the above consequence of the second assumption.

If $C(t)$ = cost of producing the item at time t, then

$$C(t) = (p_k^{1/k})^t \, C_o \tag{1}$$

[If time $\tau$ is measured in different units and with different origin, then $t = a\tau + T$ for some constants a and T. Notice that $\underline{C}\,(\tau) = C(a\tau + T) = (p_k^{1/k})^{a\tau+T} C_o = (p_k^{a/k})^\tau (p_k^{t/k})C_o$, while $\underline{C}_o = \underline{C}(0) = C(T) = p_k^{T/k} C_o$. Hence if $\pi = p_k^a$

$$\underline{C}(T) = (\pi^{1/k})^\tau \, C(0)$$

which is of the same form as (1)]

3. Y time is measured from the instant a factory goes into production, and $n(t)$ represents the number of items produced in time t, then there is a constant K such that

$$(Kt - n(t)) \to 0$$

for large enough t.

Hence, solving $n = n(t)$ for t one gets $t = t(n)$ where $(t\backslash n) - \dfrac{1}{k}n) \to 0$ for large enough n.

Notice that from (1)

$$C(t) = (p^{1/k})^{t(n)} \, C_o$$
$$\log C = \left(\frac{\log p^{1/k}}{K}\right) n + \log C_o.$$

# REVIEW OF
## *DYNAMIC EQUIPMENT POLICY*

Fame and fortune await the discoverer of a simple and complete rule prescribing the moment at which existing production equipment should be replaced. George Terborgh takes a substantial step toward this elusive objective in *Dynamic Equipment Policy*. In three words, his essential contribution is the "integration of obsolescence" into the *applied* theory of replacement. But the book also contains more. An anthology of folklore of present replacement procedures is presented, and the revelation is dismaying. Anyone who suspects that Terborgh, the director of research of the Machinery and Allied Products Institute, has been unfair in his review of current replacement policy need merely review the technical management literature for himself. He will discover that Terborgh has been overly kind in his exposé; present practice—not to be dignified with the term policy—is based on folklore and viable habits. That this is not evidence that businessmen are fools is attributable to three dominant facts: the obscurity of future machines and their operating characteristics, the sheer complexity of the formula by which costs of replacement now may be compared with deferred replacement, and the dependency of business survival upon achieved relative superiority and not upon perfection in the method of seeking an aspired objective.

Terborgh, like a guide, first points out the dangers of unguided action (Chapter 1); he then specifies the nature of the problem (Chapters 2–4); following this he states his fundamental premises which are to serve as landmarks to the guide (Chapters 5 and 6). Shortcuts and practical applications appear in Chapters 7–10. Chapters 11–14 criticize the folklore of current practice, while Chapter 15 concludes with a general summary of the analysis. Fourteen brief appendices supplement the text.

Terborgh's statement of the problem emphasizes two points. First, the cost of operating a given item must be compared with the alternative of the best available machines during the successive years of the life of the machine. As

Review of George Terborgh, *Dynamic Equipment Policy* (New York: McGraw-Hill, 1949), reprinted from *American Economic Review* (September 1950): 693–97.

better alternatives appear in the future, these must be treated as the available alternative. In other words, operating costs of various machines must be compared or measured from the best alternative—on a top-down principle. This difference, "operating inferiority," is a combination of deterioration in existing equipment and improvements in new—appearing as obsolescence in the old. Second, predictions of the future potentiality of unborn machines must be made—not exorcised.

The problem posed by Terborgh is that of minimizing this operating inferiority subject to the capital costs inherent in frequent replacement. Only by turning in machines every year could one reduce operating inferiority to zero. But this incurs large annual capital costs. By delaying replacement, even at the expense of rising actual and falling alternative operating costs, total costs may be lower because capital costs may thereby be reduced even more. The problem in replacement is to estimate the life of each machine before replacement which minimizes the discounted value of operating inferiority plus the discounted capital outlays.

Now it can be shown (but Terborgh does not do so) that the period of economic life of future assets which minimizes the discounted value of cumulated operating inferiority relative to best available equipment is the same life length that minimizes absolute total costs above a base of zero. Terborgh's ensuing recommendations would have been more understandable had he presented a clear demonstration of this fact; instead, the reader may experience some confusion. Although Terborgh's operating inferiority concept is redundant in strict logic, it has the psychological and propaganda power required to forcefully call attention to the phenomenon of obsolescence—which Terborgh shows is all too frequently ignored in many varieties of customary analysis of replacement policies, and which incidentally justifies "*Dynamic*" in the book's title.

Another minor source of possible confusion is the omission of an explicit proof of the fact that his criterion for replacement is equivalent to comparing the costs of replacement now with replacement a year later. He does state that comparing the first pieces of equipment in two long series of replacements is adequate since the rest of the series have the same adverse minimum, by assumption. But the reviewer suspects that other readers will, like this reviewer, find it difficult to understand why Terborgh's method of comparing costs gives a consistent answer. Terborgh obtains the excess of operating, depreciation and interest costs of the present machine over the operating costs (only) of the new challenging machine. This excess for the first year is compared with the minimum annuity average of the present value of the stream of operating inferiorities of future machines. If the former exceed the latter, replacement is signalled. Perhaps other readers will not be so obtuse as this reviewer, but after intensive search of the book he had to resort to paper and pencil and mathematicians in order to prove that Terborgh's method did give a consistent answer. In fact, it is exactly equivalent to comparing $(rP + g/r)$ with E, where r is the rate of interest, P is the present worth of the entire stream of minimized costs [by optimum replacement period] associated with immediate replacement, g is the annual amount by which operating costs of new machines decline (Terborgh's inferiority gradient) and E is the cost of running the defending equipment one more year (including interest and depreciation). Whether Terborgh's version of this inequality is simpler is open to question, but its consistency is not.

Since practical applications of guiding principles will be made only if simple forms of such principles are available, Terborgh derives simplified approximations by simplifying assumptions. One assumption, which can be dropped without much loss in simplicity, is that salvage or resale values of existing—defending—assets is zero. Another is the linearity assumption for the combined rates of deterioration and obsolescence. The second approximation, linearity, is the powerful element leading to the simplified formulas.

If salvage values should be large enough to be effective, an additional simple calculation is required. But there is no escape from the question of the validity of the linearity approximation. However valid the linear approximation may be, Terborgh's defense of it is the weakest part of his analysis and does not contribute to one's confidence in it. He writes: "Is any alternative assumption more reasonable? We know of none. In general, when the future cannot be foreseen, the best we can do is to project a continuation of the present. All prediction rests, in the last analysis, on the premise that the past contains elements of recurrence or continuity that will repeat themselves hereafter. In the absence of evidence to the contrary, therefore, the presumption is in favor of repetition. . . . It would still be by far the best standard assumption because of the unique simplicity . . . it makes possible" (pp. 64–65). Appeals to insufficient reason and to simplicity do not constitute justification of assumptions. In addition, the empirical data are presented in such summary form that the hypothesis of linearity cannot be tested.

Instead of straight-line approximations, one could use modified exponentials, but the equations would then be more formidable and less subject to simplification. An electronic computer would then be necessary for rapid flexible computations, but these now exist and are available for such application.

Weak as the arguments given by Terborgh for his linearity assumption may seem, his assumptions and analysis are incomparably superior to the implicit assumptions and procedures which dominate the current folklore methods of replacement analysis. For example, his discussion of the interest charge for discounting purposes exposes several fallacious practices (pp. 160–75). However, Terborgh seems to be not completely fair in his criticisms of the minimum-pay-off-period method, which requires that the new challenging machine be able to pay for itself in saving within a given number of years, e.g., three or four. Terborgh correctly states that this leads to use of equipment beyond its economic life. More economic equipment is not used, because only spectacular new innovations or machines will be sufficiently economic to be adopted. It can be argued, however, that this short pay-off period is merely a way of allowing for uncertainty in one's costs predictions. By replacing only if the savings appear very large, one is protected against large underestimates of future costs—a serious error if the manager is more afraid of losses than he is attracted by increases in profits. This is the type of behavior that is conceived by the existence of uncertainty and the observed irregular rates of obsolescence and is nurtured by a fear of losses. It is this element of uncertainty which frequently justifies caution; rules of behavior based on single-valued estimates are often fatally bad for behavior where uncertainty exists.

Terborgh could answer that this type of uncertainty should be considered explicitly by allowing for alternative estimates of future obsolescence rates; bracketing values for future deterioration and obsolescence rates should be used.

This weakness—and one that is inherent in lack of knowledge of the future—is merely another facet of the weakness of the justification for the linearity assumption. These last aspects of uncertainty indicate a major question in replacement theory. Does a formula based on certainty of foresight and solved with alternative values of the variables provide sufficient allowance for uncertainty, or is a new principle required for the actual world of uncertainty? One is reminded of the use of pure competition as an approximation to oligopolistic situations. A related aspect of the problem is the competitive element of reciprocal action between competitors—a situation in which relative advantage and survival are more important than absolute advantage and perfection of objective. Much work remains to be done with uncertainty, and replacement policy appears to be a promising field of application which may yield new insight.

Upon noting that replacement is part of gross investment, one will realize that the book makes a substantial contribution to our understanding of gross investment policy. It is no accident that the author of the *Bogey of Economic Maturity* and of *Dynamic Equipment Policy* should be the same person. Terborgh early shows that his book is an analysis of one of the major factors affecting the rate of investment and growth of an economy. Surely some of the effort now devoted to trying to predict decisions in investment policy through elaborate statistical and interview procedures should be redirected to the more mundane but influential decision process of the type studied by Terborgh.

In summary, *Dynamic Equipment Policy* is a valuable contribution to replacement policy. Its verbosity reduces comprehension time for the non-mathematically trained reader.[1] Because it is too detailed for the typical business executive, Terborgh promises to issue a manual for practical application.

---

1. The mathematician, for whom this book was not written, would be benefitted by a brief technical appendix precisely setting forth the criterion and derivation of formulas.

# MEANINGS AND USES OF EQUATIONS
# AND MODELS

A subsurface dispute about economic methodology and model making may appear, in part, to be one between the mathematically minded economists and the literary economists. At least the commonly heard comments may induce that impression. Actually, however, that is no issue. Mathematics in economics is here to stay and to grow, just as its more popular but weaker variant, graphic analysis, has stayed. Some regard it as merely quantifying the generalities (and that is really statistics' task). Some regard it as a symbolic device used to avoid waste of pencil and paper and eye muscles and semantic problems (and that at least would be agreeable to all). Some regard it as an analytical method used to develop new implications and theories.

The real issue relates to the economic substance—the applicability to real economic problems, or what I call here empirical validity—of the mathematical models. And with regard to this, it is submitted here that the mathematical analysis reveals very clearly the true scope and structure of the analysis, thereby facilitating an evaluation of its empirical validity. One may well argue that the empirical invalidity, or unrealism, of so many mathematically expressed theories and hypotheses is simply a result of their clarity, which reveals quickly the applicability of the system, whereas in literary theories it is difficult to make such an appraisal so readily. In any event the mathematical approach must not be treated as the new delivery truck was treated by the delivery man who became so absorbed in the operating characteristics of the truck that he neglected to deliver the goods.

The real dispute exists as to the usefulness and purpose of the various models—the now popular term for theories. Are they predictive devices? Or are they sources of policy recommendations? Or do they help explain in a "causal" sense the workings of the economic system so that one may specify existing cause-and-effect patterns? (And this is different from the ability to indicate which policy changes will provide corrective measures.) Or do they merely

Reprinted, by permission of the author, from *Proceedings of the 25th Annual Conference of the Pacific Coast Economic Association* (1950): 39–42.

describe a particular situation in terms of itself? If one keeps in mind these disparate objectives, one can judge better the various models by the degree to which they achieve their goal.

A model is a set of relationships. These relationships may be called equations; that is purely a matter of terminology. But the type of relationships and their scope are substantive matters. Clearly, in no case will the model be all-inclusive; it must exclude certain types of events, and the analyst must be aware of the type of excluded events. But the derived results should be consistent with observations. This is saying less than that the theory or model should include all observed events. The types of relationships used in these models can be classified tentatively into five groups for the purpose of presenting a classification that has proven useful in understanding and evaluating the various theories relating to a particular problem. Not until such an arrangement of ideas had been culled from the literature was I able to compare theories or doctrines. It is hoped that other classifications will be compared with this one so that a better one may be derived. All five types of relations have not been included explicitly in every model in economics.

First there are the definitions; these are often expressed as relationships in equation form and therefore are possibly misleading. They are true identities; both sides are the same thing. Only the names or symbols are different. Thus we have Hicks' excess demand being equal to demand minus supply.[1] It is that; it isn't merely quantitatively equal to it. Similarly, there is Keynes' investment and saving; his income and consumption plus investment; and Lange's monetary effect and excess supply.[2] These things are the same not merely in magnitude but in concept. Many examples are easy to find.

The second type of relationship (or equation) expresses a necessary connection between one concept and other concepts. Thus costs can be quantitatively associated with some function of output. The rate of consumption can be associated with some function of income, etc. These express relationships between different economic concepts. Statistics and economic substances are involved in the discovery and measurement of these relationships.

A third type of relationship expresses intertemporal connections between values of a given variable or between different variables. These are known as dynamic equations. Note that in each relation or equation different time points

---

1. J. R. Hicks, *Value and Capital*, Oxford, 1939, p. 63.

2. J. M. Keynes, *The General Theory of Employment, Interest and Money*, New York, 1936, pp. 52–65; O. Lange, *Price Flexibility and Employment*, Bloomington, Ind., 1944, Ch. IV.

are related. This is not merely dating or analyzing over a time interval. Each moment's values are tied to the values at some other moment. This expressed intertemporal association is the essential element. What happens today must be shown to be tied to what happened earlier or it must be uniquely related to some succeeding moment. This is expressed mathematically by means of differences and differential equations. In non-mathematical terms the different periods are identified by dates, and in a given relation there are at least two different dates. For example, the rate of investment in period two may be made a result in part of the rate of income of period one. This does not eliminate expectations. Rather it means that expectations are based in part upon past experience and the present situation. That dependence is specified via observable economic variables.

Period analysis is of little additional value if it does not show how the values of one period determine in part the values of succeeding periods. A relationship composed exclusively of contemporaneous values is not dynamic, even though dating is employed. A mere arraying of periods according to some time sequence is nothing but comparative statics. That is, time enters only incidentally as an arraying criterion rather than as a statement of the movement of the system over time.

Dynamic processes have been handled by periods and ex ante devices. The periods must be tied together so that from the results of one period the beginning situation of the next period is derivable. This means that a period is fundamentally a planning period; when the results of a given set of plans are realized as not matching expectations, new plans arise and are executed. The second period begins with the creation and execution of new plans. Ex ante has been used to mean both hoped-for and anticipated results, and also it has been applied to planned magnitudes—in the sense of activated plans. These are different, and the difference is important. The results of the plans put into effect are compared with expectations, and in terms of that difference it may be possible to determine the succeeding developments. Unless it is, we have no basis for dynamic analysis.

A fourth type of relation expresses an optimum condition of which there are two types. One involves the satisfactions of an individual's desires and a second involves the satisfaction of a group criterion. In the former are individual output at maximized profit, action in conformity with a given state of expectations, etc.[3] In the second category are full employment, progress, security, zero

3. F. Hayek, "Economics and Knowledge," *Economica*, January, 1937, p. 41ff.

profits, etc. To say that the latter are long run and the former short run is to miss the point.

These optimum situations are originally expressible in terms of desired results. After analysis of the whole model, they may be expressed implicitly in terms of the requisite conditions derivable from the model. For example, full employment may be the optimum situation desired. But what are the conditions that must be satisfied if it is to be reached—ignoring the important problem of maintaining it? This is the fifth type of relation. Given the model, there are certain implicit types of relations or conditions that can be derived from an analysis of the model. One of the advantages of the mathematical model is that often these derivative relations could not otherwise be obtained. At other times, the derived equations are obtained so simply that mathematical analysis is truly then nothing but impressionism.

With these various types of relations, certain ones are explicitly selected and models thereby formed. In every model there are implied all five types of relations. Unfortunately all economic analysts do not explicitly include all types! Others must search for the implied equations, and these are not always determinable unambiguously—thus the door is opened to all sorts of arguments, most of which are exceedingly tedious. The simultaneous satisfaction of all the relationships is investigated, and if that condition is met, one may say he has a solution. In economics it is called an equilibrium.

Equilibrium means the solution to a set of equations encompassing a given set of variables. If the set of equations contained all the acting forces, one would have a complete description of events as well as a chronicle of history. But in fact this is fantastic.

In a model one may be able to determine values of each of the variables in terms of the others. In this sense the model and equilibrium are determinate. Thus the Keynesian model, with its four equations and four variables, is an example of a closed or logically complete model.

The meaning and empirical significance of the equilibrium depend upon the scope of equations or relationships included in the model. If the equations include a social adjustment or group optimum condition, the existence of the equilibrium means the achievement of the optimum condition. The criticism may then be raised that the conceptual existence of an equilibrium does not explain why such an equilibrium should in fact be achieved. This criticism has two possible meanings. One may doubt the empirical significance of the model. The Keynesian incorporation of new relationships proved so successful in expanding the analysis of the operation of the economic system between the classical full employment equilibrium positions that the now popularly employed concept of equilibrium no longer carries with it the connotation of full employment. It is easy to be led to conclude that much of the strong conviction in the policies that were recommended in order to counter unemployment rested in part upon a misunderstanding of the empirical significance of the Keynesian equilibrium. The dispute as to whether there can be an underemployment equilibrium is a terminological one—yes, if you use equilibrium as Keynes did, and no, if you use it in the classical sense. This terminological confusion is not at all uncommon. That does not mean that all equilibria are equally relevant. In fact, the gist of these remarks is just the opposite. Furthermore, I am not implying that the Keynesian-classical difference is merely one of terminology.

Some economists adopting the general Keynesian relations have changed certain ones. Thus, Haberler relates the level of money wages to unemployment and introduces a factor producing a movement in the Keynesian equilibrium.[4] Haberler has thereby in his model implied a different equilibrium—that of full employment.

Pigou has presented the classical case.[5] It is difficult to tell whether the difference between Keynes and the classical case pertains to the relevance of the equilibrium or to the technique of analysis. The classical analysis given by Pigou is devoted to showing how the optimum condition of full employment will be brought about. And that introduces the second meaning of the criticism to the effect that the conceptual existence of an equilibrium does not explain its actual existence. One is asking now for the dynamic process which is implied in the model. If this latter interpretation is desired, the third type of relation (dynamic process) must be explicitly included in the model, and the equilibrium takes on a broader meaning.

When the dynamic processes are explicitly included in the model, the solution of the model is associated with particular time moments. For each moment there is an equilibrium or solution. This conforms to the Hicksian type of "expectation-plan" equilibrium within the "week." One can then trace this overt time and specify the equilibrium at some ultimate point of time at which no further changes in the value occur—if there is such an ultimate constancy of values. If there is no ultimate constancy, one can instead obtain an infinite series of equilibria, each identified by "time." These positions are called equi-

---

4. G. Haberler, *Prosperity and Depression* (3rd ed.), Geneva, 1941, pp. 491–503.

5. A. C. Pigou, *Employment and Equilibrium*, London, 1941, Part II, Ch. IV.

libria because they satisfy a certain subset of the relations involved in the model. Whether one chooses to call them disequilibria or equilibria is not as important as the necessity of understanding just which set of relations is being satisfied and which set is not when the word *equilibria* is used, and similarly if *disequilibria* is used.

The pattern of behavior of the variables in a model may be the characteristic defined by the solution of the model. Equilibrium is then used with reference to the pattern.

The above briefly outlined connections among (1) "will the equilibrium be achieved," (2) the implied meaning of "equilibrium," and (3) the dynamic process relationships lead to considerations of stability. The determination of the possibility of achieving the equilibrium position in any of the previous cases involves stability. To determine whether or not a particular equilibrium will be achieved one must determine if there are forces which will push the system toward that equilibrium position. Stability is that property of the system which implies that it will tend to achieve the equilibrium position. This implies resistance to change. Obviously, the stability can have specific meaning only with respect to the particular type of equilibrium that is being studied. Stability has no meaning when applied to equilibrium in the sense of determinateness of a set of values.

If the equilibrium refers to the set of values at some specific time or at some ultimate time, Samuelson has indicated a method for determining stability.[6] In essence the method specifies explicitly the dynamic processes, and then in conjunction with the other relationships investigates what set of values will ultimately be realized over time. If there is an ultimate set of values and if these satisfy the other relations of the model, the equilibrium may be considered stable.

Thus when the dynamic processes are included in the model, the solution of the set of equations is applicable to successive points over a time span or else to the set of values at some ultimate point of time at which no further change occurs. "No further change" may refer to (1) the value of the variables or to (2) the time pattern of the values of the variables or to (3) the set of equations producing the model.

In the last sense, one may consider a simple example. A demand curve shifts with changes in income, but if we include income in the equation we will have

6. P. Samuelson, "The Stability of Equilibrium: Comparative Statics and Dynamics," *Economics*, April, 1941, pp. 97–120.

stabilized the equation by making it a surface instead of a simple line. You can increase the scope so that there is no need to shift the equation. Apparently, it was such considerations which led Hicks to propose perfect and imperfect stability. The stability of the equilibrium, when induced by shifting relations, is called imperfect. If no shifts in the relations are required, it is called perfect. Obviously, if we were able to enlarge the model, as was illustrated in the demand curve case, imperfect stability would become perfect stability. Clearly then, it is perfect stability that we should strive for in our analyses; otherwise, we shall be required to appeal to exogenous factors. Perfect stability is especially important if the model is to be used for statistical studies.

In a given model then, there are many characteristics which may be used as criteria of stability. There is no necessity of obtaining the same answer with each. Consider the present capitalist system, with its erratic behavior. So long as business fluctuations are occurring with some sort of regularity, we may say the system is stable—if we are referring to its pattern of behavior. Or if referring to a particular set of values, we may have to conclude that it is unstable. Stability, like equilibrium, can be applied to varying types of phenomena, and neither stability nor equilibrium can be conceived independently of the defining system of key variables.

The value of such considerations as have been sketched stems from the fact that once a person has thought of these things and integrated them into a little scheme of thought on methodology, he will be better able to determine the appropriateness of various approaches to any economic problem. He will be able thereby to separate questions of (1) definition and analytical methods, (2) empirical validity (probability), and (3) empirical significance (usefulness). Problems of substance and fact are difficult enough without confusing them with considerations of analytical schemes. Any device that will permit one to know which issues can be tackled statistically or empirically and which cannot will save much confusion and effort. And furthermore, maybe we would be restrained from asking such questions as "Are you a Keynesian?" (thus more often than not revealing a complete failure to grasp the difference between analytical systems and empirical conclusions as to policy). We also may be deterred from saying, "People who build mathematical models are engaging in an interesting game either which has no real meaning for economics or which induces them to confine themselves to those problems that can so be expressed." The charge may be correct in some cases, but it is not merely because of the method. Some are guilty, but the charge may even more often be levied against literary economists whose models are so indefinite as to permit at the same time the consideration of all problems in a few irrelevant aspects and no problem with sufficient detail so as to be useful.[7]

Implicit also is a thought for those who believe that mathematics and equations, etc., are not very useful in economics because our knowledge of the quantitative aspects is crude and unprecise. If one understands mathematics as arithmetic and measurement and no more, the above objection seems valid. But mathematics is an analytical method, and it deals with very general relationships in a very precise and logical manner. Obviously the precision necessary is not that of measurement but of logic. Mathematics is not merely a precise way of measuring things or dealing with accurately measured quantities. Rather it is a precise logical way of handling very broad general conditions, and it does this so well that precise implicit conditions are quickly determinable. Furthermore, the implicit conditions in our usual very general literary statements are not usually specifically derivable. One must not blame the method of analysis for the multitude of alternative conclusions that is derivable. One should be grateful that they are thereby determined. To contend that imperfect quantitative data are justification for not using precise analytical methods is exactly the same thing as saying that we can therefore afford to be careless and unprecise in our logic and thinking since the original quantitative data are. This is not an attempt to justify all the mathematics that is in economics. Certainly, one should not resort to a more involved method of analysis than is required any more than one would hire a ten-ton truck to carry a few books home.

The considerations presented above imply no judgment whatsoever in favor of macroscopic-aggregative models rather than individual microscopic analyses. That very important dispute can be formulated adequately only by statistical distribution and probability theory. After a precise formulation on that basis, an empirical test of the relative usefulness of the two may be attempted.

The best example of the use and enlarging of a model is provided by Pigou. His first model (1933) explicitly relied upon the individual entrepreneur's adjustment to a profit maximization position as the motivating force.[8] He presented a rather detailed analysis of the operation of that force and how it produced the equilibrium which he there used. In his second model (1937),

7. A. G. Hart, "Model Building and Fiscal Policy," *American Economic Review*, September, 1945, pp. 531–59.

8. A. C. Pigou, *The Theory of Unemployment*, London, 1933, pp. 88–108.

undoubtedly provoked by Keynes, the motivating force of the individual, although present, is so subordinated to a presentation of the equilibrium position that Pigou himself does not know what the dynamic process is.[9] His third presentation (1941) is significant in the complete disappearance of the use of an adjustment or dynamic process relation.[10] Equilibrium values and the changes in them as the relations change are the prime concerns. Whether or not the equilibrium values will be achieved is almost totally ignored. The one time that he did discuss it, the answer given was the wrong one, because he failed to analyze explicitly the forces that were required to produce an equilibrium in his models. Whether Pigou's abandonment of the dynamic adjustment equation is a result of his conviction that period analysis is too complex or is merely an unfortunate aspect of the Keynesian impact is a question that still has no answer.

It is significant that even our latest non-text books dealing with problems of economic policy must have introductory sections devoted to an explanation of the meaning of the equilibrium concept and its usefulness and applicability.

From the foregoing remarks, it is obvious also that a specific model will facilitate quantitative forecasts which may readily be checked against events. Thus errors may be discovered, where they would not with less precise models.

If the purpose is to make forecasts, the type of model need not be like one which has as its purpose the study of some economic problem in order to discover in some sense its cause-and-effect operations. Unfortunately a predictive technique need have little relation to why or wherefore so long as the predictive device is working satisfactorily. The more analytical model is not so easily clothed with empirical values. For example it is still not known to what extent the separate relationships in a Pigou or a Keynes (or in any) model can be determined from multiple correlation analysis directed at each equation separately. It is logically correct to argue that multiple correlation is wrong, since the values of the constants in each of the equations is not independent of the constants in the other equations. Instead they should all be estimated together. Thus Tinbergen's method can be called wrong, particularly if one is interested in policy matters—as he was.[11] However, the one time in which I have seen the

9. A. C. Pigou, "Real and Money Wages Rates in Relation to Unemployment," *Economic Journal*, December, 1937, pp. 405–22.

10. A. C. Pigou, *Employment and Equilibrium*, London, 1941, Part II, Ch. IV.

11. J. Tinbergen, *Statistical Testing of Business Cycle Theories*, II, Geneva, 1939.

results obtained by multiple correlation analysis compared with the results obtained by the logically correct—but much more difficult—statistical procedure, the differences were so small as to be attributable to rounding off or sampling errors.[12] What shall we conclude? Is this a case of the wrong method giving the right answer or is the wrong method actually a pretty good approximation to the right method—a condition that is not unknown elsewhere in empirical mathematics and statistics?

12. G. Tintner, "Multiple Regression for Systems of Equations," *Econometrica*, January, 1946, pp. 5–37.

# REVIEW OF
## *ESSAYS IN ECONOMICS AND ECONOMETRICS:*
## *A VOLUME IN HONOR OF HAROLD HOTELLING*

The economists' respect for the contributions of Harold Hotelling is indicated by this volume of essays written by Arrow, Davis, Ferguson, Friedman, Frisch, Hurwicz, Klein, Pfouts, Samuelson, Tintner, and Vickrey. Perhaps no man has been honored with so impressive a list of contributors, all of whom were former students or associates. And like the work of Hotelling, the contributed papers deal with difficult problems in economic theory by means of relatively advanced mathematics.

Samuelson's opening essay on the structure of an equilibrium system is an exhaustive summary of its properties in exceptionally concise and abstract form. This paper follows the lines of analysis presented in his *Foundations.* Since equilibrium systems characterize the method of analysis of all the sciences, it is not surprising that this essay is a discussion of the logic of analytic methods. Unfortunately for this reviewer, the level of analysis is so advanced mathematically that he has had to accept the pedigree of the author as evidence of its validity.

The most impressive essay is co-authored by Arrow and Hurwicz. Following Samuelson's conversion of equilibrium to maximization problems, Arrow and Hurwicz continue by presenting a solution to the minimax problem of game theory—a problem that arises because a constrained maximization can be converted to a minimax. Earlier contributions of Arrow and Hurwicz to the gradient method of finding a minimax are related to the convergence to equilibrium in a decentralized system. They provide an economic, institutional interpretation to the gradient method, not only in the case of increasing costs but for decreasing costs as well. Perhaps more interesting to economists, judging by the reviewer's personal experience, is their presentation of methods of converting

Review of *Essays in Economics and Econometrics: A Volume in Honor of Harold Hotelling,* ed. Ralph W. Pfouts (Chapel Hill: University of North Carolina Press, 1960), reprinted from *American Economic Review* (March 1961): 157–58.

constrained maximum problems to saddlepoint or minimax problems by means of "concavified Lagrangian functions." This essay, like many others, is at a very high level of abstraction. As the authors warn, any implications about optimality or criteria of performance in the real world are limited to the case of a single-person utility function, rather than to a society of many individuals.

Vickrey and Ferguson attack practically the identical question with identical results. The issue is Edgeworth's so-called taxation paradox wherein an excise tax on one commodity can result in lower prices. Building on Hotelling's contribution, both authors present nearly identical analyses. Whether their papers are complements or substitutes is here as moot as for most economic goods. Ferguson generalizes to a wider range of possible results, whereas Vickrey suggests two economic examples where the "paradox" might occur. At the risk of being completely wrong, this reviewer's interpretation of their analyses is that a necessary condition for at least one of the prices to fall is that either (1) the rise in price of commodity $x$ produces a greater excess supply of commodity $y$ than of $x$, or (2) the cross price-elasticity exceeds the own price-elasticity in demand and in supply! Both are hard to swallow. Is my intellectual throat small, or the morsel oversized, or my sense of taste inadequately developed? In any event this pair of essays found the warmest welcome.

Tintner and Pfouts contribute two closely related essays. Pfouts introduces hours of work and savings as variables in a person's utility; Tintner introduces other people's consumption and income into each person's utility function. As in the case of the simpler utility functions all that can be said about the effects of a price change on quantities consumed is "an income and a substitution effect" with nothing definite about the resultant direction of effect. This holds for the interpersonal utility function of Tintner as well as for the hours-of-work and savings variables in Pfouts' analysis. It is still true that empirically refutable implications require restrictive postulates—something that some economists seem hesitant to acknowledge in the mistaken belief that one shouldn't rule out all possible kinds of behavior.

Harold Davis' paper is an extension of his earlier logical excursion into the analysis of time series of prices by means of differential equations. Frisch presents a series of definitions of input-output coefficients. These are expressed in physical, in volume, semivolume, and current value units. Space prohibits presenting the details here. Until Frisch presents a more detailed explanation of the implications of the various alternatives for input-output analysis, the results of the present essay will remain purely classificatory.

Lawrence Klein compares the efficiency and bias of various methods of estimating coefficients of an equation. He first presents an illuminating discussion of the difference between the estimates of the multiplier, for example, derived from an estimate of the simple consumption equation (the structural equation) and the estimate of the multiplier derived from (the reduced-form equation of) a system of equations. The first can be thought of as a partial analysis model, and the latter as a total model analysis. Thereafter he presents logical and empirical analyses to compare efficiencies of reduced-form equation coefficient estimates with and without a prior imposed restriction. The empirical sampling results cited support the logical analysis.

Possibly beneficial effects of destabilizing speculation are developed by Friedman in the only paper devoid of any mathematics and almost the only one not requiring extensive familiarity with matrix theory. Friedman explores some implications of the conjecture that facing or bearing uncertainty is a sort of activity for which some people are willing to pay a price (because they like to be exposed to uncertainty). He shows that if destabilizing speculation occurred frequently, it could be the result of such preferences.

Professor Hotelling's impressive bibliography (to 1958) concludes the volume.

# ECONOMIC REPLACEMENT POLICY

Reprinted from RAND Corporation #R-224, April 12, 1952.

## ACKNOWLEDGMENTS

Like most RAND studies, this report relies on the work of many people, each of whom solved special problems. In particular, the author is indebted to L. C. Antonellis, J. Beraru, M. Dresher, S. Enke, H. H. Germond, A. S. Mengel, J. Van Paddenburg, and J. W. T. Youngs for their contributions to the report.

# SUMMARY

The rate at which durable equipment is replaced determines, in part, the efficiency and productive capacity of both industrial firms and military organizations. Current replacement practice is guided by various rules of thumb, which are often applied blindly and mechanically to inappropriate situations. This report presents a practical guide for equipment replacement based on the comparison of present-value costs. The method involves only simple arithmetic calculations; it is sufficiently general to apply to a wide variety of replacement situations and is sufficiently specific to be useful in practice.

The report includes a description of the method, examples of its use, and tables of computing factors to facilitate its application.

# CONTENTS

## CHAPTER 1
## INTRODUCTION

### 1.1 The Problem

The rate at which durable equipment is replaced with new equipment is an important determinant of the efficiency and productivity of both our industrial economy and military organization. Unfortunately, current methods of determining when to replace equipment involve overgeneralized rules of thumb and conventions that are often unwittingly applied to inappropriate situations. Because of the importance of replacing equipment in the Air Force, the Office of the Air Comptroller, in its search for better procedures, suggested that RAND study the problem of equipment replacement.

For illustration, assume that a given piece of durable equipment—a truck, a typewriter, or a bulldozer—has been in operation for some time and that improved or newer equipment is available, but that still better equipment will be available in the future. Should the present equipment be replaced now or should we wait until later, when even better equipment will be available? The correct and obvious answer is that replacement should be made when the required stream of service will thereby be obtained at a lower total cost, or when the improvement in service will be worth more than the increase in cost. This principle is correct and complete, but it is sterile and too general. Currently used methods have been inadequate to translate it into practical terms. These rule-of-thumb methods usually assume special circumstances, and the appropriateness of a particular rule is usually a matter of chance, so that the results are no better than arbitrary guesses.

### 1.2 Solution to the Problem

A practical replacement guide which is believed to be greatly superior to those in current use is presented in this report. Essentially, the method ascertains *capitalized present value of costs* implicit in alternative replacement decisions and reveals the time of replacement which minimizes the total present-value cost. If we were able to assign values to the military services in monetary terms (as in industry), the difference between service values and costs could be computed and compared, thereby enabling us to make a decision which would maximize the profit or net value. The criterion is sufficiently versatile and general to include replacement problems arising from either physical deterioration or obsolescence.[1]

---

1. A generalized statement of the problem is given by G. A. D. Preinreich, "The Economic Life of Industrial Equipment," *Econometrica*, Vol. 8, No. 1, January, 1940, pp. 12–44.

All computing factors necessary for using the method are presented as appendixes to this report, and only simple arithmetic calculations are involved. The person using the method is expected to supply numerical values designed to summarize forecasts about certain elements. These are explained, illustrated, and applied to sample problems.

The method readily lends itself to modern electronic computing techniques for efficiency in making large-scale calculations.

## 1.3  Scope of the Report

Replacement theory is merely one facet of investment theory. A complete presentation and analysis of the replacement problem would, therefore, require a thorough coverage of capital theory and investment policy. But all studies have their limits of exposition, and this one confines itself to replacement principles without being drawn completely into the general investment problem. At some points in the study, the use of categorical statements which are considered valid applications of investment and capital theory is necessary.

## 1.4  The Criterion

The total cost of providing the stream of services is composed of several components: (1) current value of existing equipment; (2) net cost of switching from present equipment to new equipment; (3) total cost of replacements at projected intervals (purchase plus installation costs minus salvage value of existing equipment); (4) operating costs, including maintenance, of present equipment; and (5) operating costs of the series of future replacements. The rate of maintenance outlay is considered to be given; the determination of the optimum rate is regarded as a separate problem. (Ideally, the maintenance rate could be optimized if its effects on operating costs and depreciation were known.) In summary, the cost which we shall minimize is the present value of the above set of expenses. The replacement decision which minimizes that cost is the optimum decision.

If the stream of services can be given monetary values (as in business), then the present value of the service stream should be computed and compared with the present value of costs. The difference between these two is called the "capitalized present value of profits."

If monetary values cannot be assigned to the stream of services (as in military organizations), we have a special case of the more general approach. For this case the value of the service stream is set at some arbitrary constant value

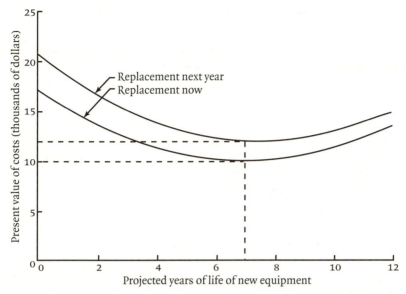

**FIG. 1.1.** *Present values of costs of immediate replacement and of replacement next year*

(zero for simplicity), and then the difference between the arbitrary value of the service and the present value of the cost stream is maximized. This means minimizing costs, which is exactly the principle stated in the preceding paragraph. The method presented in this report is equally applicable to either case.

### 1.5 How the Criterion Works

The formulation and solution simultaneously select the optimal life periods for *both* the present and future equipment to minimize total costs. By discounting, the future costs streams are converted into present value. In the determination of optimum replacement dates, the criterion also provides an economic comparison among alternative types of equipment.

Figure 1.1 shows the kind of information derivable from the procedure recommended in this report. For any given machine now in use and for any given kind of possible replacement, we shall obtain two curves which show how total cost (in present-value terms) changes with various projected operational periods of the new equipment; one curve is for immediate replacement, and the other curve is for replacement made the next year. The horizontal scale shows, in years, the alternative projected operation periods of new equipment; the vertical scale gives the capitalized present value of costs. If the present value is multiplied by the rate of interest, the result is the perpetuity annual equivalent. In the particular illustration, the immediate replacement curve is lower; hence, immediate replacement is more economical. The total present value of costs implicit in this action is minimized at $10,000 when the projected life length of new equipment is 7 years. It is noticeable that while the correct decision is to replace immediately, the costs implicit in this action depend on the projected economic life of the new equipment and that failure to select the optimal life can result in gross errors in estimated costs.

The essential feature of the criterion is its use of explicit forecasts of cost for particular service streams. The present analysis makes no attempt to derive the forecasts of cost and service elements. It states what forecasts must be made and how they are used in the replacement-decision process. Individuals familiar with the particular situation at hand must provide the forecasts. This does not, however, reduce the value of the procedure given in this report.

## 1.6 Present Values and Forecasts

The justification for using present values lies in the interdependence between current and future actions. Attempts to minimize current rates of costs (or maximize current rates of profit) may actually result in greater total costs (or losses) over a long period of time. Therefore, it is desirable to compare potential costs (and revenues) for an extended period. Meaningful present values are obtained by weighting the anticipated costs by a discounting factor. (The necessity of discounting to convert costs at different periods into comparable values is a consequence of the factors which produce interest, i.e., availability and need of capital, alternative productive possibilities, psychological preferences, etc.)

A definite responsibility is placed on the analyst to obtain the proper data. If forecasts used in the problem are wrong, the decision may be wrong. This is true of any valid replacement determination. No method exists which covers uncertainty. In short-cut methods where specific forecasts are not explicitly required, the forecasts are implicit in the formula itself and therefore may be inappropriate and lead to ambiguous results. It is a fundamental tenet of the present procedure that such implicit, haphazard forecasting must be avoided so that only relevant information is used in setting up the replacement problem. The procedure has been formulated to require only the necessary specific forecasts which will allow it to cover a wide range of replacement situations.

It would, in principle, be possible to introduce a probability allowance into the forecasts to measure uncertainty, but this would involve additional, complicated analyses. The present criterion, however, makes it easy to compare alternative forecasts so that consequences of decisions may be considered before making a commitment.

A margin of safety, or allowance for uncertainty, is not implicitly included in the present formulation, because safety margins depend on several factors: the degree of confidence an individual has in his estimates and forecasts, the size of the investment involved (a person is much more cautious when betting $1000 than when betting only $1), and the boldness of the individual. The present procedure will permit the forecasted consequences implicit in various replacement decisions to be determined. Allowances for degrees of uncertainty can be made after the projected outcomes and their consequences have been found.

### 1.7 Time Pattern of Service and Cost

In using the present-value-cost criterion, it is assumed that the time-pattern flow of services can be specified. The replacement problem is then divided into one of two cases, unlimited and limited, depending on the length of time for which the service is desired. For unlimited periods of service, the criterion determines the optimum time for replacement of present and successive equipment, and the future series of replacements are assumed to have uniform economic life length. For the limited period of service, the criterion allows for only one replacement, because of the computational complexity involved in multiple replacements during short periods. This is not an unreasonable simplification, since, in a wide class of limited-service-period situations, only one replacement is required.

All cost and service functions are approximated in the procedure of this report by modified exponential mathematical forms to allow a wide range of applicability and simplicity in computations.

### 1.8 Advantages over Present Methods

A method for guiding replacement is of little value if it requires difficult and extensive computations. One of the main virtues of the subject procedure is its simplicity. A glance at the tables in the appendixes for the key computing factors, followed by a few multiplications and additions, is all that is required to compute cost or profit.

There are many other advantages that the present procedure has over former methods:

1. The procedure is logically and economically correct.
2. Necessary forecasts about future revenue and cost conditions are made explicit.
3. Obsolescence and technological progress in future machines are recognized and incorporated in the forecasts and analysis. This, especially, is a very important feature; yet it is one in which most other procedures are inadequate.
4. Specifications of the forecasts are contained in a few numerical coefficients.
5. Computations for ascertaining correct replacement decisions are simple and brief.
6. Comparisons among alternative forecasts can be obtained quickly.
7. Both the absolute and relative costs (or profits) for alternative decisions are given.
8. Tables of computing factors for specified forecasts may be tailor-made for certain general classes of equipment, thus permitting easy calculations for maintenance and repair decisions in the field.
9. The general investment decision is answered, i.e., not merely when to replace, but whether to invest or to replace at all.
10. The decision to replace does not depend on an arbitrary estimate of the economic life of future replacements, but on optimum life as derived simultaneously and consistently within the general forecasts used in the present formulation.
11. There is no inherent bias toward replacing too early or too late.
12. The replacement decision is not left to chance via the haphazard process of selecting a replacement by one rule of thumb rather than by some other.
13. A peripheral advantage of the present formulation is its adaptability to modern electronic computers when it is desired to compare many alternative forecasts for their effects on replacement decisions. With such computers, forecasts need not be restricted to mathematical approximations. A graphic drawing of future values may be fed into a computer to obtain the solution.
14. The optimum maintenance expenditure, an associated investment

problem, can be solved after some slight modifications of the present procedure.

The present procedure determines the optimum life of machines. Usually, this is believed to be preliminary information that must be put into the analysis rather than derived from it. And sometimes the replacement decision is said to be relatively unaffected by the contemplated economic life of new equipment just as long as the machines promise to pay off in the contemplated period. In simple problems where only one kind of machine can possibly be used as a replacement, this may not cause frequent and disastrous error. Where more than one replacement is available, the costs of using each machine should be compared after its minimum-cost economic life has been determined. Failure to derive the optimum life can lead to selection of the poorer replacement items as well as possibly the wrong replacement decision.

# CHAPTER 2
## ELEMENTS OF THE REPLACEMENT PROBLEM

*The mathematically trained reader may turn directly to Chap. 3 for a mathematical state-ment of the problem and its solution. Other readers will probably prefer to read Chap. 2 and omit Chap. 3.*

### 2.1 Costs

Within the general context delineated in the preceding chapter, we detail now the specific problem and the required forecasts.

Assume, for example, that a machine is currently in use, but that we consider replacing it. What are the costs which must be considered? They are:

1. The cost of operating and maintaining the present machine.
2. The outlays required for buying and installing the new equipment.
3. The operating and maintenance costs of the new equipment.
4. Interest costs—these are accounted for by the use of present values.
5. Depreciation, which is accounted for by treating the outlays for new equipment in item (2) as net outlays over and above the turn-in or salvage value of the old equipment.

By converting these costs to present values, we may add them, regardless of their timing, and obtain the present value of the total costs of the required service stream. We denote this present value of costs by E.

A little reflection will reveal that all is not yet in order. The loss in salvage value, commonly called depreciation, which is a part of the cost of having and using new equipment, depends on how long the new item is kept. Thus, it becomes obvious that whether it is cheaper to replace the old machine now or later depends, in part, on how long the new machine will be kept once it has been acquired. And, in turn, this period depends on the characteristics of the new machines anticipated in the more distant future. The customary way to end this never-ending chase is arbitrarily to assume some operating period for the new equipment. If the period assumed is correct, all will be well; but if it is wrong, the decision to replace or to delay can be inappropriate.

In the procedure of this report, we do not resort to this dangerous simplification. Instead, we face the problem and correctly incorporate it into our solution. The resulting formulation and solution yields *two* answers: one tells when to replace the current item, and the other indicates the cost-minimizing operating period for the new equipment. In other words, the present procedure

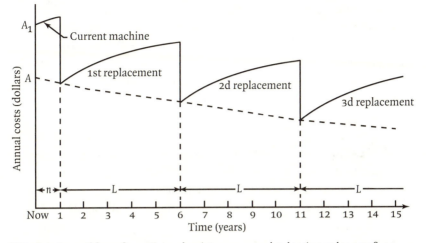

**FIG. 2.1.** *Assumed form of operating and maintenance costs related to time and to age of equipment*

solves for the most efficient economic life of the new equipment, using as a basis the anticipated rate at which the characteristics of the future machines improve. We can summarize by saying that we recognize the existence of technological progress and obsolescence and properly account for them in our replacement decision.

To this end, it is convenient to introduce symbols for these two components of our answer. We denote by $n$ the number of years before the existing machine should be replaced in its present function, and we denote by $L$ the number of years of projected life of the successor equipment. We assume that the operating periods of all items of equipment in the successor chain are equal. It can be shown, under reasonable assumptions, that this is a correct condition. The constrained-to-uniformity optimum period of the successor equipment is what we denote by $L$.

We assume that these costs are exponential functions of historical time as well as of the age of the particular machines. The meaning of this assumption is indicated in Fig. 2.1, which shows the stream of operating and maintenance costs over time for some rate of operation if the present equipment is retained for 1 year more before being replaced. At the end of the first year, new equipment is obtained. Its operating and maintenance costs will start at a lower level and will then slowly increase according to the curved cost line. When this new machine is ultimately replaced, $L$ years after its purchase, the new equipment will have even lower operating and maintenance costs—because of technological advance. But once a machine is purchased, operating and maintenance costs will again start to rise, and so on for as long as the service is needed. Thus, it is seen that the costs vary with historical time, as well as with the age of particular machines. In addition, at each replacement date there will be a capital outlay or purchase cost for the new equipment.

The sum of these acquisition and operating-maintenance costs constitutes the total costs which must be discounted to present values for comparison. To specify these two cost elements more precisely, capital costs—or the costs of acquiring the equipment—are dependent on the price of the new equipment (including installation costs) and on the turn-in or salvage value of old equipment, assuming that for any kind of new equipment the purchase price is constant over time.

We further assume that upon purchase and installation of a machine, a fraction of the initial value is lost because the item is no longer "new" nor in a formal market place, that the remaining value slowly depreciates at some constant percentage rate, and that each new machine in the series of replacements has the same depreciation characteristics.

As for operating and maintenance costs, it is assumed that the initial operating and maintenance costs of new machines decline over time because of technological advances. This decline is assumed to occur at a constant percentage rate. The dotted line in Fig. 2.1 is a trace of how initial operating and maintenance costs decline as machines improve. This improvement contributes to obsolescence in old machines and is reflected in their depreciation in salvage value.

Once a machine has been acquired, its operating and maintenance costs rise to some upper limit. Fig. 2.1 illustrates the historical sequence of operating costs of the machines in a replacement series. It is assumed that the operating costs rise each year by a constant percentage rate of the amount between the existing operating costs and the upper-limiting rate. An upper-limiting rate seems to be a realistic assumption. Of course it may be a very high limit, but, nevertheless, it seems inappropriate to assume no upper limit.

Operating and maintenance costs of the present machine whose replacement is under consideration are probably quite different from those of the new available machines. Whatever the costs of the old machine are, they are assumed to be still higher if kept for another year, and the salvage value is assumed to continue to decline.

The procedure which we use for computation enables us to take account of several factors: the operating-maintenance costs, the decline in salvage values, the change in technological advance in reducing operating-maintenance costs of future machines, and the acquisition costs of new equipment. For the currently used old equipment, the operating-maintenance costs for another year of service and the changes in salvage value consequent to such use are explicitly included in the procedure.

## 2.2 Service Streams

So far we have sought to obtain most efficiently some given service stream. However, in many cases a monetary valuation can be placed on the service stream. In industry, of course, this is essential. In general, services which enter into the market acquire a monetary value; for those organizations which do not sell their service, e.g., military and most government agencies, such a valuation is impossible. We shall intersperse this presentation of the formulation and solution of the replacement problem with details of the solution for the case in which service valuation is possible. Those organizations for which service valuations are impossible may simply ignore all the discussion explaining the service-valuation procedure. The validity of the criterion for the nonvalued service-stream problem is in no way dependent on or affected by the ability of the present procedure to account also for values of service where they are available and essential.

With a service stream that has monetary values attached to its services, the monetary values can be converted to present values and then compared with costs in order to maximize the difference, called profits. The present value of the services is denoted by R and is composed of two parts: (1) present value of services from existing equipment and (2) present value of services from future equipment.

Maximizing profits (R − E) is equivalent to minimizing E, but *only if* R is constant or if no service valuation is possible, as in the case of governmental agencies. In all other cases, minimizing E usually will not lead to a maximum of profits, R − E.

The assumptions we make about the time shape of the values of the service streams are shown in Fig. 2.2. The solid line is the historical sequence of rates of service values ordered by the series of machines. For the existing machine, it is assumed that the rate of income for the current year slowly declines during the year at some percentage rate. For the new equipment, it is assumed that the initial first-year rates of service or income rise steadily but to a limiting value as a result of technological advances. However, once a machine is acquired, the

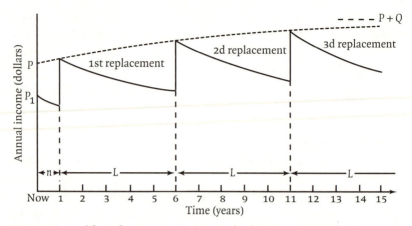

**FIG. 2.2.** *Assumed form of revenue or service income related to time and to age of equipment*

rate at which it renders services declines by a constant annual percentage amount.

The dotted line in Fig. 2.2 marks the path of increasing initial-year rates of service, while the solid lines trace the realized rates from acquired machines. Each upward vertical surge in the saw-tooth profile occurs at the time that a new machine is acquired. The area under the saw-tooth curve is the total value of the services, except that it must be discounted to present values. Similarly, the area under the saw-tooth curve in the cost diagram, plus the acquisition costs, represents the total costs. The problem is to determine when to have the first replacement—defined symbolically by $n$, the number of years remaining before replacing the old item—and to determine how far apart to space new acquisitions—denoted symbolically by $L$, the economic life length of new equipment.

### 2.3 Computational Procedure

All that is needed in order to solve the problem of the optimum replacement date is detailed in Chap. 4. The entire computational procedure is also given there. It is sufficient to emphasize here that, once the requisite forecasts are made about costs and services of old and new machines, not over 10 minutes should be necessary to complete the required computations.

In some relatively simple cases, it may be desired to know only how much cheaper (or more profitable) immediate replacement is when compared with delayed replacement. The absolute level of costs (or profits or losses) in either case is of *no* concern at this time. For this problem, the computations are very easy, even easier than for finding the absolute cost levels. Chapter 5 illustrates the required forecasts and presents the computations required, along with special tables to assist in quickly solving the problem.

## 2.4 Electronic Computer Solutions

For large-scale computations in which it is desired to compare many alternative forecasts for their effects on replacement decisions, the use of modern electronic computing may be appropriate. The Reeves Electronic Analogue Computer (REAC) is ideally suited to this problem, and it has been successfully used by RAND. The REAC is an expensive computer and requires trained operators; for these reasons it will not be readily available to most persons or organizations. However, service arrangements with organizations possessing a REAC may be worthwhile, particularly if exceptionally large investment programs are contemplated and if it is desired to compare many alternative forecasts for very many future service life lengths.

Another virtue of the REAC computer is that it will permit the use of any type of forecast that may be desired; there is no restriction to linear or exponential approximations. A graphic drawing of future costs can be read into the machine to obtain the solution.

Undoubtedly we are approaching the point in our computational skill at which simplifications are being made, not for purposes of facilitating computations, but rather to facilitate forecasts about future cost and revenue conditions. This is almost a complete reversal of past practice.

## 2.5 Limited Period of Service

Some types of services may not be needed for an indefinitely long period, and some agencies may view themselves as being appropriately concerned only with the truncated future, perhaps only with the next 20 or 30 years.

If the truncated period is fairly long, e.g., 50 years, the effect of discounting to present values reduces distant elements to negligible proportions. In final effect, the solution weights heavily the nearer years and, as a result, is an approximation to the truncated-service-period requirement.

However, for periods shorter than 50 years, a special formula will yield more reliable results. The main source of difficulty here is that if we were to select the optimal replacement periods for a set of, say, three replacements in 30 years, we would have an enormous number of alternative combinations of life lengths of first, second, and third replacements. To reduce the problem to manageable proportions, the following simplification is used: within the limited period of service requirement, only one replacement is considered, and we desire to know when that one replacement should occur. This is not so extreme a simplification, since in a wide class of equipment the situation is a plausible one.

The first problem in any finite period of required service is to determine whether the *one-replacement* assumption is a reasonable one. To verify this, we should first apply the unlimited-service-period formula, ignoring momentarily the fact that actually we are concerned with a limited period. The reason for doing this is to find the optimum uniform life lengths of the equipment in the replacement series. If these life lengths are so short, relative to our requirement for the *limited* period of service, that it takes at least two replacements to span the limited period, we can assume that our service-period requirement is long relative to machine lives. Therefore, in such cases we should use the results of this unlimited-period formula to decide when to replace existing equipment in the limited-period problem.

If, however, the service life of the new machines in the replacement series is more than half as long as the limited period of service requirement, it is apparent that it would pay to have only one replacement and to stretch out its life— as well as that of the currently used machine—to span the period. This is the procedure recommended in this report. Thus, having applied the unlimited period of service requirement and having obtained a life length for new machines so long that only one replacement seems to be called for, we may resort to a formula using only one replacement within the limited period of service. This formula will yield an answer which will tell how long to keep the presently used item before replacing it with the one replacement to be made before the expiration of the limited service period.

This point may be made more explicit by the following conclusions, which were derived from an illustrative case. As the length of service requirement increased, the number of years of economic life remaining in the currently used machine increased. The life length of the new machine also increased and was, of course, equal to the difference between the service requirement and the life of the currently used item.

In most situations, knowledge of the machines and their characteristics may make obvious the fact that one replacement will be adequate for the limited service period (or that it will not be adequate). In this event, the appropriate formula can be used at the first stage.

Chapter 3 contains a mathematical statement of the limited period of service with *one* replacement, and Chap. 5 illustrates the method of solving it.

Tables of computing factors are included in the appendixes, making them and Chap. 5 a self-contained exposition of the application of the method.

## 2.6 Discrete Changes

The present procedure has been directed toward determining whether to replace now or later, the forecasts of the future being describable by linear or exponential functional forms. However, it is possible to solve for optimum replacement decisions where a discrete jump or change in technology or styles (and hence in costs and revenue) is expected at some future date. Even if the date at which the discrete change is to occur is not known, a date may be set tentatively, and the limited-service-requirement formula may be used for a period of time extending from the current instant to that hypothesized future date. If the limited-service formula indicates immediate replacement of current equipment, the replacement should be made; otherwise it should be delayed. Another test can be made a year later.

If the date of the discrete change is not confidently known, it may be varied forward and backward to see if any change in action is indicated. If none is indicated, the uncertainty regarding the date is not critical in its effects on the decision. After having taken the action indicated by the formula, we can wait until the discrete change occurs (if it does) and at that future time use the unlimited-service formula, if appropriate, to determine optimal action at that future date. One precaution must be observed. The salvage value of a replacement, as well as of the existing item, must be varied to allow for the expected discrete change in the future. This implied depreciation rate bears the major burden of the forecasted effects of the discrete change.

## CHAPTER 3
## MATHEMATICAL FORMULATION

### 3.1 Introduction

The preceding chapters have discussed the replacement problem and the principles of its formulation and solution. Chapter 3 presents the same information in precise and concise mathematical form. First, the notation is presented, followed by the general mathematical expressions for the present value of costs and for the present value of revenues. Secondly, the exponential forms representing the cost and revenue streams are specified. Thirdly, these expressions are simplified into computational forms. Finally, the same procedure is carried out for the limited-service-period problem.

The reader who is not trained in mathematics would probably be well advised to skip this chapter. Chapter 4 gives in detail the step-by-step procedure to be followed in actual applications.

### 3.2 Notation in Mathematical Formulation

$A =$ initial annual rate of operating and maintenance costs of new item now available

$A_1 =$ current annual rate of operating and maintenance costs of incumbent item

$A + B =$ limiting annual rate of operating and maintenance costs (deterioration) of new item

$A_1 + B_1 =$ limiting rate for operating and maintenance costs of incumbent item

$C =$ purchase price of new items

$C_0 =$ salvage value of currently used item

$d =$ coefficient related to rate of decline of salvage value of new items

$d_1 =$ coefficient related to rate of decline of salvage value of current item

$g =$ coefficient for rate at which $P + Q$ is approached

$k =$ percentage of $C$ remaining as salvage value immediately after purchase ($1 - k =$ loss due to acquisition and installation)

$L =$ projected replacement period of new equipment

$n =$ economic life of currently used equipment

$P =$ initial annual rate of revenue of new item

$P_1 =$ current annual rate of revenue of current item

$P + Q =$ limit approached by initial rate of revenue (prices of services and technological changes in new machines) as time passes

$r$ = rate of interest

$s$ = coefficient for rate at which annual revenue of a new machine changes with age of a machine

$s_1$ = coefficient related to rate of change of annual revenue of current item

$u$ = coefficient related to rate at which B changes because of new technology and prices

$w$ = coefficient of rate at which operating and maintenance costs of any new item approach the limiting rate (because of deterioration)

$w_1$ = coefficient of rate at which $A_1 + B_1$ is approached (because of deterioration)

$z$ = coefficient related to the rate at which the initial operating and maintenance costs, A, fall as new items are developed

The following list explains the symbols used in the general functional expressions for cost and revenue:

$C_0(t)$ = turn-in value of present machine $t$ years from now

$A_1(t)$ = rate of operating and maintenance costs of present machine in year $t$

$D(T)$ = turn-in value of successor machines at age T as a fraction of C

$A(t, T)$ = rate of operating and maintenance costs, per year, of a machine purchased at time $t$ for the Tth year of its age

$e^{-rt}$ = present value of one dollar $t$ years hence at force of interest $r$ (continuously compounded), where the annual compounded rate is $r' = e^r - 1$; for small values, the difference may be regarded as negligible

$t$ = time in year-units

$j + 1$ = number of items in series of machines; $j = 0$ for the current or first machine

$V_1(t)$ = value of annual rate of services in the year $t$ for an existing machine

$V(t, T)$ = value of annual services in the Tth year of life of operation of a machine installed $[n + L(j - 1)]$ years from now

The following general expression for the present value of the aggregate of costs E is obtained by converting all costs to present worths and by adding:

$$E = [C - C_0(n)]e^{-rn} + C[1 - D(L)] \sum_{j=1}^{\infty} e^{-r(n+jL)} + C_0 + \int_0^n A_1(t)e^{-rt}\, dt$$

$$+ \sum_{j=1}^{\infty} \int_0^L A[n + L(j-1), T]e^{-r[n+L(j-1)+T]}\, dT. \tag{1}$$

The first term on the right-hand side is the cost of switching from the existing to a new machine. The second term is the present worth of the future costs of switching to new successor machines. The fourth term, added to $C_0$ (the present salvage value of existing equipment), is the present worth of the costs of operating and maintaining the existing machine. The last term is the present worth of the operating and maintenance costs of future machines in the series of replacements. It will be noted that historical time is measurable by $n + Lj$, since $n$ is the time before replacement of the present machine and $Lj$ is the elapsed time between subsequent replacements. Thus, we are able to indicate the passage of time in terms of the number of machines used.

The revenue or value of service function can be denoted by the following expression:

$$R = \int_0^n V_1(t)e^{-rt}\, dt + \sum_{j=1}^{\infty} \int_0^L V[n + L(j-1), T]e^{-r[n+L(j-1)+T]}\, dT. \tag{2}$$

We now specify exponential forms for the functions. In Eq. (1) we shall replace each general term by the specific exponential form. The first term on the right-hand side is the present value of the cost of replacing the incumbent machine $n$ years hence. This becomes

$$(C - C_0 e^{-d_1 n})e^{-rn},$$

where $C_0$ = salvage or turn-in value of the machine now,

$C$ = purchase price of the new machine,

$d_1$ = a coefficient related to the annual percentage decline in salvage value.

The second term is the present value of the future replacements at L-year periods. This term becomes

$$C(1 - ke^{-dL})\sum_{j=1}^{\infty} e^{-r(n+Lj)},$$

where $k$ is the percentage of the original cost of the machine remaining, immediately after purchase, as potential turn-in value, and $d$ is a coefficient related to the annual percentage rate of decline of salvage or turn-in value thereafter.

The fourth term is the present worth of operation and maintenance costs of the incumbent machine until it is turned in $n$ years hence. It becomes

$$\int_0^n [A_1 + B_1(1 - e^{-w_1 t})]e^{-rt} \, dt,$$

where $A_1$ = current annual rate of costs of incumbent machine,

$A_1 + B_1$ = upper limit approached by this cost rate,

$\quad w_1$ = a coefficient related to annual percentage rate at which the upper limit is approached.

This percentage applies to the difference $B_1$ between the existing rate and the upper limit.

The fifth term is the present worth of the operating and maintenance costs of all the future machines. It becomes

$$\sum_{j=0}^{\infty} \int_0^L [Ae^{-z(n+Lj)} + B(1 - e^{-wT})u^{Lj}]e^{-r(n+Lj+T)} \, dT,$$

where $A$ = initial rate of operation and maintenance costs of the machine considered as the present replacement,

$\quad z$ = a coefficient related to the annual percentage rate at which initial operating and maintenance costs fall as new machines are developed,

$A + B$ = upper limit of operation and maintenance costs for a machine,

$\quad w$ = a coefficient related to the percentage rate at which $B + A$ is approached from the value $A$,

$\quad u$ = a factor whose complement $(1 - u)$ is the annual percentage rate at which the increment, $B$, of operating and maintenance costs of *future* machines decreases.

In all the terms, $t$ is a running variable to denote time and $T$ denotes the age of a machine. Equation (1) now becomes

$$E = \int_0^n [A_1 + B_1(1 - e^{-w_1 t})]e^{-rt} \, dt + (C - C_0 e^{-d_1 n})e^{-rn} + C(1 - ke^{-dL}) \sum_{j=1}^{\infty} e^{-r(n+Lj)}$$

$$+ \sum_{j=0}^{\infty} \int_0^L [Ae^{-z(n+jL)} + B(1 - e^{-wT})u^{Lj}]e^{-r(n+jL+T)} \, dt + C_0. \tag{3}$$

Next we need to specify the revenue function. Equation (2) is changed as follows. The first term is the present value of the revenue stream of the incumbent machine during the remaining $n$ years of its life. This term becomes

$$\int_0^n (P_1 e^{-s_1 t}) e^{-rt}\, dt,$$

where $P_1$ is the current rate of revenue, and $s_1$ is the rate at which the current rate of revenue changes.

The second term is the present value of revenue from all future machines; this is

$$\sum_{j=0}^{\infty} \int_0^L [P + Q(1 - e^{-g(n+Lj)})] e^{-sT - r(n+Lj+T)}\, dT,$$

where $P$ = initial rate of revenue of a machine in its first year,

$P + Q$ = upper limit of initial rates of revenue due to technological advances,

$g$ = rate at which the upper limit ($P + Q$) is approached,

$s$ = rate at which annual service of a given machine changes with the age of a machine.

Combining these two revenue components gives

$$R = \int_0^n (P_1 e^{-s_1 t}) e^{-rt}\, dt + \sum_{j=0}^{\infty} \int_0^L [P + Q(1 - e^{-g(n+Lj)})] e^{-sT - r(n+Lj+T)}\, dT. \qquad (4)$$

### 3.3 Exponential Approximation—Computational Methods

In order to facilitate the computation of $R - E$, we integrate $R$ and $E$ and combine the results. We now integrate Eq. (3) and obtain

$$E = E_1 + E_2 + E_3 + E_4 + E_5 + E_6, \qquad (5)$$

where

$$E_1 = (A_1 + B_1)\left[ \frac{(1 - e^{-rn})}{r} \right],$$

$$E_2 = -B_1\left[ \frac{(1 - e^{-(w_1 + r)n})}{w_1 + r} \right],$$

$$E_3 = C_0[1 - e^{-(r+d_1)n}],$$

$$E_4 = C\left[ e^{-rn}\left( 1 + \frac{(1 - ke^{-dL})e^{-rL}}{1 - e^{-rL}} \right) \right],$$

$$E_5 = A\left[\frac{(e^{-n(r+z)})(1 - e^{-rL})}{r(1 - e^{-(r+z)L})}\right],$$

$$E_6 = B\left[e^{-rn}\left(\frac{(1 - e^{-rL})}{r(1 - u^{t}e^{-rL})} - \frac{(1 - e^{-(w+r)L})}{(w - r)(1 - u^{t}e^{-rL})}\right)\right];$$

$E_1 + E_2 + E_3$ represents the present worth of the depreciation and operating costs of the present machine, $E_4$ represents the present worth of acquisition costs for future machines, and $E_5 + E_6$ represents the present worth of operating and maintenance costs of successor machines.

A similar integration of Eq. (4) yields

$$R = P_1\left[\frac{1 - e^{-(s_1+r)n}}{s_1 + r}\right] + \left[\left(\frac{P + Q}{1 - e^{-rL}}\right) - \frac{Qe^{-gn}}{1 - e^{-L(g+r)}}\right]\left[\frac{1 - e^{-(s+r)L}}{s + r}\right]e^{-rn}. \quad (6)$$

Combining Eqs. (6) and (5) gives $R - E$.

### 3.4 Limited Period of Service

In Eqs. (1) and (2), hold j to 1, i.e., to one replacement. Specify that n plus L must add up to the service length requirement, $L_0$. These specifications define the limited-service requirement.

For the exponential approximation, Eq. (4) becomes

$$R = \int_0^n (P_1 e^{-s_1 t})\, e^{-rt}\, dt + \int_n^{L_0} [P + Q(1 - e^{-gn})]e^{-(s+r)t}\, dt; \quad (7)$$

and Eq. (3) becomes

$$E = \int_0^n [A_1 + B_1(1 - e^{-w_1 t})]e^{-rt}\, dt + C_0(1 - e^{-(d_1+r)n})$$

$$+ \int_n^{L_0} [Ae^{-zn} + B(1 - e^{-wt})u^n]e^{-rt}\, dt + C(e^{-rn} - e^{-d(L_0-n)-rL_0}). \quad (8)$$

Maximizing the difference, $R - E$, as a function of the replacement date can best be done by maximizing an equivalent function. Unfortunately, there is no known practical way to evaluate the derivative of $R - E$. As with the infinitely long service requirement, successive values of $R - E$ for alternative combinations of n and L must be computed. In the present instance, however, since n and L total to $L_0$, only one variable need be tested:

$$R - E = P_1\left[\frac{1 - e^{-(s_1 + r)n}}{s_1 + r}\right] + P\left[\frac{e^{-(s+r)n} - e^{-(s+r)L_0}}{s + r}\right]$$

$$+ Q\left[\frac{(1 - e^{-gn})(e^{-(s+r)n} - e^{-(s+r)L_0})}{s + r}\right] - A_1\left[\frac{1 - e^{-rn}}{r}\right]$$

$$- B_1\left[\frac{1 - e^{-rn}}{r} - \frac{1 - e^{-(w_1 + r)n}}{w_1 + r}\right] - A\left[\frac{(e^{-rn} - e^{-rL_0})e^{-zn}}{r}\right]$$

$$- B\left[u^n\left(\frac{e^{-rn} - e^{-rL_0}}{r} - \frac{e^{-(w+r)n} - e^{-(w+r)L_0}}{w + r}\right)\right]$$

$$- C_0[1 - e^{-(d_1 + r)n}] - C[e^{-rn} - e^{-d(L_0 - n) - rL_0}]. \tag{9}$$

Equation (9) gives the present value of the net-income stream. This equation is the sum of nine products. By assigning numerical values to the forecasting variables, the products can be computed with the aid of Table 16, on page 112, where the values of the factors in the brackets in Eq. (9) are listed. If no revenue stream is involved, Eq. (9) reduces to the following expression for E:

$$E = A_1\left[\frac{1 - e^{-rn}}{r}\right] + B_1\left[\frac{1 - e^{-rn}}{r} - \frac{1 - e^{-(w_1 + r)n}}{w_1 + r}\right]$$

$$+ A\left[\frac{(e^{-rn} - e^{-rL_0})e^{-zn}}{r}\right] + B\left[u^n\left(\frac{e^{-rn} - e^{-rL_0}}{r}\right) - \frac{e^{-(w+r)n} - e^{-(w+r)L_0}}{w + r}\right]$$

$$+ C_0[1 - e^{-(d_1 + r)n}] + C[e^{-rn} - e^{-d(L_0 - n) - rL_0}]. \tag{10}$$

Whether to replace immediately or later can be judged by computing the value of R − E for n = 0 and for n = 1 (for the appropriate value of $L_0$). If R − E is smaller for n = 0 than for n = 1, delay replacement; if R − E is larger for n = 0, replace now.

### 3.5 Nonanalytic Functional Forms

If it is preferable to graph out predictions about the future rather than to submit to restrictions of analytic types, such as exponential and linear forms, electronic computing machines can, within limits, be usefully applied to the problem. Preliminary study indicates that difficulties may quickly arise, but as yet no extensive or intensive attempts have been made to treat this problem. The following constraints seem to be dominant: If the last term of Eq. (1) can be written as either

$$\sum_{j=1}^{\infty} \int_0^L \{s_1[n + L(j - 1)] + s_2(T)\}e^{-r[n+L(j-1)+T]}\, dt,$$

or

$$\sum_{j=1}^{\infty} \int_0^L \{s_1[n + L(j - 1)] \times s_2(T)\}e^{-r[n+L(j-1)+T]}\, dt,$$

i.e., $A[n + L(j - 1), T]$ is a separable function, a solution on the Reeves Electronic Analogue Computer (REAC) is possible for *any* form of $s_2(T)$, but care must be taken to select a proper approximation for $s_1[n + L(j - 1)]$. Sufficient care means using a form which can be easily summed outside the integral. However, there is little or no aid, as far as a REAC solution is concerned, in making $D_o(n)$, $A_o(t)$, $D(L)$, etc., exponentials. These can easily be graphed on REAC input tables. To summarize, the only expression for which an exponential form facilitates REAC computations is $s_1(n + Lj)$.

# CHAPTER 4
## SPECIFIC ASSUMPTIONS, FORECASTS,
## AND COMPUTATIONS

### 4.1 Introduction

The essence of the replacement decision is the making of forecasts about cost and service streams. The temptation to assume that some ready-made formula will alleviate this responsibility should be resisted. These predictions *are* the factors which separate one situation from another; they are the distinguishing essentials of any problem. All that the formula does is to combine the forecasts so as to derive their implications for alternative present decisions. The procedure presented in this report tries to reduce the necessary forecasts to as small a number as possible, consistent with its applicability to a wide variety of types of equipment.

The forecasts are summarized in terms of a few key variables. For the most general type of problem, there are 21 variables. This, at first, seems to be an enormous number, but in most problems several of them drop out or are very easily estimated. As soon as the nature of the assumptions about the *shapes* of the cost and service streams are understood, it will be seen that making estimates about the position, heights, or slopes of these general shapes is not a difficult task. It should be stressed that these forecasts are not made necessary by the particular formula used here. They are necessary under any replacement procedure whatsoever. In those procedures where there is ostensibly no necessity for making such forecasts, it would be discovered, upon investigation, that the forecasts have been implicitly made by the formula, and there are available as many different formulas as there are possible forecasts. In such a case, the selection of the formula would determine the particular forecasts implicit in a replacement decision.

It is a fundamental tenet of the present report that such implicit haphazard forecasting is exactly what we seek to avoid in order to bring to bear the maximum amount of relevant information in the correct way.

To return to the principal problem, the 21 forecasts that must be made can probably best be understood from a graphic presentation. In the graphs described in the following sections, time is on the horizontal scale with the origin at the present moment; the vertical scale is always in dollars.

## 4.2  Capital and Acquisition Cost Forecasts

### 4.2.1  Currently Used Equipment

Figure 4.1 shows the salvage value of the existing machine plotted against time. The present salvage value is $C_0$, but this value declines over time along one of the curves originating at $C_0$. Each of the curves corresponds to a different annual percentage rate of decline; this rate of decline is shown in parentheses adjacent to each curve. We must estimate $C_0$ and select one of the declining salvage-value curves. Having made this estimate, we have, in effect, selected the values of $C_0$ and $d_1$.

The value of $d_1$ is equal to the percentage rate of annual decline, *if* the percentage rate is less than 0.10. For larger rates of annual decline, the numerical value of $d_1$ will diverge. This divergence is due to the fact that we have used the exponential approximation, assuming a *continuous* change rather than annual or semiannual jumps. This is analogous to interest compounded annually or semiannually versus interest compounded continuously. As is well known, compounding interest once a year at 15 per cent is equivalent (at the end of each year) to compounding it continuously at a slightly lower rate. In the present case, we are speaking of rates of decrease, and it will follow that the nu-

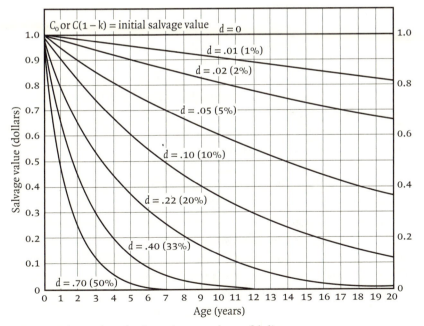

**FIG. 4.1.** *Salvage values related to various annual rates of decline*

merical value of the coefficient will be larger than the numerical value of the rate of annual percentage decreases. To facilitate the conversion of annual rates of decrease to the appropriate values of the coefficients, Table 1 lists the values of annual percentage rates of change and the matching values of the coefficients to be used. In general, for values of rates of annual change of less than 0.15 per cent, no large error results from using the same magnitude for the coefficient; but for larger values, the divergence becomes substantial, and the correct value should be used.

### 4.2.2 New Equipment

For the new machine being considered as a replacement, we must estimate the purchase and installation costs, $C$, and the rate at which salvage value of the new machines will decline (depreciation).

For this prediction there are three numbers to specify. First, there are purchase and initial installation costs; secondly, it is well known that once an item is purchased it loses value merely by virtue of its no longer being "new" and also by virtue of its having been removed from a routine marketing channel. This initial and abrupt decline can be large or small, depending on circumstances. It is accounted for here by the simple device of expressing the post-purchase and installation value as a percentage of the original acquisition and installation costs. For example, if an item costs 100 to acquire and 20 to install and immediately after installation is worth 60 in redeemable net salvage either for resale or scrap or alternative use elsewhere, one-half of the original cost remains as salvage value. The variable, $k$, used for this purpose here has a value of 0.5. Thirdly, the salvage value continues to decline, because of deterioration and obsolescence, along one of the curves shown in Fig. 4.1. A different constant annual rate of decline corresponds to each curve. The applicable curve must be selected, and, with this selection made, a unique value of $d$ is thus obtained.

In the case of the indefinitely long service period, it should be remembered that the new machine itself will someday be replaced by a new one, etc. It is assumed in the present procedure that these future machines will have the same values of $C$, $k$, and $d$. It would be desirable to vary these, but the price of doing so would be very high in computational costs as well as in the required amount of research. It is suspected that even if the computational burden were trivial, the current assumption would have to be adopted anyway.

TABLE 1. Annual rates of change and corresponding values for coefficients expressing that rate of change*

| Percentage rate of annual decline | Value of coefficient |
| --- | --- |
| .00 | .00 |
| .01 | .00 |
| .02 | .02 |
| .03 | .03 |
| .04 | .04 |
| .05 | .05 |
| .06 | .06 |
| .07 | .07 |
| .08 | .08 |
| .09 | .09 |
| .10 | .10 |
| .11 | .12 |
| .12 | .13 |
| .14 | .15 |
| .20 | .22 |
| .25 | .30 |
| .30 | .35 |
| .33 | .40 |
| .40 | .50 |
| .45 | .60 |
| .50 | .70 |
| .65 | 1.00 |
| .70 | 1.20 |
| .80 | 1.60 |
| .90 | 2.30 |
| .95 | 3.00 |
| .999 | 6.00 |

*For the coefficients $d_1$, $d$, $z$, $w_1$, $w$, $s_1$, $s$, and $g$ (but not for $u$ and $k$).

## 4.3 Operating-Costs Forecasts

### 4.3.1 Currently Used Equipment

Operating costs are defined in a similar fashion. Figure 4.2 shows the general pattern of the operating-maintenance costs that are implicit in the form of the formula used in this report. In each case, the exact height and slope of the curves will be determined by the forecasts. Again we must distinguish the cost characteristics of the present machine from those of the new machine being considered as a replacement. For the existing machine, the current rate of costs per year is given by $A_1$, and the limiting rate to which it can rise is $B_1$ higher. The rate at which that inevitable increase in operating costs is incurred is indicated by the slope of the cost curve up toward the limiting value. This slope coefficient is given by $w_1$. In Fig. 4.2, several curves for various values of $w_1$ are shown, but all of them have the same $A_1$ and $B_1$ values. It should be noted that once a value of $B_1$ is selected, the shape of the curve of rising costs is identified by $w_1$ alone. The value of $A_1$ is not relevant; it is merely the starting height. The actual slope is determined by $B_1$ and $w_1$ for any given time. In Fig. 4.2, the value of $B_1$ is equivalent to the distance on the ordinate from 1.0 to 2.00. The proportion of any given value of $B_1$ by which costs rise annually is given by the curves, in accordance with the appropriate value of $w_1$.

It is to be expected that for the existing machine, if it is an old one, the value of $B_1$ will be much smaller than for a new one, since presumably operating costs have already just about reached their upper limit. But if it is a newer machine, the spread between the initial rate of operating costs and the eventual upper limit will be much greater.

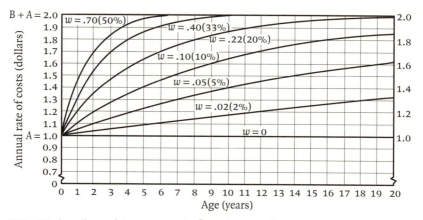

**FIG. 4.2.** Operating-maintenance costs rates for various rates of increase

4.3.2 *New Equipment*

The historical pattern of costs implicit in using an existing machine one more year, replacing it and using a new machine L years, and then, in turn, replacing that machine, and so on, was illustrated in Fig. 2.1, on page 665. It will be seen that the initial operating costs of the new machines start at lower rates as we look farther into the future and also that the upper limit of the costs declines slightly. If, instead of operating one more year, the old machine is replaced immediately, the new machine will have slightly higher initial operating costs than a machine that could be obtained a year hence. Thus, there is some advantage in delaying replacement to obtain the benefits of the reduced costs of improved machines. But this, of course, may be offset by the current higher costs of continuing to operate the old machine. This possibility is what the replacement formula evaluates. In terms of the formula, we need to express the rate at which initial operating costs, A, decline with time. The coefficient denoting this is z. In Fig. 2.1 it determines the slope of the dotted line declining from point A. Figure 4.1, page 681, can also be interpreted as a series of alternative decline (or progress) rates. Adjacent to each curve is a number denoting the annual percentage decline. For annual percentage rate of change of less than 10 per cent, the value z (instead of d) is equal to the annual percentage rate of change which is shown in the parentheses.

Whatever may be the starting point for operating and maintenance costs of some new machine, the rate at which these costs, for that machine, rise to the limiting rate is given by $w$; this is analogous to the $w_1$ coefficient for the old machine whose replacement is being considered. It is a coefficient giving the percentage rate at which the distance B is eaten up in the first year, and the rate at which the remaining distance for that machine is eaten up in the second year, and so on. Figure 4.2 illustrates this also.

The description of future operating and maintenance costs is completed by the coefficient describing the rate at which the upper-limiting rate, B, of operating and maintenance costs is reduced due to technological progress. This rate of decline is denoted by the coefficient u. When there is no reduction, its value is 1. A 10 per cent reduction gives it a value of 0.90. In other words, $1 - u$ is the annual percentage reduction in limiting rates of operating-maintenance costs resulting from better equipment.

## 4.4 Computation of Implied Present Value of Costs

If the problem at hand is one of minimizing costs, we may ignore the service function and its coefficients. In this report, a rate of 4 per cent is assumed to be the relevant discounting rate. For any particular agency, the rate is usually con-

TABLE 2. *Pairing of factors with cost or revenue magnitudes*

Unlimited Period of Service

| Computing factor and rate-of-change coefficients* | Rate of annual cost | Present value of costs |
|---|---|---|
| I | $(A_1 + B_1)$ | $E_1$ |
| II $(w_1)$ | $-B_1$ | $-E_2$ |
| III $(d_1)$ | $C_0$ | $E_3$ |
| IV $(k, d)$ | $C$ | $E_4$ |
| V $(z)$ | $A$ | $E_5$ |
| VI $(w, u)$ | $B$ | $E_6$ |
| Total | | $E$ |

| Computing factor and rate-of-change coefficients* | Rate of annual revenue | Present value of revenue |
|---|---|---|
| VII $(s)$ | $(P + Q)$ | $R_1$ |
| VIII $(s, g)$ | $-Q$ | $-R_2$ |
| IX $(s_1)$ | $P_1$ | $R_3$ |
| Total | | $R$ |

*All factors depend on the rate of interest, on n, and on L and are given in Tables 14 and 15 of Appendix I.

stant and not subject to variation over various types of equipment; in effect, then, it is a sort of once-and-for-all coefficient value. All the data in the computing tables of the appendixes are based on 4 per cent. For other rates, a new set of tables is required and, should the demand for them arise, they could be computed by The RAND Corporation.

Six of the preceding variables were dollar-value figures, and the remaining seven were rates of change of this dollar figure. An inspection of Eq. (5) for costs reveals that it consists of the sum of six terms, each a product of a term consisting of a dollar figure and a term (hereafter called a computing factor) based on the coefficients of rates of change. Hence, all that is needed is to obtain these six products and to add them. Table 2 lists the dollar terms and their associated computing factors. To obtain the six products requires only the multiplication of the two terms in each product; the first term is nothing but the dollar figure, and the second term (the computing factor) can be very quickly obtained from Tables 14 and 15 of Appendix I, pages 718 and 722, which are provided for this purpose. All that is necessary is to find the appropriate page and to note the appropriate entry. The illustration of these calculations in Chap. 5 will be sufficient to explain the process.

By computing the costs relevant to replacement now and the costs relevant to replacement a year from now ($n = 0$ and $n = 1$, respectively), for any arbitrary value of L, we can determine which is cheaper, if the particular value of L selected is the optimum value. But suppose that it is an inappropriate value of L. A range of values (for L) should be used, and for each value the costs with replacement now and with replacement later can be computed. In this manner, we ascertain how the costs will vary as the contemplated life length of the replacement series changes.

But all of this computing is not always necessary. In some cases it will be cheaper (or more expensive) to replace immediately rather than a year hence, no matter what value of L is assumed (e.g., see Fig. 1.1). In other words, usually one or the other action will be consistently better over the whole range of alternative values of L as well as for the optimum value of L. In this case, we need merely compute costs for one value of L. But if we want to be relatively safe, we can compute the present value of costs at two values of L some distance apart, say at 3 and at 20, and if it is cheaper to replace in both cases, we can feel reasonably confident that the costs of replacement now are cheaper for all values of L as well as the optimum value. Not too much should be made of this convenience, however. Quite often it is not merely a question of taking the cheaper action, but one of knowing exactly how cheap or costly the action will be. For resolving this question, we should compute costs for a few values of L in order to isolate the optimum value of L and the minimum cost that is realized at that point. At worst, this will require only a few more minutes of computing time. Hence, even in this more general case, the present formula is convenient.

## 4.5 Service Forecasts

We now continue with the more general case in which we want to maximize the difference between service revenue and costs. To do this we must compute the present value of revenues if we replace immediately and if we replace a year hence. We must first estimate the annual rate of revenue, $P_1$, for the current year if the currently owned equipment is used another year. Next, we must estimate the annual percentage rate, $s_1$, by which the annual revenue will decrease. Figure 2.2, on page 668, shows the value of the service stream if replacement is de-layed one year. The saw-tooth profile results from the fact that once a machine is bought and put into use, there is a jump to a more efficient machine which, in turn, starts to deteriorate. Each new machine is better than the previous one, and hence the initial revenue rate is higher on successive machines. The start-ing point for the new machine available today is denoted by $P$, an annual rate of income in dollars. The rate of income declines annually as the machine deteri-orates; the rate of decline is given by $s$, and for small annual rates, say less than 10 per cent, the numerical value of $s$ is equal to the numerical value of the rate of annual percentage decline. Figure 4.1 may be used as a reference to see the pattern of decline—if $s$ is substituted for $d$.

On the other hand, it will be noticed from Fig. 2.2 that the starting point for the revenue rate of new machines increases as time progresses. This is due to general technical progress. This initial rate potential increases steadily to some upper limit in the present formula. We denote the upper limit of these initial rates as time progresses by $P + Q$, with $Q$ as the amount of potential improve-ment. The rate at which $Q$ is taken up is given by $g$. Again, for small annual rates of percentage changed, the numerical values of $g$ will be equal to the percent-age rate. Figure 4.2 shows alternative patterns of rises of $g$—if $g$ is substituted for $w$. These are all the service forecasts.

### 4.6 Computation of Service Value

There are three dollar magnitudes and three parameters of rates of changes. The present value of revenue is the sum of three terms, each of which is the product of a dollar magnitude and a computing factor based on the rate-of-change coefficients. Again, by reading from Tables 14 and 15 of Appendix I, we can quickly obtain these factors and multiply them by the dollar magnitudes, and by summing these we can obtain the present value of the service stream. This is done for $n = 0$ and $n = 1$ for alternative values of L. Often, R − E will be larger for $n = 0$ than for $n = 1$ at one value of L and yet will be smaller at some other value of L. To determine this, we should compute R − E for $n = 0$ and $n = 1$ at three values of L, at least. If reversals occur, then the value of L which maximizes R − E can be isolated by using a few more values of L. If no reversals occur, there is an increased likelihood that none will occur, but this situation can be checked by computing R − E for more values of L.

We summarize the computational structure as follows: Each of the dollar magnitudes has associated with it a "computing factor" which incorporates the estimated future historical changes and which also converts that pattern of revenue or cost flow to a present value. We have, in all, nine computing factors for the indefinitely long service-requirement problem. These factors are listed in Table 2 and are designated by Roman numerals (with the particular rate-of-change coefficient on which each factor depends enclosed in adjoining parentheses). Paired with each factor in Table 2 is the dollar cost or revenue magnitude symbol by which it is to be multiplied. An example of the computational procedure is given in Chap. 5.

## 4.7  Limited Period of Service

Instead of an indefinitely long service period as considered thus far, we may contemplate a limited, or finite, period of service, after which the machine will be salvaged and the service no longer provided. In order to *solve* the problem of

TABLE 3. *Pairing of factors with cost and revenue magnitudes*

Limited Period of Service

| Computing factor and rate-of-change coefficients* | Rate of annual revenue | Present value of revenue |
|---|---|---|
| I $(s_1)$ | $P_1$ | $R_1$ |
| II $(s)$ | $P$ | $R_2$ |
| III $(s, g)$ | $Q$ | $R_3$ |
| Total | | $R$ |

| Computing factor and rate-of-change coefficients* | Rate of annual cost | Present value of costs |
|---|---|---|
| IV | $A_1$ | $E_1$ |
| V $(w_1)$ | $B_1$ | $E_2$ |
| VI $(z)$ | $A$ | $E_3$ |
| VII $(u, w)$ | $B$ | $E_4$ |
| VIII $(d_1)$ | $C_0$ | $E_5$ |
| IX $(d)$ | $C$ | $E_6$ |
| Total | | $E$ |

*All factors depend on r and are given in Table 16 of Appendix II.

minimizing costs in this limited period, some additional simplifying assumptions are necessary. The assumption of particular pertinence here is that only *one* new machine may be acquired. It may be obtained immediately or at a later date, but in any event only one, at most, will be obtained.

The reason for this restriction is that if we permitted two or three replacements in the contemplated interval, we would have an enormous number of possible combinations of replacement dates for the two or three later replacements. To keep the problem from becoming computationally forbidding, we have constrained ourselves to but one replacement. If the service period is so long that more than one replacement is *believed* to be sensible, the following "test" procedure is suggested. Use the indefinitely long service-period formula. If the optimum value of L (the life length of replacement) is about as long as the limited service period, then the limited-service-period formula with one replacement should be used instead. If, on the other hand, the length of the limited service period is two or more times as long as the optimum value of L obtained by the unlimited period of service requirement, we suggest using the results of the indefinitely long service requirement.

If only one replacement appears to be the appropriate action, the basis for action is summarized in Eqs. (9) and (10). An illustration of the computational steps is given in Chap. 5. It is sufficient for present purposes to point out that the computations required are merely those of summing six terms, each of which is the product of two terms—a dollar value and a computing-factor value. Table 3 lists the required dollar variables and their paired computing factors (each of which is associated with a variable summarizing the forecasts of future rates of change).

# CHAPTER 5
## ILLUSTRATION OF PROCEDURE

## 5.1 Indefinitely Long Service Requirement

Illustrative applications are the best way to understand the procedure recommended in this report. Therefore, we will start with the question that inevitably arose during the discussions of the replacement problem, namely, "When should I replace my present automobile?"

In answering the question as to when to replace the presently used car, it will be convenient to separate the problem into three parts. We shall ascertain first how the length of time for which a car is used affects the cost of the service, since the answer as to when to replace a presently owned car depends on how much it costs to obtain and operate newer cars. This is done in Sec. 5.1.1. Then, in Sec. 5.1.2 we shall assume that a car is already owned and that we are considering its replacement. In deciding whether or not to replace it, we must compare (1) the costs consequent to immediate replacement with (2) the costs of operating it one more year before buying and operating a new car. As we shall see from Sec. 5.1.1, the costs of these two alternatives depend on how long we contemplate using the new car before eventually replacing it in turn. Hence, our solution must take account of these different possible operating periods for the new cars. In Sec. 5.1.2 we do take this into account. Finally, in Sec. 5.1.3 we shall enlarge the problem and assume that we can attach money values to the automobile services. In that case, we are interested in profits rather than in costs only. The following new-car possibilities will be used as illustrations in the discussions of the problem:

1. Car A—a $2000 car, to be driven 10,000 miles per year.
2. Car B—a $3000 car, to be driven 10,000 miles per year.
3. Car C—a $2300 car, to be driven 20,000 miles per year.

The exact details of each of the above three examples are given in Table 4. All costs are included: purchase, depreciation, interest, operating, maintenance, insurance, and taxes.

### 5.1.1 How Contemplated Life Length Affects Cost of Service

Since the first problem concerns the relationship between cost and the length of time a car is kept, we are, in effect, assuming a new car is bought now and held for potentially alternative lengths of time.

TABLE 4. *Automobile replacement problem*

Illustrative Problem

| | Type of car | | |
|---|---|---|---|
| | A | B | C |
| Coefficients | (10,000 mi/yr) | (10,000 mi/yr) | (20,000 mi/yr) |
| C | $2000 | $3000 | $2300 |
| A | $350 | $400 | $500 |
| B | $150 | $200 | $150 |
| P | $0 | $0 | $0 |
| Q | $0 | $0 | $0 |
| k | .9 | .9 | .9 |
| d | .22 | .22 | .40 |
| z | 0 | 0 | 0 |
| u | 1.0 | 1.0 | 1.0 |
| r | .04 | .04 | .04 |
| u | .10 | .10 | .10 |

The calculations were made as follows: The values of the several coefficients were first obtained from inspection of automobile-operation records
plus some "informed estimates." This requires some time and effort—but
there is no apology for this. Any replacement formula which purports to eliminate this essential step is simply inadequate, and to use such a formula is, in
effect, to trust to accidents of fate. Our assumptions for the A-car were that it
cost $2000 to buy the car and that the first year's operating, maintenance, in-
surance, etc., outlays would be $350. These costs would rise to a limiting an-
nual rate of $500, some $150 higher than the initial rate. Thus, $C = \$2000$,
$A = \$350$, and $B = \$150$. The rate of rise in operating costs was expressed by
the estimate that about 10 per cent of the inevitable increase would be incurred the first year, and that in the second year the annual operating costs
would be still higher by 10 per cent of the then-remaining distance to the
upper limit. Each year the operating costs would increase by 10 per cent of the
remaining interval up to the limiting annual rate of operating-maintenance
costs—$500. Thus, $w = 0.10$.

It was assumed that 10 per cent of the original purchase price was lost upon purchase. This means that $k = 0.9$. Of the remaining \$1800 of value, about 20 per cent was lost each year, $d = 0.22$. In other words, except for the initial loss in value, the depreciation was 20 per cent a year.

It was estimated that the operating costs of new cars to be available in the future would be exactly the same as those currently available. Although styling and comfort might increase, there was estimated to be no decrease in operating costs. Hence, all the other coefficients were set at zero (except $u$, which is 1 for this type of estimate).

If we look at Eq. (5), page 676, or at Table 2, the top half of which is a tabular form of that equation, we shall see that it is the sum of six terms, $E_1, E_2, \ldots, E_6$, each of which is a product involving a dollar-value coefficient and an expression in brackets involving the rate-of-change coefficients. We shall compute the present value of costs with $n = 0$, since this is equivalent to starting with a new car. The first three expressions have dollar coefficients equal to zero, since we have no old equipment on hand. The first three terms may therefore be ignored in the present problem, in which we are computing the cost, not of immediate replacement, but rather of starting in at this time to have automobile service. Here the choice is how long to keep each car before replacing it. Only if we already have some older car whose cost characteristics are different from those of the currently available new car shall we have to use the first three terms, $E_1$, $E_2$, and $E_3$.

All we need to do now is to compute the last three products, $E_4$, $E_5$, and $E_6$. The dollar terms in each of the last three products are the values $C$, $A$, and $B$, i.e., the initial purchase cost, the initial annual rate of operating and maintenance costs, and the difference between the initial rate and the ultimate limiting rate as the car wears out. Factor IV, to be multiplied by $C$, depends on the value of $k$ and $d$. Since we first compute costs for $L = 1$, we turn to page 718 ($L = 1$) of Table 15 in Appendix I, find in the upper half of the page (where $n = 0$) the section labeled IV, which lists the values of computing factor IV, and read the appropriate entry corresponding to $k = 0.9$ and $d = 0.22$. The factor value is 7.8054. The value of the computing factor for the "A" term depends on $z$ and is given on the same page in the section labeled V. The value for our particular problem, in which $z = 0$, is 25.0.

The last term, $B = \$150$, has factor VI dependent on $w$ and $u$. On the same page ($L = 1$), we find the section labeled VI; for $w = 0.10$ and $u = 1.00$, the factor is 1.2014. Now, by multiplying and summing, we obtain 24,541, which is the present value of costs implicit in owning Car A, driving it 10,000 miles, and replacing it *every* year by a new car. At 4 per cent, this is equivalent to annual costs of $982.

The same process is repeated for L = 5, for which the factor values are found on the L = 5 page of Table 15. The sum is $17,851. For L = 10 and for L = 15, the sums turn out to be $15,712 and $14,768.*

This calculation of the products and their summation is an extremely simple and rapid operation. For all cases it would be desirable to design some computing sheets on which the relevant data can be recorded to facilitate computation and preservation of records. Because it is a simple task to design such a form, and because the exact form actually used would depend on the type of person and his mathematical and computing ability, no particular form will be recommended here.

The computed present values for A-cars, and also for the two other cars, are given in Table 5 and in Fig. 5.1. The heights of these curves at any point give the present value of the total costs of owning and operating automobiles, with replacements every L years, where L is the number of years each car is retained. Thus, if a new A-car is purchased every 3 years, the present value of the cost of such service is $19,640. At 4 per cent this is equivalent to a steady cost stream of $786 each and every year. If, instead, replacement takes place every 5 years, the present value of costs of such service is $17,851, which is equivalent to a steady cost stream of $714 per year. Thus, replacing every 5 years instead of every 3 years yields a saving of $72 *every* year. Turned around, this means that it costs about $70 more every year to have new A-cars every 3 years than it does to have them every 5 years.

The present values of costs have been converted into annual perpetuity equivalents by multiplying the present values by the rate of interest. The height of the curve at L = 6 gives the annual cost of automobile service when the series of cars is replaced every 6 years. Note that this is the average annual cost. The curve does not show the changing annual historical cost in each year, but, rather, the average of total costs spread over the years of service.

The curves decline substantially until they reach about 15 to 20 years of age per item. If we regard the decline remaining after that age as negligible, the cheapest policy is to replace the car every 15 or 20 years. There is little point in keeping the car longer, since practically no reduction in costs ensues. This does not mean that a car should be kept as long as that. New cars more often and

*Editor's note: Data for L > 1 not reproduced here.—DKB

TABLE 5. *Automobile ownership and service costs as function of replacement period*

Present Values and Annual Equivalents

Illustrative Problem

| L | Car A (10,000 mi/yr) | Car B (10,000 mi/yr) | Car C (20,000 mi/yr) |
|---|---|---|---|
| **Replacement-Period Present Values** | | | |
| 1 | 24,541 | 33,656 | 37,338 |
| 2 | 21,191 | 28,604 | 31,594 |
| 3 | 19,640 | 26,252 | 28,450 |
| 5 | 17,851 | 23,523 | 24,697 |
| 7 | 16,755 | 21,839 | 22,538 |
| 10 | 15,712 | 20,238 | 20,701 |
| 12 | 15,251 | 19,508 | 19,969 |
| 15 | 14,768 | 18,749 | 19,258 |
| 20 | 14,287 | 17,984 | 18,599 |
| **Equivalent Annual Rates of Cost** | | | |
| 1 | 982 | 1,346 | 1,494 |
| 2 | 848 | 1,144 | 1,264 |
| 3 | 786 | 1,050 | 1,138 |
| 5 | 714 | 941 | 988 |
| 7 | 670 | 874 | 902 |
| 10 | 628 | 810 | 828 |
| 12 | 610 | 780 | 799 |
| 15 | 591 | 750 | 770 |
| 20 | 571 | 719 | 744 |

SOURCES: Table 4 and Appendix I.

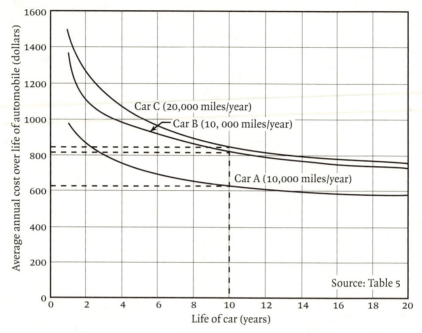

**FIG. 5.1.** *Annual cost of automobile service averaged over life of automobile (ownership and service)*

higher costs may be preferred. All we can do is, in effect, present a menu; the individual can choose his own fare.

Incidentally, the following type of comparison may be useful. According to the above estimates, it is just as cheap to have a B-car every 10 years as it is to have a new A-car every 2.5 years. One of these two alternatives could be chosen on the basis of personal preference alone. Other similar comparisons can be constructed in accordance with the interests of the individual.

### 5.1.2  *Should a Presently Owned Item Be Replaced Now?*

Now suppose that we have an older car on hand. Is it cheaper to replace it now or to wait at least a year? Let us assume that our new car under consideration is the A-car characterized in Table 4. The data presented in Table 6 are the estimated costs characterizing the continued use of the old car.

We must compute the costs of getting automobile service by replacing now ($n = 0$) and the costs of the service if we replace next year ($n = 1$). But, as we have seen in the preceding section, these two costs will depend on L, the projected use-period of the new car. This means that when we compute costs for

TABLE 6. *Cost characteristics of presently used automobiles*

Illustrative Problem

$450 = A_1$    (present annual rate operating costs)
$50 = B_1$    (amount by which annual rate of costs can rise in future)
$400 = C_0$    (present salvage value)
.22 = $d_1$    (rate of depreciation is .20 per year)[*]
.10 = $w_1$    (rate at which annual operating costs rise as applied to remaining possible cost rise)

---

[*]See Sec. 4.2, page 681, for explanation of difference between 0.20 and 0.22.

immediate replacement and for replacement next year, we should make our assumptions regarding L explicit. We can thereby see which value of L gives the minimum-cost method of obtaining automobile services and, at the same time, whether it is obtained with replacement now ($n = 0$) or a year later ($n = 1$).

Our computing procedure is as follows: We shall first select three alternative values for L, e.g., 1, 3, and 10. Then, for each of these we shall compute E for $n = 0$ and also for $n = 1$. A reference back to Table 2 will show the pairings of the cost estimates with the various computing factors (and the coefficients on which the computing factors depend). We also see from Table 2 that the present worth of total costs, E, is the sum of six products, called $E_1, E_2, \ldots, E_6$. To obtain these later products, we multiply the dollar-cost figure by the computing-factor value. With our estimates in Table 6, we can refer to Tables 14 and 15 of Appendix I to find the values of the computing factors for $n = 0$ and $L = 1$. This will give us the total present worth of costs of immediate replacement, with replacements each year thereafter. Computing factors I, II, and III *always* have values of zero when $n = 0$. Computing factors IV, V, and VI depend on the particular value of $n$ (0 or 1) and also on the particular value of L. Factors IV, V, and VI are listed in Table 15 of Appendix I, where each page corresponds to a different value of L and where the values of $n = 0$ are on the top half of the page and the $n = 1$ values are on the bottom half. It will be recalled that these same pages were used to obtain values of the computing factors in the illustration in Sec. 5.1.1. For our present example, the value of computing factor IV for $n = 0$ and $L = 1$ is obtained by finding the entry in section IV under the column and row corresponding to $k = 0.9$ and $d = 0.22$. Its value is 7.8054; this is to be multiplied by $C = \$2000$. Computing factor V, which depends on $z = 0$, has its value

TABLE 7. *Cost of service with replacement now versus replacement next year*

Illustrative Problem

| L | Present Values | |
| | Replace Now | Replace Next Year |
| (years) | ($) | ($) |
| --- | --- | --- |
| 1 | 24,541 | 24,114 |
| 2 | 21,191 | 20,895 |
| 3 | 19,640 | 19,405 |
| 5 | 17,851 | 17,687 |
| 7 | 16,755 | 16,633 |
| 10 | 15,712 | 15,631 |
| 12 | 15,251 | 15,188 |
| 15 | 14,768 | 14,724 |
| 20 | 14,287 | 14,261 |

SOURCES: Tables 4, 5, and 6, and Appendix I.

listed on the same page; its value is 25.00. This value is to be multiplied by $A = \$350$. Factor VI, on the same page, depends on $w = 0.10$ and $u = 1.0$ and may be found under the appropriate column and row. Its value is 1.2014, which is to be multiplied by $B = \$150$.

By multiplying and summing the products, the total for E—of replacement now ($n = 0$) with replacement each year thereafter ($L = 1$)—is $\$24,541$. This is listed in the second column of Table 7.

For the present worth of costs of replacement next year ($n = 1$) with annual replacement thereafter ($L = 1$), we need new values for these same computing factors. The values for factors I, II, and III are independent of L, and all of them can therefore be listed on the bottom half of the one page of Table 14, Appendix I. For this particular example, the values are 0.9803, 0.9332, and 0.2290, respectively. These values are to be multiplied by $A_1 + B_1 = \$500$, $-B_1 = -\$50$, and $C_0 = \$400$, respectively, which will give $E_1$, $E_2$, and $E_3$. The computing factors IV, V, and VI can be found in Table 15, Appendix I, for $L = 1$. Factor IV, which depends on $k = 0.9$ and $d = 0.22$, has a value of 7.4993; this is to be multiplied by $C = \$2000$. Factor V, which depends on $z = 0$, has a value of 24.0197; this is to be multiplied by $A = \$350$. Factor VI, which depends on $w = 0.10$ and $u = 1.00$, has a value of 1.1543; this is to be multiplied by $B = \$150$.

The sum of the six products is $24,114, which is to be found in the last column of Table 7.

The above process may now be repeated for L = 3 and L = 10. We show in Table 7 the results for several values of L. It will take the reader much more time to read through and understand the above steps than it will for him to work a problem through, once the procedure is understood. Actually, by arranging a work table with the dollar values at the head of each row and with the associated values of the computing factors recorded across the row in several columns, one column for each n and L combination, it is possible to perform all the recording and computing steps in but a few minutes.

The minimum-cost policy in this example is to delay replacement, since the column of costs under delayed replacement is cheaper than immediate replacement, no matter what is the contemplated life length, L, of the series of successor automobiles.

### 5.1.3 *How to Allow for Service Value*

Finally, in the indefinitely long service-period requirement, we consider also the revenue function. Using the automobile example, we shall imagine that we are providing a taxi service. We have an old used car, and we are to determine whether it is more profitable to replace now or to wait at least another year. The answer to this requires some estimates of the revenue-earning capabilities of the presently used car and also of the newly available cars, now and in the future. Equation (6), page 677—or Table 2, the bottom half of which is a tabular form of that equation—contains the variables about which estimates must be made, and it yields the present value of the revenue stream. By subtracting the present value of the cost stream from the present value of the revenue stream, we shall have the net present value of service, or present value of the profit stream. Estimates for the revenue characteristics of the present and future machines are presented in Table 8, and the paired computing factors are indicated in the lower part of Table 2.

We have estimated that the present car will yield revenue in the next year at the rate of $500 per year ($P_1$ = $500) and that this rate will decline 5 per cent ($s_1$ = 0.05) per year. The new car considered for immediate purchase will yield $1000 ($P$ = $1000) per year revenue in the first year, and this rate will decline at 10 per cent ($s$ = 0.10) per year. A *new* car *next* year will bring in $1050 per year in its first year of service. That is, the initial rate of revenue will rise each year by an amount equal to 10 per cent of the difference between the currently available initial rate and the upper-limiting rate ($P + Q$ = $1500).

TABLE 8. *Revenue characteristics of present and future automobiles*

Illustrative Problem

$500 = P_1$   (current annual rate of revenue of current item)
$1000 = P$   (initial annual rate of revenue of new item)
$500 = Q$   [equal to $(P + Q) - P$]*
.05 = $s_1$   (coefficient related to rate of change of annual revenue of current item)
.10 = $s$   (coefficient for rate at which annual revenue of new machine changes with age of machine)
.10 = $g$   (coefficient for rate at which $P + Q$ is approached)

---

*$P + Q$ = limit approached by initial rate of revenue (prices of services and technological changes in new machines) as time passes.

Three of these estimates, $P_1$, $P$, and $Q$, are the dollar annual rates of return, and three, $s_1$, $s$, and $g$, are the rates at which these dollar rates of revenue will change with time and age of the equipment. The present value of the revenue stream, $R$, is the sum of three products, each product consisting of two terms, a dollar income rate and a factor dependent on the rate of change of the income rate. These three factors are labeled VII, VIII, and IX.

Again, as in the previous section, these factor values must be obtained for the appropriate combinations of $n$ and $L$. The values of factors VII and VIII are listed in Table 15, Appendix I, where the values for $n = 0$ are on the top half of page 720 and values for $n = 1$ are on the bottom half. There is a separate page for each value of $L$. To be consistent with the detailed steps given in Sec. 5.1.2, these factors must first be obtained for the case of $n = 0$ and $L = 1$, and also for the case in which $n = 1$ and $L = 1$. In particular, the value for factor VII, which depends on $s = 0.10$, can be found in Table 15 on page 720; its value is 23.7899, which is to be multiplied by $P + Q = \$1500$. The value of factor VIII, which depends on $s = 0.10$ and $g = 0.10$, is found on the same page and, in this case, has a value of 7.1429. This must be multiplied by $-Q = -\$500$. Factor IX depends on $s_1 = 0.05$, but it just happens that factor IX does not in any way depend on $L$; hence it is listed in Table 14, Appendix I. In fact, for $n = 0$, the value of factor IX is always zero, regardless of the value of $s_1$. Factor IX is multiplied by $P_1$, but the product will be zero since the factor value is zero.

Summing the three products obtained by using factors VII, VIII, and IX gives a sum, $R$, of $32,126, and this is listed in the second column of Table 9,

TABLE 9. *Present values of revenue, cost, and net revenue as function of date of replacement and life cycles of new automobiles*

Illustrative Problem

| Life Cycle of New Cars, L (years) | R | E |
|---|---|---|
| | Replacement Now | |
| 1 | 32,126 | 24,541 |
| 3 | 28,923 | 19,640 |
| 5 | 26,184 | 17,851 |
| 7 | 23,835 | 16,755 |
| 10 | 20,913 | 15,712 |
| 15 | 17,267 | 14,768 |
| 20 | 14,702 | 14,287 |
| | Replacement Next Year | |
| 1 | 31,671 | 24,114 |
| 3 | 28,594 | 19,405 |
| 5 | 25,962 | 17,687 |
| 7 | 23,705 | 16,633 |
| 10 | 20,898 | 15,631 |
| 15 | 17,395 | 14,724 |
| 20 | 14,930 | 14,261 |

| Life Cycle of New Cars, L (years) | Net Worth | |
|---|---|---|
| | Replace Now | Replace Next Year |
| 1 | 7,585* | 7,557 |
| 3 | 9,283* | 9,189 |
| 5 | 8,333* | 8,275 |
| 7 | 7,080* | 7,072 |
| 10 | 5,201 | 5,267* |
| 15 | 2,499 | 2,671* |
| 20 | 415 | 669* |

SOURCES: Tables 4, 6, and 8, and Appendix I.
*Maximum values.

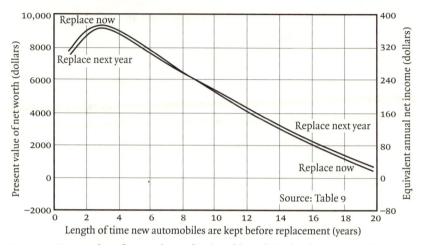

**FIG. 5.2.** *Present values of net worths as a function of date of initial replacement and of successive replacement life lengths*

opposite the value of L = 1, for replacement now. This is the present worth of the service stream.

For the present worth of the services with replacement next year (n = 1), the same factors, VII, VIII, and IX, are obtained from the bottom half of the same pages used in the preceding calculations. In this case the factor values are 22.8654, 6.2097, and 0.9563, respectively. These must be multiplied by their associated dollar-value terms (the proper pairings are shown in Table 2). The sum of these products is R = $31,671. This sum is listed in Table 9, second column, with L = 1, in the delayed replacement (n = 1) section.

It takes longer to read the above instructions than it does to perform the calculations. A convenient work table may easily be devised to facilitate the work so that only a few minutes are required.

The values of R computed for other values of L are also listed in Table 9 to illustrate the sensitivity of R to changes in L. By varying L, it is possible to change a positive value of R − E to a negative one. But the changes will be fairly smooth; hence only a few different values of L need to be tested in order to trace out a curve with adequate precision. The results for this problem are graphed in Fig. 5.2.

In this illustration immediate replacement is indicated. We can see that if we had arbitrarily *assumed* an economic life length of anything over about 8 years, the decision would have been to delay replacement. But we know now that, with this procedure, the optimum L is 3 years and that the replacement should be made now. This line of action will lead to larger profits than if we arbitrarily assumed a life of over 8 years.

It is true that in the example the increased profits realized by making the correct replacement decision is only very small, but this is merely a fortuitous consequence of the particular example. However, we see in the example that the projected life length of the new equipment is an important variable in its effect on the size of the expected present value of profits and on the decision to replace now or later. The present procedure enables us to test quickly and simply for the appropriate value of L and at the same time to make the correct replacement decision according to that optimal projected life length.

### 5.1.4 Summary

By nothing more than a series of simple multiplications, we can ascertain the minimum costs or maximum-profit service lives for a series of machines, even when none is possessed now. Similarly, when a machine is now possessed and its replacement is being considered, an answer is readily available. The variation in the present value of costs or profits implied by various replacement life lengths may be ascertained. The decision to replace now or later in the light of the effect on costs or profits can be made in conjunction with the best projected service life of the new machines, rather than with an arbitrary life length. This combination of speed, simplicity, and generality, hitherto not achieved in replacement-decision procedures, is one of the chief merits of the procedure recommended in this report.

## 5.2 Limited Period of Service

When the service is desired for only a relatively short future period, the appropriate computations are based on Eq. (9), page 678. We illustrate this situation with the following example.

Let us assume that we want to obtain automobile service for 20 years and that we now possess a car 6 years old. Should we replace it, and if so, when? We first make the necessary estimates of costs and their rates of change. These are listed in Table 10. Next, we refer to Table 3, page 689, which identifies and pairs the dollar values and the computing factors.

We obtain the value of each cost factor by reading the entries in Table 16 of Appendix II, on the page for $L_0 = 20$. The values for $n = 0$ and $n = 1$ (for $L_0 = 20$) are used. The first set for $n = 0$ (on the upper half of the page in Table 16) yields, when multiplied by the paired terms, the cost implicit in replacing now and using the replacement for the full 20 years. The second set, for $n = 1$, yields

TABLE 10. *Cost characteristics of currently used machine*

Limited Period of Service

$200 = B_1     [equal to $(A_1 + B_1) - A_1$]*
$500 = A_1     (current annual rate of operating and maintenance costs of incumbent item)
$1000 = C_0    (salvage value of currently used item)
$200 = B       [equal to $(A + B) - A$]†
$400 = A       (initial annual rate of operating and maintenance costs of new item now available)
$2000 = C      (purchase price of new items)
.02 = w_1      (coefficient of rate at which $A_1 + B_1$ is approached, because of deterioration)
.10 = d_1      (coefficient related to rate of decline of salvage value of current item)
.02 = w        (coefficient of rate at which operating and maintenance costs of any new item approach the limiting rate, because of deterioration)
1.00 = u       (coefficient related to rate at which B changes because of new technology and prices)
.10 = z        (coefficient related to rate at which initial operating and maintenance costs, A, fall as new items are developed)
.10 = d        (coefficient related to rate of decline of salvage value of new items)

---

*$A_1 + B_1$ = limiting rate for operating and maintenance costs of incumbent item.
†$A + B$ = limiting annual rate of operating maintenance costs.

the cost of replacing a year hence and using the replacement for the remaining 19 years. If the latter action is cheaper, do not replace now.[1]

In the current illustration, the values of E for $n = 0$ and $n = 1$ are $7809 for immediate replacement and $7460 if replacement is delayed a year.

The total time required to obtain the entries from Table 16 and obtain the final values of E was 4 minutes. The time could be reduced substantially for cer-

---

1. If immediate replacement is cheaper, it does not necessarily mean that immediate replacement is called for. It is conceivable that a 2- or 3-year delay will prove to be cheaper than a 1-year delay—and even cheaper than immediate replacement. In other words, the

tain classes of equipment by using tables with a smaller set of alternatives more appropriate to that class of equipment.

If a revenue value can be assigned to the service, we should maximize the present value of net profits rather than minimize costs. Equation (11) yields the present value of the revenue stream. It is the sum of three terms, each being a product of a dollar magnitude and a factor accounting for rates of change and converting to present values. The required forecasts are listed below:

$$P_1 = \$1000 \qquad\qquad s_1 = .05$$
$$P = \$1500 \qquad\qquad s = .05$$
$$Q = \$500 \qquad\qquad g = .05$$

Table 16 contains the values of the factors I, II, and III, by which $P_1$, $P$, and $Q$ are multiplied. Again we determine these values for $L_0 = 20$, for $n = 0$ and $n = 1$. Factor I associated with $P_1$ depends on $s_1$ and, in this case, has a value of 0.00 for $n = 0$ and a value of 0.95632 for $n = 1$. Factor II associated with $P$ depends on $s$ and has a value of 0.92745 for $n = 0$ and a value of 8.31814 for $n = 1$. Factor III associated with $Q$ depends on $s$ and $g$ and, for this case, has a value of 0.00 for $n = 0$ and 0.40568 for $n = 1$. By multiplying the factors by the appropriate terms and by adding, we obtain the present value of the revenue stream. The difference between this and the cost values gives the present worth of profits. Listed below are the values of R, E, and R − E for $n = 0$ and $n = 1$.[2]

|  Immediate Replacement | Delayed Replacement |
|---|---|
| ($n = 0$) | ($n = 1$) |
| R = $13,912 | R = $13,636 |
| E =    7,809 | E =    7,460 |
| R − E = $  6,103 | R − E = $  6,176 |

fact that immediate replacement is cheaper than delaying it 1 year does not necessarily mean that it is cheaper than a greater delay. However, it is extremely unlikely that that would be the case. So far, in all the test cases in which the present method has been used, no reversal has occurred. If an invention leading to a major and discrete change in costs or revenues is expected to become available in 2 or more years, a reversal is possible. But such developments, if suspected, can be given appropriate consideration separately. See Sec. 2.6, above.

2. The entire time required to ascertain factor values and record and compute final R's and E's in this example was 7 minutes. This excludes the time required to make the forecasts.

It can be seen that replacement should be delayed until next year, when the replacement decision should be posed again. The reason for reopening the question of replacement *next* year is to allow for the best action at that time in the event of changed conditions, i.e., erroneous forecasts today. Even if the decision was to replace immediately, the question should be reopened for the then 1-year-old equipment.

## CHAPTER 6
## SOME ISSUES COMMON TO ALL APPLICATIONS

### 6.1 Introduction

However neat and formally correct an analysis or recommended procedure may be, there inevitably remain difficulties attendant on its application. The present analysis is no exception. We will now present some of the side problems of application to show that the present method is pliable and not restricted in applicability.

Difficulties of application are usually caused by factors which cannot be generalized in such a form as to be treated explicitly as a variable in the problem. These difficulties must be treated as special aspects of each problem and must be handled with judgment and common sense; in other words, they must be left in the realm of difficulties that cannot be specifically defined independent of the context of the particular problem.

### 6.2 Service Valuation

Let us first consider the evaluation of services rendered. It was assumed in some of the preceding analyses that we could attach a monetary measure of value to the services of the machine. In many cases this is impossible. For example, the Air Force would have an impossible task if it tried to value its services. Where values cannot be attached to the services, the appropriate solution seems to be to omit them explicitly from the present calculations and to compute the costs of the operation. This is not a counsel of despair, nor is it of small value.

Decisions will be made in any event. Half the necessary information is not as helpful as all the information, but it is very useful and is better than none. Prices on a menu are of enormous importance and aid in the selection of dinners even in the absence of a numerical scale of satisfactions.

A few *obiter dicta* on the problem of ascertaining the military worth of equipment are submitted here. First, the utility aspects of Air Force equipment are not different from consumers' goods in the sense that their utility depends on what someone else has. Combat value of equipment clearly depends on the quality and quantity of the enemy's equipment. If the enemy improves his materiel, ours will perforce become less valuable. Secondly, even if we had a way of measuring the military worth, there would still remain the problem of aggregating values of different dates. (Where a monetary evaluation derived from a market place is permissible, the rate of interest will enable us to make inter-time comparisons by the discounting process. If the service is valued in other ways, no revaluation or aggregating by an interest rate is possible.)

## 6.3 What Rate of Interest?

A second question of application stems from the first one. What is the appropriate rate of interest to use in the time discounting process?

At this point it is very desirable to avoid becoming entangled in the complexities of investment theory. In particular, if the answer to be given to the above question were to be thoroughly justified, we should have to devote a long section to capital theory. We shall, instead, simply adopt the generalizations derivable from that theory. The discount rate to be used is the rate that reflects the relative value or availability of capital. This is the rate at which funds can be borrowed or loaned in the capital or lending market; and it will probably vary among persons and among institutions. But the rate that the investing unit must pay for borrowing funds or will receive for lending them, whatever that rate may be, is the rate to be used for discounting. This is the applicable principle, whether the unit has to borrow more funds to make the investment or whether it has the funds on hand.

If the interest rate which the unit has to pay in order to borrow funds is not the same as that which it can earn from alternative investments of available funds, the question of the appropriate discounting rate must be faced. The principle and the computations are relatively simple. Suppose the following situation existed: An investment under consideration required $10,000. Six thousand dollars are possessed, and the best alternative use of it would yield 4 per cent. To borrow $4000 would necessitate paying 8 per cent. The question is whether to use 4 per cent or 8 per cent to convert future receipts and outlays to present values. The answer to the question is to include interest and principal repayments on the $4000 loan in the expense stream and to discount the net-revenue stream at 4 per cent. This will give the present worth of the profit or net-revenue stream. However, this present worth is then dependent on the particular rate of loan repayment—the faster the repayment rate, the higher profit value. In general, it seems safe to conjecture that as long as the interest rate at which we borrow is greater than the available earning rate, the most rapid repayment possible will be the most economical.

It will be noticed that in the formulation we have used a constant (over time) rate of interest for the whole life of the contemplated replacement series. To do otherwise would have transformed a calculable problem into one for which no calculation system would have been satisfactorily simple. Fortunately for the Air Force, it seems correct to state that the borrowing and lending rates coincide; therefore, all the above problems arising from different rates are avoided.

What is the rate applicable to the Air Force? It is the rate which the Government must pay for its capital funds or the rate at which it could lend them.[1] Because the Air Force is part of the Government, and since the Government is a monetary and a taxing authority, it is not completely correct to treat the Government as an ordinary borrower in the capital market. At the present time it is, by its monetary authority, playing a major role in influencing the rate of interest at which it can borrow. Whatever the source of its capital may be, however, it must discount at a rate reflecting the relative scarcity of that capital, no matter how it obtains the capital. Even for money created by the Government and used for Air Force budgets, the foregone rates of return must be considered. That is, no matter how these funds were obtained—whether by taxation or by money creation—the Government would have to recognize a measure of capital scarcity. As a social agency it should use a rate which represents the alternative use value of the funds. This report uses 4 per cent; if some other rate were considered more appropriate, the attached computing tables would have to be altered. Sets of tables for other interest rates can be provided easily, since they are easily computed and printed by modern high-speed electronic computers.[2]

1. There is a possible exception to this rule. If the Government is able to utilize its funds in investments that are returning more than the rate of interest at which it can borrow, and if it does not continue to borrow until these two rates are brought to equality, there arises the problem of allocating funds over the various departments or available investments. In this case, the rate of discount should be varied until the set of investments which are profitable are just sufficient to use up all the capital funds at the same time that marginal internal rates of return are brought to equality with the discount rate. The effect of changing the rate of discount will be the selection of a different set of investments depending on the time shape of the revenues and costs. This is counsel of perfection and, for all practical purposes, is a prescription of action beyond necessary refinements. It is just as satisfactory to use the rate of discount which reflects the price of borrowing or the forsaken return from lending and then to seek larger or smaller budgets in the succeeding fiscal periods. The effect of this is to change slightly the set of selected investments in any given year, but the change will in all probability be extremely small. This is particularly so if we depart from ideals based on perfect foresight and face the realism of uncertain estimates and foresight.

2. The tables in Appendixes I and II were all computed with the International Business Machine's Card Programmed Calculator.

## 6.4  Effect of Uncertainty of Forecasts

Probably the most important source of error arises from the presence of uncertainty regarding the future. All the data entering into replacement decisions are forecasts. If these are wrong, a wrong decision may be indicated. No logically complete and consistent method exists which incorporates uncertainty; as a result, no matter how bad or how good an individual's method or logic may be, a successful outcome in any particular case will not verify the propriety of the decision-making method, nor will failure establish the stupidity of the decision maker. A decision proves to be either fortunate or unfortunate.

Efforts have been made and are continuing to be made by various interested people to derive a rationale of optimal behavior where uncertainty and incomplete information exist. So far, little success has been achieved. For example, the standard criterion for maximizing profits or present values is unambiguous and useful for decision-making only where uncertainty is absent, but if uncertainty prevails a choice must be made from a set of subjective outcome distributions. It now becomes a matter of choice among distributions—not among single values. For example, suppose that there is a choice between replacing now or replacing next year with a particular type of asset. Table 11 lists the possible values of R and E for each action, depending on alternative forecasts of the future.

This is very much like a game. The individual in this case must choose one of the replacement actions, and nature will choose which forecast is to materialize. If one of the forecasts can be accepted with confidence, the replacement decision becomes unambiguous. However, if there is a substantial amount of doubt associated with each forecast, one decision may still stand out, *provided* that its values of R − E exceed those of all the other decisions for the various forecasts. In the above example there is no dominance. Dominance or superiority can be tested only by computing R − E for the various forecasts.

Procedures for these computations are provided by the preceding analysis. An awareness of the various possible implications of the forecasts permits such factors as gains that are possibly large to be weighted against gains that are smaller but that are possibly surer. Thus, the propensities and predispositions to loss avoidance or to large-profit realizations can be directed more accurately into appropriate actions.

It should be clearly understood that the present analysis does not try to state and cannot state what predispositions and inclinations toward risks and chances of large gains or losses should dominate an individual's actions. Instead, it merely presents a consistent vehicle for the evaluation of consequences of alternative actions under various possible environments.

TABLE 11. *Values of R, E, and R − E for alternative forecasts and alternative actions*

| | Forecasts | | | | | |
| | A | | B | | C | |
| Replacement date | R | E | R | E | R | E |
| --- | --- | --- | --- | --- | --- | --- |
| Now (n = 0) | 60 | 40 | 50 | 40 | 40 | 40 |
| 1 year hence | 55 | 46 | 50 | 40 | 45 | 38 |
| 2 years hence | 50 | 44 | 50 | 43 | 45 | 33 |

| | A | B | C |
| | R − E | R − E | R − E |
| --- | --- | --- | --- |
| Now (n = 0) | 20 | 10 | 0 |
| 1 year hence | 9 | 10 | 7 |
| 2 years hence | 6 | 7 | 12 |

A common but fallacious method of attempting to allow for uncertainty in forecasts has been to use a higher rate of discount. Raising the discount rate assumes that uncertainty increases in the future at a constant relative rate from the same absolute level of uncertainty and that uncertainty is equally applicable to all the cost and revenue components. This is a very rare situation. It is far better to shade the forecasts themselves rather than to try to use an omnibus device that is certainly inappropriate and the effects of which can be given only ambiguous interpretations. Neither as a correction for uncertainty nor as a compensation for safety margins is the use of the rate of discount a satisfactory device. It is preferable to use bracketed or shaded forecasts, which are then discounted. If safety margins are desired, the differences between prognosticated values of R and E can be considered directly in the light of the degree of confidence attached to the several forecasts.

Another type of erroneous procedure should be pointed out. In some cases both immediate replacement and replacement a year later may yield equivalent R − E values. This would appear to indicate that it makes no difference whether replacement is made now or later. Therefore, it is tempting to conclude that it is better to wait a year before making replacement, since, at no extra cost, we remain free to seize upon any new developments. The flaw in this reasoning is the assumption that any new developments which occur will be such as to make it desirable to wait a year. It is certainly possible that the newly realized developments will, instead, be such as to have made earlier replacement more desirable.

This discussion of problems likely to arise in applications of the general method presented earlier has been conducted at the level of general principles. The statement of principles is specific enough so that in any particular case no real difficulty should arise from sources other than those of obtaining empirical data for forecasts. This forces us to observe that the task of obtaining estimates and predictions for insertion in the formulas given earlier is in itself a laborious task and will constitute the essential difficulty of applications. Emphasis must again be placed on the often-ignored fact that there is absolutely no way to avoid making these necessary estimates of the future. If we use a method which does not explicitly require them, we have, in fact, selected a formula which itself implicitly contains a set of forecasts of the future. The method presented here has reduced, as far as was possible, the set of implicit forecasts of the future. These remaining implicit forecasts are: (1) exponential functions and trends, (2) a constant rate of interest for discounting, (3) equal projected life lengths for the replacements in any given series of replacements, and (4) a given rate of maintenance expenditure not subject to optimization within the problem at hand.

## 6.5 Related Investment Decisions

Other affiliated and collateral problems have a bearing on the replacement decision. The rate of maintenance has been treated as a parameter, and no attempt has been made here to regard it as a variable which could be varied in such a manner as to optimize the replacement decision. Determination of optimum rates must await a practical method of evaluating effects of alternative maintenance rates on R and E. These are not detectable by logical analysis; instead, they require statistical data and experiments.

Another related problem is that of deciding whether or not to incur a repair expense consequent to a breakdown or impending breakdown. This is essentially a replacement problem and can be handled in the following manner: (1) by computing E (or R − E) for immediate replacement without repair; (2) by computing it, also, for repair now with replacement delayed for a year; and (3) by computing it for repair and replacement at the present time. The optimum action is that having the smallest E (or maximum R − E) value.

Two other problems not covered by this presentation are those of renewal rates and inventory sizes. The former concerns the time rate at which items subject to failure should be replaced with new items. This usually involves large numbers of similar items and requires elaborate probability considerations.

## 6.6 Applicability to Air Force Equipment

Air Force items pose special problems only in the case of combat equipment. The difficulties pertaining to construction of a value index for the services of military combat equipment again appear, as is the case almost everywhere in military problems. Nevertheless, the fact that we cannot construct a measurable or definable scale of service values does not remove the need to compare qualitative use-values with quantitative cost.

At worst, the suggested procedures will permit determination of least-cost avenues of expenditure for given rates and qualities of service. At best, they will permit evaluation of the wisdom of varying the rates of service (size of air forces). In the former case, if the rate at which services are to be provided in the future can be specified, it is for this service stream that costs can be minimized with respect to replacement dates. Here, a time-related monetary-valuation weighting element—e.g., the rate of discount—is applicable only to the cost stream. The interest rate cannot, in this case, be made a measure of time utility for services, and it is extremely important to avoid this possible misapplication to combat equipment service. Only by using some time-scale index of military worth, and thereby establishing comparability of services at future dates, would it be possible to obtain a single-dimension measure of a time-scaled rate of service.

On the cost side, even if military equipment has no salvage value derivable from a market place, we should incorporate alternative use-values. If even these are absent, then the salvage-value coefficient can be set at zero.

There are other difficulties. The value of combat equipment depends on its performance in war—or in war prevention—and this depends on the enemy's combat-equipment capabilities. An airplane will have high value if it outperforms the enemy's aircraft, but the same weapon will lose much of its value if the enemy produces a superior one. The values of our equipment and their services depend on the equipment of the enemy. Attempts to value military service are therefore inextricably dependent on knowledge of enemy capabilities. Only to the extent to which these are known can any types of valuations be placed on our own equipment.

One conclusion immediately becomes obvious. The rate of replacement will be dependent on the enemy's rate of progress in producing improved equipment. The way in which these replacement rates are intertwined is suggested here by the obsolescence rate factors. But this must be the topic of a separate study of the time-phasing of combat equipment.

A further consideration is the availability of funds. The technique developed here is applicable to a larger class of military equipment. Buildings, automobiles, trucks, and training planes are examples. It may be argued that despite the revealed economy in making replacements, none will be made because of unavailability of capital funds at a particular time. This does not mean that we should therefore ignore the problem; at worst, the case for replacement expenditures can be strengthened and, at best, when funds are available, they can be spent in the most economical directions if the formulas given here are employed.

## APPENDIXES
## TABLES OF COMPUTING FACTORS

The tables of computing factors are arranged to facilitate quick entry to the appropriate term. For guidance in matching computing factors to their appropriate dollar terms, reference should be made to Table 2 (reproduced in Appendix I) and to Table 3 (reproduced in Appendix II) in which the computing factors and dollar magnitudes are paired.

In each of the tables of computing factors, the variables whose values determine the particular entry points are listed horizontally (and vertically, where two variables affect the factor value). By entering the appropriate row and column, the relevant factor values will be obtained.

# APPENDIX I
## UNLIMITED PERIOD OF SERVICE

Table 14 lists the factor values for the unlimited, or infinite, period-of-service case.

TABLE 2. *Pairing of factors with cost or revenue magnitudes*

Unlimited Period of Service

| Computing factor and rate-of-change coefficients* | Rate of annual cost | Present value of costs |
|---|---|---|
| I | $(A_1 + B_1)$ | $E_1$ |
| II $(w_1)$ | $-B_1$ | $-E_2$ |
| III $(d_1)$ | $C_0$ | $E_3$ |
| IV $(k, d)$ | $C$ | $E_4$ |
| V $(z)$ | $A$ | $E_5$ |
| VI $(w, u)$ | $B$ | $E_6$ |
| Total | | $E$ |

| Computing factor and rate-of-change coefficients* | Rate of annual revenue | Present value of revenue |
|---|---|---|
| VII $(s)$ | $(P + Q)$ | $R_1$ |
| VIII $(s, g)$ | $-Q$ | $-R_2$ |
| IX $(s_1)$ | $P_1$ | $R_3$ |
| Total | | $R$ |

*All factors depend on the rate of interest, on $n$, and on $L$ and are given in Tables 14 and 15.

TABLE 14. *Computing factors for unlimited period of service*

Cost and Revenue Factors⋆ I, II, III, and IX

$$n = 0 \left\{ \begin{array}{l} \text{Factor} \\ \text{I} \\ \text{II} \\ \text{III} \\ \text{IX} \end{array} \right.$$

For $n = 0$, these factors always equal zero.

| | | Rate-of-change Coefficients,[†] Values for $w_1$, $d_1$, and $s_1$ | | | | | | |
|---|---|---|---|---|---|---|---|---|
| | Factor[††] | .0 (.0) | .02 (.02) | .05 (.05) | .10 (.10) | .22 (.20) | .40 (.33) | .70 (.50) |
| $n = 1$ | I ($r = .04$) | .9802[‡] | | | | | | |
| | II ($w_1$) | .9802 | .9706 | .9563 | .9331 | .8806 | .8090 | .7066 |
| | III ($d_1$) | .0392 | .0582 | .0861 | .1306 | .2289 | .3559 | .5229 |
| | IX ($s_1$) | .9802 | .9706 | .9563 | .9331 | .8806 | .8090 | .7066 |

⋆Factors independent of L.

[†]Corresponding annual percentage rates of change are in parentheses. For full explanation see Sec. 4.2.

[††]Parentheses contain variables of change on which factor values depend.

[‡]A constant independent of any variables of change.

TABLE 15. Computing factors for unlimited period of service

Cost Factors IV, V, and VI  L = 1

Rate-of-Change Coefficients* for d, z, and u

| n (=) Factor | k | .o (.o) | .02 (.02) | .05 (.05) | .10 (.10) | .22 (.20) | .40 (.33) | .70 (.50) |
|---|---|---|---|---|---|---|---|---|
| 0 IV (d, k) | 1.00 | 1.0000 | 1.4851 | 2.1950 | 3.3318 | 5.8389 | 9.0782 | 13.3353 |
| | .95 | 2.2251 | 2.6861 | 3.3604 | 4.4403 | 6.8221 | 9.8995 | 13.9437 |
| | .90 | 3.4503 | 3.8870 | 4.5258 | 5.5489 | 7.8053 | 10.7207 | 14.5521 |
| | .80 | 5.9006 | 6.2888 | 6.8567 | 7.7661 | 9.7718 | 12.3632 | 15.7689 |
| | .67 | 9.0861 | 9.4111 | 9.8867 | 10.6484 | 12.3281 | 14.4985 | 17.3507 |
| | .00 | 25.5033 | 25.5033 | 25.5033 | 25.5033 | 25.5033 | 25.5033 | 25.5033 |
| V (z) | .00 | 25.0000 | 16.7549 | 11.3893 | 7.5034 | 4.2815 | 3.1696 | 1.8747 |
| | u | | | | | | | |
| VI (w, u) | 1.00 | .0000 | .2466 | .6106 | 1.2014 | 2.5424 | 4.3675 | 6.9792 |
| | .99 | .0000 | .1981 | .4904 | .9649 | 2.0421 | 3.5080 | 5.6056 |
| | .97 | .0000 | .1421 | .3519 | .6924 | 1.4653 | 2.5172 | 4.0224 |
| | .95 | .0000 | .1108 | .2744 | .5399 | 1.1426 | 1.9628 | 3.1365 |
| | .90 | .0000 | .0714 | .1769 | .3482 | .7368 | 1.2658 | 2.0227 |
| | .80 | .0000 | .0418 | .1034 | .2036 | .4308 | .7401 | 1.1827 |
| | .70 | .0000 | .0295 | .0731 | .1438 | .3044 | .5230 | .8357 |
| | .50 | .0000 | .0186 | .0460 | .0906 | .1918 | .3295 | .5266 |

| IV (d, k) | k | | | | | | |
|---|---|---|---|---|---|---|---|
| | 1.00 | .9607 | 1.4269 | 2.1089 | 3.2011 | 5.6100 | 8.7222 | 12.8124 |
| | .95 | 2.1379 | 2.5807 | 3.2286 | 4.2662 | 6.5546 | 9.5113 | 13.3969 |
| | .90 | 3.3150 | 3.7346 | 4.3484 | 5.3313 | 7.4993 | 10.3003 | 13.9815 |
| | .80 | 5.6692 | 6.0422 | 6.5878 | 7.4615 | 9.3886 | 11.8785 | 15.1506 |
| | .67 | 8.7298 | 9.0421 | 9.4991 | 10.2308 | 11.8448 | 13.9300 | 16.6704 |
| | .00 | 24.5033 | 24.5033 | 24.5033 | 24.5033 | 24.5033 | 24.5033 | 24.5033 |

| V (z) | .00 | 24.0197 | 15.7747 | 10.4090 | 6.5231 | 3.3013 | 2.1893 | .8944 |
|---|---|---|---|---|---|---|---|---|

| VI (w, u) | u | | | | | | | |
|---|---|---|---|---|---|---|---|---|
| | 1.00 | .0000 | .2370 | .5867 | 1.1543 | 2.4428 | 4.1963 | 6.7055 |
| | .99 | .0000 | .1903 | .4712 | .9271 | 1.9620 | 3.3704 | 5.3858 |
| | .97 | .0000 | .1366 | .3381 | .6652 | 1.4078 | 2.4185 | 3.8646 |
| | .95 | .0000 | .1065 | .2636 | .5187 | 1.0978 | 1.8858 | 3.0135 |
| | .90 | .0000 | .0686 | .1700 | .3345 | .7079 | 1.2162 | 1.9434 |
| | .80 | .0000 | .0401 | .0994 | .1956 | .4139 | .7111 | 1.1364 |
| | .70 | .0000 | .0283 | .0702 | .1382 | .2925 | .5024 | .8029 |
| | .50 | .0000 | .0178 | .0442 | .0871 | .1843 | .3166 | .5060 |

(continued)

TABLE 15. (continued)

Rate-of-Change Coefficients* for d, z, and u

| n (=) | Factor | g | .0 (.0) | .02 (.02) | .05 (.05) | .10 (.10) | .22 (.20) | .40 (.33) | .70 (.50) |
|---|---|---|---|---|---|---|---|---|---|
| 0 | VII (s) | .00 | 25.0000 | 24.7533 | 24.3893 | 23.7985 | 22.4575 | 21.3170 | 18.0207 |
|   | VIII (s, g) | .00 | 25.0000 | 24.7533 | 24.3893 | 23.7985 | 22.4574 | 21.3170 | 18.0207 |
|   |   | .02 | 16.8327 | 16.6666 | 16.4216 | 16.0238 | 15.1208 | 14.3529 | 12.1335 |
|   |   | .05 | 11.3893 | 11.2769 | 11.1111 | 10.8419 | 10.2310 | 9.7114 | 8.2097 |
|   |   | .10 | 7.5034 | 7.4294 | 7.3201 | 7.1428 | 6.7403 | 6.3980 | 5.4087 |
|   |   | .22 | 4.2815 | 4.2393 | 4.1770 | 4.0758 | 3.8461 | 3.6508 | 3.0863 |
|   |   | .40 | 2.7538 | 2.7266 | 2.6865 | 2.6214 | 2.4737 | 2.3481 | 1.9850 |
|   |   | .70 | 1.8747 | 1.8562 | 1.8289 | 1.7846 | 1.6840 | 1.5985 | 1.3513 |
| 1 | VII (s) | .00 | 24.0197 | 23.7827 | 23.4330 | 22.8654 | 21.5769 | 20.4811 | 17.3141 |
|   | VIII (s, g) | .00 | 24.0197 | 23.7827 | 23.4330 | 22.8653 | 21.5769 | 20.4811 | 17.3141 |
|   |   | .02 | 15.8524 | 15.6960 | 15.4652 | 15.0906 | 14.2402 | 13.5171 | 11.4269 |
|   |   | .05 | 10.4090 | 10.3063 | 10.1547 | 9.9088 | 9.3504 | 8.8756 | 7.5031 |
|   |   | .10 | 6.5231 | 6.4588 | 6.3638 | 6.2097 | 5.8597 | 5.5622 | 4.7021 |
|   |   | .22 | 3.3013 | 3.2687 | 3.2206 | 3.1426 | 2.9655 | 2.8149 | 2.3796 |
|   |   | .40 | 1.7735 | 1.7560 | 1.7302 | 1.6883 | 1.5932 | 1.5122 | 1.2784 |
|   |   | .70 | .8944 | .8856 | .8726 | .8514 | .8034 | .7626 | .6447 |

*Corresponding annual percentage rates of change are in parentheses. For full explanation see Sec. 4.2.

# APPENDIX II
## LIMITED PERIOD OF SERVICE REQUIREMENT

Table 16 lists the factor values for the limited, or finite, period-of-service case. A separate page is given for each value of $L_0$, the length of the period of time for which the service is required. Values of $L_0$ are 5, 10, 15, 20, 25, 30, 50, and 100. For a given value of $L_0$, factors related to revenue values, labeled I, II, and III, are tabulated below. Factors IV, V, VI, VII, VIII, and IX, related to costs, are tabulated on pages 722–24.

TABLE 3. *Pairing of factors with cost and revenue magnitudes*

Limited Period of Service

| Computing factor and rate-of-change coefficients* | Rate of annual revenue | Present value of revenue |
|---|---|---|
| I $(s_1)$ | $P_1$ | $R_1$ |
| II $(s)$ | $P$ | $R_2$ |
| III $(s, g)$ | $Q$ | $R_3$ |
| Total | | $R$ |

| Computing factor and rate-of-change coefficients* | Rate of annual cost | Present value of costs |
|---|---|---|
| IV | $A_1$ | $E_1$ |
| V $(w_1)$ | $B_1$ | $E_2$ |
| VI $(z)$ | $A$ | $E_3$ |
| VII $(u, w)$ | $B$ | $E_4$ |
| VIII $(d_1)$ | $C_0$ | $E_5$ |
| IX $(d)$ | $C$ | $E_6$ |
| Total | | $E$ |

*All factors depend on $r$ and are given in Table 16.

TABLE 16. *Computing factors for limited period of service*

Cost Factors IV, VI, VII, VIII, and IX

$L_o = 5$

Rate-of-Change Coefficients* for $z$, $w$, $d_1$, and $d$.

| $n$ (=) | Factor | $u$ | .0 (.0) | .02 (.02) | .05 (.05) | .10 (.10) | .22 (.20) | .40 (.33) | .70 (.50) |
|---|---|---|---|---|---|---|---|---|---|
| 0 | IV† | .00 | .0000 | .0000 | .0000 | .0000 | .0000 | .0000 | .0000 |
| | V($w_1$) | .00 | .0000 | .0000 | .0000 | .0000 | .0000 | .0000 | .0000 |
| | VI($z$) | .00 | 4.5317 | 4.5317 | 4.5317 | 4.5317 | 4.5317 | 4.5317 | 4.5317 |
| | VII($w$, $u$)†‡ | .50 | .0000 | .2120 | .5053 | .9359 | 1.7337 | 2.5108 | 3.2137 |
| | VIII($d_1$) | .00 | .0000 | .0000 | .0000 | .0000 | .0000 | .0000 | .0000 |
| | IX($d$) | .00 | .1812 | .2591 | .3623 | .5034 | .7274 | .8891 | .9752 |
| 1 | IV† | .00 | .9802 | .9802 | .9802 | .9802 | .9802 | .9802 | .9802 |
| | V($w_1$) | .00 | .0000 | .0096 | .0239 | .0471 | .0996 | .1712 | .2736 |
| | VI($z$) | .00 | 3.5514 | 3.4811 | 3.3782 | 3.2135 | 2.8501 | 2.3806 | 1.7636 |
| | VII($w$, $u$) | 1.00 | .0000 | .2023 | .4814 | .8888 | 1.6340 | 2.3395 | 2.9401 |
| | | .99 | .0000 | .2003 | .4766 | .8799 | 1.6177 | 2.3161 | 2.9107 |
| | | .97 | .0000 | .1962 | .4669 | .8621 | 1.5850 | 2.2693 | 2.8519 |
| | | .95 | .0000 | .1922 | .4573 | .8443 | 1.5523 | 2.2225 | 2.7931 |
| | | .90 | .0000 | .1821 | .4332 | .7999 | 1.4706 | 2.1056 | 2.6461 |

| g | .0 (.0) | .02 (.02) | .05 (.05) | .10 (.10) | .22 (.20) | .40 (.33) | .70 (.50) |
|---|---|---|---|---|---|---|---|
| .80 | .0000 | .1618 | .3851 | .7110 | 1.3072 | 1.8716 | 2.3521 |
| .70 | .0000 | .1416 | .3370 | .6221 | 1.1438 | 1.6377 | 2.0580 |
| .50 | .0000 | .1011 | .2407 | .4444 | .8170 | 1.1697 | 1.4700 |

| | | .0 (.0) | .02 (.02) | .05 (.05) | .10 (.10) | .22 (.20) | .40 (.33) | .70 (.50) |
|---|---|---|---|---|---|---|---|---|
| VIII ($d_1$) | .00 | .0392 | .0582 | .0860 | .1306 | .2289 | .3559 | .5228 |
| IX (d) | .00 | .1420 | .2050 | .2904 | .4119 | .6211 | .7954 | .9110 |

## Revenue Factors I, II, and III

Rate-of-Change Coefficients* $s_1$ and s

| n (=) | Factor | g | .0 (.0) | .02 (.02) | .05 (.05) | .10 (.10) | .22 (.20) | .40 (.33) | .70 (.50) |
|---|---|---|---|---|---|---|---|---|---|
| 0 | I ($s_1$) | .00 | .0000 | .0000 | .0000 | .0000 | .0000 | .0000 | .0000 |
| | II (s) | .00 | 4.5317 | 4.3196 | 4.0263 | 3.5958 | 2.7979 | 2.0209 | 1.3179 |
| | III (g, s)** | .00 | .0000 | .0000 | .0000 | .0000 | .0000 | .0000 | .0000 |
| 1 | I ($s_1$) | .00 | .9802 | .9705 | .9563 | .9331 | .8805 | .8090 | .7066 |
| | II (s) | .00 | 3.5514 | 3.3491 | 3.0700 | 2.6626 | 1.9173 | 1.2118 | .6113 |
| | III (g, s) | .00 | .0000 | .0000 | .0000 | .0000 | .0000 | .0000 | .0000 |
| | | .02 | .0703 | .0663 | .0607 | .0527 | .0379 | .0239 | .0121 |

(continued)

TABLE 16. (continued)

$L_o = 5$

Rate-of-Change Coefficients* $s_1$ and $s$

| 1 Factor | $g$ | .0 (.0) | .02 (.02) | .05 (.05) | .10 (.10) | .22 (.20) | .40 (.33) | .70 (.50) |
|---|---|---|---|---|---|---|---|---|
| | .05 | .1732 | .1633 | .1497 | .1298 | .0935 | .0591 | .0298 |
| | .10 | .3379 | .3187 | .2921 | .2533 | .1824 | .1153 | .0581 |
| | .22 | .7013 | .6613 | .6062 | .5258 | .3786 | .2393 | .1207 |
| | .40 | 1.1708 | 1.1041 | 1.0121 | .8778 | .6321 | .3995 | .2015 |
| | .70 | 1.7878 | 1.6859 | 1.5455 | 1.3404 | .9652 | .6100 | .3077 |

*Corresponding annual percentage rates of change are in parentheses. For full explanation see Sec. 4.2.

†A constant independent of any rate-of-change coefficients and of any $L_o$.

‡Independent of $u$ for $n = 0$ only.

**A constant equal to o; independent of all values of $g$ and $s$ when $n = 0$.

724

# ANALYSIS PROCEDURES

Reprinted from *Records, Analysis, and Procedures*, ed. Walter L. Deemer (Randolph Field, Texas: Army Air Force School of Aviation Medicine, 1947), 445–509.

# CHAPTER TWENTY
## PRINCIPLES OF STATISTICAL ANALYSIS

## General Principles

The principles of research used in selecting the various analytical statistical procedures in the statistical analysis unit of the headquarters, AAF Training Command, are outlined in this chapter. These principles are not necessarily in every case the ones that dominated the conduct of statistical research throughout the war. However, they are now considered to be desirable ones and are dominant in all the present postwar statistical research of the aviation psychology program. Fundamentally, these are the analytical principles of modern statistical theory. The most explicit development and statements of these principles and their applications are in the writings of R. A. Fisher, Jerzy Neyman, and E. S. Pearson, among others.[1]

It is evident therefore that this chapter will not do more than restate briefly their more elaborate writings. The intent is that the reader who is already acquainted with the general elementary techniques of statistical research may be able thereby to interpret critically the statistical procedures of the aviation psychology program and, in particular, the statistical procedures of the statistical analysis unit which are presented in the following chapters.

When one designs an experiment or research project, he is setting up a procedure which will lead from observations of a limited set of data (sample) to inferences about a larger class of existence (population). These inferences (conclusions) are either certainly true (or false) or uncertain. In statistical work they

1. J. Neyman and E. S. Pearson, Contributions to the theory of testing statistical hypotheses, *Statistical Research Memoirs*, 1–2, 1936–1937.

J. Neyman, Basic ideas and some recent results on the theory of testing statistical hypotheses, *Journal of the Royal Statistical Society*, 105, Part IV, 1942, 292–327.

J. Neyman and E. S. Pearson, On the problem of the most efficient tests of statistical hypotheses, *Philosophical Transactions of the Royal Society of London*, 231, A, 289–337.

J. Neyman, Fiducial argument and the theory of confidence intervals, *Biometrika*, 32, 1941, 128–50. Contains bibliography on fiducial-confidence intervals.

R. A. Fisher, *The Design of Experiments*, London: Oliver and Boyd, 1937.

R. A. Fisher, *Statistical Methods for Research Workers*, London: Oliver and Boyd, 1936.

W. E. Deming and R. T. Birge, On the statistical theory of errors, *Review of Modern Physics*, 6, 119–61, with additional notes of 1937 and 1938. Washington, D.C.: Graduate School, USDA, 1934.

are usually uncertain. Although the experimenter cannot be certain that his inference is true, in a well-designed procedure he may know the degree of uncertainty of his inference, or, more precisely, he may know the risk he runs of drawing an incorrect inference, given certain conditions.

This degree of risk or uncertainty is expressed as a probability. It is not the particular conclusion in any particular study about which the probability statement is made. The "conclusion" is either right or wrong. However, the procedure of drawing inferences is such that wherever and whenever it is applied the probability of drawing correct inferences can be determined.

For example, if one wishes to draw a conclusion about the difference in average stanines of graduated students and of eliminated students, he could obtain an absolutely certain answer by computing the average stanine of all graduates and of all eliminated pilots. He will then know with certainty which average is higher for the two defined sets of students. He cannot be certain that his conclusions based on the observed data will be true for a population of students still to come into training.

Our experimenter could have taken, by means of a random-sampling process, a sample of the graduated students and eliminated students. By comparing these averages he could draw conclusions about relative stanines in the population sampled, but he could not be certain that his conclusion was correct. Actually, his obtained conclusion would be either correct or wrong. No amount of study of the available sample or rephrasing of the conclusion can change that fact. Nor can he even make any statement about the probability that the graduates have higher stanines than the eliminees (other than that he doesn't know!). All he knows is that he has used a sampling process and a set of statistics which will yield correct inferences with a given determinable probability, depending upon what actually is true.

In designing an experiment, the various properties of the experiment and the statistics used will depend upon the required degree of probability of correct inferences, given the possible alternatives. Unfortunately, the higher the desired probability, the more costly and elaborate must the experiment be. Nothing short of an absolutely comprehensive study of the entire population about which information is desired will permit a statement which will be certainly correct, except in the case of certain very unusual types of hypotheses whose sample areas are mutually exclusive.

## Specific Principles

In the preceding general discussion the procedure of the experimenter has been implicitly described. Explicitly, he (1) frames a statement which he seeks to test or at least for which he seeks corroborative evidence; (2) considers other statements alternative to this one; (3) specifies the risks which he is willing to take of drawing incorrect inferences; (4) obtains data by a sampling process; (5) analyzes the data by means of statistical procedure; and (6) draws a conclusion.

### A Priori Hypotheses

The statement or hypothesis framed by the examiner must be precise in that it clearly specifies the population from which samples are to be drawn and about which inferences will be made. Extreme care must be taken to insure that inferences are not applied to other populations. The design of the experiment also requires that all the sources of variation in the population be left free to influence the sample or else that they be rigidly controlled. If uncontrolled sources of variation are not included in the test of significance, the inferences will be inapplicable.[2]

The hypothesis must also specify the possible type of evidence that might be obtained, and it must specify the probability of the various events that can occur if the hypothesis is true. In the absence of this information, the evidence cannot be weighed for or against the hypothesis.

Even if the experimenter is merely seeking to estimate some parameter, e.g., mean or standard deviation, he must still go through the process of the preceding paragraph. *Parameter* here means the true value of a coefficient of the equation of a population, while *statistic* means the estimate of that parameter value derived from a sample.

### Alternative Hypotheses

It is not sufficient that the probability of samples (evidence) be specified under the particular hypothesis alone. Unless the probabilities of the various possible samples are known under other conditions, one is unable to weigh the alternatives. And if one is unable to weigh the alternatives on the basis of samples (evidence), he is unable to know what conclusions to draw regarding the hypothesis. For example, if an observed sample is very, very improbable under the hypothesis being tested but is even less probable under the alterna-

---

2. R. A. Fisher, *The Design of Experiments*, London: Oliver and Boyd, 1935.

tives or even impossible under some of the alternatives, one could not reject the tested hypothesis simply on the basis of the low probability under the tested hypothesis. Thus, in every case, an integral part of the statement of the hypothesis involves the admissible alternatives. In fact, the most useful theory for deriving procedures of drawing conclusions from samples is based on the ratio of the probabilities under the tested hypothesis and under the admissible alternatives. This criterion is called the likelihood ratio.

### Risk of Errors

Having specified the hypothesis and the alternatives, the experimenter must select the tolerable level of risk of incorrect conclusions. An incorrect inference can arise in either of two ways. His hypothesis may actually be correct, but on the basis of the sample's evidence he concludes that the hypothesis is incorrect. A second kind of error may arise when the hypothesis is wrong (one of the alternatives is true) but he nevertheless concludes that the hypothesis is true. The probabilities of these two types of error are measurable.

The probability that a statistical test, on the basis of the observed sample, will lead to a correct decision that the tested hypothesis should be rejected (since it is wrong) is known as the power of the test. Thus for any given tested hypothesis, the probability of rejecting the hypothesis is a function of the true situation. The probability of rejecting a given hypothesis is a function of the true hypothesis; this is known as the power function. The power of a test is affected by the difference between the tested and true hypothesis, the type of statistic used, and the number of independent observations. The larger the number of independent observations, the greater the power, i.e., the smaller the detectable difference between the true and tested hypothesis. Clearly, the probability of correctly rejecting a tested hypothesis will depend upon how wrong the hypothesis is. That is, the greater the difference between the true situation and the tested hypothesis the greater should be the probability of rejecting the tested hypothesis. That statistical test which has greatest probability of correctly leading to a rejection of a wrong hypothesis (something else is true) is called the most powerful test of the particular hypothesis with respect to the particular situation that is true. If the test is most powerful with respect to all possible alternative situations it is a uniformly most-powerful test. And if, in addition, a property of the test is that the probability of correctly rejecting the hypothesis is always greater than incorrectly rejecting it, the test is unbiased. Clearly, desired characteristics of a test are high power and lack of bias.

The first type of error may be controlled by insisting on relatively more improbable events before rejecting a hypothesis. However, if one insists on very improbable samples before rejecting the hypothesis, he is likely to fail frequently to reject the hypothesis when he should in fact reject it. In other words he may be too conservative and fail to abandon his wrong hypothesis. This too is an error; in fact it is the second type of error. Obviously then the experimenter must strike a balance between (1) too severely restricting the "hypothesis denying" evidence and thereby failing to abandon an incorrect hypothesis, and (2) too greatly enlarging the hypothesis-denying evidence and thereby abandoning the hypothesis too frequently when it is true and should not have been denied.

In terms of sampling procedure, the first type of error is easily controlled by arbitrarily selecting in advance the probability of the error of the first type and selecting a set of possible samples which have that given probability of being observed. Then whenever one of these samples is observed, one will reject the hypothesis. If the observed sample is not among this predetermined set of rejection samples, the hypothesis is accepted. In this manner the probability of the first type of error is controllable by simply increasing or decreasing the range of rejection samples. The problem of which set of possible samples to consider as rejection samples (i.e., which set of samples constitute rejection sample area) is solved by selecting that rejection sample area (of fixed probability of first type of error) which has the highest probability under the alternatives. That is, the ratio of the probability of correctly rejecting the tested hypothesis to the (fixed) probability of incorrectly rejecting the tested hypothesis is maximized by properly selecting a rejection area.

The probability of correctly rejecting the tested hypothesis is called the power of the statistical test. The greater this power, the better.

The power of a statistical test may be increased by increasing the size of the rejection sample area. But since this means increasing the probability of the first type of error—that of incorrectly rejecting a true hypothesis, this is not an efficient method. A better procedure is to select for the given type of statistic that fixed-size sample rejection area which has the greatest probability of detecting the important alternative which it is desired to detect if the tested hypothesis is actually false. For example, suppose the tested hypothesis is that the population of students at a particular school has a mean height of 6 feet 0 inches. If the alternatives that it is deemed important to detect, if the hypothesis is false, are those in which the mean heights are smaller, then a certain sample rejection area will be best. The alternative that it is desirable or important to detect if the tested hypothesis is false might instead have included both the taller and shorter mean heights; then, in this case the best rejection sample area will be different from the area for the preceding set of alternatives. Specifically in the case of the t test of means the first case would have used the lower tail of the t distribution as the rejection area, whereas the latter would have used areas from both the upper and the lower tail. This is true because when one of these alternatives is true, instead of the tested hypothesis, the sample space with the highest probability of containing a sample leading to rejection of the false tested hypothesis is the lower tail area. If the alternative admits of either lower or higher means, both tails constitute the sample space with highest probability of detecting the falsity of the tested hypothesis.

Another way to increase the power of a test is to increase the size of the sample. Except for the possibility of redesigning the experiment so as to obtain the maximum information possible, the number of observations must be increased if the power is to be increased.

### Extent of Evidence by Sampling

On the basis of considerations of the hypothesis being tested, the range of alternatives for which discrimination is desired, the seriousness of the two types of error, and the types of statistical tests available, the experimenter is able to determine the size of the sample needed. In general, the larger the sample the greater will be the power of the test, thus reducing the possibility of serious error. The confidence that can be placed in the final inference will be increased.

### Analysis of Sample Data

The experimenter then decides which statistical test is to be used for the purpose of testing his hypothesis. The following chapters present the various tests used in the psychological program, and they are there discussed in terms of their power, bias, etc.

### Nature of Conclusions and Inference

The experimenter after applying his test draws an inference. The sample result will have fallen in a region of rejection or acceptance. Following this rule, he will reject if the former area contains the sample and he will know the probability of being wrong if the hypothesis were actually true. He will not reject if it does not fall in the rejection area. And he knows the probability of falsely accepting if certain alternatives are true.

If the sample leads to a rejection of the tested hypothesis, the experimenter rejects the hypothesis. It is very important to notice that this does not state anything about the probability of the tested hypothesis. If a hypothesis is rejected at the so-called 0.01 probability level it does not mean that the probability is 0.99 that the hypothesis is wrong. The hypothesis is either wrong or right. All probabilities apply to the randomly drawn samples. It is the samples obtained which are deemed more or less probable. None of the tests of statistical hypotheses will tell what the probability of a hypothesis is, except in the very exceptional cases where the possible samples under the various alternatives are mutually exclusive.

But in any given case what sort of confidence can he have that his nonrejection conclusion is correct? For any given set of a priori probabilities for the alternative hypotheses, the probability of correctly rejecting the tested hypothesis is greater, the greater the power function. In general the greater the power of the test, the greater is the confidence that the resulting inference is correct.

As was noticed earlier, an increase in the power of a test can be obtained by increasing the size of the rejection sample area, but this will reduce the probability of correctly accepting the tested hypothesis if it is true. And conversely for reductions in the size of the rejection area. The optimum size is determinable only if one is interested in maximizing the probability of correct statements of either kind and if the a priori probabilities are known. Lacking the a priori probabilities, which is the usual situation, one must arbitrarily select some rejection area on the basis of the seriousness of committing the two types of error if some selected alternatives are true.

In general then, although we may conclude that the confidence to be placed in any one of all the possible inferences is increased as the power of the test increases, we cannot make such a generalization about the effect on the confidence in an inference as a function of the size of the rejection area. The confidence may be reduced or increased as the size of the rejection area varies, and no simple generalization is applicable.

### Confidence Interval

If one knows which particular type of error of inference is most certainly to be avoided and which type of correct inference is most desirable, a criterion for the determination of the size of the rejection area is available. If the experimenter is interested in estimating the value of some parameter (that is, if he does not have a hypothesis which he wants to test) he will draw his sample and from it obtain an estimate of the parameter. This estimate may be a specific value or a range which is intended to include the true value. This range is called a confidence interval. When one sets up a confidence interval for purposes of estimation, he is saying that the confidence interval will include the true value of the parameter being estimated. The method of determining this confidence interval is such that the probability of obtaining valid confidence intervals is $x$ (between zero and one). Valid here means that the range actually includes the value of the parameter. It is important to note that the probability refers to the probability of the method yielding correctly determined intervals and not to the probability that a particular interval actually includes the true value. That is, the method yields intervals, a certain proportion of which will be correct. But for any one interval it either does or does not include the true value.

### Criteria of Estimation

There are certain properties of an estimate which are desirable. Of course the most desirable is that the estimate always be exactly correct. This is a counsel of perfection which cannot be realized short of a complete count of all cases. That is, sampling procedures will never meet this criterion. Instead it may be desirable that the average (mean) of the estimated values be equal to the true value. Such a statistic (estimate) is an unbiased mean statistic. Such statistics are available; e.g., the arithmetic mean from random samples from normal populations are unbiased.

Another desirable feature is that the standard deviation of the unbiased estimate be as small as possible, i.e., the error of estimate be as small as possible. Statistics with this character are called least-variance estimates. The smaller the variance of estimate the greater is the probability of discrimination between a tested and a true hypothesis, i.e., the greater the power of the test.

Another criterion is that of maximum likelihood; this involves estimating as the parameter value that value which will maximize the probability of having drawn at random the sample that has actually been drawn. Thus, given the randomly drawn sample, the value of the parameter (e.g., mean and standard deviation of a normal population) which maximizes the probability of the observed sample is a maximum likelihood estimate.

Maximum likelihood estimates are in some cases unbiased and with least variance, but not always. For example, the usual arithmetic mean is a maximum likelihood as well as an unbiased, least-variance statistic. The estimate of the variance obtained by dividing the sum of squares about the sample mean by $N - 1$ is the unbiased estimate of the variance.

Its square root is, however, not an unbiased estimate of the standard deviation. The maximum-likelihood estimate of the standard deviation, however, does happen to be equal to the square root of the unbiased estimate of the variance. Even though this maximum-likelihood estimate is the least-variance estimate, it is biased in giving values that still are on the average too small, for samples of less than $N = 30$. As N gets larger, the bias becomes very small. The whole preceding discussion can be translated to confidence intervals by replacing most-powerful tests by narrowest interval and by replacing biased tests by biased intervals. This holds for parametric tests only. A parametric test or hypothesis is one which specifies the value of a parameter for a given function. For example, tests of means and standard deviation in the normal-distribution function are parametric. Tests of hypotheses about the type of distribution (e.g., a chi-square test of fit to a normal distribution) are non-parametric tests.[3]

3. A. Wald, On the Principles of Statistical Inference, South Bend: Notre Dame, 1942.

H. Scheffé, Statistical inference in the nonparametric case, Annals of Mathematical Statistics, 14, 1943, 305–32.

# CHAPTER TWENTY-ONE
## UNIVARIATE ANALYSIS

The general principles used in applying statistical procedures to tests of hypotheses have been outlined in the preceding chapter. The primary purpose of this chapter is a specification of the statistics and calculation procedures used for statistical analyses of psychological data in headquarters, Army Air Forces Training Command.

The procedure will be first to specify the statistics used to estimate the parameters of the univariate normal distribution. The confidence interval will then be given, followed by the equivalent test of a statistical hypothesis. Tests of the quality of two or more populations on the basis of random samples will be given next.

Bivariate population parameters, correlation and regression coefficients, will be dealt with in chapter 22. Their estimates, confidence intervals, and tests of significance will be specified. Multisample analysis of bivariate populations will be outlined *via* the analysis of covariance.

Multivariate analytical procedures (ch. 23) for the correlation and partial regression coefficients will be the last major topic, and will be followed by certain miscellaneous problems.

It must be emphasized that a proof of the reasons for the use of the particular estimates and tests is not given. References will be made to the literature where the detailed justification may be found. In general, as indicated in the preceding chapter, either the maximum-likelihood, or the unbiased, least-variance estimate is used. Confidence intervals are the least biased and narrowest available, or in terms of tests of hypotheses, the most-powerful, least-biased tests available are used.

It is not the purpose of these chapters to enable the reader to learn statistical procedures. Rather they are designed to reveal enough detail to one already versed in statistics so that (1) the particular statistical analyses may be thoroughly understood and evaluated, (2) an interested research worker may be able to restudy projects already completed, and (3) serve as a guide to future research workers in the statistical analysis unit.

The analysis of a single variable usually requires at least the following information: (*a*) type of frequency distribution from which sample was taken, (*b*) arithmetic mean of sample, (*c*) standard deviation of sample.

*Frequency Distributions*

The frequency distribution of scores was obtained by the tabulating section from punched cards. Figure 21.1 is a sample of a frequency distribution as received from that section. This sample is the actual distribution of the experimental group. The extreme left- and right-hand columns list the scores, while the frequency of the score is in column two, with the total number of cases indicated at the bottom of the column. A cumulative frequency is in the third column, cumulated from highest score to lowest. The meaning and use of the succeeding columns is given in chapter 19, where the method of obtaining sums of squares is given. From this tabulated listing, the distribution can be typed for final reporting.

Frequently a distribution is too detailed; group intervals are then used. In general, the distributions encountered in this program were normal, or apparently so. It is not known what relative weights were given to the various factors involved in originally reaching a decision to use a nine-point normal scale. However, it may be stated now that the scale was sufficiently precise for the purposes of the program. An interval of width of one-half standard deviation unit increased the standard error by 1 percent.[1] The restriction to just nine intervals meant that the cases more than 2.0 standard deviations from the mean would be treated as being only 2.0 from the mean, thus reducing the standard deviation. The net effect of both factors was to yield a stanine standard deviation of 1.96 as computed from the restricted distribution. Other general rules and considerations followed in grouping and reporting distributions are outlined in various statistical textbooks.[2]

Distributions were also obtained by hand tallying from score rosters. Tally sheet TCJ-3 (fig. 21.2) may be used to record the tallies. Tallies in which grouped intervals are used may be tallied on regular tablet paper ruled appro-

---

1. On the basis of grouping errors, Sheppard's correction yields

$$s_g^2 = \sigma^2 + \frac{w^2}{12} = \sigma^2 + \frac{\sigma^2}{48} = \sigma^2\left(1 + \frac{1}{48}\right) = \sigma^2(1.01)^2,$$

where $s_g$ is the standard deviation computed from a grouped population, $\sigma$ is the ungrouped standard deviation, and $w$ is the width of an interval and equals $\sigma/2$.

2. F. E. Croxton and D. J. Cowden, *Applied General Statistics*, New York: Prentice Hall, 1940.

H. M. Walker and W. F. Durost, *Statistical Tables—Their Structure and Use*, New York: Teachers College, Columbia University, 1936.

H. M. Walker, *Elementary Statistical Methods*, New York: Henry Holt, 1943.

**FIGURE 21.1.** *Tally sheet (13 March 45—job 0160—group XP—distribution of reported scores—all cases deck No. 2 Inst Com 1).*

|  |  |  |  |  |  |  |
|---|---|---|---|---|---|---|
|  | 17 |  |  |  |  | 17 |
|  | 17 |  |  |  |  | 17 |
|  | 23 |  |  |  |  | 23 |
|  | 90 |  |  |  |  | 90 |

|  | X | F | CF | FX | CFX | X |
|---|---|---|---|---|---|---|
| 9 | 23 | 2 | 2 | 46 | 46 | 23 |
|  | 22 | 3 | 5 | 66 | 112 | 22 |
|  | 21 | 4 | 9 | 84 | 196 | 21 |
|  | 20 | 20 | 29 | 400 | 596 | 20 |
|  | 19 | 19 | 48 | 361 | 957 | 19 |
| 8 | 18 | 60 | 108 | 1,080 | 2,037 | 18 |
| 7 | 17 | 75 | 183 | 1,275 | 3,312 | 17 |
|  | 16 | 86 | 269 | 1,376 | 4,688 | 16 |
| 6 | 15 | 132 | 401 | 1,980 | 6,668 | 15 |
|  | 14 | 148 | 549 | 2,072 | 8,740 | 14 |
| 5 | 13 | 151 | 700 | 1,963 | 10,703 | 13 |
|  | 12 | 107 | 807 | 1,284 | 11,987 | 12 |
| 4 | 11 | 107 | 914 | 1,177 | 13,164 | 11 |
|  | 10 | 105 | 1,019 | 1,050 | 14,214 | 10 |
| 3 | 9 | 79 | 1,098 | 711 | 14,925 | 9 |
|  | 8 | 73 | 1,171 | 584 | 15,509 | 8 |
| 2 | 7 | 47 | 1,218 | 329 | 15,838 | 7 |
|  | 6 | 42 | 1,260 | 252 | 16,090 | 6 |
|  | 5 | 15 | 1,275 | 75 | 16,165 | 5 |
| 1 | 4 |  | 1,275 |  | 16,165 | 4 |
|  | 3 |  | 1,275 |  | 16,165 | 3 |
|  | 2 |  | 1,275 |  | 16,165 | 2 |
|  | 1 |  | 1,275 |  | 16,165 | 1 |
|  |  | 1,275 | 1,275 | 16,165 | 16,165 |  |

**FIGURE 21.2.** *Tally sheet.*

Job No.____ Test_____ Month_____ Unit____ Battery_____ Tallied by_____

| | | | | | |
|---|---|---|---|---|---|
| 90 | | 60 | | 30 | |
| 89 | | 59 | | 29 | |
| 88 | | 58 | | 28 | |
| 87 | | 57 | | 27 | |
| 86 | | 56 | | 26 | |
| 85 | | 55 | | 25 | |
| 84 | | 54 | | 24 | |
| 83 | | 53 | | 23 | |
| 82 | | 52 | | 22 | |
| 81 | | 51 | | 21 | |
| 80 | | 50 | | 20 | |
| 79 | | 49 | | 19 | |
| 78 | | 48 | | 18 | |
| 77 | | 47 | | 17 | |
| 76 | | 46 | | 16 | |
| 75 | | 45 | | 15 | |
| 74 | | 44 | | 14 | |
| 73 | | 43 | | 13 | |
| 72 | | 42 | | 12 | |
| 71 | | 41 | | 11 | |
| 70 | | 40 | | 10 | |
| 69 | | 39 | | 9 | |
| 68 | | 38 | | 8 | |
| 67 | | 37 | | 7 | |
| 66 | | 36 | | 6 | |
| 65 | | 35 | | 5 | |
| 64 | | 34 | | 4 | |
| 63 | | 33 | | 3 | |
| 62 | | 32 | | 2 | |
| 61 | | 31 | | 1 | |
| | | | | 0 | |

N=_____ $\Sigma x$=_____ M=_____

priately, or the tally sheet TCJ-3 may be used by striking out the printed number and writing in the desired class intervals.

### Transformations of Distributions

Distributions may be altered by making nonlinear changes in the scale of the variate. In some cases the percentile method was employed in transforming the scale of the variate. A standard score with range from one to nine, mean of five, and standard deviation of two was universally employed in reporting scores and aptitude ratings. This score was called a stanine from standard nine. Since the SD was to be two, the percentile method required raw scores containing the lowest 4 percent of cases to be given standard scores of 1, the next 7 percent to be denoted 2, the next 12 percent to be 3, the next 17 percent to be 4, the middle 20 percent to be 5, and so on symmetrically through nine.

Where a normalized standard score had to be selected for a population on the basis of one sample, the frequencies were computed in the sample and the resulting standard-score intervals were used for future samples from the same population. Other methods are available, for example, plotting a cumulative frequency curve, smoothing it by free hand, and then using the curve to determine the intervals. In general, this latter method may provide better results when performed by an experienced analyst with some *a priori* knowledge. In view of the frequent nonexistence of *a priori* knowledge the former method was used almost exclusively.

### Standardization

If a distribution is already normal, the variable may be expressed in standard units by the formula

$$\text{Standard score} = \frac{k(X - \bar{X})}{s} + k',$$

where $X$ is the original raw-score value, $\bar{X}$ is the mean, $s$ is the observed standard deviation, $k$ is the desired standard deviation in the standardized distribution, and $k'$ is equal to the desired mean of the standardized score.

Thus for the psychomotor tests where a mean of 50 and standard deviation of 10 was wanted, $k$ was equal to 10 and $k'$ equal to 50; for two-hand coordination, with a raw-score mean of 440 and a standard deviation of 85, a raw score of 500 was transformed as follows:

$$\text{Standard Score} = \frac{10(500 - 440)}{85} + 50 = \frac{600}{85} + 50 = 57.1$$

*Single Sample Analysis*

*Arithmetic Mean.* The calculating machine procedures discussed in the following paragraphs are detailed enough only to indicate the methods used; i.e., one familiar with the Marchant calculator, model AC10M, will be able to perform the operation.

Sample arithmetic means are calculated in all cases by dividing the sum of the scores by the number of cases. The sum and the N, number of cases, are obtained either from the tabulating machines or from tally sheets. In the latter case the sum is obtained with a Marchant calculator. The score value of the interval is entered in the keyboard and the frequency of that interval is entered in the multiplier column of the machine. The product appears in the lower dial. This process is repeated for each interval without clearing the dial. The score value of the interval will change uniformly, depending upon the width of the interval. In all cases, the mid-value of the interval is the value entered. The cumulated frequency appears in the upper dial.

In fixing group intervals for handling psychological test data when all scores are integral, the true lower limit of the group is generally considered to be 0.5 of a unit below the integral lower limit actually written for the step. Thus, if an interval is written 15–19, and all scores of 15–19 are tallied on this interval, the true lower limit is 14.5. To find the mid-point, one-half of the group interval should be added to the true lower limit. In this case the mid-point would be 14.5 plus 2.5 = 17. As another example consider the case in which the intervals are written 0–9; 10–19; etc. The mid-point of the first interval is −0.5 plus 5.0 or 4.5; the mid-point of the second is 9.5 plus 5.0 or 14.5, etc.

In order to determine the confidence interval or to apply a test of significance to a mean, the standard deviation of the sample is required. Therefore, the tests of significance and the method of obtaining the confidence interval of the mean will be given after the standard deviation is specified.

*Standard Deviation.* Estimates (s) of the standard deviation ($\sigma$) are based on the maximum-likelihood method. (This gives the same estimate as that derived from the square root of the *expected variance* value.) In any event, for N over thirty the other various estimates of the standard deviation converge rapidly.

$$s = \sqrt{\frac{\Sigma x^2}{N - 1}}, \text{ where } x = X - \frac{\Sigma X}{N} = X - \bar{X}.$$

Computationally, the following formula is used:

$$s^2 = \frac{\Sigma X^2 - M_x \Sigma X}{N - 1}.$$

(See the next paragraph for the method of computing the sum of squares.) The sum of squares is entered into the keyboard of a Marchant and added into the middle dials. Then the mean is entered and negatively multiplied by the sum, from which the mean was originally computed. The difference appears in the middle dials. Enter N − 1 in the keyboard and divide. In the upper dials will appear the square of the standard deviation. The square root may be obtained from a table of square roots (Barlow's Tables) or by use of the square root divisors, obtained from Marchant Table No. 56; the entire operation from the sum of squares to the standard deviation is performed on the machine without writing down any intermediary values.

Basic data are supplied by the tabulating machines or from tally sheets. The only difference is that each involves a superficially different method of obtaining the sum of the squares of the scores. Sums of squares from the tabulating machines are obtained by a cumulative summation method performed by the punch-card tabulator. A complete description of the tabulating method is given in chapter 19 of this volume.

From a hand tally sheet the sums of squares may be obtained concurrently with the sums. In addition to the interval value which is entered on the right side of the keyboard, the square of the interval score values may be entered on the extreme left. Multiplying by the frequency will cumulate the sum of squares on the left side of the middle dials, with the sums on the right, and the frequencies in the upper dial.

### Tests of Statistical Hypotheses

The several tests of statistical hypotheses outlined below do not require any more complicated arithmetical computations than those used in the preceding sections. Special work sheets useful in routinizing the calculations of certain of the tests are presented with sample problems worked on them. In those cases in which no work sheets are used, straightforward application of the formulas is recommended.

*Test of Mean: Variance Known.* For the hypothesis that a sample was drawn from a normal population whose mean is μ, where the variance of the parent population is known, the most powerful test is based on the normally distributed statistic:

$$u = \frac{(\mu - \bar{x})}{\sigma/\sqrt{N}},$$

where μ is the population mean and σ is the population standard deviation.

The calculations are simple and straightforward. The probability of obtaining larger values of u from a population whose mean is μ can be found in the table of the normal integral.

*Test of Mean: Variance Unknown.* The hypothesis that a sample was drawn from a normal population with mean, μ, and with unknown variance may be tested as follows:

The variance is estimated from the sample and the statistic t is computed:

$$t = \frac{(\mu - \bar{x})}{s/\sqrt{N}} \text{ with } N - 1 \text{ degrees of freedom,}$$

where

$$s = \sqrt{\frac{\Sigma(x - \bar{x})^2}{N - 1}}$$

This is a Student's t test. This statistic is also frequently called the critical ratio. The calculations are straightforward.

It should be noted that this test of significance involves exactly the same distribution as does the confidence interval of the mean. A confidence interval is by definition that set and only that set of parameter values giving rise to sampling distributions whose acceptance areas include the observed sample value with preassigned probability. Thus if a parameter value $\mu_o$ is not included in the confidence interval of the sample, the hypothesis that $\mu = \mu_o$ must be rejected. Conversely for any given sample value, $\bar{x}$, the confidence interval will include all the parameter points, whose acceptance areas include the observed $\bar{x}$. Thus, if any sample point, $\bar{x}$, falls in the rejection area for the hypothesized $\mu_o$, the confidence interval based on the observed mean will not include $\mu_o$. This is true whether the variance is known or estimated from the sample. It is true for all types of rejection areas provided the confidence interval is based on a similar type of area. In general there is here a one-to-one correspondence between confidence intervals and the field of parameter points which are not rejected by the observed sample point.

The exact meaning of similar types of areas will not be discussed here. The whole field of relationship between properties of confidence intervals and properties of acceptance areas is in the developmental stage in the current literature. To what extent the preceding generalizations will be affected in the case of multivariate analysis, for example, remains to be seen.

*Confidence Interval of the Arithmetic Mean: Population Variance Unknown*

$$t = \frac{(\bar{x} - \mu)}{s/\sqrt{N}}$$

is distributed as Student's t with $N - 1$ degrees of freedom, where

$\bar{x}$ is the sample mean,
$\mu$ is the population mean, and
$s$ is the standard deviation calculated from the sample.

Another way of stating this is that the inequality

$$t_{0.99} < \frac{\sqrt{N}(\bar{x} - \mu)}{s} < t_{0.01}$$

is satisfied with probability 0.98 by randomly drawn samples from a normal population with mean, $\mu$. That is, for any normal population, the $t$ as computed by the ratio from the sample's standard deviation and mean will be larger than $t_{0.99}$ with probability of 0.99 and will be smaller than $t_{0.01}$ with probability $= 0.99$ (or larger than $t_{0.01}$ with probability 0.01). This is true for any value of the parameter, $\mu$. The probability of exceeding $t_{0.99}$ is 0.99; for $t_{0.01}$ it is 0.01. Thus the probability of satisfying the inequality is 0.98. Rearranging the inequality yields

$$x + \frac{s}{\sqrt{N}} t_{0.99} > \mu_o > x + \frac{s}{\sqrt{N}} t_{0.01}.$$

This means that such inequalities are satisfied with probability equal to 0.98. It must be noted that the sampling distribution here is composed of limits and not of true parameter values. The inequality states a method of setting limits for randomly drawn samples and the probability is 0.98 that the intervals will contain the population parameter. Roughly speaking, 98 percent of all possible limits will actually include the true parameter and 2 percent will not. But which 2 percent are wrong is not determinable. Each obtained interval is either wrong or right. All we know is that the method of determining the interval will give correct limits with probability 0.98. When one has drawn a sample and set up the interval he cannot say that the probability is 0.98 that the true value lies in that particular interval.

*Confidence Interval of Arithmetic Mean: Population Variance Known.* If the population variance is known, $s$ in the above inequality is replaced by $\sigma$ and $t_{0.99}$ and $t_{0.01}$ are replaced by normal deviates. Evaluating the inequality is a simple problem. A table of $t$ values is in Fisher and Yates, *Statistical Tables*.[3] An illustration of the determination of the 2 percent limits is as follows. In a randomly drawn sample of $N = 30$ from a normal population, the mean is 3.789 and the standard deviation is 0.060. $t_{0.99}$ and $t_{0.01}$ for N equals 30, is $\pm 2.750$ respectively since the $t$ table is symmetrical about $t_{0.50} = 0$. Thus,

$$3.789 + \frac{(0.060)(2.75)}{30} = 3.789 + 0.030 = 3.819,$$

$$3.789 + \frac{(0.060)(-2.75)}{30} = 3.789 - 0.030 = 3.759,$$

$$3.759 < \mu < 3.819.$$

This means that one can have as much confidence in the interval 3.759 to 3.819 covering the true value as he can in the belief that an event with probability 0.98 will occur in a certain given trial. That is, the probability is 0.98 that an interval so derived covers the parameter value and 0.02 that it does not cover it. Thus the confidence is in the interval being in the right place, not in the parameter lying in the particular given range, 3.759 to 3.819.

*Test of Standard Deviation.* To test whether an observed sample standard deviation, $s$, differs from some hypothesized standard deviation, $\sigma$, the chi-square test based on the ratio of variances (squares of standard deviations) is used. Let $s$ be the sample standard deviation, and $\sigma$ be the hypothetical value, then

3. R. A. Fisher and F. Yates, *Statistical Tables*, London: Oliver and Boyd, 1938, 26.

$$\chi^2 = \frac{(N-1)s^2}{\sigma_o^2},$$

with $N-1$ degrees of freedom. A chi-square table will indicate the probability of drawing at random samples with chi-square greater than that observed. For example, if in some test a chi-square of 47.96 is obtained from a sample of size $N = 31$, the probability of exceeding such value is 0.02 in randomly drawn samples of size 31; this tends to increase the evidence that the observed standard deviation was from a population with a larger standard deviation than that hypothesized. Conversely an observed chi-square of 16.31 would be so small that the probability of samples of size 31 yielding smaller values is only 0.02, suggesting that the true $\sigma$ is larger than $\sigma_o$. Since this is quite unlikely under the tested hypothesis and very much more probable under the alternative that the standard deviation, $\sigma$, is larger, there is here evidence that the true standard deviation is larger than that hypothesized.

The computations are simple and direct. No special form is needed once the standard deviation has been determined.

*Confidence Interval of Standard Deviation and Variance.*  Since the standard deviation is the positive square root of the variance, its confidence limits can be determined as the square root of the variance confidence limits.

Let $\sigma^2$ be the population variance. Then,

$$\frac{(N-1)s^2}{\sigma^2}$$

is distributed as chi-square for $N-1$ degrees of freedom. Another way of saying this is that the inequality

$$\chi^2_{0.99} < \frac{(N-1)s^2}{\sigma^2} < \chi^2_{0.01}$$

(where $\chi^2_{0.99}$ is the value of chi-square beyond which lies 99 percent of the curve and $\chi^2_{0.01}$ is the value beyond which lies 1 percent of the curve) is satisfied with probability 0.98 by chi squares from randomly drawn samples from a normal population. Rearranging the inequality yields:

$$\frac{\chi^2_{0.99}}{(N-1)s^2} < \frac{1}{\sigma^2} < \frac{\chi^2_{0.01}}{(N-1)s^2},$$

$$\frac{(N-1)s^2}{\chi^2_{0.99}} > \sigma^2 > \frac{(N-1)s^2}{\chi^2_{0.01}}.$$

This means that the limits obtained from randomly drawn samples from a normal population with variance $\sigma^2$, will satisfy the inequality with probability 0.98—which is exactly what a confidence interval does. This is true for any value of the parameter, $\sigma^2$.

Taking the square root of the limits for the variance yields the limits of the standard deviation and gives the confidence interval of a standard deviation.

An example: Using the same data as was used in the illustrative sample for the confidence interval of a mean, the obtained standard deviation is .060; N is 30. Using a 98 percent confidence interval yields the following inequality:

$$\frac{(30-1)(.060)^2}{14.256} > \sigma^2 > \frac{(30-1)(.060)^2}{49.588},$$
$$.00732 > \sigma^2 > .00210,$$
$$.086 > \sigma > .046.$$

*Two Samples—One Variable*

To test the hypothesis that two samples are from normal populations whose means are equal, when the variances of the populations are known and are known to be equal, the most powerful test is based on the statistic:

$$u = \frac{(\bar{x}_1 - \bar{x}_2)}{\sigma\sqrt{\dfrac{1}{N_1} + \dfrac{1}{N_2}}},$$

where $\sigma$ is the known standard deviation. $u$ is a normally distributed variate and the probability values associated with it can be read from the normal probability tables.

If the variance is unknown, but known to be equal in the two populations, or if a test of the equality of the variances indicates homogeneity, the most powerful test is based on the following statistic:

$$t = \frac{(\bar{x}_1 - \bar{x}_2)}{s\sqrt{\dfrac{1}{N_1} + \dfrac{1}{N_2}}},$$

where $s$ is the estimate of the standard deviation based on the pooled sum of squares, i.e.,

$$s = \sqrt{\frac{\sum_i^{N_1}(X_i - \bar{x}_1)^2 + \sum_i^{N_2}(X_i - \bar{x}_2)^2}{N_1 + N_2 - 2}}$$

The required calculations are straightforward and easily obtained from the samples. No special work sheet other than that used for the determination of standard deviations from distributions is needed. The distribution of $t$ is known as Student's $t$ and probabilities may be read from the $t$ table. One must not simply assume the variances to be equal, since a failure of the assumption will bias and weaken the test for equality of the means.

The F test is used to test the equality of the variances.

$$F = \frac{s_1^2}{s_2^2},$$

where $s_1^2$ is the larger variance and $s_2^2$ is the smaller variance. Since the larger variance is always in the numerator, and since the tables of F are given only for values of $F > 1$ from sampling fluctuations in which either the numerator or denominator can be larger, the tabled probability values for F are equal to only one-half the probability of the F ratio as here defined (the larger variance in the numerator). Thus, the probability given in the F table should be doubled when using this test.

If both the equality of the means and the equality of the variances are part of the hypothesis to be tested it would at first thought appear as though one might test for the equality of the variances by the preceding test, and then if this equality is indicated, to test for the equality of the means. However, another procedure will give a more powerful test of the hypothesis of the equality of the means and of the variances where the alternatives permit differences in the means and/or variances. Let

$$\lambda = \left(\frac{s_1}{s_0}\right)^{N_1}\left(\frac{s_2}{s_0}\right)^{N_2},$$

where $s_0$ is the standard deviation of the two samples pooled together and treated as one sample, $s_1$ and $s_2$ are the standard deviations of the two samples, and $N_1$ and $N_2$ are respective sample sizes. $\lambda$ varies from one to zero, one being the value if the means and the variances are exactly equal in the samples, and zero being the limiting value of differences between the means and between the variances.

Special tables are required in order to determine the probabilities associated with values of $\lambda$.[4] If the value of $\lambda$ is so small as to indicate a denial of the tested hypothesis that the two samples are from the same normal population, either the normal populations differ in their means and/or in their variances (or a very unusual set of samples was drawn).

The statistic $\lambda$ is a unique function of the product of (1) the value of F obtained in testing the equality of the means and (2) the F obtained in testing the equality of the variances in two sampled populations. The area of rejection of the tested hypothesis is not the same as the rejection areas resulting from an application of the separate tests to the means and to the variances. The $\lambda$ test (the consolidated test) is the more powerful.[5]

The $\lambda$ test given above is a special case of the $\lambda$ test applicable to k samples of 2 variables where the hypothesis to be tested is that the means, variances, and the covariances are all equal as sets. The alternatives allow for differences in any or all of the parameters of the populations.[6]

If the tested hypothesis is that two samples are from populations with equal means, and if the standard deviations are admitted or assumed to be different, the best test depends upon the relative sizes of the two standard deviations. In the event that equality of the standard deviations cannot be assumed, and if the standard deviations are not known, no completely satisfactory test is available. The following test may be applied, if the samples are large (over 100), and of the same size:

$$ u = \frac{(\bar{x}_1 - \bar{x}_2)}{\sqrt{\dfrac{s_1^2}{N_1} + \dfrac{s_2^2}{N_2}}}, $$

where u is distributed normally.

4. James G. Smith and Acheson J. Duncan, *Sampling Statistics and Applications*, New York: McGraw-Hill Book Co., 1945, 415.

J. Neyman and E. S. Pearson, On the problem of two samples, *Bulletin International de L'Academie Polonaise des Sciences et des Lettres, Series A; Sciences mathematiques*, 1930, 92, Tables II and III.

5. From a letter from S. S. Wilks, dated 20 March 1946.

6. E. S. Pearson and S. S. Wilks, Methods of statistical analysis appropriate for k samples of two variables, *Biometrika*, 25, 1933, 354–78.

If the two samples are not equal in size, the test is biased to the extent that the two standard deviations differ. In other words, with unequal sized samples, as the standard deviations of the two populations differ, the probability of rejecting the null hypothesis when it is true will vary widely in a fairly complicated manner. For example, if the larger sample is from the population with the smaller variance, the probability of rejecting the null hypothesis that the means are equal is an increasing function of the ratio of the larger to the smaller variance.[7]

### Test of Goodness of Fit

To test the hypothesis that a sample is drawn from a specified population, the chi-square test is most commonly used.

This test is so standardized and is presented in so many textbooks that it is deemed advisable here simply to indicate the books to which reference may be made.[8] The required calculations vary from method to method, depending upon what variant of the basic formula is used. In all cases, however, the computations will involve sums and sums of squares. The machine methods for computing these quantities are outlined in the first part of this chapter. It is particularly desirable to set up a calculation table for the chi-square test of goodness of fit. These are well standardized and examples are available in the references cited.

It is extremely dangerous to attempt to determine the goodness of fit by graphic methods which involve looking at a normal curve superimposed on a histogram. What is or is not obviously a good fit will vary between observers, and the same observers may form conflicting judgments at different times. No stable criterion of fit exists when a graphic technique is used.

Attention is called to a recent suggestion that the interval used in grouping

7. P. L. Hsu, Contribution to the theory of student's t test as applied to the problem of two samples, *Statistical Research Memoirs*, 2, 1938, 1–24.

8. F. E. Croxton and D. J. Cowden, *Applied General Statistics*, New York: Prentice Hall, 1940.

J. G. Smith and A. J. Duncan, *Elementary Statistics and Application*, 1, *Sampling Statistics and Application*, 2, New York: McGraw-Hill, 1945.

A. Wald, On the choice of the number of intervals in the application of the chi-square test, *Annals of Mathematical Statistics*, 13, 1942, 306–17.

C. M. Thompson, Table of percentage points of the $\chi^2$ distribution, *Biometrika*, 1941, 32, 187–89.

L. H. C. Tippett, *The Methods of Statistics*, London: William and Norgate, 1937.

T. L. Kelley, *Statistical Method*, New York: MacMillan Co., 1924.

M. G. Kendall, *The Advanced Theory of Statistics*, 1, London: Griffin and Co., 1942.

items for the distribution be of variable width so that the proportion of the cases falling in each category will be equal; in other words, some type of percentile interval is suggested. This technique is believed to present a more powerful chi-square test.[9]

### Multisample Analysis—One Variable

When more than two samples are to be tested for the homogeneity of means the F test is used if it can be assumed that the samples are from normal populations with equal variances. Non-normality, non-randomness of sampling, and inequality of the variance would all severally or jointly prevent the applicability of the F test, with the proviso that "minor" deviations from the specifications may permit the use of F test with but slightly reduced power. However, the extent of the permissible deviation and the extent of the reduction in power have not yet been satisfactorily determined. In the event of great non-normality, transformations may be tried, e.g., the logarithmic, square root, hyperbolic tangent, etc.

No discussion will be given here of the various complex analyses of variance that have been made in the aviation psychology program. The files of the section contain all the analyses. Several references are available.[10]

There will be presented, however, an outline of the techniques used in the aviation psychology program, in applying the analyses of variance.

*Equality of Variances.* Prior to applying the F test to the means, it is advisable to test the homogeneity of the within-sample variances. Where only two samples are to be tested, the F ratio is used. Details are given earlier in this chapter. If more than two samples are to be tested the $L_1$ test[11] may be used, where

---

9. A. Wald, loc. cit.

10. R. A. Fisher, *Statistical Methods for Research Workers*, London: Oliver and Boyd, 1936.

R. A. Fisher and F. Yates, *Statistical Tables*, London: Oliver and Boyd, 1938.

L. H. C. Tippett, *The Methods of Statistics*, London: William and Norgate, 1937.

H. Freeman, *Industrial Statistics*, New York: Wiley and Sons, 1942.

E. F. Lindquist, *Statistical Analysis in Educational Research*, Boston: Houghton Mifflin Co., 1940, corrected edition.

C. H. Goulden, *Methods of Statistical Analysis*, New York: J. Wiley & Sons, 1939.

P. C. Tang, The power function of the analysis of various tests with tables and illustration of their use, *Statistical Research Memoirs*, 2, 1938, 126–49.

G. W. Snedecor, *Statistical Methods*, Ames, Iowa: Iowa State College Press, 1946.

S. S. Wilks, *Mathematical Statistics*, Princeton: Princeton University Press, 1944.

11. P. P. N. Nayer, An investigation into the application of Neyman and Pearson's $L_1$ test, with tables of percentage limits, *Statistical Research Memoirs*, 1, 1936, 38–51.

$$L_1 = \Pi_i \left(\frac{N}{n_i}\right)^{n_i/N} \Pi_i \left(\frac{\theta_i}{\Sigma \theta_i}\right)^{n_i/N}$$

$$(i = 1 \ldots \ldots s)$$

$$(s = \text{number of samples})$$

$N = \Sigma n_i$, $\theta_i$ = sum of squares around the mean within $i_{th}$ sample, and $\Pi_i$ is an operator indicating a continued product over the subscript i, $(i = 1 \ldots s)$. A full description of the test and a work sheet can be found in R. W. B. Jackson, *Application of the Analysis of Variance and Covariance Method to Educational Problems*, page 40.[12] A sample of the worksheet used in the program with an illustrative problem is given in figure 21.3. In the illustration the samples are as follows:

| Sample | N | Mean | Standard deviation |
|---|---|---|---|
| 1 | 36 | 3.278 | 0.814 |
| 2 | 78 | 3.001 | .910 |
| 3 | 43 | 2.674 | .794 |
| 4 | 51 | 4.012 | .905 |
| 5 | 66 | 2.075 | .866 |

From this set of data, or from the data necessary to determine the above statistics, the work sheet may be filled in and the value of $L_1$ computed. The work sheet is self-explanatory. $L_1$ is distributed with two arguments: k, the number of samples, and $n_a$, the average number of degrees of freedom per sample. Reference to an $L_1$ table indicates nonsignificance at the 5-percent level.[13] Therefore, the equality of the means of the populations from which these five samples were drawn may be tested by the F test. For samples smaller than $N = 20$, the method of approximating the $L_1$ distribution fails badly; hence the test should not be used in those cases.

The work sheet used for the F test in the simple one-way analysis of variance is shown as figure 21.4 with illustrative data from the preceding example. In the extreme right-hand column are the sums of squares around the means within each sample. Each of these entries is obtained in the usual manner, i.e.,

12. Toronto: University of Toronto, 1940.
13. R. W. B. Jackson, op. cit.

**FIGURE 21.3.** Computing sheet for test of differences between variances.

$$L_1 = \Pi_s \left( \frac{N}{n_s} \right)^{n_s/N} \Pi_s \left( \frac{\theta_s}{\Sigma_s \theta_s} \right)^{n_s/N} \qquad N = \Sigma_s n_s$$

$$\log L_1 = \log N - \frac{1}{N} \Sigma_s n_s \log n_s + \frac{1}{N} \Sigma_s n_s \log \theta_s - \log (\Sigma_s \theta_s)$$

$k$ = Number of samples

$\theta_s$ = sum of squares within sth group.

$\frac{1}{k} \Sigma_s \,{}^{o}\!f_s = 53.8 \cong$ degrees of freedom in the individual samples.

| k group | ${}^{o}\!f_s$ | $n_s$ | $\log n_s$ | $\theta_s$ | $\log \theta_s$ | $n_s$ |
|---|---|---|---|---|---|---|
| 1 | 35 | 36 | 1.556303 | 23.196 | 1.365493 | 36 |
| 2 | 77 | 78 | 1.892095 | 63.766 | 1.804596 | 78 |
| 3 | 42 | 43 | 1.633468 | 26.490 | 1.423082 | 43 |
| 4 | 50 | 51 | 1.707570 | 49.540 | 1.694956 | 51 |
| 5 | 65 | 66 | 1.819544 | 48.725 | 1.687752 | 66 |
| 6 | | | | | | |
| 7 | | | | | | |
| 8 | | | | | | |
| 9 | | | | | | |
| 10 | | | | | | |
| 11 | | | | | | |
| 12 | | | | | | |
| 13 | | | | | | |
| 14 | | | | | | |
| 15 | | | | | | |
| Total | 269 | 274 | 481.025416 | 211,717 | 448.94315 | |
| | | | $\Sigma_s n_s \log n_s$ | | $\Sigma_s n_s \log \theta_s$ | |

$\log N = 2.437751$ $\qquad$ $1/N \, \Sigma_s n_s \log n_s = 1.755567$

$\frac{1}{N} \Sigma_s n_s \log \theta_s = 1.638479$ $\qquad$ $\log (\Sigma_s \theta_s) = 2.325755$

Total 1 = 4.076230 $\qquad$ Total 2 = 4.081322

Total 1 − total 2 = $\log L_1$ = −.005092 $\qquad$ $L_1$ = .988; P > .05

$\log L_1 = 9.994908-10$

Reference: R. W. B. Jackson, *Application of the Analysis of Variance and Covariance Method to Educational Problems*, 1940, 40.

**FIGURE 21.4.** *Analysis of variance.*

| Group | N | $\Sigma X$ | $\Sigma X^2$ | M | $\Sigma x^2$ |
|-------|-----|------|-------|-------|---------|
| A | 36 | 118 | 410 | 3.278 | 23.196 |
| B | 78 | 234 | 766 | 3.001 | 63.766 |
| C | 43 | 115 | 334 | 2.674 | 26.490 |
| D | 51 | 205 | 872 | 4.012 | 49.540 |
| E | 66 | 137 | 333 | 2.075 | 48.725 |
| | | | | | 211.717 |
| Total | 274 | 809 | 2,715 | 2.953 | 326.023 |

| | df | Sum of squares | Mean square |
|---------|-----|----------|-----------|
| Within | 269 | 211.717 | .7871 |
| Between | 4 | 114.306 | 28.5765 |
| Total | 273 | 326.023 | |

$$F = \frac{28.577}{.787} = 36.31 \qquad .01 > P$$

$$\sum_j^{n_i} X_i^2 - M_i \sum^{n_i} X_j$$

The sum of all these is the "within-sample sum of squares." In the example this sum is 211.717. The total sums of squares around the grand mean is obtained from the equation

$$\sum_i^s \sum_j^{n_i} X_{ij}^2 - M_x \sum_i^s \sum_j^{n_i} X_{ij}$$

In the example this total is 326.023. The between-means sums of squares from the formula yields 114.306 with 4 degrees of freedom. This sum of squares is the difference between the total- and the within-sample sums of squares. Usually it is easiest to compute the "between" directly and obtain the "within" by subtraction from the "total." The F ratio from the variance of the means and the variance within samples is 36.31 with 4 degrees and 269 degrees of freedom;

this has a probability less than .01 of being exceeded by random sampling from populations with equal means.

The individual within-sample sums of squares may be computed if the homogeneity of variances is to be tested. If these are known to be homogeneous, the "within sample" sum of squares should be obtained as the difference between the total- and the between-sample sums of squares.

## Correlation Statistics

*Product-Moment Correlation Coefficient*

In the psychological program the essential problem in the analysis of two variables was that of determining their statistical relationship. The product-moment correlation coefficient has been the primary statistic used for that purpose.

Calculations of product-moment correlation coefficients for sensibly continuous data have been largely based upon summary data (sums, sums of squares, and sums of cross products) derived from IBM punch cards and tabulating machines. From these summary data the coefficients are readily computed by means of formulas adapted to such data and modern calculating machines.

Figure 22.1 is a calculating form which may be used for the calculation of the correlation coefficient, the standard deviations, and the means in a bivariate problem. The form is completely self-explanatory. All required entries are obtained from the punch-card tabulating-machine summary reports.

A small number of correlation coefficients were obtained for bivariate problems only; most of the correlation coefficients were obtained from multivariate analyses. The procedure for computing the entries in a correlation matrix is presented in the chapter on multivariate analysis (ch. 23). It was usual, if tabulating machines were not used, to obtain the sums of first powers, squares, and products from calculating machines. Given the lists of paired scores on the two variables the procedure is as follows:

(*a*) The first variable ($x$) is entered in the keyboard and the second variable ($y$) is entered via the multiplier column. The products $xy$ will cumulate in the lower dial and the sums of $y$ will appear in the upper dials.

(*b*) The sum of the "$x$ squares" is obtained by entering $x$ in both the keyboard and the multiplier column.

(*c*) The sum of the "$y$ squares" is obtained by entering $y$ in both the keyboard and the multiplier column.

(*d*) N, the total number of cases, must be counted.

(*e*) The summary data are entered on the correlation-coefficient work form and the coefficient and related statistics are computed (see fig. 22.1).

Another computational method is preferable when the number of digits in each score is not over two and the number of cases is not large, say, less than 200:

**FIGURE 22.1.** Form for computing coefficient of correlation.

(1)    $N =$          (2)    $\dfrac{1}{N} =$          (3)    $\dfrac{1}{\sqrt{N}} =$

(4)    $\Sigma X =$

(5)    $\Sigma X^2 =$

(6)    $\Sigma XY =$

(7)    $\Sigma Y =$

(8)    $\Sigma Y^2 =$

(9)    $M_X = \dfrac{\Sigma X}{N} =$

(10)    $M_Y = \dfrac{\Sigma Y}{N} =$

(11)    $\Sigma x^2 = \Sigma X^2 - (\Sigma X)(M_X) =$

(12)    $\Sigma y^2 = \Sigma Y^2 - (\Sigma Y)(M_Y) =$

(13)    $\sqrt{\Sigma x^2} =$          (13a)    $s_X = (13)\left(\dfrac{1}{\sqrt{N-1}}\right) =$

(14)    $\sqrt{\Sigma y^2} =$          (14a)    $s_Y = (14)\left(\dfrac{1}{\sqrt{N-1}}\right) =$

(15)    $(\sqrt{\Sigma x^2})\,(\sqrt{\Sigma y^2}) =$

(16)    $r = \dfrac{\Sigma XY - \Sigma X(M_Y)}{(15)} =$

(a) The x variable is entered on the extreme right of the keyboard; the y variable is entered on the extreme left.

(b) The x and the y variables are entered in the multiplier column successively, properly shifting the carriage so that when entering the x variable in the multiplier the carriage is at the left, and when multiplying by the y variable the carriage is at the right.

(c) There will accumulate in the lower carriage dials three sums; to the left will be the sum of the $y^2$, to the extreme right will be the sum of the $x^2$, and in the middle will be twice the sum of the cross products, xy.

Care must be taken to position the carriage properly so that the decimal positions will be properly aligned. The Monroe model AA-1 calculator will automatically position its carriage and is therefore preferable for this particular operation. A Marchant can be easily aligned properly if the machine has a carriage position control row at the bottom of the keyboard. Experiments with a few simple problems will quickly acquaint a proficient machine operator with the proper technique.

*Tests of Statistical Hypotheses: Correlation Coefficient.* Exact distribution tables for the correlation coefficient are available for precise tests based on random samples from a normal bivariate population.[1]

If David's tables are not available, the Fisher z transformation provides a very good approximation to the exact distribution of correlation coefficients.[2] For samples with N of 50 or more, the z computed from

$$z = \tanh^{-1}r$$

can be treated as being normally distributed with variance equal to the reciprocal of $N - 3$. Thus if in a sample of 100, a correlation of .30 is observed, it may be tested for departure from a population correlation of .50 as follows:

$$(z_{.30} - z_{.50}) \sqrt{N - 3} = u,$$
$$(.31 - .55)(9.849) = 2.37.$$

More discrepant (from the $r = .30$ hypothesis) values may be observed with probability of .02, where the alternatives to the tested hypothesis admit of either higher or lower values of the correlation parameter.

The .98 confidence interval derived from the sample using the Fisher z transformation method yields

$$.507 > \rho > .07.$$

This upper limit is expected since the confidence coefficient is .98, while the significance level was .02.

Fisher's z transformation and the accompanying test are applicable to partial or multiple correlation coefficients. In these cases the variance of z is the reciprocal of $(N - 1 - k)$ where k is the number of constants in the linear regression surface. With an ordinary zero-order correlation coefficient, k would be 2, giving $(N - 3)$, as we saw in the preceding example. With a multiple correlation coefficient between a predicted value and 8 predictor variables, k is 9. For partial correlation coefficients k is equal to 2 plus the number of variables removed. Thus for $r_{12.34}$, k is 4, so that the variance is the reciprocal of $N - 5$.

---

1. F. N. David, *Tables of the Correlation Coefficient*, Cambridge: Cambridge University Press, 1938.

2. R. A. Fisher, *Statistical Methods for Research Workers*, London: Oliver and Boyd, 1936.

Neither of the above tests is applicable unless the sample is randomly drawn from a normal bivariate population. Frequently, however, the predicting variable may not be normally distributed. An exact test of the hypothesis that the correlation is zero is provided by the statistic:

$$t = \sqrt{\frac{r^2(N-2)}{1-r^2}},$$

where t is distributed as Student's t with $N-2$ degrees of freedom. The sub-population of samples which gives rise to this t distribution is composed of samples in which one of the variables is normally distributed and in which the observed sum of squares of the other variable is constant. This test applies only to the test of the hypothesis that the correlation is zero. It is identical with the t test for regression coefficients given below in this chapter, if the hypothesized regression coefficient is zero.

The same test, basically, can be used to test a sample multiple correlation coefficient against the hypothesis that the multiple correlation of the population is zero;

$$t = \sqrt{\frac{R^2(N-m-1)}{1-R^2}}$$

is distributed as Student's t with $N-m-1$ degrees of freedom; m is the number of predicting variables; only the predicted variable needs to be normally distributed, but the subpopulation of samples giving rise to this distribution is one in which the sum of squares (around the means) of the predicting variables is constant from sample to sample, though not necessarily from variable to variable.

*Confidence Interval of the Correlation Coefficient.* David's tables giving confidence limits based on the exact sampling distribution of correlation coefficients from a normal bivariate population provide data for setting a confidence interval. The confidence intervals based on equal tails are biased. However, the bias is negligible for all practical purposes.

In the absence of David's tables, the least biased and shortest intervals are provided by the Fisher z transformation, where

$$z = \left( \log \frac{(1+r)}{(1-r)} \right) = \tanh^{-1} r.$$

For random samples from a bivariate normal population with $\rho = \rho_0$, z is practically normally distributed with

$$\text{mean } (z) = z_0 + \frac{\rho_0}{2(N-1)} \text{ plus higher order terms,}$$

and

$$\sigma_z = \frac{1}{\sqrt{N-3}}.$$

It is permissible to neglect all except the first term for mean (z). Equal tail intervals will yield approximately the same intervals that are given in David's tables, especially for $N > 50$. Even for correlations near unity, the approximation is excellent for large samples. The .98 confidence interval is, in terms of z,

$$\frac{u_{0.99}}{\sqrt{N-3}} + z > z_0 > \frac{u_{0.01}}{\sqrt{N-3}} + z.$$

*Two or More Samples: Equality of Correlation Coefficients.* To test the hypothesis that two independent samples are from populations with the same correlation coefficient when the alternatives permit of either value being the larger, Fisher's z transformation is useful. For each sample, determine the z values, $z_1$ and $z_2$. Then $z_1 - z_2$ is approximately normally distributed with standard deviation equal to

$$\sqrt{\frac{1}{N_1 - 3} + \frac{1}{N_2 - 3}}.$$

The hypothesis that two (or more) independent samples are from populations with correlation coefficients all equal to $r_0$, where the alternatives admit any other values, may be tested by compounding the independent probabilities from each sample. The procedure of compounding probabilities is applicable more generally than to just the correlation coefficients. Any statistic whose distribution function is known may be treated by the following process. David's tables are needed in order that this test may be applied to the correlation coefficients, for it is from these tables that the probabilities of each observed correlation coefficient must be obtained. For large samples, Fisher's z transformation may be used to obtain the probabilities. Multiplying together the probabilities of the independent samples (based on the particular statistic studied—in this case the correlation coefficient) yields the compound probability of observing the whole set of independent samples. However, the probability of observing samples which will give compound probabilities smaller than that observed is not the compound probability itself, but some function of it. If the probabilities are continuous, the probability of observing smaller values than that obtained by compounding the independent probabilities may be obtained as follows:

(a) Obtain the sum of twice the natural logarithm of each independent probability; change the sign of the sum, making it plus (since the p's are less than 1, the *logs* are negative).

(b) Refer to a chi-square table and obtain the probability associated with the sum obtained in (a) with 2k degrees of freedom where k is the number of independent probabilities combined.

(c) The probability obtained from the chi-square table is the probability of obtaining a compound probability smaller than that observed.

It should be emphasized that the use of the chi-square table is not based on any inherent relationship between this test and the chi-square test in general; rather the mathematical formula for evaluating the desired probability is a summation which happens to correspond to a summation formula equivalent to the special case in which chi square has two degrees of freedom.[3]

This test is an exact test when the probabilities are continuous. However its power function is not known. Consequently it cannot be completely evaluated. Fisher recommends the test in his *Statistical Methods*, paragraph 21.1. The test was developed by K. Pearson.[4] The test has been recommended for use in those cases in which no standard or better test is available; such a case is that in which nothing useful is known about the independent samples except the probabilities associated with them. For this case, no other better test is known.

Another test for the equality of two or more independently obtained correlation coefficients has been suggested by Tippett.[5] The quantity

3. W. A. Wallis, Compounding probabilities from independent significance tests, *Econometrica*, 10, 1942, 229–48.

4. K. Pearson, On a method of determining whether a sample of size N supposed to have been drawn from a parent population having unknown probability integral has probably been drawn at random, *Biometrika*, 25, 1933, 379–410.

5. L. H. C. Tippett, op. cit.

$$\sum_{i=1}^{k} (z_i - \bar{z})^2 (N_i - 3),$$

where:

$i = (1, 2, \ldots k)$ samples,

$z_i$ is the Fisher-transformed $r_i$; $z_i = \tanh^{-1} r_i$,

$N_i$ is the number of cases in the ith sample,

$$\bar{z} = \sum_{i=1}^{k} z_i (N_i - 3) \Big/ \sum_{i=1}^{k} (N_i - 3),$$

is distributed approximately as chi-square with $k - 1$ degrees of freedom.

This test is not exact, because the distribution of $z$ is not exactly normal. However for large $N_i$ (over 50) the distribution is sufficiently close to give very close approximations to the true probability. If the sample sizes are small and there is a relatively large number of samples, the bias in estimating the mean $z$ may be serious; for such cases see Fisher, *Statistical Methods*, section 36.

Although the test of the equality of the correlation coefficients may indicate that they are all drawn from normal populations with equal correlation coefficients, there may still be grounds for doubting the wisdom of combining the observed correlations into one average. Fundamentally, the populations may differ in their other characteristics (means, standard deviations, regression coefficients) while they are alike only with respect to their correlation coefficients. For example, the variances of the variables may differ from population to population. Since the coefficient is a function of the variances in those cases where the standard errors of estimate are constant, the importance and meaning to be attached to correlation coefficients will be a function of the variance of the independent (predicting) variate. A group of tests for use in analyzing these and related questions is presented later in this chapter.

### Biserial Correlation Coefficient

*One Variable Dichotomized.* If one of the variables is measured by means of a dichotomous score, then the product-moment correlation coefficient computed in the usual fashion (with only two different values for the dichotomous variable) will yield a point biserial coefficient. In other words, one simply assigns numerical values to each of the two parts of the dichotomy (the exact values don't matter, but zero and one are convenient) and computes the product-moment correlation. The result will be a point biserial correlation coefficient.

If the two categories are quantitatively scored, e.g., yes-no, pass-fail, a simple substitution of 1 for "yes" or "pass" and 0 for "no" or "fail" will quantify the variable. If $X$ is the continuous variable, the formula for the correlation coefficient then becomes

$$r_{pt.\ bis} = \frac{N_t \Sigma X_u - N_u \Sigma X_t}{N_t \Sigma X_t^2 - (\Sigma X_t)(N_u N_l)},$$

where:

$N_t$ is the size of the sample; $N_t = N_u + N_l$,
$N_u$ is the number of cases in the upper class,
$N_l$ is the number of cases in the lower class,
$\Sigma X_u$ is the sum of the $X$ (continuous variable) for the upper class,
$\Sigma X_t$ is the sum of the $X$ (continuous variable) for the whole sample,
$\Sigma X_t^2$ is the sum of squares of the $X$ variate for the whole sample.

If instead, as this statistical unit did, one regards the dichotomized variable as inherently a normally distributed continuous variable upon which a dichotomy has been forced, an estimate of the correlation can be obtained from the continuous biserial correlation coefficient, which is defined as follows:

$$\frac{M_u - M_l}{s_x} (pq/z) = r_{bis}\ \text{(continuous biserial correlation coefficient)},$$

where:

$M_u$ is the mean of the continuously quantified variable of all cases in the upper class (the choice of which class is called the upper or lower is purely arbitrary and affects only the sign of the coefficient), and $M_l$ is the mean of the other class,
$s_x$ is the standard deviation of the continuous variable,
$p$ is the percentage of cases falling in the upper class,
$q = 1 - p$,
$z$ is the ordinate of a normal curve at the abscissal point which separates the area under the curve into two proportions, $p$ and $q$.

For example, for the biserial correlation coefficient between stanine and flying proficiency where flying proficiency is measured by graduation or elimina-

**FIGURE 22.2.** *Form for computing biserial r.*

| | 1 | 2 | 3 | 4 | 5 | 6 | 7 | 8 | 9 | 10 | 11 | 12 | 13 |
|---|---|---|---|---|---|---|---|---|---|---|---|---|---|
| Variable | $N_t$ | $M_t$ | $SD_t$ | $N_g$ | $N_e$ | $\dfrac{p_e}{(4)}$ $(1)$ | $pq$ | $z$ | $(z)\,(SD)$ $(8)\,(3)$ | $M_g$ | $M_e$ | $M_g - M_e$ $(10) - (11)$ | $r$ $\dfrac{(12)\,(7)}{(9)}$ |
| Pilot stanine | 961 | 4.015 | 1.999 | 228 | 733 | 0.237 | 181 | 0.309 | 0.618 | 5.693 | 3.492 | 2.201 | 0.645 |

tion, the mean stanine for the graduated group is $M_u$ and for the eliminated group, $M_1$. $pq/z$ may be obtained from tables.[6]

The work form used in computing continuous biserial correlation coefficients is in figure 22.2. A sample problem is inserted.

If a point biserial were computed from a bivariate population in which both variables were normally distributed, but one was reported as a dichotomy, the following equation would relate the point to the continuous biserial correlation coefficient:

$$(\text{continuous } r) = (\text{point } r)(\sqrt{pq}/z)$$

The continuous is always numerically larger than the point biserial. It should be noted that the continuous biserial is an estimate of the product-moment correlation under the assumption of normality and continuity.

The standard deviation of the sampling distribution of a biserial correlation coefficient is approximately

$$S_{r_{bis}} = \frac{(\sqrt{pq}/z) - \rho^2}{\sqrt{N}}$$

The sampling distribution function of the continuous biserial coefficient is not known. In the absence of knowledge of the distribution function, sampling limits of three standard deviations may be used as confidence intervals with assurance that the interval is at least a 99 percent confidence interval if one grants the Camp-Meidel assumptions.[7] The interval may be biased, and it certainly is not the narrowest possible. To test the hypothesis that the bivariate population

6. T. L. Kelley, *Kelley Statistical Tables*, New York: Macmillan, 1938.
7. H. L. Rietz, *Mathematical Statistics*, Chicago: Open Court Publishing Co., 1927.

from which the sample was drawn has a zero correlation coefficient, the three-sigma deviation around a correlation of zero was used. This test is not exact, and its power function is not known.

*Bivariate Analysis: Double Dichotomy.* Tetrachoric correlation: Where the population is a normal bivariate but the scores on both variables are reported only in dichotomized form, the tetrachoric correlation coefficient may be used as an estimate of the sample product-moment correlation coefficient. For computing the tetrachoric, tables are available.[8]

It should be noted that the value of the tetrachoric coefficient is relatively invariant to variations in location of the dichotomizing cut-off points. Thus for a given bivariate normal correlation surface, the tetrachoric coefficient is relatively insensitive to the location of the planes which cut the surface into four parts. The standard error, on the other hand, is a function of the split. The closer the split is to the mean value the smaller is the standard error.

Significance tests of the tetrachoric coefficient were based on the three-sigma deviation level where the standard deviation of the sampling distribution of the tetrachoric coefficient, when the population correlation is zero, is

$$\frac{\sqrt{pqp'q'}}{zz'\sqrt{N}},$$

where:

$p + q = 1$ and $p$ and $q$ are proportions in the two classes of the first variable,

$p' + q' = 1$ and $p'$ and $q'$ are the proportions in the two classes or the second variable,

$z$ and $z'$ are the ordinates of the normal curve corresponding to $p$ and $p'$,

$N$ is the total number of cases.

This standard error is applicable only for tests of the hypothesis that the population correlation is zero. For other values, a more complete formula is needed.[9]

8. L. Chesire, M. Saffir, and L. Thurstone, *Computing Diagrams for the Tetrachoric Correlation Coefficient,* Chicago: University of Chicago Bookstore, 1943.

9. C. C. Peters and W. R. Van Voorhis, *Statistical Procedures and Their Mathematical Bases,* New York: McGraw-Hill, 1940.

*Chi Square: Tests of Independence.* A measure of the relationship between two truly dichotomous variables can be obtained from chi square. In the $2 \times 2$ table below, chi square may be obtained as follows:

| | | Variable 1 | | |
|---|---|---|---|---|
| | | Yes | No | |
| Variable 2 | Yes | $a$ | $b$ | $a+b$ |
| | No | $c$ | $d$ | $c+d$ |
| | | $a+c$ | $b+d$ | $N$ |

$$\text{Chi square} = \frac{(|ad - bc|)^2 (N)}{(a + c)(b + d)(a + b)(c + d)},$$

with one degree of freedom, provided the hypothetical frequencies in the cells are large, at least as large as 5. For small hypothetical frequencies the quantity will not be distributed as chi square with satisfactory closeness. Modification may be introduced which will produce a satisfactory approximation for the cases of 1 degree of freedom:

$$\text{Chi square} = \frac{(|ad - bc| - N/2)^2(N)}{(a + c)(b + d)(a + b)(c + d)}.$$

This uses the Yates' correction which involves reducing by one-half a unit the absolute difference between observed and hypothetical frequencies.[10]

The table above was called a $2 \times 2$ table because each of the variables was categorized into 2 classes. A $2 \times n$ table is one in which one of the variables is categorized into 2 classes while the other is categorized into $n$ classes. In general, an $i \times j$ table has the two variables in $i$ and $j$ classes.

No special work form was used for the $2 \times 2$ tables for computing chi square. A straightforward application of the formula above was used in all cases, even for large frequencies in the cells.

10. F. Yates, Contingency tables involving small numbers and the $\chi^2$ test, *Supp. Jour. Roy. Statist. Soc.*, 1934, 217.

For the 2 × k tables, a computational formula known as the Brandt and Snedecor method was used.[11]

$$\text{Chi square} = \frac{1}{pq} \sum_{i=1}^{k} ((a_i p_i) - n\bar{p})$$

with $k - 1$ degrees of freedom where:

$i = 1, 2, \ldots k$ categories;

$a_i$ is the frequency in category 1 of variable 1 and in category $i$ of variable 2 (which has k categories);

$b_i$ is the frequency in category 2 of variable 1 and category $i$ of variable 2;

$p_i = a_i/(a_i + b_i)$;

$\bar{p} = n_a/(n_a + n_b), \; n_a = \sum_{i=1}^{k} a_i, \; n_b = \sum_{i=1}^{k} b_i$;

$\bar{q} = (1 - p)$.

The interpretation to be placed upon the chi-square test is a function of both N and k. In a 2 × 2 table, with one degree of freedom, the probability of observing frequencies as improbable as those observed or even more improbable (with the marginal frequencies invariant), if there is no relationship between the two variables (if they are independent), may be obtained from the chi-square probability integral for one degree of freedom.

*Phi coefficient.* For noncontinuous bivariate populations which have been dichotomized in a 2 × 2 distribution the phi coefficient may be computed. The phi coefficient is defined as

$$\sqrt{\chi^2/N}.$$

*Mixed Intercorrelation Matrix: Product Moment, Tetrachoric, Phi, Chi Square.* In an intercorrelation matrix consisting of continuous variables and dichotomous variables, the product-moment correlation, the point biserial, and the phi coefficients should be used; the latter expresses the dependence in the 2 × 2 dichotomies, and the point biserial expresses the relationship between the continuous and dichotomous variables.

However, if the dichotomized variables are truly continuous and will later be

---

11. G. W. Snedecor and M. R. Irwin, *Iowa State College Journal of Science*, 8, 1933, 75.
G. W. Snedecor, *Statistical Methods*, Ames, Iowa: Iowa State College Press, 1936.

recorded as continuous variables, the tetrachoric coefficient should be used to express the correlation in the $2 \times 2$ dichotomies; similarly, the continuous biserial should be used to express the relationship between the continuous and the dichotomized continuous variable.

Of the three measures, tetrachoric, chi square, and phi, the psychological program had least occasion to use the phi coefficient. The phi coefficient was widely used in item analysis, and was a basic item validity statistic in the psychological research units. For a full discussion of the reasons and results see Report No. 5, *Printed Classification Tests*. See also Report No. 6, *The AAF Qualifying Examination*, for a discussion of other types of item statistics.

## Regression Statistics

*Regression Coefficients*

For the bivariate case, the regression coefficient, $b$, of $Y$ on $X$ in the linear regression equation, $Y = a + bX$, can be quickly and easily computed from the formula

$$b = \frac{\Sigma xy}{\Sigma x^2},$$

where $x$ and $y$ are deviations around the mean.

In terms of observed values of $X$ and $Y$, the formula may be written

$$b = \frac{\Sigma XY - M_x \Sigma Y}{\Sigma X^2 - M_x \Sigma X}.$$

This is the computation formula used for computing the regression coefficient in the simple bivariate case. On the correlation work sheet shown as figure 22.1, item (16) multiplied by item [(14)/(13)] will yield the regression coefficient.

Only on rare occasions was the regression coefficient required in the simple bivariate case. The usual situation facing the aviation psychology program was that of computing the correlation coefficients for each pair of a set of many variables. From the resulting intercorrelation matrix (giving zero-order correlation coefficients) it is a simple task to compute the zero-order regression coefficients if they are desired. The following formula is standard:

$$b_{yx} = r_{yx} \frac{\sigma_y}{\sigma_x}.$$

*Regression Coefficients: Tests of Hypotheses.*  The hypothesis that the sample was drawn from a normal bivariate population with a regression of b may be tested by the Student t statistic:

$$t = \frac{(b - B)\sqrt{\Sigma(X - \bar{x})^2}}{s},$$

with $N - 2$ degrees of freedom, where s is the standard error of estimate, i.e.,

$$\sqrt{\frac{\Sigma(Y - a - bX)^2}{N - 2}}.$$

When testing for $B = 0$, the test is identical with the test of a zero-order correlation coefficient for departure from 0.

*Confidence Interval of the Regression Coefficient.*  The confidence interval for the regression coefficient may be obtained from the t distribution since

$$t = \frac{(b - B)\sqrt{\Sigma(X - \bar{x})^2}}{s},$$

with $N - 2$ degrees of freedom, where s is the unbiased standard error of estimate; i.e., it is

$$\sqrt{\frac{\Sigma(Y - a - bX)^2}{N - 2}}.$$

It must be emphasized that the sample values of b which give rise to the t distribution are from the samples in which there is no variation in the x values from sample to sample. It is not clear to the writer whether it is the frequencies of each of the X values that are unchanged, or whether the variance of the X values is all that must be invariant. Various statements in the literature are incomplete and somewhat inconsistent. This appears to be a severe restriction to place on the sampling distribution; however without such a restriction, the variance of the x variable in the sample will enter into the distribution. The population variance is usually unknown, hence the necessity of the restriction.

Under the above restriction, then, the confidence interval is constructed from the following inequality:

$$b - \frac{st_\alpha}{\sqrt{\Sigma(X - \bar{x})^2}} \leq \beta \leq b + \frac{st_\alpha}{\sqrt{\Sigma(X - \bar{x})^2}}$$

since $t_\alpha = -t_{1-\alpha}$ where the confidence interval is for the $1 - 2\alpha$ probability level. The confidence interval is exact, and is the narrowest unbiased equal-tailed interval.

### Multisample Analysis

The hypothesis that k randomly drawn independent samples are from k bivariate populations with equal regression coefficients may be tested by means of the analysis of covariance technique. Where y and x are the two variables, and the regression coefficients are those of variable y on x, only variable y need be normally distributed and homoscedastic (i.e., of equal variance in all the x arrays). It is appropriate to recall what was said above about tests of homogeneity of correlation coefficients. If it is deemed desirable to test the sample populations for homogeneity of other parameters, the current literature contains numerous and various tests, but in most cases the power function and other properties are not known. Obviously there are many ways in which various hypotheses can be formed depending upon which parameters are tested and in what combinations they are tested.

The following pages will present the order of application of the tests of the analysis of covariance used when testing k samples from k normal bivariate populations. The reader should note that this section is not oriented to the problem of whether the adjusted means (via correlation analysis) of k samples are homogeneous; rather it is directed to the correlation statistics. In the following discussion of the analysis of covariance it is assumed that the reader is familiar with the general method. The purpose of the discussion here is to state explicitly the various hypotheses involved and to systematize the analysis. The derivation of the tests for each hypothesis is not given; the reader may refer to the fundamental references given. The synthesis given here is designed as a guide on the general analytical level. Several useful references at the general level are available.[12]

The analysis of covariance is directed at two separate but related problems. With k bivariate samples of variables y and x, one may be interested in determin-

---

12. S. S. Wilks, op. cit.; R. W. B. Jackson, op. cit.; G. W. Snedecor, op. cit.; L. H. C. Tippett, op. cit.; P. O. Johnson and J. Neyman, Tests of certain linear hypotheses and their application to some educational problems, *Statistical Research Memoirs*, 1, 1936, 57–93.

ing the correlation between $y$ and $x$ when the differences between the $k$ samples are removed. The difference is presumed to be some factor or element not related to the inherent relationship between $y$ and $x$. Thus, if $x$ were stanine and $y$ were some criterion of flying skill, it is possible that the $k$ samples represent $k$ different methods of measuring flying skill. The difference in measure of flying skill as between the $k$ samples is to be removed, so that the inherent relationship between stanine and flying skill will not be distorted by unrelated or arbitrary differences in the method of measuring flying skill. The related problems arise from the fact that differences in the means of the $y$ variable among the $k$ samples may be magnified or obscured by the differences in the associated $x$ values, where $x$ and $y$ are correlated. Thus sample 1 may have a higher mean $y$ value than sample 2 solely because of differences between the $x$ values in each sample.

If the effect of the differences in the $x$ variable is removed the $y$ values may be the same. Briefly, the problem is that of eliminating the effect of variable $x$ on variable $y$, so that the corrected values of $y$ are all comparable. This may be accomplished by the use of correlation analysis. The specific test and techniques for this problem will be covered below in the analysis of covariance. Reference to the sample problem worksheet in figure 22.3 will be made in the

| Column code | Data for each group | Computational formula | Computational procedure: Column code |
|---|---|---|---|
| a | $n_i$ | | |
| b | $\Sigma XY$ | | |
| c | $\Sigma X^2$ | | |
| d | $\Sigma Y^2$ | | |
| e | $\Sigma X$ | | |
| f | $\Sigma Y$ | | |
| g | $M_x$ | $\Sigma X/n$ | e/a |
| h | $M_y$ | $\Sigma Y/n$ | f/a |
| i | $\Sigma(X - \bar{x})(Y - \bar{y})$ | $\Sigma XY - \Sigma YM_x$ | b-fg |
| j | $\Sigma(X - \bar{x})^2$ | $\Sigma X^2 - \Sigma XM_x$ | c-eg |
| k | $\Sigma(Y - \bar{y})^2$ | $\Sigma Y^2 - \Sigma YM_y$ | d-hf |
| l | $b_{yx}\Sigma(X - \bar{x})(Y - \bar{y})$ | $(\Sigma xy)b_{yx}$ | $\dfrac{i^2}{j}$ |
| m | $\Sigma[(Y - \bar{y}) - b(X - \bar{x})]^2$ | $\Sigma y^2 - \dfrac{(\Sigma xy)^2}{\Sigma x^2}$ | k-l |

**FIGURE 22.3.** *Analysis of covariance.*

| | a | b | c | d | e | f | g | h | i | j | k | l | m | |
|---|---|---|---|---|---|---|---|---|---|---|---|---|---|---|
| Group | N | $\Sigma XY$ | $\Sigma X^2$ | $\Sigma Y^2$ | $\Sigma X$ | $\Sigma Y$ | $M_x$ | $M_y$ | $\Sigma xy$ | $\Sigma x^2$ | $\Sigma y^2$ | $(b_{yx}) \Sigma(xy)$ | $\Sigma y^2 x$ | |
| 1′ | 45 | 12,362 | 1,350 | 128,085 | 230 | 2,385 | 5.111 | 53.000 | 172.265 | 174.470 | 1680.000 | 170.088 | 1509.912 | 1′ |
| 2′ | 80 | 16,868 | 2,210 | 144,678 | 392 | 3,360 | 4.900 | 42.000 | 404.000 | 289.200 | 3558.000 | 564.371 | 2993.629 | 2′ |
| 3′ | 64 | 14,649 | 1,696 | 143,596 | 307 | 3,008 | 4.797 | 47.000 | 219.624 | 223.321 | 2220.000 | 215.988 | 2004.012 | 3′ |
| 4′ | 53 | 15,990 | 1,667 | 173,859 | 276 | 3,021 | 5.208 | 57.000 | 256.632 | 229.592 | 1662.000 | 286.857 | 1375.143 | 4′ |
| 5′ | 72 | 19,713 | 2,218 | 197,488 | 374 | 3,744 | 5.194 | 52.000 | 266.664 | 275.444 | 2800.000 | 258.164 | 2541.836 | 5′ |
| 6′ | 40 | 12,219 | 1,168 | 146,774 | 200 | 2,400 | 5.000 | 60.000 | 219.000 | 168.000 | 2774.000 | 285.482 | 2488.518 | 6′ |
| Sums | | | | | | | | | 1,538.185 | 1,360.027 | 14,694.000 | 1,780.950 | [1]12,913.050 | 1 |
| Total | 354 | 91,801 | 10,309 | 934,480 | 1,779 | 17,918 | 5.025 | 50.616 | 1,763.050 | 1,369.525 | 27,542.512 | 2,269.652 | [2]25,272.860 | 2 |
| Within | | | | | | | | | | | | 1,739.681 | [3]12,954.319 | 3 |
| | | | | | | | | | | | | | [4]41.269 | 4 |
| | | | | | | | | | | | | 1.131 | [5]12,318.541 | 5 |
| Groups | | | | | | | | | 224.865 | 9.498 | 12,848.512 | 5,323.675 | [6]7,524.837 | 6 |
| | | | | | | | | | | | | | [7]4,793.704 | 7 |

| | Degrees of freedom | | Sums of squares | Variance | Location of entry |
|---|---|---|---|---|---|
| Total, grand mean | 353 | $(N-1)$ | 27,542.512 | 77.260 | Column k, row 2 |
| Over-all regression-grand mean | 1 | 1 | 2,269.652 | 2,269.652 | Column l, row 2 |
| Total, regression-residual | 352 | $N-2$ | 25,272.860 | 71.798 | Column m, row 2 |
| Within sample-common regression coefficient-residuals | 347 | $(N-k-1)$ | 12,954.319 | 37.332 | Column m, row 3 |
| Within sample-individual regression coefficient-residuals | 342 | $(N-2k)$ | 12,913.050 | 37.757 | Column m, row 1 |
| Between individual regression coefficients | 5 | $(k-1)$ | 41.269 | 8.254 | Column m, row 4 |
| Between means adjusted by common within | 5 | $(k-1)$ | 12,318.541 | 2463.708 | Column m, row 5 |
| Means around mean regression | 4 | $(k-2)$ | 7,524.837 | 1881.209 | Column m, row 6 |
| Regression of means-common within regression | 1 | 1 | 4,793.704 | 4793.704 | Column m, row 7 |

[1]Residual from individual regression.
[2]Residual total regression.
[3]Residual common slope.
[4]Between individual slope (3-1).
[5]Means around common (2-3).
[6]Means around mean regression.
[7]Common mean regression (5-6).

following discussion and the various tests will be illustrated with the data of the sample analysis. Although the explanation is somewhat involved and detailed, the reader may easily follow the discussion if he refers at each step to the work sheet; otherwise the reader may not be able to follow the procedure. The following tabular layout explains the entries in the first k' (6') rows—there being 6 groups in the analysis.

Row 1: Summing the entries in columns i, j, k, and m will yield for each column respectively the within-sample cross products, sums of squares, and residuals within each sample around the individual regression lines. These sums are entered in row 1, which is the row immediately following 6'.

The sum of the entries in column m, rows 1' through 6' is the evaluation of

$$
\sum_{j=1}^{k}\left[\sum_{i=1}^{n_i}(Y_{ij} - \bar{y}_j)^2 - \left\{\frac{\left(\sum_{i=1}^{n_j}(X_{ij} - \bar{x}_j)(Y_{ij} - \bar{y}_j)\right)^2}{\sum_{i=1}^{n_j}(X_{ij} - \bar{x}_j)^2}\right\}\right],
\tag{22.1}
$$

$j = 1 \ldots k$ groups,
$i = 1 \ldots n_j$.

Row 2: Summing the entries in columns a through f will yield the over-all totals, which are the entries for each column in row 2.

The grand total means for columns g and h of row 2 are computed from the sums of columns e and f in row 2.

The entries for row 2, columns i, j, k, and m are computed in exactly the same manner that the corresponding entries were computed in each of rows 1' through 6'. The entries in columns i, j, and k are the sums of cross products and squares around the grand total mean. The resulting entry in column m is the sum of squares of variable y around the regression line fitted to the entire set of 6 samples—all combined. This is the evaluation of the following:

$$
\sum_{j}^{k}\sum_{i}^{n_i}(Y_{ij} - \bar{y}_j)^2 - \frac{\sum_{j}^{k}\sum_{i}^{n_i}(X_{ij} - \bar{x})(Y_{ij} - \bar{y})^2}{\sum_{j}^{k}\sum_{i}^{n_i}(X_{ij} - \bar{x})^2},
\tag{22.2}
$$

where $\bar{x}$ and $\bar{y}$ are grand means.

Row 3: Row 3 has entries for the residual sums of squares of variable y around individual regression lines, all with the same slope—the average within-sample slope. The entry in column 1 of row 3 is $i^2/j$ of row 1. This is subtracted from the entry of column k, row 1 and the result is recorded in column m of row 3. Thus $(14,694.000 - 1,739.681) = 12,954.319$. This is an evaluation of:

$$\sum_j^k \left[ \sum_i^{n_i} (Y_{ij} - \bar{y}_j)^2 \right] - \frac{\left\{ \sum_j^k \left[ \sum_i^{n_i} (X_{ij} - \bar{x}_j)(Y_{ij} - \bar{y}_j) \right] \right\}^2}{\sum^k \sum^{n_i} (X_{ij} - \bar{x}_j)^2}. \tag{22.3}$$

Row 4: Subtracting the entries of column m, row 1 from row 3 yields the entry for row 4. $(12,954.319 - 12,913.050) = 41.269$. This is the sum of squares due to the differences among the individual within-sample regression coefficients and is an evaluation of the following equation, which is equation (22.3) minus (22.1):

$$\frac{\sum_j^k \left\{ \left[ \sum_i^{n_i} (Y_{ij} - \bar{y}_j)(X_{ij} - \bar{x}_j) \right]^2 \right\}}{\sum_j^k \sum^{n_i} (X_{ij} - \bar{x}_j)^2} - \frac{\left\{ \sum_j^k \left[ \sum_i^{n_i} (X_{ij} - \bar{x}_j)(Y_{ij} - \bar{y}_j) \right] \right\}^2}{\sum_j^k \sum^{n_i} (X_{ij} - \bar{x}_j)^2} \tag{22.4}$$

Row 5: Subtracting the entry of column m, row 3 from that of column m, row 2 yields the sums of squares of the means around the regression line fitted to means but with the regression coefficient equal to the common within-sample coefficient. This is entered in column m, row 5.

Row 6: The sum of squares of the means around the regression line fitted to the means is obtained by using the following formula for the sums of squares and cross products of the means around the grand mean.

$$\sum_j^k \sum_i^n xy = \sum_j^k \left( \sum_i^n X_{ij} \bar{x}_j \right) - \bar{y} \sum_j^k \sum_i^n X_{ij},$$

$$\sum_j^k \sum_i^n x^2 = \sum_j^k \left( \sum_i^n X_{ij} \bar{x}_j \right) - \bar{x} \sum_j^k \sum_i^n X_{ij},$$

$$\sum_j^k \sum_i^n y^2 = \sum_j^k \left( \sum_i^n Y_{ij} \bar{y}_j \right) - \bar{y} \sum_j^k \sum_i^n Y_{ij},$$

where:

$\bar{y}$ and $\bar{x}$ are grand means,

$j = 1 \ldots k$ samples,

$i = 1 \ldots n_j$ items per sample.

$\Sigma xy$ is easily obtained by obtaining the sum of the products of the pairs of entries in columns f and g in each of the 6' rows and subtracting the product of the entries in columns f and g in row 2. Thus $(2385 \times 5.111) + (3360 \times 4.9000) + \ldots + (2400 \times 5.000) - (17,918 \times 5.025)$ equals 224.965, which is entered in column i of row 6.

Similarly $\Sigma x^2$ is the sum of the paired entries in columns e and g reduced by the product in the same columns in row 2. This is entered in column j of row 6.

$\Sigma y^2$ is obtained in a similar manner and entered in column k of row 6.

In column l of row 6 is $i^2/j$ which is computed from the cells of these columns in row 6. Subtracting this from the entry in column k of row 6 gives the sum of squares of the means around the regression fitted to the means, where the sum of squares is in terms of individual observations; i.e., it is weighted by the number of observations. In the example this sum of squares is 7,524,837.

(If all the samples are the same size, these sums of squares and cross products can be quickly obtained by the conventional formula treating each mean as an observation and weighting by the common sample size.)

Row 7: Subtracting the entry in column m, row 6 from the entry in column m, row 5 yields the sum of squares between the common-within-regression coefficient and the regression coefficient of the means. This is entered in column m, row 7.

*Analysis of covariance form.* Immediately below the computation form is space to record systematically the sums of squares, degrees of freedom, and variances. The source of each entry on the summary form is indicated. The final summary of the F ratios and conclusions should be presented in the manner most suitable to the problem under study. A series of hypotheses are tested by the analysis of covariance. These hypotheses are presented below in the order of testing; in each case the applicable test is indicated and the general type of conclusion is given.

The first hypothesis is $H_1$: *The residual variances around the individual regression lines of the k samples are equal.* To test this hypothesis the test for homogeneity of variances outlined above should be applied. The k residual variances are obtained from rows 1' through 6' in column m. It must be noted that these residuals are based on $n_i - 2$ degrees of freedom since they are deviations around a linear regression line. Therefore in the $L_1$ test the degrees of freedom of each residual variance is two less than the sample size. The $L_1$ table must be entered with the average degrees of freedom; if the table happens to be listed in terms of the sample sizes, the appropriate entry will be for entries under samples of size $n - 1$.

**FIGURE 22.4.** *Computing sheet for test of differences between variances.*

$$L_1 = \Pi_s\left(\frac{N}{n_s}\right)^{n_s/N} \Pi_s\left(\frac{\theta_s}{\Sigma_s\theta_s}\right)^{n_s/N} \qquad N = \Sigma_s n_s$$

$$\log L_1 = \log N - \frac{1}{N}\Sigma_s n_s \log n_s + \frac{1}{N}\Sigma_s n_s \log \theta_s - \log(\Sigma_s\theta_s)$$

$$°F = \frac{1}{k}\Sigma_s °f_s \qquad\qquad \theta_s = \text{sum of squares within sth group}$$

| k group | $°f_s$ | $n_s$ | $\log n_s$ | $\theta_s$ | $\log \theta_s$ | $n_s$ |
|---------|--------|-------|-----------|-----------|----------------|-------|
| 1 | 43 | 45 | 1.65321 | 1509.912 | 3.17874 | 45 |
| 2 | 78 | 80 | 1.90309 | 2993.629 | 3.47619 | 80 |
| 3 | 62 | 64 | 1.80618 | 2004.012 | 3.30190 | 64 |
| 4 | 51 | 53 | 1.72428 | 1375.143 | 3.13834 | 53 |
| 5 | 70 | 72 | 1.85733 | 2541.836 | 3.40514 | 72 |
| 6 | 38 | 40 | 1.60206 | 2488.518 | 3.39594 | 40 |
| Totals | 342 | 354 | 631.43417 | 12,903.973 | 1179.7998 | 354 |
|        |     |     | $\Sigma_s n_s \log n_s$ |  | $\Sigma_s n_s \log \theta_s$ |  |

Average $°F = 57$

$\log N = 2.54900$ $\qquad\qquad \frac{1}{N}\Sigma_s n_s \log n_s \qquad$ 1.78371

$\frac{1}{N}\Sigma_s n_s \log \theta_s = 3.33277 \qquad\qquad \log(\Sigma_s\theta_s) \qquad$ 4.11073

Total 1 = 5.88177 $\qquad\qquad$ Total 2 $\qquad$ 5.89444

Total 1 − total 2 = $\log L_1 = -.01267$ $\qquad L_1 = .9714 \qquad P(.9714) > .05$

Reference: R. W. B. Jackson, *Application of the Analysis of Variance and Covariance Method to Educational Problems*, 1940, 40.

In the example, figure 22.4, $L_1$ equals 0.9714 for $k = 6$ samples with average sample size of 57, or 55 degrees of freedom. References to $L_1$ tables give $P(L_1 = 0.9714) > 0.05$. The 5 percent level gives 0.969 for samples of 59 (the nearest entry to 57) degrees of freedom, and since values of $L_1$ nearer one have higher probabilities as the sample size decreases, it is clear that the obtained $L_1$ is associated with a probability slightly larger than 0.05.

If homogeneity of the residual variances could not be accepted, analysis by the following variance method would not be applicable. On the other hand, an average r could be computed by means of Fisher's z transformation if it were presumed that the sampled populations had identical correlation coefficients and if the variation in the ranges of the variables as measured by the standard deviations were regarded as unimportant. The variables of the psychological program were in general not the type that could have variances arbitrarily transformed from sample to sample: consequently, the following type of analysis is essential to a decision as to whether or not regression or correlation coefficients may be averaged.

In the example, on the basis of the test, homogeneity of the residual variances may be assumed.

$H_2$: *The regression coefficients in the populations sampled are equal.* This hypothesis is tested by applying an F test to the residual variance around the individual regressions and the variance among the individual within-sample regression coefficients. The latter variance is obtained from the difference between (1) the residual sum of squares around the average within-sample regression lines and (2) the residual sum of squares around the individual within-samples regression lines. The sum of squares of residuals around the common within-sample regression coefficient is $(14,694.000 - 1,739.681) = 12,954.319$ with $N - k - 1$ degrees of freedom. This is recorded in column m, row 3.

The residual sum of squares around the individual within-sample regression line is $(14,694.000 - 1,780.950) = 12,913.050$ with $N - 2k$ degrees of freedom. This is recorded in column m, row 1. Subtracting this latter sum of squares from the former gives $41.269$ with $k - 1$ degrees of freedom. This is the sum of squares among the individual regression coefficients and is recorded in column m, row 4. The F ratio is the ratio of the latter variance to the variance of items around the individual regression lines. Thus:

$$F = \frac{41.269/5}{12,913.050/342} = \frac{8.254}{37.757} < 1.$$

Clearly, according to this test the regression coefficients are homogeneous. Since they are now assumed to be homogenous, the best estimate of the population value is obtained by using the average within regression coefficient which is obtainable from row 1 by dividing the entry of column i by that of column j, i.e., $1538.185/1360.027 = 1.131$. This is entered in row 5, column e, if homogeneity of regression coefficients is indicated. If not, that space is left blank.

If nonhomogeneity of regression coefficients had been the conclusion drawn from the test, the samples should not be pooled for an average regression coefficient.

$H_3$: *The common within-sample regression coefficient is equal to zero.* This hypothesis may be tested by comparing: (1) the variance within samples around the individual means (this assumes the regression coefficients within samples are zero), and (2) the reduction in this variance resulting from using a regression line with the average slope. Thus:

$$F = \frac{\text{variance between "common" regression coefficient and zero slope}}{\text{variance of residuals around common regression coefficient}}.$$

These variances are obtained as follows: the denominator is the sum of squares of the residuals around the common within-sample regression line and is entered on the work sheet in column m, row 3; in the example it is 12,954.319. The numerator is found by subtracting this value from the sum of squares around the sample means. This is 1,739.681 and is found in row 3, column l. There is one degree of freedom for the numerator, it being $(N - k) - (N - k - 1) = 1$; the denominator has $(N - k - 1)$, (347), degrees of freedom. In the example problem

$$F = \frac{1,739.681/1}{12,954.319/347} = 46.60,$$

while the .01 value for 1 d. f. and 347 d. f. is about 6.7. It may be concluded that the common within-sample regression coefficient is not equal to 0.

It should be noted that this test is identical with the t test of the significance of the regression coefficient.

If nonsignificance had been indicated it would have meant that the two variables were not correlated, since the test for the regression coefficient is the same as the test of the correlation coefficient. Further analysis of the within-sample regression would not be made.

$H_4$: *The regression of the means is linear.* To test $H_4$ the following F ratio is used:

$$\frac{\text{variance of means around regression line}}{\text{variance within samples around common within-sample regression}},$$

with $k - 2$ degrees of freedom for the numerator and $N - k - 1$ degrees for the denominator. The numerator is in row 6, column m. In the example it is 7,524.837, expressed in terms of individual observations. The denominator of this test is the denominator of the test of $H_3$. In the example

$$F = \frac{7{,}524.837/4}{12{,}954.319/347} = 50.39,$$

while the .01 level of F is 3.37. Thus the hypothesis is denied and it may be concluded that the relationship between the means is nonlinear. It is, therefore, meaningless to test whether the regression coefficient of the means is different from zero, since the assumption of linearity cannot be accepted.

If on the other hand the hypothesis $H_4$ had been accepted, the next step would be to test the regression coefficient for departure from zero. This would be $H_5$.

$H_5$: *The linear regression coefficient of the means is zero.* This may be tested by the following F test if $H_4$ is accepted.

$$F = \frac{\text{variance due to the regression line of means around grand mean}}{\text{variance of the means around the regression of the means}}$$

with one degree of freedom in the numerator and $k - 2$ (4) in the denominator. This is exactly comparable to the usual test of a regression coefficient where the observations are the means.

The required data for the denominator are obtained in row 6, column m, which is the entry for the sum of squares of the means around a regression line fitted to the means, and is expressed in terms of individual observations rather than in terms of means. (That is, each mean is weighted by the number of observations.) The value in the example is 7,524.837. The entry for the numerator is obtained by subtracting the preceding sum of squares from the total of the means around the grand mean. The latter quantity is entered in row 6, column k. Thus in the example, $(12{,}848.512 - 7{,}524.837) = 5{,}323.675$ is the entry.

The F ratio is therefore

$$F = \frac{5{,}323.675/1}{7{,}524.837/4} = 2.830$$

The .05 value of F with 1 and 5 degrees of freedom is 6.61. The conclusion would then have been that the regression is not different from zero—except that the test of $H_4$ has already indicated that linearity is not acceptable. Hence, in our particular example the meaning of this test is uncertain.

If after accepting $H_4$ the hypothesis $H_5$ is also accepted, the conclusion would be that the regression of means is linear with slope equal to zero. If $H_5$

had been denied, the conclusion would be that the regression is linear with slope different from zero.

$H_6$: *The regression coefficient of the means is the same as the regression coefficient of the common within-sample regression coefficient.* $H_6$ may frequently be regarded as an alternative hypothesis to $H_5$. It is possible that both $H_5$ and $H_6$ may be accepted according to the F tests, even though the hypothesis $H_3$ (that the common within-sample regression coefficient is zero) is denied. It appears that $H_6$ may be the more appropriate hypothesis to accept in some cases and in others it may be $H_5$. If the samples are distinguished on the basis of some factor related to one of the variables, $H_6$ seems more appropriate. On the other hand, if the factor which demarks the samples is something independent of the relationship of the variables to each other, $H_5$ would seem to be the more appropriate hypothesis to accept. In any event, careful consideration must be given to the various elements of the problem before a decision is made.

If $H_4$ were accepted, then $H_6$ could be tested by the F ratio

$$\frac{\text{variance of difference between within-sample coefficient and mean coefficient}}{\text{variance within samples around common within-sample regression}}$$

with 1 degree of freedom for the numerator and $N - k - 1$ for the denominator. The numerator is obtained by subtracting the sum of squares of the residuals of the means around the mean regression line, 7,524.837 (this sum of squares is entered in row 6, column m, and is the numerator of the test of $H_4$ and also the denominator of the test of $H_5$) from the residual sums of squares of the means around the regression line with a regression coefficient equal to the "common-within" regression. This latter term is obtained from row 5 and is computed by subtracting the sums of squares within groups around the common within-sample regression (this is entered in row 3, column m) from the sums of squares around the total regression line (this is entered in row 2, column m). Thus $25{,}272.860 - 12{,}954.319 = 12{,}318.541$. The sum of squares for the numerator is $12{,}318.514 - 7{,}524.837 = 4{,}793.677$. The sum of squares for the denominator (12,954.319) is in row 3, column m. The resulting F ratio is

$$\frac{4{,}793.677/1}{12{,}954/347} = \frac{4{,}793.677}{37.303} = 128.51,$$

which is significant since the F value of the 1 percent level with 1 and 347 degrees of freedom is 6.71. The conclusion is that the slope of the means regression is different from the within-sample regression.

If $H_4$ had been denied, there would have been no justification for $H_6$. The best estimate of the regression coefficient is that within the samples.

The within-sample correlation that is computed is representative of the improvement in prediction on the basis of the predictive variable over a range (standard deviation) indicated by the standard deviation of the pooled sum of squares of the predictive variable.

*Test of Adjusted Means.* If $H_4$ were accepted but $H_6$ denied, it might seem reasonable to adjust the sample (group) means by the mean regression, and then test these adjusted means for homogeneity. The hypothesis is then: $H_7$—*The means adjusted by the mean regression are homogeneous.* However, this is actually the same hypothesis as $H_4$. If the group means vary significantly from the linear regression of the means it is obvious that they are not linearly related, by definition. Thus nonlinearity simply means that the linear relationship will not reduce the residual variance of means around the mean regression line to nonsignificant proportions.[13]

If the objective of the study is to isolate the effect of the factor which demarks the k samples (treatments, methods of teaching, etc.), and measure its effect on the y variable, the effects of variations in the variable must be removed. The purpose of covariance analysis is frequently just that—it is desired to remove the effect of variations in x on variable y so that some other factor which demarks the k samples from each other may be compared for its effects on variable y. The appropriate hypothesis may be stated as follows:

$H_8$: *The means adjusted for the common within-sample regression are homogeneous.* This may be tested by the following F ratio:

$$\frac{\text{variance of ``adjusted'' means}}{\text{error variance within-sample around common within-regression}}$$

with $k - 1$ and $N - k - 1$ degrees of freedom in the numerator and denominator respectively. The sum of squares for the numerator is entered in row 5, col. m (12,318.541), while the denominator is found in row 3, col. m (12,954.319).

Thus the F ratio is

13. R. W. B. Jackson, Analysis of covariance and educational problems, *Journal of Educational Psychology*, 32, 1941. He writes, p. 421, in an apparently contradictory statement, that a significantly large value of F may mean not nonlinearity, but merely that one or two of the array means may be out of line. It would seem, however, that this is the definition of nonlinearity.

$$\frac{12{,}318.541/5}{12{,}954.319/347} = 65.99,$$

which is significant since the 1-percent value with 5 and 347 degrees of freedom is 3.07.

This means that the difference between the $y$ values for the several samples is greater than can be accounted for by random fluctuations and by the differences in the $x$ variable. It must be noted that the sum of squares in the numerator is not the sum of squares of the means adjusted by use of the common-within-sample regression coefficient. In other words if the adjusted means are computed, their variance will not be the numerator term here. In computing the variance of the adjusted means it must be recalled that the estimate of the adjusted mean is affected by the variance of the estimate of the two parameters of a linear regression equation. For two groups, the variance of the adjusted means may be computed directly from the formula

$$S_{y.x}\left(\frac{2}{n} + \frac{(\bar{x}_1 - \bar{x}_2)^2}{\Sigma x^2}\right),$$

where $n$ is the same for both samples. The difference between the mean of the $x$ variable is involved and hence for more than 2 samples the calculations are impractical.

The justification for the F-ratio test used for this hypothesis is based on the Neyman-Pearson likelihood-ratio test, which involves the ratio of the likelihood of the obtained samples under the particular hypothesis $H_8$ to the likelihood under all admissible alternative hypotheses.[14] The Neyman-Johnson approach is fundamentally an application of the likelihood-ratio criterion, and leads to the test based on the ratio of the relative and absolute minimum of the sum of squares.

If $H_4$ and $H_6$ had both been accepted it would be appropriate to pool all the samples into one large sample for purposes of further correlational analysis. This would imply that the means adjusted by the mean regression are homogeneous; otherwise pooling or combining all samples into one large sample would not be justified.

It must be stated that as with many other widely used tests the various properties of the analysis are not commonly known. Its power and bias characteris-

---

14. P. O. Johnson and J. Neyman, loc. cit., 57–94.

tics, while known in some cases, are not easily available. Nevertheless, enough is known so that the analysis may be regarded as satisfactory and the best currently available.

*Differences in the Variances of the Sampled Population.* The variance of the dependent (predicted) variable in normal bivariate populations with equal correlation may vary as a result of any one of the following conditions:

a. the residuals around the regression lines differ,

b. the within-sample regression coefficients differ,

c. the variance of the predictive (independent) variables differs.

Condition *a* was the subject of the first hypothesis in the analysis of covariance. The equality of the regression coefficients was the second hypothesis tested. Thus if both hypotheses are accepted, conditions *a* and *b* do not exist.

Only the last condition remains; if the variances differ while the first two conditions are satisfied, the average correlation obtained by pooling the sums of cross products and squares within samples is a measure of the increase in precision of estimate when the range (as indicated by the standard deviation) is the average within-sample standard deviation. This standard deviation indicates the average dimension of the range over which prediction of the y variable is to be made. It is not the standard deviation of all k samples lumped together as one sample; rather, it is the average of the within-sample standard deviations.

# CHAPTER TWENTY-THREE
# MULTIVARIATE ANALYSIS

## Correlation Statistics

The zero-order correlation coefficients between several variables may be computed from standardized computational forms. When the sums of squares and cross products are available for all the pairs of the variables, the work form shown in figure 23.1 may be used to compute the means, standard deviations, and zero-order correlation coefficients.

It is worth emphasizing that a work sheet should be made large enough so that entries may be made without crowding. Crowding entries contributes materially to errors of transcription.

Only the upper right half (the principal diagonal and all above it) need be used for computations. The method of using the work form is as follows:

(a) At the top of the work sheet the N, its reciprocal, and the square root of its reciprocal are entered in the appropriate spaces.

(b) Above each column is recorded the name or coding of the variable, so that there is one variable for each column. Each variable is assigned the same row number as its column number. Thus, a variable in column 4 is also associated with row 4.

(c) At the head of the column i, just above row 1, the sum $X_i$, for the ith variable, is recorded.

(d) The first entry in each cell is the sum of squares or cross products; sums of squares are entered in the diagonal cell lying in the row and column associated with each variable. The sums of cross products are entered in the cells associated with the row of one variable and the column of the other. Thus the sum of cross products of variables 2 and 4 would be entered in column 4 and row 2. It would not be entered in column 2 and row 4 because only the upper half of the table is used—the table is symmetrical around the principal diagonal.

(e) No further entries need be obtained from other sources. All the remaining work is done directly from the work sheet. The means of each variable are recorded in the extreme right-hand column. These are obtained by multiplying the sums recorded at the head of each column by the reciprocal of N. The mean of variable i is entered in the cell of row i and the extreme right-hand column, there being one more column than variables. Nothing else is entered in the extreme right-hand column.

(f) The second entry in each cell of a row is $\Sigma x_i \Sigma x_j / N$ and is obtained as follows:

**FIGURE 23.1.** Correlation coefficient work sheet.

$$N = 815 \qquad \frac{1}{N} = .00122699 \qquad \frac{1}{\sqrt{N}} = .0350285$$

| 1 | 2 | 3 | 4 | | |
|---|---|---|---|---|---|
| 4119 | 4123 | 4108 | 4062 | Means | |
| 23935 | 22033 | 21365 | 21468 | | |
| 20817.38 | 20837.60 | 20761.79 | 20529.31 | | |
| 3117.62 | 1195.40 | 603.21 | 938.69 | 5.05399 | 1 |
| 55.83567 | 21.40926 | 10.80331 | 16.81166 | | |
| .01790970 | .38322 | .19348 | .29790 | | |
| 1.95584 | | | | | |
| | 23979 | 22066 | 21416 | | |
| | 20857.84 | 20781.96 | 20549.25 | | |
| | 3121.16 | 1284.04 | 866.75 | 5.05890 | 2 |
| | 55.86741 | 22.98370 | 15.51441 | | |
| | .01789952 | .41163 | .27491 | | |
| | 1.95695 | | | | |
| | | 23824 | 21917 | | |
| | | 20706.33 | 20474.47 | | |
| | | 3117.67 | 1442.53 | 5.04049 | 3 |
| | | 55.83612 | 25.83506 | | |
| | | .01790955 | .45779 | | |
| | | 1.95586 | | | |
| | | | 23430 | | |
| | | | 20245.21 | | |
| | | | 3184.79 | 4.98405 | 4 |
| | | | 56.43395 | | |
| | | | .01771983 | | |
| | | | 1.97680 | | |

Place in the keyboard of the computing machine[1] the mean value of variable 1 (entered in the last column in row 1); multiply this by the entry $\Sigma X_1$ at the head of column 1, and record the product in the second line of the cell of row 1 and column 1. Clear the dials, but not the keyboard. Multiply by the entry at

1. This explanation is adapted to the Marchant. With slight changes it can be used on any similar calculating machine.

the top of column 2, $X_2$, and record the product as the second entry in the cell of row 1, column 2. Continue across row 1.

Next fill in the second entries of the cells of row 2 beginning with the diagonal cell. This requires that the mean of variable 2 be placed in the keyboard and that successive noncumulated products be obtained by multiplying by the sums of the variables across row 2, beginning with the diagonal (variable 2).

The process is continued across all rows until the second entries of all rows are obtained.

(g) The third entry in each cell is the difference between the first and second entries. All diagonal entries will be positive but the nondiagonal may be either positive or negative and the sign must be recorded.

(h) The diagonal cells are next completed. The fourth entry in the diagonals is the square root of the third entry. The fifth entry is the reciprocal of the fourth. The sixth and last entry in each diagonal cell is the quotient of the fourth entry divided by the square root of N; or in other words it is the product of the fourth entry multiplied by the reciprocal of the square root of N. This latter item is recorded at the top of the table and by entering it in the keyboard, the products desired may be quickly obtained by a simple series of multiplications. This sixth and last entry in the diagonals is the standard deviation of the variable associated with the row and column intersecting at the particular diagonal.

(i) Return now to the nondiagonal cells. Entry four of each cell is obtained by multiplying the third entry of a cell by the fifth entry of the diagonal cell of that row. A given row of cells is completed before going to the next row.

(j) The last entry in the nondiagonal cells is the correlation coefficient and is obtained by completing *columns* successively instead of rows as heretofore. Thus, the last entry in the first cell of column 2 is obtained by multiplying its fourth entry by the fifth entry of the bottom (diagonal) cell of column 2. Similarly for column 3; the last entry in the first and second cells of this column is the fourth entry of each respective cell multiplied by the fifth entry in the bottom (diagonal) cell of that column. Continuing, all columns are completed, thereby completing the entire task.

The computations should be checked by duplicating the work form. Special care should be taken to be certain that the original entries are correctly transcribed from the sources.

### Regression Statistics

*Multiple Regression Coefficients*

Although it is shorter and more direct to proceed directly to the regression coefficients from the sums of squares and cross products, the zero-order correlation coefficients are extremely useful for extended analyses. Consequently, in all the work of the statistical unit the regression coefficients were computed from matrices of correlation coefficients. Several methods are available for computing regression coefficients from the matrix, and the method used in any situation must depend upon the size of the matrix, the degree of prior knowledge, and the extent to which use will be made of statistics other than the regression coefficients. In most cases in this unit's work the standard errors of the regression coefficients were not needed because the desirability of including particular variables had already been determined from previous knowledge or outside sources. In several cases, however, the desirability of including a new variable was tested by comparing the difference between the multiple correlation coefficients with and without the questioned variable. The test used in that case was

$$F = \frac{(R_1^2 - R_2^2)(N - m_1 - 1)}{(1 - R_1^2)(m_1 - m_2)},$$

where F is distributed with $(n - m_1 - 1)$ and $(m_1 - m_2)$ degrees of freedom in an F distribution; $R_1$ is the usual multiple correlation coefficient obtained from the $m_1$ predictive variable; $R_2$ is obtained from the $m_2$ predictive variable where $m_1$ is greater than $m_2$, and N is the total number of cases. In any one case there are $m_i + 1$ variables ($m_i$ prediction and one predicted or dependent variable). The hypothesis tested by this test is that the addition of more variables does not increase the correlation, or more specifically that the population value of $R_1$ equals the population value of $R_2$. In any sample $R_1$ will exceed $R_2$ since sample fluctuations will ensure that the use of another variable will reduce the residual sums of squares around the plane of regression, thus increasing R. The test above takes this into account by testing whether or not the difference in the observed sample values is greater than would be observed in random samples of multivariate populations where one has more variables than the other but in which the multiple R is the same. The alternative hypotheses against which the null hypothesis is tested are that the true population value of $R_1$ is greater than $R_2$. It is noteworthy that this is a case in which the error of accepting the tested hypothesis is probably more serious than erroneously rejecting the tested hypothesis; i.e., too small a region of rejection should not be used.

It is worth pointing out at this point that the sample R observed is neither the unbiased nor the maximum-likelihood estimate of the correlation parameter. The unbiased estimate is

$$R_u = \sqrt{1 - \frac{1 - R^2}{1 - \dfrac{m}{N}}}.$$

The maximum-likelihood estimate is (as first approximation)[2]

$$R_m = \sqrt{\frac{R^2(N - 1) - m}{N - m - 1}}.$$

An equivalent test is that of testing the hypothesis that the partial regression coefficient, $b_{ij} \ldots$ is zero, while the alternatives are that it is anything else.

The test is based on

$$t = \frac{b_{ij.k\ldots n}\sqrt{N}\, s_{j.k\ldots n}}{s_{i.jk\ldots n}},$$

where $t$ is distributed as Student's $t$ with $N - m$ degrees of freedom, $m$ being the number of regression statistics used in the prediction equation and $s_{i.jk\ldots n}$ is the standard error of estimate of $i$ on the other variable and $s_{j.k\ldots n}$ is the standard error of estimation of variable $j$ on $k \ldots n$ ($i$ excluded). The standard error of $b_{ij}$ is

$$\frac{s_{i.jk\ldots n}}{s_{j.k\ldots n}\sqrt{N}} = s_{b_{ij.k\ldots n}}.$$

The difficulty with this test is that the standard error of the partial regression coefficient must be computed, and that is not usually an easy task. The determination of the standard errors of the regression coefficients is a byproduct of the inverse matrix method of computing the partial regression coefficients from the correlation matrix. This method is described below.

2. J. G. Smith and A. J. Duncan, op. cit.

Another approach to the problem of deciding whether to add another variable to the set of predicting variables is to see if the correlation of the new variable with the criterion variable is high enough to increase the multiple correlation, after allowing for the correlation of the new variable with the set of previously used predicting variables. The rationale and development of the approach is given in appendix D. No allowance is made in this procedure for sampling fluctuations; consequently, if a sample result meets the suggested criterion, one must still test to see whether the criterion was met through sampling fluctuations or as a result of a real independent predictive value. This may be done by testing the hypothesis that the sample was from a population with correlation equal at least to the required correlation.

### Regression Coefficients

The weights for the tests of the classification battery were computed by first determining the Beta weights and then converting them to weights for use with nonstandardized scores by use of the following definitions:

$$\beta_{ij} = b_{ij} \frac{\sigma_i}{\sigma_j},$$

$$\beta_{ij.12\dots n} = b_{ij.12\dots n} \frac{\sigma_{i.12\dots i-1, i+1\dots n}}{\sigma_{j.12\dots i-1, i+1\dots n}}.$$

All the modern methods of computing weights from a matrix of zero-order correlation coefficients assume the use of the modern calculating machine. Essentially, the requirement is that the machine be capable of easily evaluating such expressions as $(a + bc + de + fg + ij + \dots + mn)$.

The abbreviated Doolittle solution, the Kelley-Salisbury iterative method, and the inverse matrix solution were the methods employed in this unit's work.[3] Of these the first and third are recommended for general use. If the standard errors are certainly not going to be needed, the abbreviated Doolittle method is

3. T. L. Kelley and F. S. Salisbury, An iteration method for determining multiple correlation constants, *Journal of American Statistical Association*, 21, 1926, 282–88.

P. S. Dwyer, The Doolittle technique, *Annals of Mathematical Statistics*, 12, 1941, 449–58.

P. S. Dwyer, Recent developments in correlation techniques, *Journal of American Statistical Association*, 37, 1942, 441–60.

P. S. Dwyer and F. V. Waugh, Compact computation of the inverse of a matrix, *Annals of Mathematical Statistics*, 16, 1945, 259–71.

**FIGURE 23.2.** *Sample abbreviated Doolittle method.*

| | English $X_1$ | Latin $X_2$ | Algebra $X_3$ | Chemistry $X_4$ | Criterion $X_5$ | Check |
|---|---|---|---|---|---|---|
| $X_1$ | 1.00000 | .26800 | .20100 | .30600 | .40000 | 2.17500 |
| | 1.00000 | .20800 | .20100 | .30600 | .40000 | |
| | | | | | −.27767 | |
| $X_2$ | | 1.00000 | .06600 | .10600 | .32800 | 1.76800 |
| | −.26800 | .92818 | .01213 | .02399 | .22080 | 1.18510 |
| | | | | | −.23319 | 1.18510 |
| $X_3$ | | | 1.00000 | .39500 | .21700 | 1.87900 |
| | −.20100 | −.01307 | .95944 | .33318 | .13371 | 1.42634 |
| | | | | | −.09257 | 1.42633 |
| $X_4$ | | | | 1.00000 | .28100 | 2.08800 |
| | −.30600 | −.02585 | −.34727 | .79004 | .10646 | .89649 |
| | | | | | −.13475 | .89650 |
| $X_5$ | | | | | 1.00000 | 2.22600 |
| | −.40000 | −.23778 | −.13936 | −.13475 | .75450 | .75451 |
| | | | | | | .75450 |
| Check | | −1.27690 | −1.48663 | −1.13475 | −1.00000 | |
| | | −.27680 | −.48663 | −.13475 | −.00000 | |

recommended. But since it is actually a part of the solution of the inverse matrix, only a little extra work is involved in computing the inverse matrix directly.

*Abbreviated Doolittle Method*

A brief outline of the abbreviated Doolittle method follows with an example.

1. Enter the correlation coefficients $r_{ij}$ in the appropriate spaces in the correlation table figure 23.2.

2. Copy the items in the first row directly under the original entries.

3. Divide the first entry in the first row into each of the other entries of row 1 and write the negative of the quotient, $r'_{ij}$) in the successive rows of the first column beginning with the second row.

4. Multiply the entry in the first column and second row ($r'_{21}$) by each of the entries in the first row beginning with column 2 ($r_{12}$, $r_{13}$, etc.) and add the product to the corresponding entry in the second row.

$$r'_{22} = r_{22} + r'_{21} r'_{12}$$
$$r'_{23} = r_{23} + r'_{21} r'_{13}$$

5. Divide $r'_{22}$ into the other new entries in row 2 and write the negative of the quotient in column 3 beginning with row 3 and proceeding downwards.

6. Multiply $r'_{31}$ and $r'_{32}$ by the new entries in the first and second rows respectively and add the product to the entries in row 3, writing the sum underneath the corresponding entry.

$$r'_{33} = r_{33} + r'_{31} r'_{13} + r'_{32} r'_{23}$$
$$r'_{34} = r_{34} + r'_{31} r'_{14} + r'_{32} r'_{24}$$

7. Continue as before until table is complete.

$$r'_{55} = k^2_{0.1234}$$
$$R^2 = 1 - k^2$$
$$= 1 - .75450$$
$$= .24550$$
$$= .499$$

8. Write $r'_{54}$ as the third entry in column 5 and row 4.

$$R''_{45} = r'_{54}$$

The negative of this entry is the $\beta$ coefficient for variable 4.

$$\beta_4 = -r''_{45}$$

9. Multiply $r''_{45}$ by $r'_{43}$ and add $r'_{53}$. Enter this value as the third entry in column 5 and row 3.

$$r''_{35} = r''_{45} r'_{43} + r'_{53}$$
$$\beta_3 = -r''_{35}$$

10. Continue to find the other $\beta$ coefficients

$$\beta_2 = -(r''_{35} r'_{32} + r''_{45} r'_{42} + r'_{52}) \text{ etc.}$$

In the sample exercise, the multiple correlation coefficient of English, Latin, algebra, and chemistry is .499. The β coefficients are respectively .27767, .23319, .09257, .13475.

### The Kelley-Salisbury Iterative Method

A method of approximating it are given in Report No. 3, *Research Problems and Techniques*. If the operator has some idea about the relative weights, judicious use of the Kelley iterative method will usually result in a considerable saving of time even for a poor computer. However, it is possible that the choice of weights may be such that accurate results will not be readily obtained. In case of doubt it may be wiser to resort to a somewhat longer but absolutely reliable method.

### Inverse Matrix Method

The inverse matrix for about 25 variables, including the setting up of the work form and the completion of the check can be computed by an experienced operator in about 25 hours, whereas a poor computer will have difficulty in maintaining accuracy. The method is presented in the following paragraphs. If the reader will follow each step in the sample problem by means of the work forms the procedure will be seen to be quite simple despite the apparent complexity of the explanation.

(1) Two large work sheets, Form 1 and Form 2 shown as figures 23.3 and 23.4, are required. Each is of a width and length twice that required to record conveniently the correlation matrix to five significant figures. Each form contains four matrices.

**FIGURE 23.3.** *Inverse matrix work sheet, Form no. 1.*

| | 1 | 2 | 3 | 4 | 1′ | 2′ | 3′ | 4′ | Check sum | Oper. |
|---|---|---|---|---|---|---|---|---|---|---|
| 1 | 1.000 | 0.313 | 0.280 | 0.495 | 1.000 | 0 | 0 | 0 | 3.088 | |
| 2 | | 1.000 | .652 | .650 | 0 | 1.000 | 0 | 0 | 3.015 | |
| 3 | | | 1.000 | .803 | 0 | 0 | 1.000 | 0 | 3.735 | |
| 4 | | | | 1.000 | 0 | 0 | 0 | 1.000 | 3.948 | |
| 1′ | 1.000 | .313 | .280 | .495 | 1.000 | | | | 3.088 | 3.088 |
| 2′ | | .902 | .564 | .495 | −.313 | 1.000 | | | 2.648 | 2.648 |
| 3′ | | | .569 | .355 | −.084 | −.625 | 1.000 | | 1.215 | 1.215 |
| 4′ | | | | .262 | −.271 | −.159 | −.624 | 1.000 | .208 | .208 |

**FIGURE 23.4.** *Inverse matrix work sheet, Form no. 2.*

| | 1 | 2 | 3 | 4 | 1′ | 2′ | 3′ | 4′ | Check sum | Oper. |
|---|---|---|---|---|---|---|---|---|---|---|
| 1 | 1.000 | 0 | 0 | 0 | 1.401 | −0.091 | +0.498 | −1.034 | 1.774 | 1.774 |
| 2 | 0 | 1.000 | 0 | 0 | | 1.892 | −.719 | −.607 | 1.475 | 1.475 |
| 3 | 0 | 0 | 1.000 | 0 | | | 3.243 | −2.382 | 1.640 | 1.641 |
| 4 | 0 | 0 | 0 | 1.000 | | | | 3.817 | .794 | .794 |
| 1′ | −1.000 | −.313 | −.280 | −.495 | −1.000 | | | | −3.088 | −3.088 |
| 2′ | | −1.000 | −.625 | −.549 | +.347 | −1.109 | | | −2.936 | −2.936 |
| 3′ | | | −1.000 | −.624 | +.147 | 1.098 | −1.757 | | −2.136 | −2.135 |
| 4′ | | | | −1.000 | +1.034 | .607 | 2.382 | −3.817 | −.794 | −.794 |

(2) On Form 1, in the upper left quadrant is recorded the correlation matrix with unity in the diagonals. Since the matrix is symmetrical, only the upper half need be recorded. Call this matrix 1. In the upper right matrix enter an identity matrix, i.e., 1's in the diagonal and zeros elsewhere. This is matrix 2. The last two right-hand columns are used as check columns. In the first check column, record the sum of all the entries in the row to the left that would be obtained if the correlation matrix 1 were completely filled—even below the diagonal. The second check column contains the result of operating on the appropriate figures.

(3) The bottom half of Form 1 has the rows marked by primes. This bottom half contains matrices 3 and 4. Copy the entries of row 1 into row 1′. Include the check column. Summing all the entries (except the check column) in row 1′ gives a sum check, which must equal the check column entry.

(4) On Form 2, figure 23.4, the upper left quadrant is filled in with an identity matrix, matrix 5.

(5) The entries in row 1′, Form 1, are each divided by the leading term (1.000), and the quotient *after changing its sign*, is recorded in the corresponding space in row 1′ of Form 2. In general it is recommended that five significant figures be recorded. (In the example only three have been recorded, since illustrative purposes are as well served.) Changing the sign in this case is equivalent to dividing by the leading term with the sign of the leading term changed. In the sample problem, in row 1′ of Form 2 is entered −1.000, −.313, −.280, −.495, and −1.000. Note that the operation is continued all the way across row 1 of Form 1 including the check column. The check column is treated exactly as if it were a regular column in the matrix.

(6) The entries in row 2′ of Form 1 are obtained next. To aid the computations, Form 2 should be folded vertically between cols. 1 and 2. This form is laid over Form 1 with the folded edge of Form 2 lying between col. 2 and 3 of Form 1. The paired entries in col. 2 of Form 1 and Form 2 in the upper half are multiplied together and their sum taken. Since all the entries in the upper half of col. 2 of Form 2 are zero, except for the diagonal, the upper half yields nothing but the value of the entry in col. 2 of Form 1 that is paired with the diagonal value (1.000) of the entry on Form 2. The lower paired values are multiplied together and added. Thus, in the sample problem (1.000) (1.000) + (.313) (− .313) = .902. This is entered in row 2′ of Form 1 in col. 2. The next entry of row 2′ of Form 1 is obtained by moving Form 2 one column to the right and again summing the products of the paired items of col. 3 of Form 1 and col. 2 of Form 2. In the example, (1.000) (.652) + (−.313) (.280) = .564. By another move of Form 2 to the right, there is yielded (1.000) (.650) + (−.313) (.495) = .495 which is recorded in the cell row 2′ and col. 4 of Form 1. This process is continued all the way across row 1′ through the check column. The entry for the sum-check column will be the sum of all the entries recorded in that row to the left of the check column. It must be emphasized that the entire operation for each entry is performed on a calculator by cumulating the sum of the products.

(7) The entries of row 2′ of Form 2 are obtained from the entries of row 2′ of Form 1 by dividing the latter entries by the leading term and changing the sign. Thus for row 2′ there is obtained (.902) (1.1086) = −1.000 after changing the sign. 1.1086 is the reciprocal of .902 and is used since successive multiplication is faster than division. Continuing, there is obtained (.564) (1.1086) = −.625 (changing sign) and (.495) (1.1086) = −.549 (changing the sign).

(8) Form 2 is folded again between columns 2 and 3 and placed over Form 1 with the folded edge lying between columns 3 and 4. By summing the products of the paired entries, the entries for row 3′ of Form 1 are obtained, just as for row 2′.

(9) Row 3′ of Form 1 is treated as was row 2′ of Form 1 to yield the entries for row 3′ of Form 2.

(10) This process is continued until the last row of Form 1 and 2 is completed; each time a row is completed the check column will check with the sum of entries to the left.

(11) The entries of the inverse matrix, which is matrix 6 on Form 2, may be obtained by folding Form 1 vertically between columns 4 and 1′. Lay Form 1 over Form 2 so that column 1′ of Form 1 lies just to the right of column 1′ of Form 2. The paired entries in the columns 1′ and 1′ are now multiplied and

summed and the sum is recorded in row 1 of Form 2 with the signs reversed. Thus $-1.401$ (reversed sign) equals $(-1.000)$ $(1.000)$ + $(.347)$ $(-.313)$ + $(.147)$ $(-.084)$ + $(1.034)$ $(-.271)$. The entry for column 2′, row 1 of matrix 6 in Form 2 is the sum (sign changed) of the products of the paired items of column 2′ of Form 2 and column 1′ of Form 1. These are brought into paired position by sliding Form 1 and column 1 to the right. Thus the entry is $(-1.109)$ $(-.313)$ + $(1.098)$ $(-.084)$ + $(.607)$ $(-.271)$ = $-.091$ with sign changed.

Entries of row 2 of matrix 6 are obtained by vertically folding Form 1 between columns 1′ and 2′. Placing Form 1 over Form 2 so that the folded edge is between columns 2′ and 3′ of Form 2 will pair the items to be multiplied and summed (changing signs). This sum is the first entry in row 2 of matrix No. 6. Thus $(1.000)$ $(-1.109)$ + $(1.098)$ $(-.625)$ + $(.607)$ $(-.159)$ = $1.892$ (sign changed).

Successively moving Form 1 to the right yields the other entries of row 2.

Folding Form 1 between the other columns of matrix 2 on Form 1 and placing it over Form 2 in the corresponding places will facilitate calculations of the entries for the remaining rows of matrix No. 6.

(12) The check column is treated like the other columns. The entry in the check column obtained as the sum of the paired products must equal the sum of all the entries to the left in that row including the 1.000 in matrix No. 5. It must be noted that the entries to the left of the diagonal of matrix No. 6 are not recorded—but since the inverse matrix is symmetrical these entries are in the columns above the diagonal term of each row. A check is provided by multiplying together the original matrix and the inverse matrix. A unity matrix is the product. Since both the original matrix and the inverse matrix are symmetrical, only the diagonal terms and the upper half of the product matrix need be computed.

(13) The inverse matrix is matrix 6, appearing in the upper right quadrant of Form 2. Each entry may be generally denoted by $C_{ij}$ where i is the column and j is the row. Then the following formulas are applicable.

$R_1 \ldots$ = (multiple correlation coefficient of i on all the other variables) = $1 - 1/C_{ii}$

$r_{ij} \ldots$ = (partial correlation of i on j, other variables removed linearly) = $-C_{ij}/C_{ii}C_{jj}$

$$\beta_{ij} \ldots = \text{Beta weight} = \frac{C_{ij}}{C_{ii}}$$

$$\sigma_{\beta_{ij} \ldots} = \text{standard deviation of a beta coefficient} =$$

$$\frac{C_{ii}C_{jj} - C_{ij}^2}{n'C_{ii}}$$

where $n'$ is the number of degrees of freedom.

Thus in the example

$$R_{4.123} = 1 - \frac{1}{3.817} = .859$$

$$r_{41.23} = \frac{1.034}{(-1.401)(-3.817)} = .447$$

$$\beta_{41.23} = \frac{-1.034}{3.817} = .271$$

$$\sigma_{\beta_{41.23}} = \frac{(3.817)(1.401) - (-1.034)^2}{(997)(3.817)} = .03353$$

(14) The entries in matrix 4 on Form 1 are identifiable regression coefficients. The entry of row 2′ of that matrix ($-.313$) is $-\beta_{21}$; the entries of row 3′ of that matrix ($-.084$, $-.625$) are $\beta_{31.2}$ and $-\beta_{32.1}$, respectively. The entries in row 4′ of matrix 4 are $-\beta_{41.23}$ ($-.271$), $-\beta_{42.13}$ ($-.159$), and $-\beta_{43.12}$ ($-.624$). Thus it can be seen that the regression coefficients for the complete regression equation are obtained in the process of computing the inverse matrix if the predicted variable is the variable in the extreme right column and bottom row of the correlation matrix.

(15) To eliminate a variable, the row and column containing that variable in the correlation matrix may be covered (removed) and the inverse matrix computed with only a fraction of the original amount of work. The saving will be greater if the eliminated variable is in the column just to the left of the predicted (criterion) variable, which should be to the extreme right.

(16) Certain formulas are available which permit the determination of the regression coefficients and the multiple correlation coefficients with one variable eliminated directly from the original complete inverse.[4] Thus with one variable removed the beta weights may be computed from the complete inverse matrix from the following formula:

4. P. S. Dwyer, op. cit.

$$\beta_{cj} = -\left( \frac{C_{ii}C_{jc} - C_{ic}C_{jc}}{C_{cc}C_{ii} - C_{ic}^2} \right)$$

where $c$ is the criterion (predicted) variable, and i is the variable to be excluded from the regression equation.

*Trivariate Population*

On the basis of one sample from a trivariate population it may be necessary to test the hypothesis that the correlation between variables 1 and 2 is the same as the correlation between variables 1 and 3. The alternatives are that the correlations are different, either being larger than the other. An exact test of this hypothesis is given by the following statistic:

$$t = \frac{(r_{12} - r_{13}) \sqrt{n(1 + r_{23})}}{\sqrt{2(1 - r_{12}^2 - r_{13}^2 - r_{23}^2 + 2r_{12}r_{13}r_{23})}}$$

where

$n = N - 3 =$ degrees of freedom and t is distributed as Student's t distribution with n degrees of freedom.[5]

There is one severe restriction on the application of this test. The population of samples on which this test is based is one in which the samples have the same set of values of variables 2 and 3 as in the observed sample. This restriction which is necessary to an exact solution removes the requirement of a trivariate normal distribution; only variable 1 need be distributed normally.

*Truncation; Curtailment of Range: Correction of Correlation Coefficient*

The correlation coefficient estimated from a sample is a function of the sample variance. The smaller the variance, the smaller will be the correlation coefficient, other things being constant. Appendix E outlines the aviation psychology program's method of dealing with the problem of correcting correlation coefficients for differences in the sample variance. The formulas were

---

5. H. Hotelling, The selection of variates for general use in prediction with some comments on the general problem of nuisance parameters, *Annals of Mathematical Statistics*, 11, 1940, 271–83.

**FIGURE 23.5.** *Computing form for formula 3A, Technical Bulletin 43-6*

| a | b | c | d | e | f | g | h | i | j | k |
|---|---|---|---|---|---|---|---|---|---|---|
| $S_3$ | $S_3$ | $\dfrac{b}{a}$ | $c^2 - 1$ | $\dfrac{a}{b}$ | $1 - e^2$ | $c - e$ | $r_{23}$ | $gh$ | $h^2$ | $\sqrt{1 + dj}$ |
| 1.006 | 2.000 | 1.9881 | 2.9525 | .5030 | .7470 | 1.4851 | .278 | .4129 | .0773 | 1.1083 |

| | l | m | n | o | |
|---|---|---|---|---|---|
| | $r_{12}$ | $R_{13}$ | $m^2$ | $\sqrt{1 - [\ ]*n}$ | $\dfrac{lo + [\ ]^{\ddagger}m}{[\ ]^{\#}}$ |
| Sp. Or. I | .085 | .56 | .3136 | .8751 | .276 |
| Sp. Or. II | .042 | .58 | .3364 | .8653 | .249 |
| Read. Comp. | .167 | .51 | .2601 | .8976 | .325+ |
| D. + T. | .247 | .81 | .6561 | .7141 | .461 |

*Write in f.　‡Write in k.　#Write in i.

originally derived by K. Pearson.[6] The distribution function of the corrected correlation coefficients and the extent of the bias are not known. An empirical study of the distribution of the corrected coefficients is in progress.

There will be presented here only the work sheets used in applying the formulas 3 and 3a of appendix E. The work sheets (figs. 23.5 and 23.6) are self-explanatory and are actual samples from certain statistical projects.

No special work sheets were used for the other formulas which are quite simple in form and may readily be computed on the calculators.

Another method of estimating correlation coefficients of bivariate normal populations when variable $x$ is truncated and variable $y$ is dichotomized has been presented by Gillman and Goode.[7]

The essence of the rationale of that method is as follows: The $x$ variable is

6. Karl Pearson, Mathematical contributions to the theory of evolution—XI, On the influence of natural selection on the variability and correlation of organs, *Philosophical Transactions of the Royal Society of London*, A, 200, 1903, 1–66.

7. L. Gillman and Harry H. Goode, An estimate of the correlation coefficient of a bivariate normal population when X is truncated and Y is dichotomized, *Harvard Educational Review*, 16, 1946, 52–55.

**FIGURE 23.6.** Correction for restriction of range.[1]

| | (1) | (2) | (3) | (4) | (5) | (6) | (7) | (8) | (9) | (10) | (11) | (12) | (13) | (14) | (15) |
|---|---|---|---|---|---|---|---|---|---|---|---|---|---|---|---|
| | $r_{13}$ | $r^2_{13}$ | $r_{23}$ | $r^2_{23}$ | $r_{13}r_{23}$ | $\sigma_3$ | $\dfrac{2.00}{\sigma_3}$ | $(7)^2 - 1.00$ | $(8 \times 2) + 1$ | $(8 \times 4) + 1$ | $(8 \times 5)$ | $(9 \times 10)$ | 12 | $r_{12}$ | $\dfrac{(14 + 11)}{(13)}$ |
| Figure Analogies Spa. | 0.508 | 0.258 | 0.323 | 0.104 | 0.164 | 1.658 | 1.206 | 0.455 | 1.117 | 1.047 | 0.075 | 1.169 | 1.081 | 0.175 | 0.231 |
| Visualize Apt. Test- | .478 | .228 | .588 | .346 | .281 | 1.634 | 1.224 | .498 | 1.114 | 1.172 | .140 | 1.306 | 1.143 | .215 | .311 |
| Santa Ana Picture | −.208 | .043 | .379 | .144 | −.079 | 1.371 | 1.459 | 1.128 | 1.049 | 1.162 | −.089 | 1.219 | 1.104 | .056 | −.030 |
| Integra | .323 | .104 | .313 | .098 | .101 | 1.405 | 1.423 | 1.026 | 1.107 | 1.101 | .104 | 1.219 | 1.104 | .203 | .278 |

[1]Subscripts to variables in table may be identified as follows: 1 = Test. 2 = Graduation-elimination. 3 = Pilot stanine.

categorized and in each category the proportion in the upper and lower $y$ dichotomy is obtained. In each category the proportion is converted to a normal deviate. If the correlation is zero, the normal deviate will be equal in all categories except for sampling fluctuations. For positive correlation the proportion in the upper category (e.g., high stanine) will increase as variable $x$ increases. The normal deviate of that proportion will vary linearly with the $x$ variable. Thus, if a straight line is fitted to the normal deviates, by least squares, the slope will be indicative of the correlation.

There is difficulty involved in applying this technique if all persons in one of the $x$ categories pass (or fail). The value of the normal deviate would then be infinity, which would result in an indeterminate answer. A normal deviate of 2.5 or 3 has been suggested, and it seems to be an acceptable solution in validating stanines against training. But whether it is satisfactory for all cases is not known. Other possibilities are to combine these categories with the adjoining to make a category in which less than 100 percent pass or fail.

## Multisample, Multivariate Analysis

R. A. Fisher, H. Hotelling, J. Neyman, E. S. Pearson, S. S. Wilks, and J. Wishart have developed the distribution of $k$ samples from multivariate normal populations.[8] Most of the preceding tests (the Student's $t$ test, $\chi^2$ F, L, the distribution of the correlation coefficients) are special cases of these generalized distributions.

In general these generalized tests cover the equality of sets of multivariate populations, or the satisfaction of certain *a priori* parameter values (e.g., independence of sets of variables). The statistical analysis unit rarely had occasion to use these more generalized tests and distributions.

8. E. S. Pearson and J. Neyman, On the problem of two samples, *Bulletin International de l'Academie Polonaise Des Sciences, A Sciences Mathematiques*, 1930, 73–96.

J. Neyman and E. S. Pearson, On the problem of $k$ samples, *Bulletin International de l'Academie Polonaise Des Sciences, A Science Mathematiques*, 1931–32, 460–81.

E. S. Pearson and S. S. Wilks, Methods of statistical analysis appropriate for $k$ samples of two variables, *Biometrika*, 25, 1933, 354–78. (Issued by the Biometrika Office, Univ. Col. London.)

K. Pearson, *Tables of the Incomplete Beta Function*, London: Biometrika Office, 1934.

K. Pearson, *Tables of the Incomplete Gamma Function*, London: Biometrika Office, 1934.

# AUTHORS CITED

# SUBJECT INDEX

This book is set in Quadraat, a typeface designed by Fred Smeijers and released in various weights and forms in the 1990s. Quadraat is a modern interpretation of the old-style Dutch faces of the eighteenth century, which were noted for their readability and clarity. Early in his career, Smeijers learned the now nearly lost craft of cutting metal type punches by hand, giving him an understanding of how the process of making the physical type affects the individuality of the letters. Quadraat is a striking example of a digital face that unifies these distinctive features in a harmonious whole. Its narrow, upright italic is unusual but works well with the roman text.

TheSerif, designed by Luc de Groot and introduced in 1994, is used in its bold and plain variations for much of the display type.

This book is printed on paper that is acid-free and meets the requirements of the American National Standard for Permanence of Paper for Printed Library Materials, z39.48-1992. ∞

Book design by Richard Hendel, Chapel Hill, North Carolina
Typography by Graphic Composition, Inc., Athens, Georgia
Printed and bound by Edwards Brothers, Inc., Ann Arbor, Michigan